GRE

GRADUATE
RECORD
EXAMINATION
GENERAL (APTITUDE)
TEST

GRE

GRADUATE RECORD EXAMINATION GENERAL (APTITUDE) TEST

Complete Preparation for the *NEW* Test

Gino Crocetti
National Program Director
Sexton Educational Programs

ARCO PUBLISHING, INC.
New York

First Edition, Fourth Printing, 1985

Published by Arco Publishing, Inc.
215 Park Avenue South, New York, N.Y. 10003

Copyright © 1983 by Arco Publishing, Inc.

Library of Congress Cataloging in Publication Data

Crocetti, Gino.
   Complete preparation for the graduate record
examination general (aptitude) test (GRE).

   1. Graduate record examination—Study guides.
I. Title.
LB2367.4.C76   1982   378′.1664   82-18475
ISBN 0-668-05479-4 (pbk.)

Printed in the United States of America

CONTENTS

GRE

GRADUATE
RECORD
EXAMINATION
GENERAL (APTITUDE)
TEST

ABOUT THE GRADUATE RECORD EXAMINATION GENERAL (APTITUDE) TEST AND TEST-TAKING SKILLS

HOW TO USE THIS BOOK

HOW THIS BOOK WILL HELP YOU GET A BETTER GRE SCORE

The book that you hold in your hand is different from other preparation books in several ways that will help you get a better GRE score.

First, there is much more instructional material in this book than in other preparation books. The Instructional Overviews for each type of question are substantial reviews of what the question type is all about and how to master it. They are not just filled out with more drill work. They really teach you something.

Second, the answer explanations are not only longer than usual, but they discuss all the answer choices—including the reasons that the wrong choices were attractive. There are no one-sentence explanations. There are, after all, four wrong answers to cope with for every right answer.

Third, this book offers a complete program of preparation including both general test-taking hints and specific hints for each type of question in the Instructional Overviews and in the answer explanations, many of which are longer than the questions they explain.

Fourth, there is a separate Attack Strategy for each question type, including detailed timing recommendations on sections and question types where students have had trouble in the past.

Fifth, the problems in the five practice tests are just like the test. There will be no surprises.

Sixth, there is nothing in the book that is not going to be on the test. There are no "extras" that only fill up the book without helping your score. Everything you need is here, while anything you don't is not.

For all these reasons we want to tell you how to get the full value of this book towards getting the best possible GRE score.

THE IMPORTANCE OF THE GRE SCORE

You know that the GRE score is important to your admission to graduate school. It is used both as a cutoff for some programs and as one of the two major criteria in evaluating your application in most other programs. The other criterion is usually your grade point average.

Since the GRE is used by so many different types of programs, there are many ways in which the three GRE scores—Verbal, Quantitative, and Analytic—are used. Some programs will emphasize one score, and some another. The use of the Analytic score is discussed in your GRE Bulletin, and further in the next section, "All About the GRE."

WHY AND HOW PREPARATION IS EFFECTIVE

The GRE is intended by its makers to test mental and academic skills that they regard as taking a long time to develop. These skills are usually referred to as "the ability to read, understand, and reason" but are somewhat narrower than that designation might imply. There are three separate ways that preparation can raise your score.

1. UNDERSTANDING THE TEST: Preparation will help you to know what each section of the test is about. Good preparation will also analyze each subtype of question and explain what it is asking. Also included in this area of benefit are such technical matters as knowing whether to guess (yes on the GRE), how the timing works, etc.

2. IMPROVING YOUR TEST-TAKING SKILLS: Good test-taking skills improve the efficiency of your other academic and mental

skills. There are many different test-taking skills. One of the most difficult to master is knowing just which other skills should be used for different question types. That skill is fully explained in this book. Other test-taking skills include the order in which parts of the section should be read and the emphasis to be given to each, how to tell the answer choices apart, key words to beware of, what you DON'T have to worry about, and how to avoid various common errors.

3. IMPROVING YOUR "ABILITY TO READ, UNDERSTAND, AND REASON": Or at least the mental and academic skills that go by that name on the GRE. Reading, reasoning, and problem-solving are skills that you use every day, and which, like all skills, can be improved. One of the most effective ways of improving any skill, and the one used in this book, is clear identification of errors and the appropriate times to use these skills.

Perhaps an analogy to a "physical" skill will help (no skill is purely physical; there is always a major mental element). A tennis player may have a dozen excellent shots but still play poorly because he does not know when to use them to best advantage or because he lacks one shot that he needs.

You may be in a similar position. You have spent years learning a large number of mental and academic skills, but if you don't know which ones to use on which parts of the test, you won't do as well as you should. Similarly, you can probably benefit from brushing up on, or perhaps learning in the first place, some of the skills needed for the GRE.

We won't pretend that a five-year-old could pick up this book and then get a perfect score on the GRE. But you are not five years old and you don't need a perfect score, just a better one. A better score is just what you will get if you master the skills presented in this book.

WHAT YOU NEED TO DO

How, then, shall you use this book? We will give you guidance in three areas: how to evaluate your needs and resources, how to set up a workable study plan, and how to study this sort of material effectively. Naturally there is some overlap between these three areas.

The first and most important thing that you need to do is take this book seriously. If you are just going to read a page here and there, casually do some problems without regard to timing, and never read the explanations—well, in that case you are not going to benefit nearly as much as you could. It takes work and commitment—YOUR work and YOUR commitment.

Now, having been stirred to action, here is what you do.

Evaluating your Needs and Resources

The most valuable resource you have in this work is your time. You may have a great deal of time or you may have only a little. You need to set priorities so that you can get the most return for the time invested.

Actually, your needs are not too complicated to evaluate. You should assume that you need to study closely each of the Instructional Overviews, unless you are previously both familiar AND successful with the kinds of questions it treats (but you should, in any case, see the special discussion of the Analytical score in the next section, "All About the GRE"). If you think you don't need to study one or two of the Instructional Overviews, do the appropriate sections in the first practice test as a check. Unless you get over 85% right, study the Overview. By the way, as a first exercise in logical reasoning, note that the use of 85% as a criterion in this context does not mean you should expect to get 85% of every section right on the test. As is explained in the next chapter, the GRE scoring doesn't require that criterion. Even if you can get 85% right without help, you could still probably benefit from further study.

In addition to the overviews, every student should read the next two chapters on the nature of the GRE and general test-taking strategies. You should also read the first part of the chapter on anxiety just to check yourself out, and read all of it if you find that you have even a small overanxiety problem.

That leaves the practice tests. You must take at least one test as a full-dress rehearsal. That is the highest priority after the instructional material. It is good to do all of the practice tests, but if time does not permit, you can do extra sections of the question types that give you difficulty.

As you study and do the practice tests, you will develop a list of your problem areas, which will direct your further studying. The development of this list is described later, in the section on effective studying.

Now consider your time. Do not overestimate how much time you have. If you think you have four hours every day, say instead that you have two hours five days a week. If you actually have the extra time, you can always do more studying, but if you plan on more than you actually have, you will feel bad and your priorities may become distorted. Be conservative.

Even if it is just 45 minutes a day, that is fine. Just make sure that it is actually 45 minutes and not 20 minutes of telephone calls and only 25 minutes of study. Regular study in small amounts is much better than occasional larger periods. The practice tests that you take as complete tests should be done in one sitting.

Take a piece of paper right now and write down all the time you want to dedicate to studying for the GRE between now and the test date. If you don't know the test date, consult the official GRE bulletin.

Setting Up a Workable Study Plan

Once you know how much time you have, you are halfway to having a plan that will work. Each week, you should plan exactly on which topics or tests you will work. You cannot plan the entire process at the beginning because you won't know how long things take until you have done some of them. Allow TWICE as much time as your best estimate of the time it really takes. If you actually do finish quicker, you'll feel good and there is no harm done. You will find your margin used up very quickly.

Never plan two things for the same time. For the best results, your study time must be totally dedicated to study. If you can do some extra review of your notes while commuting, so much the better, but make that extra time, not prime time.

In sum then, the keys to setting up a workable plan are dedicated time, conservative estimation, and advance planning in writing. Aside from helping you to remember when you are to study for the GRE, putting the plan in writing will remind you to reschedule those hours that will inevitably be superseded by some "emergency" or special event.

Effective Studying for the GRE

In addition to the organizing ideas just mentioned, there are several studying hints that are particularly helpful with this type of material.

1. ALWAYS HAVE A POSITIVE ATTITUDE. Start every session with the thought of how much better off you will be because you will know even more after studying than you did before.

2. STUDY IN SHORT SEGMENTS, with rest breaks in between. Most people should study in 20-minute segments with a five-minute review at the end for a total of 25 minutes of studying. Then completely relax yourself and think of nothing at all for two minutes or so. If you rush right into another topic, even another GRE topic, your memory of the first topic will not be as good. No one should go more than 40 minutes without stopping, reviewing, and resting. It just isn't efficient. You will learn better in short periods.

3. TAKE MEANINGFUL NOTES. Take notes in a separate notebook and not in the margins of this book. Don't rely only on highlighting. Write complete notes that will mean something to you at a later time.

4. PREVIEW, READ, WRITE, AND REMEMBER. Rapidly preview the chapter you are studying. Then read it carefully, taking good notes. Finally, after you are finished, close the book and try to recall all the major ideas of the chapter. If you have any difficulties, check yourself against your notes. If they are unclear or incomplete, check the book. The very act of trying to remember will engrave the material in your memory far better than merely rereading it once or even twice.

5. DO EACH EXERCISE OR PRACTICE TEST BY THE "TRAC" METHOD. The initials TRAC stand for Timed, Rework, Analyze, and Check for clues:

Timed:	First do the exercise or test in the time limit. However, mark the questions carefully to indicate the answer choices you have eliminated and the choices and questions about which you felt unsure.

Rework: Before you check your answers, rework all of the questions about which you were unsure and indicate to yourself whether you came up with the same answer or a different one.

Analyze: Now check the answer key and try to analyze any remaining errors for yourself, armed with the knowledge of the right answer. Do a full analysis.

Check for clues: Now read the answer explanations for all of the questions which gave you trouble the first time through the material—not just the ones of which you are still unsure. Look for the clues in the problem and the answer choices which you missed the first time through. Try to see how you might have worked your way to them, or seen them more easily.

This entire process will usually take from two to four times as long as the time limit for the section.

NOTE: The key to improvement in reviewing the exercises is NOT merely understanding the explanation of why the right answer was correct, but, just as important, you must try to see exactly what clues in the problem lead you to the right explanation and the right answer. After all, on the day of the test that is what you will have to do—find the answers, not just understand someone else's explanations of them.

6. LEARN ATTACK STRATEGIES AND TIMINGS. These are the basic summaries of the application of the material in the Instructional Overviews. Consciously use them whenever you are doing problems, even if you think the problem is easy.

7. VIVID IMAGES ARE EASY TO REMEMBER. Whenever you want to remember something from this book or elsewhere, you will find a vivid image easier to remember. For instance, if you want to remember the TRAC method, you might think of yourself "tracking" across a giant book and savagely cutting away the wrong answers, leaving only correct answers and uncertain questions. Then a new round of conquests without the clock shining overhead as a sun, and fewer problems still can withstand your glorious assault. . . . You get the idea. The stranger the image, the easier it is to remember. Don't worry if it is a little weird—you don't have to tell anyone about it, just use it to help remember something.

8. REST. This has been mentioned, but is worth repeating. Rest for at least two to five minutes at the end of each study session. Don't think of anything, or just imagine yourself at your favorite secluded spot, alone, gazing at the sky.

GOOD LUCK AND GOOD STUDYING!

ALL ABOUT THE NEW GRE

PURPOSE OF THE GRE

The GRE is a standardized test intended to assist graduate schools in making admissions decisions by giving a standard assessment of mental and academic skills considered to be important to graduate study. The GRE scores are designed to be a measure of the ability to read, understand, and reason.

The purpose of a standard measure is to permit admissions decisions to be based, at least in part, on an "objective" comparison of all the candidates—no matter what their college or background. There has been some controversy about the degree to which the laudable goal of "objectivity and total evenhandedness" has been met. There is no similar disagreement about the importance that schools place on the GRE scores in making their admissions decisions. At base, the purpose of the GRE is to be part of the criteria for graduate school admissions, and your purpose in taking it is to do as well as you can so you will have the best possible chance of getting into the graduate school of your choice.

THE FORMAT OF THE GRE

The GRE has undergone a number of changes in the past few years. First the Analytical Section was added and then it was thoroughly changed. The Quantitative and Verbal sections were changed from one long section each to two shorter sections each. Finally, the scoring system was changed so that there is no longer any penalty for a wrong answer. (The GRE Advanced Tests still do subtract for wrong answers.)

The sum of all these changes is that the GRE now has seven 30-minute sections as illustrated in the chart on the next page. Six of the sections will count toward determining your three GRE scores. There will be two counting sections of each type. The seventh section, which may not in

fact be Section 7 on the exam, will be either a repeat of one of the other types of sections or some entirely different sort of question. In any case, the extra section will not count toward your scores. It is merely your opportunity to assist in the development of future tests.

One of the major reasons that all of the sections are the same length is to make it all but impossible for you to identify the experimental sections as such. Unless the experimental section consists of a completely different type of question than any of the other sections, you will generally not be able to tell which six sections actually count.

For example, you might have a test that gives you two sections of Analytical and two sections of Quantitative and three sections of Verbal questions. You know that one of the Verbal sections is experimental, but you will not know which one. If the extra section was a question type not discussed in either this book or the GRE Bulletin, then you can be assured that it does not count. Usually, however, the experimental sections are composed of the same sort of questions as the ones that do count.

THE THREE GRE SCORES

When you get your report back from the Educational Testing Service (ETS), you will have three scores reported for your GRE test. The three scores are: Verbal, Quantitative (Math), and Analytical Reasoning, usually referred to as Analytical.

The Verbal score is based on your answers to two Verbal sections that will ask you a total of 76 questions of four types. The types of questions are discussed later in this section and every type of question on the test is thoroughly discussed in its own Instructional Overview in the next part of the book.

The Quantitative, or Math, score is based on your answers to two Quantitative sections that will ask you a total of 60 questions in two formats, covering what amounts to high school algebra, geometry and word problems.

The Analytical Reasoning score is based on your answers to two Analytical sections that will ask you a total of 50 questions of two types.

Different graduate programs will give different weights to the different scores. Most programs give some weight to the Verbal score, and language-oriented programs such as English and Literature would usually give it the primary weight. The Quantitative score is naturally important in the hard sciences, though the Verbal score is often counted significantly as well.

The Analytic score is not usually given the same weight as the other two sections, primarily because it is relatively new and has been undergoing a number of changes in format and content. However, with the new norms that are being established for the Analytic score, there will be programs that do give considerable weight to it. Some psychology programs in particular are likely to use this score. The best way to find out in what your particular program is interested is to ask them. While they will not always give you an informative answer, many programs have rather specific ideas about the use of the various GRE scores, including the advanced tests. When you ask your question, make it clear that you are not asking what score you need to be assured of admission, since most programs are reluctant to make such promises. What you are asking is whether there are any parts of the GRE score that they do not look at at all, or only in a very insignificant way.

If your program tells you authoritatively that they are not interested in one or more of the scores, this can save you a lot of work and anxiety. Unfortunately, if you are applying to a wide variety of programs, or have not selected your area yet, you will probably have to pay some attention to all of the scores.

While it is perfectly possible to do effective work on every part of the test, you will generally be better off if you do not spend time on a score that will not count. On the other hand, you should absolutely not ignore a score unless you are certain that the admissions officers will also ignore the score. When in doubt, study.

THE QUESTION TYPES ASKED ON THE GRE

The GRE will ask four types of Verbal problems, two formats of Math problems and two formats of Analytic problems. Each of these eight types of questions are discussed thoroughly in its own Instructional Overview. The following review is merely to give you an overview of the types of questions on the test.

Verbal Questions

ANTONYM questions give you a word and ask you to select one of the five answer choices which

FORMAT OF THE GRADUATE RECORD EXAM
(Order of Sections May Vary)

Section	Section Type	No. of Questions	Time		No. each Question Type
1	Verbal	38	30	each	7 Sentence Completion / 9 Analogy / 11 Reading Comprehension / 11 Antonym
2	Verbal	38	30		
3	Quantitative	30	30	each	15 General Mathematics
4	Quantitative	30	30		15 Quantitative Comparison
5	Analytic	25	30	each	4–6 Logical Reasoning
6	Analytic	25	30		19–21 Analytical Reasoning
7	Variable	??	30		Any of the above

There will be one 10 to 15-minute break, usually after sections 3 or 4.

is the best *opposite*. While this is primarily a test of vocabulary, making educated guesses on the more difficult words can help your score.

ANALOGY questions give you one pair of words which have some relationship between them, and ask you to select one of the five pairs given as answer choices that best replicates that relationship. The relationships can be abstract or concrete, and may vary in other ways. This type of question has a large vocabulary element, but many mistakes can be avoided by familiarity with the most common sorts of relationships and errors.

SENTENCE-COMPLETION questions give you a sentence with one or two blanks in it. You are to select an answer choice with the word(s) that best complete(s) the sentence and convey(s) its intended meaning. This is not generally very dependent on vocabulary. The structure of the sentence is usually the key clue, as will be discussed in the Instructional Overview.

READING COMPREHENSION questions are based on a reading passage and ask you to demonstrate your understanding of the passage by answering questions about the structure, meaning, and implications of the passage. Similar questions appear on several other standardized exams, such as the SAT, GMAT, and LSAT.

Quantitative Questions

REGULAR MATH FORMAT questions present a mathematical situation and ask a question. There are five answer choices and you must select the one that represents the proper answer to the question asked. There is little numerical calculation, and the major issue is usually the connections between mathematical ideas—often of an everday nature.

QUANTITATIVE COMPARISON FORMAT questions give you two quantities, one in Column A and one in Column B, and ask you to compare them and determine whether one is definitely larger than the other, they are equal, or their relationship cannot be definitely determined based on the information given.

Analytic Questions

LOGICAL REASONING questions are based on very short arguments. You are asked to demonstrate your understanding of the arguments by choosing answers that describe the argument, weaken or strengthen it, identify its premises, or state its conclusions or implications. This question type also appears on the LSAT.

ANALYTICAL REASONING questions are based on a set of information which you must organize in order to answer the questions. Diagrams of various sorts are helpful. This is also referred to as "logical games" and is not dissimilar to games found in various magazines. A similar version of this question type appears on the LSAT.

SCORING OF THE GRE

There are two issues related to scoring which are worth discussing briefly. First, how your score is derived from the answers you give to the questions. Second, how that score is expressed on the scoring scales.

There will be no penalty for wrong answers on the GRE General Test. (Note: The scoring formula for the GRE Subject Tests *will* still penalize wrong answers.) *Since there will be no penalty for wrong answers, you will definitely answer every question on the test, even if it is a guess.* You will answer, in fact, even those questions you have not read.

Your answer sheet will usually have more answer spaces than there are questions on a particular section. If you are unsure of the number of questions on a section, you should fill in a random answer for every answer space. Even if there are only 25 questions in a section and you fill in through number 42 or 50 on the answer sheet, there will be no penalty.

Since Quantitative Comparison questions only have four possible answer choices—A through D—you should avoid randomly guessing answer choice E. This is particularly true if you are filling in the random guesses after the section is over.

On other tests given by ETS, and previously for the GRE, you were allowed to clean up your answer sheet at the end of the test. This is no longer the case. Therefore, you should make sure that you have filled in all the proper places on the answer sheet at the end of each section.

The three GRE scores are all reported for a range of 200–800. This range is slightly misleading, since virtually all scores are much less than 800, and 99% of the scores for each type of score are usually below 750.

REGISTRATION FOR THE GRE

You can obtain registration materials for the GRE and the Minority Graduate Student Locator Service in the same package either from your college's career advisor or dean, or by writing to:

Graduate Record Examinations
Box 955
Princeton, NJ 08541

You should register well in advance of the test and should get your materials as soon as possible. The registration booklet also contains a full-length sample test which you should do as part of your preparation. While this test lacks answer explanations, it does have an answer key. It is very useful in the later stages of your preparation.

SPECIAL ADMINISTRATIONS OF THE GRE

Special arrangements can be made for the physically and visually handicapped, for persons whose religious beliefs forbid taking the test on a Saturday, and for some persons with other special needs. The key to making satisfactory arrangements is time. If you want to make any special arrangements for taking the GRE, communicate immediately with the Educational Testing Service at the address just given.

GENERAL TEST-TAKING STRATEGIES

In the chapter, "All About the GRE," we discussed the intellectual skills needed to do well in each specific section (see also our chapter on "How to Recognize and Reduce Test Anxiety" for further hints). Later we will provide attack strategies aimed at each section. At this point, we need to take up the more general problem of working within the limits of a standardized test such as the GRE. The GRE is to a very large extent a game—a game with its own rules—and the winners and the losers are selected within that framework. This artificiality produces some surprising anomalies. For example, it is conceivable, though extremely unlikely, that a person could score a perfect GRE just by guessing, and it is also conceivable that a person could turn in a very low score because he picked not the best but the second-best answer on every problem. The test, you see, has this very large blind spot: The machine reads only correct answers—those little black marks on the answer sheet. No one receives any credit for the "thinking" that went into solving the problem. Unless the mark is there in the appropriate spot, the machine will assume the student simply could not answer the question (no partial credit is given for an "almost" answer).

Four Points to Remember

Since you are aware of the limitations of the GRE, you can turn those limitations to your own advantage. We make the following four suggestions regarding taking the GRE: (1) preview sections, (2) be attentive to the time, (3) guess when necessary, and (4) watch carefully how you enter your answers on the answer sheet. Let us develop each one of these in a little more detail.

Previewing sections. When the proctor announces that it is time to begin work on a section (remember each section is separately timed and you will not be allowed to work ahead in other sections, nor will you be allowed to return to a section once time has been called on that section), take a few seconds to preview the material. This procedure is beneficial in two ways. First, it has a calming effect. Instead of beginning work in a frantic manner, you can take a deep breath and remind yourself of the strategy which you have learned for approaching that particular section. Your eye may fall onto a question stem which looks familiar and this will trigger associations. In other words, you will be in a better state of mind to begin work in a systematic fashion. A second benefit of previewing is that you guard against the unexpected. In this book we have followed faithfully the layout which ETS (Educational Testing Service) has officially announced for the GRE. ETS is under no legal or moral compunction, however, to abide by every detail of this information. To be sure, ETS is not likely to spring a whole new test or new question type on students (that is inconceivable), but it is not out of the realm of possibility that they could make some last minute adjustments in the test format. For example, it is just conceivable that ETS could add two Verbal questions to a section, bringing the total number of questions to forty. If you make it a practice to preview the section before you begin work, you cannot be caught out by any such adjustments in the test.

Timing. A second very important point, which should be always on your mind, is the critical nature of timing. Remember the computer which grades your paper has no mechanism for judging the depth of your thought. It gives the same credit for a lucky guess as it gives for a well-thought-out answer, and it gives the same credit for a tentative "I'm not sure about this" answer as it gives for a firm "This has to be it" answer. So your entire effort must be aimed at maximizing the *total number of correct answers*—without regard to incorrect answers and without regard to the amount of thought which went into finding the answer.

To make this clear, let us compare the performances of two hypothetical students. One student is a very meticulous thinker. He attacks the Analytical Reasoning section in a very careful manner, checking his work. At the end of the thirty minutes, he has answered only eighteen questions, but he has gotten fifteen of those correct—missing only three. Another student works more quickly—not that he is careless; it is just that he knows the importance of the time limit—and attempts to answer all twenty-five of the questions. Some of them he sees immediately, so he does not bother to recheck his work. Others he can see would take a long time to solve, so he makes his best guess. On still others, he was able to limit his choice to two of the five possibilities, and once he reached that point he knew it would be a bad investment of his time to keep working toward a certainty which he knew might never materialize. Our second student answered twenty-five questions, but he missed eight questions, giving him a total of seventeen questions answered correctly. Now, at first glance it might seem that our careful student is the better student, and under different circumstances (in the real world) that may be so. But on the GRE, our second student is the better performer—by a total of two questions, seventeen correct as compared with only fifteen correct. This demonstrates the importance of careful attention to the time limit. To guide you in learning how quickly you must work, keep the following points in mind:

1. Do not spend too much time on any one problem. Remember, each question on the test counts the same; the difficult questions are not extra-credit questions. It just does not pay to spend extra time answering a hard question when there may be some easy questions left for you to answer.

2. Do not look for certainty. There will be many times when you have eliminated all but two answers. At that point you will probably want to work some more on the problem, thinking to yourself, "If I give this another minute or so, I will definitely figure it out." *This is a mistake*. If you use that minute in answering another problem (taking your chances with a fifty-fifty guess on the first one), you will be better off in the long run than if you try answering only one problem with certainty.

3. Do not try to be "super" accurate. While it is true that the GRE places a premium on careful reading and attention to detail, you must still work quickly. Rest assured that there are no cheap tricks, such as words written in invisible ink, that you have to find. Try for comprehension, but learn to do it quickly.

4. Finally, there is obviously some trade-off between accuracy and speed, and the optimal point will vary from individual to individual. The best thing to do in preparing for this test is to work to find that point for yourself—remembering that it is the number of correct answers, not the accuracy rate, which determines the GRE scores.

Guessing. The third point of general strategy is: when in doubt, GUESS—and this rule applies equally to problems you did not have time to do. The scoring mechanism of the GRE differs from other standardized tests you may have taken in that it does not penalize you for an incorrect answer. Obviously, since there is no penalty for a guess, and since there is a chance that you will happen across the correct answer, you should always enter an answer for every question.

Answer sheets. Finally, it goes without saying that you must be attentive to the mechanics of the testing process; specifically, you must be careful in your management of your answer sheet. As obvious as this is, some students will make a coding error in completing the answer sheet, e.g., putting the answer intended for question twenty-four in the slot for the answer to question twenty-five. Interestingly enough, this kind of mistake seems to be randomly distributed across the scoring range—that is, the very best students seem just as likely to make this kind of error as their colleagues who did not score as well. In order to avoid making this error, we suggest:

1. Keep a separate record of answers in the test booklet (yes, you may write in the test booklet). You get no credit for marks made in the test booklet (only for those answers coded on the answer sheet), but circling the answer you believe to be correct and placing a question mark by those you intend to come back to will provide you with a separate record of your choices. Should you then discover that you have made an error in coding answers, you can retrieve the information more easily.

2. Code answers in blocks. Rather than coding answers one-by-one (which requires needless paper shuffling), work a group of problems, say four or five, without coding answers (keeping your independent record in the test booklet). Then, when you find a convenient breaking point, e.g., turning a page, take that opportunity to record those answers. Coding in blocks will minimize the danger of a coding error, and it will also save time. Obviously, it is important to watch the time. Make absolutely certain that the proctor does not call time before you have had the opportunity to record answers. It may be a good idea, as time draws to a close, to record answers one by one. In any event, you should practice this technique at home before attempting to use it on the actual GRE.

HOW TO RECOGNIZE AND REDUCE TEST ANXIETY

HOW TO USE THIS CHAPTER

This chapter will help you to recognize, minimize, and control test anxiety while you prepare for and take the GRE.

Many students are tense and anxious about the GRE. Indeed, you need a certain amount of adrenaline flowing in order to do your best on the exam. However, too much tension can be a serious problem for some students. Overanxious students are often unable to think clearly, read quickly and precisely, or remember accurately during the exam. Needless to say, their scores suffer.

This chapter provides a step-by-step program for discovering and addressing these problems. Even if you do not have a severe overanxiety problem, you will probably benefit from following the guidelines contained in this chapter. We will first discuss the nature and sources of anxiety. Then we will analyze the elements of anxiety and give you some hints on how to reduce these problems during your preparation for the test. This is followed by some specific hints on how to recognize and control tension during the test itself.

WHAT IS ANXIETY AND WHERE DOES IT COME FROM?

One definition of anxiety calls it a state of "uncertainty, agitation or dread, and brooding fear." This pretty well describes the feelings of all too many test-takers. Anxious students may find themselves sweating, trembling, or gripped with muscle tension, racing hearts, and pounding pulses.

One critical fact about anxiety that most students don't know or ignore is that it is not solely a phenomenon of the testing room. The seeds of anxiety are sown long before the test and some of the best weeding-out of anxiety can also be done before the test—as part of your preparation for the GRE.

CONTROLLING ANXIETY BEFORE THE TEST

Let's take each part of the definition of anxiety and see how you can control and minimize it.

UNCERTAINTY: Standardized tests such as the GRE ask the test-taker to be definite and precise. While speed is not the major problem on the GRE, most of the problems have to be done fairly quickly.

The best way to combat uncertainty on the GRE is to focus your study time on issue recognition, which is one major skill required by graduate students and asked for by the test. Many students study problem explanations simply to see if they can follow along with the explanation. Certainly that is required, but it is just as important to look for the clues in the question or the passage which tell you that a certain approach or issue is important in this particular problem. This book tries to help you to do that in the discussions of the basic problem types and in the answer explanations. For Analytical Reasoning problems, for instance, you will learn how to tell map problems from names and occupations problems, and in knowing what the problem type is you will know how it should be approached.

But there is another, deeper level of uncertainty with which you must cope. When you first read a problem, there will ALWAYS be a moment of ignorance when you don't know what to do. Sometimes the moment is very short, and other times noticeably long. Many anxious students feel this moment of ignorance and become convinced that they can never do the problem. If they take too long to talk themselves out of this defeatist attitude, they lose valuable time.

Let's do an experiment. What is 2 + 2?

"Four," you said to yourself so rapidly it seemed instantaneous.

What is 19 + 19?

For most people this takes a little longer than 2 + 2. However, you have little doubt that you can do the addition so you get right to work and in a few seconds you have the answer. The fact that there was a moment of ignorance when you were asked to add 19 + 19 was absolutely no indication that you could not do it. All it meant was that you had to work it out rather than pull it directly from memory like 2 + 2.

GRE problems are more complicated than 19 + 19, but the same principle applies—JUST BECAUSE THE ANSWER OR APPROACH DOESN'T COME IMMEDIATELY TO MIND HAS PRACTICALLY NOTHING TO DO WITH WHETHER YOU CAN GET THE ANSWER OR NOT.

The antidote to uncertainty has three parts:

1. Carefully studying the instructions and different types of problems so that you can recognize what they require for solution. This should take the form of outlined notes and memorized attack strategies and problem recognition clues.

2. Becoming tolerant of your moment of ignorance.

3. Learning that perfection is not the goal. The GRE scoring system was explained earlier in this book. It is expected that everyone will miss some questions, and a very respectable score may well be the result of a situation where you are certain of fewer than half the questions. If you do not remember this clearly, reread that section of the chapter describing the GRE.

AGITATION: This is essentially the physical part of the anxiety syndrome—the muscle tension, trembling hands, sweaty palms or brows, pounding pulse, and shortness of breath. Few students experience all of these symptoms, but the significance of these physical symptoms is that they will let you know that you are overanxious and that it is time to do something about it.

Agitation is rarely severe, even on the day of the test. The most common part of the agitation syndrome is muscle tension, usually in the neck, shoulders, arms, or lower back. Such tensions can tire you out and distract you from the task at hand—scoring your best on the test.

In your study sessions prior to the GRE the best way to reduce tensions is to always be totally relaxed before and during your study sessions. The simplest and most direct way to relax is to follow these steps:

1. Sit in a comfortable chair (your study chair should be comfortable) in a reasonably undisturbed location.

2. Close your eyes, roll your head and shoulders, and take a deep breath—letting it out slowly.

3. Starting with your toes, tense each muscle in your body slowly and then relax it—along with its tension—in a slow rhythm.

4. Once you have relaxed your body just float there for a minute or two, breathing slowly but deeply.

It is also a good idea to do a relaxation exercise at the end of your study session. If you have had successful experiences with other methods of relaxation, you can certainly use them either in addition to or in place of the ones described here. However, a method which is not focused on relaxation so much as some other object such as on a mantra, a center, etc., is not as likely to be helpful in this particular context.

Using this technique regularly will help you to apply the following anxiety-reducing technique for your use during the test.

DREAD AND BROODING FEAR: While this is much more extreme than most students will ever feel, fear of the test is usually the result of a lack of confidence, from whatever source. If you have previously had bad experiences with tests, you should remind yourself each time you study for this test that you are better prepared this time.

Another trick that some students play on themselves is to always focus on their difficulties with a problem and their errors. Although it is true that studying your errors can help you to correct them, it is also true that you should always keep in mind the things you are doing right. Many times you can be making life tough for yourself by using the wrong standard to measure your performance. Perfection is not, as was previously mentioned, the proper reference point.

As the song says, "Accentuate the positive."

CONTROLLING ANXIETY DURING THE TEST

Your main job during the test is to answer questions. Sometimes, you may be a little over-anxious. If you are, it can be helpful to recognize the signs of overanxiety and take action to relieve the anxiety during the test so that it doesn't become a problem. There are three signs of overanxiety during the test and three ways of relieving it.

Recognizing Overanxiety

1. As previously noted, the most common sign of anxiety is muscle tension. While you can expect to be a little stiff from sitting in a chair for several hours, you will notice excess tension if it is present.
2. If you find yourself reading and rereading sentences or questions without really grasping what you have read, this is the result of overanxiety and not your inability to read the material on the test.
3. Assuming that you have not been so foolish as to have been up late partying the night before the test, any sleepiness that you might feel is the result of anxiety and not fatigue.

Reducing Overanxiety

If you find that you might be becoming a little overanxious, you can do the following things:

1. Remember that you are well prepared. You know a lot about all the types of problems and you CAN work on them.
2. Reduce the tension by moving your muscles. Stretch, rotate, shake your arms. Be sure to get up and move during the break in the test. Don't worry how it looks, just do it.
3. Do a relaxation exercise. You shouldn't take the time during the test to do a full-dress exercise, but you can do a shorter version which can be very effective.
—Take a deep breath and hold it for just one second.
—Close your eyes, blank your mind, and let out the breath while you relax your upper body (without falling off your chair).

The whole thing should take only four or five seconds. Don't take any longer. If you keep it short, you can do it as often as you need to, even after every question if you need to. You should practice this exercise before the day of the test.

AN OUNCE OF PREVENTION

When you are at the test you may be near someone who is very nervous. Don't talk about the test. Similarly, you should not talk about the test during the break. Use the break to stretch, drink, go to the bathroom, and relax. If you want to calmly review your guidelines for a section which has not yet appeared, that is fine. Just don't give anyone else an opportunity to make themselves feel good by telling you what they think you have done wrong.

PART TWO

REVIEW OF GRE QUESTION TYPES

GENERAL HINTS FOR THE GRE MATHEMATICS SECTIONS

There are many specific hints in the Mathematics Review about the shortest and best approaches to specific types of problems that you will see on the GRE. The answer explanations to the mathematical questions in the five practive GRE tests also contain many hints. You should read the explanations even if you got the problem right, since there are often alternative solutions which take less time or are more accurate or both.

The following hints focus on some of the most common errors that students make in approaching the Mathematics sections of the GRE. Read them carefully and try to follow them conscientiously throughout your preparation and, of course, on the test itself. Although some are very simple, they can all be very helpful.

Do not compute most of the time. Quantitative Comparison problems can be done with little or no computation or algebraic manipulation. Even the regular mathematics format questions require less computation than most students make. The Educational Testing Service consciously designs the GRE to have relatively little computation on it. The numbers almost always come out neatly and evenly, with perhaps the occasional square root (which should almost never be computed as a number, but left as a square root). They assume, rightly or wrongly, that you know how to compute with numbers by now, so that is not the point of any of the GRE mathematics questions.

Estimate on Chart Questions. You will probably have a few chart questions. Research indicates that students who feel uncomfortable with math tend to skip chart questions, or only give them a minimum effort. You should do the chart questions whenever you can because they have no mathematics in them beyond simple arithmetic. Again, do not compute, but estimate.

Focus on what you need to answer the question. This sounds so obvious that you may wonder why we mention it at all. When having trouble with a problem, most people go over and over the given information, hoping for a spark to light the way. Sometimes it does, of course, but often it doesn't—and it becomes a waste of time.

On some problems you will just see what is going on right away. But on the ones where you don't, work backward from the real question. For example, if a percentage is asked for, think: "In order to get to a percentage, I need a number and a base. Where are they?"

In some questions the needed information is just lying around waiting to be picked up, but in longer, more difficult questions you will sometimes find that you have to figure out one of the items needed for the final solution of the problem. For example, in the above percentage problem, you might find that the base is given, but you need to find the number of whatever it is by using another percentage and another base.

Illustration: There are 150 boys and 250 girls in a school. If two-thirds of the boys are ten years old or older, what percentage of the total students are boys under ten years old?

SOLUTION: 1. To get the percentage of boys under ten years old, you need:

$$\frac{\text{number of boys under ten years old}}{\text{total student body}} = \% \text{ boys under ten.}$$

2. To find total student body, you add boys and girls: $150 + 250 = 400$.

3. To find the number of boys under ten, you have to link this to the given information, which is in terms of total boys and boys TEN AND OVER, thus: boys under ten = total boys − boys ten and over. But you don't know the number of boys ten and over. You have to figure that out.

4. Number of boys ten and over = % or proportion of boys over ten × number total boys, which is $(\frac{2}{3})(150) = 100$.

5. Boys under ten = $150 - 100 = 50$

6. % boys under ten of total school = $\frac{50}{400} = \frac{1}{8} = 12\frac{1}{2}\%$.

Answer: $12\frac{1}{2}\%$.

An alternative to steps 4 and 5 would be to note that if $\frac{2}{3}$ of the boys are ten and over, $\frac{1}{3}$ are under ten and $(\frac{1}{3})(150) = 50$.

The major virtues of this approach are (a) that it will actually get you the correct answer quickly and (b) that it will prevent you from pulling numbers out of the air—getting the problem wrong even when you know perfectly well how to calculate a percentage.

Don't skip geometry. As with chart questions, research indicates that many students simply give up on geometry problems that they could solve using their years of experience with the real world of shapes and objects. You do need to know a few formulas, but the questions are primarily testing your ability to see the connections between different parts of the problem. Again, some backward thinking might be helpful. If asked the area of a triangle, there is one, and only one, formula—height times base divided by two = area. So, go look for the base and the height.

Also, in Quantitative Comparison format geometry problems, look for points, lines and angles that are not tied down, that move or stretch within the given information. This might show you that no definite answer is possible (Answer D) or, conversely, lead you to another answer by seeing the limits of the movement.

On Quantitative Comparison problems watch exponents: Whenever you see an exponent, especially on Quantitative Comparison questions, check to see the effects of having the base be a negative number or a fraction. See the Powers and Roots section of the Mathematics Review for more on this key issue. Several problems will turn on these issues.

General Hints for the GRE Quantitative Sections

The Quantitative sections of the GRE have two forms of math questions—Quantitative Comparison and General Mathematics—combined in each section. The Quantitative Comparison problems will come first and are *not* differentiated as Part A, with the other math questions as Part B.

The recommended timing allowances are:

OPTIMUM TIME ALLOWANCES BY QUESTION TYPE FOR GRE QUANTITATIVE SECTIONS

Order in Section	Question Type	No. of Questions	Time Allowance
First	Quantitative Comparison	15	10 minutes
Second	General Mathematics	15	20 minutes

Total Section 30 Questions 30 Minutes

Students find Quantitative Comparison questions easier than General Mathematics questions. One of the reasons the Quantitative Comparison Questions seem easier is that they are shorter. In order to make the best use of your time, you must allow enough time for the General Mathematics questions. If you spend all of your time on the Quantitative Comparison problems, you may not have enough time for even the easier General Mathematics problems.

MATHEMATICS REVIEW FOR THE GRE

In order to solve a mathematical problem, it is essential to know the mathematical meaning of the words used. There are many expressions having the same meaning in mathematics. These expressions may indicate a relationship between quantities or an operation (addition, subtraction, multiplication, division) to be performed. This chapter will help you to recognize some of the mathematical synonyms commonly found in word problems.

Equality

The following expressions all indicate that two quantities are equal (=):

> is equal to
> is the same as
> the result is
> yields
> gives

Also, the word "is" is often used to mean "equals," as in "8 *is* 5 more than 3," which translates to "8 = 5 + 3".

Addition

The following expressions all indicate that the numbers A and B are to be added:

A + B	**2 + 3**
the sum of A and B	the sum of 2 and 3
the total of A and B	the total of 2 and 3
A added to B	2 added to 3
A increased by B	2 increased by 3
A more than B	2 more than 3
A greater than B	2 greater than 3

Subtraction

The following expressions all indicate that the number B is to be subtracted from the number A:

A − B	**10 − 3**
A minus B	10 minus 3
A less B	10 less 3
the difference of A and B	the difference of 10 and 3
from A subtract B	from 10 subtract 3
A take away B	10 take away 3
A decreased by B	10 decreased by 3
A diminished by B	10 diminished by 3
B is subtracted from A	3 is subtracted from 10
B less than A	3 less than 10

Multiplication

If the numbers A and B are to be multiplied (A × B), the following expressions may be used.

A × B	**2 × 3**
A multiplied by B	2 multiplied by 3
the product of A and B	the product of 2 and 3

The parts of a multiplication problem are indicated in the example below:

$$
\begin{array}{r}
15 \quad \text{(multiplicand)} \\
\times\ 10 \quad \text{(multiplier)} \\
\hline
150 \quad \text{(product)}
\end{array}
$$

Other ways of indicating multiplication are:

Parentheses: A × B = (A)(B)
Dots: A × B = A · B
In algebra, letters next to each other: A × B = AB

A **coefficient** is a number that shows how many times to multiply a variable, such as in 3B, where 3 is the coefficient.

Inequalities

When two numbers are not necessarily equal to each other, this idea can be expressed by using the "greater than" symbol ($>$) or the "less than" symbol ($<$). The wider part of the wedge is always towards the greater number.

A is greater than B	A is less than B
$A > B$	$A < B$
A is greater than or equal to B	A is less than or equal to B
$A \geq B$	$A \leq B$

An **integer** can be defined informally as a whole number, either positive or negative, including zero, e.g., $+5$, -10, 0, $+30$, -62, etc.

A **prime number** can be defined informally as a whole number (positive only) that is evenly divisible only by itself and 1, e.g., 1, 2, 3, 5, 7, 11, 13, 17, 19, etc.

Division

Division of the numbers A and B (in the order $A \div B$) may be indicated in the following ways. (See also the discussion of fractions.)

$A \div B$	$14 \div 2$
A divided by B	14 divided by 2
the quotient of A and B	the quotient of 14 and 2

The parts of a division problem are indicated in the example below:

$$
\text{(divisor)} \quad 7\,\overline{)\,36\,} \quad \begin{matrix} 5\frac{1}{7} & \text{(quotient)} \\ & \text{(dividend)} \end{matrix}
$$
$$
\begin{matrix} \underline{35} \\ 1 \end{matrix} \quad \text{(remainder)}
$$

Factors and Divisors

The relationship $A \times B = C$, for any whole numbers A, B, and C, may be expressed as:

$A \times B = C$	$2 \times 3 = 6$
A and B are factors of C	2 and 3 are factors of 6
A and B are divisors of C	2 and 3 are divisors of 6
C is divisible by A and by B	6 is divisible by 2 and by 3
C is a multiple of A and of B	6 is a multiple of 2 and of 3

Symbols

Common symbols used on the exam are*:

$\neq$	is not equal to
$>$	is greater than ($3 > 2$)
$<$	is less than ($2 < 3$)
$\geq$	is greater than or equal to
$\leq$	is less than or equal to
: and ::	is to; the ratio to (see also section on ratios)
$\sqrt{}$	radical sign—used without a number, it indicates the square root of ($\sqrt{9} = 3$) or with an index above the sign to indicate the root to be taken if the root is not a square root ($\sqrt[3]{8} = 2$) (see also section on powers and roots).
$|x|$	absolute value of (in this case x) (see section on basic properties of numbers, item 6).

BASIC PROPERTIES OF NUMBERS

1. A number greater than zero is called a **positive number.**

2. A number smaller than zero is called a **negative number.**

3. When a negative number is added to another number, this is the same as subtracting the equivalent positive number.

   Example: $2 + (-1) = 2 - 1 = 1$

4. When two numbers of the same sign are multiplied together, the result is a positive number.

   Example: $2 \times 2 = 4$

   Example: $(-2)(-3) = +6$

*Geometric symbols are reviewed in the section on geometry.

5. When two numbers of different signs are multipled together, the result is a negative number.

    Example: $(+5)(-10) = -50$

    Example: $(-6)(+8) = -48$

6. The **absolute value** of a number is the equivalent positive value.

    Example: $|+2| = +2$

    Example: $|-3| = +3$

7. An even number is an integer that is divisible evenly by two. Zero would be considered an even number for practical purposes.

8. An odd number is an integer that is not an even number.

9. An even number times any integer will yield an even number.

10. An odd number times an odd number will yield an odd number.

11. Two even numbers or two odd numbers added together will yield an even number.

12. An odd number added to an even number will yield an odd number.

FRACTIONS

Fractions and Mixed Numbers

1. A **fraction** is part of a unit.

    a. A fraction has a **numerator** and a **denominator.**

    Example: In the fraction $\frac{3}{4}$, 3 is the numerator and 4 is the denominator.

    b. In any fraction, the numerator is being divided by the denominator.

    Example: The fraction $\frac{2}{7}$ indicates that 2 is being divided by 7.

    c. In a fraction problem, the whole quantity is 1, which may be expressed by a fraction in which the numerator and denominator are the same number.

    Example: If the problem involves $\frac{1}{8}$ of a quantity, then the whole quantity is $\frac{8}{8}$, or 1.

2. A **mixed number** is an integer together with a fraction such as $2\frac{3}{5}$, $7\frac{3}{8}$, etc. The integer is the integral part, and the fraction is the fractional part.

3. An **improper fraction** is one in which the numerator is equal to or greater than the denominator, such as $\frac{19}{6}$, $\frac{25}{4}$, or $\frac{10}{10}$.

4. To change a mixed number to an improper fraction:

    a. Multiply the denominator of the fraction by the integer.

    b. Add the numerator to this product.

    c. Place this sum over the denominator of the fraction.

    Illustration: Change $3\frac{4}{7}$ to an improper fraction.

    SOLUTION: $7 \times 3 = 21$
    $$21 + 4 = 25$$
    $$3\tfrac{4}{7} = \tfrac{25}{7}$$

    Answer: $\frac{25}{7}$

5. To change an improper fraction to a mixed number:

    a. Divide the numerator by the denominator. The quotient, disregarding the remainder, is the integral part of the mixed number.

    b. Place the remainder, if any, over the denominator. This is the fractional part of the mixed number.

    Illustration: Change $\frac{36}{13}$ to a mixed number.

    SOLUTION:
    $$13 \overline{)\ 36} \quad {}^{2}$$
    $$\underline{26}$$
    $$10 \quad \text{remainder}$$
    $$\tfrac{36}{13} = 2\tfrac{10}{13}$$

    Answer: $2\frac{10}{13}$

6. The numerator and denominator of a fraction may be changed, without affecting the

value of the fraction, by multiplying both by the same number.

Example: The value of the fraction $\frac{2}{5}$ will not be altered if the numerator and the denominator are multiplied by 2, to result in $\frac{4}{10}$.

7. The numerator and the denominator of a fraction may be changed, without affecting the value of the fraction, by dividing both by the same number. This process is called **reducing the fraction.** A fraction that has been reduced as much as possible is said to be in **lowest terms.**

Example: The value of the fraction $\frac{3}{12}$ will not be altered if the numerator and denominator are divided by 3, to result in $\frac{1}{4}$.

Example: If $\frac{6}{30}$ is reduced to lowest terms (by dividing both numerator and denominator by 6), the result is $\frac{1}{5}$.

8. As a final answer to an exam question, it may be necessary to:
   a. reduce a fraction to lowest terms
   b. convert an improper fraction to a mixed number
   c. convert a mixed number to an improper fraction

Addition of Fractions

9. **Fractions cannot be added unless the denominators are all the same.**
   a. If the denominators are the same, add all the numerators and place this sum over the common denominator. In the case of mixed numbers, follow the above rule for the fractions and then add the integers.
   Example: The sum of $2\frac{3}{8} + 3\frac{1}{8} + \frac{3}{8} = 5\frac{7}{8}$.
   b. If the denominators are not the same, the fractions, in order to be added, must be converted to ones having the same denominator. The lowest common denominator is often the most convenient common denominator to find, but any common denominator will work. You can cancel out the extra numbers after the addition.

10. The **lowest common denominator** (henceforth called the L.C.D.) is the lowest num-

ber that can be divided evenly by all the given denominators. If no two of the given denominators can be divided by the same number, then the L.C.D. is the product of all the denominators.

Example: The L.C.D. of $\frac{1}{2}$, $\frac{1}{3}$, and $\frac{1}{5}$ is $2 \times 3 \times 5 = 30$.

11. To find the L.C.D. when two or more of the given denominators can be divided by the same number:
   a. Write down the denominators, leaving plenty of space between the numbers.
   b. Select the smallest number (other than 1) by which one or more of the denominators can be divided evenly.
   c. Divide the denominators by this number, copying down those that cannot be divided evenly. Place this number to one side.
   d. Repeat this process, placing each divisor to one side until there are no longer any denominators that can be divided evenly by any selected number.
   e. Multiply all the divisors to find the L.C.D.

Illustration: Find the L.C.D. of $\frac{1}{5}$, $\frac{1}{7}$, $\frac{1}{10}$, and $\frac{1}{14}$.

SOLUTION:

2) 5	7	10	14
5) 5	7	5	7
7) 1	7	1	7
1	1	1	1

$7 \times 5 \times 2 = 70$

Answer: The L.C.D. is 70.

12. To add fractions having different denominators:
   a. Find the L.C.D. of the denominators.
   b. Change each fraction to an equivalent fraction having the L.C.D. as its denominator.
   c. When all of the fractions have the same denominator, they may be added, as in the example following item 9a.

Illustration: Add $\frac{1}{4}$, $\frac{3}{10}$, and $\frac{2}{5}$.

SOLUTION: Find the L.C.D.:

$$2\ )\ \underline{4 \quad\quad 10 \quad\quad 5}$$
$$2\ )\ \underline{2 \quad\quad 5 \quad\quad 5}$$
$$5\ )\ \underline{1 \quad\quad 5 \quad\quad 5}$$
$$1 \quad\quad 1 \quad\quad 1$$

L.C.D. $= 2 \times 2 \times 5 = 20$

$$\frac{1}{4} = \quad \frac{5}{20}$$
$$\frac{3}{10} = \quad \frac{6}{20}$$
$$+\ \frac{2}{5} = +\ \frac{8}{20}$$
$$\frac{19}{20}$$

Answer: $\frac{19}{20}$

13. To add mixed numbers in which the fractions have different denominators, add the fractions by following the rules in item 12 above, then add the integers.

Illustration: Add $2\frac{5}{7}$, $5\frac{1}{2}$, and 8.

SOLUTION: L.C.D. $= 14$
$$2\frac{5}{7} = \quad 2\frac{10}{14}$$
$$5\frac{1}{2} = \quad 5\frac{7}{14}$$
$$+\ 8 = +\ 8$$
$$15\frac{17}{14} = 16\frac{3}{14}$$

Answer: $16\frac{3}{14}$

Subtraction of Fractions

14. a. Unlike addition, which may involve adding more than two numbers at the same time, subtraction involves only two numbers.

   b. In subtraction, as in addition, the denominators must be the same.

15. To subtract fractions:

   a. Find the L.C.D.

   b. Change both fractions so that each has the L.C.D. as the denominator.

   c. Subtract the numerator of the second fraction from the numerator of the first, and place this difference over the L.C.D.

   d. Reduce, if possible.

Illustration: Find the difference of $\frac{5}{8}$ and $\frac{1}{4}$.

SOLUTION: L.C.D. $= 8$
$$\frac{5}{8} = \quad \frac{5}{8}$$
$$-\ \frac{1}{4} = -\ \frac{2}{8}$$
$$\frac{3}{8}$$

Answer: $\frac{3}{8}$

16. To subtract mixed numbers:

   a. It may be necessary to "borrow," so that the fractional part of the first term is larger than the fractional part of the second term.

   b. Subtract the fractional parts of the mixed numbers and reduce.

   c. Subtract the integers.

Illustration: Subtract $16\frac{4}{5}$ from $29\frac{1}{3}$.

SOLUTION: L.C.D. $= 15$
$$29\frac{1}{3} = \quad 29\frac{5}{15}$$
$$-\ 16\frac{4}{5} = -\ 16\frac{12}{15}$$

Note that $\frac{5}{15}$ is less than $\frac{12}{15}$. Borrow 1 from 29, and change to $\frac{15}{15}$.

$$29\frac{5}{15} = \quad 28\frac{20}{15}$$
$$-\ 16\frac{12}{15} = -\ 16\frac{12}{15}$$
$$12\frac{8}{15}$$

Answer: $12\frac{8}{15}$

Multiplication of Fractions

17. a. To be multiplied, fractions need not have the same denominators.

   b. A whole number can be thought of as having a denominator of 1: $3 = \frac{3}{1}$.

18. To multiply fractions:

   a. Change the mixed numbers, if any, to improper fractions.

   b. Multiply all the numerators, and place this product over the product of the denominators.

   c. Reduce, if possible.

Illustration: Multiply $\frac{2}{3} \times 2\frac{4}{7} \times \frac{5}{9}$.

SOLUTION:
$$2\frac{4}{7} = \frac{18}{7}$$
$$\frac{2}{3} \times \frac{18}{7} \times \frac{5}{9} = \frac{180}{189}$$
$$= \frac{20}{21}$$

Answer: $\frac{20}{21}$

19. a. **Cancellation** is a device to facilitate multiplication. To cancel means to divide a numerator and a denominator by the same number in a multiplication problem.

Example: In the problem $\frac{4}{7} \times \frac{5}{6}$, the numerator 4 and the denominator 6 may be divided by 2.

$$\frac{\overset{2}{4}}{7} \times \frac{5}{\underset{3}{6}} = \frac{10}{21}$$

b. With fractions (and percentages), the word "of" is often used to mean "multiply."

Example: $\frac{1}{2}$ of $\frac{1}{2} = \frac{1}{2} \times \frac{1}{2} = \frac{1}{4}$

20. To multiply a whole number by a mixed number:

a. Multiply the whole number by the fractional part of the mixed number.

b. Multiply the whole number by the integral part of the mixed number.

c. Add both products.

Illustration: Multiply $23\frac{3}{4}$ by 95.

SOLUTION:
$$\frac{95}{1} \times \frac{3}{4} = \frac{285}{4}$$
$$= 71\frac{1}{4}$$
$$95 \times 23 = 2185$$
$$2185 + 71\frac{1}{4} = 2256\frac{1}{4}$$

Answer: $2256\frac{1}{4}$

Division of Fractions

21. The **reciprocal** of a fraction is that fraction inverted.

a. When a fraction is inverted, the numerator becomes the denominator and the denominator becomes the numerator.

Example: The reciprocal of $\frac{3}{8}$ is $\frac{8}{3}$.

Example: The reciprocal of $\frac{1}{3}$ is $\frac{3}{1}$, or simply 3.

b. Since every whole number has the denominator 1 understood, the reciprocal of a whole number is a fraction having 1 as the numerator and the number itself as the denominator.

Example: The reciprocal of 5 (expressed fractionally as $\frac{5}{1}$) is $\frac{1}{5}$.

22. To divide fractions:

a. Change all the mixed numbers, if any, to improper fractions.

b. Invert the second fraction and multiply.

c. Reduce, if possible.

Illustration: Divide $\frac{2}{3}$ by $2\frac{1}{4}$.

SOLUTION:
$$2\frac{1}{4} = \frac{9}{4}$$
$$\frac{2}{3} \div \frac{9}{4} = \frac{2}{3} \times \frac{4}{9}$$
$$= \frac{8}{27}$$

Answer: $\frac{8}{27}$

23. A **complex fraction** is one that has a fraction as the numerator, or as the denominator, or as both.

Example: $\dfrac{\frac{2}{3}}{5}$ is a complex fraction.

24. To clear (simplify) a complex fraction:

a. Divide the numerator by the denominator.

b. Reduce, if possible.

Illustration: Clear $\dfrac{\frac{3}{7}}{\frac{5}{14}}$.

SOLUTION:
$$\frac{3}{7} \div \frac{5}{14} = \frac{3}{7} \times \frac{14}{5} = \frac{42}{35}$$
$$= \frac{6}{5}$$
$$= 1\frac{1}{5}$$

Answer: $1\frac{1}{5}$

Comparing Fractions

25. If two fractions have the same denominator, the one having the larger numerator is the greater fraction.

Example: $\frac{3}{7}$ is greater than $\frac{2}{7}$.

26. If two fractions have the same numerator, the one having the larger denominator is the smaller fraction.

Example: $\frac{5}{12}$ is smaller than $\frac{5}{11}$.

27. To compare two fractions having different numerators and different denominators:

    a. Change the fractions to equivalent fractions having their L.C.D. as their new denominator.

    b. Compare, as in the example following item 25, for the largest denominator.

    Illustration: Compare $\frac{4}{7}$ and $\frac{5}{8}$.

    SOLUTION: L.C.D. $= 7 \times 8 = 56$
    $$\frac{4}{7} = \frac{32}{56}$$
    $$\frac{5}{8} = \frac{35}{56}$$

    Answer: Since $\frac{35}{56}$ is larger than $\frac{32}{56}$, $\frac{5}{8}$ is larger than $\frac{4}{7}$.

    Note: Actually, any common denominator will work, not only the L.C.D.

28. To compare two fractions, multiply the denominators of the left fraction by the numerator of the right fraction and write the result above the right fraction. Then multiply the denominator of the right fraction by the numerator of the left fraction and write the result over the left fraction. If the number over the left fraction is larger than the number over the right fraction, the left fraction is larger. If the number over the right fraction is larger, the right fraction is larger. If the numbers over the two fractions are equal, the fractions are equal.

    Illustration: Compare $\frac{5}{7}$ and $\frac{3}{4}$.

    SOLUTION: $\overset{20}{}\ \overset{21}{}$
    $$\frac{5}{7} \underset{}{\times} \frac{3}{4}$$
    $$4 \times 5 = 20$$
    $$3 \times 7 = 21$$
    $$20 < 21$$

    Answer: $\frac{5}{7} < \frac{3}{4}$. This method will only determine which fraction is larger. It cannot be used to tell you the size of the difference.

Fraction Problems

29. Most fraction problems can be arranged in the form: "What fraction of a number is another number?" This form contains three important parts:

    • The fractional part
    • The number following "of"
    • The number following "is"

    a. If the fraction and the "of" number are given; multiply them to find the "is" number.

    Illustration: What is $\frac{3}{4}$ of 20?

    SOLUTION: Write the question as "$\frac{3}{4}$ of 20 is what number?" Then multiply the fraction $\frac{3}{4}$ by the "of" number, 20:

    $$\frac{3}{4} \times \overset{5}{\underset{1}{20}} = 15$$

    Answer: 15

    b. If the fractional part and the "is" number are given, divide the "is" number by the fraction to find the "of" number.

    Illustration: $\frac{4}{5}$ of what number is 40?

    SOLUTION: To find the "of" number, divide 40 by $\frac{4}{5}$:

    $$40 \div \frac{4}{5} = \overset{10}{\underset{1}{\frac{40}{1}}} \times \frac{5}{4}$$
    $$= 50$$

    Answer: 50

    c. To find the fractional part when the other two numbers are known, divide the "is" number by the "of" number.

    Illustration: What part of 12 is 9?

    SOLUTION: $9 \div 12 = \frac{9}{12}$
    $$= \frac{3}{4}$$

    Answer: $\frac{3}{4}$

Practice Problems Involving Fractions

1. Reduce to lowest terms: $\frac{60}{108}$.
   (A) $\frac{1}{48}$
   (B) $\frac{1}{3}$
   (C) $\frac{5}{9}$
   (D) $\frac{10}{18}$
   (E) $\frac{15}{59}$

2. Change $\frac{27}{7}$ to a mixed number.
   (A) $2\frac{1}{7}$
   (B) $3\frac{6}{7}$
   (C) $6\frac{1}{3}$

(D) $7\frac{1}{2}$

(E) $8\frac{1}{7}$

3. Change $4\frac{2}{3}$ to an improper fraction.

   (A) $\frac{10}{3}$

   (B) $\frac{11}{3}$

   (C) $\frac{14}{3}$

   (D) $\frac{24}{3}$

   (E) $\frac{42}{3}$

4. Find the L.C.D. of $\frac{1}{6}$, $\frac{1}{10}$, $\frac{1}{18}$, and $\frac{1}{21}$.

   (A) 160

   (B) 330

   (C) 630

   (D) 890

   (E) 1260

5. Add $16\frac{3}{8}$, $4\frac{4}{5}$, $12\frac{3}{4}$, and $23\frac{5}{6}$.

   (A) $57\frac{91}{120}$

   (B) $57\frac{1}{4}$

   (C) 58

   (D) 59

   (E) $59\frac{91}{120}$

6. Subtract $27\frac{5}{14}$ from $43\frac{1}{6}$.

   (A) 15

   (B) $15\frac{5}{84}$

   (C) $15\frac{8}{21}$

   (D) $15\frac{15}{20}$

   (E) $15\frac{17}{21}$

7. Multiply $17\frac{5}{8}$ by 128.

   (A) 2256

   (B) 2305

   (C) 2356

   (D) 2368

   (E) 2394

8. Divide $1\frac{2}{3}$ by $1\frac{1}{9}$.

   (A) $\frac{2}{3}$

   (B) $1\frac{1}{2}$

   (C) $1\frac{23}{27}$

   (D) 4

   (E) 6

9. What is the value of $12\frac{1}{6} - 2\frac{3}{8} - 7\frac{2}{3} + 19\frac{3}{4}$?

   (A) 21

   (B) $21\frac{7}{8}$

   (C) $21\frac{1}{8}$

   (D) 22

   (E) $22\frac{7}{8}$

10. Simplify the complex fraction $\dfrac{\frac{4}{9}}{\frac{2}{5}}$.

    (A) $\frac{1}{2}$

    (B) $\frac{9}{10}$

    (C) $\frac{2}{5}$

    (D) 1

    (E) $1\frac{1}{9}$

11. Which fraction is largest?

    (A) $\frac{9}{16}$

    (B) $\frac{7}{10}$

    (C) $\frac{5}{8}$

    (D) $\frac{4}{5}$

    (E) $\frac{1}{2}$

12. One brass rod measures $3\frac{5}{16}$ inches long and another brass rod measures $2\frac{3}{4}$ inches long. Together their length is

    (A) $6\frac{9}{16}$ in.

    (B) $6\frac{1}{16}$ in.

    (C) $5\frac{1}{8}$ in.

    (D) $5\frac{1}{16}$ in.

    (E) $5\frac{1}{32}$ in.

13. The number of half-pound packages of tea that can be weighed out of a box that holds $10\frac{1}{2}$ lb. of tea is

    (A) 5

    (B) $10\frac{1}{2}$

    (C) 11

    (D) $20\frac{1}{2}$

    (E) 21

14. If each bag of tokens weighs $5\frac{3}{4}$ pounds, how many pounds do 3 bags weigh?

    (A) $7\frac{1}{4}$

    (B) $15\frac{3}{4}$

    (C) $16\frac{1}{2}$

    (D) $17\frac{1}{4}$

    (E) $17\frac{1}{2}$

15. During one week, a man traveled $3\frac{1}{2}$, $1\frac{1}{4}$, $1\frac{1}{6}$, and $2\frac{3}{8}$ miles. The next week he traveled $\frac{1}{4}$, $\frac{3}{8}$, $\frac{9}{16}$, $3\frac{1}{16}$, $2\frac{5}{8}$, and $3\frac{3}{16}$ miles. How many more miles did he travel the second week than the first week?

    (A) $1\frac{37}{48}$

    (B) $1\frac{1}{2}$

    (C) $1\frac{3}{4}$

    (D) 1

    (E) $\frac{47}{48}$

16. A certain type of board is sold only in lengths of multiples of 2 feet. The shortest board sold is 6 feet and the longest is 24 feet. A builder needs a large quantity of this type of board in $5\frac{1}{2}$-foot lengths. For minimum waste the lengths to be ordered should be
    (A) 6 ft
    (B) 12 ft
    (C) 22 ft
    (D) 24 ft
    (E) 26 ft

17. A man spent $\frac{15}{16}$ of his entire fortune in buying a car for $7500. How much money did he possess?
    (A) $6000
    (B) $6500
    (C) $7000
    (D) $8000
    (E) $8500

18. The population of a town was 54,000 in the last census. It has increased $\frac{2}{3}$ since then. Its present population is
    (A) 18,000
    (B) 36,000
    (C) 72,000
    (D) 90,000
    (E) 108,000

19. If $\frac{1}{3}$ of the liquid contents of a can evaporates on the first day and $\frac{3}{4}$ of the remainder evaporates on the second day, the fractional part of the original contents remaining at the close of the second day is
    (A) $\frac{5}{12}$
    (B) $\frac{7}{12}$
    (C) $\frac{1}{6}$
    (D) $\frac{1}{2}$
    (E) $\frac{4}{7}$

20. A car is run until the gas tank is $\frac{1}{8}$ full. The tank is then filled to capacity by putting in 14 gallons. The capacity of the gas tank of the car is
    (A) 14 gal
    (B) 15 gal
    (C) 16 gal
    (D) 17 gal
    (E) 18 gal

Fraction Problems—Correct Answers

1.	(C)	6.	(E)	11.	(D)	16.	(C)
2.	(B)	7.	(A)	12.	(B)	17.	(D)
3.	(C)	8.	(B)	13.	(E)	18.	(D)
4.	(C)	9.	(B)	14.	(D)	19.	(C)
5.	(A)	10.	(E)	15.	(A)	20.	(C)

Problem Solutions—Fractions

1. Divide the numerator and denominator by 12:

$$\frac{60 \div 12}{108 \div 12} = \frac{5}{9}$$

One alternate method (there are several) is to divide the numerator and denominator by 6 and then by 2:

$$\frac{60 \div 6}{108 \div 6} = \frac{10}{18}$$

$$\frac{10 \div 2}{18 \div 2} = \frac{5}{9}$$

Answer: **(C)** $\frac{5}{9}$

2. Divide the numerator (27) by the denominator (7):

$$\begin{array}{r} 3 \\ 7 \overline{)\, 27} \\ 21 \\ \hline 6 \quad \text{remainder} \end{array}$$

$\frac{27}{7} = 3\frac{6}{7}$

Answer: **(B)** $3\frac{6}{7}$

3.

$$4 \times 3 = 12$$
$$12 + 2 = 14$$
$$4\frac{2}{3} = \frac{14}{3}$$

Answer: **(C)** $\frac{14}{3}$

4.

$$2\ \underline{)\ 6 \quad 10 \quad 18 \quad 21} \quad \text{(2 is a divisor of 6, 10, and 18)}$$
$$3\ \underline{)\ 3 \quad 5 \quad 9 \quad 21} \quad \text{(3 is a divisor of 3, 9, and 21)}$$
$$3\ \underline{)\ 1 \quad 5 \quad 3 \quad 7} \quad \text{(3 is a divisor of 3)}$$
$$5\ \underline{)\ 1 \quad 5 \quad 1 \quad 7} \quad \text{(5 is a divisor of 5)}$$
$$7\ \underline{)\ 1 \quad 1 \quad 1 \quad 7} \quad \text{(7 is a divisor of 7)}$$
$$\quad\ \ 1 \quad 1 \quad 1 \quad 1$$

L.C.D. $= 2 \times 3 \times 3 \times 5 \times 7 = 630$

Answer: **(C)** 630

5. L.C.D. = 120

$$16\tfrac{3}{8} = \quad 16\tfrac{45}{120}$$
$$4\tfrac{4}{5} = \quad 4\tfrac{96}{120}$$
$$12\tfrac{3}{4} = \quad 12\tfrac{90}{120}$$
$$+\ 23\tfrac{5}{6} = +\ 23\tfrac{100}{120}$$
$$55\tfrac{331}{120} = 57\tfrac{91}{120}$$

Answer: **(A)** $57\tfrac{91}{120}$

6. L.C.D. = 42

$$43\tfrac{1}{6} = \quad 43\tfrac{7}{42} = \quad 42\tfrac{49}{42}$$
$$-\ 27\tfrac{5}{14} = -\ 27\tfrac{15}{42} = -\ 27\tfrac{15}{42}$$
$$15\tfrac{34}{42} = 15\tfrac{17}{21}$$

Answer: **(E)** $15\tfrac{17}{21}$

7.
$$17\tfrac{5}{8} = \tfrac{141}{8}$$
$$\tfrac{141}{8} \times \tfrac{\cancel{128}^{16}}{1} = 2256$$

Answer: **(A)** 2256

8.
$$1\tfrac{2}{3} \div 1\tfrac{1}{9} = \tfrac{5}{3} \div \tfrac{10}{9}$$
$$= \tfrac{\cancel{5}^{1}}{\cancel{3}^{1}} \times \tfrac{\cancel{9}^{3}}{\cancel{10}^{2}}$$
$$= \tfrac{3}{2}$$
$$= 1\tfrac{1}{2}$$

Answer: **(B)** $1\tfrac{1}{2}$

9. L.C.D. = 24

$$12\tfrac{1}{6} = \ 12\tfrac{4}{24} = \ 11\tfrac{28}{24}$$
$$-\ 2\tfrac{3}{8} = -\ 2\tfrac{9}{24} = -\ 2\tfrac{9}{24}$$
$$9\tfrac{19}{24} = \qquad 9\tfrac{19}{24}$$
$$-\ 7\tfrac{2}{3} = -\ 7\tfrac{16}{24}$$
$$2\tfrac{3}{24} = \qquad 2\tfrac{3}{24}$$
$$+19\tfrac{3}{4} = +19\tfrac{18}{24}$$
$$21\tfrac{21}{24}$$

$$21\tfrac{21}{24} = 21\tfrac{7}{8}$$

Answer: **(B)** $21\tfrac{7}{8}$

10. To simplify a complex fraction, divide the numerator by the denominator:

$$\tfrac{4}{9} \div \tfrac{2}{5} = \tfrac{4}{9} \times \tfrac{5}{\cancel{2}^{1}}^{2}$$
$$= \tfrac{10}{9}$$
$$= 1\tfrac{1}{9}$$

Answer: **(E)** $1\tfrac{1}{9}$

11. Write all of the fractions with the same denominator. L.C.D. = 80

$$\tfrac{9}{16} = \tfrac{45}{80}$$
$$\tfrac{7}{10} = \tfrac{56}{80}$$
$$\tfrac{5}{8} = \tfrac{50}{80}$$
$$\tfrac{4}{5} = \tfrac{64}{80}$$
$$\tfrac{1}{2} = \tfrac{40}{80}$$

Answer: **(D)** $\tfrac{4}{5}$

12.
$$3\tfrac{5}{16} = \quad 3\tfrac{5}{16}$$
$$+\ 2\tfrac{3}{4} = +\ 2\tfrac{12}{16}$$
$$5\tfrac{17}{16}$$
$$= \quad 6\tfrac{1}{16}$$

Answer: **(B)** $6\tfrac{1}{16}$ in.

13.
$$10\tfrac{1}{2} \div \tfrac{1}{2} = \tfrac{21}{2} \div \tfrac{1}{2}$$
$$= \tfrac{21}{\cancel{2}} \times \tfrac{\cancel{2}}{1}$$
$$= 21$$

Answer: **(E)** 21

14.
$$5\tfrac{3}{4} \times 3 = \tfrac{23}{4} \times \tfrac{3}{1}$$
$$= \tfrac{69}{4}$$
$$= 17\tfrac{1}{4}$$

Answer: **(D)** $17\tfrac{1}{4}$

15. First week:
L.C.D. = 24

$$3\tfrac{1}{2} = \quad 3\tfrac{12}{24} \text{ miles}$$
$$1\tfrac{1}{4} = \quad 1\tfrac{6}{24}$$
$$1\tfrac{1}{6} = \quad 1\tfrac{4}{24}$$
$$+\ 2\tfrac{3}{8} = +\ 2\tfrac{9}{24}$$
$$7\tfrac{31}{24} = 8\tfrac{7}{24} \text{ miles}$$

Second week:
L.C.D. = 16

$$\tfrac{1}{4} = \quad \tfrac{4}{16} \text{ miles}$$
$$\tfrac{3}{8} = \quad \tfrac{6}{16}$$
$$\tfrac{9}{16} = \quad \tfrac{9}{16}$$
$$3\tfrac{1}{16} = \quad 3\tfrac{1}{16}$$
$$2\tfrac{5}{8} = \quad 2\tfrac{10}{16}$$
$$+\ 3\tfrac{3}{16} = +\ 3\tfrac{3}{16}$$
$$8\tfrac{33}{16} = 10\tfrac{1}{16} \text{ miles}$$

L.C.D. = 48

$$10\tfrac{1}{16} = \quad 9\tfrac{51}{48} \text{ miles second week}$$
$$-\ 8\tfrac{7}{24} = -\ 8\tfrac{14}{48} \text{ miles first week}$$
$$1\tfrac{37}{48} \text{ miles more traveled}$$

Answer: **(A)** $1\tfrac{37}{48}$

16. Consider each choice:
    Each 6-ft board yields one $5\frac{1}{2}$-ft board with $\frac{1}{2}$ ft waste.
    Each 12-ft board yields two $5\frac{1}{2}$-ft boards with 1 ft waste ($2 \times 5\frac{1}{2} = 11$; $12 - 11 = 1$ ft waste).
    Each 24-ft board yields four $5\frac{1}{2}$-ft boards with 2 ft waste ($4 \times 5\frac{1}{2} = 22$; $24 - 22 = 2$ ft waste).
    Each 22 ft board may be divided into four $5\frac{1}{2}$-ft boards with no waste ($4 \times 5\frac{1}{2} = 22$ exactly).

    Answer: **(C)** 22 ft

17. $\frac{15}{16}$ of fortune is $7500.
    Therefore, his fortune $= 7500 \div \frac{15}{16}$
    $$= \frac{\overset{500}{\cancel{7500}}}{1} \times \frac{16}{\underset{1}{\cancel{15}}}$$
    $$= 8000$$

    Answer: **(D)** $8000

18. $\frac{2}{3}$ of 54,000 = increase

    $$\text{Increase} = \frac{2}{3} \times \overset{18,000}{\cancel{54,000}}$$
    $$= 36,000$$
    $$\text{Present population} = 54,000 + 36,000$$
    $$= 90,000$$

    Answer: **(D)** 90,000

19. First day: $\frac{1}{3}$ evaporates
    $\frac{2}{3}$ remains

    Second day: $\frac{3}{4}$ of $\frac{2}{3}$ evaporates
    $\frac{1}{4}$ of $\frac{2}{3}$ remains

    The amount remaining is
    $$\frac{1}{\underset{2}{\cancel{4}}} \times \frac{\overset{1}{\cancel{2}}}{3} = \frac{1}{6} \text{ of original contents}$$

    Answer: **(C)** $\frac{1}{6}$

20. $\frac{7}{8}$ of capacity = 14 gal
    Therefore, capacity $= 14 \div \frac{7}{8}$
    $$= \frac{\overset{2}{\cancel{14}}}{1} \times \frac{8}{\underset{1}{\cancel{7}}}$$
    $$= 16 \text{ gal}$$

    Answer: **(C)** 16 gal

DECIMALS

1. A **decimal,** which is a number with a decimal point (.), is actually a fraction, the denominator of which is understood to be 10 or some power of 10.

   a. The number of digits, or places, after a decimal point determines which power of 10 the denominator is. If there is one digit, the denominator is understood to be 10; if there are two digits, the denominator is understood to be 100, etc.

   Example: $.3 = \frac{3}{10}$, $.57 = \frac{57}{100}$, $.643 = \frac{643}{1000}$

   b. The addition of zeros after a decimal point does not change the value of the decimal. The zeros may be removed without changing the value of the decimal.

   Example: $.7 = .70 = .700$ and, vice versa, $.700 = .70 = .7$

   c. Since a decimal point is understood to exist after any whole number, the addition of any number of zeros after such a decimal point does not change the value of the number.

   Example: $2 = 2.0 = 2.00 = 2.000$

Addition of Decimals

2. Decimals are added in the same way that whole numbers are added, with the provision that the decimal points must be kept in a vertical line, one under the other. This determines the place of the decimal point in the answer.

   Illustration: Add 2.31, .037, 4, and 5.0017

   SOLUTION:

   $$
   \begin{array}{r}
   2.3100 \\
   .0370 \\
   4.000 \\
   + \; 5.0017 \\
   \hline
   11.3487
   \end{array}
   $$

   Answer: 11.3487

Subtraction of Decimals

3. Decimals are subtracted in the same way that whole numbers are subtracted, with the provision that, as in addition, the decimal points must be kept in a vertical line, one under the other. This determines the place of the decimal point in the answer.

Illustration: Subtract 4.0037 from 15.3

SOLUTION:

$$\begin{array}{r} 15.3000 \\ -\ 4.0037 \\ \hline 11.2963 \end{array}$$

Answer: 11.2963

Multiplication of Decimals

4. Decimals are multiplied in the same way that whole numbers are multiplied.

   a. The number of decimal places in the product equals the sum of the decimal places in the multiplicand and in the multiplier.

   b. If there are fewer places in the product than this sum, then a sufficient number of zeros must be added in front of the product to equal the number of places required, and a decimal point is written in front of the zeros.

Illustration: Multiply 2.372 by .012

SOLUTION:

$$\begin{array}{r} 2.372 \quad \text{(3 decimal places)} \\ \times\ .012 \quad \text{(3 decimal places)} \\ \hline 4744 \\ 2372 \quad\quad \\ \hline .028464 \quad \text{(6 decimal places)} \end{array}$$

Answer: .028464

5. A decimal can be multiplied by a power of 10 by moving the decimal point to the *right* as many places as indicated by the power. If multiplied by 10, the decimal point is moved one place to the right; if multiplied by 100, the decimal point is moved two places to the right; etc.

   Example:
   .235 × 10 = 2.35
   .235 × 100 = 23.5
   .235 × 1000 = 235

Division of Decimals

6. There are four types of division involving decimals:

   • When the dividend only is a decimal.
   • When the divisor only is a decimal.
   • When both are decimals.
   • When neither dividend nor divisor is a decimal.

   a. When the dividend only is a decimal, the division is the same as that of whole numbers, except that a decimal point must be placed in the quotient exactly above that in the dividend.

Illustration: Divide 12.864 by 32

SOLUTION:

$$\begin{array}{r} .402 \\ 32\ \overline{)\ 12.864} \\ 12\ 8\quad\quad \\ \hline 64 \\ 64 \\ \hline \end{array}$$

Answer: .402

   b. When the divisor only is a decimal, the decimal point in the divisor is omitted and as many zeros are placed to the right of the dividend as there were decimal places in the divisor.

Illustration: Divide 211327 by 6.817

SOLUTION:

$$6.817\ \overline{)\ 211327}$$
(3 decimal places)

$$= 6817\ \overline{)\ 211327000} \quad\quad\ \begin{array}{l} 31000 \\ \end{array}$$

$$\begin{array}{r} 20451\quad \text{(3 zeros added)} \\ \hline 6817 \\ 6817 \\ \hline \end{array}$$

Answer: 31000

   c. When both divisor and dividend are decimals, the decimal point in the divisor is omitted and the decimal point in the dividend must be moved to the right as many decimal places as there were in the divisor. If there are not enough places in the dividend, zeros must be added to make up the difference.

Illustration: Divide 2.62 by .131

SOLUTION: .131) 2.62 = 131) 2620
$$\frac{20}{262}$$

Answer: 20

d. In instances when neither the divisor nor the dividend is a decimal, a problem may still involve decimals. This occurs in two cases: when the dividend is a smaller number than the divisor; and when it is required to work out a division to a certain number of decimal places. In either case, write in a decimal point after the dividend, add as many zeros as necessary, and place a decimal point in the quotient above that in the dividend.

Illustration: Divide 7 by 50.

SOLUTION: 50) 7.00
```
    .14
50 ) 7.00
     5 0
     2 00
     2 00
```

Answer: .14

Illustration: How much is 155 divided by 40, carried out to 3 decimal places?

SOLUTION:
```
      3.875
40 ) 155.000
     120
      35 0
      32 0
       3 00
       2 80
         200
```

Answer: 3.875

7. A decimal can be divided by a power of 10 by moving the decimal to the *left* as many places as indicated by the power. If divided by 10, the decimal point is moved one place to the left; if divided by 100, the decimal point is moved two places to the left; etc. If there are not enough places, add zeros in front of the number to make up the difference and add a decimal point.

Example: .4 divided by 10 = .04
.4 divided by 100 = .004

Rounding Decimals

8. To round a number to a given decimal place:

   a. Locate the given place.

   b. If the digit to the right is less than 5, omit all digits following the given place.

   c. If the digit to the right is 5 or more, raise the given place by 1 and omit all digits following the given place.

Examples:

4.27   = 4.3 to the nearest tenth
.71345 = .713 to the nearest thousandth

9. In problems involving money, answers are usually rounded to the nearest cent.

Conversion of Fractions to Decimals

10. A fraction can be changed to a decimal by dividing the numerator by the denominator and working out the division to as many decimal places as required.

Illustration: Change $\frac{5}{11}$ to a decimal of 2 places.

SOLUTION: $\frac{5}{11}$ = 11) 5.00
```
      .45 5/11
11 ) 5.00
     4.44
       60
       55
        5
```

Answer: $.45\frac{5}{11}$

11. To clear fractions containing a decimal in either the numerator or the denominator, or in both, divide the numerator by the denominator.

Illustration: What is the value of $\frac{2.34}{.6}$?

SOLUTION: $\frac{2.34}{.6}$ = .6) 2.34 = 6) 23.4
```
       3.9
6 ) 23.4
    18
     5 4
     5 4
```

Answer: 3.9

Conversion of Decimals to Fractions

12. Since a decimal point indicates a number having a denominator that is a power of 10, a decimal can be expressed as a fraction, the numerator of which is the number itself and the denominator of which is the power indicated by the number of decimal places in the decimal.

    Example: $.3 = \frac{3}{10}, .47 = \frac{47}{100}$

13. When the decimal is a mixed number, divide by the power of 10 indicated by its number of decimal places. The fraction does not count as a decimal place.

    Illustration: Change $.25\frac{1}{3}$ to a fraction.

    SOLUTION: $.25\frac{1}{3} = 25\frac{1}{3} \div 100$
    $$= \frac{76}{3} \times \frac{1}{100}$$
    $$= \frac{76}{300} = \frac{19}{75}$$

    Answer: $\frac{19}{75}$

14. When to change decimals to fractions:

    a. When dealing with whole numbers, do not change the decimal.

    Example: In the problem $12 \times .14$, it is better to keep the decimal:
    $$12 \times .14 = 1.68$$

    b. When dealing with fractions, change the decimal to a fraction.

    Example: In the problem $\frac{3}{5} \times .17$, it is best to change the decimal to a fraction:
    $$\frac{3}{5} \times .17 = \frac{3}{5} \times \frac{17}{100} = \frac{51}{500}$$

15. Because decimal equivalents of fractions are often used, it is helpful to be familiar with the most common conversions.

$\frac{1}{2} = .5$	$\frac{1}{3} = .3333$
$\frac{1}{4} = .25$	$\frac{2}{3} = .6667$
$\frac{3}{4} = .75$	$\frac{1}{6} = .1667$
$\frac{1}{5} = .2$	$\frac{1}{7} = .1429$
$\frac{1}{8} = .125$	$\frac{1}{9} = .1111$
$\frac{1}{16} = .0625$	$\frac{1}{12} = .0833$

    Note that the left column contains exact values. The values in the right column have been rounded to the nearest ten-thousandth.

Practice Problems Involving Decimals

1. Add 37.03, 11.5627, 3.4005, 3423, and 1.141. _____

2. Subtract 4.64324 from 7. _____

3. Multiply 27.34 by 16.943. _____

4. How much is 19.6 divided by 3.2, carried out to 3 decimal places? _____

5. What is $\frac{5}{11}$ in decimal form (to the nearest hundredth)? _____

6. What is $.64\frac{2}{3}$ in fraction form? _____

7. What is the difference between $\frac{3}{5}$ and $\frac{9}{8}$ expressed decimally? _____

8. A boy saved up $4.56 the first month, $3.82 the second month, and $5.06 the third month. How much did he save altogether? _____

9. The diameter of a certain rod is required to be 1.51 ± .015 inches. The rod's diameter must be between _____ and _____.

10. After an employer figures out an employee's salary of $190.57, he deducts $3.05 for social security and $5.68 for pension. What is the amount of the check after these deductions? _____

11. If the outer radius of a metal pipe is 2.84 inches and the inner radius is 1.94 inches, the thickness of the metal is _____.

12. A boy earns $20.56 on Monday, $32.90 on Tuesday, $20.78 on Wednesday. He spends half of all that he earned during the three days. How much has he left? _____

13. The total cost of $3\frac{1}{2}$ pounds of meat at $1.69 a pound and 20 lemons at $.60 a dozen will be _____.

14. A reel of cable weighs 1279 lb. If the empty reel weighs 285 lb and the cable weighs 7.1

lb per foot, the number of feet of cable on the reel is _____.

15. 345 fasteners at $4.15 per hundred will cost _____.

Problem Solutions—Decimals

1. Line up all the decimal points one under the other. Then add:

$$
\begin{array}{r}
37.03 \\
11.5627 \\
3.4005 \\
3423.0000 \\
+ \quad 1.141 \\
\hline
3476.1342
\end{array}
$$

Answer: 3476.1342

2. Add a decimal point and five zeros to the 7. Then subtract:

$$
\begin{array}{r}
7.00000 \\
- \ 4.64324 \\
\hline
2.35676
\end{array}
$$

Answer: 2.35676

3. Since there are two decimal places in the multiplicand and three decimal places in the multiplier, there will be 2 + 3 = 5 decimal places in the product.

$$
\begin{array}{r}
27.34 \\
\times \ 16.943 \\
\hline
8202 \\
1\ 0936 \\
24\ 606 \\
164\ 04 \\
273\ 4 \\
\hline
463.22162
\end{array}
$$

Answer: 463.22162

4. Omit the decimal point in the divisor by moving it one place to the right. Move the decimal point in the dividend one place to the right and add three zeros in order to carry your answer out to three decimal places, as instructed in the problem.

$$
\begin{array}{r}
6.125 \\
3.2. \overline{)\ 19.6.000} \\
19\ 2 \\
\hline
4\ 0 \\
3\ 2 \\
\hline
80 \\
64 \\
\hline
160 \\
160 \\
\hline
\end{array}
$$

Answer: 6.125

5. To convert a fraction to a decimal, divide the numerator by the denominator:

$$
\begin{array}{r}
.454 \\
11\ \overline{)\ 5.000} \\
4\ 4 \\
\hline
60 \\
55 \\
\hline
50 \\
44 \\
\hline
6
\end{array}
$$

Answer: .45 to the nearest hundredth

6. To convert a decimal to a fraction, divide by the power of 10 indicated by the number of decimal places. (The fraction does not count as a decimal place.)

$$
\begin{aligned}
64\tfrac{2}{3} \div 100 &= \tfrac{194}{3} \div \tfrac{100}{1} \\
&= \tfrac{194}{3} \times \tfrac{1}{100} \\
&= \tfrac{194}{300} \\
&= \tfrac{97}{150}
\end{aligned}
$$

Answer: $\tfrac{97}{150}$

7. Convert each fraction to a decimal and subtract to find the difference:

$$\tfrac{9}{8} = 1.125 \qquad \tfrac{3}{5} = .60 \qquad
\begin{array}{r}
1.125 \\
- \ \ .60 \\
\hline
.525
\end{array}$$

Answer: .525

8. Add the savings for each month:

$$
\begin{array}{r}
\$4.56 \\
3.82 \\
+ \ \ 5.06 \\
\hline
\$13.44
\end{array}
$$

Answer: $13.44

9.
$$\begin{array}{r} 1.51 \\ + \ .015 \\ \hline 1.525 \end{array} \qquad \begin{array}{r} 1.510 \\ - \ .015 \\ \hline 1.495 \end{array}$$

Answer: The rod may have a diameter of from 1.495 inches to 1.525 inches inclusive.

10. Add to find total deductions:

$$\begin{array}{r} \$3.05 \\ + \ 5.68 \\ \hline \$8.73 \end{array}$$

Subtract total deductions from salary to find amount of check:

$$\begin{array}{r} \$190.57 \\ - \ 8.73 \\ \hline \$181.84 \end{array}$$

Answer: \$181.84

11. Outer radius minus inner radius equals thickness of metal:

$$\begin{array}{r} 2.84 \\ - \ 1.94 \\ \hline .90 \end{array}$$

Answer: .90 in

12. Add daily earnings to find total earnings:

$$\begin{array}{r} \$20.56 \\ 32.90 \\ + \ 20.78 \\ \hline \$74.24 \end{array}$$

Divide total earnings by 2 to find out what he has left:

$$2 \overline{)\ \$74.24}\ \ \ \$37.12$$

Answer: \$37.12

13. Find cost of $3\frac{1}{2}$ pounds of meat:

$$\begin{array}{r} \$1.69 \\ \times \ 3.5 \\ \hline 845 \\ 5\ 07 \\ \hline \$5.915 \end{array} = \$5.92 \text{ to the nearest cent}$$

Find cost of 20 lemons:
$.60 \div 12 = \$.05$ (for 1 lemon)
$.05 \times 20 = \$1.00$ (for 20 lemons)

Add cost of meat and cost of lemons:

$$\begin{array}{r} \$5.92 \\ + \ 1.00 \\ \hline \$6.92 \end{array}$$

Answer: \$6.92

14. Subtract weight of empty reel from total weight to find weight of cable:

$$\begin{array}{r} 1279 \text{ lb} \\ - \ 285 \text{ lb} \\ \hline 994 \text{ lb} \end{array}$$

Each foot of cable weighs 7.1 lb. Therefore, to find the number of feet of cable on the reel, divide 994 by 7.1:

$$7.1 \overline{)\ 994.0\ }\ \ \ 14\ 0.$$
$$\begin{array}{r} 71 \\ \hline 284 \\ 284 \\ \hline 0\ 0 \end{array}$$

Answer: 140

15. Each fastener costs:

$$\$4.15 \div 100 = \$.0415$$

345 fasteners cost:

$$\begin{array}{r} 345 \\ \times \ .0415 \\ \hline 1725 \\ 345 \\ 13\ 80 \\ \hline 14.3175 \end{array}$$

Answer: \$14.32

PERCENTS

1. The **percent symbol (%)** means "parts out of a hundred." Thus a percent is really a fraction—25% is 25 parts out of a hundred, or $\frac{25}{100}$, which reduces or simplifies to $\frac{1}{4}$, or one part out of four. Some problems involve expressing a fraction or a decimal as a percent. In other problems it is necessary to express a percent as a fraction or decimal in order to perform the calculations efficiently. When you have a percent (or decimal) which

converts to a common fraction ($25\% = .25 = \frac{1}{4}$), it is usually best to do any multiplying or dividing by first converting the percent or decimal to the common fraction, since the numbers are usually smaller and will work better. For adding and subtracting, percentages and decimals are often easier.

2. To change a whole number or a decimal to a percent:

 a. Multiply the number by 100.

 b. Affix a % sign.

 Illustration: Change 3 to a percent.

 SOLUTION: $3 \times 100 = 300$
 $$3 = 300\%$$

 Answer: 300%

 Illustration: Change .67 to a percent.

 SOLUTION: $.67 \times 100 = 67$
 $$.67 = 67\%$$

 Answer: 67%

3. To change a fraction or a mixed number to a percent:

 a. Multiply the fraction or mixed number by 100.

 b. Reduce, if possible.

 c. Affix a % sign.

 Illustration: Change $\frac{1}{7}$ to a percent.

 SOLUTION: $\frac{1}{7} \times 100 = \frac{100}{7}$
 $$= 14\frac{2}{7}$$
 $$\frac{1}{7} = 14\frac{2}{7}\%$$

 Answer: $14\frac{2}{7}\%$

 Illustration: Change $4\frac{2}{3}$ to a percent.

 SOLUTION: $4\frac{2}{3} \times 100 = \frac{14}{3} \times 100 = \frac{1400}{3}$
 $$= 466\frac{2}{3}$$
 $$4\frac{2}{3} = 466\frac{2}{3}\%$$

 Answer: $466\frac{2}{3}\%$

4. To remove a % sign attached to a decimal, divide the decimal by 100. If necessary, the resulting decimal may then be changed to a fraction.

Illustration: Change .5% to a decimal and to a fraction.

SOLUTION: $.5\% = .5 \div 100 = .005$
$$.005 = \frac{5}{1000} = \frac{1}{200}$$

Answer: $.5\% = .005$
$$.5\% = \frac{1}{200}$$

5. To remove a % sign attached to a fraction or mixed number, divide the fraction or mixed number by 100, and reduce, if possible. If necessary, the resulting fraction may then be changed to a decimal.

Illustration: Change $\frac{3}{4}\%$ to a fraction and to a decimal.

SOLUTION: $\frac{3}{4}\% = \frac{3}{4} \div 100 = \frac{3}{4} \times \frac{1}{100}$
$$= \frac{3}{400}$$

$$\frac{3}{400} = 400 \overline{)\begin{array}{c} .0075 \\ 3.0000 \end{array}}$$

Answer: $\frac{3}{4}\% = \frac{3}{400}$
$$\frac{3}{4}\% = .0075$$

6. To remove a % sign attached to a decimal that includes a fraction, divide the decimal by 100. If necessary, the resulting number may then be changed to a fraction.

Illustration: Change $.5\frac{1}{3}\%$ to a fraction.

SOLUTION: $.5\frac{1}{3}\% = .005\frac{1}{3}$
$$= \frac{5\frac{1}{3}}{1000}$$
$$= 5\frac{1}{3} \div 1000$$
$$= \frac{16}{3} \times \frac{1}{1000}$$
$$= \frac{16}{3000}$$
$$= \frac{2}{375}$$

Answer: $.5\frac{1}{3}\% = \frac{2}{375}$

7. Some fraction-percent equivalents are used so frequently that it is helpful to be familiar with them.

$\frac{1}{25} = 4\%$	$\frac{1}{5} = 20\%$
$\frac{1}{20} = 5\%$	$\frac{1}{4} = 25\%$
$\frac{1}{12} = 8\frac{1}{3}\%$	$\frac{1}{3} = 33\frac{1}{3}\%$
$\frac{1}{10} = 10\%$	$\frac{1}{2} = 50\%$
$\frac{1}{8} = 12\frac{1}{2}\%$	$\frac{2}{3} = 66\frac{2}{3}\%$
$\frac{1}{6} = 16\frac{2}{3}\%$	$\frac{3}{4} = 75\%$

Solving Percent Problems

8. Most percent problems involve three quantities:

   • The rate, R, which is followed by a % sign.
   • The base, B, which follows the word "of."
   • The amount of percentage, P, which usually follows the word "is."

   a. If the rate (R) and the base (B) are known, then the percentage (P) = R × B.

   Illustration: Find 15% of 50.

   SOLUTION: Rate = 15%
   Base = 50
   $$P = R \times B$$
   $$P = 15\% \times 50$$
   $$= .15 \times 50$$
   $$= 7.5$$

   Answer: 15% of 50 is 7.5.

   b. If the rate (R) and the percentage (P) are known, then the base (B) = $\frac{P}{R}$.

   Illustration: 7% of what number is 35?

   SOLUTION: Rate = 7%
   Percentage = 35
   $$B = \frac{P}{R}$$
   $$B = \frac{35}{7\%}$$
   $$= 35 \div .07$$
   $$= 500$$

   Answer: 7% of 500 is 35.

   c. If the percentage (P) and the base (B) are known, the rate (R) = $\frac{P}{B}$.

   Illustration: There are 96 men in a group of 150 people. What percent of the group are men?

   SOLUTION: Base = 150
   Percentage (amount) = 96
   Rate = $\frac{96}{150}$
   $$= .64$$
   $$= 64\%$$

   Answer: 64% of the group are men.

Illustration: In a tank holding 20 gallons of solution, 1 gallon is alcohol. What is the strength of the solution in percent?

SOLUTION:

   Percentage (amount) = 1 gallon
   Base = 20 gallons
   Rate = $\frac{1}{20}$
   $$= .05$$
   $$= 5\%$$

Answer: The solution is 5% alcohol.

9. In a percent problem, the whole is 100%.

   Example: If a problem involves 10% of a quantity, the rest of the quantity is 90%.

   Example: If a quantity has been increased by 5%, the new amount is 105% of the original quantity.

   Example: If a quantity has been decreased by 15%, the new amount is 85% of the original quantity.

10. Percent change, percent increase, or percent decrease are special types of percent problems in which the difficulty is in making sure to use the right numbers to calculate the percent. The full formula is:

$$\frac{\text{(New Amount)} - \text{(Original Amount)}}{\text{(Original Amount)}} \times 100 = \text{percent change}$$

Where the new amount is less than the original amount, the number on top will be a negative number and the result will be a **percent decrease.** When a percent decrease is asked for, the negative sign is omitted. Where the new amount is greater than the original amount, the percent change is positive and is called a **percent increase.**

The percent of increase or decrease is found by putting the amount of increase or decrease over the original amount and changing this fraction to a percent by multiplying by 100.

Illustration: The number of automobiles sold by the Cadcoln Dealership increased from 300 one year to 400 the following year. What was the percent of increase?

SOLUTION: There was an increase of 100, which must be compared to the original 300.

$$\frac{100}{300} = \frac{1}{3} = 33\frac{1}{3}\%$$

Answer: $33\frac{1}{3}\%$

Practice Problems Involving Percents

1. 10% written as a decimal is
   (A) 1.0
   (B) 0.1
   (C) 0.01
   (D) 0.010
   (E) 0.001

2. What is 5.37% in fraction form?
   (A) $\frac{537}{10,000}$
   (B) $\frac{537}{1000}$
   (C) $5\frac{37}{10,000}$
   (D) $5\frac{37}{100}$
   (E) $\frac{537}{10}$

3. What percent is $\frac{3}{4}$ of $\frac{5}{6}$?
   (A) 60%
   (B) 75%
   (C) 80%
   (D) 90%
   (E) 111%

4. What percent is 14 of 24?
   (A) $62\frac{1}{4}\%$
   (B) $58\frac{1}{3}\%$
   (C) $41\frac{2}{3}\%$
   (D) $33\frac{3}{5}\%$
   (E) 14%

5. 200% of 800 equals
   (A) 4
   (B) 16
   (C) 200
   (D) 800
   (E) 1600

6. If John must have a mark of 80% to pass a test of 35 items, the number of items he may miss and still pass the test is
   (A) 7
   (B) 8

   (C) 11
   (D) 28
   (E) 35

7. The regular price of a TV set that sold for $118.80 at a 20% reduction sale is
   (A) $158.60
   (B) $148.50
   (C) $138.84
   (D) $95.04
   (E) $29.70

8. A circle graph of a budget shows the expenditure of 26.2% for housing, 28.4% for food, 12% for clothing, 12.7% for taxes, and the balance for miscellaneous items. The percent for miscellaneous items is
   (A) 79.3
   (B) 70.3
   (C) 68.5
   (D) 29.7
   (E) 20.7

9. Two dozen shuttlecocks and four badminton rackets are to be purchased for a playground. The shuttlecocks are priced at $.35 each and the rackets at $2.75 each. The playground receives a discount of 30% from these prices. The total cost of this equipment is
   (A) $7.29
   (B) $11.43
   (C) $13.58
   (D) $18.60
   (E) $19.40

10. A piece of wood weighing 10 ounces is found to have a weight of 8 ounces after drying. The moisture content was
   (A) 80%
   (B) 40%
   (C) $33\frac{1}{3}\%$
   (D) 25%
   (E) 20%

11. A bag contains 800 coins. Of these, 10 percent are dimes, 30 percent are nickels, and the rest are quarters. The amount of money in the bag is
   (A) less than $150
   (B) between $150 and $300

(C) between $301 and $450
(D) between $450 and $800
(E) more than $800

12. Six quarts of a 20% solution of alcohol in water are mixed with 4 quarts of a 60% solution of alcohol in water. The alcoholic strength of the mixture is
(A) 80%
(B) 40%
(C) 36%
(D) $33\frac{1}{3}$%
(E) 10%

13. A man insures 80% of his property and pays a $2\frac{1}{2}$% premium amounting to $348. What is the total value of his property?
(A) $19,000
(B) $18,000
(C) $18,400
(D) $17,400
(E) $13,920

14. A clerk divided his 35-hour work week as follows: $\frac{1}{5}$ of his time was spent in sorting mail; $\frac{1}{2}$ of his time in filing letters; and $\frac{1}{7}$ of his time in reception work. The rest of his time was devoted to messenger work. The percent of time spent on messenger work by the clerk during the week was most nearly
(A) 6%
(B) 10%
(C) 14%
(D) 16%
(E) 20%

15. In a school in which 40% of the enrolled students are boys, 80% of the boys are present on a certain day. If 1152 boys are present, the total school enrollment is
(A) 1440
(B) 2880
(C) 3600
(D) 5400
(E) 5760

16. Mrs. Morris receives a salary raise from $25,000 to $27,500. Find the percent of increase.
(A) 9
(B) 10
(C) 90

(D) 15
(E) $12\frac{1}{2}$

17. The population of Stormville has increased from 80,000 to 100,000 in the last 20 years. Find the percent of increase.
(A) 20
(B) 25
(C) 80
(D) 60
(E) 10

18. The value of Super Company Stock dropped from $25 a share to $21 a share. Find the percent of decrease.
(A) 4
(B) 8
(C) 12
(D) 16
(E) 20

19. The Rubins bought their home for $30,000 and sold it for $60,000. What was the percent of increase?
(A) 100
(B) 50
(C) 200
(D) 300
(E) 150

20. During the pre-holiday rush, Martin's Department Store increased its sales staff from 150 to 200 persons. By what percent must it now decrease its sales staff to return to the usual number of salespersons?
(A) 25
(B) $33\frac{1}{3}$
(C) 20
(D) 40
(E) 75

Percent Problems—Correct Answers

1.	(B)	6.	(A)	11.	(A)	16.	(B)
2.	(A)	7.	(B)	12.	(C)	17.	(B)
3.	(D)	8.	(E)	13.	(D)	18.	(D)
4.	(B)	9.	(C)	14.	(D)	19.	(A)
5.	(E)	10.	(E)	15.	(C)	20.	(A)

Problem Solutions—Percents

1. $10\% = .10 = .1$

    Answer: **(B)** 0.1

2. $5.37\% = .0537 = \dfrac{537}{10,000}$

    Answer: **(A)** $\dfrac{537}{10,000}$

3. Base (number following "of") $= \frac{5}{6}$
    Percentage (number following "is") $= \frac{3}{4}$,

    Rate $= \dfrac{\text{Percentage}}{\text{Base}}$

    $= $ Percentage $\div$ Base

    Rate $= \frac{3}{4} \div \frac{5}{6}$

    $= \frac{3}{4} \times \frac{\overset{3}{\cancel{6}}}{\underset{2}{}5}$

    $= \frac{9}{10}$

    $\frac{9}{10} = .9 = 90\%$

    Answer: **(D)** 90%

4. Base (number following "of") $= 24$
    Percentage (number following "is") $= 14$

    Rate $= $ Percentage $\div$ Base
    Rate $= 14 \div 24$

    $= .58\frac{1}{3}$

    $= 58\frac{1}{3}\%$

    Answer: **(B)** $58\frac{1}{3}\%$

5. 200% of $800 = 2.00 \times 800$

    $= 1600$

    Answer: **(E)** 1600

6. He must answer 80% of 35 correctly. Therefore, he may miss 20% of 35.
    20% of $35 = .20 \times 35$

    $= 7$

    Answer: **(A)** 7

7. Since $118.80 represents a 20% reduction, $118.80 = 80% of the regular price.

    Regular price $= \dfrac{\$118.80}{80\%}$

    $= \$118.80 \div .80$

    $= \$148.50$

    Answer: **(B)** $148.50

8. All the items in a circle graph total 100%. Add the figures given for housing, food, clothing, and taxes:

    $$\begin{array}{r} 26.2\% \\ 28.4\% \\ 12\ \ \% \\ +\ 12.7\% \\ \hline 79.3\% \end{array}$$

    Subtract this total from 100% to find the percent for miscellaneous items:

    $$\begin{array}{r} 100.0\% \\ -\ \ 79.3\% \\ \hline 20.7\% \end{array}$$

    Answer: **(E)** 20.7%

9. Price of shuttlecocks $= 24 \times \$.35 = \$\ 8.40$
    Price of rackets $\quad = 4 \times \$2.75 = \$11.00$
    Total price $\qquad\qquad = \qquad\quad \$19.40$

    Discount is 30%, and $100\% - 30\% = 70\%$

    Actual cost $= 70\%$ of 19.40
    $= .70 \times 19.40$
    $= 13.58$

    Answer: **(C)** $13.58

10. Subtract weight of wood after drying from original weight of wood to find amount of moisture in wood:

    $$\begin{array}{r} 10 \\ -\ \ 8 \\ \hline \end{array}$$
    2 ounces of moisture in wood

    Moisture content $= \dfrac{2 \text{ ounces}}{10 \text{ ounces}} = .2 = 20\%$

    Answer: **(E)** 20%

11. Find the number of each kind of coin:

    10% of $800 = .10 \times 800 = 80$ dimes
    30% of $800 = .30 \times 800 = 240$ nickels
    60% of $800 = .60 \times 800 = 480$ quarters

    Find the value of the coins:

    $\ \ 80$ dimes $= \ \ 80 \times .10 = \$\ \ \ 8.00$
    240 nickels $= 240 \times .05 = \ \ \ 12.00$
    480 quarters $= 480 \times .25 = \ \ 120.00$
    $\qquad\qquad\qquad\qquad$ Total $\quad \$140.00$

    Answer: **(A)** less than $150

12. First solution contains 20% of 6 quarts of alcohol.

$$\text{Alcohol content} = .20 \times 6$$
$$= 1.2 \text{ quarts}$$

Second solution contains 60% of 4 quarts of alcohol.

$$\text{Alcohol content} = .60 \times 4$$
$$= 2.4 \text{ quarts}$$

Mixture contains: $1.2 + 2.4 = 3.6$ quarts alcohol

$6 + 4 = 10$ quarts liquid

$$\text{Alcoholic strength of mixture} = \frac{3.6}{10} = 36\%$$

Answer: **(C)** 36%

13. $2\frac{1}{2}\%$ of insured value = $348

$$\text{Insured value} = \frac{348}{2\frac{1}{2}\%}$$
$$= 348 \div .025$$
$$= \$13,920$$

$13,920 is 80% of total value

$$\text{Total value} = \frac{\$13,920}{80\%}$$
$$= \$13,920 \div .80$$
$$= \$17,400$$

Answer: **(D)** $17,400

14. $\frac{1}{5} \times 35 = 7$ hr sorting mail
$\frac{1}{2} \times 35 = 17\frac{1}{2}$ hr filing
$\frac{1}{7} = 35 = \underline{\;\;5\;\;}$ hr reception
$29\frac{1}{2}$ hr accounted for

$35 - 29\frac{1}{2} = 5\frac{1}{2}$ hr left for messenger work

% spent on messenger work:

$$= \frac{5\frac{1}{2}}{35}$$
$$= 5\frac{1}{2} \div 35$$
$$= \frac{11}{2} \times \frac{1}{35}$$
$$= \frac{11}{70}$$
$$= .15\frac{5}{7}$$
$$= 15\frac{5}{7}\%$$

Answer: **(D)** most nearly 16%

15. 80% of the boys = 1152

$$\text{Number of boys} = \frac{1152}{80\%}$$
$$= 1152 \div .80$$
$$= 1440$$

40% of students = 1440

$$\text{Total number of students} = \frac{1440}{40\%}$$
$$= 1440 \div .40$$
$$= 3600$$

Answer: **(C)** 3600

16. Amount of increase = $2500

$$\text{Percent of increase} = \frac{\text{amount of increase}}{\text{original}}$$

$$\frac{2500}{25,000} = \frac{1}{10} = 10\%$$

Answer: **(B)** 10%

17. Amount of increase = 20,000

$$\text{Percent of increase} = \frac{20,000}{80,000} = \frac{1}{4} = 25\%$$

Answer: **(B)** 25%

18. Amount of decrease = $4

$$\text{Percent of decrease} = \frac{4}{25} = \frac{16}{100} = 16\%$$

Answer: **(D)** 16%

19. Amount of increase $30,000

$$\text{Percent of increase} = \frac{30,000}{30,000} = 1 = 100\%$$

Answer: **(A)** 100%

20. Amount of decrease = 50

$$\text{Percent of decrease} = \frac{50}{200} = \frac{1}{4} = 25\%$$

Answer: **(A)** 25%

SHORTCUTS IN MULTIPLICATION AND DIVISION

There are several shortcuts for simplifying multiplication and division. Following the description of each shortcut, practice problems are provided.

Dropping Final Zeros

1. a. A zero in a whole number is considered a "final zero" if it appears in the units column or if all columns to its right are filled with zeros. A final zero may be omitted in certain kinds of problems.

    b. In decimal numbers, a zero appearing in the extreme right column may be dropped with no effect on the solution of a problem.

2. In multiplying whole numbers, the final zero(s) may be dropped during computation and simply transferred to the answer.

    Examples:

$$
\begin{array}{r} 2310 \\ \times\ 150 \\ \hline 1155 \\ 231 \\ \hline 346500 \end{array}
\qquad
\begin{array}{r} 129 \\ \times\ 210 \\ \hline 129 \\ 258 \\ \hline 27090 \end{array}
$$

$$
\begin{array}{r} 1760 \\ \times\ 205 \\ \hline 880 \\ 352 \\ \hline 360800 \end{array}
$$

Practice Problems

Solve the following multiplication problems, dropping the final zeros during computation.

1.
$$
\begin{array}{r} 230 \\ \times\ 12 \\ \hline \end{array}
$$

2.
$$
\begin{array}{r} 175 \\ \times\ 130 \\ \hline \end{array}
$$

3.
$$
\begin{array}{r} 203 \\ \times\ 14 \\ \hline \end{array}
$$

4.
$$
\begin{array}{r} 621 \\ \times\ 140 \\ \hline \end{array}
$$

5.
$$
\begin{array}{r} 430 \\ \times\ 360 \\ \hline \end{array}
$$

6.
$$
\begin{array}{r} 132 \\ \times\ 310 \\ \hline \end{array}
$$

7.
$$
\begin{array}{r} 350 \\ \times\ 24 \\ \hline \end{array}
$$

8.
$$
\begin{array}{r} 520 \\ \times\ 410 \\ \hline \end{array}
$$

9.
$$
\begin{array}{r} 634 \\ \times\ 120 \\ \hline \end{array}
$$

10.
$$
\begin{array}{r} 431 \\ \times\ 230 \\ \hline \end{array}
$$

Solutions to Practice Problems

1.
$$
\begin{array}{r} 230 \\ \times\ 12 \\ \hline 46 \\ 23 \\ \hline 2760 \end{array}
$$

2.
$$
\begin{array}{r} 175 \\ \times\ 130 \\ \hline 525 \\ 175 \\ \hline 22750 \end{array}
$$

3.
$$
\begin{array}{r} 203 \\ \times\ 14 \\ \hline 812 \\ 203 \\ \hline 2842 \end{array}
$$
(no final zeros)

4.
$$
\begin{array}{r} 621 \\ \times\ 140 \\ \hline 2484 \\ 621 \\ \hline 86940 \end{array}
$$

5.
$$
\begin{array}{r} 430 \\ \times\ 360 \\ \hline 258 \\ 129 \\ \hline 154800 \end{array}
$$

6.
```
      132
  ×  310
      132
      396
    40920
```

7.
```
      350
  ×   24
      140
       70
     8400
```

8.
```
      520
  ×  410
       52
      208
   213200
```

9.
```
      634
  ×  120
     1268
      634
    76080
```

10.
```
      431
  ×  230
     1293
      862
    99130
```

Multiplying Whole Numbers by Decimals

3. In multiplying a whole number by a decimal number, if there are one or more final zeros in the multiplicand, move the decimal point in the multiplier to the right the same number of places as there are final zeros in the multiplicand. Then cross out the final zero(s) in the multiplicand.

Examples:
```
   27500        275
 ×   .15   =  ×  15
```

```
    1250        125
  × .345     × 3.45
```

Practice Problems

Rewrite the following problems, dropping the final zeros and moving decimal points the appro-

priate number of spaces. Then compute the answers.

1.
```
      2400
  ×    .02
```

2.
```
       620
  ×    .04
```

3.
```
       800
  ×   .005
```

4.
```
       600
  ×   .002
```

5.
```
       340
  ×    .08
```

6.
```
       480
  ×     .4
```

7.
```
       400
  ×    .04
```

8.
```
      5300
  ×     .5
```

9.
```
       930
  ×     .3
```

10.
```
      9000
  ×   .001
```

Solutions to Practice Problems

The rewritten problems are shown, along with the answers.

1.
```
       24
  ×     2
       48
```

2.
$$\begin{array}{r} 62 \\ \times\ .4 \\ \hline 24.8 \end{array}$$

3.
$$\begin{array}{r} 8 \\ \times\ .5 \\ \hline 4.0 \end{array}$$

4.
$$\begin{array}{r} 6 \\ \times\ .2 \\ \hline 1.2 \end{array}$$

5.
$$\begin{array}{r} 34 \\ \times\ .8 \\ \hline 27.2 \end{array}$$

6.
$$\begin{array}{r} 48 \\ \times\ 4 \\ \hline 192 \end{array}$$

7.
$$\begin{array}{r} 4 \\ \times\ 4 \\ \hline 16 \end{array}$$

8.
$$\begin{array}{r} 530 \\ \times\ 5 \\ \hline 2650 \end{array}$$

9.
$$\begin{array}{r} 93 \\ \times\ 3 \\ \hline 279 \end{array}$$

10.
$$\begin{array}{r} 9 \\ \times\ 1 \\ \hline 9 \end{array}$$

Dividing by Whole Numbers

4. a. When there are final zeros in the divisor but no final zeros in the dividend, move the decimal point in the dividend to the left as many places as there are final zeros in the divisor, then omit the final zeros.

Example: 2700. $)\ \overline{37523.}$ = 27. $)\ \overline{375.23}$

b. When there are fewer final zeros in the divisor than there are in the dividend, drop the same number of final zeros from the dividend as there are final zeros in the divisor.

Example: 250. $)\ \overline{45300.}$ = 25. $)\ \overline{4530.}$

c. When there are more final zeros in the divisor than there are in the dividend, move the decimal point in the dividend to the left as many places as there are final zeros in the divisor, then omit the final zeros.

Example: 2300. $)\ \overline{690.}$ = 23. $)\ \overline{6.9}$

d. When there are no final zeros in the divisor, no zeros can be dropped in the dividend.

Example: 23. $)\ \overline{690.}$ = 23. $)\ \overline{690.}$

Practice Problems

Rewrite the following problems, dropping the final zeros and moving the decimal points the appropriate number of places. Then compute the quotients.

1. 600. $)\ \overline{72.}$
2. 310. $)\ \overline{6200.}$
3. 7600 $)\ \overline{1520.}$
4. 46. $)\ \overline{920.}$
5. 11.0 $)\ \overline{220.}$
6. 700. $)\ \overline{84.}$
7. 90. $)\ \overline{8100.}$
8. 8100. $)\ \overline{1620.}$
9. 25. $)\ \overline{5250.}$
10. 41.0 $)\ \overline{820.}$
11. 800. $)\ \overline{96.}$
12. 650. $)\ \overline{1300.}$
13. 5500. $)\ \overline{110.}$
14. 36. $)\ \overline{720.}$
15. 87.0 $)\ \overline{1740.}$

Rewritten Practice Problems

1. 6.) .72

2. 31.) 620.

3. 76.) 15.2

4. 46.) 920.

5. 11.) 220.

6. 7.) .84

7. 9.) 810.

8. 81.) 16.2

9. 25.) 5250.

10. 41.) 820.

11. 8.) .96

12. 65.) 130.

13. 55.) 1.1

14. 36.) 720.

15. 87.) 1740.

Solutions to Practice Problems

1.
```
    .12
6. ) .72
```

2.
```
    20
31. ) 620.
     62
     ──
     00
```

3.
```
    .2
76. ) 15.2
     15 2
     ────
     0 0
```

4.
```
    20
46. ) 920.
     92
     ──
     00
```

5.
```
    20
11. ) 220.
     22
     ──
     00
```

6.
```
    .12
7. ) .84
```

7.
```
    90
9. ) 810.
    81
    ──
    00
```

8.
```
    .2
81. ) 16.2
     16 2
     ────
      0 0
```

9.
```
    210
25. ) 5250.
     50
     ──
     25
     25
     ──
     00
```

10.
```
    20
41. ) 820.
     82
     ──
     00
```

11.
```
    .12
8. ) .96
```

12.
```
    2
65. ) 130.
     130
     ───
     00
```

13.
```
    .02
55. ) 1.10
     1 10
     ────
      00
```

14.
```
    20
36. ) 720.
     72
     ──
     00
```

15.
```
    20
87. ) 1740.
     174
     ───
     00
```

Division by Multiplication

5. Instead of dividing by a particular number, the same answer is obtained by multiplying by the equivalent multiplier.

6. To find the equivalent multiplier of a given divisor, divide 1 by the divisor.

   Example: The equivalent multiplier of $12\frac{1}{2}$ is $1 \div 12\frac{1}{2}$ or .08. The division problem $100 \div 12\frac{1}{2}$ may be more easily solved as the multiplication problem $100 \times .08$. The answer will be the same. This can be helpful when you are estimating answers.

7. Common divisors and their equivalent multipliers are shown below:

Divisor	Equivalent Multiplier
$11\frac{1}{9}$	.09
$12\frac{1}{2}$	.08
$14\frac{2}{7}$	.07
$16\frac{2}{3}$	.06
20	.05
25	.04
$33\frac{1}{3}$	.03
50	.02

8. A divisor may be multiplied or divided by any power of 10, and the only change in its equivalent multiplier will be in the placement of the decimal point, as may be seen in the following table:

Divisor	Equivalent Multiplier
.025	40.
.25	4.
2.5	.4
25.	.04
250.	.004
2500.	.0004

Practice Problems

Rewrite and solve each of the following problems by using equivalent multipliers. Drop the final zeros where appropriate.

1. $100 \div 16\frac{2}{3} =$

2. $200 \div 25 =$

3. $300 \div 33\frac{1}{3} =$

4. $250 \div 50 =$

5. $80 \div 12\frac{1}{2} =$

6. $800 \div 14\frac{2}{7} =$

7. $620 \div 20 =$

8. $500 \div 11\frac{1}{9} =$

9. $420 \div 16\frac{2}{3} =$

10. $1200 \div 33\frac{1}{3} =$

11. $955 \div 50 =$

12. $900 \div 33\frac{1}{3} =$

13. $275 \div 12\frac{1}{2} =$

14. $625 \div 25 =$

14. $244 \div 20 =$

16. $350 \div 16\frac{2}{3} =$

17. $400 \div 33\frac{1}{3} =$

18. $375 \div 25 =$

19. $460 \div 20 =$

20. $250 \div 12\frac{1}{2} =$

Solutions to Practice Problems

The rewritten problems and their solutions appear below:

1. $100 \times .06 = 1 \times 6 = 6$

2. $200 \times .04 = 2 \times 4 = 8$

3. $300 \times .03 = 3 \times 3 = 9$

4. $250 \times .02 = 25 \times .2 = 5$

5. $80 \times .08 = 8 \times .8 = 6.4$

6. $800 \times .07 = 8 \times 7 = 56$

7. $620 \times .05 = 62 \times .5 = 31$

8. $500 \times .09 = 5 \times 9 = 45$

9. $420 \times .06 = 42 \times .6 = 25.2$

10. $1200 \times .03 = 12 \times 3 = 36$

11. $955 \times .02 = 19.1$

12. $900 \times .03 = 9 \times 3 = 27$

13. $275 \times .08 = 22$

14. $625 \times .04 = 25$

15. $244 \times .05 = 12.2$

16. $350 \times .06 = 35 \times .6 = 21$

17. $400 \times .03 = 4 \times 3 = 12$

18. $375 \times .04 = 15$

19. $460 \times .05 = 46 \times .5 = 23$

20. $250 \times .08 = 25 \times .8 = 20$

Multiplication by Division

9. Just as some division problems are made easier by changing them to equivalent multiplication problems, certain multiplication problems are made easier by changing them to equivalent division problems.

10. Instead of arriving at an answer by multiplying by a particular number, the same answer is obtained by dividing by the equivalent divisor.

11. To find the equivalent divisor of a given multiplier, divide 1 by the multiplier.

12. Common multipliers and their equivalent divisors are shown below:

Multiplier	Equivalent Divisor
$11\frac{1}{9}$	.09
$12\frac{1}{2}$	.08
$14\frac{2}{7}$	.07
$16\frac{2}{3}$	.06
20	.05
25	.04
$33\frac{1}{3}$	.03
50	.02

Notice that the multiplier-equivalent divisor pairs are the same as the divisor-equivalent multiplier pairs given earlier.

Practice Problems

Rewrite and solve each of the following problems by using division. Drop the final zeros where appropriate.

1. $77 \times 14\frac{2}{7} =$

2. $81 \times 11\frac{1}{9} =$

3. $475 \times 20 =$

4. $42 \times 50 =$

5. $36 \times 33\frac{1}{3} =$

6. $96 \times 12\frac{1}{2} =$

7. $126 \times 16\frac{2}{3} =$

8. $48 \times 25 =$

9. $33 \times 33\frac{1}{3} =$

10. $84 \times 14\frac{2}{7} =$

11. $99 \times 11\frac{1}{9} =$

12. $126 \times 33\frac{1}{3} =$

13. $168 \times 12\frac{1}{2} =$

14. $654 \times 16\frac{2}{3} =$

15. $154 \times 14\frac{2}{7} =$

16. $5250 \times 50 =$

17. $324 \times 25 =$

18. $625 \times 20 =$

19. $198 \times 11\frac{1}{9} =$

20. $224 \times 14\frac{2}{7} =$

Solutions to Practice Problems

The rewritten problems and their solutions appear below:

1. $.07 \overline{)\ 77.} = 7 \overline{)\ 7700.}$ $1100.$

2. $.09 \overline{)\ 81.} = 9 \overline{)\ 8100.}$ $900.$

3. $.05 \overline{)\ 475.} = 5 \overline{)\ 47500.}$ $9500.$

4. $.02 \overline{)\ 42.} = 2 \overline{)\ 4200.}$ $2100.$

5. $.03 \overline{)\ 36.} = 3 \overline{)\ 3600.}$ $1200.$

6. $.08 \overline{)\ 96.} = 8 \overline{)\ 9600.}$ $1200.$

7. $.06 \overline{)\ 126.} = 6 \overline{)\ 12600.}$ $2100.$

8. $.04 \overline{)\ 48.} = 4 \overline{)\ 4800.}$ $1200.$

9. $.03 \overline{)\ 33.} = 3 \overline{)\ 3300.}$ $1100.$

10. $.07 \overline{)\ 84.} = 7 \overline{)\ 8400.}$ $1200.$

11. $.09 \overline{)\ 99.} = 9 \overline{)\ 9900.}$ $1100.$

12. $.03 \overline{)\ 126.} = 3 \overline{)\ 12600.}$ $4200.$

13. $.08 \overline{)\ 168.} = 8 \overline{)\ 16800.}$ $2100.$

14. $.06 \overline{)\ 654.} = 6 \overline{)\ 65400.}$ $10900.$

15. $.07 \overline{)\ 154.} = 7 \overline{)\ 15400.}$ $2200.$

16. $.02 \overline{)\ 5250.} = 2 \overline{)\ 525000.}$ $262500.$

17. $.04 \overline{)\ 324.} = 4 \overline{)\ 32400.}$ $8100.$

18. $.05 \overline{)\ 625.} = 5 \overline{)\ 62500.}$ $12500.$

19. $.09 \overline{)\ 198.} = 9 \overline{)\ 19800.}$ $2200.$

20. $.07 \overline{)\ 224.} = 7 \overline{)\ 22400.}$ $3200.$

AVERAGES

1. a. The term average can technically refer to a variety of mathematical ideas, but on the test it refers to the **arithmetic mean.** It is found by adding the numbers given and then dividing this sum by the number of items being averaged.

Illustration: Find the arithmetic mean of 2, 8, 5, 9, 6, and 12.

SOLUTION: There are 6 numbers.

$$\text{Arithmetic mean} = \frac{2 + 8 + 5 + 9 + 6 + 12}{6}$$

$$= \frac{42}{6}$$

$$= 7$$

Answer: The arithmetic mean is 7.

b. If a problem calls for simply the average or the mean, it is referring to the arithmetic mean.

2. If a group of numbers is arranged in order, the middle number is called the **median.** If there is no single middle number (this occurs when there is an even number of items), the median is found by computing the arithmetic mean of the two middle numbers.

Example: The median of 6, 8, 10, 12, and 14 is 10.

Example: The median of 6, 8, 10, 12, 14, and 16 is the arithmetic mean of 10 and 12.

$$\frac{10 + 12}{2} = \frac{22}{2} = 11.$$

3. The **mode** of a group of numbers is the number that appears most often.

Example: The mode of 10, 5, 7, 9, 12, 5, 10, 5 and 9 is 5.

4. When some numbers among terms to be averaged occur more than once, they must be given the appropriate weight. For example, if a student received four grades of 80 and one of 90, his average would not be the average of 80 and 90, but rather the average of 80, 80, 80, 80, and 90.

To obtain the average of quantities that are weighted:

a. Set up a table listing the quantities, their respective weights, and their respective values.

b. Multiply the value of each quantity by its respective weight.

c. Add up these products.

d. Add up the weights.

e. Divide the sum of the products by the sum of the weights.

Illustration: Assume that the weights for the following subjects are: English 3, History 2, Mathematics 2, Foreign Languages 2, and Art 1. What would be the average of a student whose marks are: English 80, History 85, Algebra 84, Spanish 82, and Art 90?

SOLUTION:

Subject	Weight	Mark
English	3	80
History	2	85
Algebra	2	84
Spanish	2	82
Art	1	90

English	3 × 80 = 240
History	2 × 85 = 170
Algebra	2 × 84 = 168
Spanish	2 × 82 = 164
Art	1 × 90 = 90
	832

Sum of the weights: 3 + 2 + 2 + 2 + 1 = 10

832 ÷ 10 = 83.2

Answer: Average = 83.2

Note: On the test, you might go directly to a list of the weighted amounts, here totalling 832, and divide by the number of weights; or you might set up a single equation.

Illustration: Mr. Martin drove for 6 hours at an average rate of 50 miles per hour and for 2 hours at an average rate of 60 miles per hour. Find his average rate for the entire trip.

SOLUTION:

$$\frac{6(50) + 2(60)}{8} = \frac{300 + 120}{8} = \frac{420}{8} = 52\tfrac{1}{2}$$

Answer: $52\tfrac{1}{2}$

Since he drove many more hours at 50 miles per hour than at 60 miles per hour, his average rate should be closer to 50 than to 60, which it is. In general, average rate can always be found by dividing the total distance covered by the time spent traveling.

Practice Problems Involving Averages

1. The arithmetic mean of 73.8, 92.2, 64.7, 43.8, 56.5, and 46.4 is
   (A) 60.6
   (B) 62.9
   (C) 64.48
   (D) 75.48
   (E) 82.9

2. The median of the numbers 8, 5, 7, 5, 9, 9, 1, 8, 10, 5, and 10 is
   (A) 5
   (B) 7
   (C) 8
   (D) 9
   (E) 10

3. The mode of the numbers 16, 15, 17, 12, 15, 15, 18, 19, and 18 is
   (A) 15
   (B) 16
   (C) 17
   (D) 18
   (E) 19

4. A clerk filed 73 forms on Monday, 85 forms on Tuesday, 54 on Wednesday, 92 on Thursday, and 66 on Friday. What was the average number of forms filed per day?
   (A) 60
   (B) 72
   (C) 74
   (D) 92
   (E) 370

5. The grades received on a test by twenty students were: 100, 55, 75, 80, 65, 65, 85, 90, 80, 45, 40, 50, 85, 85, 85, 80, 80, 70, 65, and 60. The average of these grades is
   (A) 70
   (B) 72
   (C) 77
   (D) 80
   (E) 100

6. A buyer purchased 75 six-inch rulers costing 15¢ each, 100 one-foot rulers costing 30¢ each, and 50 one-yard rulers costing 72¢ each. What was the average price per ruler?
   (A) $26\frac{1}{8}$¢
   (B) $34\frac{1}{3}$¢
   (C) 39¢
   (D) 42¢
   (E) $77\frac{1}{4}$¢

7. What is the average of a student who received 90 in English, 84 in Algebra, 75 in French, and 76 in Music, if the subjects have the following weights: English 4, Algebra 3, French 3, and Music 1?
   (A) 81

(B) $81\frac{1}{2}$
(C) 82
(D) $82\frac{1}{2}$
(E) 83

Questions 8–11 refer to the following information:

A census shows that on a certain block the number of children in each family is 3, 4, 4, 0, 1, 2, 0, 2, and 2, respectively.

8. Find the average number of children per family.
   (A) 4
   (B) 3
   (C) $3\frac{1}{2}$
   (D) 2
   (E) $1\frac{1}{2}$

9. Find the median number of children.
   (A) 1
   (B) 2
   (C) 3
   (D) 4
   (E) 5

10. Find the mode of the number of children.
    (A) 0
    (B) 1
    (C) 2
    (D) 3
    (E) 4

Averages Problems—Correct Answers

1.	**(B)**	6.	**(B)**
2.	**(C)**	7.	**(E)**
3.	**(A)**	8.	**(D)**
4.	**(C)**	9.	**(B)**
5.	**(B)**	10.	**(C)**

Problem Solutions—Averages

1. Find the sum of the values:

   $73.8 + 92.2 + 64.7 + 43.8 + 56.5 + 46.4 = 377.4$

   There are 6 values.

   $$\text{Arithmetic mean} = \frac{377.4}{6} = 62.9$$

   Answer: **(B)** 62.9

2. Arrange the numbers in order:

    1, 5, 5, 5, 7, 8, 8, 9, 9, 10, 10

    The middle number, or median, is 8.

    Answer: **(C)** 8

3. The mode is that number appearing most frequently. The number 15 appears three times.

    Answer: **(A)** 15

4. Average = $\dfrac{73 + 85 + 54 + 92 + 66}{5}$

    $= \dfrac{370}{5}$

    $= 74$

    Answer: **(C)** 74

5. Sum of the grades = 1440.

    $\dfrac{1440}{20} = 72$

    Answer: **(B)** 72

6. $75 \times 15¢ = 1125¢$
   $100 \times 30¢ = 3000¢$
   $\underline{\;50 \times 72¢ = 3600¢}$
   $225 \qquad\quad 7725¢$

    $\dfrac{7725¢}{225} = 34\frac{1}{3}¢$

    Answer: **(B)** $34\frac{1}{3}¢$

7.

Subject	Grade	Weight
English	90	4
Algebra	84	3
French	75	3
Music	76	1

    $(90 \times 4) + (84 \times 3) + (75 \times 3) + (76 \times 1)$
    $360 + 252 + 225 + 76 = 913$
    Weight = $4 + 3 + 3 + 1 = 11$
    $913 \div 11 = 83$ average

    Answer: **(E)** 83

8. Average = $\dfrac{3 + 4 + 4 + 0 + 1 + 2 + 0 + 2 + 2}{9}$

    $= \dfrac{18}{9}$

    $= 2$

    Answer: **(D)** 2

9. Arrange the numbers in order:

    0, 0, 1, 2, 2, 2, 3, 4, 4

    Of the 9 numbers, the fifth (middle) number is 2.

    Answer: **(B)** 2

10. The number appearing most often is 2.

    Answer: **(C)** 2

RATIO AND PROPORTION

Ratio

1. A **ratio** expresses the relationship between two (or more) quantities in terms of numbers. The mark used to indicate ratio is the colon (:) and is read "to."

    Example: The ratio 2:3 is read "2 to 3."

2. A ratio also represents division. Therefore, any ratio of two terms may be written as a fraction, and any fraction may be written as a ratio.

    Example: $3:4 = \frac{3}{4}$
    $\frac{5}{6} = 5:6$

3. To simplify any complicated ratio of two terms containing fractions, decimals, or percents:

    a. Divide the first term by the second.

    b. Write as a fraction in lowest terms.

    c. Write the fraction as a ratio.

    Illustration: Simplify the ratio $\frac{5}{6} : \frac{7}{8}$

    SOLUTION: $\frac{5}{6} \div \frac{7}{8} = \frac{5}{6} \times \frac{8}{7} = \frac{20}{21}$
    $\frac{20}{21} = 20:21$

    Answer: 20:21

4. To solve problems in which the ratio is given:

    a. Add the terms in the ratio.

    b. Divide the total amount that is to be put into a ratio by this sum.

c. Multiply each term in the ratio by this quotient.

Illustration: The sum of $360 is to be divided among three people according to the ratio 3:4:5. How much does each one receive?

SOLUTION: $3 + 4 + 5 = 12$
$$\$360 \div 12 = \$30$$
$$\$30 \times 3 = \$90$$
$$\$30 \times 4 = \$120$$
$$\$30 \times 5 = \$150$$

Answer: The money is divided thus: $90, $120, $150.

Proportion

5. a. A **proportion** indicates the equality of two ratios.

Example: 2:4 = 5:10 is a proportion. This is read "2 is to 4 as 5 is to 10."

b. In a proportion, the two outside terms are called the **extremes,** and the two inside terms are called the **means.**

Example: In the proportion 2:4 = 5:10, 2 and 10 are the extremes, and 4 and 5 are the means.

c. Proportions are often written in fractional form.

Example: The proportion 2:4 = 5:10 may be written $\frac{2}{4} = \frac{5}{10}$.

d. In any proportion, the product of the means equals the product of the extremes. If the proportion is a fractional form, the products may be found by cross-multiplication.

Example: In $\frac{2}{4} = \frac{5}{10}$, $4 \times 5 = 2 \times 10$.

e. The product of the extremes divided by one mean equals the other mean; the product of the means divided by one extreme equals the other extreme.

6. Many problems in which three terms are given and one term is unknown can be solved by using proportions. To solve such problems:

a. Formulate the proportion very carefully according to the facts given. (If any term is misplaced, the solution will be incorrect.) Any symbol may be written in place of the missing term.

b. Determine by inspection whether the means or the extremes are known. Multiply the pair that has both terms given.

c. Divide this product by the third term given to find the unknown term.

Illustration: The scale on a map shows that 2 cm represents 30 miles of actual length. What is the actual length of a road that is represented by 7 cm on the map?

SOLUTION: The map lengths and the actual lengths are in proportion—that is, they have equal ratios. If m stands for the unknown length, the proportion is:

$$\frac{2}{7} = \frac{30}{m}$$

As the proportion is written, m is an extreme and is equal to the product of the means, divided by the other extreme:

$$m = \frac{7 \times 30}{2}$$
$$m = \frac{210}{2}$$
$$m = 105$$

Answer: 7 cm on the map represents 105 miles.

Illustration: If a money bag containing 500 nickels weighs 6 pounds, how much will a money bag containing 1600 nickels weigh?

SOLUTION: The weights of the bags and the number of coins in them are proportional. Suppose w represents the unknown weight. Then

$$\frac{6}{w} = \frac{500}{1600}$$

The unknown is a mean and is equal to the product of the extremes, divided by the other mean:

$$w = \frac{6 \times 1600}{500}$$
$$w = 19.2$$

Answer: A bag containing 1600 nickels weighs 19.2 pounds.

Practice Problems Involving Ratio and Proportion

1. The ratio of 24 to 64 is
   (A) 1:64
   (B) 1:24
   (C) 20:100
   (D) 24:100
   (E) 3:8

2. The Baltimore Colts won 8 games and lost 3. The ratio of games won to games played is
   (A) 11:8
   (B) 8:3
   (C) 8:11
   (D) 3:8
   (E) 3:11

3. The ratio of $\frac{1}{4}$ to $\frac{3}{5}$ is
   (A) 1 to 3
   (B) 3 to 20
   (C) 5 to 12
   (D) 3 to 4
   (E) 5 to 4

4. If there are 16 boys and 12 girls in a class, the ratio of the number of girls to the number of children in the class is
   (A) 3 to 4
   (B) 3 to 7
   (C) 4 to 7
   (D) 4 to 3
   (E) 7 to 4

5. 259 is to 37 as
   (A) 5 is to 1
   (B) 63 is to 441
   (C) 84 is to 12
   (D) 130 is to 19
   (E) 25 is to 4

6. 2 dozen cans of dog food at the rate of 3 cans for $1.45 would cost
   (A) $10.05
   (B) $10.20
   (C) $11.20

(D) $11.60
(E) $11.75

7. A snapshot measures $2\frac{1}{2}$ inches by $1\frac{7}{8}$ inches. It is to be enlarged so that the longer dimension will be 4 inches. The length of the enlarged shorter dimension will be
   (A) $2\frac{1}{2}$ in
   (B) 3 in
   (C) $3\frac{3}{8}$ in
   (D) 4 in
   (E) 5 in

8. Men's white handkerchiefs cost $2.29 for 3. The cost per dozen handkerchiefs is
   (A) $27.48
   (B) $13.74
   (C) $9.16
   (D) $6.87
   (E) $4.58

9. A certain pole casts a shadow 24 feet long. At the same time another pole 3 feet high casts a shadow 4 feet long. How high is the first pole, given that the heights and shadows are in proportion?
   (A) 18 ft
   (B) 19 ft
   (C) 20 ft
   (D) 21 ft
   (E) 24 ft

10. The actual length represented by $3\frac{1}{2}$ inches on a drawing having a scale of $\frac{1}{8}$ inch to the foot is
    (A) 3.5 ft
    (B) 7 ft
    (C) 21 ft
    (D) 28 ft
    (E) 120 ft

11. Aluminum bronze consists of copper and aluminum, usually in the ratio of 10:1 by weight. If an object made of this alloy weighs 77 lb, how many pounds of aluminum does it contain?
    (A) 0.7
    (B) 7.0
    (C) 7.7
    (D) 70.7
    (E) 77.0

12. It costs 31 cents a square foot to lay vinyl flooring. To lay 180 square feet of flooring, it will cost
    (A) $16.20
    (B) $18.60
    (C) $55.80
    (D) $62.00
    (E) $180.00

13. If a per diem worker earns $352 in 16 days, the amount that he will earn in 117 days is most nearly
    (A) $3050
    (B) $2575
    (C) $2285
    (D) $2080
    (E) $1170

14. Assuming that on a blueprint $\frac{1}{8}$ inch equals 12 inches of actual length, the actual length in inches of a steel bar represented on the blueprint by a line $3\frac{3}{4}$ inches long is
    (A) $3\frac{3}{4}$
    (B) 30
    (C) 36
    (D) 360
    (E) 450

15. A, B, and C invested $9,000, $7,000 and $6,000, respectively. Their profits were to be divided according to the ratio of their investment. If B uses his share of the firm's profit of $825 to pay a personal debt of $230, how much will he have left?
    (A) $30.50
    (B) $32.50
    (C) $34.50
    (D) $36.50
    (E) $37.50

Ratio and Proportion Problems—Correct Answers

1.	**(E)**	6.	**(D)**	11.	**(B)**
2.	**(C)**	7.	**(B)**	12.	**(C)**
3.	**(C)**	8.	**(C)**	13.	**(B)**
4.	**(B)**	9.	**(A)**	14.	**(D)**
5.	**(C)**	10.	**(D)**	15.	**(B)**

Problem Solutions—Ratio and Proportion

1. The ratio 24 to 64 may be written 24:64 or $\frac{24}{64}$. In fraction form, the ratio can be reduced:

   $$\frac{24}{64} = \frac{3}{8} \quad \text{or} \quad 3:8$$

   Answer: **(E)** 3:8

2. The number of games played was $3 + 8 = 11$. The ratio of games won to games played is 8:11.

   Answer: **(C)** 8:11

3. $\frac{1}{4}:\frac{3}{5} = \frac{1}{4} \div \frac{3}{5}$
   $= \frac{1}{4} \times \frac{5}{3}$
   $= \frac{5}{12}$
   $= 5:12$

   Answer: **(C)** 5 to 12

4. There are $16 + 12 = 28$ children in the class. The ratio of number of girls to number of children is 12:28.

   $$\frac{12}{28} = \frac{3}{7}$$

   Answer: **(B)** 3 to 7

5. The ratio $\frac{259}{37}$ reduces by 37 to $\frac{7}{1}$. The ratio $\frac{84}{12}$ also reduces to $\frac{7}{1}$. Therefore, $\frac{259}{37} = \frac{84}{12}$ is a proportion.

   Answer: **(C)** 84 is to 12

6. The number of cans are proportional to the price. Let p represent the unknown price:

   Then
   $$\frac{3}{24} = \frac{1.45}{p}$$
   $$p = \frac{1.45 \times 24}{3}$$
   $$p = \frac{34.80}{3}$$
   $$= \$11.60$$

   Answer: **(D)** $11.60

7. Let s represent the unknown shorter dimension:

$$\frac{2\frac{1}{2}}{4} = \frac{1\frac{7}{8}}{s}$$

$$s = \frac{4 \times 1\frac{7}{8}}{2\frac{1}{2}}$$

$$= \frac{\overset{1}{\cancel{4}} \times \frac{15}{8}\,_{2}}{2\frac{1}{2}}$$

$$= \frac{15}{2} \div 2\frac{1}{2}$$
$$= \frac{15}{2} \div \frac{5}{2}$$
$$= \frac{15}{2} \times \frac{2}{5}$$
$$= 3$$

Answer: **(B)** 3 in

8. If p is the cost per dozen (12):

$$\frac{3}{12} = \frac{2.29}{p}$$

$$p = \frac{\overset{4}{\cancel{12}} \times 2.29}{\underset{1}{\cancel{3}}}$$

$$= 9.16$$

Answer: **(C)** $9.16

9. If f is the height of the first pole, the proportion is:

$$\frac{f}{24} = \frac{3}{4}$$

$$f = \frac{\overset{6}{\cancel{24}} \times 3}{\underset{1}{\cancel{4}}}$$

$$= 18$$

Answer: **(A)** 18 ft

10. If y is the unknown length:

$$\frac{3\frac{1}{2}}{\frac{1}{8}} = \frac{y}{1}$$

$$y = \frac{3\frac{1}{2} \times 1}{\frac{1}{8}}$$

$$= 3\frac{1}{2} \div \frac{1}{8}$$
$$= \frac{7}{2} \times \frac{8}{1}$$
$$= 28$$

Answer: **(D)** 28 ft

11. Since only two parts of a proportion are known (77 is total weight), the problem must be solved by the ratio method. The ratio 10:1 means that if the alloy were separated into equal parts, 10 of those parts

would be copper and 1 would be aluminum, for a total of 10 + 1 = 11 parts.

$$77 \div 11 = 7 \text{ lb per part}$$

The alloy has 1 part aluminum.

$$7 \times 1 = 7 \text{ lb aluminum}$$

Answer: **(B)** 7.0

12. The cost (c) is proportional to the number of square feet.

$$\frac{\$.31}{c} = \frac{1}{.180}$$

$$c = \frac{\$.31 \times 180}{1}$$

$$= \$55.80$$

Answer: **(C)** $55.80

13. The amount earned is proportional to the number of days worked. If a is the unknown amount:

$$\frac{\$352}{a} = \frac{16}{117}$$

$$a = \frac{\$352 \times 117}{16}$$

$$a = \$2574$$

Answer: **(B)** $2575

14. If n is the unknown length:

$$\frac{\frac{1}{8}}{3\frac{3}{4}} = \frac{12}{n}$$

$$n = \frac{14 \times 3\frac{3}{4}}{\frac{1}{8}}$$

$$= \frac{\overset{3}{\cancel{12}} \times \frac{15}{4}\,_{1}}{\frac{1}{8}}$$

$$= \frac{45}{\frac{1}{8}}$$

$$= 45 \div \frac{1}{8}$$
$$= 45 \times \frac{8}{1}$$
$$= 360$$

Answer: **(D)** 360

15. The ratio of investment is:

$$9,000:7,000:6,000 \quad \text{or} \quad 9:7:6$$

$$9 + 7 + 6 = 22$$
$$\$825 \div 22 = \$37.50 \text{ each share of profit}$$
$$7 \times \$37.50 = \$262.50 \text{ B's share of profit}$$

$$\begin{array}{r} \$262.50 \\ -\ 230.00 \\ \hline \$\ 32.50 \end{array} \text{ amount B has left}$$

Answer: **(B)** $32.50

WORK AND TANK PROBLEMS

Work Problems

1. a. In work problems, there are three items involved: the number of people working, the time, and the amount of work done.

    b. The number of people working is directly proportional to the amount of work done; that is, the more people on the job, the more the work that will be done, and vice versa.

    c. The number of people working is inversely proportional to the time; that is, the more people on the job, the less time it will take to finish it, and vice versa.

    d. The time expended on a job is directly proportional to the amount of work done; that is, the more time expended on a job, the more work that is done, and vice versa.

Work at Equal Rates

2. a. When given the time required by a number of people working at equal rates to complete a job, multiply the number of people by their time to find the time required by one person to do the complete job.

    Example: If it takes 4 people working at equal rates 30 days to finish a job, then one person will take 30 × 4 or 120 days.

    b. When given the time required by one person to complete a job, to find the time required by a number of people working at equal rates to complete the same job, divide the time by the number of people.

    Example: If 1 person can do a job in 20 days, it will take 4 people working at equal rates 20 ÷ 4 or 5 days to finish the job.

3. To solve problems involving people who work at equal rates:

    a. Multiply the number of people by their time to find the time required by 1 person.

    b. Divide this time by the number of people required.

Illustration: Four workers can do a job in 48 days. How long will it take 3 workers to finish the same job?

SOLUTION: One worker can do the job in 48 × 4 or 192 days.
3 workers can do the job in 192 ÷ 3 = 64 days.

Answer: It would take 3 workers 64 days.

4. In some work problems, the rates, though unequal, can be equalized by comparison. To solve such problems:

    a. Determine from the facts given how many equal rates there are.

    b. Multiply the number of equal rates by the time given.

    c. Divide this by the number of equal rates.

Illustration: Three workers can do a job in 12 days. Two of the workers work twice as fast as the third. How long would it take one of the faster workers to do the job himself?

SOLUTION: There are two fast workers and one slow worker. Therefore, there are actually five slow workers working at equal rates.

1 slow worker will take 12 × 5 or 60 days.
1 fast worker = 2 slow workers; therefore, he will take 60 ÷ 2 or 30 days to complete the job.

Answer: It will take 1 fast worker 30 days to complete the job.

5. Unit time is expressed in terms of 1 minute, 1 hour, 1 day, etc.

6. The rate at which a person works is the amount of work he can do in **unit time.**

7. If given the time it will take one person to do a job, then the reciprocal of the time is the part done in unit time.

   Example: If a worker can do a job in 6 days, then he can do $\frac{1}{6}$ of the work in 1 day.

8. The reciprocal of the work done in unit time is the time it will take to do the complete job.

   Example: If a worker can do $\frac{3}{7}$ of the work in 1 day, then he can do the whole job in $\frac{7}{3}$ or $2\frac{1}{3}$ days.

9. If given the various times at which each of a number of people can complete a job, to find the time it will take to do the job if all work together:

   a. Invert the time of each to find how much each can do in unit time.

   b. Add these reciprocals to find what part all working together can do in unit time.

   c. Invert this sum to find the time it will take all of them together to do the whole job.

   Illustration: If it takes A 3 days to dig a certain ditch, whereas B can dig it in 6 days, and C in 12, how long would it take all three to do the job?

   SOLUTION: A can do it in 3 days; therefore, he can do $\frac{1}{3}$ in one day. B can do it in 6 days; therefore, he can do $\frac{1}{6}$ in one day. C can do it in 12 days; therefore, he can do $\frac{1}{12}$ in one day.

   $$\frac{1}{3} + \frac{1}{6} + \frac{1}{12} = \frac{7}{12}$$

   A, B, and C can do $\frac{7}{12}$ of the work in one day; therefore, it will take them $\frac{12}{7}$ or $1\frac{5}{7}$ days to complete the job.

   Answer: A, B, and C, working together, can complete the job in $1\frac{5}{7}$ days.

10. If given the total time it requires a number of people working together to complete a job, and the times of all but one are known, to find the missing time:

    a. Invert the given times to find how much each can do in unit time.

b. Add the reciprocals to find how much is done in unit time by those whose rates are known.

c. Subtract this sum from the reciprocal of the total time to find the missing rate.

d. Invert this rate to find the unknown time.

Illustration: A, B, and C can do a job in 2 days. B can do it in 5 days, and C can do it in 4 days. How long would it take A to do it himself?

SOLUTION: B can do it in 5 days; therefore, he can do $\frac{1}{5}$ in one day. C can do it in 4 days; therefore, he can do $\frac{1}{4}$ in one day. The part that can be done by B and C together in 1 day is:

$$\frac{1}{5} + \frac{1}{4} = \frac{9}{20}$$

The total time is 2 days; therefore, all can do $\frac{1}{2}$ in one day.

$$\frac{1}{2} - \frac{9}{20} = \frac{1}{20}$$

A can do $\frac{1}{20}$ in 1 day; therefore, he can do the whole job in 20 days.

Answer: It would take A 20 days to complete the job himself.

11. In some work problems, certain values are given for the three factors—number of workers, the amount of work done, and the time. It is then usually required to find the changes that occur when one or two of the factors are given different values.

    One of the best methods of solving such problems is by directly making the necessary cancellations, divisions and multiplications.

    In this problem it is easily seen that more workers will be required since more houses are to be built in a shorter time.

    Illustration: If 60 workers can build 4 houses in 12 months, how many workers would be required to build 6 houses in 4 months?

    SOLUTION: To build 6 houses instead of 4 in the same amount of time, we would need $\frac{6}{4}$ of the number of workers.

    $$\frac{6}{4} \times 60 = 90$$

    Since we now have 4 months where previously we needed 12, we must triple the number of workers.

$$90 \times 3 = 270$$

Answer: 270 workers will be needed to build 6 houses in 4 months.

12. In general, a work problem in which the workers work at different rates can be fitted into the following formula for combining their work:

$$\frac{\text{work done by worker A}}{\text{time taken by worker A}}$$

$$+ \frac{\text{work done by worker B}}{\text{time taken by worker B}}$$

$$= \frac{\text{Total work done}}{\text{Total time taken}}$$

The problem will, directly or indirectly, give you five of the above six items. Plug in the known quantities and calculate the unknown one.

Note: Be sure your units of work and time are consistent throughout the formula.

Illustration: A can do the job in 4 hours. B can do it in 5. How long do they take together?

SOLUTION:
$$\frac{1 \text{ job}}{4 \text{ hrs.}} + \frac{1 \text{ job}}{5 \text{ hrs.}} = \frac{1 \text{ job}}{x \text{ hrs.}}$$
$$\frac{1}{4} + \frac{1}{5} = \frac{1}{x}$$
$$\frac{5}{20} + \frac{4}{20} = \frac{1}{x}$$
$$\frac{9}{20} = \frac{1}{x}$$
$$\frac{20}{9} = \frac{x}{1}$$
$$2\frac{2}{9} = x$$

Answer: A and B together take $2\frac{2}{9}$ hours to do the job.

Tank Problems

13. The solution of tank problems is similar to that of work problems. Completely filling (or emptying) a tank may be thought of as completing a job.

14. a. If given the time it takes a pipe to fill or empty a tank, the reciprocal of the time will represent that part of the tank that is filled or emptied in unit time.

Example: If it takes a pipe 4 minutes to fill a tank, then $\frac{1}{4}$ of the tank is filled in one minute.

b. The amount that a pipe can fill or empty in unit time is its **rate.**

15. If given the part of a tank that a pipe or a combination of pipes can fill or empty in unit time, invert the part to find the total time required to fill or empty the whole tank.

Example: If a pipe can fill $\frac{2}{5}$ of a tank in 1 minute, then it will take $\frac{5}{2}$ or $2\frac{1}{2}$ minutes to fill the entire tank.

16. To solve tank problems in which only one action (filling or emptying) is going on:

a. Invert the time of each pipe to find how much each can do in unit time.

b. Add the reciprocals to find how much all can do in unit time.

c. Invert this sum to find the total time.

Illustration: Pipe A can fill a tank in 3 minutes whereas B can fill it in 4 minutes. How long would it take both pipes, working together, to fill it?

SOLUTION: Pipe A can fill it in 3 minutes; therefore, it can fill $\frac{1}{3}$ of the tank in one minute. Pipe B can fill it in 4 minutes; therefore, it can fill $\frac{1}{4}$ of the tank on one minute.

$$\frac{1}{3} + \frac{1}{4} = \frac{7}{12}$$

Pipe A and Pipe B can fill $\frac{7}{12}$ of the tank in one minute; therefore, they can fill the tank in $\frac{12}{7}$ or $1\frac{5}{7}$ minutes.

Answer: Pipes A and B, working together, can fill the tank in $1\frac{5}{7}$ minutes.

17. In problems in which both filling and emptying actions are occurring:

a. Determine which process has the faster rate.

b. The difference between the filling rate and the emptying rate is the part of the tank that is actually being filled or emptied in unit time. The fraction representing the slower action is subtracted from the fraction representing the faster process.

c. The reciprocal of this difference is the time it will take to fill or empty the tank.

Illustration: A certain tank can be filled by Pipe A in 12 minutes. Pipe B can empty the tank in 18 minutes. If both pipes are open, how long will it take to fill or empty the tank?

SOLUTION: Pipe A fills $\frac{1}{12}$ of the tank in 1 minute.
Pipe B empties $\frac{1}{18}$ of the tank in 1 minute.

$$\frac{1}{12} = \frac{3}{36}$$
$$\frac{1}{18} = \frac{2}{36}$$

Since $\frac{1}{12}$ is greater than $\frac{1}{18}$, the tank will ultimately be filled. In 1 minute, $\frac{3}{36} - \frac{2}{36} = \frac{1}{36}$ of the tank is actually filled. Therefore, the tank will be completely filled in 36 minutes.

Answer: It will take 36 minutes to fill the tank if both pipes are open.

Work and Tank Practice Problems

1. If 314 clerks filed 6594 papers in 10 minutes, what is the number filed per minute by the average clerk?
   (A) .2
   (B) 1.05
   (C) 2.1
   (D) 2.5
   (E) 21

2. Four men working together can dig a ditch in 42 days. They begin, but one man works only half-days. How long will it take to complete the job?
   (A) 38 days
   (B) 42 days
   (C) 43 days
   (D) 44 days
   (E) 48 days

3. A clerk is requested to file 800 cards. If he can file cards at the rate of 80 cards an hour,

the number of cards remaining to be filed after 7 hours of work is
   (A) 140
   (B) 240
   (C) 260
   (D) 560
   (E) 800

4. If it takes 4 days for 3 machines to do a certain job, it will take two machines
   (A) 6 days
   (B) $5\frac{1}{2}$ days
   (C) 5 days
   (D) $4\frac{1}{2}$ days
   (E) 2 days

5. A stenographer has been assigned to place entries on 500 forms. She places entries on 25 forms by the end of half an hour, when she is joined by another stenographer. The second stenographer places entries at the rate of 45 an hour. Assuming that both stenographers continue to work at their respective rates of speed, the total number of hours required to carry out the entire assignment is
   (A) 5
   (B) $5\frac{1}{2}$
   (C) $6\frac{1}{2}$
   (D) 7
   (E) $7\frac{1}{14}$

6. If in 5 days a clerk can copy 125 pages, 36 lines each, 11 words to the line, how many pages of 30 lines each and 12 words to the line can he copy in 6 days?
   (A) 145
   (B) 155
   (C) 160
   (D) 165
   (E) 175

7. A and B do a job together in two hours. Working alone A does the job in 5 hours. How long will it take B to do the job alone?
   (A) 2 hrs
   (B) $2\frac{1}{3}$ hrs
   (C) $2\frac{1}{2}$ hrs
   (D) 3 hrs
   (E) $3\frac{1}{3}$ hrs

8. A stenographer transcribes her notes at the rate of one line typed in ten seconds. At this

rate, how long (in minutes and seconds) will it take her to transcribe notes, which will require seven pages of typing, 25 lines to the page?
(A) 29 min 10 sec
(B) 20 min 30 sec
(C) 17 min 50 sec
(D) 15 min
(E) 9 min 30 sec

9. A group of five clerks have been assigned to insert 24,000 letters into envelopes. The clerks perform this work at the following rates of speed: Clerk A, 1100 letters an hour; Clerk B, 1450 letters an hour; Clerk C, 1200 letters an hour; Clerk D, 1300 letters an hour; Clerk E, 1250 letters an hour. At the end of two hours of work, Clerks C and D are assigned to another task. From the time that Clerks C and D were taken off the assignment, the number of hours required for the remaining clerks to complete this assignment is
(A) less than 2 hr
(B) more than 2 hr, but less than 4 hr
(C) more than 4 hr, but less than 6 hr
(D) more than 6 hr
(E) none of the above

10. If a certain job can be performed by 18 workers in 26 days, the number of workers needed to perform the job in 12 days is
(A) 24
(B) 30
(C) 39
(D) 45
(E) 52

11. A steam shovel excavates 2 cubic yards every 40 seconds. At this rate, the amount excavated in 45 minutes is
(A) 90 cu yd
(B) 135 cu yd
(C) 270 cu yd
(D) 1200 cu yd
(E) 3600 cu yd

12. If a plant making bricks turns out 1250 bricks in 5 days, the number of bricks that can be made in 20 days is
(A) 5000
(B) 6250

(C) 12,500
(D) 25,000
(E) none of the above

13. A tank is $\frac{3}{4}$ full. Fillpipe A can fill the tank in 12 minutes. Drainpipe B can empty it in 8 minutes. If both pipes are open, how long will it take to empty the tank?
(A) 8 min
(B) 12 min
(C) 16 min
(D) 18 min
(E) 24 min

14. A tank that holds 400 gallons of water can be filled by one pipe in 15 minutes and emptied by another in 40 minutes. How long would it take to fill the tank if both pipes are functioning?
(A) 20 min
(B) 21 min
(C) 23 min
(D) 24 min
(E) 28 min

15. An oil burner in a housing development burns 76 gallons of fuel oil per hour. At 9 A.M. on a very cold day the superintendent asks the housing manager to put in an emergency order for more fuel oil. At that time, he reports that he has on hand 266 gallons. At noon, he again comes to the manager, notifying him that no oil has been delivered. The maximum amount of time that he can continue to furnish heat without receiving more oil is
(A) $\frac{1}{2}$ hr
(B) 1 hr
(C) $1\frac{1}{2}$ hr
(D) 2 hr
(E) none of the above

Work and Tank Problems—Correct Answers

1.	**(C)**	6.	**(D)**	11.	**(B)**
2.	**(E)**	7.	**(E)**	12.	**(A)**
3.	**(B)**	8.	**(A)**	13.	**(D)**
4.	**(A)**	9.	**(B)**	14.	**(D)**
5.	**(B)**	10.	**(C)**	15.	**(A)**

Work and Tank Problem Solutions

1. 6594 papers ÷ 314 clerks = 21 papers per clerk in 10 minutes
   21 papers ÷ 10 minutes = 2.1 papers per minute filed by average clerk

   Answer: **(C)** 2.1

2. It would take 1 man 42 × 4 = 168 days to complete the job, working alone.
   If $3\frac{1}{2}$ men are working (one man works halfdays, the other 3 work full days), the job would take 168 ÷ $3\frac{1}{2}$ = 48 days.

   Answer: **(E)** 48 days

3. In 7 hours the clerk files 7 × 80 = 560 cards. Since 800 cards must be filed, there are 800 − 560 = 240 remaining.

   Answer: **(B)** 240

4. It would take 1 machine 3 × 4 = 12 days to do the job. Two machines could do the job in 12 ÷ 2 = 6 days.

   Answer: **(A)** 6 days

5. At the end of the first half-hour, there are 500 − 25 = 475 forms remaining. If the first stenographer completed 25 forms in half an hour, her rate is 25 × 2 = 50 forms per hour. The combined rate of the two stenographers is 50 + 45 = 95 forms per hour. The remaining forms can be completed in 475 ÷ 95 = 5 hours. Adding the first half-hour, the entire job requires $5\frac{1}{2}$.

   Answer: **(B)** $5\frac{1}{2}$

6. 36 lines × 11 words = 396 words on each page
   125 pages × 396 words = 49,500 words in 5 days
   49,500 ÷ 5 = 9900 words in 1 day
   12 words × 30 lines = 360 words on each page
   9900 ÷ 360 = $27\frac{1}{2}$ pages in 1 day
   $27\frac{1}{2}$ × 6 = 165 pages in 6 days.

   Answer: **(D)** 165

7. If A can do the job alone in 5 hours, A can do $\frac{1}{5}$ of the job in 1 hour. Working together, A and B can do the job in 2 hours, therefore in 1 hour they do $\frac{1}{2}$ the job.
   In 1 hour, B alone does
   $$\frac{1}{2} - \frac{1}{5} = \frac{5}{10} - \frac{2}{10}$$
   $$= \frac{3}{10} \text{ of the job.}$$
   It would take B $\frac{10}{3}$ hours = $3\frac{1}{3}$ hours to do the whole job alone.

   Answer: **(E)** $3\frac{1}{3}$ hr

8. She must type 7 × 25 = 175 lines. At the rate of 1 line per 10 seconds, it will take 175 × 10 = 1750 seconds.
   1750 seconds ÷ 60 = $29\frac{1}{6}$ minutes
   = 29 min 10 sec

   Answer: **(A)** 29 min 10 sec

9. | Clerk | Number of letters per hr |
   |-------|--------------------------|
   | A | 1100 |
   | B | 1450 |
   | C | 1200 |
   | D | 1300 |
   | E | + 1250 |
   | Total = | 6300 |

   All 5 clerks working together process a total of 6300 letters per hour. After 2 hours, they have processed 6300 × 2 = 12,600. Of the original 24,000 letters there are

   $$\begin{array}{r} 24,000 \\ -\ 12,600 \\ \hline 11,400 \text{ letters remaining} \end{array}$$

   Clerks A, B, and E working together process a total of 3800 letters per hour. It will take them

   $$11,400 \div 3800 = 3 \text{ hours}$$

   to process the remaining letters.

   Answer: **(B)** more than 2 hr, but less than 4 hr

10. The job could be performed by 1 worker in 18 × 26 days = 468 days. To perform the job in 12 days would require 468 ÷ 12 = 39 workers.

    Answer: **(C)** 39

11. The shovel excavates 1 cubic yard in 20 seconds.

    There are $45 \times 60 = 2700$ seconds in 45 minutes.

    In 2700 seconds the shovel can excavate $2700 \div 20 = 135$ cubic yards.

    Answer: **(B)** 135 cu yd

12. In 20 days the plant can produce four times as many bricks as in 5 days.

    $$1250 \times 4 = 5000 \text{ bricks}$$

    Answer: **(A)** 5000

13. Pipe A can fill the tank in 12 min or fill $\frac{1}{12}$ of the tank in 1 min. Pipe B can empty the tank in 8 min or empty $\frac{1}{8}$ of the tank in 1 min. In 1 minute, $\frac{1}{8} - \frac{1}{12}$ of the tank is emptied (since $\frac{1}{8}$ is greater than $\frac{1}{12}$).

    $$\begin{array}{r} \frac{1}{8} \\ - \frac{1}{12} \end{array} = \begin{array}{r} \frac{3}{24} \\ - \frac{2}{24} \\ \hline \frac{1}{24} \end{array}$$ of the tank is emptied per minute

    It would take 24 min to empty whole tank, but it is only $\frac{3}{4}$ full:

    $$\frac{3}{4} \times \overset{6}{\underset{1}{24}} = 18 \text{ minutes}$$

    Answer: **(D)** 18 min

14. The first pipe can fill $\frac{1}{15}$ of the tank in 1 minute. The second pipe can empty $\frac{1}{40}$ of the tank in 1 minute. With both pipes open, $\frac{1}{15} - \frac{1}{40}$ of the tank will be filled per minute.

    $$\begin{array}{r} \frac{1}{15} \\ - \frac{1}{40} \end{array} = \begin{array}{r} \frac{8}{120} \\ - \frac{3}{120} \\ \hline \frac{5}{120} = \frac{1}{24} \end{array}$$

    In 1 minute, $\frac{1}{24}$ of the tank is filled; therefore, it will take 24 mintues for the entire tank to be filled.

    Answer: **(D)** 24 min

15. If 76 gallons are used per hour, it will take $266 \div 76 = 3\frac{1}{2}$ hours to use 266 gallons.

    From 9 a.m. to noon is 3 hours; therefore, there is only fuel for $\frac{1}{2}$ hour more.

    Answer: **(A)** $\frac{1}{2}$ hr

DISTANCE PROBLEMS

1. In distance problems, there are usually three quantities involved: the distance (in miles), the rate (in miles per hour—mph), and the time (in hours).

    a. To find the distance, multiply the rate by the time: distance = rate × time.

    Example: A man traveling 40 miles an hour for 3 hours travels 40×3 or 120 miles.

    b. The rate is the distance traveled in unit time. To find the rate, divide the distance by the time.

    Example: If a car travels 100 miles in 4 hours, the rate is $100 \div 4$ or 25 miles an hour.

    c. To find the time, divide the distance by the rate.

    Example: If a car travels 150 miles at the rate of 30 miles an hour, the time is $150 \div 30$ or 5 hours.

Combined Rates

2. a. When two people or objects are traveling towards each other, the rate at which they are approaching each other is the sum of their respective rates.

    b. When two people or objects are traveling in directly opposite directions, the rate at which they are separating is the sum of their respective rates.

3. To solve problems involving combined rates:

    a. Determine which of the three factors is to be found.

    b. Combine the rates and find the unknown factor.

    Illustration: A and B are walking towards each other over a road 120 miles long. A walks at a rate of 6 miles an hour, and B walks at a rate of 4 miles an hour. How soon will they meet?

SOLUTION: The factor to be found is the time.

Time = distance ÷ rate
Distance = 120 miles
Rate = 6 + 4 = 10 miles an hour
Time = 120 ÷ 10 = 12 hours

Answer: They will meet in 12 hours.

Illustration: Joe and Sam are walking in opposite directions. Joe walks at the rate of 5 miles an hour, and Sam walks at the rate of 7 miles an hour. How far apart will they be at the end of 3 hours?

SOLUTION: The factor to be found is distance.

Distance = time × rate
Time = 3 hours
Rate = 5 + 7 = 12 miles an hour
Distance = 12 × 3 = 36 miles

Answer: They will be 36 miles apart at the end of 3 hours.

4. To find the time it takes a faster person or object to catch up with a slower person or object:

a. Determine how far ahead the slower person or object is.

b. Subtract the slower rate from the faster rate to find the distance the faster person or object gains per unit time.

c. Divide the slower person or object's lead by the difference in rates (b).

Illustration: Two automobiles are traveling along the same road. The first one, which travels at the rate of 30 miles an hour, starts out 6 hours ahead of the second one, which travels at the rate of 50 miles an hour. How long will it take the second one to catch up with the first one?

SOLUTION: The first automobile starts out 6 hours ahead of the second. Its rate is 30 miles an hour. Therefore, it has traveled 6 × 30 or 180 miles by the time the second one starts. The second automobile travels at the rate of 50 miles an hour. Therefore, its gain is 50 − 30 or 20 miles an hour. The second auto has to cover 180 miles. There-fore, it will take 180 ÷ 20 or 9 hours to catch up with the first automobile.

Answer: It will take the faster auto 9 hours to catch up with the slower one.

Average of Two Rates

5. In some problems, two or more rates must be averaged. When the times are the same for two or more different rates, add the rates and divide by the number of rates.

Example: If a man travels for 2 hours at 30 miles an hour, at 40 miles an hour for the next 2 hours, and at 50 miles an hour for the next 2 hours, then his average rate for the 6 hours is (30 + 40 + 50) ÷ 3 = 40 miles an hour.

6. When the times are not the same, but the distances are the same:

a. Assume the distance to be a convenient length.

b. Find the time at the first rate.

c. Find the time at the second rate.

d. Find the time at the third rate, if any.

e. Add up all the distances and divide by the total time to find the average rate.

Illustration: A boy travels a certain distance at the rate of 20 miles an hour and returns at the rate of 30 miles an hour. What is his average rate for both trips?

SOLUTION: The distance is the same for both trips. Assume that it is 60 miles. The time for the first trip is 60 ÷ 20 = 3 hours. The time for the second trip is 60 ÷ 30 = 2 hours. The total distance is 120 miles. The total time is 5 hours. Average rate is 120 ÷ 5 = 24 miles an hour.

Answer: The average rate is 24 miles an hour.

7. When the times are not the same and the distances are not the same:

a. Find the time for the first distance.

b. Find the time for the second distance.

c. Find the time for the third distance, if any.

d. Add up all the distances and divide by the total time to find the average rate.

Illustration: A man travels 100 miles at 20 miles an hour, 60 miles at 30 miles an hour, and 80 miles at 10 miles an hour. What is his average rate for the three trips?

SOLUTION: The time for the first trip is $100 \div 20 = 5$ hours. The time for the second trip is $60 \div 30 = 2$ hours. The time for the third trip is $80 \div 10 = 8$ hours. The total distance is 240 miles. The total time is 15 hours. Average rate is $240 \div 15 = 16$.

Answer: The average rate for the three trips is 16 miles an hour.

Gasoline Problems

8. Problems involving miles per gallon (mpg) of gasoline are solved in the same way as those involving miles per hour. The word gallon simply replaces the word hour.

9. Miles per gallon = distance in miles ÷ no. of gallons

   Example: If a car can travel 100 miles using 4 gallons of gasoline, then its gasoline consumption is $100 \div 4$, or 25 mpg.

Practice Problems Involving Distance

1. A ten-car train took 6 minutes to travel between two stations that are 3 miles apart. The average speed of the train was
   (A) 20 mph
   (B) 25 mph
   (C) 30 mph
   (D) 35 mph
   (E) 40 mph

2. A police car is ordered to report to the scene of a crime 5 miles away. If the car travels at an average rate of 40 miles per hour, the time it will take to reach its destination is
   (A) 3 min

(B) 7.5 min
(C) 10 min
(D) 13.5 min
(E) 15 min

3. If the average speed of a train between two stations is 30 miles per hour and the two stations are $\frac{1}{2}$ mile apart, the time it takes the train to travel from one station to the other is
   (A) 1 min
   (B) 2 min
   (C) 3 min
   (D) 4 min
   (E) 5 min

4. A car completes a 10-mile trip in 20 minutes. If it does one-half the distance at a speed of 20 miles an hour, its speed for the remainder of the distance must be
   (A) 25 mph
   (B) $33\frac{1}{3}$ mph
   (C) 40 mph
   (D) 50 mph
   (E) 60 mph

5. An express train leaves one station at 9:02 and arrives at the next station at 9:08. If the distance traveled is $2\frac{1}{2}$ miles, the average speed of the train (mph) is
   (A) 15 mph
   (B) 20 mph
   (C) 25 mph
   (D) 40 mph
   (E) 50 mph

6. A motorist averaged 60 miles per hour in going a distance of 240 miles. He made the return trip over the same distance in 6 hours. What was his average speed for the entire trip?
   (A) 40 mph
   (B) 48 mph
   (C) 50 mph
   (D) 60 mph
   (E) 64 mph

7. A city has been testing various types of gasoline for economy and efficiency. It has been found that a police radio patrol car can travel 18 miles on a gallon of Brand A

gasoline, costing $1.30 a gallon, and 15 miles on a gallon of Brand B gasoline, costing $1.25 a gallon. For a distance of 900 miles, Brand B will cost
(A) $10 more than Brand A
(B) $10 less than Brand A
(C) $100 more than Brand A
(D) $100 less than Brand A
(E) the same as Brand A

8. A suspect arrested in New Jersey is being turned over by New Jersey authorities to two New York City police officers for a crime committed in New York City. The New York officers receive their prisoner at a point 16 miles from their precinct station house, and travel directly toward their destination at an average speed of 40 miles an hour except for a delay of 10 minutes at one point because of a traffic tie-up. The time it should take the officers to reach their destination is, most nearly,
(A) 16 min
(B) 18 min
(C) 24 min
(D) 30 min
(E) 34 min

9. The Mayflower sailed from Plymouth, England, to Plymouth Rock, a distance of approximately 2800 miles, in 63 days. The average speed was closest to which one of the following?
(A) $\frac{1}{2}$ mph
(B) 1 mph
(C) 2 mph
(D) 3 mph
(E) 4 mph

10. If a vehicle is to complete a 20-mile trip at an average rate of 30 miles per hour, it must complete the trip in
(A) 20 min
(B) 30 min
(C) 40 min
(D) 50 min
(E) 60 min

11. A car began a trip with 12 gallons of gasoline in the tank and ended with $7\frac{1}{2}$ gallons. The car traveled 17.3 miles for each gallon of gasoline. During the trip gasoline was

bought for $10.00, at a cost of $1.25 per gallon. The total number of miles traveled during this trip was most nearly
(A) 79
(B) 196
(C) 216
(D) 229
(E) 236

12. A man travels a total of 4.2 miles each day to and from work. The traveling consumes 72 minutes each day. How many hours would he save in 129 working days if he moved to another residence so that he would travel only 1.7 miles each day, assuming he travels at the same rate?
(A) 98.3
(B) 97.0
(C) 95.6
(D) 93.2
(E) 90.3

13. A man can travel a certain distance at the rate of 25 miles an hour by automobile. He walks back the same distance on foot at the rate of 10 miles an hour. What is his average rate for both trips?
(A) $14\frac{2}{7}$ mph
(B) $15\frac{1}{3}$ mph
(C) $17\frac{1}{2}$ mph
(D) $28\frac{4}{7}$ mph
(E) 35 mph

14. Two trains running on the same track travel at the rates of 25 and 30 miles an hour. If the first train starts out an hour earlier, how long will it take the second train to catch up with it?
(A) 2 hr
(B) 3 hr
(C) 4 hr
(D) 5 hr
(E) 6 hr

15. Two ships are 1550 miles apart sailing towards each other. One sails at the rate of 85 miles per day and the other at the rate of 65 miles per day. How far apart will they be at the end of 9 days?
(A) 180 mi
(B) 200 mi
(C) 220 mi

(D) 785 mi
(E) 1350 mi

Distance Problems—Correct Answers

1.	(C)	6.	(B)	11.	(C)
2.	(B)	7.	(A)	12.	(E)
3.	(A)	8.	(E)	13.	(A)
4.	(E)	9.	(C)	14.	(D)
5.	(C)	10.	(C)	15.	(B)

Problem Solutions—Distance

1.
$$6 \text{ min} = \tfrac{6}{60} \text{ hr} = .1 \text{ hr}$$
$$\text{Speed (rate)} = \text{distance} \div \text{time}$$
$$\text{Speed} = 3 \div .1 = 30 \text{ mph}$$

Answer: **(C)** 30 mph

2.
$$\text{Time} = \text{distance} \div \text{rate}$$
$$\text{Time} = 5 \div 40 = .125 \text{ hr}$$
$$.125 \text{ hr} = .125 \times 60 \text{ min}$$
$$= 7.5 \text{ min}$$

Answer: **(B)** 7.5 min

3.
$$\text{Time} = \text{distance} \div \text{rate}$$
$$\text{Time} = \tfrac{1}{2} \text{ mi} \div 30 \text{ mph}$$
$$= \tfrac{1}{60} \text{ hr}$$
$$\tfrac{1}{60} \text{ hr} = 1 \text{ min}$$

Answer: **(A)** 1 min

4. First part of trip $= \tfrac{1}{2}$ of 10 miles $= 5$ miles
Time for first part $= 5 \div 20$
$$= \tfrac{1}{4} \text{ hour}$$
$$= 15 \text{ minutes}$$

Second part of trip was 5 miles, completed in $20 - 15$ minutes, or 5 minutes.

$$5 \text{ minutes} = \tfrac{1}{12} \text{ hour}$$
$$\text{Rate} = 5 \text{ mi} \div \tfrac{1}{12} \text{ hr}$$
$$= 60 \text{ mph}$$

Answer: **(E)** 60 mph

5. Time is 6 minutes, or .1 hour

$$\text{Speed} = \text{distance} \div \text{time}$$
$$= 2\tfrac{1}{2} \div .1$$
$$= 2.5 \div .1$$
$$= 25 \text{ mph}$$

Answer: **(C)** 25 mph

6.
$$\text{Time for first 240 mi} = 240 \div 60$$
$$= 4 \text{ hours}$$
$$\text{Time for return trip} = 6 \text{ hours}$$
$$\text{Total time for round trip} = 10 \text{ hours}$$
$$\text{Total distance for round trip} = 480 \text{ mi}$$
$$\text{Average rate} = 480 \text{ mi} \div 10 \text{ hr}$$
$$= 48 \text{ mph}$$

Answer: **(B)** 48 mph

7.
$$\text{Brand A requires } 900 \div 18 = 50 \text{ gal}$$
$$50 \text{ gal} \times \$1.30 \text{ per gal} = \$65$$

$$\text{Brand B requires } 900 \div 15 = 60 \text{ gal}$$
$$60 \text{ gal} \times \$1.25 \text{ per gal} = \$75$$

Answer: **(A)** Brand B will cost $10 more than Brand A

8.
$$\text{Time} = \text{distance} \div \text{rate}$$
$$\text{Time} = 16 \text{ mi} \div 40 \text{ mph}$$
$$= \tfrac{4}{10} \text{ hrs}$$
$$= \tfrac{4}{10} \times 60 \text{ minutes}$$
$$= 24 \text{ minutes}$$
$$24 + 10 = 34 \text{ minutes}$$

Answer: **(E)** 34 min

9.
$$63 \text{ days} = 63 \times 24 \text{ hours}$$
$$= 1512 \text{ hours}$$
$$\text{Speed} = 2800 \text{ mi} \div 1512 \text{ hr}$$
$$= 1.85 \text{ mph}$$

Answer: **(C)** 2 mph

10.
$$\text{Time} = 20 \text{ mi} \div 30 \text{ mph}$$
$$= \tfrac{2}{3} \text{ hr}$$
$$\tfrac{2}{3} \text{ hr} = \tfrac{2}{3} \times 60 \text{ min} = 40 \text{ min}$$

Answer: **(C)** 40 min

11. The car used

$$12 - 7\tfrac{1}{2} = 4\tfrac{1}{2} \text{ gal, plus}$$
$$\$10.00 \div \$1.25 = 8 \text{ gal,}$$

for a total of $12\tfrac{1}{2}$ gal, or 12.5 gal.

$$12.5 \text{ gal} \times 17.3 \text{ mpg} = 216.25 \text{ mi}$$

Answer: **(C)** 216

12.
$$72 \text{ min} = \tfrac{72}{60} \text{ hr} = 1.2 \text{ hr}$$
$$\text{Rate} = 4.2 \text{ mi} \div 1.2 \text{ hr} = 3.5 \text{ mph}$$

At this rate it would take 1.7 mi $\div$ 3.5 mph

= .5 hours (approx.) to travel 1.7 miles. The daily savings in time is 1.2 hr − .5 hr = .7 hr.

$$.7 \text{ hr} \times 129 \text{ days} = 90.3 \text{ hr}$$

Answer: **(E)** 90.3

13. Assume a convenient distance, say, 50 mi.

Time by automobile = 50 mi ÷ 25 mph
= 2 hr
Time walking = 50 mi ÷ 10 mph
= 5 hr
Total time = 7 hours
Total distance = 100 mi
Average rate = 100 mi ÷ 7 hr
= $14\frac{2}{7}$ mph

Answer: **(A)** $14\frac{2}{7}$ mph

14.   30 mi − 25 mi = 5 mi gain per 1 hr

During first hour, the first train travels 25 miles.

$$25 \text{ mi} \div 5 \text{ mph} = 5 \text{ hr}$$

Answer: **(D)** 5 hr

15.   85 mi × 9 da = 765 mi
65 mi × 9 da = 585 mi
———
1350

1550 mi − 1350 = 200 miles apart at end of 9 days.

Answer: **(B)** 200 mi

INTEREST

1. **Interest (I)** is the price paid for the use of money. There are three items considered in interest:

a. The **principal (p),** which is the amount of money-bearing interest.

b. The **interest rate (r),** expressed in percent on an annual basis.

c. The **time (t)** during which the principal is used, expressed in terms of a year.

2. The basic formulas used in interest problems are:

a. I = prt

b. $p = \dfrac{I}{rt}$

c. $r = \dfrac{I}{pt}$

d. $t = \dfrac{I}{pr}$

3. a. For most interest problems, the year is considered to have 360 days. Months are considered to have 30 days, unless a particular month is specified.

b. To use the interest formulas, time must be expressed as part of a year.

Examples: 5 months = $\frac{5}{12}$ year

36 days = $\frac{36}{360}$ year, or $\frac{1}{10}$ year

1 year 3 months = $\frac{15}{12}$ year

c. In reference to time, the prefix semi- means every half. The prefix bi- means every two.

Examples: Semiannually means every half-year (every 6 months).
Biannually means every 2 years.
Semimonthly means every half-month (every 15 days, unless the month is specified).
Biweekly means every 2 weeks (every 14 days).

4. There are two types of interest problems:

a. **Simple interest,** in which the interest is calculated only once over a given period of time.

b. **Compound interest,** in which interest is recalculated at given time periods based on previously earned interest.

Simple Interest

5. To find the interest when the principal, rate, and time are given:

a. Change the rate of interest to a fraction.

b. Express the time as a fractional part of a year.

c. Multiply all three items.

Illustration: Find the interest on $400 at $11\frac{1}{4}\%$ for 3 months and 16 days.

SOLUTION: $11\frac{1}{4}\% = \frac{45}{4}\% = \frac{45}{400}$

3 months and 16 days = 106 days
(30 days per month)
106 days = $\frac{106}{360}$ of a year = $\frac{53}{180}$ year
(360 days per year)

$$\overset{1}{\cancel{400}} \times \frac{45}{\cancel{400}} \times \frac{53}{\cancel{180}} = \frac{53}{4}$$

$$= 13.25$$

Answer: Interest = $13.25

6. To find the principal if the interest, interest rate, and time are given:

   a. Change the interest rate to a fraction.

   b. Express the time as a fractional part of a year.

   c. Multiply the rate by the time.

   d. Divide the interest by this product.

Illustration: What amount of money invested at 6% would receive interest of $18 over $1\frac{1}{2}$ years?

SOLUTION: $\qquad 6\% = \frac{6}{100}$

$1\frac{1}{2}$ years = $\frac{3}{2}$ years

$$\overset{3}{\frac{6}{100}} \times \frac{3}{2} = \frac{9}{100}$$

$$\$18 \div \frac{9}{100} = \$\overset{2}{\cancel{18}} \times \frac{100}{\cancel{9}} = \$200$$

$$= \$200$$

Answer: Principal = $200

7. To find the rate if the principal, time, and interest are given:

   a. Change the time to a fractional part of a year.

   b. Multiply the principal by the time.

   c. Divide the interest by this product.

   d. Convert to a percent.

Illustration: At what interest rate should $300 be invested for 40 days to accrue $2 in interest?

SOLUTION: 40 days = $\frac{40}{360}$ of a year

$$\overset{5}{\cancel{300}} \times \frac{\overset{20}{\cancel{40}}}{\cancel{360}} = \frac{100}{3}$$

$$\$2 \div \frac{100}{3} = \overset{1}{\cancel{2}} \times \frac{3}{\underset{50}{\cancel{100}}}$$

$$= \frac{3}{50}$$

$$\frac{3}{50} = 6\%$$

Answer: Interest rate = 6%

8. To find the time (in years) if the principal, interest, and interest rate are given:

   a. Change the interest rate to a fraction (or decimal).

   b. Multiply the principal by the rate.

   c. Divide the interest by this product.

Illustration: Find the length of time for which $240 must be invested at 5% to accrue $16 in interest.

SOLUTION: $\qquad 5\% = .05$

$$240 \times .05 = 12$$

$$16 \div 12 = 1\frac{1}{3}$$

Answer: Time = $1\frac{1}{3}$ years

Compound Interest

9. Interest may be computed on a compound basis; that is, the interest at the end of a certain period (half-year, full year, or whatever time stipulated) is added to the principal for the next period. The interest is then computed on the new increased principal, and for the next period the interest is again computed on the new increased principal. Since the principal constantly increases, compound interest yields more than simple interest.

10. To find the compound interest when given the principal, the rate, and time period:

    a. Calculate the interest as for simple interest problems, using the period of compounding for the time.

    b. Add the interest to the principal.

    c. Calculate the interest on the new principal over the period of compounding.

d. Add this interest to form a new principal.

e. Continue the same procedure until all periods required have been accounted for.

f. Subtract the original principal from the final principal to find the compound interest.

Illustration: Find the amount that $200 will become if compounded semiannually at 8% for $1\frac{1}{2}$ years.

SOLUTION: Since it is to be compounded semiannually for $1\frac{1}{2}$ years, the interest will have to be computed 3 times:

Interest for the first period: $.08 \times \frac{1}{2} \times \$200 = \$8$
First new principal: $\$200 + \$8 = \$208$

Interest for the second period: $.08 \times \frac{1}{2} \times \$208 = \$8.32$
Second new principal: $\$208 + \$8.32 = \$216.32$

Interest for the third period: $.08 \times \frac{1}{2} \times \$216.32 = \$8.6528$
Final principal: $\$216.32 + \$8.6528 = \$224.9728$

Answer: $224.97 to the nearest cent

Bank Discounts

11. A **promissory note** is a commitment to pay a certain amount of money on a given date, called the **date of maturity.**

12. When a promissory note is cashed by a bank in advance of its date of maturity, the bank deducts a discount from the principal and pays the rest to the depositor.

13. To find the bank discount:

a. Find the time between the date the note is deposited and its date of maturity, and express this time as a fractional part of a year.

b. Change the rate to a fraction.

c. Multiply the principal by the time and the rate to find the bank discount.

d. If required, subtract the bank discount from the original principal to find the amount the bank will pay the depositor.

Illustration: A $400 note drawn up on August 12, 1980, for 90 days is deposited at the bank on September 17, 1980. The bank charges a $6\frac{1}{2}$% discount on notes. How much will the depositor receive?

SOLUTION: From August 12, 1980, to September 17, 1980, is 36 days. This means that the note has 54 days to run.

$$54 \text{ days} = \tfrac{54}{360} \text{ of a year}$$
$$6\tfrac{1}{2}\% = \tfrac{13}{2}\% = \tfrac{13}{200}$$
$$\$400 \times \tfrac{13}{200} \times \tfrac{54}{360} = \tfrac{39}{10}$$
$$= \$3.90$$
$$\$400 - \$3.90 = \$396.10$$

Answer: The depositor will receive $396.10.

Practice Problems Involving Interest

1. What is the simple interest on $460 for 2 years at $8\frac{1}{2}$%? _____

2. For borrowing $300 for one month, a man was charged $6.00. The rate of interest was _____.

3. At a simple interest rate of 5% a year, the principal that will give $12.50 interest in 6 months is _____.

4. Find the interest on $480 on $10\frac{1}{2}$% for 2 months and 15 days. _____

5. The interest on $300 at 6% for 10 days is _____.

6. The scholarship board of a certain college loaned a student $200 at an annual rate of 6% from September 30 until December 15. To repay the loan and accumulated interest the student must give the college _____.

7. If $300 is invested at simple interest so as to yield a return of $18 in 9 months, the amount of money that must be invested at the same rate of interest so as to yield a return of $120 in 6 months is _____.

8. When the principal is $600, the difference in one year between simple interest at 12% per annum and interest compounded semiannually at 12% per annum is _____.

9. What is the compound interest on $600, compounded quarterly, at 6% for 9 months? _____.

10. A 90-day note for $1200 is signed on May 12. Seventy-five days later the note is deposited at a bank that charges 8% discount on notes. The bank discount is _____.

Problem Solutions—Interest

1.
$$\text{Principal} = \$460$$
$$\text{Rate} = 8\tfrac{1}{2}\% = .085$$
$$\text{Time} = 2 \text{ years}$$
$$\text{Interest} = \$460 \times .085 \times 2$$
$$= \$78.20$$

Answer: $78.20

2.
$$\text{Principal} = \$300$$
$$\text{Interest} = \$6$$
$$\text{Time} = \tfrac{1}{12} \text{ year}$$
$$\$300 \times \tfrac{1}{12} = \$25$$
$$\$6 \div \$25 = .24 = 24\%$$

Answer: 24%

3.
$$\text{Rate} = 5\% = .05$$
$$\text{Interest} = \$12.50$$
$$\text{Time} = \tfrac{1}{2} \text{ year}$$
$$.05 \times \tfrac{1}{2} = .025$$
$$\$12.50 \div .025 = \$500.00$$

Answer: $500

4. Time:

2 months 15 days = 75 days or $\tfrac{75}{360}$ of a year

Rate:
$$10\tfrac{1}{2}\% = \tfrac{21}{2}\% = \tfrac{21}{200}$$

Interest:
$$480 \times \tfrac{21}{200} \times \tfrac{75}{360} = \tfrac{21}{2} = 10.50$$

Answer: $10.50

5.
$$\text{Principal} = \$300$$
$$\text{Rate} = .06 = \tfrac{6}{100}$$
$$\text{Time} = \tfrac{10}{360} = \tfrac{1}{36}$$
$$\text{Interest} = \$\overset{3}{\cancel{300}} \times \tfrac{\overset{1}{\cancel{6}}}{\cancel{100}} \times \tfrac{1}{\underset{6}{\cancel{36}}}$$
$$= \tfrac{3}{6} = \$.50$$

Answer: $.50

6.
$$\text{Principal} = \$200$$
$$\text{Rate} = .06 = \tfrac{6}{100}$$

Time from Sept. 30 until Dec. 15 is 76 days. (31 days in October, 30 days in November, 15 days in December)

$$76 \text{ days} = \tfrac{76}{360} \text{ year}$$
$$\text{Interest} = \$\overset{2}{\cancel{200}} \times \tfrac{\overset{1}{\cancel{6}}}{\cancel{100}} \times \tfrac{76}{\underset{60}{\cancel{360}}}$$
$$= \$\tfrac{152}{60} = \$2.53$$
$$\$200 + \$2.53 = \$202.53$$

Answer: closest to $202.50

7.
$$\text{Principal} = \$300$$
$$\text{Interest} = \$18$$
$$\text{Time} = \tfrac{9}{12} \text{ years} = \tfrac{3}{4} \text{ year}$$
$$\$300 \times \tfrac{3}{4} = \$225$$
$$\$18 \div \$225 = .08$$

Rate is 8%.

To yield $120 at 8% in 6 months,

$$\text{Interest} = \$120$$
$$\text{Rate} = .08$$
$$\text{Time} = \tfrac{1}{2} \text{ year}$$
$$.08 \times \tfrac{1}{2} = .04$$
$$\$120 \div .04 = \$3000 \text{ must be invested}$$

Answer: $3000

8. Simple interest:
$$\text{Principal} = \$600$$
$$\text{Rate} = .12$$
$$\text{Time} = 1$$
$$\text{Interest} = \$600 \times .12 \times 1$$
$$= \$72.00$$

Compound interest:
$$\text{Principal} = \$600$$
$$\text{Period of compounding} = \tfrac{1}{2} \text{ year}$$
$$\text{Rate} = .12$$

For the first period,
$$\text{Interest} = \$600 \times .12 \times \tfrac{1}{2}$$
$$= \$36$$
$$\text{New principal} = \$600 + \$36$$
$$= \$636$$

For the second period,
$$\text{Interest} = \$636 \times .12 \times \tfrac{1}{2}$$
$$= \$38.16$$
$$\text{New principal} = \$636 + \$38.16$$
$$= \$674.16$$

Total interest = $74.16
Difference = $74.16 − 72.00
= $2.16

Answer: $2.16

9.   Principal = $600
             Rate = 6% = $\frac{6}{100}$
Time (period of
compounding) = $\frac{3}{12}$ year = $\frac{1}{4}$ year

In 9 months, the interest will be computed 3 times.

For first quarter,
Interest = $600 × $\frac{6}{100}$ × $\frac{1}{4}$
= $9

New principal at end of first quarter:
$600 + $9 = $609

For second quarter,
Interest = $609 × $\frac{6}{100}$ × $\frac{1}{4}$
= $$\frac{3654}{400}$ = $9.135,
or $9.14

New principal at end of second quarter:
$609 + $9.14 = $618.14

For third quarter,
Interest = $618.14 × $\frac{6}{100}$ × $\frac{1}{4}$
= $$\frac{3708.84}{400}$
= $9.27

Total interest for the 3 quarters:
$9 + $9.14 + $9.27 = $27.41

Answer: $27.41

10.   Principal = $1200
             Time = 90 days − 75 days
             = 15 days
15 days = $\frac{15}{360}$ year
Rate = 8% = $\frac{8}{100}$
Bank discount = $\overset{12}{\cancel{\$1200}} × \frac{\overset{1}{\cancel{8}}}{\cancel{100}} × \frac{15}{\underset{45}{\cancel{360}}}$
= $$\frac{180}{45}$ = $4

Answer: $4.00

TAXATION

1. a. Taxation problems are a form of percent-age or fraction problems since the tax rate is often expressed as a percentage

(parts per hundred) or as another sort of fraction such as tax per $100,000, etc.

   b. Taxation problems may also be a form of table or chart problem when the rate of taxation is not a single rate, but changes in accordance with something else, such as total to be taxed, time, etc.

2. In taxation, there are usually three items involved: the amount taxable, henceforth called the base, the tax rate, and the tax itself.

3. To find the tax when given the base and the tax rate in percent:

   a. Change the tax rate to a decimal.

   b. Multiply the base by the tax rate.

   Illustration: How much would be realized on $4000 if taxed 15%?

   SOLUTION: 15% = .15
                      $4000 × .15 = $600

   Answer: Tax = $600

4. To find the tax rate in percent form when given the base and the tax:

   a. Divide the tax by the base.

   b. Convert to a percent.

   Illustration: Find the tax rate at which $5600 would yield $784.

   SOLUTION: $784 ÷ $5600 = .14
                      .14 = 14%

   Answer: Tax rate = 14%

5. To find the base when given the tax rate and the tax:

   a. Change the tax rate to a decimal.

   b. Divide the tax by the tax rate.

   Illustration: What amount of money taxed 3% would yield $75?

   SOLUTION: 3% = .03
                      $75 ÷ .03 = $2500

   Answer: Base = $2500

6. When the tax rate is fixed and expressed in terms of money, take into consideration the denomination upon which it is based; that is, whether it is based on every $100, or $1000, etc.

7. To find the tax when given the base and the tax rate in terms of money:

   a. Divide the base by the denomination upon which the tax is based.

   b. Multiply this quotient by the tax rate.

   Illustration: If the tax rate is $3.60 per $1000, find the tax on $470,500.

   SOLUTION:

   $$470,500 \div \$1000 = 470.5$$
   $$470.5 \times \$3.60 = \$1,693.80$$

   Answer: $1,693.80

8. To find the tax rate based on a certain denomination when given the base and the tax derived:

   a. Divide the base by the denomination indicated.

   b. Divide the tax by this quotient.

   Illustration: Find the tax rate per $100 that would be required to raise $350,000 on $2,000,000 of taxable property.

   SOLUTION: $2,000,000 \div \$100 = 20,000$
   $$\$350,000 \div 20,000 = \$17.50$$

   Answer: Tax rate = $17.50 per $100

9. Since a surtax is an additional tax besides the regular tax, to find the total tax:

   a. Change the regular tax rate to a decimal.

   b. Multiply the base by the regular tax rate.

   c. Change the surtax rate to a decimal.

   d. Multiply the base by the surtax rate.

   e. Add both taxes.

   Illustration: Assuming that the tax rate is $2\frac{1}{3}\%$ on liquors costing up to $3.00, and 3% on those costing from $3.00 to $6.00, and $3\frac{1}{2}\%$ on those from $6.00 to $10.00, what would be the tax on a bottle costing $8.00 if there is a surtax of 5% on all liquors above $5.00?

   SOLUTION: An $8.00 bottle falls within the category of $6.00 to $10.00. The tax rate on such a bottle is

   $$3\tfrac{1}{2}\% = .035$$
   $$\$8.00 \times .035 = \$.28$$
   $$\text{surtax rate} = 5\% = .05$$
   $$\$8.00 \times .05 = \$.40$$
   $$\$.28 + \$.40 = \$.68$$

   Answer: Total tax = $.68

Practice Problems Involving Taxation

1. Mr. Jones' income for a year is $15,000. He pays $2250 for income taxes. The percent of his income that he pays for income taxes is _____.

2. If the tax rate is $3\frac{1}{2}\%$ and the amount to be raised is $64.40, what is the base? _____

3. What is the tax rate per $1000 if a base of $338,500 would yield $616.07? _____

4. A man buys an electric light bulb for 54¢, which includes a 20% tax. What is the cost of the bulb without tax? _____

5. What tax rate on a base of $3650 would raise $164.25? _____

6. A piece of property is assessed at $22,850 and the tax rate is $4.80 per thousand. What is the amount of tax that must be paid on the property? _____

7. $30,000 worth of land is assessed at 120% of its value. If the tax rate is $5.12 per $1000 assessed valuation, the amount of tax to be paid is _____.

8. Of the following real estate tax rates, which is the largest?
   $31.25 per $1000
   $3.45 per $100
   32¢ per $10
   3¢ per $1

9. A certain community needs $185,090.62 to cover its expenses. If its tax rate is $1.43 per $100 of assessed valuation, what must be the assessed value of its property? _____

10. A man's taxable income is $14,280. The state tax instructions tell him to pay 2% on the first $3000 of his taxable income, 3% on each of the second and third $3000, and 4% on the remainder. What is the total amount of income tax that he must pay? _____

Problem Solutions—Taxation

1.
$$\text{Tax} = \$2250$$
$$\text{Base} = \$15,000$$
$$\text{Tax rate} = \text{Tax} \div \text{Base}$$
$$\text{Tax rate} = \$2250 \div \$15,000 = .15$$
$$\text{Tax rate} = .15 = 15\%$$

Answer: 15

2.
$$\text{Tax rate} = 3\tfrac{1}{2}\% = .035$$
$$\text{Tax} = \$64.40$$
$$\text{Base} = \text{Tax} \div \text{Tax rate}$$
$$\text{Base} = \$64.40 \div .035$$
$$= \$1840$$

Answer: $1840

3.
$$\text{Base} = \$338,500$$
$$\text{Tax} = \$616.07$$
$$\text{Denomination} = \$1000$$
$$\$338,500 \div \$1000 = 338.50$$
$$\$616.07 \div 338.50 = \$1.82 \text{ per } \$1000$$

Answer: $1.82

4. 54¢ is 120% of the base (cost without tax)

$$\text{Base} = 54 \div 120\%$$
$$= 54 \div 1.20$$
$$= 45$$

Answer: 45¢

5.
$$\text{Base} = \$3650$$
$$\text{Tax} = \$164.25$$
$$\text{Tax rate} = \text{Tax} \div \text{Base}$$
$$= \$164.25 \div \$3650$$
$$= .045$$
$$= 4\tfrac{1}{2}\%$$

Answer: $4\tfrac{1}{2}\%$

6.
$$\text{Base} = \$22,850$$
$$\text{Denomination} = \$1000$$
$$\text{Tax rate} = \$4.80 \text{ per thousand}$$
$$\frac{\$22,850}{\$1000} = 22.85$$
$$22.85 \times \$4.80 = \$109.68$$

Answer: $109.68

7.
$$\text{Base} = \text{Assessed val.} = 120\% \text{ of } \$30,000$$
$$= 1.20 \times \$30,000$$
$$= \$36,000$$

$$\text{Denomination} = \$1000$$
$$\text{Tax rate} = \$5.12 \text{ per thousand}$$
$$\frac{\$36,000}{\$1000} = 36$$
$$36 \times \$5.12 = \$184.32$$

Answer: $184.32

8. Express each tax rate as a decimal:

$$\$31.25 \text{ per } \$1000 = \frac{31.25}{1000} = .03125$$

$$\$3.45 \text{ per } \$100 = \frac{3.45}{100} = .0345$$

$$32¢ \text{ per } \$10 = \frac{.32}{10} = .0320$$

$$3¢ \text{ per } \$1 = \frac{.03}{1} = .0300$$

The largest decimal is .0345

Answer: $3.45 per $100

9.
$$\text{Tax rate} = \$1.43 \text{ per } \$100$$
$$= \frac{1.43}{100} = .0143$$
$$= 1.43\%$$
$$\text{Tax} = \$185,090.62$$
$$\text{Base} = \text{Tax} \div \text{rate}$$
$$= 185,090.62 \div .0143$$
$$= \$12,943,400$$

Answer: $12,943,400

10.

First $3000:	.02 × $3000 = $ 60.00
Second $3000:	.03 × $3000 = $ 90.00
Third $3000:	.03 × $3000 = $ 90.00
Remainder ($14,280 − $9000):	.04 × $5280 = $211.20
	Total tax = $451.20

Answer: $451.20

PROFIT AND LOSS

1. The following terms may be encountered in profit and loss problems:

   a. The **cost price** of an article is the price paid by a person who wishes to sell it again.

   b. There may be an **allowance** or **trade discount** reducing the cost price.

   c. The **list price** or **marked price** is the price at which the article is listed or marked to be sold.

   d. There may be a **discount** or **series of discounts** (usually expressed as a percent) on the list price.

   e. The **selling price** or **sales price** is the price at which the article is finally sold.

   f. If the selling price is greater than the cost price, there has been a **profit.**

   g. If the selling price is lower than the cost price, there has been a **loss.**

   h. If the article is sold at the same price as the cost, there has been no loss or profit.

   i. A percentage profit or loss may be based either on the cost price or on the selling price.

   j. Profit or loss may be stated in terms of dollars and cents, or in terms of percent.

   k. **Overhead** expenses include such items as rent, salaries, etc., and may be added to cost price or to the profit to increase the selling price.

2. The basic formulas used in profit and loss problems are:

   > Selling price = cost price + profit
   > Selling price = cost price − loss

   Example: If the cost of an article is $2.50, and the profit is $1.50, then the selling price is $2.50 + $1.50 = $4.00.

   Example: If the cost of an article is $3.00, and the loss is $1.20, then the selling price is $3.00 − $1.20 = $1.80.

3. a. To find the profit in terms of money, subtract the cost price from the selling price, or selling price − cost price = profit.

   Example: If an article costing $3.00 is sold for $5.00, the profit is $5.00 − $3.00 = $2.00.

   b. To find the loss in terms of money, subtract the selling price from the cost price, or: cost price − selling price = loss.

   Example: If an article costing $2.00 is sold for $1.50, the loss is $2.00 − $1.50 = $.50.

4. To find the selling price if the profit or loss is expressed in percent based on cost price:

   a. Multiply the cost price by the percent of profit or loss to find the profit or loss in terms of money.

   b. Add this product to the cost price if a profit is involved, or subtract for a loss.

   Illustration: Find the selling price of an article costing $3.00 that was sold at a profit of 15% of the cost price.

   SOLUTION: 15% of $3.00 = .15 × $3.00
   = $.45 profit
   $3.00 + $.45 = $3.45

   Answer: Selling price = $3.45

   Illustration: If an article costing $2.00 is sold at a loss of 5% of the cost price, find the selling price.

   SOLUTION: 5% of $2.00 = .05 × $2.00
   = $.10 loss
   $2.00 − $.10 = $1.90

   Answer: Selling price = $1.90

5. To find the cost price when given the selling price and the percent of profit or loss based on the selling price:

   a. Multiply the selling price by the percent of profit or loss to find the profit or loss in terms of money.

   b. Subtract this product from the selling price if a profit, or add the product to the selling price if a loss.

Illustration: If an article sells for $12.00 and there has been a profit of 10% of the selling price, what is the cost price?

SOLUTION:

$$10\% \text{ of } \$12,00 = .10 \times \$12.00$$
$$= \$1.20 \text{ profit}$$
$$\$12.00 - \$1.20 = \$10.80$$

Answer: Cost price = $10.80

Illustration: What is the cost price of an article selling for $2.00 on which there has been a loss of 6% of the selling price?

SOLUTION: $6\% \text{ of } \$2.00 = .06 \times \$2.00$
$$= \$.12 \text{ loss}$$
$$\$2.00 + \$.12 = \$2.12$$

Answer: Cost price = $2.12

6. To find the percent of profit or percent of loss based on cost price:

   a. Find the profit or loss in terms of money.

   b. Divide the profit or loss by the cost price.

   c. Convert to a percent.

Illustration: Find the percent of profit based on cost price of an article costing $2.50 and selling for $3.00.

SOLUTION: $3.00 - \$2.50 = \$.50$ profit

$$2.50\overline{)\,.50} = 250\overline{)\,50.00}^{\,.20}$$
$$.20 = 20\%$$

Answer: Profit = 20%

Illustration: Find the percent of loss based on cost price of an article costing $5.00 and selling for $4.80.

SOLUTION: $5.00 - \$4.80 = \$.20$ loss

$$5.00\overline{)\,.20} = 500\overline{)\,20.00}^{\,.04}$$
$$.04 = 4\%$$

Answer: Loss = 4%

7. To find the percent of profit or percent of loss on selling price:

   a. Find the profit or loss in terms of money.

   b. Divide the profit or loss by the selling price.

   c. Convert to a percent.

Illustration: Find the percent of profit based on the selling price of an article costing $2.50 and selling for $3.00.

SOLUTION:

$$\$3.00 - \$2.50 = \$.50 \text{ profit}$$
$$3.00\overline{)\,.50} = 300\overline{)\,50.00} = .16\tfrac{2}{3}$$
$$= 16\tfrac{2}{3}\%$$

Answer: Profit = $16\tfrac{2}{3}\%$

Illustration: Find the percent of loss based on the selling price of an article costing $5.00 and selling for $4.80.

SOLUTION:

$$\$5.00 - \$4.80 = \$.20 \text{ loss}$$
$$4.80\overline{)\,.20} = 480\overline{)\,20.00} = .04\tfrac{1}{6}$$
$$= 4\tfrac{1}{6}\%$$

Answer: Loss = $4\tfrac{1}{6}\%$

8. To find the cost price when given the selling price and the percent of profit based on the cost price:

   a. Establish a relation between the selling price and the cost price.

   b. Solve to find the cost price.

Illustration: An article is sold for $2.50, which is a 25% profit of the cost price. What is the cost price?

SOLUTION: Since the selling price represents the whole cost price plus 25% of the cost price,

$$2.50 = 125\% \text{ of the cost price}$$
$$2.50 = 1.25 \text{ of the cost price}$$
$$\text{Cost price} = 2.50 \div 1.25$$
$$= 2.00$$

Answer: Cost price = $2.00

9. To find the selling price when given the profit based on the selling price:

   a. Establish a relation between the selling price and the cost price.

   b. Solve to find the selling price.

Illustration: A merchant buys an article for $27.00 and sells it at a profit of 10% of the selling price. What is the selling price?

SOLUTION: $27.00 + \text{profit} = \text{selling price}$

Since the profit is 10% of the selling price, the cost price must be 90% of the selling price.

$$27.00 = 90\% \text{ of the selling price}$$
$$= .90 \text{ of the selling price}$$
$$\text{Selling price} = 27.00 \div .90$$
$$= 30.00$$

Answer: Selling price = $30.00

Trade Discounts

10. A **trade discount,** usually expressed in percent, indicates the part that is to be deducted from the list price.

11. To find the selling price when given the list price and the trade discount:

   a. Multiply the list price by the percent of discount to find the discount in terms of money.

   b. Subtract the discount from the list price.

   Illustration: The list price of an article is $20.00. There is a discount of 5%. What is the selling price?

   SOLUTION: $20.00 \times 5\%$
   $$= 20.00 \times .05 = \$1.00 \text{ discount}$$
   $$\$20.00 - \$1.00 = \$19.00$$

   Answer: Selling price = $19.00

   An alternate method of solving the above problem is to consider the list price to be 100%. Then, if the discount is 5%, the selling price is $100\% - 5\% = 95\%$ of the list price. The selling price is

   $$95\% \text{ of } \$20.00 = .95 \times \$20.00$$
   $$= \$19.00$$

Series of Discounts

12. There may be more than one discount to be deducted from the list price. These are called a **discount series.**

13. To find the selling price when given the list price and a discount series:

   a. Multiply the list price by the first percent of discount.

   b. Subtract this product from the list price.

   c. Multiply the difference by the second discount.

   d. Subtract this product from the difference.

   e. Continue the same procedure if there are more discounts.

   Illustration: Find the selling price of an article listed at $10.00 on which there are discounts of 20% and 10%.

   SOLUTION:

   $$\$10.00 \times 20\% = 10.00 \times .20 = \$2.00$$
   $$\$10.00 - \$2.00 = \$8.00$$
   $$\$8.00 \times 10\% = 8.00 \times .10 = \$.80$$
   $$\$8.00 - \$.80 = \$7.20$$

   Answer: Selling price = $7.20

14. Instead of deducting each discount individually, it is often more practical to find the single equivalent discount first and then deduct. It does not matter in which order the discounts are taken.

15. The single equivalent discount may be found by assuming a list price of 100%. Leave all discounts in percent form.

   a. Subtract the first discount from 100%, giving the net cost factor (NCF) had there been only one discount.

   b. Multiply the NCF by the second discount. Subtract the product from the NCF, giving a second NCF that reflects both discounts.

   c. If there is a third discount, multiply the second NCF by it and subtract the product from the second NCF, giving a third NCF that reflects all three discounts.

   d. If there are more discounts, repeat the process.

   e. Subtract the final NCF from 100% to find the single equivalent discount.

Illustration: Find the single equivalent discount of 20%, 25%, and 10%.

SOLUTION:

$$
\begin{array}{rl}
& 100\% \\
- & 20\% \text{ first discount} \\
\hline
& 80\% \text{ first NCF}
\end{array}
$$

$$
-25\% \text{ of } 80\% = \underline{\quad 20\%\quad}
$$
$$
60\% \text{ second NCF}
$$

$$
-10\% \text{ of } 60\% = \underline{\quad 6\%\quad}
$$
$$
54\% \text{ third NCF}
$$

$$
100\% - 54\% = 46\% \text{ single equivalent discount}
$$

Answer: 46%

Illustration: An article lists at $750.00. With discounts of 20%, 25%, and 10%, what is the selling price of this article?

SOLUTION: As shown above, the single equivalent discount of 20%, 25%, and 10% is 46%.

$$
46\% \text{ of } \$750 = .46 \times \$750
$$
$$
= \$345
$$
$$
\$750 - \$345 = \$405
$$

Answer: Selling price = $405

Practice Problems Involving Profit and Loss

1. Dresses sold at $65.00 each. The dresses cost $50.00 each. The percentage of increase of the selling price over the cost is _____.

2. A dealer bought a ladder for $27.00. What must it be sold for if he wishes to make a profit of 40% on the selling price? _____

3. A typewriter was listed at $120.00 and was bought for $96.00. What was the rate of discount? _____

4. A dealer sells an article at a loss of 50% of the cost. Based on the selling price, the loss is _____.

5. What would be the marked price of an article if the cost was $12.60 and the gain was 10% of the cost price? _____

6. A stationer buys note pads at $.75 per dozen and sells them at 25 cents apiece. The profit based on the cost is _____.

7. An article costing $18 is to be sold at a profit of 10% of the selling price. The selling price will be _____.

8. A calculating maching company offered to sell a city agency 4 calculating machines at a discount of 15% from the list price, and to allow the agency $85 for each of two old machines being traded in. The list price of the new machines is $625 per machine. If the city agency accepts this offer, the amount of money it will have to provide for the purchase of these 4 machines is _____.

9. Pencils are purchased at $9 per gross and sold at 6 for 75 cents. The rate of profit based on the selling price is _____.

10. The single equivalent discount of 20% and 10% is _____.

Problem Solutions—Profit and Loss

1.
$$
\begin{aligned}
\text{Selling price} - \text{cost} &= \$65 - \$50 \\
&= \$15
\end{aligned}
$$
$$
\frac{\$15}{\$50} = .30 = 30\%
$$

Answer: 30%

2. Cost price = 60% of selling price, since the profit is 40% of the selling price, and the whole selling price is 100%.

$$
\$27 = 60\% \text{ of selling price}
$$
$$
\begin{aligned}
\text{Selling price} &= \$27 \div 60\% \\
&= \$27 \div .6 \\
&= \$45
\end{aligned}
$$

Answer: $45

3. The discount was $120 - $96 = $24

$$
\text{Rate of discount} = \frac{\$24}{\$120} = .20
$$
$$
= 20\%
$$

Answer: 20%

4. Loss = cost − selling price.

   Considering the cost to be 100% of itself, if the loss is 50% of the cost, the selling price is also 50% of the cost. (50% = 100% − 50%)

   Since the loss and the selling price are therefore the same, the loss is 100% of the selling price.

   Answer: 100%

5.
$$\text{Gain (profit)} = 10\% \text{ of } \$12.60$$
$$= .10 \times \$12.60$$
$$= \$1.26$$

$$\text{Selling price} = \text{cost} + \text{profit}$$
$$= \$12.60 + \$1.26$$
$$= \$13.86$$

   Answer: $13.86

6. Each dozen note pads cost $.75 and are sold for
$$12 \times \$.25 = \$3.00$$
   The profit is $\$3.00 - \$.75 = \$2.25$
$$\text{Profit based on cost} = \frac{\$2.25}{\$.75}$$
$$= 3$$
$$= 300\%$$

   Answer: 300%

7.
$$\text{If profit} = 10\% \text{ of selling price,}$$
$$\text{then cost} = 90\% \text{ of selling price}$$
$$\$18 = 90\% \text{ of selling price}$$
$$\text{Selling price} = \$18 \div 90\%$$
$$= \$18 \div .90$$
$$= \$20$$

   Answer: $20.00

8. Discount for each new machine:
$$15\% \text{ of } \$625 = .15 \times \$625$$
$$= \$93.75$$

   Each new machine will cost
$$\$625 - \$93.75 = \$531.25$$

   Four new machines will cost
$$\$531.25 \times 4 = \$2125$$

   But there is an allowance of $85 each for 2 old machines:
$$\$85 \times 2 = 170$$

   Final cost to city:
$$\$2125 - \$170 = \$1955$$

   Answer: $1955

9.
$$1 \text{ gross} = 144 \text{ units}$$
$$\text{Selling price for 6 pencils} = \$.75$$
$$\text{Selling price for 1 pencil} = \frac{\$.75}{6}$$
$$\begin{array}{r}\text{Selling price for 1 gross} \\ \text{of pencils}\end{array} = \frac{\$.75}{\overset{}{6}} \times \overset{24}{\cancel{144}}$$
$$= \$18.00$$
$$\text{Cost for 1 gross of pencils} = \$9.00$$
$$\text{Profit for 1 gross of pencils} = \$18.00 - \$9.00$$
$$= \$9.00$$
$$\frac{\text{profit}}{\text{selling price}} = \frac{\$9.00}{\$18.00}$$
$$= .5 = 50\%$$

   Answer: 50%

10.
$$\begin{array}{r} 100\% \\ - \ \ 20\% \\ \hline 80\% \end{array}$$
$$-10\% \text{ of } 80\% = \begin{array}{r} - \ \ 8\% \\ \hline 72\% \end{array}$$

   100% − 72% = 28% single equivalent discount

   Answer: 28%

TABLES

1. **Tables** are used to organize information in easily understandable form. The key to understanding tables is to read the title and the margins, or stubs as they are sometimes called. These items, plus the footnotes to the table, if any, will tell you what the numbers in the table mean. The numbers themselves have no meaning without the writing. For example, consider the following arrangement of numbers:

300	500	800
400	600	1000
700	1100	1800

   You may think that the bottom row and the right-hand column represent totals since things seem to add up that way. It is possible that this is correct, but unless there is written information to tell you this, you do not know it to be true.

2. You should be particularly alert to the units that are used in a table, which may be

different from the units asked for in the problem. For example, a table may give you information in tons and the problem might ask for pounds.

3. Other than the fact that the information is presented in a table, there is nothing about a table problem that is different from any of the other sorts of problems which have been discussed.

4. As in other arithmetic computational problems, it is usually a good idea to estimate the numbers that you have to use from a table rather than using them in their printed form. Generally the first and second digits are all that is needed.

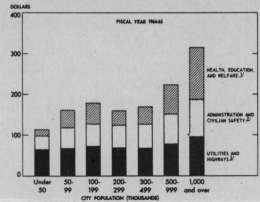

Municipal Expenditures, Per Capita

1/PUBLIC WELFARE, EDUCATION, HOSPITALS, HEALTH, LIBRARIES, AND HOUSING AND URBAN RENEWAL.
2/POLICE AND FIRE PROTECTION, FINANCIAL ADMINISTRATION, GENERAL CONTROL, GENERAL PUBLIC BUILDINGS, INTEREST ON GENERAL DEBT, AND OTHER.
3/HIGHWAYS, SEWERAGE, SANITATION, PARKS AND RECREATION, AND UTILITIES.
SOURCE: DEPARTMENT OF COMMERCE.

GRAPHS

1. **Graphs** illustrate comparisons and trends in statistical information. The most commonly used graphs are **bar graphs, line graphs, circle graphs,** and **pictographs.** The fundamental idea about graphs is that they all use some distance or area to represent value. The distance may be length, width, etc., and the value may be dollars, percents, etc. The graphs are always labelled to show what part of the graph means what value. So read the labels, margins, and notes of each graph carefully.

Bar Graphs

2. **Bar graphs** are used to compare various quantities. Each bar may represent a single quantity or may be divided to represent several quantities.

3. Bar graphs may have horizontal or vertical bars.

Illustration (next column):

Question 1: What was the approximate municipal expenditure per capita in cities having populations of 200,000 to 299,000?

Answer: The middle bar of the seven shown represents cities having populations from 200,000 to 299,000. This bar reaches about halfway between 100 and 200. Therefore, the per capita expenditure was approximately $150.

Question 2: Which cities spent the most per capita on health, education, and welfare?

Answer: The bar for cities having populations of 1,000,000 and over has a larger striped section than the other bars. Therefore, those cities spent the most.

Question 3: Of the three categories of expenditures, which was least dependent on city size?

Answer: The expenditures for utilities and highways, the darkest part of each bar, varied least as city size increased.

Line Graphs

4. **Line graphs** are used to show trends, often over a period of time.

5. A line graph may include more than one line, with each line representing a different item.

Illustration:

The graph below indicates, at 5 year-intervals, the number of citations issued for various offenses from the year 1960 to the year 1980.

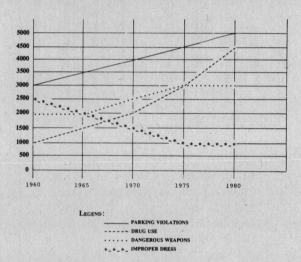

LEGEND:
——————— PARKING VIOLATIONS
- - - - - - DRUG USE
· · · · · · DANGEROUS WEAPONS
*_*_*_ IMPROPER DRESS

Question 4: Over the 20-year period, which offense shows an average rate of increase of more than 150 citations per year?

Answer: Drug-use citations increased from 1000 in 1960 to 4500 in 1980. The average increase over the 20-year period is $\frac{3500}{20}$ = 175.

Question 5: Over the 20-year period, which offense shows a constant rate of increase or decrease?

Answer: A straight line indicates a constant rate of increase or decrease. Of the four lines, the one representing parking violations is the only straight one.

Question 6: Which offense shows a total increase or decrease of 50% for the full 20-year period?

Answer: Dangerous weapons citations increased from 2000 in 1960 to 3000 in 1980, which is an increase of 50%.

Circle Graphs

6. **Circle graphs** are used to show the relationship of various parts of a quantity to each other and to the whole quantity.

7. Percents are often used in circle graphs. The 360 degrees of the circle represents 100%.

8. Each part of the circle graph is called a **sector.**

Illustration:

The following circle graph shows how the federal budget of $300.4 billion was spent.

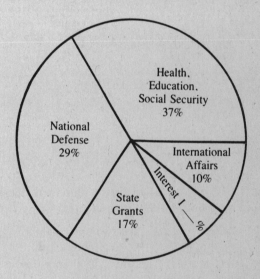

Question 7: What is the value of I?

Answer: There must be a total of 100% in a circle graph. The sum of the other sectors is:

$$17\% + 29\% + 37\% + 10\% = 93\%$$

Therefore, I = 100% − 93% = 7%.

Question 8: How much money was actually spent on national defense?

Answer: 29% × $300.4 billion
= $87.116 billion
= $87,116,000,000

Question 9: How much more money was spent on state grants than on interest?

Answer: 17% − 7% = 10%
10% × $300.4 billion
= $30.04 billion
= $30,040,000,000

Pictographs

9. **Pictographs** allow comparisons of quantities by using symbols. Each symbol represents a given number of a particular item.

Illustration:

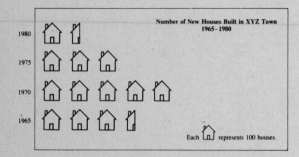

Question 10: How many more new houses were built in 1970 than in 1975?

Answer: There are two more symbols for 1970 than for 1975. Each symbol represents 100 houses. Therefore, 200 more houses were built in 1970.

Question 11: How many new houses were built in 1965?

Answer: There are 3½ symbols shown for 1965; 3½ × 100 = 350 houses.

Question 12: In which year were half as many houses built as in 1975?

Answer: In 1975, 3 × 100 = 300 houses were built. Half of 300, or 150, houses were built in 1980.

Practice Problems Involving Graphs

Questions 1–4 refer to the graph in the next column:

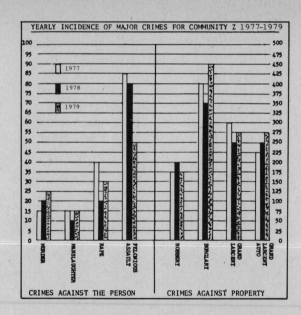

YEARLY INCIDENCE OF MAJOR CRIMES FOR COMMUNITY Z 1977-1979

1. In 1979, the incidence of which of the following crimes was greater than in the previous two years?
   (A) murder
   (B) grand larceny
   (C) rape
   (D) robbery
   (E) manslaughter

2. If the incidence of burglary in 1980 had increased over 1979 by the same number as it had increased in 1979 over 1978, then the average for this crime for the four-year period from 1977 through 1980 would be most nearly
   (A) 100
   (B) 400
   (C) 425
   (D) 440
   (E) 550

3. The above graph indicates that the *percentage* increase in grand larceny auto from 1978 to 1979 was:
   (A) 5%
   (B) 10%
   (C) 15%
   (D) 20%
   (E) 25%

4. Which of the following cannot be determined because there is not enough information in the above graph to do so?
   (A) For the three-year period, what percentage of all "Crimes Against the Person" involved murders committed in 1978?
   (B) For the three-year period, what percentage of all "Major Crimes" was committed in the first six months of 1978?
   (C) Which major crimes followed a pattern of continuing yearly increases for the three-year period?
   (D) For 1979, what was the ratio of robbery, burglary, and grand larceny crimes?
   (E) What was the major crime with the greatest annual incidence for the period 1977–1979?

Questions 5–7 refer to the following graph:

In the graph below, the lines labeled "A" and "B" represent the cumulative progress in the work of two file clerks, each of whom was given 500 consecutively numbered applications to file in the proper cabinets over a five-day work week.

5. The day during which the largest number of applications was filed by both clerks was
   (A) Monday
   (B) Tuesday
   (C) Wednesday
   (D) Thursday
   (E) Friday

6. At the end of the second day, the percentage of applications still to be filed was
   (A) 25%
   (B) 30%
   (C) 50%
   (D) 66%
   (E) 75%

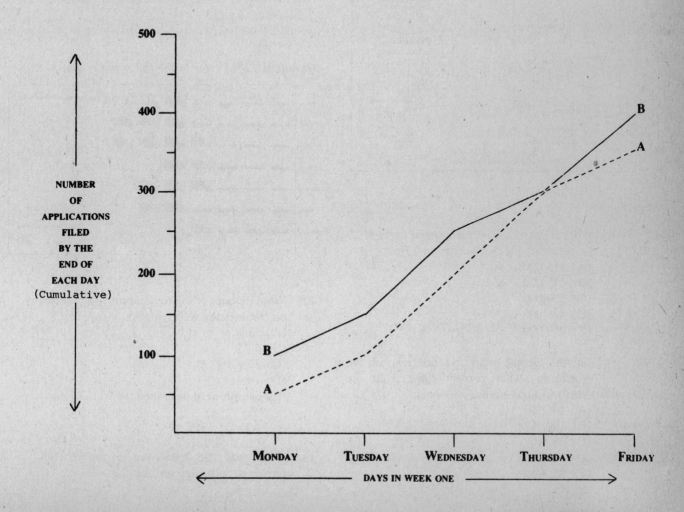

7. Assuming that the production pattern is the same the following week as the week shown in the chart, the day on which Clerk B will finish this assignment will be
(A) Monday
(B) Tuesday
(C) Wednesday
(D) Thursday
(E) Friday

Questions 8–11 refer to the following graph:

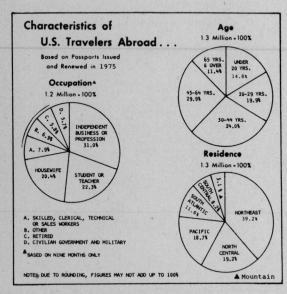

8. Approximately how many persons aged 29 or younger traveled abroad in 1975?
(A) 175,000
(B) 245,000
(C) 350,000
(D) 415,000
(E) 450,000

9. Of the people who did *not* live in the Northeast, what percent came from the North Central states?
(A) 19.2%
(B) 19.9%
(C) 26.5%
(D) 31.6%
(E) 38.7%

10. The fraction of travelers from the four smallest occupation groups is most nearly equal to the fraction of travelers
(A) under age 20, and 65 and over, combined
(B) from the North Central and Mountain states
(C) between 45 and 64 years of age
(D) from the Housewife and Other categories
(E) Northeast and Pacific states

11. If the South Central, Mountain, and Pacific sections were considered as a single classification, how many degrees would its sector include?
(A) 30°
(B) 67°
(C) 108°
(D) 120°
(E) 180°

Questions 12–15 refer to the following graph:

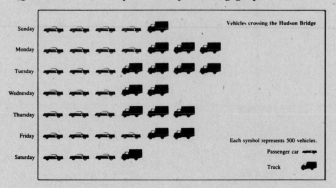

12. What percent of the total number of vehicles on Wednesday were cars?
(A) 85%
(B) 60%
(C) 30%
(D) 10%
(E) cannot be determined

13. What was the total number of vehicles crossing the bridge on Tuesday?

(A) 7
(B) 700
(C) 1500
(D) 2000
(E) 3500

14. How many more trucks crossed on Monday than on Saturday?
    (A) 200
    (B) 1000
    (C) 1500
    (D) 2000
    (E) 3500

15. If trucks paid a toll of $1.00 and cars paid a toll of $.50, how much money was collected in tolls on Friday?
    (A) $400
    (B) $750
    (C) $2000
    (D) $2500
    (E) $3000

Graphs—Correct Answers

1.	**(A)**	6.	**(E)**	11.	**(C)**
2.	**(D)**	7.	**(A)**	12.	**(B)**
3.	**(B)**	8.	**(E)**	13.	**(E)**
4.	**(B)**	9.	**(D)**	14.	**(B)**
5.	**(C)**	10.	**(A)**	15.	**(C)**

Problem Solutions—Graphs

1. The incidence of murder increased from 15 in 1977 to 20 in 1978 to 25 in 1979.

   Answer: **(A)** murder

2. The incidence of burglary in 1977 was 400; in 1978 it was 350; and in 1979 it was 450. The increase from 1978 to 1979 was 100. An increase of 100 from 1979 gives 550 in 1980.
   The average of 400, 350, 450, and 550 is

   $$\frac{400 + 350 + 450 + 550}{4} = \frac{1750}{4}$$
   $$= 437.5$$

   Answer: **(D)** 440

3. The incidence of grand larceny auto went from 250 in 1978 to 275 in 1979, an increase of 25.
   The percent increase is

   $$\frac{25}{250} = .10 = 10\%$$

   Answer: **(B)** 10%

4. This graph gives information by year, not month. It is impossible to determine from the graph the percentage of crimes committed during the first six months of any year.

   Answer: **(B)**

5. For both A and B, the greatest increase in the cumulative totals occurred from the end of Tuesday until the end of Wednesday. Therefore, the largest number of applications was filed on Wednesday.

   Answer: **(C)** Wednesday

6. By the end of Tuesday, A had filed 100 applications and B had filed 150, for a total of 250. This left 750 of the original 1000 applications.

   $$\frac{750}{1000} = .75 = 75\%$$

   Answer: **(E)** 75%

7. During Week One, Clerk B files 100 applications on Monday, 50 on Tuesday, 100 on Wednesday, 50 on Thursday, and 100 on Friday, a total of 400. On Monday of Week Two, he will file numbers 401 to 500.

   Answer: **(A)** Monday

8. 20–29 yrs.:   19.9%
   Under 20 yrs.:   +14.8%
                          34.7%

   34.7% × 1.3 million = .4511 million
                         = 451,100

   Answer: **(E)** 450,000

9. 100% − 39.2% = 60.8% did not live in Northeast.

   19.2% lived in North Central

   $$\frac{19.2}{60.8} = .316 \text{ approximately}$$

   Answer: **(D)** 31.6%

10. Four smallest groups of occupation:

$$7.9 + 6.9 + 5.8 + 5.7 = 26.3$$

Age groups under 20 and over 65:

$$14.8 + 11.4 = 26.2$$

Answer: **(A)**

11. South Central: 8.2%
    Mountain: 3.1%
    Pacific: 18.7%
    ────────
           30.0%

$$30\% \times 360° = 108°$$

Answer: **(C)** 108°

12. There are 5 vehicle symbols, of which 3 are cars.

$$\tfrac{3}{5} = 60\%$$

Answer: **(B)** 60%

13. On Tuesday, there were $3 \times 500 = 1500$ cars and $4 \times 500 = 2000$ trucks. The total number of vehicles was 3500.

Answer: **(E)** 3500

14. The graph shows 2 more truck symbols on Monday than on Saturday. Each symbol represents 500 trucks, so there were $2 \times 500 = 1000$ more trucks on Monday.

Answer: **(B)** 1000

15. On Friday there were

$$4 \times 500 = 2000 \text{ cars}$$
$$2 \times 500 = 1000$$

Car tolls: $2000 \times \$ .50 = \quad \$1000$
Truck tolls: $1000 \times \$1.00 = + \$1000$
Total tolls: $\$2000$

Answer: **(C)** $2000

POWERS AND ROOTS

1. The numbers that are multiplied to give a product are called the **factors** of the product.

   Example: In $2 \times 3 = 6$, 2 and 3 are factors.

2. If the factors are the same, an **exponent** may be used to indicate the number of times the factor appears.

   Example: In $3 \times 3 = 3^2$, the number 3 appears as a factor twice, as is indicated by the exponent 2.

3. When a product is written in exponential form, the number the exponent refers to is called the **base.** The product itself is called the **power.**

   Example: In 2^5, the number 2 is the base and 5 is the exponent.
   $2^5 = 2 \times 2 \times 2 \times 2 \times 2 = 32$, so 32 is the power.

4. a. If the exponent used is 2, we say that the base has been **squared,** or raised to the second power.

   Example: 6^2 is read "six squared" or "six to the second power."

   b. If the exponent used is 3, we say that the base has been **cubed,** or raised to the third power.

   Example: 5^3 is read "five cubed" or "five to the third power."

   c. If the exponent is 4, we say that the base has been raised to the fourth power. If the exponent is 5, we say the base has been raised to the fifth power, etc.

   Example: 2^8 is read "two to the eighth power."

5. A number that is the product of a whole number squared is called a **perfect square.**

   Example: 25 is a perfect square because 25 $= 5^2$.

6. a. If a number has exactly two equal factors, each factor is called the **square root** of the number.

   Example: $9 = 3 \times 3$; therefore, 3 is the square root of 9.

   b. The symbol $\sqrt{}$ is used to indicate square root.

Example: $\sqrt{9} = 3$ means that the square root of 9 is 3, or $3 \times 3 = 9$.

c. In principle, all numbers have a square root. Although many square roots cannot be calculated exactly, they can be found to whatever degree of accuracy is needed (see item 8). Thus the square root of 10, $\sqrt{10}$, is *by definition* the number that equals 10 when it is squared—$\sqrt{10} \times \sqrt{10} = 10$.

d. If a number has exactly three equal factors, each factor is called a **cube root.** The symbol $\sqrt[3]{}$ is used to indicate a cube root.

Example: $8 = 2 \times 2 \times 2$; thus $2 = \sqrt[3]{8}$

e. In general, the nth root is indicated as $\sqrt[n]{}$

7. The square root of the most common perfect squares may be found by using the following table, or by trial and error; that is, by finding the number that, when squared, yields the given perfect square.

Number	Perfect Square	Number	Perfect Square
1	1	10	100
2	4	11	121
3	9	12	144
4	16	13	169
5	25	14	196
6	36	15	225
7	49	20	400
8	64	25	625
9	81	30	900

Example: To find $\sqrt{81}$, note that 81 is the perfect square of 9, or $9^2 = 81$. Therefore, $\sqrt{81} = 9$.

8. On the GRE you will only rarely have to find the square root of a number that is not a perfect square. The two most common square roots with which you will have to deal with are $\sqrt{2}$, which equals approximately 1.4, and $\sqrt{3}$, which equals approximately 1.7. Most times you will not have to convert these square roots to their equivalents since the answer choices will be in terms of the square roots, e.g., (A) $4\sqrt{3}$, etc.

The following method is the way to compute square roots of numbers that are not perfect squares. It is very effective, but it is long and you are unlikely to actually need it on the GRE.

a. Locate the decimal point.

b. Mark off the digits in groups of two in both directions beginning at the decimal point.

c. Mark the decimal point for the answer just above the decimal point of the number whose square root is to be taken.

d. Find the largest perfect square contained in the left-hand group of two.

e. Place its square root in the answer. Subtract the perfect square from the first digit or pair of digits.

f. Bring down the next pair.

g. Double the partial answer.

h. Add a trial digit to the right of the doubled partial answer. Multiply this new number by the trial digit. Place the correct new digit in the answer.

i. Subtract the product.

j. Repeat steaps f–i as often as necessary.

You will notice that you get one digit in the answer for every group of two you marked off in the original number.

Illustration: Find the square root of 138,384.

SOLUTION:

$$\begin{array}{r} 3 \\ \sqrt{13'83'84.} \\ 3^2 = \quad 9 \\ \hline 4\ 83 \end{array}$$

$$\begin{array}{r} 3\ \ 7\ \ 2. \\ \sqrt{13'83'84.} \\ 3^2 = \quad 9 \\ \hline 4\ 83 \\ 7 \times 67 = \quad 4\ 69 \\ \hline 14\ 84 \\ 2 \times 742 = \quad 14\ 84 \\ \hline \end{array}$$

The number must first be marked off in groups of two figures each, beginning at the decimal point, which, in the case of a whole number, is at the right. The number of figures in the root will be the same as the number of groups so obtained.

The largest square less than 13 is 9. $\sqrt{9} = 3$

Place its square root in the answer. Subtract the perfect square from the first digit or pair of digits. Bring down the next pair. To form our trial divisor, annex 0 to this root "3" (making 30) and multiply by 2.

$483 \div 60 = 80$. Multiplying the trial divisor 68 by 8, we obtain 544, which is too large. We then try multiplying 67 by 7. This is correct. Add the trial digit to the right of the doubled partial answer. Place the new digit in the answer. Subtract the product. Bring down the final group. Annex 0 to the new root 37 and multiply by 2 for the trial divisor:

$$2 \times 370 = 740$$
$$1484 \div 740 = 2$$

Place the 2 in the answer.

Answer: The square root of 138,384 is 372.

Illustration: Find the square root of 3 to the nearest hundredth.

SOLUTION:

```
                          1. 7  3  2
                     √3.00′00′00
            1² =        1
            20        2 00
      7 × 27 =        1 89
          340        11 00
    3 × 343 =        10 29
         3460         71 00
    2 × 3462 =        69 24
```

Answer: The square root of 3 is 1.73 to the nearest hundredth.

9. When more complex items are raised to powers, the same basic rules apply.

   a. To find the power of some multiplied item, find the power of each multiplicand and multiply those powers together.

Example: $(4x)^2 = (4x)(4x) = (4)(4)(x)(x) = (4)^2(x)^2 = 16x^2$

Example: $(2xy)^4 = (2)^4(x)^4(y)^4 = 16x^4y^4$

   b. To find the power of some divided item or fraction, find the power of each part of the fraction and then divide in the manner of the original fraction.

Example: $\left(\dfrac{2}{x}\right)^2 = \left(\dfrac{2}{x}\right)\left(\dfrac{2}{x}\right) = \left(\dfrac{4}{x^2}\right)$

   c. To find the result when two powers of the same base are multiplied together, *add* the exponents. You add the exponents because you are adding to the length of the string of the same base all being multiplied together.

Example: $(x^2)(x^3) = (x)(x) \cdot (x)(x)(x) = xxxxx = x^{(2+3)} = x^5$

Example: $2^a \cdot 2^b = 2^{(a+b)}$

   d. To find the result when a power is raised to an exponent, *multiply* the exponents. You multiply the exponents together because you are multiplying the length of the string of the same base all being multiplied together.

Example: $(x^2)^3 = (x^2)(x^2)(x^2) = xxxxxx = x^{(2\cdot3)} = x^6$

   e. When a power is divided by another power of the same base, the result is found by subtracting the exponent in the denominator (bottom) from the exponent in the numerator (top).

Example: $\dfrac{x^3}{x^2} = \dfrac{xxx}{xx} = x^{(3-2)} = x^1 = x$

Note: Any base to the first power, x^1, equals the base.

Example: $\dfrac{x^9}{x^6} = x^{(9-6)} = x^3$

Example: $\dfrac{x^2}{x^2} = \dfrac{xx}{xx} = x^{(2-2)} = x^0 = 1$

Note: Any base to the "zero-th" power, x^0, equals 1.

Example: $\dfrac{x^3}{x^4} = \dfrac{xxx}{xxxx} = \dfrac{1}{x} = x^{(3-4)} = x^{-1}$

f. **A negative exponent** is a reciprocal, as discussed in the earlier section on fractions.

Example: $z^{-3} = \left(\dfrac{z}{1}\right)^{-3} = \left(\dfrac{1}{z}\right)^{+3} = \dfrac{1^3}{z^3} = \dfrac{1}{z^3}$

Example: $(3p)^{-2} = \dfrac{1}{(3p)^{+2}} = \dfrac{1}{9p^2}$

Example: $(r^{-3})^{-6} = \dfrac{1}{(r^{-3})^{+6}} = \dfrac{1}{\left(\dfrac{1}{r^3}\right)^6} = \dfrac{1}{\dfrac{1}{r^{18}}}$

$= (1)\left(\dfrac{r^{18}}{1}\right) = r^{18}$

or $(r^{-3}) = r^{(-3)(-6)} = r^{+18}$

10. Some problems require that different powers be grouped together. Depending on the relationships, they can be grouped by doing the processes explained in #9 in the reverse direction.

Example: $9x^2 = 3^2 \cdot x^2 = (3x)^2$

Example: $\dfrac{81}{y^2} = \dfrac{9^2}{y^2} = \left(\dfrac{9}{y}\right)^2$

Example: $m^{12} = (m^5)(m^7)$ or $(m^{10})(m^2)$ etc.

Example: $z^{24} = (z^6)^4$ or $(z^8)^3$ etc.

11. The conditions under which radicals can be added or subtracted are much the same as the conditions for letters in an algebraic expression. The radicals act as a label, or unit, and must therefore be exactly the same. In adding or subtracting, we add or subtract the coefficients, or rational parts and carry the radical along as a label, which does not change.

Example: $\sqrt{2} + \sqrt{3}$ cannot be added
$\sqrt{2} + \sqrt[3]{2}$ cannot be added
$4\sqrt{2} + 5\sqrt{2} = 9\sqrt{2}$

Often, when radicals to be added or subtracted are not the same, simplification of one or more radicals will make them the same. To simplify a radical, we remove any perfect square factors from underneath the radical sign.

Example: $\sqrt{12} = \sqrt{4}\sqrt{3} = 2\sqrt{3}$
$\sqrt{27} = \sqrt{9}\sqrt{3} = 3\sqrt{3}$

If we wish to add $\sqrt{12} + \sqrt{27}$, we must first

simplify each one. Adding the simplified radicals gives a sum of $5\sqrt{3}$.

Example: $\sqrt{125} + \sqrt{20} - \sqrt{500}$

SOLUTION:

$\sqrt{25}\,\sqrt{5} + \sqrt{4}\,\sqrt{5} - \sqrt{100}\,\sqrt{5}$
$5\sqrt{5} + 2\sqrt{5} - 10\sqrt{5}$
$-3\sqrt{5}$

Answer: $-3\sqrt{5}$

12. In multiplication and division we again treat the radicals as we would letters in an algebraic expression. They are factors and must be treated as such.

Example: $(\sqrt{2})\,(\sqrt{3}) = \sqrt{(2)(3)} = \sqrt{6}$

Example: $4\sqrt{2} \cdot 5\sqrt{3} = 20 \cdot \sqrt{6}$

Example: $(3\sqrt{2})^2 = 3\sqrt{2} \cdot 3\sqrt{2} = 9 \cdot 2 = 18$

Example: $\dfrac{\sqrt{8}}{\sqrt{2}} = \sqrt{4} = 2$

Example: $\dfrac{10\sqrt{20}}{\sqrt{4}} = \dfrac{\overset{5}{\cancel{10}}\sqrt{20}}{\cancel{2}} = 5\sqrt{20}$

Example: $\sqrt{2}\,(\sqrt{8} + \sqrt{18}) = \sqrt{16} + \sqrt{36}$
$= 4 + 6 = 10$

13. In simplifying radicals that contain several terms under the radical sign, we must combine terms before taking the square root.

Example: $\sqrt{16 + 9} = \sqrt{25} = 5$

Note: It is not true that $\sqrt{16 + 9} = \sqrt{16} + \sqrt{9}$, which would be $4 + 3$, or 7.

Example: $\sqrt{\dfrac{x^2}{16} - \dfrac{x^2}{25}} = \sqrt{\dfrac{25x^2 - 16x^2}{400}}$

$= \sqrt{\dfrac{9x^2}{400}} = \dfrac{3x}{20}$

Practice Problems Involving Roots

1. Combine $4\sqrt{27} - 2\sqrt{48} + \sqrt{147}$
(A) $27\sqrt{3}$
(B) $-3\sqrt{3}$
(C) $9\sqrt{3}$

(D) $10\sqrt{3}$
(E) $11\sqrt{3}$

2. Combine $\sqrt{80} + \sqrt{45} - \sqrt{20}$
   (A) $9\sqrt{5}$
   (B) $5\sqrt{5}$
   (C) $-\sqrt{5}$
   (D) $3\sqrt{5}$
   (E) $-2\sqrt{5}$

3. Combine $6\sqrt{5} + 3\sqrt{2} - 4\sqrt{5} + \sqrt{2}$
   (A) 8
   (B) $2\sqrt{5} + 3\sqrt{2}$
   (C) $2\sqrt{5} + 4\sqrt{2}$
   (D) $5\sqrt{7}$
   (E) 5

4. Combine $\frac{1}{2}\sqrt{180} + \frac{1}{3}\sqrt{45} - \frac{2}{5}\sqrt{20}$
   (A) $3\sqrt{10} + \sqrt{15} + 2\sqrt{2}$
   (B) $\frac{16}{5}\sqrt{5}$
   (C) $\sqrt{97}$
   (D) $\frac{24}{5}\sqrt{5}$
   (E) none of these

5. Combine $5\sqrt{mn} - 3\sqrt{mn} - 2\sqrt{mn}$
   (A) 0
   (B) 1
   (C) $\sqrt{mn}$
   (D) mn
   (E) $-\sqrt{mn}$

6. Multiply and simplify: $2\sqrt{18} \cdot 6\sqrt{2}$
   (A) 72
   (B) 48
   (C) $12\sqrt{6}$
   (D) $8\sqrt{6}$
   (E) 36

7. Find $(3\sqrt{3})^3$
   (A) $27\sqrt{3}$
   (B) $81\sqrt{3}$
   (C) 81
   (D) $9\sqrt{3}$
   (E) 243

8. Multiply and simplify: $\frac{1}{2}\sqrt{2}\,(\sqrt{6} + \frac{1}{2}\sqrt{2})$
   (A) $\sqrt{3} + \frac{1}{2}$
   (B) $\frac{1}{2}\sqrt{3}$
   (C) $\sqrt{6} + 1$
   (D) $\sqrt{6} + \frac{1}{2}$
   (E) $\sqrt{6} + 2$

9. Divide and simplify: $\dfrac{\sqrt{32b^3}}{\sqrt{8b}}$
   (A) $2\sqrt{b}$
   (B) $\sqrt{2b}$
   (C) $2b$
   (D) $\sqrt{2b^2}$
   (E) $b\sqrt{2b}$

10. Divide and simplify: $\dfrac{15\sqrt{96}}{5\sqrt{2}}$
    (A) $7\sqrt{3}$
    (B) $7\sqrt{12}$
    (C) $11\sqrt{3}$
    (D) $12\sqrt{3}$
    (E) $40\sqrt{3}$

11. Simplify $\sqrt{\dfrac{x^2}{9} + \dfrac{x^2}{16}}$
    (A) $\dfrac{25x^2}{144}$
    (B) $\dfrac{5x}{12}$
    (C) $\dfrac{5x^2}{12}$
    (D) $\dfrac{x}{7}$
    (E) $\dfrac{7x}{12}$

12. Simplify $\sqrt{36y^2 + 64x^2}$
    (A) $6y + 8x$
    (B) $10xy$
    (C) $6y^2 + 8x^2$
    (D) $10x^2y^2$
    (E) cannot be simplified

13. Simplify $\sqrt{\dfrac{x^2}{64} - \dfrac{x^2}{100}}$
    (A) $\dfrac{x}{40}$
    (B) $-\dfrac{x}{2}$
    (C) $\dfrac{x}{2}$
    (D) $\dfrac{3x}{40}$
    (E) $\dfrac{3x}{80}$

14. Simplify $\sqrt{\dfrac{y^2}{2} - \dfrac{y^2}{18}}$
    (A) $\dfrac{2y}{3}$

(B) $\dfrac{y\sqrt{5}}{3}$

(C) $\dfrac{10y}{3}$

(D) $\dfrac{y\sqrt{3}}{6}$

(E) cannot be simplified

15. $\sqrt{a^2 + b^2}$ is equal to
   (A) $a + b$
   (B) $a - b$
   (C) $\sqrt{a^2} + \sqrt{b^2}$
   (D) $(a + b)(a - b)$
   (E) none of these

16. Which of the following square roots can be found exactly?
   (A) $\sqrt{.4}$
   (B) $\sqrt{.9}$
   (C) $\sqrt{.09}$
   (D) $\sqrt{.02}$
   (E) $\sqrt{.025}$

Root Problems—Correct Answers

1.	**(E)**	9.	**(C)**
2.	**(B)**	10.	**(D)**
3.	**(C)**	11.	**(B)**
4.	**(B)**	12.	**(E)**
5.	**(A)**	13.	**(D)**
6.	**(A)**	14.	**(A)**
7.	**(B)**	15.	**(E)**
8.	**(A)**	16.	**(C)**

Problem Solutions—Roots

1. $4\sqrt{27} = 4\sqrt{9}\sqrt{3} = 12\sqrt{3}$
   $2\sqrt{48} = 2\sqrt{16}\sqrt{3} = 8\sqrt{3}$
   $\sqrt{147} = \sqrt{49}\sqrt{3} = 7\sqrt{3}$
   $12\sqrt{3} - 8\sqrt{3} + 7\sqrt{3} = 11\sqrt{3}$

   Answer: **(E)** $11\sqrt{3}$

2. $\sqrt{80} = \sqrt{16}\sqrt{5} = 4\sqrt{5}$
   $\sqrt{45} = \sqrt{9}\sqrt{5} = 3\sqrt{5}$
   $\sqrt{20} = \sqrt{4}\sqrt{5} = 2\sqrt{5}$
   $4\sqrt{5} + 3\sqrt{5} - 2\sqrt{5} = 5\sqrt{5}$

   Answer: **(B)** $5\sqrt{5}$

3. Only terms with the same radical may be combined.
   $$6\sqrt{5} - 4\sqrt{5} = 2\sqrt{5}$$
   $$3\sqrt{2} + \sqrt{2} = 4\sqrt{2}$$
   Therefore we have $2\sqrt{5} + 4\sqrt{2}$

   Answer: **(C)** $2\sqrt{5} + 4\sqrt{2}$

4. $\frac{1}{2}\sqrt{180} = \frac{1}{2}\sqrt{36}\sqrt{5} = 3\sqrt{5}$
   $\frac{1}{3}\sqrt{45} = \frac{1}{3}\sqrt{9}\sqrt{5} = \sqrt{5}$
   $\frac{2}{3}\sqrt{20} = \frac{2}{3}\sqrt{4}\sqrt{5} = \frac{4}{3}\sqrt{5}$
   $3\sqrt{5} + \sqrt{5} - \frac{4}{3}\sqrt{5} = 4\sqrt{5} - \frac{4}{3}\sqrt{5} = 3\frac{1}{3}\sqrt{5} = \frac{16}{3}\sqrt{5}$

   Answer: **(B)** $\frac{16}{3}\sqrt{5}$

5. $5\sqrt{mn} - 5\sqrt{mn} = 0$

   Answer: **(A)** 0

6. $2\sqrt{18} \cdot 6\sqrt{2} = 12\sqrt{36} = 12 \cdot 6 = 72$

   Answer: **(A)** 72

7. $3\sqrt{3} \cdot 3\sqrt{3} \cdot 3\sqrt{3} = 27(3\sqrt{3}) = 81\sqrt{3}$

   Answer: **(B)** $81\sqrt{3}$

8. Using the distributive law, we have
   $$\tfrac{1}{2}\sqrt{12} + \tfrac{1}{4} \cdot 2 = \tfrac{1}{2}\sqrt{4}\sqrt{3} + \tfrac{1}{2} = \sqrt{3} + \tfrac{1}{2}$$
   Answer: **(A)** $\sqrt{3} + \frac{1}{2}$

9. Dividing the numbers in the radical sign, we have $\sqrt{4b^2} = 2b$

   Answer: **(C)** 2b

10. $3\sqrt{48} = 3\sqrt{16}\sqrt{3} = 12\sqrt{3}$

   Answer: **(D)** $12\sqrt{3}$

11. $\sqrt{\dfrac{16x^2 + 9x^2}{144}} = \sqrt{\dfrac{25x^2}{144}} = \dfrac{5x}{12}$

   Answer: **(B)** $\dfrac{5x}{12}$

12. The terms cannot be combined and it is not possible to take the square root of separated terms.

   Answer: **(E)** cannot be done

13. $\sqrt{\dfrac{100x^2 - 64x^2}{6400}} = \sqrt{\dfrac{36x^2}{6400}} = \dfrac{6x}{80} = \dfrac{3x}{40}$

   Answer: **(D)** $\dfrac{3x}{40}$

14. $\sqrt{\dfrac{18y^2 - 2y^2}{36}} = \sqrt{\dfrac{16y^2}{36}} = \dfrac{4y}{6} = \dfrac{2y}{3}$

   Answer: **(A)** $\dfrac{2y}{3}$

15. It is not possible to find the square root of separate terms.

   Answer: **(E)** none of these

16. In order to take the square root of a decimal, it must have an even number of decimal places so that its square root will have exactly half as many. In addition to this, the digits must form a perfect square ($\sqrt{.09} = .3$).

   Answer: **(C)** $\sqrt{.09}$

ALGEBRAIC FRACTIONS

1. In reducing algebraic fractions, we must divide the numerator and denominator by the same factor, just as we do in arithmetic. We can never cancel terms, as this would be adding or subtracting the same number from the numerator and denominator, which changes the value of the fraction. When we reduce $\dfrac{6}{8}$ to $\dfrac{3}{4}$, we are really saying that $\dfrac{6}{8} = \dfrac{2 \cdot 3}{2 \cdot 4}$ and then dividing numerator and denominator by 2. We do not say $\dfrac{6}{8} = \dfrac{3+3}{3+5}$ and then say $\dfrac{6}{8} = \dfrac{3}{5}$. This is faulty reasoning in algebra as well. If we have $\dfrac{6t}{8t}$, we can divide numerator and denominator by 2t, giving $\dfrac{3}{4}$ as an answer. However, if we have $\dfrac{6 + t}{8 + t}$, we can do no more, as there is no factor that divides into the *entire* numerator as well as the *entire* denominator. Cancelling terms is one of the most frequent student errors. Don't get caught! Be careful!

Example: Reduce $\dfrac{3x^2 + 6x}{4x^3 + 8x^2}$ to its lowest terms.

SOLUTION: Factoring the numerator and denominator, we have $\dfrac{3x(x + 2)}{4x^2(x + 2)}$. The factors common to both numerator and denominator are x and (x + 2). Dividing these out, we arrive at $\dfrac{3}{4x}$.

Answer: $\dfrac{3}{4x}$

2. In adding or subtracting fractions, we must work with a common denominator and the same shortcuts we used in arithmetic.

Example: Find the sum of $\dfrac{1}{a}$ and $\dfrac{1}{b}$.

SOLUTION: Remember to add the two cross products and put the sum over the denominator product.

Answer: $\dfrac{b + a}{ab}$

Example: Add: $\dfrac{2n}{3} + \dfrac{3n}{2}$

SOLUTION: $\dfrac{4n + 9n}{6} = \dfrac{13n}{6}$

Answer: $\dfrac{13n}{6}$

3. In multiplying or dividing fractions, we may cancel a factor common to any numerator and any denominator. Always remember to invert the fraction following the division sign. Where exponents are involved, they are added in multiplication and subtracted in division.

Example: Find the product of $\dfrac{a^3}{b^2}$ and $\dfrac{b^3}{a^2}$.

SOLUTION: We divide a^2 into the first numerator and second denominator, giving $\dfrac{a}{b^2} \cdot \dfrac{b^2}{1}$. Then we divide b^2 into the first denominator and second numerator, giving $\dfrac{a}{1} \cdot \dfrac{b}{1}$. Finally, we multiply the resulting fractions, giving an answer of ab.

Answer: ab

Example: Divide $\dfrac{6x^2y}{5}$ by $2x^3$.

SOLUTION: $\dfrac{6x^2y}{5} \cdot \dfrac{1}{2x^3}$. Divide the first numerator and second denominator by $2x^2$, giving $\dfrac{3y}{5} \cdot \dfrac{1}{x}$. Multiplying the resulting fractions, we get $\dfrac{3y}{5x}$.

Answer: $\dfrac{3y}{5x}$

4. Complex algebraic fractions are simplified by the same methods used in arithmetic. Multiply *each term* of the complex fraction by the lowest quantity that will eliminate the fraction within the fraction.

Example: $\dfrac{\dfrac{1}{a} + \dfrac{1}{b}}{ab}$

SOLUTION: We must multiply *each term* by ab, giving $\dfrac{b + a}{a^2b^2}$ Since no reduction beyond this is possible, $\dfrac{b + a}{a^2b^2}$ is our final answer. Remember *never* to cancel terms unless they apply to the entire numerator or the entire denominator.

Answer: $\dfrac{b + a}{a^2b^2}$

Practice Problems Involving Algebraic Fractions

1. Find the sum of $\dfrac{n}{6} + \dfrac{2n}{5}$.
   (A) $\dfrac{13n}{30}$
   (B) $17n$
   (C) $\dfrac{3n}{30}$
   (D) $\dfrac{17n}{30}$
   (E) $\dfrac{3n}{11}$

2. Combine into a single fraction: $1 - \dfrac{x}{y}$
   (A) $\dfrac{1 - x}{y}$
   (B) $\dfrac{y - x}{y}$
   (C) $\dfrac{x - y}{y}$
   (D) $\dfrac{1 - x}{1 - y}$

(E) $\dfrac{y - x}{xy}$

3. Divide $\dfrac{x - y}{x + y}$ by $\dfrac{y - x}{y + x}$.
   (A) 1
   (B) -1
   (C) $\dfrac{(x-y)^2}{(x+y)^2}$
   (D) $-\dfrac{(x-y)^2}{(x+y)^2}$
   (E) 0

4. Simplify: $\dfrac{1 + \dfrac{1}{x}}{\dfrac{y}{x}}$
   (A) $\dfrac{x + 1}{y}$
   (B) $\dfrac{x + 1}{x}$
   (C) $\dfrac{x + 1}{xy}$
   (D) $\dfrac{x^2 + 1}{xy}$
   (E) $\dfrac{y + 1}{y}$

5. Find an expression equivalent to $\left(\dfrac{2x^2}{y}\right)^3$.
   (A) $\dfrac{8x^5}{3y}$
   (B) $\dfrac{6x^6}{y^3}$
   (C) $\dfrac{6x^5}{y^3}$
   (D) $\dfrac{8x^5}{y^3}$
   (E) $\dfrac{8x^6}{y^3}$

6. Simplify: $\dfrac{\dfrac{1}{x} + \dfrac{1}{y}}{3}$
   (A) $\dfrac{3x + 3y}{xy}$
   (B) $\dfrac{3xy}{x + y}$
   (C) $\dfrac{xy}{3}$
   (D) $\dfrac{x + y}{3xy}$
   (E) $\dfrac{x + y}{3}$

7. $\dfrac{1}{a} + \dfrac{1}{b} = 7$ and $\dfrac{1}{a} - \dfrac{1}{b} = 3$.

Find $\dfrac{1}{a^2} - \dfrac{1}{b^2}$.

(A) 10
(B) 7
(C) 3
(D) 21
(E) 4

Algebraic Fractions—Correct Answers

1.	**(D)**	5.	**(E)**
2.	**(B)**	6.	**(D)**
3.	**(B)**	7.	**(D)**
4.	**(A)**		

Solutions—Algebraic Fractions

1. $\dfrac{n}{6} + \dfrac{2n}{5} = \dfrac{5n + 12n}{30} = \dfrac{17n}{30}$

   Answer: **(D)** $\dfrac{17n}{30}$

2. $\dfrac{1}{1} - \dfrac{x}{y} = \dfrac{y - x}{y}$

   Answer: **(B)** $\dfrac{y - x}{y}$

3. $\dfrac{x - y}{x + y} \cdot \dfrac{y + x}{y - x}$
   Since addition is commutative, we may cancel x + y with y + x, as they are the same quantity. However, subtraction is not commutative, so we may not cancel x − y with y − x, as they are *not* the same quantity. We can change the form of y − x by factoring out a − 1. Thus, y − x = (−1)(x − y). In this form, we can cancel x − y, leaving an answer of $\dfrac{1}{-1}$, or −1.

   Answer: **(B)** −1

4. Multiply every term in the fraction by x, giving $\dfrac{x + 1}{y}$.

   Answer: **(A)** $\dfrac{x + 1}{y}$

5. $\dfrac{2x^2}{y} \cdot \dfrac{2x^2}{y} \cdot \dfrac{2x^2}{y} = \dfrac{8x^6}{y^3}$

   Answer: **(E)** $\dfrac{8x^6}{y^3}$

6. Multiply every term of the fraction by xy, giving $\dfrac{y + x}{3xy}$.

   Answer: **(D)** $\dfrac{y + x}{3xy}$

7. $\dfrac{1}{a^2} - \dfrac{1}{b^2}$ is equivalent to $\left(\dfrac{1}{a} + \dfrac{1}{b}\right)\left(\dfrac{1}{a} - \dfrac{1}{b}\right)$.
   We therefore multiply 7 by 3 for an answer of 21.

   Answer: **(D)** 21

PROBLEM-SOLVING IN ALGEBRA

1. In solving verbal problems, the most important technique is to read accurately. Be sure you understand clearly what you are asked to find. Then try to evaluate the problem in common-sense terms; use this to eliminate answer choices.

   Example: If two people are working together, their combined speed is greater than either one, but not more than twice as fast as the fastest one.

   Example: The total number of the correct answers cannot be greater than the total number of answers. Thus if x questions are asked and you are to determine from other information how many correct answers there were, they cannot come to 2x.

2. The next step, when common sense alone is not enough, is to translate the problem into algebra. Keep it as simple as possible.

   Example: 24 = what % of 12?

   Translation: $24 = x\% \cdot 12$
   or $24 = x\tfrac{1}{100} \cdot 12$
   or $24 = \tfrac{x}{100} \cdot \tfrac{12}{1}$

   Divide both sides by 12.

   $$2 = \tfrac{x}{100}$$

   Multiply both sides by 100.

   $$200 = x \text{ IN PERCENT}$$

3. Be alert for the "hidden equation." This is' some necessary information so obvious in the stated situation that the question assumes that you know it.

Example: Boys plus girls = total class

Example: Imported wine plus domestic wine = all wine.

Example: The wall and floor, or the shadow and the building, make a right angle (thus permitting use of the Pythagorean Theorem).

4. Always remember that a variable (letter) can have any value whatsoever within the terms of the problem. Keep the possibility of fractional and negative values constantly in mind.

5. **Manipulating Equations.** You can perform any mathematical function you think helpful to one side of the equation, *provided* you do precisely the same thing to the other side of the equation. You can also substitute one side of an equality for the other in another equation.

6. **Manipulating Inequalities.** You can add to or subtract from both sides of an inequality without changing the direction of the inequality.

Example: $8 > 5$
$8 + 10 > 5 + 10$
$18 > 15$

Example: $3x > y + z$
$3x + 5 > y + z + 5$

You can also multiply or divide both sides of the inequality by any POSITIVE number without changing the direction of the inequality.

Example: $12 > 4$
$3(12) > 3(4)$
$36 > 12$

Example: $x > y$
$3x > 3y$

If you multiply or divide an inequality by a NEGATIVE number, you REVERSE the direction of the inequality.

Example: $4 > 3$
$(-2)(4) < (-2)(3)$
$-8 < -6$

Example: $x^2y > z^2x$
$-3(x^2y) < -3(z^2x)$

7. **Solving Equations.** The first step is to determine what quantity or letter you wish to isolate. Solving an equation for x means getting x on one side of the equals sign and everything else on the other.

Example: $5x + 3 = y$
Subtract 3.
$5x = y - 3$
Divide by 5.
$x = \dfrac{y - 3}{5}$

Aside from factoring, discussed later in this review, unwrapping an equation is a matter of performing three steps. These rules are stated in terms of *x*, but apply equally to all variables or variable expressions.

Put all x on one side of the equation, if not already there. This can be done by adding, subtracting, dividing or multiplying. Sometimes other quantities come along.

Example: $4x + 2 = 29 + bxy$
Subtract bxy.
$4x + 2 - bxy = 29$
(continued below)

Unpeel x by considering the structure of the whole side x is on as a single expression and perform the opposite operation. Addition and subtraction are opposites; multiplication and division are opposites; raising to powers and taking roots are opposites.

Example: $14k + 8 = 22$
Left is addition, so subtract 8.
$14k = 14$
Divide by 14.
$k = 1$

Continue step b until only terms with x in them are left.

Example: (from above)

$4x + 2 - bxy = 29$
Subtract 2.
$4x - bxy = 29 - 2 = 27$

If only one x term is left, unravel to just x.

Example: 8x = 24
                     Divide by 8.
                         x = 3

Example: $4x^2 = 36$
                     Divide by 4.
                         $x^2 = 9$
                     Take square root. Note ±.
                         x = ±3

If more than one term with x in it is left, try to factor. While, in principle, many things are not factorable, on the GRE most polynomials will be factorable. (Factoring and polynomial multiplication are discussed in the next section of the math review.)

8. If there are two variables in an equation, it may be helpful to put all expressions containing one variable on one side and all the others on the other.

9. Expressing x in terms of y means having an equation with x alone on one side and some expression of y on the other, such as $x = 4y^2 + 3y + 4$.

10. We will review some of the frequently encountered types of algebra problems, although not every problem you may get will fall into one of these categories. However, thoroughly familiarizing yourself with the types of problems that follow will help you to translate and solve all kinds of verbal problems.

A. Coin Problems

In solving coin problems, it is best to change the value of all monies involved to cents before writing an equation. Thus, the number of nickels must be multiplied by 5 to give their value in cents; dimes must be multiplied by 10; quarters by 25; half-dollars by 50; and dollars by 100.

Example: Richard has $3.50 consisting of nickels and dimes. If he has 5 more dimes than nickels, how many dimes does he have?

SOLUTION:

Let x = the number of nickels
x + 5 = the number of dimes
5x = the value of the nickels in cents
10x + 50 = the value of the dimes in cents
350 = the value of the money he has in cents
5x + 10x + 50 = 350
15x = 300
x = 20

Answer: He has 20 nickels and 25 dimes.

In a problem such as this, you can be sure that 20 would be among the multiple-choice answers. You must be sure to read carefully what you are asked to find and then continue until you have found the quantity sought.

B. Consecutive Integer Problems

Consecutive integers are one apart and can be represented by x, x+1, x+2, etc. Consecutive even or odd integers are two apart and can be represented by x, x+2, x+4, etc.

Illustration: Three consecutive odd integers have a sum of 33. Find the average of these integers.

Solution: Represent the integers as x, x+2 and x+4. Write an equation indicating the sum is 33.

3x + 6 = 33
3x = 27
x = 9

The integers are 9, 11, and 13. In the case of evenly spaced numbers such as these, the average is the middle number, 11. Since the sum of the three numbers was given originally, all we really had to do was to divide this sum by 3 to find the average, without ever knowing what the numbers were.

Answer: 11

C. Age Problems

Problems of this type usually involve a comparison of ages at the present time, several years from now, or several years ago. A person's age x years from now is found by adding x to his present age. A person's age x years ago is found by subtracting x from his present age.

Illustration: Michelle was 12 years old y years ago. Represent her age b years from now.

SOLUTION: Her present age is $12 + y$. In b years. her age will be $12 + y + b$.

Answer: $12 + y + b$

D. Interest Problems

The annual amount of interest paid on an investment is found by multiplying the amount of principal invested by the rate (percent) of interest paid.

$$\text{Principal} \cdot \text{Rate} = \text{Interest income}$$

Illustration: Mr. Strauss invests $4,000, part at 6% and part at 7%. His income from these investments in one year is $250. Find the amount invested at 7%.

SOLUTION: Represent each investment. Let x = the amount invested at 7%. Always try to let x represent what you are looking for.

$4000 - x$ = the amount invested at 6%
$.07x$ = the income from the 7% investment
$.06(4000 - x)$ = the income from the 6% investment

$$.07x + .06(4000 - x) = 250$$
$$7x + 6(4000 - x) = 25000$$
$$7x + 24000 - 6x = 25000$$
$$x = 1000$$

Answer: He invested $1,000 at 7%.

E. Mixture

There are two kinds of mixture problems with which you could be familiar. These problems are rare, so this is best regarded as an extra-credit section and not given top priority. The first is sometimes referred to as dry mixture, in which we mix dry ingredients of different values, such as nuts or coffee.

Also solved by the same method are problems such as those dealing with tickets at different prices. In solving this type of problem, it is best to organize the data in a chart of three rows and three columns, labeled as illustrated in the following problem.

Illustration: A dealer wishes to mix 20 pounds of nuts selling for 45 cents per pound with some more expensive nuts selling for 60 cents per pound, to make a mixture that will sell for 50 cents per pound. How many pounds of the more expensive nuts should he use?

SOLUTION:

	No. of lbs.	Price/lb.	= Total Value
Original	20	.45	.45(20)
Added	x	.60	.60(x)
Mixture	20 + x	.50	.50(20+x)

The value of the original nuts plus the value of the added nuts must equal the value of the mixture. Almost all mixture problems require an equation that comes from adding the final column.

$$.45(20) + .60(x) = .50(20 + x)$$
Multiply by 100 to remove decimals.
$$45(20) + 60(x) = 50(20 + x)$$
$$900 + 60x = 1000 + 50x$$
$$10x = 100$$
$$x = 10$$

Answer: He should use 10 lbs. of 60-cent nuts.

In solving the second type, or chemical, mixture problem, we are dealing with percents rather than prices, and amounts instead of value.

Illustration: How much water must be added to 20 gallons of solution that is 30% alcohol to dilute it to a solution that is only 25% alcohol?

SOLUTION:

	No.of gals.	% alcohol	= Amt. alcohol
Original	20	.30	.30(20)
Added	x	0	0
New	20 + x	.25	.25(20 + x)

Note that the percent of alcohol in water is 0. Had we added pure alcohol to strengthen the solution, the percent would have been 100. The equation again comes from the last column. The amount of alcohol added (none in this case) plus the amount we had to start with must equal the amount of alcohol in the new solution.

$$.30(20) = .25(20 + x)$$
$$30(20) = 25(20 + x)$$
$$600 = 500 + 25x$$
$$100 = 25x$$
$$x = 4$$

Answer: 4 gallons.

F. Motion Problems

The fundamental relationship in all motion problems is that Rate · Time = Distance. The problems at the level of this examination usually derive their equation from a relationship concerning distance. Most problems fall into one of three types.

Motion in opposite directions. When two objects start at the same time and move in opposite directions, or when two objects start at points at a given distance apart and move toward each other until they meet, then the distance the second travels will equal the total distance covered.

In either of the above cases, $d^1 + d^2 =$ Total distance.

Motion in the same direction. This type of problem is sometimes called the "catch-up" problem. Two objects leave the same place at different times and different rates, but one "catches up" to the other. In such a case, the two distances must be equal.

Round trip. In this type of problem, the rate going is usually different from the rate returning. The times are also different. But if we go somewhere and then return to the starting point, the distances must be the same.

To solve any motion problem, it is helpful to organize the data in a box with columns for rate, time, and distance. A separate line should be used for each moving object. Remember that if the rate is given in *miles per hour,* the time must be in *hours* and the distance in *miles.*

Illustration: Two cars leave a restaurant at 1 P.M., with one car traveling east at 60 miles per hour and the other west at 40 miles per hour along a straight highway. At what time will they be 350 miles apart?

SOLUTION:

	Rate	Time	= Distance
Eastbound	60	x	60x
Westbound	40	x	40x

Notice that the time is unknown, since we must discover the number of hours traveled. However, since the cars start at the same time and stop when they are 350 miles apart, their times are the same.

$$60x + 40x = 350$$
$$100x = 350$$
$$x = 3\frac{1}{2}$$

Answer: In $3\frac{1}{2}$ hours, it will be 4:30 P.M.

Illustration: Gloria leaves home for school, riding her bicycle at a rate of 12 MPH. Twenty minutes after she leaves, her mother sees Gloria's English paper on her bed and leaves to bring it to her. If her mother drives at 36 MPH, how far must she drive before she reaches Gloria?

SOLUTION:

	Rate	Time	=	Distance
Gloria	12	x		12x
Mother	36	$x - \frac{1}{3}$		$36(x - \frac{1}{3})$

Notice that 20 minutes has been changed to $\frac{1}{3}$ of an hour. In this problem the times are not equal, but the distances are.

$$12x = 36(x - \frac{1}{3})$$
$$12x = 36x - 12$$
$$12 = 24x$$
$$x = \frac{1}{2}$$

Answer: If Gloria rode for $\frac{1}{2}$ hour at 12 m.p.h., the distance covered was 6 miles.

Illustration: Judy leaves home at 11 A.M. and rides to Mary's house to return her bicycle. She travels at 12 miles per hour and arrives at 11:30 A.M. She turns right around and walks home. How fast does she walk if she returns home at 1 P.M.?

SOLUTION:

	Rate ·	Time	=	Distance
Going	12	$\frac{1}{2}$		6
Return	x	$1\frac{1}{2}$		$\frac{3}{2}x$

The distances are equal.

$$6 = \frac{3}{2}x$$
$$12 = 3x$$
$$x = 4$$

Answer: She walked at 4 m.p.h.

G. Work Problems

In most work problems, a complete job is broken into several parts, each representing a fractional part of the entire job. For each fractional part, which represents the portion completed by one man, one machine, one pipe, etc., the numerator should represent the time actually spent working, while the denominator should represent the total time needed to do the entire job alone. The sum of all the individual fractions should be 1.

Illustration: John can wax his car in 3 hours. Jim can do the same job in 5 hours. How long will it take them if they work together?

SOLUTION: If multiple-choice answers are given, you should realize that the correct answer must be smaller than the shortest time given, for no matter how slow a helper may be, he does do part of the job and therefore it will be completed in less time.

	John	Jim	
Time spent	$\frac{x}{3}$	$\frac{x}{5}$	
Total time needed to do job alone	3	5	= 1

Multiply by 15 to eliminate fractions.

$$5x + 3x = 15$$
$$8x = 15$$
$$x = 1\frac{7}{8} \text{ hours}$$

11. In general, you need as many equations as you have unknowns in order to get a unique numerical solution.

12. The two methods for coping with two or more equations are called **substitution** and **simultaneous.** They overlap. You have used both many times.

Substitution. Whenever one unknown equals something, you can substitute that something for it.

Example: (1) $2x + 3y = 14$ } given
(2) $x = 2y$

Substitute 2y for x in first equation.

$$2(2y) + 3y = 14$$
$$4y + 3y = 14$$

Add up y's; divide by 7.

$$7y = 14$$
$$y = 2$$

Substitute for y in second equation.

$$x = 2(2)$$
$$x = 4$$

Simultaneous. Sometimes adding or subtracting whole equations is shorter.

Example: (1) $5x + 3y = 13$
(2) $2x + 3y = 7$

Subtract (2) from (1).

$$5x + 3y = 13$$
$$- [2x + 3y = 7]$$
$$[5x - 2x] + [3y - 3y] = [13 - 7]$$
$$3x = 6$$

Divide by 3.

$$x = 2$$
$$y = 1 \quad \text{by substitution}$$

Practice Problems—Algebra

1. Sue and Nancy wish to buy a gift for a friend. They combine their money and find they have $4.00, consisting of quarters, dimes, and nickels. If they have 35 coins and the number of quarters is half the number of nickels, how many quarters do they have?
   (A) 5
   (B) 10
   (C) 20
   (D) 3
   (E) 6

2. Three times the first of three consecutive odd integers is 3 more than twice the third. Find the third integer.
   (A) 9
   (B) 11
   (C) 13
   (D) 15
   (E) 7

3. Robert is 15 years older than his brother Stan. However, y years ago Robert was twice as old as Stan. If Stan is now b years old and b > y, find the value of b − y.
   (A) 13
   (B) 14
   (C) 15
   (D) 16
   (E) 17

4. How many ounces of pure acid must be added to 20 ounces of a solution that is 5% acid to strengthen it to a solution that is 24% acid?
   (A) $2\frac{1}{2}$
   (B) 5
   (C) 6
   (D) $7\frac{1}{2}$
   (E) 10

5. A dealer mixes a lbs. of nuts worth b cents per pound with c lbs. of nuts worth d cents per pound. At what price should he sell a pound of the mixture if he wishes to make a profit of 10 cents per pound?
   (A) $\dfrac{ab + cd}{a + c} + 10$
   (B) $\dfrac{ab + cd}{a + c} + .10$
   (C) $\dfrac{b + d}{a + c} + 10$
   (D) $\dfrac{b + d}{a + c} + .10$
   (E) $\dfrac{b + d + 10}{a + c}$

6. Barbara invests $2,400 in the Security National Bank at 5%. How much additional money must she invest at 8% so that the total annual income will be equal to 6% of her entire investment?
   (A) $2,400
   (B) $3,600
   (C) $1,000
   (D) $3,000
   (E) $1,200

7. Frank left Austin to drive to Boxville at 6:15 P.M. and arrived at 11:45 P.M. If he averaged 30 miles per hour and stopped one hour for dinner, how far is Boxville from Austin?
   (A) 120
   (B) 135
   (C) 180
   (D) 165
   (E) 150

8. A plane traveling 600 miles per hour is 30 miles from Kennedy Airport at 4:58 P.M. At what time will it arrive at the airport?
   (A) 5:00 P.M.
   (B) 5:01 P.M.
   (C) 5:02 P.M.
   (D) 5:20 P.M.
   (E) 5:03 P.M.

9. Mr. Bridges can wash his car in 15 minutes, while his son Dave takes twice as long to do the same job. If they work together, how many minutes will the job take them?
   (A) 5
   (B) $7\frac{1}{2}$
   (C) 10
   (D) $22\frac{1}{2}$
   (E) 30

10. The value of a fraction is $\frac{2}{5}$. If the numerator is decreased by 2 and the denominator increased by 1, the resulting fraction is equivalent to $\frac{1}{4}$. Find the numerator of the original fraction.
   (A) 3
   (B) 4
   (C) 6
   (D) 10
   (E) 15

Algebra Problem-Solving— Correct Answers

1.	**(B)**	6.	**(E)**
2.	**(D)**	7.	**(B)**
3.	**(C)**	8.	**(B)**
4.	**(B)**	9.	**(C)**
5.	**(A)**	10.	**(C)**

Problem Solutions—Algebra Problem-Solving

1. Let x = number of quarters
    $2x$ = number of nickels
    $35 - 3x$ = number of dimes
    Write all money values in cents.
    $25(x) + 5(2x) + 10(35 - 3x) = 400$
    $25x + 10x + 350 - 30x = 400$
    $5x = 50$
    $x = 10$

    Answer: **(B)** 10

2. Let x = first integer
    $x + 2$ = second integer
    $x + 4$ = third integer
    $3(x) = 3 + 2(x + 4)$
    $3x = 3 + 2x + 8$
    $x = + 11$
    The third integer is 15.

    Answer: **(D)** 15

3. b = Stan's age now
    $b + 15$ = Robert's age now
    $b - y$ = Stan's age y years ago
    $b + 15 - y$ = Robert's age y years ago
    $b + 15 - y = 2(b - y)$
    $b + 15 - y = 2b - 2y$
    $15 = b - y$

    Answer: **(C)** 15

4.

	No. of oz.	% acid	=	Amt. acid
Original	20	.05		1
Added	x	1.00		x
Mixture	20 + x	.24		.24(20 + x)

   $1 + x = .24(20 + x)$ Multiply by 100 to eliminate decimal.
   $100 + 100x = 480 + 24x$
   $76x = 380$
   $x = 5$

   Answer: **(B)** 5

5. The a lbs. of nuts are worth a total of ab cents. The c lbs. of nuts are worth a total of cd cents. The value of the mixture is $ab + cd$ cents. Since there are $a + c$ pounds, each pound is worth $\frac{ab + cd}{a + c}$ cents.

   Since the dealer wants to add 10 cents to each pound for profit, and the value of each pound is in cents, we add 10 to the value of each pound.

   Answer: **(A)** $\frac{ab + cd}{a + c} + 10$

6. If Barbara invests x additional dollars at 8%, her total investment will amount to $2400 + x$ dollars.
    $.05(2400) + .08(x) = .06(2400 + x)$
    $5(2400) + 8(x) = 6(2400 - x)$
    $12,000 + 8x = 14400 + 6x$
    $2x = 2400$
    $x = 1200$

    Answer: **(E)** $1,200

7. Total time elapsed is $5\frac{1}{2}$ hours. However, one hour was used for dinner. Therefore, Frank drove at 30 m.p.h. for $4\frac{1}{2}$ hours, covering 135 miles.

    Answer: **(B)** 135

8. Time $= \dfrac{\text{Distance}}{\text{Rate}} = \dfrac{30}{600} = \dfrac{1}{20}$ hour, or 3 minutes.

    Answer: **(B)** 5:01 P.M.

9. Dave takes 30 minutes to wash the car alone.

    $$\dfrac{x}{15} + \dfrac{x}{30} = 1$$
    $$2x + x = 30$$
    $$3x = 30$$
    $$x = 10$$

    Answer: **(C)** 10

10. Let $2x$ = original numerator
    $5x$ = original denominator

    $$\dfrac{2x - 2}{5x + 1} = \dfrac{1}{4} \text{ Cross multiply}$$
    $$8x - 8 = 5x + 1$$
    $$3x = 9$$
    $$x = 3$$

    Original numerator is 2(3), or 6.

    Answer: **(C)** 6

POLYNOMIAL MULTIPLICATION AND FACTORING

1. A polynomial is any expression with two or more terms, such as $2x + y$ or $3z + 9m^2$.

2. A single term multiplied by another expression must multiply *every* term in the second expression.

    Example: $4(x + y + 2z) = 4x + 4y + 8z$

3. The same holds true for division.

    Example: $\dfrac{(a + b + 3c)}{3} = \dfrac{a}{3} + \dfrac{b}{3} + \dfrac{3c}{3}$
    $$= \dfrac{a}{3} + \dfrac{b}{3} + c$$

4. The FOIL method should be used when multiplying two binomials together.

    Example: $(x + y)(x + y)$

    First $(x + y)(x + y) = x^2$

    Outer $(x + y)(x + y) = xy$

    Inner $(x + y)(x + y) = xy$

    Last $(x + y)(x + y) = y^2$

    $(x + y)(x + y) = x^2 + 2xy + y2$

5. You should know these three equivalencies by heart for the GRE.

    $(x + y)^2 = (x + y)(x + y) = x^2 + 2xy + y^2$
    $(x - y)^2 = (x - y)(x - y) = x^2 - 2xy + y^2$
    $(x + y)(x - y) = x^2 - y^2$

    Work all three out with the FOIL method. The x or y could stand for a letter, a number, or an expression.

    Example: $(m + 3)^2 = m^2 + 2 \cdot 3 \cdot m + 3^2$
    $$= m^2 + 6m + 9$$

    Example: $(2k - p)^2 = (2k)^2 - 2 \cdot 2k \cdot p + p^2$
    $$= 4k^2 - 4kp + p^2$$

6. You will not need much factoring on the exam. Most of what you do need was covered in the preceding points—if you just reverse the process of multiplication.

    Example: $3x + 6xy = 3x(1 + 2y)$

    Example: $2xyz + 4xy = 2xy(z + 2)$

7. One special situation (called a quadratic equation) occurs when an algebraic multiplication equals zero. Since zero can only be achieved in multiplication by multiplying by zero itself, one of the factors must be zero.

    Example: $(x + 1)(x + 2) = 0$
    Therefore, either $x + 1 = 0$, $x = -1$
    or $x + 2 = 0$, $x = -2$.

    In such a situation you simply have to live with two possible answers. This uncertainty may be important in Quantitative Comparison questions.

8. You may also need to factor to achieve a quadratic format.

Example: $x^2 + 2x + 1 = 0$

$(x + 1)(x + 1) = 0$

Thus, $x + 1 = 0$

$x = -1$ since both factors are the same.

GEOMETRY

Symbols

The most common symbols used in GRE geometry problems are listed below. The concepts behind the symbols will be explained in this section.

Angles

∠ or ∢   angle (∠ C = angle C or ∢ C = angle C)

∟   right angle (90°)

Lines

⊥   perpendicular, at right angles to

∥   parallel (line B ∥ line C)

$\overline{BD}$ line or line segment BD

Circles

⊙   circle

$\overset{\frown}{AC}$ arc AC

Angles

1. a. An **angle** is the figure formed by two lines meeting at a point.

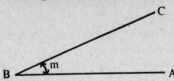

b. The point B is the **vertex** of the angle and the lines BA and BC are the **sides** of the angle.

2. There are three common ways of naming an angle:

a. By a small letter or figure written within the angle, as ∢m.

b. By a capital letter at its vertex, as ∢B.

c. By three capital letters, the middle letter being the vertex letter, as ∠ABC.

3. a. When two straight lines intersect (cut each other), four angles are formed. If these four angles are equal, each angle is a **right angle** and contains 90°. The symbol ∟ is used to indicate a right angle.

Example:

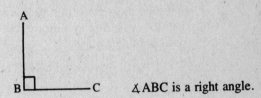

∢ABC is a right angle.

b. An angle less than a right angle is an **acute angle.**

c. If the two sides of an angle extend in opposite directions forming a straight line, the angle is a **straight angle** and contains 180°.

d. An angle greater than a right angle (90°) and less than a straight angle (180°) is an **obtuse angle.**

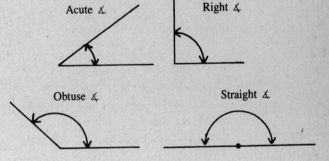

4. a. Two angles are **complementary** if their sum is 90°.

b. To find the complement of an angle, subtract the given number of degrees from 90°.

Example: The complement of 60° is 90° − 60° = 30°.

5. a. Two angles are **supplementary** if their sum is 180°.

b. To find the supplement of an angle, subtract the given number of degrees from 180°.

Example: The supplement of 60° is 180° − 60° = 120°.

Lines

6. a. Two lines are **perpendicular** to each other if they meet to form a right angle. The symbol ⊥ is used to indicate that the lines are perpendicular.

   Example: ∠ABC is a right angle. Therefore, AB ⊥ BC.

   b. Lines that do not meet no matter how far they are extended are called **parallel lines.** Parallel lines are always the same perpendicular distance from each other. The symbol ‖ is used to indicate that two lines are parallel.

   Example: AB ‖ CD

Triangles

7. A **triangle** is a closed, three-sided figure. The figures below are all triangles.

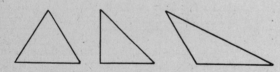

8. a. The sum of the three angles of a triangle is 180°.

   b. To find an angle of a triangle when you are given the other two angles, add the given angles and subtract their sum from 180°.

   Illustration: Two angles of a triangle are 60° and 40°. Find the third angle.

   SOLUTION: 60° + 40° = 100°
   180° − 100° = 80°

   Answer: The third angle is 80°.

9. a. A triangle that has two equal sides is called an **isosceles triangle.**

   b. In an isosceles triangle, the angles opposite the equal sides are also equal.

10. a. A triangle that has all three sides equal is called an **equilateral triangle.**

    b. Each angle of an equilateral triangle is 60°.

11. a. A triangle that has a right angle is called a **right triangle.**

    b. In a right triangle, the two acute angles are complementary.

    c. In a right triangle, the side opposite the right angle is called the **hypotenuse** and is the longest side. The other two sides are called **legs.**

    Example: AC is the hypotenuse.
    AB and BC are the legs.

12. The **Pythagorean Theorem** states that in a right triangle the square of the hypotenuse equals the sum of the squares of the legs. In the triangle above, this would be expressed as $\overline{AB}^2 + \overline{BC}^2 = \overline{AC}^2$. The simplest whole number example is $3^2 + 4^2 = 5^2$.

13. a. To find the hypotenuse of a right triangle when given the legs:

    a. Square each leg.

    b. Add the squares.

    c. Extract the square root of this sum.

    Illustration: In a right triangle the legs are 6 inches and 8 inches. Find the hypotenuse.

    SOLUTION: $6^2 = 36$ $8^2 = 64$
    $36 + 64 = 100$
    $\sqrt{100} = 10$

    Answer: The hypotenuse is 10 inches.

b. To find a leg when given the other leg and the hypotenuse of a right triangle:

   a. Square the hypotenuse and the given leg.

   b. Subtract the square of the leg from the square of the hypotenuse.

   c. Extract the square root of this difference.

Illustration: One leg of a right triangle is 12 feet and the hypotenuse is 20 feet. Find the other leg.

SOLUTION: $12^2 = 144$ $20^2 = 400$
$$400 - 144 = 256$$
$$\sqrt{256} = 16$$

Answer: The other leg is 16 feet.

14. Within a given triangle, the largest side is opposite the largest angle; the smallest side is opposite the smallest angle; and equal sides are opposite equal angles.

Quadrilaterals

15. a. A **quadrilateral** is a closed, four-sided figure in two dimensions. Common quadrilaterals are the **parallelogram, rectangle,** and **square.**

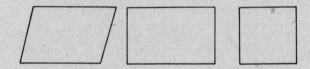

   b. The sum of the four angles of a quadrilateral is 360°.

16. a. A **parallelogram** is a quadrilateral in which both pairs of opposite sides are parallel.

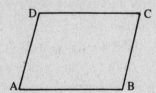

   b. Opposite sides of a parallelogram are also equal.

   c. Opposite angles of a parallelogram are equal.

17. A **rectangle** has all of the properties of a parallelogram. In addition, all four of its angles are right angles.

18. A **square** is a rectangle having the additional property that all four of its sides are equal.

Circles

19. A **circle** is a closed plane curve, all points of which are equidistant from a point within called the **center.**

20. a. A **complete circle** contains 360°.

   b. A **semicircle** contains 180°.

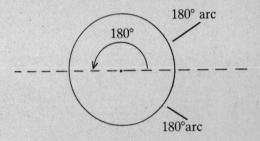

21. a. A **chord** is a line segment connecting any two points on the circle.

   b. A **radius** of a circle is a line segment connecting the center with any point on the circle.

   c. A **diameter** is a chord passing through the center of the circle.

   d. A **secant** is a chord extended in either one or both directions.

   e. A **tangent** is a line touching a circle at one and only one point.

   f. The **circumference** is the curved line bounding the circle.

   g. An **arc** of a circle is any part of the circumference.

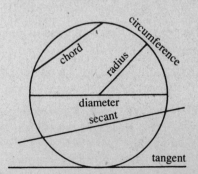

Note: The terms secant and chord are rarely used on the test.

22. a. A **central angle,** as ∠AOB in the figure below, is an angle whose vertex is the center of the circle and whose sides are radii. A central angle is equal to, or has the same number of degrees as, its intercepted arc.

   b. An **inscribed angle,** as ∠MNP, is an angle whose vertex is on the circle and whose sides are chords. An inscribed angle has half the number of degrees as its intercepted arc. ∠MNP intercepts arc MP and has half the degrees of arc MP.

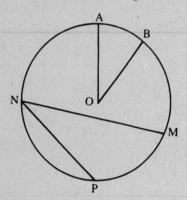

Perimeter

23. The **perimeter** of a two-dimensional figure is the distance around the figure.

Example: The perimeter of the figure above is 9 + 8 + 4 + 3 + 5 = 29.

24. a. The perimeter of a triangle is found by adding all of its sides.

   Example: If the sides of a triangle are 4, 5, and 7, its perimeter is 4 + 5 + 7 = 16.

   b. If the perimeter and two sides of a triangle are given, the third side is found by adding the two given sides and subtracting this sum from the perimeter.

Illustration: Two sides of a triangle are 12 and 15, and the perimeter is 37. Find the other side:

SOLUTION: 12 + 15 = 27
             37 − 27 = 10

Answer: The third side is 10.

25. The perimeter of a rectangle equals twice the sum of the length and the width. The formula is P = 2(l + w).

   Example: The perimeter of a rectangle whose length is 7 feet and width is 3 feet equals 2 × 10 = 20 feet.

26. The perimeter of a square equals one side multiplied by 4. The formula is P = 4s.

   Example: The perimeter of a square, one side of which is 5 feet, is 4 × 5 feet = 20 feet.

27. a. The circumference of a circle is equal to the product of the diameter multiplied by π. The formula is C = πd.

   b. The number π (pi) is approximately equal to $\frac{22}{7}$, or 3.14 (3.1416 for greater accuracy). A problem will usually state which value to use; otherwise, express the answer in terms of "pi," π.

   Example: The circumference of a circle whose diameter is 4 inches = 4π inches; or, if it is stated that $\pi = \frac{22}{7}$, the circumference is $4 \times \frac{22}{7} = \frac{88}{7} = 12\frac{4}{7}$ inches.

   c. Since the diameter is twice the radius, the circumference equals twice the radius multiplied by π. The formula is C = 2πr.

   Example: If the radius of a circle is 3 inches, then the circumference = 6π inches.

   d. The diameter of a circle equals the circumference divided by π.

   Example: If the circumference of a circle is 11 inches, then, assuming

$$\pi = \frac{22}{7},$$
$$\text{diameter} = 11 \div \frac{22}{7} \text{ inches}$$
$$= \overset{1}{11} \times \frac{7}{\underset{2}{22}} \text{ incheses}$$
$$= \frac{7}{2} \text{ inches, or } 3\frac{1}{2} \text{ inches}$$

Area

28. a. In a figure of two dimensions, the total space within the figure is called the **area.**

    b. Area is expressed in square denominations, such as square inches, square centimeters, and square miles.

    c. In computing area, all dimensions must be expressed in the same denomination.

29. The area of a square is equal to the square of the length of any side. The formula is A = s^2.

    Example: The area of a square, one side of which is 6 inches, is 6 × 6 = 36 square inches.

30. a. The area of a rectangle equals the product of the length multiplied by the width. The length is any side; the width is the side next to the length. The formula is A = l × w.

    Example: If the length of a rectangle is 6 feet and its width 4 feet, then the area is 6 × 4 = 24 square feet.

    b. If given the area of a rectangle and one dimension, divide the area by the given dimension to find the other dimension.

    Example: If the area of a rectangle is 48 square feet and one dimension is 4 feet, then the other dimension is 48 ÷ 4 = 12 feet.

31. a. The altitude, or height, of a parallelogram is a line drawn from a vertex perpendicular to the opposite side, or base.

    Example: DE is the height.
    AB is the base.

    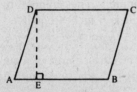

    b. The area of a parallelogram is equal to the product of its base and its height: A = b × h.

Example: If the base of a parallelogram is 10 centimeters and its height is 5 centimeters, its area is 5 × 10 = 50 square centimeters.

c. If given one of these dimensions and the area, divide the area by the given dimension to find the base or the height of a parallelogram.

Example: If the area of a parallelogram is 40 square inches and its height is 8 inches, its base is 40 ÷ 8 = 5 inches.

32. a. The altitude, or height, of a triangle is a line drawn from a vertex perpendicular to the opposite side, called the base. Each triangle has three sets of altitudes and bases.

    b. The area of a triangle is equal to one-half the product of the base and the height: A = $\frac{1}{2}$b × h.

    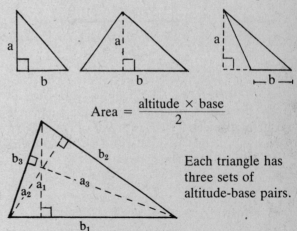

    $$\text{Area} = \frac{\text{altitude} \times \text{base}}{2}$$

    Each triangle has three sets of altitude-base pairs.

    Example: The area of a triangle having a height of 5 inches and a base of 4 inches is $\frac{1}{2}$ × 5 × 4 = $\frac{1}{2}$ × 20 = 10 square inches.

    c. In a right triangle, one leg may be considered the height and the other leg the base. Therefore, the area of a right triangle is equal to one-half the product of the legs.

    Example: The legs of a right triangle are 3 and 4. Its area is $\frac{1}{2}$ × 3 × 4 = 6 square units.

33. a. The area of a circle is equal to the radius squared, multiplied by π: A = πr^2.

    Example: If the radius of a circle is 6 inches, then the area = 36π square inches.

b. To find the radius of a circle given the area, divide the area by π and find the square root of the quotient.

Example: To find the radius of a circle of area 100π:

$$\frac{100\pi}{\pi} = 100$$
$$\sqrt{100} = 10 = \text{radius.}$$

34. Some figures are composed of several geometric shapes. To find the area of such a figure it is necessary to find the area of each of its parts.

Illustration: Find the area of the figure below:

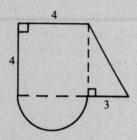

SOLUTION: The figure is composed of three parts: a square of side 4, a semi-circle of diameter 4 (the lower side of the square), and a right triangle with legs 3 and 4 (the right side of the square).

Area of square = 4^2 = 16
Area of triangle = $\frac{1}{2} \times 3 \times 4$ = 6
Area of semicircle is $\frac{1}{2}$ area of circle = $\frac{1}{2}\pi r^2$
Radius = $\frac{1}{2} \times 4$ = 2
Area = $\frac{1}{2}\pi r^2$
     = $\frac{1}{2} \times \pi \times 2^2$
     = 2π

Answer: Total area = $16 + 6 + 2\pi = 22 + 2\pi$.

Three-Dimensional Figures

35. a. In a three-dimensional figure, the total space contained within the figure is called the **volume;** it is expressed in **cubic denominations.**

b. The total outside surface is called the **surface area;** it is expressed in **square denominations.**

c. In computing volume and surface area, all dimensions must be expressed in the same denomination.

36. a. A **rectangular solid** is a figure of three dimensions having six rectangular faces meeting each other at right angles. The three dimensions are length, width and height.

   The figure below is a rectangular solid; "l" is the length, "w" is the width, and "h" is the height.

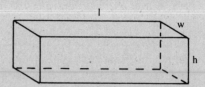

b. The volume of a rectangular solid is the product of the length, width, and height; $V = l \times w \times h$.

Example: The volume of a rectangular solid whose length is 6 feet, width 3 feet, and height 4 feet is $6 \times 3 \times 4 = 72$ cubic feet.

37. a. A **cube** is a rectangular solid whose edges are equal. The figure below is a cube; the length, width, and height are all equal to "e."

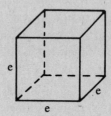

b. The volume of a cube is equal to the edge cubed: $V = e^3$.

Example: The volume of a cube whose height is 6 inches equals $6^3 = 6 \times 6 \times 6 = 216$ cubic inches.

c. The surface area of a cube is equal to the area of any side multiplied by 6.

Example: The surface area of a cube whose length is 5 inches = $5^2 \times 6 = 25 \times 6 = 150$ square inches.

38. The volume of a **circular cylinder** is equal to the product of π, the radius squared, and the height.

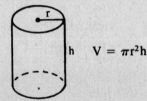

$$V = \pi r^2 h$$

Example: A circular cylinder has a radius of 7 inches and a height of $\frac{1}{2}$ inch. Using $\pi = \frac{22}{7}$, its volume is

$$\frac{22}{7} \times 7 \times 7 \times \frac{1}{2} = 77 \text{ cubic inches}$$

39. The volume of a **sphere** is equal to $\frac{4}{3}$ the product of π and the radius cubed.

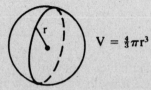

$$V = \frac{4}{3}\pi r^3$$

Example: If the radius of a sphere is 3 cm, its volume in terms of π is

$$\frac{4}{3} \times \pi \times 3 \text{ cm} \times 3 \text{ cm} \times 3 \text{ cm} = 36\pi \text{ cm}^3$$

Practice Problems Involving Geometry

1. If the perimeter of a rectangle is 68 yards and the width is 48 feet, the length is
   (A) 10 yd
   (B) 18 yd
   (C) 20 ft
   (D) 46 ft
   (E) 56 ft

2. The total length of fencing needed to enclose a rectangular area 46 feet by 34 feet is
   (A) 26 yd 1 ft
   (B) $26\frac{2}{3}$ yd
   (C) 48 yds
   (D) 52 yd 2 ft
   (E) $53\frac{1}{3}$ yd

3. An umbrella 50″ long can lie on the bottom of a trunk whose length and width are, respectively,
   (A) 26″, 30″

(B) 39″, 36″
(C) 31″, 31″
(D) 40″, 21″
(E) 40″, 30″

4. A road runs 1200 ft from A to B, and then makes a right angle going to C, a distance of 500 ft. A new road is being built directly from A to C. How much shorter will the new road be?
   (A) 400 ft
   (B) 609 ft
   (C) 850 ft
   (D) 1000 ft
   (E) 1300 ft

5. A certain triangle has sides that are, respectively, 6 inches, 8 inches, and 10 inches long. A rectangle equal in area to that of the triangle has a width of 3 inches. The perimeter of the rectangle, expressed in inches, is
   (A) 11
   (B) 16
   (C) 22
   (D) 24
   (E) 30

6. A ladder 65 feet long is leaning against the wall. Its lower end is 25 feet away from the wall. How much further away will it be if the upper end is moved down 8 feet?
   (A) 60 ft
   (B) 52 ft
   (C) 14 ft
   (D) 10 ft
   (E) 8 ft

7. A rectangular bin 4 feet long, 3 feet wide, and 2 feet high is solidly packed with bricks whose dimensions are 8 inchs, 4 inches, and 2 inches. The number of bricks in the bin is
   (A) 54
   (B) 320
   (C) 648
   (D) 848
   (E) none of these

8. If the cost of digging a trench is $2.12 a cubic yard, what would be the cost of digging a trench 2 yards by 5 yards by 4 yards?
   (A) $21.20
   (B) $40.00

(C) $64.00
(D) $84.80
(E) $104.80

9. A piece of wire is shaped to enclose a square, whose area is 121 square inches. It is then reshaped to enclose a rectangle whose length is 13 inches. The area of the rectangle, in square inches, is
(A) 64
(B) 96
(C) 117
(D) 144
(E) 234

10. The area of a 2-foot-wide walk around a garden that is 30 feet long and 20 feet wide is
(A) 104 sq ft
(B) 216 sq ft
(C) 680 sq ft
(D) 704 sq ft
(E) 1416 sq ft

11. The area of a circle is 49π. Find its circumference, in terms of π.
(A) 14π
(B) 28π
(C) 49π
(D) 98π
(E) 147π

12. In two hours, the minute hand of a clock rotates through an angle of
(A) 90°
(B) 180°
(C) 360°
(D) 720°
(E) 1080°

13. A box is 12 inches in width, 16 inches in length, and 6 inches in height. How many square inches of paper would be required to cover it on all sides?
(A) 192
(B) 360
(C) 720
(D) 900
(E) 1440

14. If the volume of a cube is 64 cubic inches, the sum of its edges is
(A) 48 in

(B) 32 in
(C) 24 in
(D) 16 in
(E) 12 in

Geometry Problems—Correct Answers

1.	**(B)**	6.	**(C)**	11.	**(A)**
2.	**(E)**	7.	**(C)**	12.	**(D)**
3.	**(E)**	8.	**(D)**	13.	**(C)**
4.	**(A)**	9.	**(C)**	14.	**(A)**
5.	**(C)**	10.	**(B)**		

Problem Solutions—Geometry

1.

48' □ 48'

Perimeter = 68 yards
Each width = 48 feet = 16 yards
Both widths = 16 yd + 16 yd = 32 yd
Perimeter = sum of all sides
Remaining two sides must total 68 − 32 = 36 yards.
Since the remaining two sides are equal, they are each 36 ÷ 2 = 18 yards.

Answer: **(B)** 18 yd

2. Perimeter = 2(46 + 34) feet
   = 2 × 80 feet
   = 160 feet
160 feet = 160 ÷ 3 yards = $53\frac{1}{3}$ yards

Answer: **(E)** $53\frac{1}{3}$ yd

3. The umbrella would be the hypotenuse of a right triangle whose legs are the dimensions of the trunk.

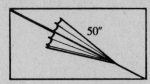

50"

The Pythagorean Theorem states that in a right triangle, the square of the hypotenuse equals the sum of the squares of the legs. Therefore, the sum of the dimensions of the trunk squared must at least equal the length of the umbrella squared, which is 50^2 or 2500.

The only set of dimensions filling this condition is **(E)**:

$$40^2 = 30^2 = 1600 + 900$$
$$= 2500$$

Answer: **(E)** 40″, 30″

4. The new road is the hypotenuse of a right triangle, whose legs are the old road.

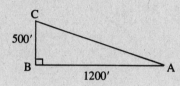

$$AC^2 = AB^2 + BC^2$$
$$AC = \sqrt{500^2 + 1200^2}$$
$$= \sqrt{250,000 + 1,440,000}$$
$$= \sqrt{1,690,000}$$
$$= 1300 \text{ feet}$$
$$\text{Old road} = 1200 + 500 \text{ feet}$$
$$= 1700 \text{ feet}$$
$$\text{New road} = 1300 \text{ feet}$$
$$\text{Difference} = 400 \text{ feet}$$

Answer: **(A)** 400 ft

5. Since $6^2 + 8^2 = 10^2$ (36 + 64 = 100), the triangle is a right triangle. The area of the triangle is $\frac{1}{2} \times 6 \times 8 = 24$ square inches. Therefore, the area of the rectangle is 24 square inches.

If the width of the rectangle is 3 inches, the length is $24 \div 3 = 8$ inches. Then the perimeter of the rectangle is $2(3 + 8) = 2 \times 11 = 22$ inches.

Answer: **(C)** 22

6. The ladder forms a right triangle with the wall and the ground.

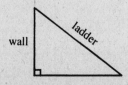

First, find the height that the ladder reaches when the lower end of the ladder is 25 feet from the wall:

$$65^2 = 4225$$
$$25^2 = 625$$
$$65^2 - 25^2 = 3600$$
$$\sqrt{3600} = 60$$

The ladder reaches 60 feet up the wall when its lower end is 25 feet from the wall.

If the upper end is moved down 8 feet, the ladder will reach a height of $60 - 8 = 52$ feet.

The new triangle formed has a hypotenuse of 65 feet and one leg of 52 feet. Find the other leg:

$$65^2 = 4225$$
$$52^2 = 2704$$
$$65^2 - 52^2 = 1521$$
$$\sqrt{1521} = 39$$

The lower end of the ladder is now 39 feet from the wall. This is $39 - 25 = 14$ feet further than it was before.

Answer: **(C)** 14 ft

7. Convert the dimensions of the bin to inches:

$$4 \text{ feet} = 48 \text{ inches}$$
$$3 \text{ feet} = 36 \text{ inches}$$
$$2 \text{ feet} = 24 \text{ inches}$$
$$\text{Volume of bin} = 48 \times 36 \times 24 \text{ cubic inches}$$
$$= 41,472 \text{ cubic inches}$$
$$\text{Volume of}$$
$$\text{each brick} = 8 \times 4 \times 2 \text{ cubic inches}$$
$$= 64 \text{ cubic inches}$$
$$41,472 \div 64 = 648 \text{ bricks}$$

Answer: **(C)** 648

8. The trench contains

$$2 \text{ yd} \times 5 \text{ yd} \times 4 \text{ yd} = 40 \text{ cubic yards}$$
$$40 \times \$2.12 = \$84.80$$

Answer: **(D)** $84.80

9. Find the dimensions of the square: If the area of the square is 121 square inches, each side is $\sqrt{121} = 11$ inches, and the perimeter is $4 \times 11 = 44$ inches.

Next, find the dimensions of the rectangle: The perimeter of the rectangle is the same as the perimeter of the square, since the same length of wire is used to enclose either figure. Therefore, the perimeter of the rectangle is 44 inches. If the two lengths are each 13 inches, their total is 26 inches, and 44 − 26 inches, or 18 inches, remain for the two widths. Each width is equal to 18 ÷ 2 = 9 inches.

The area of a rectangle with length 13 in and width 9 in is 13 × 9 = 117 sq in.

Answer: **(C)** 117

10.

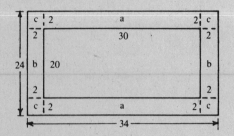

The walk consists of:

a. 2 rectangles of length 30 feet and width 2 feet.

Area of each rectangle = 2 × 30 = 60 sq ft
Area of both rectangles: = 120 sq ft

b. 2 rectangles of length 20 feet and width 2 feet.

Area of each = 2 × 20 = 40 sq ft
Area of both = 80 sq ft

c. 4 squares, each having sides measuring 2 feet.

Area of each square = 2^2 = 4 sq ft
Area of 4 squares = 16 sq ft

Total area of walk = 120 + 80 + 16
= 216 sq ft

Alternate solution:

Area of walk = Area of large rectangle
− area of small rectangle
= 34 × 24 − 30 × 20
= 816 − 600
= 216 sq ft

Answer: **(B)** 216 sq ft

11. If the area of a circle is 49π, its radius is $\sqrt{49}$

= 7. Then, the circumference is equal to 2 × 7 × π = 14π.

Answer: **(A)** 14π

12. In one hour, the minute hand rotates through 360°. In two hours, it rotates through 2 × 360° = 720°.

Answer: **(D)** 720°

13. Find the area of each surface:

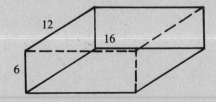

Area of top = 12 × 16 = 192 sq in
Area of bottom = 12 × 16 = 192 sq in
Area of front = 6 × 16 = 96 sq in
Area of back = 6 × 16 = 96 sq in
Area of right side = 6 × 12 = 72 sq in
Area of left side = 6 × 12 = + 72 sq in
Total surface area = 720 sq in

Answer: **(C)** 720

14. For a cube, V = e^3. If the volume is 64 cubic inches, each edge is $\sqrt[3]{64}$ = 4 inches.

A cube has 12 edges. If each edge is 4 inches, the sum of the edges is 4 × 12 = 48 inches.

Answer: **(A)** 48 in

COORDINATE GEOMETRY

Perhaps the easiest way to understand the coordinate axis system is as an analog to the points of the compass. If we take a plot of land, we can divide it into quadrants:

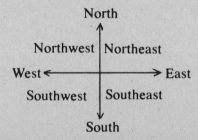

Now, if we add measuring units along each of the directional axes, we can actually describe any location on this piece of land by two numbers. For example, point P is located at 4 units East and 5 units North. Point Q is located at 4 units West and 5 units North. Point R is located at 5 units West and 2 units South. And Point T is located at 3 units East and 4 units South.

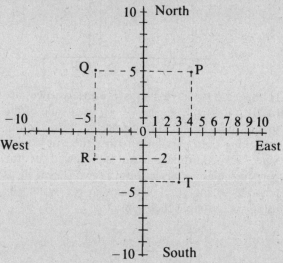

The coordinate system used in coordinate geometry differs from our map of a plot of land in two respects. First, it uses x and y axes divided into negative and positive regions.

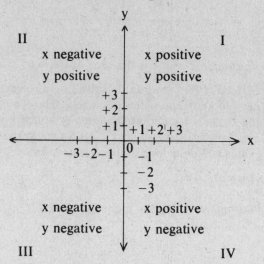

It is easy to see that Quadrant I corresponds to our Northeast quarter, and in it the measurements on both the x and y axes are positive. Quadrant II corresponds to our Northwest quarter, and in it the measurements on the x axis are negative and the measurements on the y axis

are positive. Quadrant III corresponds to the Southwest quarter, and in it both the x axis measurements and the y axis measurements are negative. Finally, Quadrant IV corresponds to our Southeast quarter, and there the x values are positive while the y values are negative.

Second, mathematicians adopt a convention called **ordered pairs** to eliminate the necessity of specifying each time whether one is referring to the x axis or the y axis. An ordered pair of coordinates has the general form (a, b). The first element always refers to the x value (distance left or right of the *origin*, or intersection, of the axes) while the second element gives the y value (distance up or down from the origin).

To make this a bit more concrete, let us *plot* some examples of ordered pairs, that is, find their locations in the system: Let us start with the point (3, 2). We begin by moving to the positive 3 value on the x axis. Then from there we move up two units on the y axis.

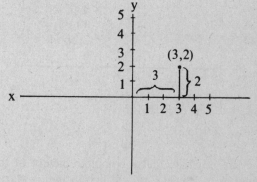

An alternative way of speaking about this is to say that the point (3, 2) is located at the intersection of a line drawn through the x value 3 parallel to the y axis and a line drawn through the y value 2 parallel to the x axis:

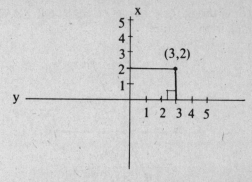

Both methods locate the same point. Let us now use the ordered pairs (−3, 2), (−2, −3) and (3, −2):

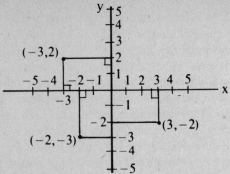

One important use of the coordinate axis system is that it can be used to draw a picture of an equation. For example, we know that the equation x = y has an infinite number of solutions:

$$\begin{array}{c|ccccccc} x & 1 & 2 & 3 & 5 & 0 & -3 & -5 \\ \hline y & 1 & 2 & 3 & 5 & 0 & -3 & -5 \end{array} \text{ etc.}$$

We can plot these pairs of x and y on the axis system:

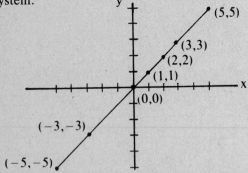

We can now see that a complete picture of the equation x = y is a straight line including all the real numbers such that x is equal to y.

Similarly, we might graph the equation x = 2y

$$\begin{array}{c|ccccccc} x & -4 & -2 & -1 & 0 & 1 & 2 & 4 \\ \hline y & -8 & -4 & -2 & 0 & 2 & 4 & 8 \end{array}$$

After entering these points on the graph, we can complete the picture:

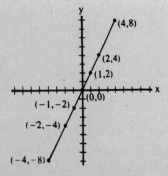

It too is a straight line, but it rises at a more rapid rate than does x = y.

A final use one might have for the coordinate system on the GRE is in graphing geometric figures:

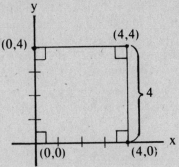

In this case we have a square whose vertices are (0, 0), (4, 0), (4, 4) and (0, 4). Each side of the square must be equal to 4 since each side is four units long (and parallel to either the x or y axis). Since all coordinates can be viewed as the perpendicular intersection of two lines, it is possible to measure distances in the system by using some simple theorems.

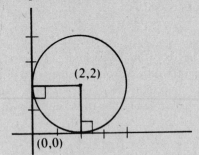

Illustration: What is the area of circle 0?

SOLUTION: In order to solve this problem, we need to know the radius of circle 0. The center of the circle is located at the intersection of x = 2 and y = 2, or the point (2, 2). So we know the radius is 2 units long and the area is 4π.

Answer: 4π

Illustration: What is the length of PQ?

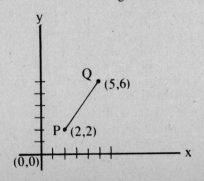

SOLUTION: We can find the length of PQ by constructing a triangle:

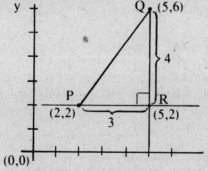

Now, we see that PR runs from (5, 6) to (5, 2) and so it must be 4 units long. We see that QR runs from (2, 2) to (5, 2) so it is 3 units long. We then use the Pythogorean Theorem to determine that PQ, which is the hypotenuse of our triangle, is 5 units long.

Answer: 5 units

It is actually possible to generalize on this example. Let us take any two points on the graph (for simplicity's sake we will confine the discussion to the First Quadrant, but the method is generally applicable, that is, will work in all quadrants and even with lines covering two or more quadrants) P and Q. Now let us assign the value (x_1, y_1) to P and (x_2, y_2) to Q.

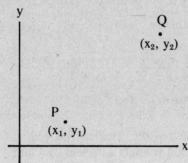

Then, following our method above, we construct a triangle so that we can use the Pythagorean Theorem:

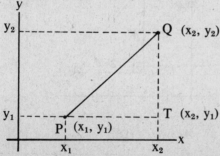

Point T now has the coordinates (x_2, y_1). Side PT will be $x_2 - x_1$ units long (the y coordinate does not change, so the length is only the distance moved on the x axis), and QT will be $y_2 - y_1$ (again, the distance is purely vertical, moving up from y_1 to y_2, with no change in the x value). Using the Pythagorean Theorem:

$$PQ^2 = PT^2 + QT^2$$
$$PQ^2 = (x_2 - x_1)^2 + (y_2 - y_1)^2$$
$$PQ = \sqrt{(x_2 - x_1)^2 + (y_2 - y_1)^2}$$

And we have just derived what is called the **Distance Formula.** We can find the length of any straight line segment drawn in a coordinate axis system (that is, the distance between two points in the system) using this formula.

Illustration: What is the distance between P and Q?

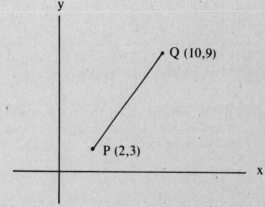

SOLUTION: Point P has the coordinates (2,3) and Q the coordinates (10,9). Using the formula:

$$PQ^2 = \sqrt{(10 - 2)^2 + (9 - 3)^2}$$
$$PQ = \sqrt{8^2 + 6^2}$$
$$PQ = \sqrt{64 + 36}$$
$$PQ = \sqrt{100}$$
$$PQ = 10$$

Answer: 10

For those students who find the Distance Formula a bit too technical, be reassured that the Pythagorean Theorem (which is more familiar) will work just as well on the GRE. In fact, as a general rule, any time one is asked to calculate a distance which does not move parallel to one of the axes, the proper attack is to use the Pythagorean Theorem.

Practice Problems Involving Coordinate Geometry

1. AB is the diameter of a circle whose center is O. If the coordinates of A are (2,6) and the coordinates of B are (6,2), find the coordinates of O.
   (A) (4,4)
   (B) (4,−4)
   (C) (2,−2)
   (D) (0,0)
   (E) (2,2)

2. AB is the diameter of a circle whose center is O. If the coordinates of O are (2,1) and the coordinates of B are (4,6) find the coordinates of A.
   (A) $(3,3\frac{1}{2})$
   (B) $(1,2\frac{1}{2})$
   (C) $(0,-4)$
   (D) $(2\frac{1}{2},1)$
   (E) $(-1,-2\frac{1}{2})$

3. Find the distance from the point whose coordinates are (4,3) to the point whose coordinates are (8,6).
   (A) 5
   (B) 25
   (C) $\sqrt{7}$
   (D) $\sqrt{67}$
   (E) 15

4. The vertices of a triangle are (2,1), (2,5), and (5,1). The area of the triangle is
   (A) 12
   (B) 10
   (C) 8
   (D) 6
   (E) 5

5. The area of a circle whose center is at (0,0) is 16π. The circle passes through each of the following points *except*
   (A) (4,4)
   (B) (0,4)
   (C) (4,0)
   (D) (−4,0)
   (E) (0,−4)

Coordinate Geometry Problems— Correct Answers

1. (A)
2. (C)
3. (A)
4. (D)
5. (A)

Problem Solutions— Coordinate Geometry

1. Find the midpoint of AB by averaging the x coordinates and averaging the y coordinates.
   $$\left(\frac{6+2}{2}, \frac{2+6}{2}\right) = (4, 4)$$
   Answer: (A) (4,4)

2. O is the midpoint of AB.
   $$\frac{x+4}{2} = 2 \quad x + 4 = 4 \quad x = O$$
   $$\frac{y+6}{2} = 1 \quad y + 6 = 2 \quad y = -4$$
   A is the point (0,−4)
   Answer: (C) (0,−4)

3. $d = \sqrt{(8-4)^2 + (6-3)^2} = \sqrt{4^2 + 3^2} = \sqrt{16+9} = \sqrt{25} = 5$
   Answer: (A) 5

4. Sketch the triangle and you will see it is a right triangle with legs of 4 and 3.

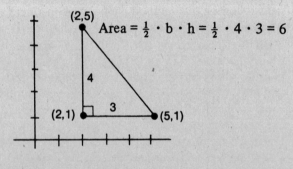

Area $= \frac{1}{2} \cdot b \cdot h = \frac{1}{2} \cdot 4 \cdot 3 = 6$

Answer: (D) 6

5. Area of a circle = πr^2

    $\pi r^2 = 16\pi$ r = 4

    Points B, C, D, and E are all 4 units from the origin. Point A is not.

    Answer: **(A)** (4, 4)

QUANTITATIVE COMPARISONS

Quantitative Comparison questions give you two quantities, one in Column A and one in Column B. For some of the questions, there is common information that is centered between the two columns. Your task is to decide how the two quantities compare. The quantities may be numbers, arithmetic expressions, letters, algebraic expressions, line segments, angles, coordinates on a coordinate geometry graph, elements of a chart, table, or graph or any expression which could be reduced to numerical terms. Any variable or term used in both columns of the same problem has the same value in both columns.

There are four answer choices, (A) through (D). If the quantity in Column A is ALWAYS greater than the quantity in Column B, the answer is (A). If the quantity in Column B is ALWAYS greater than the quantity in Column A, (B) is the answer. If the two quantities are ALWAYS equal, (C) is the answer. You will answer (D) when there is not enough information to decide that one or the other is ALWAYS greater or that the two are ALWAYS equal. Sometimes the information given will not really tell you anything about one or both of the quantities, so D is the correct choice. Sometimes you may know a great deal about the quantities in the columns, but there is enough uncertainty in one or both so that you cannot state that they will ALWAYS be in a given relationship.

On the other hand, there will be many times when you cannot state exactly what the quantity is in one or both of the columns, but you do know that one column is always greater than or less than or equal to the other. For example, if x is a positive number, Column A is x and Column B is 2x, then B will always be greater. However, if you do not know that x is positive, then the answer would be (D), since twice a negative number is a more

negative number—e.g., 2(−5) = −10—which is smaller. If x = 0, then x = 2x, since 2(0) = 0.

This type of question can really test your ability to work quickly. Unnecessary involvement with tedious computation can slow you down here. Always remember that if you are doing lengthy written work in finding an answer, there must be an easier way.

1. No problems should involve multiplication or division with large numbers.

    Illustration: A   B
    $$\frac{(8)(45)(17)}{(462)(8)} \qquad \frac{(17)(9)(42)}{(231)(16)}$$

    SOLUTION: The denominators of both fractions are equal, since 462 is 231 times 2, making both denominators (231)(2)(8). The numerator of B is larger than A, as they both have a factor of 17, but (9)(42) is greater than (8)(45). Therefore, B is the greater fraction—a conclusion reached with no major computation at all.

    Answer: **(B)** B is greater

2. Another important concept to remember is that the product of any number of factors will be zero if and only if one of the factors is 0.

    Illustration: x > 0, y > 0, z = 0
    A   B
    3z(2x + 5y)   3x(2z + 5y)

    SOLUTION: If z = 0, then 3z = 0 and the product of the factors in Column A is 0. In Column B, the product will be (3x)(5y), which is positive. Therefore, B is greater.

    Answer: **(B)** B is greater.

    Illustration: x < 0, y > 0, z = 0
    A   B
    3z(2x + 5y)   3x(2z + 5y)

    SOLUTION: Again, the product of the factors in Column A will be 0, since 3z = 0. In Column B, 3x will be negative, 5y will be positive, so their product will be a negative number. This time, A is greater.

    Answer: **(A)** A is greater.

3. When making comparisons in this type of question, be sure to consider all possibilities.

Illustration: $x^2 = 81$
                   $y^2 = 64$

A	B
x	y

SOLUTION: Remember that a quadratic equation has two roots. If $x^2 = 81$, x may be 9 or −9. If $y^2 = 64$, y may be 8 or −8. If x is 9 while y is 8, x will be greater. But if x is −9 while y is −8, y will be greater. Therefore, the correct answer is (D), not enough information.

Answer: **(D)** not enough information

Illustration:

A	B
x^3	x^2

SOLUTION: If x is greater than 1, A is greater. If x is a fraction between 0 and 1, or any negative number, B is greater. If x is 0 or 1, both A and B are equal. Therefore, the correct answer is (D).

Answer: **(D)** not enough information

Illustration: $1 < x < 3$
                   $1 < y < 99$

A	B
x	y

SOLUTION: If x and y are both 2, A and B are equal. If x is $2\frac{1}{2}$ and y is 2, A is greater. If x is 2 and y is 17, B is greater. Again, the correct answer is (D).

Answer: **(D)** not enough information

In each of the above examples, it is important to consider all possible values of the variable before jumping to a conclusion.

Triangle relationships in geometry also lend themselves to this type of question.

Illustration:

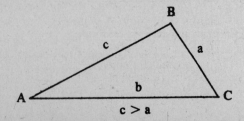

c > a

COLUMN A	COLUMN B
1. ∠A	∠C
2. ∠A	∠B
3. a + b	c

SOLUTION:
1. If two sides of a triangle are unequal, the angles opposite are unequal, with the greater angle opposite the greater side. Therefore, the correct answer is (B).
2. Since we do not know whether a or b is greater, we can not tell which angle is greater. The correct answer is (D).
3. The sum of any two sides of a triangle must always be greater than the third. Therefore, the correct answer is (A).

Answer: **(A)**

Because these questions cover all work previously reviewed, and it is important that you have sufficient practice with them, 50 practice exercises follow.

Practice Problems Involving Quantitative Comparisons

Compare the two quantities in Column A and Column B and determine whether:
    (A) the quantity is greater in Column A
    (B) the quantity is greater in Column B
    (C) both quantities are equal
    (D) no comparison can be made with the information given after working out the problem in the space provided.

Write in your answer next to the question number.

Notes: (1) Information concerning one or both of the compared quantities will be centered between the two columns when given.

(2) Symbols that appear in both columns represent the same thing in Column A as in Column B.

(3) Letters such as x, n, and k are symbols for real numbers.

	COLUMN A	COLUMN B
1.	$\frac{2}{3} \div 2$	30%
2.	$\frac{4}{17}$	$\frac{2}{15}$
3.	$3\frac{1}{2}$ expressed as a percent	3.5%
4.	$\sqrt{25.1}$	5.1
5.	Cost per egg if 2 dozen cost $1.90	9¢
6.	$(2 + .2)(2 - .2)(\frac{1}{5})$	$(.2)(1.8)(2.2)$
7.	$\sqrt{\frac{1}{4} + \frac{1}{9}}$	$\frac{1}{2} + \frac{1}{3}$

$$m = 3, n = -2$$

	COLUMN A	COLUMN B
8.	$(m + n)^2$	$(m - n)^2$

9.	The distance from A to B is 3 miles. The distance from B to C is 4 miles.	
	5 miles	The distance from A to C.
10.	x^5	x^2

11.	The area of a circle is 16π.	
	Diameter of the circle	16

12.	The average of 5 numbers is 20.	
	The sum of the five numbers	110

	COLUMN A	COLUMN B
13.	$\frac{1}{.5}$	$\frac{1}{.05}$
14.	$.1\pi$	$\sqrt{.81}$
15.	Area of a square having perimeter 32	Area of circle having radius 5

COLUMN A	COLUMN B

16.
$$y^2 - 1 = 8$$

8	y

17.
$$a^2 = 49$$

a	7

18.
$$a > b > 0$$

$\dfrac{1}{a}$	$\dfrac{1}{b}$

19.
$$(2)(2)(a) = (3)(3)(3)$$

a	2

20.
$$-4 < x < -2$$

$\dfrac{1}{x^4}$	$\dfrac{1}{x^5}$

21.

(16)(351)(10)	(15)(351)(11)

22.
$$a^2 > 0$$

a	0

23.

A single discount of 10%	Two successive discounts of 5% and 5%.

24.

50%	$\dfrac{1}{.02}$

25.

Time elapsed from 11:50 P.M. to 12:02 A.M.	$\frac{1}{3}$ hour

The diagram below applies to problems 26–29.

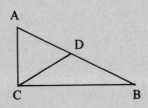

$$AC = CD = AD \qquad AC \perp CB$$

26.	CD	DB
27.	$\angle A$	$\angle B$
28.	CD	CB
29.	AD	DB

COLUMN A	COLUMN B

Questions 30–31 refer to the figure below.

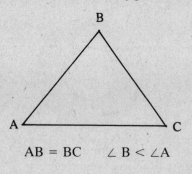

AB = BC   ∠ B < ∠A

	COLUMN A	COLUMN B
30.	∠B	∠C
31.	AB	AC

Questions 32–34 refer to the figure below.

EC ⊥ AD

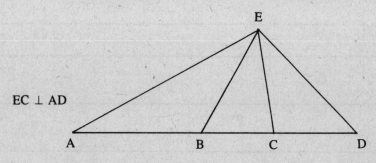

	COLUMN A	COLUMN B
32.	EC	ED
33.	∠EBA	∠ECD
34.	∠A	∠ECB

Questions 35–37 refer to the figure below.

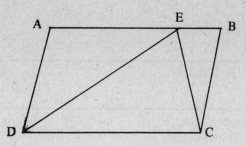

ABCD is a parallelogram.
E is any point on AB.

	COLUMN A	COLUMN B
35.	Twice the area of triangle DEC	Area of parallelogram
36.	∠A	∠B
37.	AD	DC

COLUMN A	COLUMN B

Questions 38–40 apply to the figure below.

Radius of outer circle = 10
Radius of inner circle = 5

	COLUMN A	COLUMN B
38.	Twice area of inner circle	Area of shaded portion
39.	Area of inner circle	75
40.	Circumference of inner circle	50% of circumference of outer circle

	COLUMN A	COLUMN B
41.	105% of 200	50% of 400

	COLUMN A	COLUMN B
43.	35%	$\dfrac{0.7}{2}$

43.
$$6x = 3y = 2z$$

x	z

44.
$$a > b > c$$

2a	b + c

45.
$$\frac{1}{x} > 1$$

x	1

46.
$$\frac{1}{x} < 0$$

x	0

	COLUMN A	COLUMN B
47.	The percent of increase from $10 to $12	The percent of increase from $20 to $22
48.	Sylvia's average rate if she drives 100 miles in 2 hours 30 minutes	Gloria's average rate if she drives 20 miles in 30 minutes

49.
$$m > 0, n > 0$$

$(m + n)^2$	$m^2 + n^2$

50.
$$a > 0, b > 0, \frac{a}{b} < 1$$

a	b

Answer Key to Quantitative Comparison Practice Exercise

1.	**(A)**	26.	**(C)**
2.	**(A)**	27.	**(A)**
3.	**(A)**	28.	**(B)**
4.	**(B)**	29.	**(C)**
5.	**(B)**	30.	**(B)**
6.	**(C)**	31.	**(A)**
7.	**(B)**	32.	**(B)**
8.	**(B)**	33.	**(A)**
9.	**(D)**	34.	**(B)**
10.	**(D)**	35.	**(C)**
11.	**(B)**	36.	**(D)**
12.	**(B)**	37.	**(D)**
13.	**(B)**	38.	**(B)**
14.	**(B)**	39.	**(A)**
15.	**(B)**	40.	**(C)**
16.	**(A)**	41.	**(A)**
17.	**(D)**	42.	**(C)**
18.	**(B)**	43.	**(D)**
19.	**(A)**	44.	**(A)**
20.	**(A)**	45.	**(B)**
21.	**(B)**	46.	**(B)**
22.	**(D)**	47.	**(A)**
23.	**(A)**	48.	**(C)**
24.	**(B)**	49.	**(A)**
25.	**(B)**	50.	**(B)**

Problem Solutions— Quantitative Comparisons

1. **(A)** $\frac{2}{3} \div 2 = \frac{2}{3} \cdot \frac{1}{2} = \frac{1}{3} = 33\frac{1}{3}\%$

2. **(A)** For two positive fractions, to compare $\frac{a}{b}$ with $\frac{c}{d}$, compare ad with bc.

   If $ad < bc$, then the first fraction is smaller. If $ad = bc$, the fractions are equal. If $ad > bc$, then the first fraction is larger. 4 times 15 is greater than 17 times 2. Therefore, the first fraction is greater.

3. **(A)** $3\frac{1}{2} = 3.5 = 350\%$

4. **(B)** Since both columns are positive, square both. $(\sqrt{25.1}$; or $)^2 = 25.1$; or $(5.1)^2 = 26.01$

5. **(B)** There are 24 eggs in 2 dozen.

   $$24\overline{)1.90}^{.07} \text{ or } 24 \times .09 = \$2.16$$
   $$\frac{1\ 68}{22}$$

   Each egg costs almost 8 cents.

6. **(C)** $2 + .2 = 2.2$
   $2 - .2 = 1.8$
   $\frac{1}{5} = .2$

   Factors on both sides are the same.

7. **(B)** $\sqrt{\frac{1}{4} + \frac{1}{9}} = \sqrt{\frac{13}{36}} = \frac{\sqrt{13}}{6}$

   $\frac{1}{2} + \frac{1}{3} = \frac{5}{6}; 5 > \sqrt{13}$

8. **(B)** $(m + n)^2 = (1)^2 = 1$
   $(m - n)^2 = (5)^2 = 25$

9. **(D)** There is no indication as to the direction from B to C. It may not be a right angle triangle.

10. **(D)** If $x > 1$, A is bigger. If $x = 1$, A and B are equal. If $x < 0$, B is bigger.

11. **(B)** Area of circle $= \pi r^2$
    $16\pi = \pi r^2$
    $16 = r^2$; $r = 4$; diameter $= 8$

12. **(B)** If the average is 20, then the 5 numbers were added and the sum divided by 5 to give 20. The sum must be 100.

13. **(B)** $\frac{1}{.5} = \frac{10}{5} = 2$ tops are equal
    $\frac{1}{.05} = \frac{100}{5} = 20$ or   but bottom of B smaller.

14. **(B)** $.1(3.14) = .314$
    $\sqrt{.81} = .9$

15. **(B)** Each side of the square is 8. Area of the square is 64. Area of the circle is 25π. $25(3.14)$ is greater than 64.

16. **(A)** $8 = y^2 - 1$
    $9 = y^2$
    $y = 3$ or -3
    8 is greater than either value of y.

17. **(D)** a may be either 7 or − 7.

18. **(B)** When fractions have equal numerators, the fraction having the smaller denominator has the greater value.

19. **(A)** $4a = 27 \qquad a = 6\frac{3}{4}$

20. **(A)** Any even power of x is positive, but since x is negative any odd power of x is negative.

21. **(B)** (16)(10) is less than (15)(11)

22. **(D)** a^2 must be positive; a can be either negative or positive.

23. **(A)** Consider a marked price of $100. A single discount of 10% gives $10 off. An initial discount of 5% gives $5 off, making the new price $95. The second 5% discount is 5% of only $95 or $4.75, making the total discount only $5 + $4.75 or $9.75.

24. **(B)** $50\% = \frac{1}{2}$

    $$\frac{1}{.02} = \frac{100}{2} = 50$$

25. **(B)** From 11:50 P.M. to 12:02 A.M. is 12 minutes. $\frac{1}{3}$ of an hour is 20 minutes.

26. **(C)**

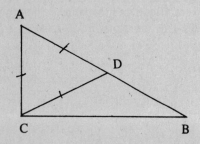

Triangle ACD is equilateral, making each angle 60°. Angle DCB is then 30°, and angle CDB is 120°, leaving 30° for angle B. Therefore, triangle DCB is isosceles.

27. **(A)** Angle A is 60°, angle B is 30°.

28. **(B)** In triangle CDB, CD is opposite a 30° angle, while CB is opposite 120°.

29. **(C)** Both of these segments are equal to CD.

30. **(B)** Since ∠A and ∠C must be equal, because the sides opposite are congruent, ∠B is also less than ∠C.

31. **(A)** Since ∠B is less than ∠C, AC will be less than AB.

32. **(B)** The shortest distance from a point to a line is the perpendicular.

33. **(A)** Angle EBA is an exterior angle of triangle EBC and is therefore greater than angle ECB. Since angle ECD is also a right angle, angle EBA will be greater than angle ECD.

34. **(B)** Triangle ECA has a right angle. Since there will be 90° left to divide between the two remaining angles, angle A must be less than 90°.

35. **(C)** The altitude of triangle EDC is equal to the altitude of the parallelogram. Both the triangle and the parallelogram have the same base. Since the area of a triangle is $\frac{1}{2}$bh and the area of a parallelogram is bh, these quantities are equal.

36. **(D)** There is no way to tell which is greater.

37. **(D)** There is no way to tell which is greater.

38. **(B)** Area of outer circle = $\pi r^2 = 100\pi$
    Area of inner circle = 25π
    Shaded portion is outer circle minus inner circle, or 75π.

39. **(A)** Area of inner circle = $\pi r^2 = 25\pi$
    25(3.14) is more than 75.

40. **(C)** Circumference = πd
    Circumference of outer circle = $\pi(20)$
    Circumference of inner circle = $\pi(10)$
    $50\% = \frac{1}{2}$; $\frac{1}{2}$ of outer circumference = 10π

41. **(A)** 105% of 200 is more than 200.
    50% or $\frac{1}{2}$ of 400 is 200.

42. **(C)** $35\% = .35$

$$\frac{0.7}{2} = .35$$

43. **(D)** If $6x = 2z$, then $3x = z$, or $x = \frac{1}{3}z$. If either x or z is zero, both quantities are equal; if both are positive, z is larger. If both are negative, x is larger.

44. **(A)**
$$\begin{array}{c} a > b \\ a > c \\ \hline 2a > b + c \end{array}$$

45. **(B)** If $\frac{1}{x} > 1$, we multiply each side by x and have $1 > x$. There should be no concern about reversing the inequality, as x must be positive if $\frac{1}{x} > 1$.

46. **(B)** If $\frac{1}{x}$ is to be negative, x must be negative, since a positive number divided by a negative number gives a negative quotient. 0 is larger than any negative number.

47. **(A)** Percent of increase = $\frac{\text{Amount of increase}}{\text{Original}} \cdot 100$. The percent of increase in A is $\frac{2}{10} \cdot 100$. The percent of increase in B is $\frac{2}{20}$ or $\frac{1}{10} \cdot 100$.

48. **(C)** Average rate = $\frac{\text{Total distance}}{\text{Total time}}$

Sylvia's average rate = $\frac{100}{2.5} = 40$

Gloria's average rate = $\frac{20}{.5} = 40$

49. **(A)** $(m + n)^2 = m^2 + 2mn + n^2$. Since m and n are both positive, $2mn$ is positive.

50. **(B)** If $\frac{a}{b} < 1$, the denominator must be greater than the numerator.

GENERAL HINTS FOR GRE
VERBAL SECTIONS

The Verbal Section contains 38 questions. These 38 questions are of four types: Antonyms, Analogies, Sentence Completion, and Reading Comprehension. Although these types of questions are probably familiar to you from other tests, it is a good idea to read carefully the Instructional Overviews for each question type before doing the practice tests. The explanations of the problems in the practice tests contain many comments on technique, pattern recognition and the like, but the Instructional Overviews present this sort of material in a much more concise and organized fashion.

It is worth noting here that although Antonym and Analogy questions do test the extent of your vocabulary and the precision with which you can define words, there is a considerable amount of problem-solving skill even in those question types. You are therefore best advised to give at least a small amount of thought even to those questions that at first appear to contain totally unfamiliar words. It is important to make sure that you take your best shot at as many of the questions as possible.

TIMING HINTS

It is very helpful to keep control of your time as you do a GRE Verbal Section because the four types of questions (Sentence Completion, Analogy, Antonym, and Reading Comprehenssion) should not all be done at the same rate. The optimum timings for the average student on the verbal sections are as follows:

OPTIMUM TIME ALLOWANCES BY QUESTION TYPE FOR GRE VERBAL SECTIONS

Order in Section	Question Type	No. of Questions	Time Allowance
First	Sentence Completion	7	5 minutes
Second	Analogy	9	6 minutes
Third	Reading Comprehension	11*	13 minutes*
Fourth	Antonyms	11	6 minutes
Total Section		38 Questions	30 Minutes

*A Reading Comprehension passage with 3 questions should be allowed 4 minutes; one with 8 question should be allowed 9 minutes.

Use of Time Allowance Chart

The most important part of the time allowance chart is the recommendation that you leave adequate time for the antonym questions that appear at the end of the section. If you spend too much time on the earlier questions, especially the Reading Comprehension questions, which is easy to do, you will forfeit your chance to get several relatively easy antonym questions in the last sub-part of the section.

Your Reading Comprehension questions will probably be divided into two passages of *unequal length* and with *different numbers of questions*. You will probably have one shorter passage with three questions and one longer passage with eight questions. You should allow yourself three or four minutes to read the shorter passage and answer its questions, and nine or ten minutes to read the longer passage and answer its questions.

More detailed timing hints on the division of time between reading and answering questions, and the like are found in the Instructional Overview for Reading Comprehension.

If you have difficulty in controlling your timing on the Reading Comprehension passages so that you are consistently "shortchanging" the Antonym questions, you might consider doing the questions in a different order. When you finish the Analogy questions, go directly to the Antonym questions. Do them in their allotted time and then leave the last 13 minutes for the two Reading Comprehension passages. It is better if you can discipline yourself and not have to shuffle the extra pages forward and backward, but the bottom line is that you must leave enough time for the Antonym questions.

THE READING QUESTIONS

READING COMPREHENSION INSTRUCTIONAL OVERVIEW

INTRODUCTION

"Reading comprehension?" you snort. "I know how to read." And you do. But somehow you still make errors on reading comprehension problems.

While reading is a skill that you have practiced nearly all your life, it is one that you—like almost everyone else—could probably improve greatly. We don't mean just speed, or even primarily speed, but COMPREHENSION—getting the meaning, the whole meaning, and nothing but the meaning. Having made that global statement, let us focus on the much narrower and simpler task of improving your score on the Reading Comprehension questions on the GRE.

We will approach this task by first describing how the Reading Comprehension question appears in the GRE; second, by identifying different kinds of reading tasks and approaches that you will need on the test; third, by analyzing the types of questions you will be asked and the answer choices among which you will be choosing; and, fourth, by developing an attack strategy.

STRUCTURE AND TIMING OF READING COMPREHENSION QUESTIONS

The Reading Comprehension questions on the GRE will be based on four passages. In each of the two Verbal Sections that count you will have 11 Reading Comprehension questions. Usually 3 questions will be based on a shorter passage of from 125 to 175 words in length. The other 8 questions are usually based on a longer passage of from 450–550 words in length.

The passages will usually be writings that are, or could be, from textbooks, journal articles, academic essays, and the like. While they will not often be intrinsically interesting to you personally, they are fairly well written with definite structure and considerable implicit meaning. Later we will discuss this further. The topics presented will range widely and will usually include passages from the humanities and social sciences, with some fairly technical-sounding passages from such fields as economics, psychology, and occasionally even physical sciences. The topics are not really important since in principle you can always answer all of the questions even if you have no knowledge of the field other than what the passage says.

You will often, correctly, be told: THE RC SECTION IS NOT A TEST OF KNOWLEDGE, BUT ONLY OF READING SKILLS. While this is basically true, it is also true that you are expected to use two general areas of knowledge—language and common sense. The linguistic knowledge required is not knowledge of esoteric vocabulary, but the ability to read closely and know the precise relationships expressed by common words. Common sense knowledge is merely what any reasonably alert college graduate could be expected to know. For example:

Cows are the source of beef, cows are deliberately raised by humans for food and not simply harvested like fish, China is a country, theology has to do with God, etc.

Many students are very worried that their reading speed is inadequate for the test. They

128

often base this feeling on the experience of having wanted more time than was available for the reading sections of this or other tests. READING SPEED IS NOT THE KEY TO THE GRE. You will only have to read about 115 words per minute, perhaps less, for the whole section, including passages, questions, and answer choices. This is well within the capacities of virtually any college graduate. Of course there is one other little matter—you have to think about the questions and answer them.

The overall timing recommendations for the Verbal Section are given in the Verbal Strategy Overview. For Reading Comprehension passages, you should allocate approximately four minutes for a three-question passage and nine minutes for an eight-question passage. This time is best divided as shown in the chart below:

TIMING FOR READING COMPREHENSION PASSAGES

Three-Question Passage

Previewing Questions	15 seconds
Reading Passage	1 minute 30 seconds
Answering Questions	2 minutes 15 seconds
Total	4 minutes

Eight-Question Passage

Previewing	45 seconds
Reading Passage	3 minutes 30 seconds
Answering Questions	4 minutes 45 seconds
Total	9 minutes

This works out to approximately 5 seconds per question for the previewing, 25–30 seconds per question for reading the passage, and 30–35 seconds per question for answering the questions.

Occasionally, there is a Verbal Section in which the reading is divided into a four-question passage and a seven-question passage. Five minutes and eight minutes would be good rules of thumb for such a distribution.

The most important thing for you to remember about this timing recommendation is that it is not rigid. It is certain that you will not follow it exactly for most passages, so don't worry. The second most important thing is that you spend more time answering the questions than reading the passage. While this will not always be possible with a longer or more obscure passage, it is the goal you should strive for. The questions and answers between them will usually have even more words to read than the passage, words that are not all connected together. In addition, you will have to think about the answer choices to the questions since many are rather close, as we will discuss later. While it is true that you have to think about the passage while you read it, there is still more work to be done with the questions than with the passage. Furthermore, your natural impulse is to feel that if you could memorize the passage all your troubles would be over and the questions would answer themselves. Nothing could be further from the truth. Practically none of the RC questions will merely ask you to parrot back what was in the passage. At the least, you will need to use different words and often you will need to work from underlying structures and implicit ideas, again as we will discuss later. All of this means that your goal is to read the passage carefully but briskly once, thinking all the while, and then to work the problems briskly but carefully.

The previewing of the question stem that we recommend is a very quick reading of just the part of the question which asks the question, not the answer choices or roman numeral propositions, if any. There are three purposes to this preview. First, it can alert you to most of the questions that concern details or have references to specific parts of the passage ("line 20" or "first paragraph," etc.); this foreknowledge can save you time and improve accuracy, though it only applies to a few questions. Second, it can give you some idea of the topic and approach of the passage so that you can more easily follow it; this can be particularly helpful when the passage has a broad range, or a beginning that is quite different from its body. Third, by giving you some clues and structure for your reading of the passage, this preview can combat both fatigue and boredom. As interested as you are in your score, you may find the passages less than thrilling. If you can persuade yourself that it is a detective game— which it is, of sorts—you might keep up your interest and do better.

Most students find previewing the questions very helpful and reassuring. Try this technique on the practice tests in this book. If you personally find that you are not comfortable with it and you can do well without previewing the questions, then don't do it.

Another issue that affects timing is the question of referring back to the passage while considering a particular question. Naturally, it is quickest to answer a question without referring back to the passage. You should make as much progress as possible in eliminating answer choices and choosing the correct answer before you let yourself refer back to the passage. You should be able to answer most questions without having to refer to the passage—provided you have done a reasonably good job in reading the passage in the first place. On some questions, you will need to refer back to the passage to distinguish between a few answer choices or to get a handle on a particular idea or phrase.

When you do need to refer back to the passage it is very important to do so efficiently. You certainly do not have time to re-read the entire passage for each question. Before you go back to the passage, try to be clear in your mind just which part or parts of the passage are relevant. This can be deduced from the overall structure of the passage and your understanding of where the idea you are checking fits into that structure. For instance, a passage may trace the chronological development of theories of electricity. If the question asks about Galvani's ideas, you may remember that Galvani was fairly early on and thus go to the earlier parts of the passage. A few seconds (two or three) spent in fixing the position of the idea you are checking in the structure of the passage will not only save time in the review, but also improve your ability to understand the material you are reviewing.

If you have no idea where or how the idea in the question relates to the passage, leave the question to the end of the time allotted for that passage and do the rereading only if you do have time after answering the other questions.

DIFFERENT KINDS OF READING AND HOW TO DO THEM

Four aspects of reading will concern us here.
1. literal versus implicit meaning
2. precision versus imprecision
3. active versus passive reading
4. "test reading" versus "real-world" reading

These are not entirely separate ideas, nor will you find them strange. You have been reading suc-

cessfully for many years and all we will try to do in this section is help you to improve by making you conscious of and emphasizing the reading skills most used on the GRE.

We will use the following short passage as the basis of our discussions of both the different kinds of reading and the different kinds of questions on the GRE. Whenever a question is asked about the passage, try to answer it before you read the explanation.

> One dependable characteristic of the cattle cycle is the biologic time lag in the production process.
>
> Heifers are not bred for their first calf until they are 14 to 18 months old. Then the gestation period is 9 months. The calf, in turn, won't reach mature slaughter weight for another 17 to 19 months, depending on the individual calf's rate of gain and the feeding program.
>
> Consequently, it takes up to 4 years from the time a cattle producer's heifer is born until her offspring reaches slaughter weight. If this offspring is retained to expand the herd rather than sent to slaughter, it could be about 5½ years from the time the first calf is retained in the herd until an offspring reaches slaughter.
>
> Because of the time lag, beef production continues to increase well beyond the time price signals change. This happened in the 1974–76 period. Beef production kept increasing despite the large financial losses to cattle producers.

Literal Versus Implicit Meaning

Literal meaning is the meaning of the passage that is explicitly stated. For instance:

1. What is the period of gestation in cattle?

The answer is found by looking up the period in the second paragraph of the passage (or by memory) and noting that it is 9 months.

2. What happened to beef production and prices during 1974–76?

In the last paragraph it is stated that the production kept increasing despite lower prices and large losses.

Although it is hard to do anything with a passage if you do not even see its literal meaning, most of the questions and most of the information in a passage—even one as simple and descriptive as this one—is carried in the implicit meanings. There are many kinds of implicit meanings, but they are all essentially the same idea. The connections between the different parts of the passage and the fact that the specific literal ideas are presented in particular orders and with particular emphases and relationships conveys additional meaning. There is, of course, no absolute dividing line between explicit and implicit. Some ideas can be understood in several ways.

3. What is a heifer?

A young female of the cattle species. This could be known by prior knowledge (not much of that on the GRE, though) or you could see that it is implied from the statement in the passage that heifers are the cattle which give birth, hence female by our common knowledge of mammalian reproduction, and are young since it is the earliest they can be bred. The latter is a little less sure than the former.

4. What is the cattle cycle referred to in the first sentence?

Here we begin to get into what the answer is not. The cattle cycle is not the generations of cattle or the process of getting one cow from another. That would be the biologic cycle perhaps. We know this because if something (the biologic cycle) is a characteristic of something else (the cattle cycle), then the characteristic is not likely to be the whole thing.

What, then, is the cattle cycle? The last paragraph tells us that there is a price movement as well, and that the price movement and the biologic movement have been out of synchrony. This leads to the idea that the cattle cycle is some sort of cycle involving the prices, the production or number of cattle, and the biologic cycle of cattle. Since it is referred to as a cycle, it presumably goes up and down. Therefore, we might see a further question of this sort.

5. What probably happened to beef prices and cattle supplies after 1976?

Since the cycle had been on a down price and up cattle supplies part of the cycle through 1976,

one would expect a reduction in herd size and an increase in prices after 1976. This would be followed by a natural desire for the cattle producers to increase their herds to take advantage of the higher prices (deduced from the cyclic nature of things, reinforced by common sense applied to basic business). This would gradually lead to a general increase in cattle supplies and an eventual decrease in prices, thus completing the cycle.

6. How long does a cattle cycle probably take?

This is not a question that can be answered with great confidence. One would actually have to work with the answer choices to some extent as will be described in the section on questions. However, we CAN imply from the passage that the cycle must involve at least 6 years or more since it will take at least that long for the herds to have increased through two generations. An answer choice of less than 5 years would be too short to allow really major changes in cattle supplies and one longer than 15 years (maybe 10) would not be good since it would not recognize the building up of oversupply. The upper limit is much less certain than the lower.

We will leave this topic now, though it will be carried forward further in the discussion of the kinds of questions which you will be asked, and the proper approaches to them. Many examples of this sort of reading are explained in the answer explanations for the practice test RC questions.

Precision in Reading

Many of the implications which you will be called upon to see in the passages on the test will be strong or weak or even possible because of the precise wording of the passage. It is very important, however, to remember that precision is not the same as subtlety. An example of precision is the difference between *can* and *will* in these two sentences:

Inflation can be controlled.
Inflation will be controlled.

These sentences have very different meanings. The first states that it is possible to control inflation, while the second states that not only can it be controlled, but also that this happy outcome will occur. The difference is not subtle in any way, even though it turns on a single word.

In the passage about cattle, the first sentence used the word cycle, and we were able to learn a lot from the fact that the cattle situation was a cycle. If the sentence had only referred to a problem or an industry we would have known much less about what was happening.

There are too many possible sentences for us to hope to classify them all for you, nor is that needed. There is one fundamental idea which you need to apply: EVERYTHING COUNTS.

In order to fully understand this injunction that everything counts, let us remember just what the test-writers are interested in and with what sorts of passages you will be dealing. The test-writers want to see how well you can get the fullest understanding—comprehension—from a passage. To permit a good test of that skill, they will usually give you passages that—unlike much writing—are highly structured and fairly well written. We must immediately point out that interest, vitality, and style are not within the scope of the writing we are now describing, though some passages have those qualities. What we are referring to is the fact that the authors of the passages have thought about the structure of their sentences and paragraphs and about their choice of words rather carefully. We may assume that whatever words or structures are in the passages are intended to convey every bit of meaning that can reasonably be wrung from them.

Thus, if the word cycle is used, you must conclude that it was precisely a cycle that was meant and not merely an event, period, or circumstance.

How, you may be wondering, can the reader possibly catch all of this precision in less than 39 readings of the passage? The answer to this reasonable qustion is contained in the third aspect of reading we will treat in this section.

Many words are particularly important in terms of understanding the strength or scope of a statement, such as: some, all, every, etc. The significance of these words is fully discussed in Instructional Overviews for both Logical Reasoning and Analytical Reasoning problems.

Active Versus Passive Reading

Every piece of reading is done differently. If you are reading a book in bed at night in order to relax and go to sleep, you will probably read more slowly and without as much attention to detail than if you were studying the same book in order to write a major analytic paper on it. But no matter how fast or with how much concentration you are reading, you are always thinking about what you are reading as you are reading it.

When you are watching television or looking up at the clouds after a summer picnic, you may be doing practically nothing but passively receiving visual stimuli.

When you read, however, your understanding depends on how much thinking you are doing while you are reading. Indeed, even pure memorization of a passage will be improved if you have done some good thinking about it while you were reading.

Active reading, then, is reading accompanied by sustained, intense thought about the passage being read: not a conscious counterpoint to the passage, but just feeling the gears whirring underneath, where most thought occurs.

As we have mentioned, it is the structure and implicit meanings of the passage that will be the major subjects of the questions on the test. Therefore, you will want to be constantly trying to "dig the bones" of the passage. Here are some of the questions you should be considering as you read:

—How is this idea connected to previous ones in the passage?
—What is likely to follow (from) this idea?
—What is the author's purpose in making this particular statement at this particular place in the passage?
—What does this prove, exemplify, demonstrate, etc.?
—Is this a continuation of some previous idea or the introduction of a new line of thought?

Connections, connections—that is always your concern. Always working while you are reading is your method of finding them in the time available. You do this all the time; all that you need to do on the GRE is do this a little bit more.

"Test Reading" versus "Real-world" Reading

When you are reading an article in the real world you will be trying to link what the article is telling you to everything else that you know. This is the most powerful sort of reading that you can do. In practice, of course, you don't quite manage to make a complete cross-referencing to everything you know about every topic, but you probably pretty well cross-reference to a lot of what you know about the specific topic of the passage and related topics.

On the test you don't do the same thing. The GRE is not a test of your previous knowledge of the topic of the passage, nor of any particular previous knowledge at all except language and reading skills. All the test is concerned with is the INTERNAL linkages within the passage. This makes your job much easier. All you have to do is correlate all of the parts of the passage with each other and understand whatever can be implied from that. While there are hard and easy questions, you will find after a while that the difficulty of the questions is largely a matter of the range of answer choices and not so much a matter of the passage's difficulty. Focusing on the internal linkages within the passage actually reduces the work a great deal.

ANSWERING THE DIFFERENT TYPES OF RC QUESTIONS

We will analyze RC questions in two ways: Formal structure and linkage to the passage. In the latter we will analyze the different types of question stems and what they are asking of you. Then we will discuss the fundamental rules for answering RC questions prior to developing an attack strategy in the next section.

Formal Structure

The directions ask you to select the best answer choice out of the five available. This means just what it says. The correct answer choice will be better than any of the others. It may be all but perfect and surrounded by other good choices, or it may be fairly poor and surrounded by totally unacceptable choices. While all of the correct answer choices have merit, there are wrong answer choices which also have merit and some correct ones whose main claim is the poverty of their competition. For this reason you always read all of the answer choices.

The question stem for the RC question, as for most verbal questions, sets up a criterion by which to judge the answer choices. Any answer choice may relate to the criterion in three basic ways: definitely meets the criterion, definitely fails the criterion, or it is not known how it relates to the criterion. Therefore, when the question asks which answer choice is, for example, true, the incorrect answer choices may be either false or indeterminate. In addition, two or more of the answer choices may have some measure of truth and you have to choose the one which is most strongly deducible.

When the question states that all of the answers are, for example, agreeable to the author EXCEPT . . . THEN the incorrect answers are agreeable, though the agreeableness of some may be more strongly supported than that of others, and the correct answer choice may be either known to be disagreeable or something whose agreeableness is not determinable.

The proper approach to roman numeral-format questions is discussed in the Instructional Overview for Analytical Reasoning problems, where they are more frequent.

The strength and scope of the questions and the answer choices is very important, and as noted in the Precision Reading section, this issue is discussed in other Instructional Overviews in even more detail.

Linkage to the Passage

Each and every question that you face on the test has the unstated introductory clause "In light of what the passage says or implies. . . . " Some questions actually say "according to the passage," or "according to the author," etc. But you will always have that in your mind whether it is said or not.

While it is possible to consider every question to be asking for you to make some sort of inference, we shall first sort out some other slightly more restricted sorts of questions before addressing the general topic of inference questions as the residual category of questions. We will discuss the following kinds of questions:

—Specific details (0–2)
—Purpose (1–3)

—Tone (1–3)
—Identity of author or other person (0–2)
—Use of evidence (2–5)
—Main idea, including title (4–7)
—Logical reasoning or method of argument (1–3)
—Inference, implication, author agree, trend, or stated or implied (5–8)

The numbers in parentheses following each question type are a very approximate indication of the typical range of frequency for that question type between both Verbal Sections. The types are not utterly distinct, and some variants, combinations, or just plain oddball questions are perfectly possible, but there won't be many.

Specific details questions. There may be a few questions which essentially ask you to report something which is specifically stated in the passage. These would be questions such as questions 1, 2, or 3 previously discussed. If you see this sort of question, be very careful in checking the answer choices for qualifiers and limiters that may be the difference between one choice and another. Also, more than one quality or descriptor may go with a particular idea and the correct answer choice may be somewhat more comprehensive than the incorrect ones.

Purpose of the passage or author. If the passage is just a description of something, then the purpose will be to describe whatever the passage describes. The purpose can also be explanatory of some aspect of the passage which is implicit. In the illustrative passage abut the cattle cycle, for example, you might have the following:

7. What is the author's purpose in writing the passage?
   (A) To describe the problems of ranchers.
   (B) To justify the cattle cycle.
   (C) To explain how the cattle cycle can lead to apparently irrational actions by cattle producers.

(A) has the merit of saying that some problem is being explained, which is true of the passage. It is not, however, especially the problem of ranchers, but of cattle producers. This is a matter of precision reading.

(B) has the merit of referring to the cattle cycle, which is certainly a major part of the passage.

However, justify means to show why something is good, usually in spite of appearances to the contrary. The cycle just is, and the author isn't in favor of it.

(C) is the best answer since it amounts to saying that the purpose of the passage is to justify the cattle producers' actions as being not irrational in the least because of the lag time. Justify might be too strong anyway, so the use of explain in (C) is better.

Thus, a purpose must match the passage as precisely and completely as possible. Generally, it will reflect the bulk of the passage similar to the way a main idea problem does as discussed in the "Tone of Passage" section below.

The only exception would be a passage which makes a specific proposal for some change. In that case, the purpose of the passage was to make the proposal.

Tone of the passage. As in any other question, the answer chosen must have a basis—preferably a strong one—in the passage. This passage might be described as factual, objective, explanatory, and so on. It would be too strong to call it apologetic or alarmed or worried. Some tone questions have single-word answer choices; others have longer choices. The longer the choices, the more accurately they can reflect the texture of the passage—factual but concerned.

Identity of author or other person. Usually this is a matter of time and job description. Typically the inferences are a bit on the thin side, and frequently fall far short of perfection. In the illustrative passage, the perfect description might be "an agricultural economist writing in the late 1970's." The time could not be before 1977, and the job must be something to do with economics or agriculture. An answer choice such as "Congressional aide" is tempting, but there is nothing "Congressional" about the passage. There is no basis.

Use of evidence. This question type asks you to identify the role of some piece of evidence or sub-argument in the overall scheme of things. Occasionally, the role of a piece of evidence in the development of a sub-argument or a quoted argument may be sought. The basic type would be of this sort:

8. What does the author demonstrate by referring to "large financial losses" in the last paragraph?
   (A) foolishness of cattle producers

(B) financial weakness of cattle pro-
      ducers
(C) poor prospects of small cattle pro-
      ducers
(D) inevitability of the biologic time lag
(E) futility of trying to plan anything in
      cattle production

As discussed for 7, the author does not feel that the cattle producers are especially foolish, but is explaining the difficulties they face, hence (A) is inadequate. (B) has a superficial appeal since large losses surely cannot strengthen the financial strength of the cattle producers, but that is not related to the flow of the actual passage, which is concerned with explaining the interactions of the cattle and biologic cycles. (C) fails on precision reading grounds since nothing is said in the passage about small producers as such. The prospects of all cattle producers are tainted by the seeming unavoidability of the cattle cycle, but "small" is unfounded.

(D) is the best answer because of the author's purpose in mentioning the losses (and low prices) is to show just how inevitable the biologic lag is. Even when they lose money, they still have to increase the production of beef (slaughter) since they started growing the animals years previously. This highlights the need ALWAYS to consider your answer in light of the actual passage.

(E) is appealing because it captures the feeling of inevitability just referred to in (D). However, the word anything is far too strong since the passage is only describing a part of the cattle production process.

Main idea including title. In the previous two problems we had different statements of the main idea of the passage. It is important in the longer passages that you will see on the test that you make certain that the main idea answer choice that you choose covers as much of the passage as possible. No significant part should be left out if it can be avoided. Typically, several of the answer choices in this type of problem are quite good and you have to examine the differences between the various answer choices closely in order to choose the correct one. Any outright error would eliminate an answer choice, but scope and fit are usually the final issues you must consider. Always be aware of how well the answer choices reflect the range of ideas, generality, causality, or other connecting ideas and strength of the passage.

A title question is treated the same way except that the potential titles are usually shorter than the answer choices in a main idea question, which means that the fit to the passage will be somewhat rougher.

Logical reasoning or method of argument. You will occasionally have a question that is essentially a Logical Reasoning question. Treat it the same way you would if it appeared on the Logical Reasoning section. Method-of-argument and premises questions would be the most likely.

Inference, implication, etc. This large class of questions is unified not so much by the varied question stems as by the method of attack. Questions 4, 5, and 6 are all examples of this question type. Let us take one more example:

9. All of the following may be inferred from
     the passage EXCEPT
     (A) Weight is a more important determi-
           nant of a calf's readiness for slaughter
           than age.
     (B) Successful cattle producers usually
           have either considerable ready capi-
           tal or substantial lines of credit.
     (C) The cattle cycle is a dependable
           phenomenon and will continue
           indefinitely.
     (D) It would be an improvement over
           current practice if market prices coor-
           dinated with beef supplies.
     (E) The 1974–76 period was not an un-
           usual one for cattle producers.

(A) can be inferred from the second paragraph. This is practically stated since the only reference to "slaughterability" is in terms of weight. (B) is much more implicit and derives from some of the same considerations as (E). The passage makes it clear that the cattle cycle is a cycle—a repetitive event. The biologic lag is dependable and it was the biologic lag which led to the mismatch between prices and supplies, and thus the losses. Therefore, cyclical losses (presumably offset by gains at other times) are typical of cattle produc-ing, hence (E). If cyclical losses are typical, then any successful cattle producer must have some way of surviving these losses, hence (B).

(C) and (D) are both candidates for not being inferable, but by definition of the problem, one will turn out to be inferable and the other won't. (C) has two ideas in it about the cattle cycle. One is that the cycle AS A WHOLE is dependable and the other is that it will continue indefinitely. The first is only very weakly supported. The fact that it is a cycle is all that we needed for (E) and (B). (C) adds the modifier dependable. The only thing which is known to be dependable is the biologic lag (cycle) which, while important to the cattle cycle, is not necessarily the whole thing. Furthermore, we must see what the author means by dependable in the passage. When he refers to the biologic lag, he means that it is both necessary and of fairly well-defined duration. While the cattle cycle appears to be occurring, neither its necessity nor the regularity of its timing are known to be.

(D), on the other hand, has a somewhat weaker claim, which is thus easier to infer. (D) holds that the current situation, where the market prices and beef supplies are not in synchrony, is not as good as one where they would be in synchrony. This is supported by the last paragraph's reference to price signaling change in beef production (thus, one should follow the other) and, to a lesser extent, by the author's basically sympathetic view of the cattle producers' problems.

On a test, many of these ideas will not come to you neatly sorted out in reference to each answer choice, but will derive from a close examination of each choice and its differences from the other answer choices.

ATTACK STRATEGY FOR READING COMPREHENSION

The final section of the Instructional Overview will review a number of tips, tricks, and traps for RC questions. Here we will summarize our discussion in the form of an attack strategy for this type of question.

1. **Do each passage separately.** Do not jump back and forth for each passage.
2. **Preview the question stems only.** Become alert to specific references and idea of passage.
3. **Read passage actively, briskly, precisely.** See linkages, structural clues, and flow.

Checkmark specific references known from preview.
4. **Read question and all answer choices.** Read precisely and actively. Watch for key words. Identify question type.
5. **Choose answer choice by elimination and contrast.** Focus on differences between answers to eliminate. Resolve close calls by strength of inference and closeness to main idea of passage.
6. **Refer back to passage only when necessary or for specific-detail questions.**
7. **Do not get hung up on one question.**

Tips, Tricks, and Traps

This section is a listing of hints that may help to improve your speed or accuracy on RC passages.

1. **Topic sentences.** Most paragraphs will have a topic sentence giving the idea of the paragraph. This sentence is usually the first or last sentence.

2. **Structural clues in passage.** The following items are all clues to the structure of a paragraph or passage and should be noted by you as you read. In each case ask yourself how this structural clue advances the ideas of the passage.
   —Comparison (finding similarities, what is basis)
   —Contrast (finding differences, what is basis)
   —Causes (exactly what causes what, and how)
   —Sequences (order and basis of order)
   —Processes (steps and underlying idea, what next)
   —Metaphors or images (how do they work, what in the image represents what in the world, what does it prove, where does it lead)
   —Quotations and examples (what does it prove, why is it at this point in the passage)
   —Numbers and dates (don't memorize, do they connect to anything else, do they limit the other ideas)
   —Generality and specificity (is this a universal situation, limited, limited to what, how)
   —Modifiers (why is it this kind of thing, what is the significance of the modifier, what else also is this way)
   —Where is the evidence/conclusion (if one is given look for the other, either can be first)

—Definitions (do you understand it and how it works in the development of the passage's ideas)

—Buzzwords, jargon, technical terms (what you need to know about them is in the passage, but the definition might be implicit—note if it isn't defined)

3. Flow of the argument. It is usually important to notice when the argument is definitely continuing in the same vein or when it is making a change. The change may only be within a sentence or it may be a basic change in the flow of the entire passage. Many words and phrases indicate these ideas, but here are a few examples:

—Flow continuers: *and, also, in addition to, moreover, thus, since, because, then,* etc.

—Flow changers: *instead, on the other hand, unless, despite, although, but,* etc.

4. Key words. The following words are the kinds of words which are likely to be important in interpreting questions, answers, and passages. This list is only exemplary, not exhaustive: *always, never, ever, possible, definite, impossible, exactly, precisely, necessar(y)(ily), primar(y)(ily), most, least, unless, without, entire, all, no, part(ial)(ly),* etc.

5. Reading speed and speed reading. It is better to read faster with the same or increased comprehension. It is true that many persons do not read as fast as they could, even maintaining the same comprehension. Many people report increased comprehension as well as speed with a speed reading course. Leaving aside the question of the comprehension tests having been given by the speed reading schools, this is reasonable since the essence of speed reading is better concentration and mental and physical discipline. Both of those should increase speed and also comprehension.

However, the key limit on the GRE is comprehension, not speed. Just as the increased concentration resulting from speed study often yields increased comprehension, the increased concentration resulting from comprehension study almost always results in increased speed. If you have only a few weeks to study for the GRE, you should concentrate on improving your comprehension through practicing precise and active reading. If you make sure that you don't let yourself slack off on the speed, you will probably find that your speed has increased along with your comprehension.

One of the key fallacies that many people believe about reading is that a good reader just sails through the material at top speed and understands it. This may be true for fairly easy material. However, it is often the poor reader who will finish a particular passage most quickly, but with very little understanding. A good reader will slow down his reading speed to suit the difficulty of the particular sentence, or part of a sentence, and then speed up when the going is easier. The key difference between a good reader and a poor reader in terms of speed and comprehension is that a good reader will be constantly checking himself while he is reading to make sure that he is understanding at least the basic flow of ideas and will take the time *during* the reading process to get it right the first time. A poor reader, in a time pressure situation such as the GRE, will frequently feel that he does not have the time to get it really right and thus goes so fast that he does not understand very much at all. In other words, doing the job correctly the first time is more efficient than trying to do it quickly and then fixing it up later.

Do not worry if you find yourself subvocalizing some of the more difficult parts of the passage (you don't need to subvocalize the whole thing). This is just a way of concentrating on the material, and can even be helpful.

On the other hand, you do not need to pore over every word for ten minutes. Every passage consists of a series of thoughts and your only job is to interpret the sentences one by one to see this structure.

6. Eyes. Physically we can all read a thousand words a minute unless there is something wrong with our eyes. Mentally, that is usually not so practical. The point is that if you feel eyestrain or have a lot of trouble physically reading, you should go to an ophthalmologist or optometrist and have your eyes checked. It probably is the tension of studying, but if you do need glasses or some other treatment, get it at once.

7. Practice makes better, but only if it is practice of the right things. For everything that you read from now to the test, especially the practice tests in this book, analyze them carefully and check any errors you might make to see which clue(s) you missed—so you won't miss them next time.

SENTENCE COMPLETION INSTRUCTIONAL OVERVIEW

INTRODUCTION

Each Verbal section of the GRE will contain a subsection of Sentence Completion questions. Typically, this subsection is the first part of the Verbal section and contains 7 questions. The Sentence Completion questions are considered to be more closely related to the Reading Comprehension questions than to the Antonym and Analogy questions. This kinship derives from the fact that the Sentence Completion questions are primarily concerned with the structure of sentences and the implications that can be drawn from those structures. There is much less vocabulary in the Sentence Completion question than in the Antonym and Analogy questions.

Format

The Sentence Completion question presents you with a sentence that contains one or two blanks. The answer choices provide alternative words with which to fill in the blanks in the sentence. Approximately half of the problems that you will see will have two blanks, and the rest will have one blank. There is no particular difference in difficulty between questions with one blank or two, though there are some procedural differences caused by the fact of having one or two blanks to fill.

Directions

The directions for the Sentence Completion questions simply ask that you fill in the blank with the answer that best fits in with the meaning of the sentence as a whole. These instructions are significant in two ways. First, the injunction to select the *best* answer means, as always, that the correct answer need not be perfect and that some incorrect answers may have some merit. Second, the whole of the sentence must be considered in answering the question. Frequently, the keys to the problem are not next to the blank, but at the other end of the sentence.

1 Blank Versus 2 Blanks

As noted above, there is no basic difference between questions with one blank and those with two. When there are two blanks, you have two opportunities to eliminate answers, but you will usually find that the correct answer is the best way of filling *both* blanks. Sometimes one or more of the incorrect answers will acceptably fill one of the blanks. In such a case you can "triangulate" toward the correct answer by eliminating first on the basis of one blank and then on the basis of the other. You will also find that some problems need to be approached by considering how the two blanks work together. For example:

1. The decision was handed down in _____ circumstances that were a(n) _____ to the spectators.

Example 1, above, shows a sentence that could be filled in with a large number of pairs of words, since the two words work with each other. For instance, it might be filled in to read: The decision was handed down in suspicious circumstances that were a scandal to the spectators. Alternatively, the sentence might have been completed this way: The decision was handed down in dignified circumstances that were a lesson to the spectators.

To be sure, the second version seems less satisfactory than the first one. The reason for this is that whenever there is a qualification or explanation of something, it is usually an indica-

138

tion that the situation is unusual in some way. One would normally expect a decision to be handed down in a dignified way; thus, the fact that the circumstances need to be specified would lead you to suppose that the circumstances were probably not dignified. Other sorts of sentence structures will, of course, lead to different relationships between the two blanks.

KEYS TO SENTENCE COMPLETION QUESTIONS

No short list can exhaust the variety and richness of English sentence structure nor the clues which that structure can provide in the solution of Sentence Correction problems. Several common keys can be identified. It is convenient to separate these keys into structural and verbal keys, although there is considerable overlap between the categories.

As noted before, all of the clues and reading hints described in the Reading Comprehension Instructional Overview apply with full force to Sentence Completion questions.

Verbal Keys

Any word that indicates the strength or quality of a relationship is likely to provide a clue to the types of words which should fill in the blanks. In analyzing a sentence you should also pay attention to the words that actually tell you what is going on. In the sentence above, the words decision and spectator give you pegs in the real world on which to hang the meaning of the sentence.

Structural Keys

Antonym and synonym relationships: In many sentences there will be an opposition or similarity between two or more parts of the sentence. Some of the most common structures that give this feeling use words such as: but, although, instead, in preference to, etc. Similarity can be indicated by the use of words such as: and, like, such as.

These same ideas can be expressed in purely structural terms. For example:

2. Since he was able to _____, he did not need the _____.

In this sentence one could fill in the blanks by saying: Since he was able to swim, he did not need the float.

A related structure might be: Since he was unable to cry, he did not need the handkerchief.

Lists and parallel construction: Whenever the blank is in a list of any sort, this is a very important clue. The blank will not repeat any other item in the list, but will be the same sort of idea as the other items in the list. Sometimes the listing will be a progression:

3. After the battle, the exhausted armies buried their dead, cared for their wounded, and _____ their stores.

What we need in this sentence is the next step in the progression of recuperation by the armies. After the dead and wounded are taken care of, the stores need to be replenished or restocked, which is a similar concept except applied to stores of goods; it is also the next step in the recuperation process.

Another way of having a list or a parallel construction is to have an explanation or definition. For example:

Johnny is a(n) _____, he cannot read or write.

The blank is defined by the clause that follows it. Thus the blank must be filled with the word illiterate, which means "unable to read or write." The defining clause or phrase can also precede the blank or be in an entirely different part of the sentence.

Modifying words, phrases and clauses: Any type of modifier, whether directly relating to a blank or relating to some other part of the sentence—and through that, relating to the blank—is likely to have some impact on answering the question. In the example above, the fact that the armies were exhausted helps to tell you that they were in need of replenishment, though there are other clues in that particular sentence.

4. Impressed with the power of the argument, he _____.

In Example 4, "he" has a particular quality—he is impressed with the power of the argument. If one is impressed with the power of an argument, then one is likely to agree with it, or capitulate, give in, or take action.

Images, comparisons and metaphors: Many of the sentences that you will be asked to complete will use some sort of image to make their point or will liken one thing to another. When this occurs, it can be a very powerful tool to help you complete the sentence. Always be careful to try and follow through on the image or comparison that is being suggested.

   5.   Like a cloud before the sun, family discord can _____ the happiest life.

The best completion of problem 5 would be something like darken or shadow because the image of a cloud being before the sun would naturally imply that there was less light. In a sentence like that, you would probably see incorrect answer choices such as upset, disarray, or some other word that is not intrinsically a bad way to refer to the effect of family discord on a happy life, but which would be wrong because it does not fit in with the style or expresion used in the particular sentence.

Punctuation: Although this is not the most common key, it does help in many sentences, and it is critically important in a few sentences. Remember that a semicolon (;) is a greater separation than a comma. This means that a sentence with a semicolon in the middle of it might have two levels of parallel or opposite construction. One level would be between the parts separated by the semicolon and the other would be within each part. For example:

   As an artist, his duty was to beauty and truth; as a patriot, his obligation was to his _____.

The proper filler for this blank is clearly country. The overall sentence has a parallel structure for each part of the sentence and also within each part. Sometimes the overall sentence is parallel, but each part may have an oppositeness. For example: I could not love you so much, loved I not honor more.

ATTACK STRATEGY FOR SENTENCE COMPLETION QUESTIONS

Although the fundamental idea is to consider how each answer choice might fit into the blank(s), merely reading the sentence five times with the different answer choices is not always enough to give you the answer, and it is often not the most efficient approach. We recommend the following approach:

1. Read the sentence through, being sure to say "something" or "blank" to yourself as you read the sentence; this ensures that you preserve the space and do not accidentally construct the meaning of the sentence in your mind so as to exclude the missing word altogether.

2. Read the answer choices quickly and see if any of the choices strikes you as definitely wrong or definitely right. If so, check it with a quick reading of the sentence with your selection in the blank. This will not guarantee that you have the best answer, but it is some insurance against totally inappropriate answers.

3. Examine the sentence quickly for any of the structural or verbal clues discussed in this overview, or any other INTERNAL CONNECTION to be found between the blank and other parts of the sentence.

4. After identifying the keys in the particular sentence, use them to eliminate answer choices until the best one emerges. If a sentence appears to have no suitable answer choice at all, you are either misreading the sentence's meaning or there is some meaning of one of the answer choices that you have not considered. This is similar to the problem of the single-facet meaning of words as discussed in the Antonym Instructional Overview.

5. If time permits, it is wise to test your selection by reading the sentence, using your selection in the blank. As noted above, this is only a minimum check, but it can be helpful when the sentence is long and involved and you may have been unintentionally focusing on one part of it to the confusion of the meaning of the whole sentence.

Following these simple steps will help you to focus your mind on the issues that are important in the Sentence Completion questions: the keys that connect the blank to the rest of the sentence. It is important to review all of the Sentence Completion problems in the practice tests carefully and to identify consciously all of the keys in each sentence so that your recognition of keys improves. Do this for the problems that you answered correctly as well as for the ones that gave you trouble.

A FINAL NOTE ON USAGE

In some Sentence Completion problems there are incorrect answers that are simply incorrect because they are inappropriate usage. By inappropriate usage we mean that the word that is being suggested for the blank is simply not the kind of word that is used in normal English discourse in that particular situation. Similarly, the correct answer may sometimes consist of words that are especially appropriate because they apply to that particular situation. For example, a speaker might introduce an idea in order to make a point, but he would not greet the idea in order to make a point. On the other hand, he might greet an idea with scorn.

ANTONYM INSTRUCTIONAL OVERVIEW

INTRODUCTION

Each of the Verbal Sections of the GRE will contain one subsection of Antonym questions. Typically these questions will be at the end of the section, though it is possible for them to be located anywhere. Each subsection will typically consist of 11 Antonym questions arranged, generally, from easiest to hardest. This ordering is the result of statistical analysis performed by the Educational Testing Service, but it is not a strict ordering. First of all, the fact that a problem is statistically harder for all the people who take the GRE does not mean that it will be harder for you on the day of the exam. To take a trivial example, you might have had cause to look the word up the night before the exam. Also, the questions are not put in strict order of their statistical difficulty. The first three or four will be somewhat easier, and the last three or four somewhat harder, but the fourth one might be the hardest and the fourth-from-last the easiest.

The significance to you of the fact that the questions are in this general order—from easier to harder—is twofold. First, you will expect this arrangement and consequently will be neither distracted or discouraged by it. Secondly, you will be able to plan to have a little time in hand when you get to the last few questions, since they may require a little extra pondering.

FORMAT

All Antonym questions on the test will have the same format. In each case there will be a capitalized word, called the stem word, followed by a colon. This will be followed by five answer choices, which are in lower-case letters. The answer choices will be either short phrases or single words, usually only one or the other and only rarely combined. Thus there is not much reading to do for an Antonym question.

There are two ways in which antonyms will appear to be different: (1) type of antonym relationship and (2) mysteriousness. The mysteriousness of the problem is the degree of familiarity that you have with the stem word and the words in the answer choices. As will be discussed later, even when you are not very familiar with the words, you can sometimes make some progress on the question and make an educated, rather than random, guess. On the other hand, there may well be times when you will only be able to make a random guess.

DIRECTIONS

The directions for the Antonym questions are straightforward in that they simply ask you to pick out the answer choice that is most nearly opposite in meaning to the stem word. ETS is not trying to be tricky. All they are interested in is the meaning of the words. However, the phraseology most nearly should remind you that antonym problems, like all verbal problems, are looking for the best of the five available answers and not the one and only perfect answer. This means that some of the wrong answers will have some merit and many of the correct answer choices will fall short of perfection. As usual, you must read all of the answer choices and work with the differences between the answer choices in order to decide close choices.

TYPES OF ANTONYMS

We will analyze the possible antonym relationships as being of three types: total antonyms, single-facet antonyms, and special-case antonyms. It is fairly important to keep all three of these possibilities in mind since our intuitive understanding of antonyms is usually limited at first to the concept of total antonyms. In order to make the differences between these three types of antonyms clear, it is critically important that you realize that all words are designed to be used in sentences, and that their meanings are best understood in the context of a sentence. Thus, the overall idea of word X being an antonym of word Y is that there is some sentence using the word X that would have essentially the opposite meaning if Y were substituted for X in the sentence.

The significance of this definition is that it makes clear the fact that antonyms are closely related words since they will work in the same sentence, even in a complex sentence. This leads to:

FUNDAMENTAL DEFINITION OF AN ANTONYM: An antonym of word X is a word that refers to the same thing as X, but in an opposite way.

This means that the correct answer will have a definite connection to the stem word, if you can only see it, and that totally unrelated words are not antonyms. Milk and frog are not opposites, since their meanings are essentially unrelated.

Another consequence of this idea is that the GRE does not use synonyms as incorrect answer choices, though there are occasional words that have some equivalence of meaning. This means that the first question you ask of an answer choice is whether it is connected at all to the stem word, and the second question is if it is the precise opposite in one of the three ways discussed below.

Total Antonyms

Total antonyms are the sort of opposites that one usually thinks of when asked to name a pair of antonyms. We call them total antonyms because they will work as opposites in virtually every sentence one might write using the words interchangeably. Examples abound: strong:weak, slow:fast, in:out, push:pull. You would have no hesitation in identifying any of these pairs as antonyms. An example in proper format is shown as problem 1:

1. HIGH:
   (A) sunken
   (B) flat
   (C) low
   (D) medium
   (E) common

(C) is the answer, of course, but even with this easy problem other choices have some merit (as discussed below).

Single-Facet Antonyms

A single-facet antonym is one in which the relevant meaning of the word is one separate meaning of the word, and perhaps not the most common meaning. This situation derives from the fact that many words, often common ones, have several different meanings. Roughly speaking, the different meanings can be considered as either separate or related, though the distinction is not always precise. A separate meaning would be something like the word shed meaning both a small building and to take off some covering. Many times these different meanings will correspond to a different part of speech, as we have just seen with shed, which can be either a noun or a verb. Sometimes the two meanings can be the same part of speech, as in an ear of corn and a human ear. We are not talking about relationships in terms of the historical derivation of the words, but merely their current meanings.

Even common words, like those given as examples of total opposites above, can have other meanings. Fast can mean a state of not eating, and pull can mean influence, though the latter is considered somewhat "low-level" usage.

Let us consider example 1 again and examine the sorts of echoes and connections that several of the wrong answer choices might have with high. Answer choice (A), sunken, has some feeling of oppositeness since a sunken place is not a high place. The difficulties can be seen when we compare sunken with low. A sunken place is lower than it was, but not necessarily low. The top of a volcanic mountain like Mt. St. Helen's may be sunken, but it is not low. The opposite to sunken would be risen or raised.

Answer choice (B), flat, is less seductive than (A). Although valleys and other low places may be more likely to be flat than are high places, this is not necessarily so. Flat refers to the type of surface and high refers to the altitude; therefore, they are not the same thing in an opposite way, and thus not antonyms. Flat has another connotation, which is the definition in music of a note that is lower in pitch than it should be; but the opposite in that context is sharp. We will discuss this case in greater detail in a few paragraphs.

Answer choice (D), medium, might have some appeal, since high status is different from medium status, but substituting medium for high will only give you a different meaning, not an opposite one.

Answer choice (E), common, can also have some feeling of oppositeness in the sense of a high-born person being the opposite of a common person. This sort of error can easily creep up on you if you permit yourself to add words to the stem or the answer choice. You must work only with the meaning of the actual words given and be very sparing about adding any extraneous ideas to them. Since you will often need to see some context in order to be sure of an answer choice, this means that you need to be very clear in your own mind as to the difference between the meaning of the word you are analyzing and the context in which you might be considering it. In the case of common, for instance, a common man is not the opposite of a high man. It is natural to want to add the word born to the high and thus achieve a good antonym pair. However, the conclusion that you should draw from seeing common:high born as an antonym pair is that common:high is NOT an antonym pair. The type of connection which we have seen between high and the four incorrect answer choices can be characterized as *derived meanings*. This defines a goodly portion of the wrong answer choices, and you must be careful with them.

A single-facet opposite, then, is a total opposite to just one of several meanings of a particular word, when the meanings themselves are rather distinct. Where the various meanings of a word are all essentially related, the general meaning of the word is most likely to be used.

Special-Case Antonyms

A special-case antonym is a type of single-facet antonym in the sense that a pair of special-case antonyms will give opposite meanings only in some special cases or contexts. The example of flat and sharp is an excellent illustration. These words are only opposite in the context of music, but within that context they are true antonyms. These sorts of antonym relationships can sometimes result in rather difficult antonym problems concerning relatively well-known words, and they deserve special consideration (see Attack Strategy for Antonyms below).

ANALYZING THE WORD STEM

Two basic situations may arise concerning your knowledge of the stem word: In one situation you know the word, either well or to some small degree; in the other situation you have no idea what the word means. It is important to group together words of which you have some knowledge with the words that you know well because the same approach will apply to both cases—you will want to make the most of what you do know. This does not mean that you cannot improve your memory of a word by using some of the techniques we recommend for words you don't know at all, but making the most of what you know is the best way to increase your score.

Strengthening your Grip on a Word's Meaning

When you have some idea of what the stem word means but need to improve or refine that understanding, two things will most likely assist you in calling up the correct associations. The first is the fact that one of the answers is in fact an antonym of the stem word; this means that one of the answers is in the same area of meaning as the stem word. This connection will not be slim, but substantial. Thus you can use the answer choices by defining for yourself their specific areas and asking if the stem word seems to be in one of those areas. If you did not know the full meaning of allay, perhaps an answer choice such as make worse might help you to remember that allay means to make something change, but for the better, not for the worse. This approach is particularly helpful when the answer choices are short phrases. Phrases occur in only ¼ to ⅓ or so of the questions. Even antonym questions with single-word answer choices can yield to this approach.

The second assist you can give to yourself is to try to use the stem word in a sentence and see if any context suggests itself. Since you most likely first encountered the word in a sentence, trying to recreate that situation might jog your memory. You can also try and put the stem word and the answer choices into the same sentence in a way that makes the meaning of the sentence depend on the oppositeness of the word pair. For example, you might say, "X could not apply to this situation (or person or thing), because it was Y." Of course, no single formulation of an English sentence will serve to encompass all words; the language is too flexible and varied for that. You might need to say that it was or was not X, or phrase it some other way. Naturally, the same ideas can be used to help you understand the meaning of an answer choice that is unfamiliar to you. The only difference is that you cannot be assured that the stem word is supposed to make a sentence with the unfamiliar answer choice.

The test will often ask about unusual forms of words that you do know. Prompt is a common word, but promptitude is not as common (it means the quality of being prompt). Not all words that look like other words actually have the same meanings, but most of the time there is some relationship and it may help you to make your choice.

Making the Best Guess when a Word is Totally Unknown

There is some difference in the significance between a stem word that is totally unknown and an answer choice that is totally unknown. When the stem word is totally unknown, the best that you can do is make a reasonable and somewhat educated guess. When only an answer choice is unknown, you will probably be able to answer the question as well as if you did know the word. If both stem word and answer choices are totally unknown, then just guess and go on to the next question.

In both cases, the first line of attack is to use word parts such as the ones that are delineated in the word part list in this book or any others that you may know. Using word parts is only an educated guess, but that's much better than a random guess and will, all in all, help your score considerably. The more complex a word sounds, the more likely it is that word parts will be helpful. Many simple words have been used so much that their meanings have shifted or become specialized over the years. Wholesome, for instance, does not mean whole, but homophone does mean same sound. Be very certain that the word part actually is present in the whole word. Also be careful of the word parts that have two meanings, such as homo-, which means man (from the Latin) and same (from the Greek). If you only know one part of the word, that is much less helpful than if you can identify two or more parts. If the only part of the word that you are able to identify is a prefix, this is very weak evidence in which to base an answer.

ATTACK STRATEGY FOR ANTONYMS

The attack strategy for antonyms has the following steps:

1. Read the stem word and take ONE second to let its meaning come to you.
2. Read all the answer choices, looking for (in order of priority):
   a. total antonyms
   b. one-fact antonyms
   c. special-case antonyms
3. When you are unsure of the oppositeness or of the meaning of a word, try to use the word (or pair of words) in a sentence.
4. Use elimination and contrast as you do for any verbal problem.
5. Use word parts to make educated guesses about words that are totally unknown to you, or to modify the meanings of words whose roots or other forms you do know.

Let us apply this to a relatively simple example:

2. SHORT:
   (A) rather large
   (B) well endowed
   (C) stretched thin
   (D) solidly connected
   (E) very trustworthy

When you first approach this problem, you might anticipate seeing long as the opposite to the extent that you will choose stretched thin as the answer, since that is the only choice which has anything to do with length at all. However, the real meaning of stretched thin is that it is thin and it is made thin by stretching, which is not at all the same sort of thing as being short. The stem merely states the length, while choice (C) tells how the length has been changed. These are rather different, and you should not accept (C) as an answer without some additional thought.

If you can avoid the trap of forcing a total opposite when one is not there, you will next be looking for some sort of one-facet or special-case usage of the stem word to give you the answer. Using the answer choices, you might ask yourself whether there is any usage of short that has anything to do with size as (A) does. None comes readily to mind. Next, you ask whether any usage dealing with endowment or money suggests itself. One does exist, and that is the expression short of money, meaning lacking funds. Being well endowed can mean having a lot of money, so there is an opposite relationship here after all. It is not the strongest antonym relationship that can be imagined, but it will work well enough. More importantly, it is the best available answer in this particular problem. (D) might suggest something about electricity, since a short is a wrong connection, but it is not a weak connection and thus D is inadequate. (E) has no relationship to suggest.

A FINAL NOTE

Many students fare much more poorly on the Antonyms section than they should because they adopt a fatalistic attitude and seem to feel that they will either know the answer instantly or not at all. This is simply false. It is true that there are a few very difficult and unusual words on the test. But there are also many more words whose opposites you can get if you work at it. It is true that you do not have an excess of time for Antonym questions (see the discussion on timing in the Overview for the entire Verbal section), which is all the more reason for not simply waiting for inspiration, but going to work right away. You may be assured that the antonym is one of the five answers, and you can probably come much closer than you think with a little work.

ANALOGIES INSTRUCTIONAL OVERVIEW

INTRODUCTION

Each Verbal section of the test will have a subsection of Verbal Analogies questions. Typically this subsection will be the second subsection and will consist of 10 Analogy questions. As with the other subparts of the Verbal sections, the questions will generally be a little easier at the beginning of the subsection and a little harder towards the end. This does not really affect your work, except to reassure you that there is such a progression.

The Analogy questions are considered to have a significant vocabulary element. This means that one of the things that is being tested is your knowledge of the meanings of words, so you can expect to encounter some rather unusual or difficult words in the Analogy questions. However, since the completed analogy contains four words, as described below, you will usually be able to make an educated guess even on the questions that have difficult vocabulary. The suggestions for jogging your memory and thereby making the most of the words that you do know, which are described in the Instructional Overview for Antonym Questions, also apply to Analogy questions.

We will first describe the format of the Analogy question and the fundamental idea of an Analogy question. Then we will discuss several ways in which the answer choices can relate to the original analogy. This is followed by a review of some of the most common analogy relationships to be found within analogy pairs on the exam, and then an attack strategy.

FORMAT OF THE ANALOGY QUESTION

The format of the Analogy questions consists of a capitalized pair of words with a colon between

them and two colons following them, and five answer choices, each being a pair of lower-case words with a colon between them. You are to select the word-pair whose relationship is most similar to the relationship between the original, or stem, pair.

FUNDAMENTAL CONCEPT OF THE ANALOGY QUESTION

Every Analogy question has a fundamental or *primary relationship* that can be expressed this way:

PRIMARY RELATIONSHIP: $1 : 2 :: 3 : 4$

The first word is related to the second word in the same way as the third word is related to the fourth word. Thus, the Analogy question can be seen as giving you a definite first pair and offering you a selection of second pairs. The arrows are included to indicate that the order of the relationship does matter very much. The relationship of a horse to a blacksmith is absolutely not the same as the relationship of a blacksmith to a horse. Certain people nail horseshoes to the hooves of horses, but horses do not nail horseshoes to the feet of certain people. It is perfectly true that the relationship between a horse and a blacksmith is the same whether you say the blacksmith shoes the horse or the horse is shoed by the blacksmith, but most of the analogies that you will encounter on the test do have a definite direction that should be kept in mind when answering the question. You should always strive for as much precision as possible in your description of the relationship.

Example: GLOVE : HAND :: shoe : foot

The example shows an analogy in which the direction is perfectly clear. A glove is a protective covering for the hand, and a shoe is a protective covering for a foot. The example also shows clearly a *secondary relationship,* which can be very helpful in answering some analogy questions but which must be considered to be totally secondary to the primary relationship just described.

Secondary Relationship: 1 : 2 :: 3 : 4

The first and third words have the same relationship to each other as the second and fourth words. We can see, for instance, that a glove and a shoe are both protective coverings for parts of the body, and that a hand and a foot are both parts of the body commonly covered with such coverings.

A word of caution: this secondary relationship is to be used ONLY after a general idea of the primary relationship has been grasped or as a means of making an educated guess either when the primary relationship is not clear to you or when one of the words in the analogy is unknown to you. GLOVE : HAND :: hat : foot is an example of the nonsense that you might end up with if you use only a secondary relationship. You are always trying to get to the primary relationship, and sometimes the secondary relationship can help you do that. Sometimes it can't.

Similarly, the direction of the relationship must be preserved from the stem pair to the answer choice. GLOVE : HAND :: foot : shoe is not a valid analogy, though there are not many incorrect answer choices on the test that are incorrect only because they are backward.

TYPES OF ANALOGOUS RELATIONSHIPS

We will discuss the analogous relationships that appear on the test only in terms of content and form. The content of an analogous relationship is the specific type of relationships that can link the meanings of two words, such as size, kind, degree and function. The form of an analogy question is the general nature of the linkages in the sense of being abstract or concrete or mixed or of the type of linkage between the pairs that are referred to as being overlapping or independent.

Content of Analogous Relationships

While this listing cannot be considered to describe every question that you might see on the test, most of the analogy questions will have relationships of these sorts. It is important to note that many analogous relationships contain more than one of the elements described in this listing. Indeed, several of the examples given can be described in more than one way. This occurs because the connections between real objects and real ideas are more often complex than simple.

Degree. A relationship of degree will have two words that mean somewhat the same thing, but one of the words signifies a different degree of the activity or concept than the other.

Example: WHISPER : SHOUT :: tap : pummel

In the first pair we have a soft speaking and a loud or extreme speaking; in the second pair we have a soft or slight touching and a severe touching. Note that there is not much of a secondary relationship in this particular analogy.

Kind. A relationship of kind can be of two types. One of the words can be a general grouping of some sort with the other word being a member of that grouping; order is significant.

Example: HORSE : THOROUGHBRED :: bird : eagle

Example: DAY : WEEK :: letter : alphabet

Alternatively, both of the words can be subkinds of the same thing; order is probably not significant.

Example: BASEBALL : FOOTBALL :: poker : roulette

Quality. A relationship of this sort is between some person or object and a quality that it typically or archetypically possesses or lacks; here order is significant.

Example: TRAITOR : LOYALTY :: perjurer : truthfulness

Example: STONE : HARD :: feather : soft

Some of these relationships derive from common usages, such as hard as stone or soft as a feather.

Function. Many words describe people or objects in terms of a specific function. The relationship may be expressed by stating the object and the function or the person and the field.

Example: TONGS : HOLD :: scissors : cut

Sometimes the idea of function can be approached by relating the functional person or object to the place where the function occurs, the objects of the function, or other circumstances connected to the exercise of the function.

Example: IRONWORKER : FOUNDRY :: astronaut : space

Example: TAILOR : CLOTHES :: reporter : news story

Example: LAWYER : COURT :: jockey : racetrack

It is often important to keep in mind the particular nature of the function because that is often required in order to sort out the wrong answers from the right one.

Illustration: CHAIRMAN : COMMITTEE ::
    (A)   president : country
    (B)   referee : players
    (C)   teacher : schoolroom
    (D)   manager : production line
    (E)   attorney : office

SOLUTION: All of the answer choices have some functional relationship between the first and second words. However, the precise function of a chairman in relation to a committee is to make sure that the rules are observed by the committee and that the work is done. This is very similar to the function of the referee in regard to the players of a game. The other four answer choices all refer to the physical location of the functioner, while the stem pair and (B) refer to people with whom the function is performed. It is rarely enough merely to note that there is some sort of relationship. Precision is required for most Analogy questions.

Answer: (B)

Sequence. Closely related to function is the idea of sequence. The sequence analogy may have one word that describes the general sequence and another that refers to some particular part of the sequence. The description of the general idea of the sequence may refer to a game, process or other functional unit.

Example: TENNIS : SERVE :: baseball : pitch

The analogy pair may also refer to two parts of the sequence, in which case order and the particular part of the sequence is very important. The name of a person or object typical of the part of the process may also be used.

Example: HORSE : COLT :: man : boy

The process here is one of growth and development, which could also be referred to as a relationship of age, under physical characteristics.

Physical characteristics. Any two persons, objects or situations that have a similar quality can, as noted earlier, form the basis of an analogy. Analogies of physical characteristics can be seen as a variety of that analogy, but it is useful to consider them as their own kind of analogy.

Example: TREE : SEEDLING :: cow : calf (age, size)

Example: POTATO : ROOT :: tea : leaf (part of plant)

Physical characteristics are seldom the only sort of analogous relationship operating in a problem. They sometimes work to refine or sharpen some other analogy. For instance, a rope goes around a pulley, as well as being used with a pulley.

Causal relationships. A causal relationship can overlap one of the other relationships, but often has its own special flavor.

Example: FIRE : ASHES :: smelting : slag

This example overlaps a sequence and a characteristic as well as being a causal relationship.

Form of Analogous Relationships

The words used in constructing an analogous relationship can be concrete terms such as cannon, water, or corn. They can also be abstract terms such as anger, conflict, legality. Approximately one-third of the analogy questions will concern concrete relating to concrete; one-third are abstract to abstract; and one-third concern concrete to abstract. Usually the answer choice will have the same form, in terms of concrete and abstract, as the stem pair.

Another aspect of the analogy question is the relationship between the two pairs in terms of whether they share any meaning or only share in separate, but analogous, relationships. Sometimes a word in the answer choice may overlap in meaning with a word in the stem pair. Usually there is no overlap and, as discussed earlier in this overview, the secondary relationship is purely secondary.

One additional aspect of a number of analogies is the positive or negative character of the actions or objects being used. It would be very unusual to have a negative quality or person analogized to a positive one. For example, if a traitor lacks loyalty, that relationship will not usually be analogized to a humble man lacking vanity. Traitor is negative and loyalty positive, while the opposite relationship exists in the second pair. The idea of positive and negative will never be the whole story for any analogy, but it might help you to start identifying the relationships. Legality and illegality can also be aspects of an analogy.

Don't Worry About "Garbage" Relationships

You may have heard awful tales about Analogy problems based on such obscure ideas as rhyming, anagrams, one word being part of another word, general knowledge and a number of other ideas that do not derive from the dictionary meanings of the words. This is not done on the GRE. While some of the words may be rather specialized, such as epaulet being a decoration on a shoulder, every single analogy on a test is derivable from the meanings of the words. That is absolutely all with which you need to concern yourself.

ATTACK STRATEGY

Many students can get the general idea of the relationship that is being used in a particular problem, but they then fail to refine this idea sufficiently to get the final answer. If you have an idea that works for all or most of the answer choices, it means that it is probably the right idea, but it needs to be refined by asking how, or in what way, or with what other things, or under what circumstances, or some similar question.

In a like manner, if you have an idea for a relationship for the stem pair that does not have any connection to the answer choices, you will need to start over with a new relationship. The steps in approaching an analogy question are:

1. Read the stem pair and describe as specific a relationship as you can in a few seconds.
2. Read the answer choices, looking for all the pairs that have any substantial aspect of the relationship you have discovered in the stem pair.
3. If only one choice has the same relationship AND that relationship is a detailed and substantial one, choose it. If several choices satisfy the relationship, refine it further, using either the answer choices or the stem pair to suggest refinements. Remember that the stem pair is the guide. If none of the answer choices really fits the relationship, go back and try to find a new one.
4. If you do not know one of the words,
    — try to jog your memory as described for Antonyms
    — work around it with a secondary relationship
    — remember that an answer with an unknown word is not a good guess if one of the other choices has merit; one with an unknown word *is* a good guess if the other choices seem poor.

VOCABULARY BUILDING

You may feel that your vocabulary is a weak link in preparation for the GRE, or even for graduate school itself. There is a definite testing of vocabulary in Antonym and Analogy questions, but Sentence Completion and Reading Comprehension questions are much less vocabulary-oriented.

Nevertheless, approximately half of the questions in the Verbal sections of the GRE do depend significantly on vocabulary. Therefore you may wish to try to improve your vocabulary between now and the test date. Naturally, the more time you can devote to preparation of all sorts, the better your results will be. This is particularly true of vocabulary building.

It is very difficult to remember words by themselves, out of sentence context. Thus, simply trying to quickly memorize the word parts that we provide is not likely to be very helpful to your score. The approach that we recommend is based on the fact that you do not either know a word perfectly or know nothing at all about it. Many of the difficult words on the GRE will not be totally unfamiliar to you, but are, rather, words you have heard or read only a few times and therefore do not know very well, or they are unfamiliar versions of words you do know.

PROCEDURE FOR USING THE WORD PARTS LIST

The word parts are valuable because they let you multiply your vocabulary by letting your knowledge of one word lead to an understanding of many others. For example, the root word gram means writing. An audiogram would therefore be a writing that represented some sound (audio), and a petrogram would represent something in writing about rocks (petro). These are somewhat esoteric examples.

Do not merely read over the word parts list. Somehow you must make it yours. While the list is extensive, the best way to study this sort of material is to do it in small chunks. For each word part you will find both its definition and some word in which it is used. You should try to think of as many other words as you can that use the word part. Try to think of at least two for each word part. This need not take a great deal of time. There is space in the word parts list for you to write down your extra words. The vocabulary building is *in addition to* the mastery of the other materials in this book and cannot replace it. However, it is important to not focus on building your vocabulary to the detriment of complete understanding of the Instructional Overviews for each type of problem.

PROCEDURE FOR LEARNING NEW WORDS

This procedure is applicable to any words in the Verbal Skills exercises that may be unfamiliar to you, or any other new words you want to learn.

Five Steps to Vocabulary Building

1. **Examine each word** and its definition and classify the word into one of three categories:

   a. Familiar, but not well understood—go to step 2.

   b. New or unfamiliar, but containing one or more familiar word parts—go to step 3.

   c. New or unfamiliar and containing no recognizable word part—go to step 4.

2. **Familiar, but not well understood.** Check the definition and compose two sentences, preferably in writing, using the word in a clear way. For example, if the word is recalcitrant, meaning stubborn or unwilling, do not say "He is recalcitrant," because that tells

you nothing. Rather say something like this: "Fighting and resisting all the way to the bathtub, the recalcitrant dog refused to be bathed."

Do not slide over any words merely because you know them a little. Making sure of the words that are only somewhat familiar to you is probably more helpful to your score than trying to learn many totally new words in a short time.

3. **New or unfamiliar, but containing one or more familiar word parts.** Take the word apart and "translate" the root and other parts with your knowledge of word parts gained from studying our listing of word parts and from your general knowledge. Understanding the structure and background of the word will make it much easier to remember. Check the definition and the word parts list for any parts that are unfamil-

iar to you and compose a sentence, using the word as described in step 2.

4. **New or unfamiliar and containing no recognizable word part.** In this case, you have no prior knowledge with which to hook the word into your memory, so it is largely a case of pure memorization. If time permits, compose a sentence or two, using the word and expressing your understanding of it.

5. For all words on which you need to work, it is very useful to write down the sentences you compose, preferably in a notebook devoted to that purpose and that is small enough to be carried with you at all times. Try to review the sentences the day after you composed them, three days after that, and three weeks after that, if that is possible. This pattern of review is very helpful to memorization for most students.

WORD PARTS

PREFIXES

Prefix	Meaning	Examples
a-	in, on, of, to	abed—in bed
a-, ab-, abs-	from, away	abrade—wear off absent—away, not present
a-, an-	lacking, not	asymptomatic—showing no symptoms anaerobic—able to live without air
ad-, ac-, af-, ag-, al-, an-, ap-, ar-, as-, at-	to, toward	accost—approach and speak to adjunct—something added to aggregate—bring together
ambi, amphi-	around, both	ambidextrous—using both hands equally amphibious—living both in water and on land
ana-	up, again, anew, throughout	analyze—loosen up, break up into parts anagram—word spelled by mixing up letters of another word
ante-	before	antediluvian—before the Flood
anti-	against	antiwar—against war
arch-	first, chief	archetype—first model
auto-	self	automobile—self-moving vehicle
bene-, ben-	good, well	benefactor—one who does good deeds
bi-	two	bilateral—two-sided
circum-	around	circumnavigate—sail around
com-, co-, col-, con-, cor-	with, together	concentrate—bring closer together cooperate—work with collapse—fall together
contra-, contro-, counter-	against	contradict—speak against counterclockwise—against the clock
de-	away from, down, opposite of	detract—draw away from
demi-	half	demitasse—half cup
di-	twice, double	dichromatic—having two colors
dia-	across, through	diameter—measurement across

dis-, di-	not, away from	dislike—to not like digress—turn away from the subject
dys-	bad, poor	dyslexia—poor reading
equi-	equal	equivalent—of equal value
ex-, e-, ef-	from, out	expatriate—one who lives outside his native country emit—send out
extra-	outside, beyond	extraterrestrial—from beyond the earth
fore-	in front of, previous	forecast—tell ahead of time foreleg—front leg
geo-	earth	geography—science of the earth's surface
homo-	same, like	homophonic—sounding the same
hyper-	too much, over	hyperactive—overly active
hypo-	too little, under	hypothermia—state of having too little body heat
in-, il-, ig-, im-, ir-	not	innocent—not guilty ignorant—not knowing illogical—not logical irresponsible—not responsible
in-, il-, im-, ir-,	on, into, in	impose—place on invade—go into
inter-	between, among	interplanetary—between planets
intra-, intro-,	within, inside	intrastate—within a state
mal-, male-	bad, wrong, poor	maladjust—adjust poorly malevolent—ill-wishing
mis-	badly, wrongly	misunderstand—understand wrongly
mis-, miso-	hatred	misogyny—hatred of women
mono-	single, one	monorail—train that runs on a single rail
neo-	new	neolithic—of the New Stone Age
non-	not	nonentity—a nobody
ob-	over, against, toward	obstruct—stand against
omni-	all	omnipresent—present in all places
pan-	all	panorama—a complete view
peri-	around, near	periscope—device for seeing all around
poly-	many	polygonal—many-sided
post-	after	postmortem—after death

pre-	before, earlier than	prejudice—judgment in advance
pro-	in favor of, forward, in front of	proceed—go forward prowar—in favor of war
re-	back, again	rethink—think again reimburse—pay back
retro-	backward	retrospective—looking backward
se-	apart, away	seclude—keep away
semi-	half	semiconscious—half conscious
sub-, suc-, suf-, sug-, sus-	under, beneath	subscribe—write underneath suspend—hang down suffer—undergo
super-	above, greater	superfluous—overflowing, beyond what is needed
syn-, sym-, syl-, sys-	with, at the same time	synthesis—a putting together sympathy—a feeling with
tele-	far	television—machine for seeing far
trans-	across	transport—carry across a distance
un-	not	uninformed—not informed
vice-	acting for, next in rank to	viceroy—one acting for the king

SUFFIXES

Suffix	Meaning	Examples
-able, -ble,	able, capable	acceptable—able to be accepted
-acious, -cious	characterized by, having the quality of	fallacious—having the quality of a fallacy
-age	sum, total	mileage—total number of miles
-al	of, like, suitable for	theatrical—suitable for theater
-ance, -ancy	act or state of	disturbance—act of disturbing
-ant, -ent	one who	defendant—one who defends himself
-ary, -ar	having the nature of, concerning	military—relating to soldiers polar—concerning the pole
-cy	act, state, or position of	presidency—position of president ascendency—state of being raised up
-dom	state, rank, that which belongs to	wisdom—state of being wise
-ence	act, state, or quality of	dependence—state of depending
-er, -or	one who, that which	doer—one who does conductor—that which conducts
-escent	becoming	obsolescent—becoming obsolete

-fy	to make	pacify—make peaceful
-hood	state, condition	adulthood—state of being adult
-ic, -ac	of, like	demonic—of or like a demon
-il, -ile	having to do with, like, suitable for	civil—having to do with citizens tactile—having to do with touch
-ion	act or condition of	operation—act of operating
-ious	having, characterized by	anxious—characterized by anxiety
-ish	like, somewhat	foolish—like a fool
-ism	belief or practice of	racism—belief in racial superiority
-ist	one who does, makes or is concerned with	scientist—one concerned with science
-ity, -ty, -y	character or state of being	amity—friendship jealousy—state of being jealous
-ive	of, relating to, tending to	destructive—tending to destroy
-logue, -loquy	speech or writing	monologue—speech by one person colloquy—conversation
-logy	speech, study of	geology—study of the earth
-ment	act or state of	abandonment—act of abandoning
-mony	a resulting thing, condition, or state	patrimony—property inherited from one's father
-ness	act or quality	kindness—quality of being kind
-ory	having the quality of; a place or thing for	compensatory—having the quality of a compensation lavatory—place for washing
-ous, -ose	full of, having	glamorous—full of glamor
-ship	skill, state of being	horsemanship—skill in riding ownership—state of being an owner
-some	full of, like	frolicsome—playful
-tude	state or quality of	rectitude—state of being morally upright
-ward	in the direction of	homeward—in the direction of home
-y	full of, like, somewhat	wily—full of wiles

ROOTS

Root	Meaning	Examples
acr	bitter	acrid, acrimony
act, ag	do, act, drive	action, react, agitate

acu	sharp, keen	acute, acumen
agog	leader	pedagogue, demagogic
agr	field	agronomy, agriculture
ali	other	alias, alienate, inalienable
alt	high	altitude, contralto
alter, altr	other, change	alternative, altercation, altruism
am, amic	love, friend	amorous, amiable
anim	mind, life, spirit	animism, animate, animosity
annu, enni	year	annual, superannuated, biennial
anthrop	man	anthropoid, misanthropy
apt, ept	fit	apt, adapt, ineptitude
aqu	water	aquatic, aquamarine
arbit	judge	arbiter, arbitrary
arch	chief	anarchy, matriarch
arm	arm, weapon	army, armature, disarm
art	skill, a fitting together	artisan, artifact, articulate
aster, astr	star	asteroid, disaster, astral
aud, audit, aur	hear	auditorium, audition, auricle
aur	gold	aureate, aureomycin
aut	self	autism, autograph
bell	war	antebellum, belligerent
ben, bene	well, good	benevolent, benefit
bibli	book	bibliography, bibliophile
bio	life	biosphere, amphibious
brev	short	brevity, abbreviation
cad, cas, cid	fall	cadence, casualty, occasion, accident
cand	white, shining	candid, candle, incandescent
cant, chant	sing, charm	cantor, recant, enchant
cap, capt, cept, cip	take, seize, hold	capable, captive, accept, incipient
capit	head	capital, decapitate, recapitulate
carn	flesh	carnal, incarnate
cede, ceed, cess	go, yield	secede, exceed, process, intercession
cent	hundred	percentage, centimeter
cern, cert	perceive, make certain, decide	concern, certificate, certain
chrom	color	monochrome, chromatic
chron	time	chronometer, anachronism
cide, cis	cut, kill	genocide, incision

cit	summon, impel	cite, excite, incitement
civ	citizen	uncivil, civilization
clam, claim	shout	clamorous, proclaim, claimant
clar	clear	clarity, clarion, declare
clin	slope, lean	inclination, recline
clud, clus, clos	close, shut	seclude, recluse, closet
cogn	know	recognize, incognito
col, cul	till	colony, cultivate, agriculture
corp	body	incorporate, corpse
cosm	order, world	cosmetic, cosmos, cosmopolitan
crac, crat	power, rule	democrat, theocracy
cre, cresc, cret	grow	increase, crescent, accretion
cred	trust, believe	credit, incredible
crux, cruc	cross	crux, crucial, crucifix
crypt	hidden	cryptic, cryptography
culp	blame	culprit, culpability
cur, curr, curs	run, course	occur, current, incursion
cura	care	curator, accurate
cycl	wheel, circle	bicycle, cyclone
dec	ten	decade, decimal
dem	people	demographic, demagogue
dent	tooth	dental, indentation
derm	skin	dermatitis, pachyderm
di, dia	day	diary, quotidian
dic, dict	say, speak	indicative, edict, dictation
dign	worthy	dignified, dignitary
doc, doct	teach, prove	indoctrinate, docile, doctor
domin	rule	predominate, domineer, dominion
dorm	sleep	dormitory, dormant
du	two	duo, duplicity, dual
duc, duct	lead	educate, abduct, ductile
dur	hard, lasting	endure, obdurate, duration
dyn	force, power	dynamo, dynamite
ego	I	egomania, egotist
equ	equal	equation, equitable
erg, urg	work, power	energetic, metallurgy, demiurge
err	wander	error, aberrant
ev	time, age	coeval, longevity

fac, fact, fect, fic	do, make	facility, factual, perfect, artifice
fer	bear, carry	prefer, refer, conifer, fertility
ferv	boil	fervid, effervesce
fid	belief, faith	infidelity, confidant, perfidious
fin	end, limit	finite, confine
firm	strong	reaffirm, infirmity
flect, flex	bend	reflex, inflection
flor	flower	florescent, floral
flu, fluct, flux	flow	fluid, fluctuation, influx
form	shape	formative, reform, formation
fort	strong	effort, fortitude
frag, fract	break	fragility, infraction
fug	flee	refuge, fugitive
fus	pour, join	infuse, transfusion
gam	marry	exogamy, polygamous
ge, geo	earth	geology, geode, perigee
gen	birth, kind, race	engender, general, generation
gest	carry, bear	gestation, ingest, digest
gon	angle	hexagonal, trigonometry
grad, gress	step, go	regress, gradation
gram	writing	grammar, cryptogram
graph	writing	telegraph, graphics
grat	pleasing, agreeable	congratulate, gratuitous
grav	weight, heavy	gravamen, gravity
greg	flock, crowd	gregarious, segregate
habit, hibit	have, hold	habitation, inhibit, habitual
heli	sun	helium, heliocentric, aphelion
hem	blood	hemoglobin, hemorrhage
her, hes	stick, cling	adherent, cohesive
hydr	water	dehydration, hydrofoil
iatr	heal, cure	pediatrics, psychiatry
iso	same, equal	isotope, isometric
it	journey, go	itinerary, exit
ject	throw	reject, subjective, projection
jud	judge	judicial, adjudicate
jug, junct	join	conjugal, juncture, conjunction
jur	swear	perjure, jurisprudence

labor	work	laborious, belabor
leg	law	legal, illegitimate
leg, lig, lect	choose, gather, read	illegible, eligible, select, lecture
lev	light, rise	levity, alleviate
liber	free	liberal, libertine
liter	letter	literate, alliterative
lith	rock, stone	eolithic, lithograph
loc	place	locale, locus, allocate
log	word, study	logic, biology, dialogue
loqu, locut	talk, speech	colloquial, loquacious, interlocutor
luc, lum	light	translucent, pellucid, illumine, luminous
lud, lus	play	allusion, ludicrous, interlude
magn	large, great	magnificent, magnitude
mal	bad, ill	malodorous, malinger
man, manu	hand	manifest, manicure, manuscript
mar	sea	maritime, submarine
mater, matr	mother	matrilocal, maternal
medi	middle	intermediary, medieval
mega	large, million	megaphone, megacycle
ment	mind	demented, mental
merg, mers	plunge, dip	emerge, submersion
meter, metr, mens	measure	chronometer, metronome, geometry, commensurate
micr	small	microfilm, micron
min	little	minimum, minute
mit, miss	send	remit, admission, missive
mon, monit	warn	admonish, monument, monitor
mor	custom	mores, immoral
mor, mort	death	mortify, mortician
morph	shape	amorphous, anthropomorphic
mov, mob, mot	move	removal, automobile, motility
multi	many	multiply, multinational
mut	change	mutable, transmute
nasc, nat	born	native, natural, nascent, innate
nav	ship, sail	navy, navigable
necr	dead, die	necropolis, necrosis
neg	deny	renege, negative
neo	new	neologism, neoclassical

nomen, nomin	name	nomenclature, cognomen, nominate
nomy	law, rule	astronomy, antinomy
nov	new	novice, innovation
ocul	eye	binocular, oculist
omni	all	omniscient, omnibus
onym	name	pseudonym, eponymous
oper	work	operate, cooperation, inoperable
ora	speak, pray	oracle, oratory
orn	decorate	adorn, ornate
orth	straight, correct	orthodox, orthopedic
pan	all	panacea, pantheon
pater, patr	father	patriot, paternity
path, pat, pass	feel, suffer	telepathy, patient, compassion, passion
ped	child	pedagogue, pediatrics
ped, pod	foot	pedestrian, impede, tripod
pel, puls	drive, push	impel, propulsion
pend, pens	hang	pendulous, suspense
pet, peat	seek	petition, impetus, repeat
phil	love	philosopher, Anglophile
phob	fear	phobic, agoraphobia
phon	sound	phonograph, symphony
phor	bearing	semaphore, metaphor
phot	light	photograph, photoelectric
pon, pos	place, put	component, repose, postpone
port	carry	report, portable, deportation
pot	power	potency, potential
press	press	pressure, impression
prim	first	primal, primordial
proto, prot	first	proton, protagonist
psych	mind	psychic, metempsychosis
pyr	fire	pyrite, pyrophobia
quer, quir, quis, ques	ask, seek	query, inquiry, inquisitive, quest
reg, rig, rect	straight, rule	regulate, dirigible, corrective
rid, ris	laugh	deride, risible, ridiculous
rog	ask	rogation, interrogate
rupt	break	erupt, interruption, rupture
sanct	holy	sacrosanct, sanctify, sanction

sci, scio	know	nescient, conscious, omniscience
scop	watch, view	horoscope, telescopic
scrib, script	write	scribble, proscribe, description
sed, sid, sess	sit, seat	sedate, residence, session
seg, sect	cut	segment, section, intersect
sent, sens	feel, think	nonsense, sensitive, sentient, dissent
sequ, secut	follow	sequel, consequence, consecutive
sign	sign, mark	signature, designate, assign
sol	alone	solitary, solo, desolate
solv, solu, solut	loosen	dissolve, soluble, absolution
somn	sleep	insomnia, somnolent
son	sound	sonorous, unison
soph	wise, wisdom	philosophy, sophisticated
spec, spic, spect	look	specimen, conspicuous, spectacle
spir	breathe	spirit, conspire, respiration
stab, stat	stand	unstable, status, station, establish
stead	place	instead, steadfast
string, strict	bind	astringent, stricture, restrict
stru, struct	build	construe, structure, destructive
sum, sumpt	take	presume, consumer, assumption
tang, ting, tact, tig	touch	tangent, contingency, contact, tactile, contiguous
tax, tac	arrange, arrangement	taxonomy, tactic
techn	skill, art	technique, technician
tele	far	teletype, telekinesis
tempor	time	temporize, extemporaneous
ten, tain, tent	hold	tenant, tenacity, retention, contain
tend, tens, tent	stretch	contend, extensive, intent
tenu	thin	tenuous, attenuate
term	end	terminal, terminate
terr, ter	land, earth	inter, terrain
test	witness	attest, testify
the	god	polytheism, theologist
therm	heat	thermos, isotherm
tom	cut	atomic, appendectomy
tort, tors	twist	tortuous, torsion, contort
tract	pull, draw	traction, attract, protract
trib	assign, pay	attribute, tribute, retribution

trud, trus	thrust	obtrude, intrusive
turb	agitate	perturb, turbulent, disturb
umbr	shade	umbrella, penumbra, umbrage
uni	one	unify, disunity, union
urb	city	urbane, suburb
vac	empty	vacuous, evacuation
vad, vas	go	invade, evasive
val, vail	strength, worth	valid, avail, prevalent
ven, vent	come	advent, convene, prevention
ver	true	aver, veracity, verity
verb	word	verbose, adverb, verbatim
vert, vers	turn	revert, perversion
vest	dress	vestment
vid, vis	see	video, evidence, vision, revise
vinc, vict	conquer	evince, convict, victim
viv, vit	life	vivid, revive, vital
voc, vok	call	vociferous, provocative, revoke
vol	wish	involuntary, volition
volv, volut	roll, turn	involve, convoluted, revolution
vulg	common	divulge, vulgarity
zo	animal	zoologist, paleozoic

GENERAL HINTS FOR THE
GRE ANALYTICAL SECTIONS

Each of the two Analytical sections will contain 25 questions. Nineteen or twenty of the questions will be of the Analytical Reasoning (AR), or logical game, variety and the remaining five or six will be of the Logical Reasoning variety (LR). The Instructional Overviews for these question types describe them very thoroughly and give instructions on the best approaches to each type of question as well as how to tell one type of question from the other. Detailed timing hints for the different questions are also given.

The order of problems can vary from section to section, but the most likely order will be as follows:

TYPICAL QUESTION ORDER
FOR ANALYTIC SECTION

Question Number	Type
1–4	1 Analytical Reasoning question set
5–7	3 Logical Reasoning questions
8–22	3 or 4 Analytical Reasoning question sets
23–25	3 Logical Reasoning questions

Since this order may vary, you will need to check your own test carefully. Most students are best advised to work right through the section, skipping only those questions which, on inspection, prove to be too time-consuming or difficult. Remember to put an answer for all questions since *there is no penalty for a wrong answer.*

Some students find themselves particularly fearful of the Analytical section because it contains problems not usually encountered on standardized tests. Although familiarity may not breed contempt, you will find that the mystery and difficulty of these problems will fade as you become better acquainted with them. Therefore, conscientious study of these question types—beginning with a careful reading of the Instructional Overviews—is very important. It is absolutely essential that you read the Instructional overview for the AR question type before attempting to do the practice tests.

The Logical Reasoning Instructional overview contains many important insights into the structure of verbal reasoning that are helpful in answering Reading Comprehension, Analytical Reasoning, and Logical Reasoning questions, and should therefore not be omitted, even though there are relatively few "official" Logical Reasoning problems.

ANALYTICAL REASONING
INSTRUCTIONAL OVERVIEW

FUNDAMENTAL CONCEPTS OF ANALYTICAL REASONING PROBLEMS

As mentioned in the general description of the test, the Analytic section will contain 18–20 Analytical Reasoning questions and 5–6 Logical Reasoning questions. While these questions are sufficiently different in structure and approach to merit separate Instructional Overviews, they are similar enough to be included in the same section and score. It is important that you read both the Logical Reasoning and Analytical Reasoning Instructional Overviews. They are designed to work together, and the Logical Reasoning Overview can also be helpful for Reading Comprehension questions.

Analytical Reasoning problems (hereafter, AR problems) can be distinguished from Logical Reasoning problems in two ways. First, the AR problems will come in problem sets of from three to seven problems based on information given or a short passage, while Logical Reasoning problems will usually be single or in pairs. Occasional trios of Logical Reasoning problems do occur, however, but never more than that. Logical Reasoning problems will be based on short passages that present logical arguments and will often have question stems about weakening, strengthening and finding the assumptions of the arguments in the passages.

AR questions are fundamentally matters of organizing a system of conditions, or being able to see and use the structure of some set of information. In other words, it is the linkages within the information that are the focus of the questions. The set of information will consist of a series of statements which may be a simple listing—numbered—accompanied by a further explanatory paragraph or presented in paragraph form or a combination of these formats. The information set will be accompanied by from three to six, or even seven, problems.

We will now discuss the kinds of information which are included in an AR problem set and the kinds of questions that are asked about that information. Then we will discuss methods of attack which apply to all AR questions, preliminary to discussing the detailed approaches to the major kinds of AR questions. It is very important that you be familiar with the basic ideas which apply to all AR questions before you study the special techniques for specific kinds of AR problems.

Nature of the Information Set

In addition to the preceding remarks, it is useful to analyze a little more closely just what is occurring with AR information sets, so that you can more confidently, accurately, and quickly attack these problems. There are three kinds of information that can be given to you in an information set: outline, linkages, and specifics. ALL ARE IMPORTANT to answering the questions.

The **outline** is that portion of the information which tells you generally what sort of situation it is. For example:

> Three sailors are assigned to three different ships.
> The chief of a tribe is selecting hunters and trackers for a hunting expedition.
> Twelve people are seated in a restaurant at four tables.

This outline information is usually presented first, and it is the first step in understanding the problem. If three sailors are on three different ships, then each goes to one ship and our task is clearly to figure out who goes where, or some such. If people are seated in a restaurant, then only one person sits in a given seat and they would generally be expected to face the table so you can tell left from right by considering them all facing the table. The hunting expedition will require some hunters and some trackers, and they are probably going to be different people.

The point is that the situations will usually be everyday in their outlines and the common sense nature of the situation can give you useful—indeed necessary—information about the problems. Do not feel that the purpose of the problem is to trick you, for that is absolutely not true. Some outlines and situations have more realism than others, and a few may be totally abstract.

The linkages, conditions, or relationships are the connections between the various parts of the problem. These usually contain the bulk of the information given in the information set, and they will often be the major items with which you will work. You must, however, not divorce them from the outline. Sometimes, to be sure, the outline is not critical, but even when not necessary, most test-takers find it helpful in keeping track of things. Most of the substance of the diagrams that you will draw will be derived from the linkages given in the problem.

A linkage and the outline can sometimes overlap a bit. In the hunting party, the requirement that there be at least two hunters on the trip can be viewed as either a linkage or as part of the outline. It doesn't really matter, so long as you don't forget about it. THERE WILL BE VERY LITTLE INFORMATION GIVEN WHICH IS NOT USED FOR ANY OF THE PROBLEMS. (*Little,* but not necessarily *none.*)

A more typical linkage would be: If tracker X goes, hunter Y cannot go. Sometimes the reason for the linkage will be explained and sometimes it won't. If it is, then the same reasoning may be used implicitly in a problem or for setting up a further linkage.

> Tracker X can't go with Hunter Y, because two members of the same family may not be risked on a single trip.

If this linkage was followed with the detail that P and Q were in the same family, then you would know that P and Q couldn't both go on the trip either.

Linkages can be of different sorts and they can also be of different strengths. We are not referring here to the variations in the specific situations you will see on the exam, but rather LOGICAL variations, since AR questions rely on basic logical relationships, usually not even as advanced as those found in the harder of the Logical Reasoning problems. The variations of linkages are of several types:

COMMON TYPES OF VARIATION
IN LINKAGES
Exclusion/Inclusion
All the time/Part of the time
Can/Will
Some/All
Likes, prefers, desires/Must, cannot, etc.
Relative in position or reference/Absolute in position or reference

Naturally, these elements are usually combined in a given linkage.

> Mary must sit two seats to the left of George.

This is absolute in connecting George to Mary, but relative in the placement of Mary in that her position is stated as relative to George rather than at any particular seat—as George moves, so does Mary. The direction from George to Mary is definitely left (as opposed to simply two seats in either direction).

The key to linkages is that they are very precise as to what they say and what they do not say. More will be said of this later.

Specifics are NOT unimportant. They are items which are not connections between one item and another but absolute statements, such as: Jim is on the third boat; or M is a hunter. They are not dissimilar to an absolute linkage involving only one characteristic of one item.

Completeness of the Information

In most AR problem sets, the information given will not be totally complete, though this can vary from problem set to problem set. Sometimes the information will be virtually complete; once you have delved its final depths, only a few of the possible interrelationships are not specified in full. Often the information will not be very complete at all, with only a small number of possible relationships being specified and the rest left to the manipulation of the questions. All you have to do is be willing to cope with whatever level of completeness the particular problem happens to have.

What AR Questions Do

Having erected some sort of system of linkages in the information set, there are several different kinds of questions which the test can ask you. Each has its own charms. The major types of questions are: analysis, new specifics, new conditions, partial information, and changed or deleted conditions or linkages. Some questions combine these basic forms, and there are always a few seemingly oddball questions which can be combinations of the major types, perhaps with information from the outline being required.

The most common AR questions are the analysis, new specifics, and new conditions questions—with the first two probably being the more numerous. (Remember that the distinction between a condition and a specific is somewhat arbitrary.)

Analysis questions are ones which explore the given information. The more complete the information that is given, the greater the number of analysis questions which are likely to be asked, which is only common sense. Why set up a whole structure if they are not going to ask you about it? Having figured out the seating arrangement mandated by a problem set, for example, an analysis problem will simply ask who sits next to Aunt Jane or who sits three chairs from Harry, etc. A variant of the analysis problem is one which either asks how many possibilities there are, or asks you to identify possible or impossible combinations, arrangements, orders, etc.

New specifics questions are usually the most common when the information set is not very complete. In these problems a new specific is given, such as "X will go on the hunting trip." You are then asked to analyze who else can or cannot go, or how many possibilities are left for tracker, etc.

New conditions questions introduce a new

condition and then ask for an analysis of the situation. Usually the new condition is no more complex than the ones already present in the problem.

Each of the three question types just described absolutely require that, in principle, you consider all of the information given in the information set. The two to be described next use only part of the information given in the information set.

Partial information questions will usually occur when the information set has numbered statements that the question can clearly refer to. This type of question will ask what could be known from only some of the original information statements. For example, it might ask what would follow from statements I, III, and V. It is efficient to do this sort of question first since the final structure of linkages that you construct from all of the information may not be helpful. The final structure might, for instance, exclude a possibility which is still available when only part of the information is used.

Changed or deleted conditions or linkages questions do just what their name implies: They ask you to analyze the situation that would result if one of the conditions was changed or deleted. A deleted conditions or linkages question can be handled by putting together all of the other information first, answering this question, and then adding in the linkage in order to address the rest of the questions. Often the changed or deleted conditions question can just as easily be done in its listed order. When a linkage is modified, it is usually easiest to start with the completed structure and modify it as indicated by the question—though occasionally a fresh start is easier, time permitting.

GENERAL APPROACHES TO ANSWERING AR PROBLEMS

The overall approach is to separate the tasks of arranging the information and answering the questions. In cases where the information is complete, or nearly so, the arrangement of the information will naturally take much longer than when relatively little original information is given. We will first discuss overall timing for AR questions. Then we will discuss the fundamental rules of arranging information for AR questions. In the next section we will discuss the identification and treatment of specific types of information by creating diagrams suitable to that particular information.

Timing

Timing is an important issue on all sections of the test, but many students find that they need to watch their time most closely when doing AR questions. The Analytical section has 25 questions in 30 minutes, which averages about 72 seconds per question. That is not too helpful a piece of information, however, without some interpretation. It does, however, give the measure of the time available for each problem set. This total time for each set needs to be further divided. You have two tasks to accomplish within the time allotted for each set of problems: arrangement of the information into usable form, and answering the questions. While no hard and fast rules can be laid down, since the problems vary in several ways, a general idea of how your time should be divided can be gleaned from a VERY brief preview of the question stems, that is to say, the part of the question which asks the question—not the answer choices, and not any roman numeral statements which may be running around in the question (technically they are part of the answer choices).

The purpose of the preview is very limited. Like the preview in Logical Reasoning and Reading Comprehension, the purpose is to get information to plan the assault on the problem.

Unlike those sections, no specific information about the actual problem is sought. All that the preview can usefully give you is two things: (1) an idea about how to divide your time between arranging and answering and (2) advanced knowledge of partial information, and deleted or changed conditions questions which may best be answered out of order as previously discussed. THAT IS IT! Don't try to memorize the questions. Anything like that is generally a waste of time.

THE PREVIEW SHOULD TAKE NO MORE THAN 5 SECONDS PER QUESTION! If you don't have the discipline to skim them that fast, only preview two of them in 10 seconds and if you don't have the discipline to do that, don't preview at all. You can't possibly do the problems until you have the information organized, so anything but a skim is a complete waste.

The findings of the preview can be evaluated as follows. If all of the questions, or all but one, are "if" questions, then it is likely that the information is not very complete and most of your time will be spent with the questions. If few or none of the questions are "if" questions, then probably most of your time should be spent on arranging the information. The main reason for even bothering to find out how your time should be spent is to avoid anxiety in complete information problems when $\frac{1}{2}$ to $\frac{2}{3}$ of your time might be spent on organizing the information.

If you find partial information or deleted or changed conditions questions, then you should do those questions first, especially the partial information ones.

SHORT AND LONG TIME ALLOTMENTS FOR AR PROBLEM SETS
(in minutes)

NUMBER OF QUESTIONS	COMPLETE INFORMATION		PARTIAL INFORMATION		TOTAL TIME
	ARRANGING	ANSWERING	ARRANGING	ANSWERING	
3	2	1½	1	2½	3½
4	2⅔	2	1⅓	3⅓	4⅔
5	4	2	1⅔	4⅓	6
6	4¼	3	2¼	5	7¼
7	5	3½	2½	6	8½

Note: See the section on Timing and General Hints for the Analytic Sections.

Lest this chart seem too overwhelming, remember that it is only a guide and its main purpose is to impress upon you that the division of time between arranging and answering information is very variable indeed. The only fairly ironclad timing is the total time for a problem set.

Fundamental Rules for Arranging AR Information

Arranging the information in the AR question set is at least as important as the answering of the questions, since the latter depends on the former. In addition, all of the rules and understandings which are necessary for proper arrangement of the information are equally necessary for manipulating the information for all of the questions, except perhaps the pure analysis question.

The instructions for the Analytic section indicate that "it may be helpful to draw a diagram." While it is true that some students do not need to draw diagrams for some of the AR problem sets, these are few and far between, and they usually will be mentally making some sort of diagram or organizing structure. That is fine if you are both very good at these sorts of problems and very experienced at them. But everyone, whether they make diagrams or not, should abide by the following fundamental rules for arranging the information. You probably already follow them instinctively, but a review will ensure that you do so consistently and completely.

There are five rules. Three of the rules are general, and apply in similar ways to some of the other sections of the test. Two of the rules primarily apply to AR. You can remember them as PLICC (pronounced "plick").

—Precise reading is always necessary, but no tricks.
—Logical rules should always be followed as shown in the Logical Reasoning Instructional Overview.
—Independence criterion applies totally. Carry nothing from one question to the next.
—Chain your information together, one item at a time.
—Cherish your ignorance. Knowing what you don't know is at least as important as knowing what you do know.

Let us examine each of these principles by itself.

PRECISE READING does not mean paranoia. As mentioned in the other Instructional Overviews, precise reading means paying attention to what each sentence actually says. The GRE warns you to be particularly alert to words that describe or limit relationships or linkages. Words particularly important in AR information sets are: *only, exactly, never, always, must be/can be/cannot be, some, all, no, entire, each, every, except, but, unless, none, if, more/less, before/after, possible/impossible, different/same, taller/shorter, lighter/heavier, least/most,* any superlative (*-est*), maximum (*at most*), minimum (*at least*).

There are many others and you should be particularly alert for words which derive their meaning from the specific situation—the outline—because they are ones which you may easily miss because of their unique character.

The proper approach to all the reading on the AR section is one of bland but analytical acceptance. You are not disputing what is said at all, you are merely analyzing it for just precisely what it does say so that you can file it away properly and draw the proper conclusions from it.

The LOGIC on the AR section is all essentially deductive logic. There is virtually no inductive work to be done at all. Some of the questions might possibly seem to require some sort of generalization, but only do this if it is clearly required by the question. The only complication is that most of the time you will not have everything tied down completely, but will need to constantly consider different contingencies or possibilities.

The INDEPENDENCE CRITERION applies to all GRE questions. It is absolutely critical that you never carry anything forward from one question to the next. To be sure, the test-makers usually try to avoid having questions which change the basic conditions in different ways right next to each other, but there are many ways that you might carry things forward. The most common is by making alterations to your basic diagram for a particular problem, and then forgetting that the alteration is based on information that applies only to one problem and using it in another problem. The solution to this is to either not make marks on your main diagram at all, or be prepared to redraw all or part of it for a couple of questions. This need not be as onerous as it sounds, since the redrawing is usually only required in situations where the original information was not too complete anyway.

Another facet of the independence criterion is that you only look for the items, people, and things which are actually stated in the problem. If they ask how many people could possibly be on the porch, you only consider the persons mentioned in the problem and not your cousin Sue and your Uncle Mike. Keep within the problem's parameters. Also be careful not to make any unnecessary, and thus unwarranted assumptions about the connections being discussed in the passage: Taller does not necessarily mean heavier; a husband is not necessarily older than his wife; a woman is not necessarily smaller or lighter or weaker than a man; staying at a party longer does not necessarily mean that one drank more. In other words, be careful NOT to make ordinary inductions about the situation which are not required by the problem itself.

CHAIN your information together. This is *critical* in both the arrangement of the information into a diagram, and the interpretation of the diagram for the solution of problems. More mistakes are probably made on AR questions through improper chaining than from any other single cause.

The process of chaining has three parts: break-down, linking and review. The first step is **breaking down** the information to be arranged into individual items of information. Frequently, the original information set will contain sentences which have several items of information in them. You cannot enter all of these items at once, but must separate them and enter them one at a time into the diagram which you will be constructing. For example:

> Mary will not sit at the same table as Bob or Jane.

This sentence contains two items of information: (1) Mary is not at the same table as Bob, and (2) Mary is not at the same table as Jane. These should be entered separately and should be reviewed separately because each one may have separate implications that need to be followed through separately.

Linking means that you cannot enter an item

into the diagram unless you have something to hook it on to. Here is a simple example:

> I.   A is larger than B.
> II. C is larger than D.
> III. B is larger than C.

If we make a diagram in which we say that left is smaller and right is bigger, then we can enter these items as follows:

←SMALLER————LARGER→

Enter I   B   A

If you now try to enter II at once, there is no way to link it to the information you have about B and A, since II concerns neither, and there is no information in the diagram yet about either C or D. Try entering II yourself and see that wherever you enter it into the diagram it isn't very helpful. All you could do would be to indicate that there is no real connection between I and II, and you have essentially two separate diagrams. While there are some problems which do end up with something of that sort, you do not want to do it unless you have to, because you might be missing some deductions you need in order to answer problems. For example, if we make two lines on our diagram:

←SMALLER————LARGER→

         B   A

         ←D   C→

Even this is open to misinterpretation since we might accidentally suppose that B = D or A = C or that C > B.

You should hold off entering II until you have some sort of linkage.

←SMALLER————————LARGER→

Enter III instead   C   B   A

Now II can be entered   D   C   B   A

Which gives the final relationship for these three items of information. Note that there are many deductions which can be made from the diagram listed: D < B, D < A, C < A. One of the virtues of a diagram of this sort is that when it can be made—and it is not always appropriate—it saves you having to write down all the deductions without running any risk of not seeing them if you need them for the solution of a problem.

There are some sorts of diagrams, as we shall see, where the outline of the problem can be used to set up a structure that immediately guarantees that all information can be usefully entered, or where there is so little information that all that can be diagrammed is a few linkages. In these cases you still have to be very careful to separate each item of information from others and to enter it only as it can be linked, but the linkage requirement is much less onerous and would not usually require holding off on entering any items.

Review is the process of evaluating the possible deductions that can be made between the item of information which is under review and every other single item of information already entered and every other possible combination of the items already entered. This doubtless sounds like a terrific amount of work, and it sometimes is, but if you use a little common sense you will only be doing the work necessary for the problems. The key here, as in all test problems, is to look for connections. In this case it is connections between the item of information you are reviewing and the other items already entered into your diagram or structure. If your item says Bob is the son of Mary, you can look for the following connectors:

> Mary, or other relatives of Mary, who will also be relatives of Bob. Bob not being the husband or sibling of Mary, etc.
> Anything to do with being male.
> Anything to do with being younger than someone else since Bob must be younger than Mary.
> Anything to do with being a son in general.

Examples of previously coded items that could relate to the preceding item using these ideas are:

> Mary is married to Andy; thus, Andy is Bob's (step)father.
> Mary is younger than Jim; thus, Jim is older than Bob.
> The pilot is a female; thus, Bob is not the pilot.
> John is an only child; thus, John is not Bob's brother, and not the son of Mary.

The point of all this is that it is the easiest thing in the world to overlook a deduction in the heat of the test. You can guard against making that serious error by developing the ironbound habit of always reviewing carefully each item as you use it. It will save you many errors and much wasted effort in the AR section.

CHERISHING YOUR IGNORANCE is primarily a matter of not tricking yourself into thinking you know more than you do. There is a natural pressure to get the last drop of deduction out of the information, but many questions turn as much on clearly knowing the limits of your knowledge in the situation as on having made all possible deductions. In fact, the two often work together, with some answer choices being wrong for one reason and some for the other.

The review of logic which is contained in the Logical Reasoning Instructional Overview has many valuable pointers on logic and you should be as careful to use good reasoning in the AR section as you are in the Logical Reasoning section. However, let us review some particularly pertinent points of logic here as well, to warn you of some of the errors that might make you accidentally fail to cherish your ignorance.

1. SOME only means at least one, and there is no implication whatever that because "some elephants are gray" there are some (any) elephants which are not gray. All elephants might be gray. From "some X are Y" you cannot conclude that "some X are not Y." If you are told that "not all Q are S," then you can conclude that "some Q are not S."

2. "All A are B" does not tell you anything about the B which are not A. There may be B which are not A, or maybe not; it is just a possibility.

3. "Only D are E" equals "All E are D" and the same strictures apply.

4. "Mary cannot work with George" is the same as "if Mary, then not George," which is the same as "if George, then not Mary." Error can creep in when there are several statements of this sort:

> Mary cannot work with George.
> George cannot work with Tom.

You have to be a little careful with this situation. While it is true that if George is included, both

Mary and Tom cannot be included, there being no other linkage between Mary and Tom. Mary CAN work with Tom, but is not required to be with him as far as these two statements alone are concerned.

5. TRANSFORMATIONS often occur in AR problems. When a couple marries, they may become the caste/tribe/etc. of the husband or the wife, or they may be arbitrarily assigned some designation. Thus, "a woman of caste N becomes caste P upon marriage" means that the woman may be referred to as either "a pre-marriage caste N woman" or "a married caste P woman." This kind of multiple referencing can also occur in any problem where more than one characteristic is assigned to an individual person or thing. If the biggest dog lives in the third house with Jim, then they might ask you about the location of Jim's dog or the size of Jim's dog or the location or owner of the biggest dog, etc.

6. NECESSARY VERSUS SUFFICIENT: Just because all elephants must be gray doesn't mean that everything that is gray is an elephant. Classifications into groups are typically done on the basis of more than one characteristic. This is easy to spot in real life since we know perfectly well that there are other gray things, even other gray animals such as squirrels and donkeys. When the situation is abstract or unrealistic, we don't have that reality check and have to ask logically and consciously if the condition of being a Z is sufficient to make something automatically a W, or if it is an open question, or if it is even impossible.

7. COUNTING POSSIBILITIES: You will sometimes be asked to count the number of possible different arrangements of some situation. There are two thorns of which to beware. First, you must determine whether it is just bunches of things that are at issue or whether order matters in some way. For example, if you are making up the hunting party referred to earlier in the chapter, it does not seem to matter whether the trackers are Bob and Jane, or Jane and Bob, so that is just *one* possibility. On the other hand, if the question is discussing the slate of officers for an election, it is quite different if Jane is president and Bob vice-president, or the other way around. That would be *two* possibilities. There can also be an issue of physical rotation, as discussed later when seating-type diagrams are discussed.

DRAWING THE RIGHT DIAGRAM FOR EACH AR PROBLEM

Almost every problem will require a diagram (for most students) as previously discussed. We strongly recommend that you practice drawing diagrams of all sorts so that you will always be prepared for any problem you might see on the test. If you get to the actual test and you can easily keep it all in your head, fine! Do it! But most people at least need to keep a few notes, and a diagram is usually the most efficient way to keep the notes.

We will now be discussing several different types of diagrams and ways of deciding which one is best for a particular problem. Although it is helpful to start with the best diagram, the choice of diagramming method is not something that you should spend a very long time over. If you are paying the proper attention to the information in the problem set, you will generally find yourself being guided to the right diagramming technique because it will be the one that fits. Thus, it is important to have some familiarity with several different techniques. In addition to the material presented in the Instructional Overview, you should definitely review the explanations for all of the AR questions in the practice tests and closely follow the construction of the diagrams there.

Using the Outline

The outline of the problem is the statement of the general situation as discussed in the early part of this Instructional Overview. The outline is the first piece of evidence to be used in deciding which type of diagram will be most efficient for a particular set of AR problems. The second piece of evidence is the nature of the linkages which are given in the problem. A third important piece of evidence is sometimes provided by the form of the questions in the AR problem set. First, we shall discuss these three types of evidence and explain how to interpret them; then we will detail the different types of diagrams.

The outline is usually the most important piece of evidence leading you to the correct form of diagram. In every case, the purpose of the diagram is to arrange the information in the AR problem set in the most natural and useful way. It is only common sense that the proper arrangement depends on the nature of the information being arranged.

If the situation is a seating arrangement, then a diagram of the table is indicated, though other things may also be needed. If the situation is colors and sizes and fuels of six trucks, then you know that you will need to make a table or two to correlate all the information. If the situation is one in which a process is described whereby persons change status or location according to given rules, then you need to make a chart which will allow you to make the required transformations quickly and accurately, forwards and backwards. The outline is also usually the key to identifying the special types of diagram situations described below.

The linkages are helpful in diagnosing the problem because they may be the point in the presentation at which the various possibilities are raised. You know there are six trucks, but you don't know that their fuel is an issue until a linkage raises it. There are sometimes problem sets where the major issues are limited, but the linkages deal with additional issues. For example, if the issue is which sailor goes with which boat, there might be a linkage telling you that one of the boats is bigger than another, or one of the sailors is blond. As such, these are not major arranging issues, but subsidiary ones that help to limit possibilities.

The questions are often helpful in deciding about the arrangement of the information. As previously noted, if there are many "if" questions, it is likely that there is not too much information being given, and that it will not completely describe the situation. This means that most of the information will be linkages and a few parameters, such as in the hunting party situation described briefly at the beginning of this Instructional Overview. In such cases the diagram is usually limited to a pure linkage format as described in the following paragraphs. If the questions ask about an issue—Which sailor had the red hair?—then you know that you are going to have to know something about red hair, or at least hair color in general. A large number of analysis questions usually indicates that a table or physical analog diagram is likely to be helpful, though this is not always the case.

Specific Diagramming Techniques

We shall discuss three major categories—Physical Analog, Pure Linkage, and Tables—and the combination of the last two types. Pure linkage and table diagrams apply, in principle, to virtually all problems. The physical analog diagrams apply to some special cases that may appear and which are most efficiently handled with these special techniques. Let us deal with the special situations first.

Physical analog. All this means is that the diagram you will make is a picture of the situation in some direct way. One simple example would be a problem set where the issue (or one of the issues) was the relative weight of a group of individuals. What you do is establish some direction as representing heavier and the opposite direction as representing lighter. This could be up and down or left and right or even diagonally if that seems good at the time (though we don't recommend that). For example:

$$\leftarrow \text{LIGHTER} \text{——} \text{HEAVIER} \rightarrow.$$

Sometimes there may be more than one such parameter in a problem, such as louder/quieter and faster/slower, or whatever it may be. These are simple problems provided that you remember the fundamental rules for diagramming (PLICC).

Sometimes there is a residuum of uncertainty in the problem. This can occur in two ways. First consider the propositions:

$$\leftarrow \text{LIGHTER} \text{——} \text{HEAVIER} \rightarrow.$$

I. A is heavier than B.   B   A

II. A is heavier than C.   C   A

The problem is how to indicate that you do NOT know the relationship between B and C. Use arrows to indicate ranges of possibilities:

$$\leftarrow \text{LIGHTER} \text{——} \text{HEAVIER} \rightarrow.$$
$$\text{B} \quad \text{A}$$
$$\leftarrow \text{C} \rightarrow$$

This accurately notes that B might be greater than, less than, or equal to C. If we add to this another proposition that "C is heavier than D," we end up with two somewhat separate lines, which can still be used to answer questions.

$$\leftarrow\text{LIGHTER}\text{——}\text{HEAVIER}\rightarrow.$$

$$B \quad A$$

$$\leftarrow\text{D}\text{——}\text{C}\rightarrow$$

Another example of a physical analog diagram is when there is a situation that is a map; that is, there are directions north, east, west, and south just like a map, and the issue is to draw the map so that questions can be answered. Again, close adherence to the fundamental rules of diagramming is essential—indeed, it is always essential, and the failure to repeat this warning for every problem type is simply to save you reading the same thing ten times, but do remember it.

With a map situation, you will either be making a map of streets, avenues, lanes, etc., or ones of towns, blocks, areas, etc. In either case, you should always assume that the map is a rectilinear grid or checkerboard unless something in the problem says otherwise. Always interpret any direction given as precisely that direction. North means directly north. Precise directions should always be used in making the diagram. In answering the questions always use precise directions, unless there is no possible answer that way—in which case you can use northwards instead of north. This is very rare. Do not assume that you know how long any streets are unless you are told. Also, be careful to observe the same sort of care with double references that you have to do with heavier/lighter diagrams as was discussed in the preceding paragraphs.

A third kind of physical analog is the Venn diagram (circles to represent categories or groups), which is explained in detail in the Logical Reasoning Instructional Overview. The Venn should be used when the situation is primarily one of interacting or overlapping groups with only some individuals in the problem. Typical propositions for such questions are "no X are Y," "only M can be Y," etc. Remember that Venns cannot be used with more than three groups at once. The relationships among four groups cannot be adequately represented by four circles on a flat piece of paper. If there is this sort of question on your test and it seems to have four groups, just make the Venn for the three most discussed groups and then fit in the fourth one verbally as you need it.

A fourth common type of physical analog diagram is the seating diagram. This actually applies to any situation where a physical arrangement is at issue: beds, lines, shelves, seats, cars, garages, etc. Typically, a seating problem will have a combined diagram with several linkages being used as well as the seating diagram. In fact, it is common for you to have to construct a different seating chart for each question based on the requirements of the linkages and the question.

A problem often encountered with seating diagrams is when more than one arrangement is possible. For example:

I. F, G, H, and J are sitting at a four-sided table, one on each side.
II. F is opposite G and H is opposite J.

There are two basic arrangements:

$$
\begin{array}{ccccc}
 & F & & & F \\
H & \quad J & & J & \quad H \\
 & G & & & G
\end{array}
$$

Also, F could be sitting in any one of the four seats, as far as we know at this time, so there could be $2 \times 4 = 8$ arrangements. It also matters whether it is a case of just who is there, or how they are arranged.

Pure linkage. These diagrams are used when all, or virtually all, of the information is in the form of linkages. This situation is usually accompanied by questions primarily of the added detail or condition type. Therefore, what you need is a diagram that will quickly and accurately let you travel through the linkages, both forward and backward, in order to ascertain the results of the added details or conditions.

The "classic" pure linkage problem would be one such as the hunting party situation we have mentioned at several points in this overview. Let us lay this out as if it were a full problem.

> The chief of the Inagway tribe is selecting a hunting party, which will consist of two hunters and two trackers.
>
> G, H, J, and K are hunters and M, N, and P are trackers.
>
> G and P cannot go on the trip together because they are from the same family, and P does not get along with M so the chief cannot send both P and M together.

1. If P goes on the trip, who else must go?

2. If G goes on the trip, who else cannot go?

We see that we have to be concerned in this instance with the linkages among a group of seven individuals who are subdivided into two groups—hunters and trackers. While it would be all right to just have the seven listed as a single group, it makes sense to have them sorted out as much as possible. We know that the hunter/tracker designation will matter since there are limits placed on the situation based on that division—two of each. (Of course, if there were no sub-groups, then you would treat the whole group together.)

As we analyze the outline we see that we should have the two groups just mentioned—hunter and trackers. We also see that the only other information is in the form of linkages—who cannot go with whom—and a condition that there must be two of each in the party. The "if" questions—added details or conditions—confirm that linkage is the major issue.

There are several methods that can be used to chart the linkages we have been given. The two simplest are *labelled arrows* and *pseudo-algebra*. Don't let the names put you off—we had to call them something—and it doesn't matter what you call the diagram so long as you get the questions right.

Most people prefer the labelled arrows method, so let us describe that first. After you have the outline in mind—here the idea that there are two groups to interrelate—you just draw arrows from individual to individual to indicate their linkages. Here are several sample arrows with labels:

X←NEVER WITH→Y   X←ALWAYS WITH→Y

X←ONLY WITH→Y   X←BEFORE—TWO DAYS—AFTER→Y

X←WITH ONLY ONE OF   →Y
                      OR
                      →Z

Note that while most arrows will point both ways, it is possible for a condition or linkage to be stated so that the arrow only works one way. If a condition states that X could only go if Y could go too, that is only one way. Y might go even if X did not. In the hunting party case we would draw the following diagram:

HUNTERS	TRACKERS
Choose two	Choose two
G←NOT WITH	P←NOT WITH→M
H	N
J	
K	

This diagram makes it easy to answer the questions.

1. If P goes, then neither M nor G can go. This means that since two trackers are required, N must go. However, on the hunter side we have three candidates for two seats, and cannot say who MUST go.

2. If G goes, then only P is excluded; M and N must go, but that isn't what the question asked.

Two additional points about labelled arrows. You may easily find that the arrows are not straight as an arrow. That is just fine. All you are interested in is what the linkage is as shown by the arrow. The direction means nothing here since you have not assigned it any meaning (unlike some of the physical analog diagrams). As a corollary of that point, you may find that your arrows sometimes cross. That is OK, too. If direction means nothing, then the fact that the arrows cross means nothing, since crossing is a function of direction.

Pseudo-algebra is just a fancy way of saying that you can borrow some algebraic notation, such as "=," "not=," etc., and use it for your own purposes and with your own meanings. If you are not comfortable with math, you should definitely use the labelled arrow method. Pseudo-algebra is not really quite as good since we are using signs which have other meanings, and that multiplicity of meaning can sometimes confuse us.

In the hunting party example, we would do the following:

HUNTERS	TRACKERS
G NOT=	P NOT= M
H	N
J	
K	

You can see the similarities between this method and the other. The question answering is the same.

One difficulty with the pseudo-algebra is when two items must go together (in whatever way things go together in that problem set). You indicate this by X=Y, and you have to be careful to remember that that symbolism does NOT mean that X and Y are the same thing.

If you have your own methods and they work, fine. They are probably essentially the same idea as these, but just using your own symbols.

Tables. Tables (and scorecards) are particularly helpful when your task is to sort out some situation where, in principle, there is only one actual arrangement but you may not have been given enough information to complete the sorting out. For example:

I. There are three sailors, F, G, and H, who are a bosun, gunner, and cook on ships 101, 201, and 301, not necessarily in that order.

II. G and H are in a different navy than F, but in the same navy as each other.

III. Yesterday the bosun was transferred from ship 101, where he was serving with the gunner, to ship 201.

1. Who serves on ship 301?

2. The rank of which sailor(s) is (are) not definitely known?

The information seems fairly complete and the two questions are both analysis questions. Thus, we expect to be able to develop a fairly complete picture of the situation, though question 2 indicates that there might still be uncertainties—even when all the available information is arranged. Since it is a "sorting out" type of situation, a table or scorecard is likely to be helpful. We will have a table that will have three columns and four rows for the three locations or individuals, and the four types of information we know about each individual—name, rank, boat, and navy.

The reason that we have referred to a scorecard will become clear as we use the table. The purpose of a scorecard is to enable you to figure out who the players are. Similarly, the purpose of the table or scorecard here is to enable you to figure out who the "players" are.

The second part of proposition III tells us that the gunner is on 101. While it is "true" in the real world that he might have been transferred since yesterday, the real world is not the only (or even the main) guide. The problem says nothing of the gunner's being transferred; therefore, he was not transferred. Let us enter what we know so far into the diagram:

NAME	F	G	H
RANK		gunner or	bosun
BOAT		101 or	201
NAVY	different	same as H	same as G

There is still much to be deduced from this situation by the review of the interactions of all of the now-known items. Since we know that the three different sailors all had different boats and different ranks, the process of elimination lets us reach two more deductions: (5) F is the cook, and (6) F is on 301. Entering this we get the final diagram:

NAME	F	G	H
RANK	cook	gunner or	bosun
BOAT	301	101 or	201
NAVY	different	same as H	same as G

We are now in a position to answer any questions that might be asked about this situation. To answer the particular questions previously raised:

1. F serves on ship 301.

2. The ranks of G and H are not definitely known.

If you have a problem set which does not concern the piecing together of the real identity and characteristics of some set of individual persons or things, then you might find yourself using a straight table method in which you would list all of the different kinds of information which you expect to have to arrange (and add to this table as you need to), and then carefully enter each item and check it against every other entry that you have made. The straight table method is the most generally applicable method, and can in principle be used for every kind of problem, but it is not nearly as efficient as the other methods—for the problems to which the other methods apply.

In the case of the sailors, for example, you would have made the following headings for your set of tables:

RANK	NAME	BOAT					
(1 EACH TYPE)	(INDIVIDUALS)	(1 EACH TYPE)					
BOSUN COOK GUNNER	F	G	H	101	201	301	

You would probably not make a separate table for navy, though you could. The method of execution is simply to enter each and every item and deduction in the tables. The tedious BUT ABSOLUTELY NECESSARY part is that you have to enter many connections in two places. When you find out that F is on boat 301, you have to enter "on 301" under F and "F" under 301. This double connection is noted in the scorecard form of table by the fact that F and 301 are in the same column. If you don't put everything in, you almost might as well not bother. You also have to be very disciplined in making sure that you follow these rules of entry, derived from the fundamental rules of diagramming:

1. Consider only one piece of information at a time.
2. Cross-check that piece with every other entry already in the table, looking for deductions or for connections to yet other entries.
3. Whenever a deduction is found, it must be entered at once, and then BOTH the deduction and the original piece of information must be checked against every piece of information starting from the beginning again. It is tedious but it works. Do it!

Combinations. Combining the table or scorecard method with the linkage method is common. Sometimes it is merely a matter of it being more convenient to record as a linkage some slightly out-of-the-way piece of information, such as navy status in the preceding example. Other times there is fairly complete information about one aspect of the situation and only linkage information about another. Do not hesitate to record something as a linkage, even if you end up putting it into a table later when there is some further deduction or other information on the same point.

SUMMARY REVIEW OF ATTACK STRATEGY FOR AR PROBLEM SETS

FOR EACH PROBLEM SET you should follow this attack strategy. Remember, however, that this one listing is only a summary of the ideas of the previous pages, and you cannot substitute reading this outline for reading the entire overview.

1. Quickly preview the question stems only. (Five seconds each.) Note the partial information questions.
2. Skim the information set quickly to get an idea of the outline of the situation. (Fifteen seconds.)
3. Evaluate the outline of the situation. (Ten seconds.)
4. Quickly decide on the basic diagram method you will use. Note, for your peace of mind, the completeness of the information and the likely proportions of arranging and answering times.
   - Physical analog—greater/lesser
     - —mapping
     - —Venn diagrams (circles)
     - —seating
   - Linkages—few analysis questions, incomplete information
   - Scorecard—tables with definite outcome
   - Tables—most general method
5. Enter the information using PLICC. Enter in order given, except enter first the propositions used for partial information questions.
   - —Precise reading
   - —Logical rules
   - —Independence criterion
   - —Chain information
   - —Cherish ignorance
6. Answer the questions, remembering the different types.
   - —Analysis
   - —Partial information
   - —Deleted or changed conditions or linkages
   - —New conditions
   - —New specifics
7. Watch time closely. Don't spend too much on one problem and don't run overtime for the problem set.

LOGICAL REASONING
INSTRUCTIONAL OVERVIEW

PRELIMINARIES

Logical Reasoning questions are a part of the Analytic sections on the GRE. As noted earlier in this book, each Analytic section will have 5 or 6 Logical Reasoning problems and 19 or 20 Analytical Reasoning problems. While the total of 10 or 12 Logical Reasoning problems may not seem very many, they do constitute almost a quarter of that score. Even more importantly, the discussion of reasoning methods and ideas contained in this overview can be important in answering both Analytical Reasoning *and* Reading Comprehension questions.

Now, the very title of this question—*Logic*al Reasoning—causes some students to worry, for it suggests to them that they will be tested on the formal rules of logic. They imagine that they will encounter problems using Latin terms and mathematical symbols and notations. Fortunately, this is not the case. Doing well on these questions does not depend upon having had any official instruction in logic, such as a college course in Symbolic Logic, and the official GRE bulletin stresses this point, saying that "no knowledge of the terminology of formal logic is presupposed."

Instead, two skills are really being tested— reading ability and reasoning power—both of which are essential to graduate study. Of course, it cannot be denied that a student who has had formal training in non-symbolic logic, for example, the standard introduction to logic offered by most college philosophy departments, may find occasion to put that training to use here, but many brilliant thinkers have never received so much as a single hour of instruction in the rules of thinking.

The value of a course in logic is not so much that it teaches a student anything new—after all, we all *do think* even if we do not *know how* it is that we think. Rather, the value of a logic course is that it brings some order or structure to what we do quite naturally. Perhaps an analogy drawn from athletics might make the point clear. Some people are natural sprinters and can run very fast. Nonetheless, a good coach can show even the most gifted runners how they can improve their performances. The same is true of thinking. Some people are naturally brilliant thinkers, others are not; but whatever the level of natural ability, everyone could definitely benefit from "coaching" in this area. In this Instructional Overview, we will try to offer some hints on how to sharpen up your analytical abilities. It must be emphasized, however, that the material we present is not new. This is not like a course in organic chemistry, where a student can get a good grade simply by memorizing all the formulas. Instead, we are just trying to make you *aware* of what you have always done—to put you in touch with your thought processes. As you read this material, then, you should try to make it your own by fitting it into your own thought patterns. For example, we may use a newspaper ad to illustrate the danger of not attending to detail.

> Seventy-three percent of the doctors surveyed said they would, if asked by a patient, recommend Lite Cigarettes with their low tar and nicotine for patients who smoke.

Does the ad claim that many *doctors* are encouraging people to smoke Lite Cigarettes? Not exactly, for the claim made by the ad is carefully qualified in several respects. First, the ad speaks of a certain *percentage* of doctors without saying how many doctors were questioned. Second, the doctors who did respond did not say they *do* recommend Lite Cigarettes; the ad says specifically they *would* recommend Lite Cigarettes *if* a patient asked them about cigarette smoking. And third, the final phrase of the ad also makes a very important qualification: The doctors would make such a recommendation for those patients who *do* smoke already. We can see from this very simple illustration that there is a great difference between the general impression created by this advertisement and what the advertisement really says. And this is one skill you need to develop: careful reading with attention to detail.

It should be obvious, then, that it does absolutely no good to memorize the rules. Read carefully! As you study these materials, make cross-connections to similar material which you have encountered, for example, another advertisement. Also, you should practice being alert. Someone who is really aware of the importance of careful reading is always attending to detail. This is not to suggest that good thinkers are paranoid about people trying to trick or deceive them, and the GRE does not require paranoia; the problems do not involve cute tricks. But careful thinkers are always paying attention. Learning to be a careful thinker involves practice. We would never imagine that an athlete could learn to run faster or jump higher by just listening to a lecture on muscle structure. We know very well that the athlete has to take that information and incorporate it into his training regimen. Fortunately, the practice field for logical thinking is everyday life. Think carefully about everything you hear or read.

Our approach here will not be limited to classifying actual GRE Logical Reasoning problems. Instead, we will try to give a highly condensed course in basic logic, pointing out the most common argument forms and fallacies that appear on the GRE. Then, in our answer explanations to the practice tests that follow, we will study the question stems ETS uses in the Logical Reasoning questions to test whether a candidate can recognize these forms and fallacies. If you feel you would benefit from further reading in logic and have the time to pursue these studies, we recommend the standard college textbook on elementary logic: *Introduction to Logic,* Irving M. Copi (Macmillan Publishing Co.: NY, 5th ed., 1978), particularly chapters one through seven.

STRUCTURE OF AN ARGUMENT

An *argument* is a group of statements or assertions, one of which, the *conclusion*, is supposed to follow from the others, the *premises*. Some arguments are very short and simple:

Premise: No fish are mammals.
Conclusion: No mammals are fish.

Others are extremely lengthy and complex, taking up entire volumes. Some arguments are good, some are bad. Scientists use arguments to justify a conclusion regarding the cause of some natural phenomenon; politicians use arguments to reach conclusions about the desirability of government policies. But even given this wide variety of structures and uses, arguments fall into one of two general categories, depending on the kind of *inference* which is required to get *from the premises to the conclusion.* An inference which depends solely on the meanings of the terms used in the argument is called a *deductive* argument. All other arguments are termed *inductive*. So all arguments have three parts—premise(s), inference, conclusion; and the difference between deduction and induction is the kind of inference. Let us take a look at some examples.

A *deductive* argument is one in which the inference is guaranteed by the meanings of the terms:

Premises: All bats are mammals.
               All mammals are warm-
               blooded.
Conclusion: Therefore, all bats are warm-
               blooded.

We know that this argument has to be correct just by looking at it. No research is necessary to show us that the conclusion *follows automatically* from the premises. This argument is what the logicians call a *valid argument,* by which they mean that the conclusion does follow from the premises; or more precisely, *if* the premises are true, then the conclusion must also be true. We must be careful to distinguish "truth" from "validity." Logic is an "arm-chair" science. The logician is concerned with the *connection* between the assertions. He is concerned only incidentally, if at all, with the ultimate truth of those assertions.

We might think of logic then as analogous in function to a computer. The computer generates outputs on the basis of inputs; if the input is correct (and the computer is functioning properly), then the output will also be correct. But if the input is wrong, then the output will be correct only as a matter of luck. So, too, the logical thinker takes the input which is given to him and he processes it; he says, in effect, "I myself know nothing about bats personally; but if the information you have given me is correct, then the conclusion is also correct." In deductive logic, we speak of arguments as being logical or illogical or, using the more technical terms, we speak of them as being valid or invalid. We never refer to an *argument* as being true or false. The statements used in making the argument may be true or false, but the deductive argument itself—the inference from premises to conclusion—can only be valid or invalid, logical or illogical, good or bad, but never true or false.

An *inductive* argument also moves from premises to a conclusion, but it uses a different kind of inference: a probable inference. For example:

Premise: My car will not start and the fuel gauge reads "empty."
Conclusion: Therefore, the car is probably out of gas.

Notice that here, unlike in our deductive argument, the conclusion does not follow with certainty; it is not guaranteed. The conclusion does seem to be likely or probable, but there are some gaps in the argument. It is possible, for example, that the fuel gauge is broken, or that there is fuel in the tank and the car will not start because something else is wrong. Since we have used the terms valid and invalid to apply to deductive arguments, we will not want to use them to apply to inductive arguments. Instead, we will speak of inductive inferences as being strong or weak, and we realize that no conclusion which follows inductively is guaranteed. Some inductive conclusions are very strong:

Premise: This is an ordinary coin I am tossing.
Conclusion: Therefore, it will not come to rest on its edge.

It is of course possible that the coin will land on its edge—but very, very unlikely. Some inductive conclusions are very weak:

Premise: This year the July Fourth picnic was rained out.

Conclusion: Therefore, every year the July Fourth picnic is rained out.

But regardless of the relative strength of the argument, both of these examples have the same inductive form. The conclusions do not follow from the premises as a matter of logic.

FINDING THE CONCLUSION

Locating the conclusion of an argument and defining its exact scope is the first step in evaluating the strength of any argument. You cannot begin to look for fallacies or other weaknesses in a line of reasoning or even find the line of reasoning until you have clearly identified the point the author wishes to prove. Any attempt to skip over this important step can only result in misunderstanding and confusion. We have all had the experience of discussing a point for some length of time only to say finally, "Oh, now I see what you were saying, and I agree with you." Of course, sometimes such misunderstandings are the fault of the speaker, who perhaps did not clearly state his position in the first place. This is particularly true in less formal discourse, such as conversation, where we have not carefully prepared our remarks before the discussion begins; but it can also occur in writing, though in the case of writing the proponent of a claim generally has the opportunity to consider his words carefully, and is therefore, one would hope, less likely to misstate his point. Often, however, the misunderstanding cannot be charged to the speaker or writer and the blame must be placed on the listener or the reader.

Careful thinkers will obviously want to know precisely what is being claimed in an argument they are examining. They know it is a waste of their mental energy to attack a point which has not been advanced by their opponents but is only the product of their own failure to pay careful attention. In order to help you become more sensitive to the importance of finding the exact point of an argument, we will discuss conclusions in two steps: (1) locating the main point of an argument, and (2) defining exactly the main point of any argument.

Locating the Main Point

Sometimes the main point of an argument is fairly easy to find—it is the last statement in the paragraph:

> Since this watch was manufactured in Switzerland, and all Swiss watches are reliable, <u>this watch must be reliable</u>.

Here the conclusion or the point of the line of reasoning is the part that is underlined. The argument also contains two premises: "This watch was manufactured in Switzerland" and "all Swiss watches are reliable." The same argument could be made, however, with the statements presented in a different order:

> <u>This watch must be reliable</u> since it was manufactured in Switzerland and all Swiss watches are reliable.
>
> or
>
> Since this watch was manufactured in Switzerland, <u>it must be reliable</u> because all Swiss watches are reliable.

So we cannot always count on the conclusion of the argument being the last sentence of the paragraph even though sometimes it is.

Instead, it is always necessary to ask, "What is the main point of this argument?" Or perhaps, "What is the author trying to prove here?" If the conclusion is not the last statement in a passage, it may be *signaled* by indicator words. We often use transitional words or phrases such as *therefore, hence, thus, so, it follows that, as a result,* and *consequently* to announce to the reader or listener that we are making an inference, that is, that we are moving from our premise(s) to our conclusion. For example:

> Ms. Slote has a Masters in Education, and she has twenty years of teaching experience, <u>therefore</u> (hence, thus, etc.) she is a good teacher.

Here the conclusion is "she is a good teacher," and the premises are "Ms. Slote has a Masters in Education" and "she has twenty years of teaching experience."

In some arguments the premises rather than the conclusion are signalled. Words which signal premises include *since, because, for,* and others which normally connect a dependent clause to an independent one. For example:

> <u>Since</u> Rex has been with the company twenty years and does such a good job, he <u>will probably receive a promotion</u>.
>
> or
>
> <u>Rex will probably receive a promotion</u> <u>because</u> he has been with the company twenty years and he does such a good job.
>
> or
>
> <u>If</u> Rex has been with the company twenty years and has done a good job, <u>he will probably receive a promotion</u>.

In each of the three examples just presented, the conclusion is "Rex will probably receive a promotion" and the premise is that "he has been with the company twenty years and does a good job."

Not all arguments, however, are broken down by the numbers, so to speak. Sometimes inattention on the part of the author or speaker or sometimes matters of style result in an argument which does not include a prominent signal of any sort. In such a case, the readers or listeners must use their judgments to answer the question, "What is the author or speaker trying to prove?" For example:

> We must reduce the amount of money we spend on space exploration. Right now, the Soviet Union is launching a massive military buildup, and we need the additional money to purchase military equipment to match the anticipated increase in Soviet strength.

In this argument there are no key words to announce the conclusion, nor is the conclusion the last sentence or statement made in the passage. Instead, the reader must ask, "What is the author trying to prove?" Is the author trying to *prove* that the Soviet Union is beginning a military buildup? No, because that statement is used as a premise in the larger argument, so it cannot be the conclusion. Is the main point that we must match the Soviet buildup? Again the answer is "no," because that, too, is an intermediate step on the way to some other conclusion. Is the author trying to prove that we must cut back on the budget for space exploration? The answer is "yes, that is the author's point." The other two statements are premises that lead the author to conclude that a cutback in space exploration is necessary.

Sometimes an argument may contain arguments within the main argument. Thus, the argument about the need for military expenditures might have included this sub-argument:

> The Soviets are now stockpiling titanium, a metal which is used in building airplanes. And each time the Soviet Union has stockpiled titanium it has launched a massive military buildup. So, right now, the Soviet Union is launching a massive military buildup.

Notice that now one of the premises of an earlier argument is the conclusion of a sub-argument. The conclusion of the sub-argument is "the Soviet Union . . . buildup," which has two explicit premises: "The Soviets are now stockpiling titanium" and "a stockpiling of titanium means a military buildup." So, in trying to find the main point of an argument one must also be alert to the possibility that an intermediate conclusion may also function as a premise in the main argument.

Defining the Main Point

Once the main point of the argument has been isolated it is necessary to take the second step of exactly defining that point. In particular, one must be attentive to any qualifying remarks made by the author. In this regard it will be helpful to ask three questions: (1) How great a claim (or limited a claim) is the author making? (2) Precisely what is the author talking about? And (3) What is the author's intention in making the claim?

The first of these questions reminds us that authors will frequently qualify their claims by using words such as some, all, none, never, always, everywhere, and sometimes. Thus, there is a big difference in the claims:

> <u>All</u> mammals live on land.
> <u>Most</u> mammals live on land.

The first is false, the second is true. Compare also:

> The United States and Russia have always been enemies.
> <u>For the past thirty years</u>, the United States and Russia have been enemies.

Again, the first statement is false and the second is true. Finally, compare:

> It is raining and the temperature is predicted to drop below 32° F; therefore it will *surely* snow.
> It is raining and the temperature is predicted to drop below 32° F; therefore it will *probably* snow.

The first is a much less cautious claim than the second, and if it failed to snow, the first claim would have been proved false, though not the second. The second statement claims only that it is probable that snow will follow, not that it definitely will. So someone could make the second claim and defend it when the snow failed to materialize by saying, "Well, I allowed for that in my original statement."

The second group of elements to pay attention to are the descriptive words used in a passage. Here we cannot even hope to provide a list, so the best we can do is present some examples.

> In nations which have a bicameral legislature, the speed with which legislation is passed is largely a function of the strength of executive leadership.

Notice here that the author makes a claim about "nations," so (at least without further information to license such an extension) it would be wrong to apply the author's reasoning to *states* (such as New York) which also have bicameral legislatures. Further, we would not want to conclude that the author believes that bicameral legislatures pass different laws from those passed by unicameral legislatures. The author mentions only the "speed" with which the laws are passed—not their content. Let us take another example:

> All of the passenger automobiles manufactured by Detroit automakers since 1975 have been equipped with seat belts.

We would not want to conclude from this statement that all *trucks* have also been equipped with seat belts since the author makes a claim only about *passenger automobiles*, nor would we want to conclude that *imported cars* have seat belts, for the author mentions Detroit-made cars only. Finally, here is yet another example in which the descriptive terms in the claim are intended to restrict the claim:

> No other major department store offers you a low price and a seventy-five-day warranty on parts and labor on this special edition of the XL-30 color television.

The tone of the ad is designed to create a very large impression on the hearer, but the precise claim made is fairly limited. First, the ad's claim is specifically restricted to a comparison of *department* stores, and *major* department stores at that. It is possible that some non-major department store offers a similar warranty and price; also it may be that another type of retail store, say, an electronics store, makes a similar offer. Second, other stores, department or otherwise, may offer a better deal on the product, say, a low price with a three-month warranty, and still the claim would stand—so long as no one else offered exactly a *seventy-five-day* warranty. Finally, the ad is restricted to a *special edition* of the television, so, depending on what that means, the ad may be even more restrictive in its claim.

The final point in understanding the conclusion is to be careful to distinguish between claims of fact and proposals of change. Do not assume that if an author claims to have found a problem, he also knows how to solve it. An author can make a claim about the cause of some event without believing that the event can be prevented or even that it ought to be prevented. For example, from the argument:

> Since the fifth-ward vote is crucial to Gordon's campaign, if Gordon fails to win over the ward leaders, he will be defeated in the election.

You cannot conclude that the author believes Gordon should or should not be elected. The author gives only a factual analysis, without endorsing or condemning either possible outcome. Also, from the argument:

> Each year the rotation of Earth slows a few tenths of a second. In several million years it will have stopped altogether, and life as we know it will no longer be able to survive on Earth.

You cannot conclude that the author wants to find a solution for the slowing of Earth's rotation. For all we know, the author thinks that the process is inevitable, or even desirable.

To summarize this discussion of conclusions, remember you must find the conclusion the author is aiming at by uncovering the structure of the argument. (Did the author try to prove this, and if so, did he use this as a premise of a further argument?) Then pay careful attention to the precise claim made by the conclusion.

FINDING THE PREMISES

In our discussion of conclusions, we implicitly treated the problem of finding the premises of an argument, for in separating the conclusion from the remainder of the paragraph, we also isolated those premises explicitly used by the author in constructing his chain of reasoning. In this section, we do not need to redo that analysis, but it will be useful if we describe three important kinds of assumptions an author might make—value judgments, factual assumptions, and definitional assumptions. Then we will discuss the significance of assumptions.

One very important kind of assumption is the *value judgment*. For example, if we argue that the city government should spend money to hire a crossing guard to protect schoolchildren walking to school, we have implicitly assumed that the lives of schoolchildren are important and, further that protecting these lives is a proper function of city government. Another kind of assumption is the *factual assumption*. For example, "The ball struck the window and the glass shattered." So the person who threw the ball broke the window. Here the explanation uses the factual assumption that it was the ball that broke the glass—and not some super ray fired by a Martian at the same time. Finally, a third group of assumptions, *definitional assumptions,* are those called into play when we use vague terms. For example, the person who threw the ball is to blame for the broken window, because a person is responsible for his misdeeds. Here the conclusion rests upon the assumption that throwing the ball is, by definition (at least under the circumstances), a misdeed.

With this in mind, we can turn to a discussion of the importance of assumptions in evaluating an argument. In our discussion of conclusions, we noticed that the conclusion of one argument may function as a premise of yet a further argument. With a little imagination, we could construct an argument in which there might be twenty, thirty, or even more intermediate links in the chain of reasoning joining the initial premise and the final conclusion. Of course, in practice our arguments are hardly ever so complicated. Usually, we require only three or four steps. For example, we may reason:

> Since there is snow on the ground, it must have snowed last night. If it snowed last night, then the temperature must have dropped below 32° F. The temperature drops below 32° F only in the winter. So, since there is snow on the ground, it must be winter here.

We can easily imagine also extending this string of situational assumptions in either direction. Instead of starting with "there is snow on the ground," we might have backed up one further step and reasoned, "If there is a snowman on the front lawn, it must be because there is snow on the ground"; and from the presence of the snowman on the front lawn we could have reached the conclusion that "it is winter here." Or we might extend the argument to yet another conclusion. Using the additional premise "If it is winter here, it is summer in Australia," we could reason from "there is a snowman on the front lawn" to "it is summer in Australia."

In practice, however, we do not extend our arguments indefinitely in either direction. We stop at the conclusion we had hoped to prove, and we begin from what seems to us to be a convenient and secure starting point: "If there is snow on the ground, then it must have snowed last night." Now it is obvious that the strength of an argument depends in a very important way upon the legitimacy of its assumptions; in fact, defeating an assumption is the most effective way of attacking any argument. Let us consider examples of arguments using our three types of assumptions.

A very simple factual assumption is the following:

Premises: If there is gasoline in the tank, my car will start.
I checked and there is gasoline in the tank.
Conclusion: Therefore, my car will start.

A very effective attack on this argument can be aimed at the first premise. One would want to object that the situational premise "if gas, then car starts" is unacceptable because it ignores the fact that there are other reasons the car may fail to start, e.g., the battery is dead, the distributor cap is wet, the engine was stolen. Now the conclusion "my car will start" no longer has any support. Of course it is possible that the car will start, but whether it does or not will not be determinable from the specific argument we have just defeated.

An example of a value judgment is the following:

Premises: The government should help people who might hurt themselves.
Cigarette smoking is harmful to people.
Conclusion: Therefore, the government ought to prevent people from smoking.

One way of attacking this argument is to attack the value judgment that the government ought to protect people from themselves. That might be done by talking about freedom or individual rights, and it will not be possible to clearly *defeat* the assumption of value. In our first argument, the assumption was a question of fact—causal laws in the physical universe—and could be resolved by empirical evidence. In arguments resting on value judgments, it may never be possible to get final agreement. But for purposes of evaluating the strength of an argument, one way of *pursuing the issue,* which is to say, one way of objecting to the argument, is to reject the value judgment upon which it rests.

Finally, a definitional assumption is similar to a valuational one:

Premises:　　An inexperienced person will not make an effective Supreme Court Justice.

A person with only ten years of legal practice is inexperienced.

Conclusion:　Therefore, a person with only ten years of legal practice will not make an effective Supreme Court Justice.

This argument is a valid deductive argument, but that does not mean it is unassailable as it applies to the real world. One way of attacking the argument is to question its second premise by insisting that ten years is long enough to make a person experienced. Of course, that might be disputed, but at least that is a possible line of attack on the argument. After all, if it could be *proved* that ten years of practice makes one experienced, then the conclusion of the argument must be considered to have been defeated.

Hidden Premises

In each of our three examples, the attack on the argument was fairly easy to find. To be sure, there were others available to us; but at the very least we knew one way of attacking the argument would be to question the assumptions on which it rested. Unfortunately, the attack is not always this easy to find because many times arguments are built upon hidden or concealed assumptions, and this is not necessarily because the proponent of the argument is intentionally hiding something which he knows will weaken his argument. Since an argument could be extended backward indefinitely (But why do you believe that? So why do you think that? What is your reason for that?), the starting point of an argument is always a bit arbitrary. Even someone who is giving what he thinks to be a correct and honest argument will make some assumptions that he does not explicitly acknowledge.

Argument:　　The ground is damp, so it must have rained last night.

Hidden premise:　Rain is the only thing that can cause the ground to become damp.

Argument:　　Homosexuality is a sin; therefore, there should be laws against such practices.

Hidden premise:　The government ought to enforce morality.

Argument:　　John is the perfect husband; he never cheats on his wife.

Hidden premise:　Any husband who does not cheat on his wife is a perfect husband.

So, in evaluating an argument, it is always important to be aware of the possibility of hidden assumptions which might be open to attack. This is particularly true if one finds an argument which on the surface appears to be logically correct, but reaches a conclusion which seems factually impossible, or one which seems valuationally or judgmentally absurd. In such a situation, it is a good idea to look for a hidden assumption which makes the argument work. Of course, even though the conclusion seems strange, it might just be correct, in which case careful thinkers admit that their initial reactions to the argument were wrong, and they change their minds. Similarly, a reasonable-appearing conclusion can be based on inadequate or wrong argumentation.

With regard to premises, then, we have learned that every argument rests upon them. An explanation of events usually rests upon factual premises, and a proposal for action rests upon value judgments. And both kinds of arguments will make definitional assumptions. It should also be kept in mind that since a complex argument is made of sub-arguments, a final factual conclusion may ultimately have a value judgment somewhere in the argument supporting it, and, by the same token, a final value judgment may have a factual premise somewhere in the argument supporting it. Many times the assumptions of an argument will not be explicitly mentioned by the author; they may be hidden. But whether an assumption is explicit or just implicit, it is of critical importance to the argument, and for this reason attacks on premises can be very powerful.

EVALUATING INFERENCES (INDUCTIVE)

In the preceding two sections, we described the importance of finding the conclusion and the premises of an argument. We now turn our attention to techniques for evaluating the inference which is supposed to link the conclusion to the premises. Our discussion of inductive inferences is a checklist of the most important kinds of fallacies that appear on the GRE. You should not, however, allow yourself to think that you can memorize the list and apply it mechanically to Logical Reasoning problems. The classification we present is somewhat artificial, and discretion is required in using it. We will discuss seven fallacies: the *ad hominem* attack, circular reasoning, appeals to irrelevant considerations, false cause, hasty generalization, ambiguity, and false analogy.

Ad Hominem Attack

This is any argument which is directed against the source of the claim rather than the claim itself. Since there are times when such attacks are useful, as when the credibility of the speaker is at issue, we must be careful to distinguish the illegitimate *ad hominem* attack from the legitimate attack on a person's credibility. An illegitimate *ad hominem* argument is one which ignores the merits of the issue in favor of an attempt to discredit the source of the argument where the credibility of the speaker is not at issue. For example:

> We should not accept Professor Smith's analysis of the causes of traffic accidents because we know that she has been unfaithful to her husband.

Setting aside such outlandish speculations as the possibility that Professor Smith has killed her husband in a fake accident, we can see that there is no connection between Smith's analysis of accidents and her infidelity to her husband. So this is an illegitimate attack. A student who wants to see further examples of such attacks need only read the daily newspaper with particular attention

to any political campaign or other political struggle. On the other hand, there are attacks on the credibility of speakers which are legitimate. We are all suspicious of the claims made by salespersons, and rightly so! More generally, it is legitimate to take account of any possible self-interest in making a statement. For example:

General: The Army needs more and bigger tanks. Even though they are expensive, they are vital to the nation's security.

Politician: And if I am elected governor, I will cut taxes and put an end to crime.

In these cases, it is not wrong to point out that the speaker's vision may be clouded by his own interest in the outcome of the matter.

Circular Reasoning

A second common fallacy is that of circular reasoning. Any argument which includes the conclusion it hopes to prove as one of its premises is fallacious because it is circular. For example:

> Beethoven was the greatest composer of all time because he wrote the greatest music of any composer, and he who composes the greatest music must be the greatest composer.

The conclusion of this argument is that Beethoven was the greatest composer of all time, but one of the premises of the argument is that he composed the greatest music, and the other premise states that that is the measure of greatness. The argument is fallacious, for there is really no argument for the conclusion at all, just a restatement of the conclusion.

Appeals to Irrelevant Considerations

A third type of fallacy which you might encounter is any appeal to irrelevant considerations. For example, an argument which appeals to the popularity of a position to prove the position is fallacious. For example:

Frederick must be the best choice for chairman because most people believe that he is the best person for the job.

That many people hold an opinion obviously does not guarantee its correctness—after all, many people once thought airplanes couldn't fly. Another appeal to an irrelevant consideration might be an illegitimate appeal to authority. For example:

The theory of evolution is only so much hogwash, and this is clearly proved by the fact that Professor Edwards, who got an M.A. in French Literature from Yale University, says so.

In this case, the authority is not an authority on the topic for which authority is needed. Now, there may be legitimate appeals to authority. For example:

Inflation erodes the standard of living of those persons who are retired and have fixed incomes such as savings or pensions; and Professor Jones, an economist who did a study on the harms of inflation, concluded that over 75% of retired people live on fixed incomes.

In this case, the appeal to authority is legitimate. We often must defer to the expertise of others, but we must be careful to select our sources of authority so that we find ones which are unbiased and truly expert.

False Cause

A fourth type of fallacy, and one of which ETS is fond, is the fallacy of the false cause. An argument which commits this error attributes a causal relationship between two events where none exists—or at least the relationship is misidentified. For example:

Every time the doorbell rings I find there is someone at the door. Therefore, it must be the case that the doorbell calls these people to my door.

Obviously, the causal link suggested here is backward. It is the presence of the person at the door which then leads to the ringing of the bell, not vice versa. A more serious example of the fallacy of the false cause is:

There were more air traffic fatalities in 1979 than there were in 1969; therefore, the airways are more dangerous today than they were ten years ago.

The difficulty with this argument is that it attributes the increase to a lack of safety when, in fact, it is probably attributable to an increase in air travel generally.

Hasty Generalization

A fifth fallacy is that of hasty generalization. In our discussion about the structure of an argument, where we distinguished inductive from deductive arguments, we remarked that the best one can hope for in an inductive argument is that it will *probably* be true. We pointed out that some arguments are very strong, while some are weak. A common weakness in an inductive argument is the hasty generalization—that is, basing a large conclusion on too little data. For example:

All four times I have visited Chicago it has rained; therefore, Chicago probably gets very little sunshine.

The rather obvious difficulty with the argument is that it moves from a small sample—four visits—to a very broad conclusion: Chicago gets little sunshine. Of course, generalizing on the basis of a sample or limited experience can be legitimate:

All five of the buses manufactured by Gutmann which we inspected have defective wheel mounts; therefore, some other buses manufactured by Gutmann probably have similar defects.

Admittedly this argument is not airtight. Perhaps the other uninspected buses do not have the same defect, but this second argument is much stronger than the first.

Ambiguity

A sixth fallacy is that of ambiguity. Anytime there is a shifting in the meaning of terms used in an argument, the argument has committed a fallacy of ambiguity. For example:

> Man is only one million years old. John is a man. Therefore, John is only one million years old.

The error of the argument is that it uses the word man as two different meanings. In the first occurrence man is used as a group; in the second occurrence man designates a particular individual. Another, less playful example:

> Sin occurs only when man fails to follow the will of God. But since God is all-powerful, what He wills must actually be. Therefore, it is impossible to deviate from the will of God, so there can be no sin in the world.

The equivocation here is in the word will. The first time it is used, the author intends that the will of God is God's wish and implies that it *is* possible to fail to comply with those wishes. In the second instance, the author uses the word will in a way which implies that such deviation is *not* possible. The argument reaches the conclusion that there is no sin in the world only by playing on these two senses of "will of God."

False Analogy

A seventh, and final, fallacy is that of false analogy. We do sometimes present legitimate arguments from analogy. For example:

> The government should pay more to its diplomats who work in countries with unstable governments. The work is more dangerous there than in stable countries. This is very similar to paying soldiers combat premiums if they are stationed in a war zone.

The argument here relies on an analogy between diplomats in a potentially dangerous country and soldiers in combat areas. Of course, the analogy is not perfect—no analogy can be more than an analogy—but some analogies are clearly so imperfect that they have no persuasive force. For example:

> People should have to be licensed before they are allowed to have children. After all, we require people who operate automobiles to be licensed.

In this case, the two situations—driving and having children—are so dissimilar that we would probably want to say they are not analogous at all—having children has nothing to do with driving.

While the ingenuity of the test-makers can result in Logical Reasoning problems that do not precisely fit these fallacies of induction, there will be very few problems on the test which have any other sort of inductive reasoning errors. The practice tests in this book contain many illustrations of each kind of problem, with full explanations. There are also problems that show how these different errors can be combined in one problem.

EVALUATING INFERENCES (DEDUCTIVE)

In the last section, we discussed some common inductive fallacies; in this section, we turn our attention to deductive reasoning. You will recall from the first section that a deductive inference differs from an inductive inference in that the deductive inference—if it is valid—is guaranteed by the meanings of the terms used in the argument. The argument form we most often associate with the study of logic is the syllogism, a term which will be familiar to anyone who has studied basic logic:

> All trees are plants.
> All redwoods are trees.
> Therefore, all redwoods are plants.

Ancient and medieval thinkers devoted a great deal of study to the various forms of syllogisms and other logical structures, and their treatments are full of technicalities—technicalities which we can safely ignore. All that one requires for the GRE is a working knowledge of the forms without all the jargon. Thus, although we have employed some technical terms in these materials, this was strictly for purposes of organization, and you need not commit these to memory. Our discussion will treat four groups of deductive arguments: direct inferences, syllogisms, implications, and relational sequences.

Direct Inferences

By a direct inference, we mean a conclusion which follows from a single premise. For example, from the statement "no birds are mammals" we can conclude "no mammals are birds," since there is no individual which is a member of both the group bird and the group mammal. From "no birds are mammals" we could also reach the conclusion that "all birds are not mammals," but this is really nothing more than a grammatical restructuring of the original form, whereas the statement "no mammals are birds" is actually an inference (it is a totally new claim).

Setting aside possible variations in grammatical structure ("no B are M" = "all B are not M," "some B are M" = "some B are not non-M," etc.), we may organize such assertions into four groups, depending on whether they make a claim about "some" on the one hand or, on the other hand, either "all" or "no" members of groups and whether they are "affirmative" or "negative." In order to save space and also to show that our techniques are generally applicable—that is, not dependent on any particular content—we will find it convenient to use capital letters as substitutes for terms. Thus, "all birds are mammals" becomes "all B are M," which could also stand for "all bats are myopic," but nothing is lost in the translation since we are concerned with the formal relations and not the actually substantive or content relations between sentences. Using capital letters, we set up the following scheme so that we have sentences which make affirmative claims about all of a group, negative claims about all of a group, affirmative claims about part of a group, and negative claims about part of a group.

General

Affirmative { All A are B.   No A are B.   Some A are B.   Some A are not B } Negative

Specific

Before we proceed any further, there is one very important point regarding use of the word

some which we must make. The GRE follows the logician in using the word some to mean only at least one. So a statement of the sort "some A are B" means *only* that there is at least one A which is also a B. The statement does *not* imply, as well, that there are some A's which are not B's. Similarly, the statement "some A are not B" means that there is at least one A which is not a B; it does *not* imply that there are also some A's which are B's. Notice that this is at variance with our ordinary conversational usage of the word some. In conversation a person who states "some of the students have not turned in their term papers" probably wants us to understand that some students have turned in their papers, but this additional implication depends upon the context in which the statement is made. Strictly speaking, as a matter of logic, the statement "some students have not turned in their term papers" means just that—some students have not turned in their term papers—and does not further mean that some students have turned in their term papers. It is conceivable that no student has turned in a term paper; still, the statement "some students have not turned in their term papers" would be accurate. Even though it only partially describes the situation—*some* as opposed to *all*—it does give an accurate description of that part it describes.

Perhaps a little thought experiment will clarify the point. Imagine that you are standing in front of an opaque container with marbles in it, and you are asked to pick marbles blindly from the container. You pick a marble which happens to be red. At that point we ask you to describe the color or colors of the marbles in the container. You can say, "some of the marbles are red" (setting aside the difficulty that the red marble is no longer in the container, for we are talking about the marble population without regard to such technicalities). This statement is obviously true since you hold the proof in your hand. Now, if you draw the remaining marbles from the container, one of two situations will develop. Either all of the remaining marbles will prove to be red, in which case you can say, "all of the marbles are red," or not all of the remaining marbles will prove to be red in which case you can say, "some of the marbles are not red." But since our first statement, "some of the marbles are red," was proven to be true by the fact that you held a red marble in your hand, and since a true statement does not become false with the passing of time (again, setting aside such difficulties as demonstrative pronouns, such as "this is a live cat," and time-dependent statements, such as "Nixon is *now* President"), the statement "some marbles are red" remains true even if it should turn out that "all marbles are red." What this shows is that the statement "some marbles are red" is not logically inconsistent with—does not contradict—the statement "all marbles are red." Similarly, "all M are R" not only does not contradict "some M are R," but the latter statement must actually follow from the former. A moment's reflection will also show that a similar relationship exists between the statements of the negative form, "some M are not R" and "no M are R." The only possible exception would be a Logical Reasoning question which consists of a discussion, in the form of a transcript, between two persons. If the tone is *very* conversational, one of the speakers *might* mean some in its everyday sense.

To return to our four kinds of statements:

Using Venn or circle diagrams. It is also fairly apparent that there are interrelationships among all the statement forms. For example, if "all A are B" is true, then both "no A are B" and "some A are not B" must be false. One way of exhibiting these relationships is through the use of Venn or circle diagrams. (These are also used in Analytical Reasoning problems.) We will use a circle to mark off a "logical area." So a circle which we label "A" separates the field of the page into two spaces, A and not-A. The interior of the circle is the space where all A's are located, and anything located outside the circle is not an A (it is a non-A):

Diagram 1:

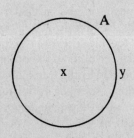

In Diagram 1, *x* is an A, but *y* is not an A, which is to say *y* is a non-A. Now, if we draw two overlapping circles, we can represent not only two groups, A and B, but also the intersection of those groups:

Diagram 2:

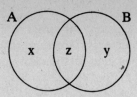

In Diagram 2, *x* is an A, which is not, however, a B; *y* is a B, which is not, however, an A; and *z* is something that is both A and B. Using diagrams, we can draw up a table to exhibit the interrelationships of our four statements: If it is true that "all A are B," then it is not possible for something to be an "A but not also a B," so we blot out that portion of our circle diagrams which contains the area "A but not also B":

Diagram 3:

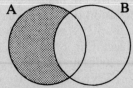

Now, if it is true that "all A are B," then:

"no A are B" is false. (All the A are B.)
"some A are B" is true. (All the A are within the B circle.)
"some A are not B" is false. (That area is eliminated.)

If it is false that "all A are B," that might be because "no A are B":

Diagram 4:

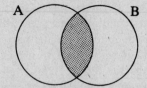

However, it might also be because "some, though not all, A are not B":

Diagram 5:

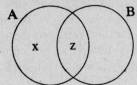

Both situations are consistent with "all A are B" being a false statement. So, if it is false that "all A are B," then:

"no A are B" might be true or false. (We cannot choose between Diagram 4 and Diagram 5.)
"some A are B" might be true or false. (We have no basis for choice.)
"some A are not B" is true. (This is the case with both Diagram 4 and Diagram 5.)

If it is true that "no A are B," then there is no overlap between the two:

Diagram 6:

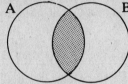

So, "all A are B" is false. (There is no overlap.)
"some A are B" is false. (There is no overlap.)
"some A are not B" is true. (That part is left open.)

But if "no A are B" is false, that might be because "all A are B":

Diagram 7:

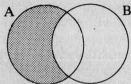

But it might equally well be because "some, though not all, A are B":

Diagram 8:

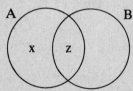

Therefore, "all A are B" might be true or false. (There is no basis for choice.)
"some A are B" is true. (See Diagrams 7 and 8.)
"some A are not B" might be true or false. (There is no basis for choice between diagrams.)
If it is true that "some A are B,"

Diagram 9:

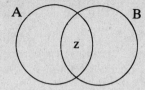

then, "all A are B" might be true or false. (See discussion of *some.*)
"no A are B" is false. (See Diagram 9.)
"some A are not B" might be true or false. (See discussion of *some.*)
If it is false that "some A are B," this can only be because there is no overlap between the two circles:

Diagram 10:

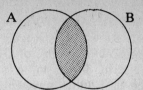

Therefore, "all A are B" is false. (There is no overlap at all.)
"no A are B" is true. (See Diagram 10.)
"some A are not B" is true. (That area is left open.)
If it is true that "some A are not B":

Diagram 11:

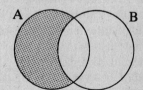

then, "all A are B" is false. (Shown by the *x* in Diagram 11.)
"no A are B" might be true or false. (The *x* does not close off the overlap of A and B, but then again we do not know that there are individuals with the characteristic A and B.)
"some A are B" might be true or false. (See the reasoning just given for "no A are B.")
If it is false, that "some A are not B":

Diagram 12:

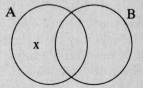

then the area of the A circle which does not overlap the B circle is empty, as shown by Diagram 12. Therefore:

"all A are B" is true. (The one is contained in the other.)
"no A are B" is false. (The one is contained in the other.)
"some A are B" is true. (In fact, all are, but see our discussion of *some.*)

A word of caution: Do not memorize all the relationships just presented. The circle diagrams will provide an aid for thought and practice, and they will also prove useful in our study of the second form of deductive inference: the syllogism.

Syllogisms. Technically, a syllogism is supposed to be constructed from three statements, two of which are assumptions, and the third the conclusion. However, since the test is not a test of technical knowledge of logical forms, it may use the term "syllogism" in a looser way, applying that term to an argument with four, or perhaps even five, statements. For example:

> All trees are plants.
> All redwoods are trees.
> This tree is a redwood.
> Therefore, this tree is a plant.

If we analyzed this argument in a technical way, we would say it includes not one, but two syllogisms—the conclusion of the first forming a premise of the second:

> All trees are plants.
> All redwoods are trees.
> Therefore, all redwoods are plants.

> All redwoods are plants.
> This tree is a redwood.
> Therefore, this tree is a plant.

But for purposes of the test, you can call the first argument a syllogism as well.

Of course, a syllogism can be constructed using negative statements as well. Now, depending on which statement forms are used and how the terms are arranged, we can construct many different syllogisms. Not all of these, however, would be valid. For example, the following syllogism is valid:

> All A are B.
> No B are C.
> Therefore, no A are C.

We can show its validity by using a variation on our circle diagrams. Now we have three terms instead of two. Remember that two terms or groups might be related in three ways: an A which is not a B, a B which is not an A, and something which is both A and B. When we add our third term, C, we have to allow for something which is a C, but not an A or B; something which is a C and B, but not an A; something which is a C and A, but not a B; and something which is C, B, and A. In other words, there are seven possible combinations.

1. an A, but not a B or C
2. a B, but not an A or C
3. an A and B, but not a C
4. a C, but not an A or B
5. an A and C, but not a B
6. a B and C, but not an A
7. an A, B and C

These seven possibilities can be shown on a three-circle diagram:

Diagram 13:

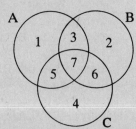

Using our three-circle diagrams, we can show the validity of the syllogism constructed at the beginning of this paragraph. Since our first premise states that "all A are B," we can eliminate the areas of the diagram that are within the A circle but not within the B circle. This corresponds to areas 1 and 5 in Diagram 13.

Diagram 14:

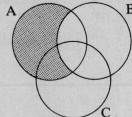

Our second premise states that "no B are C," so we must eliminate those areas corresponding to 6 and 7 on Diagram 13, which allow that something might be a B and a C. (Notice that something which is an A, B, and C—area 7—is automatically something which is a B and a C.)

Diagram 15:

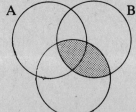

Now if we enter both premises one and two on the same diagram, we have:

Diagram 16:

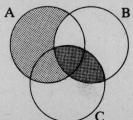

The conclusion of our syllogism asserts that "no A are C," and our diagram confirms this. The only area of A left open is within the B circle; all A but non-B areas have been erased.

Another example of a valid syllogism is:

All A are B.
Some C are A.
Therefore, some C are B.

In a syllogism in which one of the propositions uses some and the other proposition uses all or no, it is a good idea to enter the all or no information first. So we enter first, "all A are B":

Diagram 17:

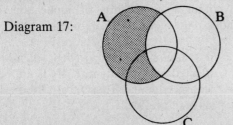

Then we enter "some C are A" by putting an *x* in the area of C and A. Since there is only one such area left, the *x* must be placed so:

Diagram 18:

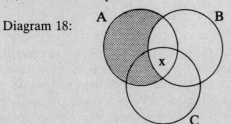

Now the diagram shows the validity of our syllogism: there is at least one C which is also a B.

An example of an *invalid* deductive argument is the syllogism which has the form:

No A are B.
No B are C.
Therefore, no A are C.

We enter the first and second premises:

Diagram 19:

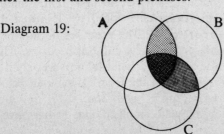

But then we observe that the overlap of A and C is still open, so our conclusion that "no A are C" is not warranted, that is, it does not definitely follow from our premises. So, too, the following argument is invalid:

Some A are B.
Some B are not C.
Therefore, some A are not C.

Since there is no premise which begins with all or no, we are forced to start with a premise which begins with some. We take premise number one first, "some A are B," but we have no way of determining whether or not the A's which are B's are also C's. So we will leave open those possibilities:

Diagram 20:

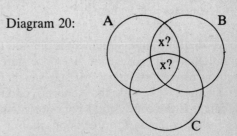

Now we add the information "some B are not C," again keeping open the possibility that that something might be a B and an A or a B but not an A:

Diagram 21:

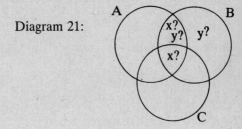

Diagram 21 shows that the conclusion, "some A are not C," does not follow from our premises because we do not definitely know the locations of our *x*'s or *y*'s, as indicated by the question marks.

Implications

Thus far, we have treated deductive inferences which involved relationships among terms. Now we treat a group of deductive arguments, which we will call implications, that are based on the connections of *sentences* as opposed to *terms*. An example of an implication argument is:

> If John is elected president, Mary is elected vice-president, and if Mary is elected vice-president, Paul is elected secretary. Therefore, if John is elected president, Paul is elected secretary.

If we employ our capital letters again, this time using each letter to stand for a clause (or sentence), we can see that our argument has the form:

> If J, then M.
> If M, then P.
> Therefore, if J, then P.

Notice that our entire argument is phrased in the conditional. Our conclusion does not state that "Paul is elected secretary." It states rather that "*if* J, then P," and that entire conditional statement is the conclusion of our argument.

Another common form of implication is illustrated by the argument:

> If John is elected president, Mary is elected vice-president. John is elected president. Therefore, Mary is elected vice-president.

The form of the argument is:

> If J, then M.
> J.
> Therefore, M.

Notice that this argument differs from our conditional argument, for our second premise definitely asserts "John is elected president." Now, since the validity of an argument is dependent only upon its form, it is clear that any argument which has this form is valid. This form of argument must not, however, be confused with the superficially similar but invalid form:

> If A, then B.
> B.
> Therefore, A.

The first premise asserts only that A is followed by B, it does not assert that an occurrence of situation B is necessarily preceded by an occurrence of situation A. For example, the following argument is not valid.

> If an object is made of clay, it will not burn. This object will not burn. Therefore, this object is made of clay.

There are many objects which will not burn and which are not made of clay—those made of steel for example. So *any* argument which has this form is invalid.

Another common form of implication that is valid is illustrated by the argument:

> If John is elected president, then Mary is elected vice-president. Mary is not elected vice-president. Therefore, John is not elected president.

It has the form:

> If J, then M.
> Not M.
> Therefore, not J.

Since the first premise states that an occurrence of situation J will be followed by an occurrence of situation M, and since the second premise tells us that situation M did not occur, we can logically conclude that situation J did not occur, for if J had occurred, so, too, M would have occurred. A similar, but invalid, argument form is illustrated by the argument:

> If John is elected president, then Mary is elected vice-president. John is not elected president. Therefore, Mary is not elected vice-president.

That this argument is invalid is demonstrated by the consideration that the first premise states only that an occurrence of J is followed by an occurrence of M. The premises do not establish that M can occur *only* if J also occurs. The first premise says "if J, then M," not "M only if J." So any argument of the form "If A, then B. Not A. Therefore, not B" is *invalid*.

Not all valid implicational forms have been

shown; our illustrations are intended to illustrate the technique of substituting capital letters for sentences. This allows us to isolate the general *form* of an argument, which makes analyzing or comparing that form easier.

Relational Sequences

There is a final group of deductive arguments, which we call relational sequences. A simple example is provided by the argument:

A is greater than B.
B is greater than C.
Therefore, A is greater than C.

Since these arguments are susceptible to treatment by using pictorial devices, we have treated them in the section on Analytical Reasoning, where such devices are introduced.

LOGICAL REASONING TEST STRATEGY

As we indicated earlier, the difficulty with the Logical Reasoning question is that there is such a variety of question stems that it is difficult to provide a mechanical procedure for approaching such problems. The following tips, however, may help make our somewhat abstract discussion of logic easier to apply to actual problems.

Logical Reasoning questions will usually be either by themselves or in pairs. This means that there will be one short passage or paragraph and one or two questions associated with it. Occasionally, there might be three Logical Reasoning questions based on one short passage, but that is rare. In any case, the Logical Reasoning questions can be distinguished from the Analytical Reasoning questions by the fact that the passage associated with them will be some sort of argument, while the Analytical Reasoning question sets will be based on some descriptive situation with several conditions, relationships or propositions.

Preview question stem. The first point of attack in the Logical Reasoning question is to read the question stem (the part to which the question mark is attached) before reading the paragraph or sample argument. The reason for this suggestion is easily explained. There are many different questions which one might ask about an argument: "How can it be strengthened?" "How can it be weakened?" "What are its assumptions?" "How is the argument developed?" and so on. If you read an argument without focusing your attention on some aspect of it, all of these aspects of argumentation (and even more) are likely to come to mind. Unfortunately, this is distracting. The most efficient way to handle the Logical Reasoning questions is to read the stem of the question first. Let that guide you in what to look for as you read.

Find the conclusion. This is always helpful, even when it is merely a descriptive statement. Keep in mind the importance of finding the exact conclusion for structuring the argument and assessing its strengths or weaknesses.

Attack the answer choices. The differences between the answer choices often help you isolate the issues in the problem. Attack the answer choices by:

1. always reading all the answer choices
2. eliminating obviously incorrect choices
3. contrasting remaining choices to isolate the relevant issues

Remember that you are only trying to choose the best answer. The best is often not perfect, and the less than best—and thus incorrect—answers often have some merit.

For special Logical Reasoning questions. Many of the Logical Reasoning questions are straightforward questions about how to attack and defend arguments. Some questions, however, are ETS' inventions and involve special twists of thinking. To assist you in answering some of these, keep in mind the following points:

• For a question that asks, "Which of the following arguments is most similar?" remember that you are not supposed to correct the argument. You are supposed to find an answer choice with a similar structure—even if the original argument contains a fallacy. Also, be careful to notice exactly what is to be paralleled—all of an argument, one speaker, or whatever.

- For a question involving deductive reasoning, try using a Venn (circle) diagram, a relational line, or some other pictorial device. Venns may also be helpful for some AR question sets.

- When the question stem asks for the identification of assumptions, it is seeking implicit or unstated premises, which—like all premises— are necessary to the argument.

- When the question stem asks for weakening ideas, it is usually a matter of attacking implicit assumptions that justify the application of the evidence to the conclusion(s).

- When the question stem asks for strengthening ideas, the correct answer might be merely an explicit statement of a previously implicit premise.

- When the question stem asks what the second person in an exchange has interpreted the first person to mean, two things are important: (1) The second person has *mis*interpreted the first person and, thus, (2) the correct answer must relate to the second person's comments, not to those of the first.

- *Cave Distractum:* Watch out for *superficial* similarities of subject matter between answer choices and argument. Wrong answers often mention irrelevant details.

PART THREE

5 FULL-LENGTH PRACTICE EXAMINATIONS

ANSWER SHEET—PRACTICE EXAMINATION 1

Section I

1 Ⓐ Ⓑ Ⓒ Ⓓ Ⓔ   8 Ⓐ Ⓑ Ⓒ Ⓓ Ⓔ   15 Ⓐ Ⓑ Ⓒ Ⓓ Ⓔ   22 Ⓐ Ⓑ Ⓒ Ⓓ Ⓔ   29 Ⓐ Ⓑ Ⓒ Ⓓ Ⓔ   36 Ⓐ Ⓑ Ⓒ Ⓓ Ⓔ

2 Ⓐ Ⓑ Ⓒ Ⓓ Ⓔ   9 Ⓐ Ⓑ Ⓒ Ⓓ Ⓔ   16 Ⓐ Ⓑ Ⓒ Ⓓ Ⓔ   23 Ⓐ Ⓑ Ⓒ Ⓓ Ⓔ   30 Ⓐ Ⓑ Ⓒ Ⓓ Ⓔ   37 Ⓐ Ⓑ Ⓒ Ⓓ Ⓔ

3 Ⓐ Ⓑ Ⓒ Ⓓ Ⓔ   10 Ⓐ Ⓑ Ⓒ Ⓓ Ⓔ   17 Ⓐ Ⓑ Ⓒ Ⓓ Ⓔ   24 Ⓐ Ⓑ Ⓒ Ⓓ Ⓔ   31 Ⓐ Ⓑ Ⓒ Ⓓ Ⓔ   38 Ⓐ Ⓑ Ⓒ Ⓓ Ⓔ

4 Ⓐ Ⓑ Ⓒ Ⓓ Ⓔ   11 Ⓐ Ⓑ Ⓒ Ⓓ Ⓔ   18 Ⓐ Ⓑ Ⓒ Ⓓ Ⓔ   25 Ⓐ Ⓑ Ⓒ Ⓓ Ⓔ   32 Ⓐ Ⓑ Ⓒ Ⓓ Ⓔ

5 Ⓐ Ⓑ Ⓒ Ⓓ Ⓔ   12 Ⓐ Ⓑ Ⓒ Ⓓ Ⓔ   19 Ⓐ Ⓑ Ⓒ Ⓓ Ⓔ   26 Ⓐ Ⓑ Ⓒ Ⓓ Ⓔ   33 Ⓐ Ⓑ Ⓒ Ⓓ Ⓔ

6 Ⓐ Ⓑ Ⓒ Ⓓ Ⓔ   13 Ⓐ Ⓑ Ⓒ Ⓓ Ⓔ   20 Ⓐ Ⓑ Ⓒ Ⓓ Ⓔ   27 Ⓐ Ⓑ Ⓒ Ⓓ Ⓔ   34 Ⓐ Ⓑ Ⓒ Ⓓ Ⓔ

7 Ⓐ Ⓑ Ⓒ Ⓓ Ⓔ   14 Ⓐ Ⓑ Ⓒ Ⓓ Ⓔ   21 Ⓐ Ⓑ Ⓒ Ⓓ Ⓔ   28 Ⓐ Ⓑ Ⓒ Ⓓ Ⓔ   35 Ⓐ Ⓑ Ⓒ Ⓓ Ⓔ

Section II

1 Ⓐ Ⓑ Ⓒ Ⓓ Ⓔ   8 Ⓐ Ⓑ Ⓒ Ⓓ Ⓔ   15 Ⓐ Ⓑ Ⓒ Ⓓ Ⓔ   22 Ⓐ Ⓑ Ⓒ Ⓓ Ⓔ   29 Ⓐ Ⓑ Ⓒ Ⓓ Ⓔ   36 Ⓐ Ⓑ Ⓒ Ⓓ Ⓔ

2 Ⓐ Ⓑ Ⓒ Ⓓ Ⓔ   9 Ⓐ Ⓑ Ⓒ Ⓓ Ⓔ   16 Ⓐ Ⓑ Ⓒ Ⓓ Ⓔ   23 Ⓐ Ⓑ Ⓒ Ⓓ Ⓔ   30 Ⓐ Ⓑ Ⓒ Ⓓ Ⓔ   37 Ⓐ Ⓑ Ⓒ Ⓓ Ⓔ

3 Ⓐ Ⓑ Ⓒ Ⓓ Ⓔ   10 Ⓐ Ⓑ Ⓒ Ⓓ Ⓔ   17 Ⓐ Ⓑ Ⓒ Ⓓ Ⓔ   24 Ⓐ Ⓑ Ⓒ Ⓓ Ⓔ   31 Ⓐ Ⓑ Ⓒ Ⓓ Ⓔ   38 Ⓐ Ⓑ Ⓒ Ⓓ Ⓔ

4 Ⓐ Ⓑ Ⓒ Ⓓ Ⓔ   11 Ⓐ Ⓑ Ⓒ Ⓓ Ⓔ   18 Ⓐ Ⓑ Ⓒ Ⓓ Ⓔ   25 Ⓐ Ⓑ Ⓒ Ⓓ Ⓔ   32 Ⓐ Ⓑ Ⓒ Ⓓ Ⓔ

5 Ⓐ Ⓑ Ⓒ Ⓓ Ⓔ   12 Ⓐ Ⓑ Ⓒ Ⓓ Ⓔ   19 Ⓐ Ⓑ Ⓒ Ⓓ Ⓔ   26 Ⓐ Ⓑ Ⓒ Ⓓ Ⓔ   33 Ⓐ Ⓑ Ⓒ Ⓓ Ⓔ

6 Ⓐ Ⓑ Ⓒ Ⓓ Ⓔ   13 Ⓐ Ⓑ Ⓒ Ⓓ Ⓔ   20 Ⓐ Ⓑ Ⓒ Ⓓ Ⓔ   27 Ⓐ Ⓑ Ⓒ Ⓓ Ⓔ   34 Ⓐ Ⓑ Ⓒ Ⓓ Ⓔ

7 Ⓐ Ⓑ Ⓒ Ⓓ Ⓔ   14 Ⓐ Ⓑ Ⓒ Ⓓ Ⓔ   21 Ⓐ Ⓑ Ⓒ Ⓓ Ⓔ   28 Ⓐ Ⓑ Ⓒ Ⓓ Ⓔ   35 Ⓐ Ⓑ Ⓒ Ⓓ Ⓔ

Section III

1 Ⓐ Ⓑ Ⓒ Ⓓ Ⓔ   6 Ⓐ Ⓑ Ⓒ Ⓓ Ⓔ   11 Ⓐ Ⓑ Ⓒ Ⓓ Ⓔ   16 Ⓐ Ⓑ Ⓒ Ⓓ Ⓔ   21 Ⓐ Ⓑ Ⓒ Ⓓ Ⓔ   26 Ⓐ Ⓑ Ⓒ Ⓓ Ⓔ

2 Ⓐ Ⓑ Ⓒ Ⓓ Ⓔ   7 Ⓐ Ⓑ Ⓒ Ⓓ Ⓔ   12 Ⓐ Ⓑ Ⓒ Ⓓ Ⓔ   17 Ⓐ Ⓑ Ⓒ Ⓓ Ⓔ   22 Ⓐ Ⓑ Ⓒ Ⓓ Ⓔ   27 Ⓐ Ⓑ Ⓒ Ⓓ Ⓔ

3 Ⓐ Ⓑ Ⓒ Ⓓ Ⓔ   8 Ⓐ Ⓑ Ⓒ Ⓓ Ⓔ   13 Ⓐ Ⓑ Ⓒ Ⓓ Ⓔ   18 Ⓐ Ⓑ Ⓒ Ⓓ Ⓔ   23 Ⓐ Ⓑ Ⓒ Ⓓ Ⓔ   28 Ⓐ Ⓑ Ⓒ Ⓓ Ⓔ

4 Ⓐ Ⓑ Ⓒ Ⓓ Ⓔ   9 Ⓐ Ⓑ Ⓒ Ⓓ Ⓔ   14 Ⓐ Ⓑ Ⓒ Ⓓ Ⓔ   19 Ⓐ Ⓑ Ⓒ Ⓓ Ⓔ   24 Ⓐ Ⓑ Ⓒ Ⓓ Ⓔ   29 Ⓐ Ⓑ Ⓒ Ⓓ Ⓔ

5 Ⓐ Ⓑ Ⓒ Ⓓ Ⓔ   10 Ⓐ Ⓑ Ⓒ Ⓓ Ⓔ   15 Ⓐ Ⓑ Ⓒ Ⓓ Ⓔ   20 Ⓐ Ⓑ Ⓒ Ⓓ Ⓔ   25 Ⓐ Ⓑ Ⓒ Ⓓ Ⓔ   30 Ⓐ Ⓑ Ⓒ Ⓓ Ⓔ

Section IV

1 Ⓐ Ⓑ Ⓒ Ⓓ Ⓔ 6 Ⓐ Ⓑ Ⓒ Ⓓ Ⓔ 11 Ⓐ Ⓑ Ⓒ Ⓓ Ⓔ 16 Ⓐ Ⓑ Ⓒ Ⓓ Ⓔ 21 Ⓐ Ⓑ Ⓒ Ⓓ Ⓔ 26 Ⓐ Ⓑ Ⓒ Ⓓ Ⓔ

2 Ⓐ Ⓑ Ⓒ Ⓓ Ⓔ 7 Ⓐ Ⓑ Ⓒ Ⓓ Ⓔ 12 Ⓐ Ⓑ Ⓒ Ⓓ Ⓔ 17 Ⓐ Ⓑ Ⓒ Ⓓ Ⓔ 22 Ⓐ Ⓑ Ⓒ Ⓓ Ⓔ 27 Ⓐ Ⓑ Ⓒ Ⓓ Ⓔ

3 Ⓐ Ⓑ Ⓒ Ⓓ Ⓔ 8 Ⓐ Ⓑ Ⓒ Ⓓ Ⓔ 13 Ⓐ Ⓑ Ⓒ Ⓓ Ⓔ 18 Ⓐ Ⓑ Ⓒ Ⓓ Ⓔ 23 Ⓐ Ⓑ Ⓒ Ⓓ Ⓔ 28 Ⓐ Ⓑ Ⓒ Ⓓ Ⓔ

4 Ⓐ Ⓑ Ⓒ Ⓓ Ⓔ 9 Ⓐ Ⓑ Ⓒ Ⓓ Ⓔ 14 Ⓐ Ⓑ Ⓒ Ⓓ Ⓔ 19 Ⓐ Ⓑ Ⓒ Ⓓ Ⓔ 24 Ⓐ Ⓑ Ⓒ Ⓓ Ⓔ 29 Ⓐ Ⓑ Ⓒ Ⓓ Ⓔ

5 Ⓐ Ⓑ Ⓒ Ⓓ Ⓔ 10 Ⓐ Ⓑ Ⓒ Ⓓ Ⓔ 15 Ⓐ Ⓑ Ⓒ Ⓓ Ⓔ 20 Ⓐ Ⓑ Ⓒ Ⓓ Ⓔ 25 Ⓐ Ⓑ Ⓒ Ⓓ Ⓔ 30 Ⓐ Ⓑ Ⓒ Ⓓ Ⓔ

Section V

1 Ⓐ Ⓑ Ⓒ Ⓓ Ⓔ 6 Ⓐ Ⓑ Ⓒ Ⓓ Ⓔ 11 Ⓐ Ⓑ Ⓒ Ⓓ Ⓔ 16 Ⓐ Ⓑ Ⓒ Ⓓ Ⓔ 21 Ⓐ Ⓑ Ⓒ Ⓓ Ⓔ

2 Ⓐ Ⓑ Ⓒ Ⓓ Ⓔ 7 Ⓐ Ⓑ Ⓒ Ⓓ Ⓔ 12 Ⓐ Ⓑ Ⓒ Ⓓ Ⓔ 17 Ⓐ Ⓑ Ⓒ Ⓓ Ⓔ 22 Ⓐ Ⓑ Ⓒ Ⓓ Ⓔ

3 Ⓐ Ⓑ Ⓒ Ⓓ Ⓔ 8 Ⓐ Ⓑ Ⓒ Ⓓ Ⓔ 13 Ⓐ Ⓑ Ⓒ Ⓓ Ⓔ 18 Ⓐ Ⓑ Ⓒ Ⓓ Ⓔ 23 Ⓐ Ⓑ Ⓒ Ⓓ Ⓔ

4 Ⓐ Ⓑ Ⓒ Ⓓ Ⓔ 9 Ⓐ Ⓑ Ⓒ Ⓓ Ⓔ 14 Ⓐ Ⓑ Ⓒ Ⓓ Ⓔ 19 Ⓐ Ⓑ Ⓒ Ⓓ Ⓔ 24 Ⓐ Ⓑ Ⓒ Ⓓ Ⓔ

5 Ⓐ Ⓑ Ⓒ Ⓓ Ⓔ 10 Ⓐ Ⓑ Ⓒ Ⓓ Ⓔ 15 Ⓐ Ⓑ Ⓒ Ⓓ Ⓔ 20 Ⓐ Ⓑ Ⓒ Ⓓ Ⓔ 25 Ⓐ Ⓑ Ⓒ Ⓓ Ⓔ

Section VI

1 Ⓐ Ⓑ Ⓒ Ⓓ Ⓔ 6 Ⓐ Ⓑ Ⓒ Ⓓ Ⓔ 11 Ⓐ Ⓑ Ⓒ Ⓓ Ⓔ 16 Ⓐ Ⓑ Ⓒ Ⓓ Ⓔ 21 Ⓐ Ⓑ Ⓒ Ⓓ Ⓔ

2 Ⓐ Ⓑ Ⓒ Ⓓ Ⓔ 7 Ⓐ Ⓑ Ⓒ Ⓓ Ⓔ 12 Ⓐ Ⓑ Ⓒ Ⓓ Ⓔ 17 Ⓐ Ⓑ Ⓒ Ⓓ Ⓔ 22 Ⓐ Ⓑ Ⓒ Ⓓ Ⓔ

3 Ⓐ Ⓑ Ⓒ Ⓓ Ⓔ 8 Ⓐ Ⓑ Ⓒ Ⓓ Ⓔ 13 Ⓐ Ⓑ Ⓒ Ⓓ Ⓔ 18 Ⓐ Ⓑ Ⓒ Ⓓ Ⓔ 23 Ⓐ Ⓑ Ⓒ Ⓓ Ⓔ

4 Ⓐ Ⓑ Ⓒ Ⓓ Ⓔ 9 Ⓐ Ⓑ Ⓒ Ⓓ Ⓔ 14 Ⓐ Ⓑ Ⓒ Ⓓ Ⓔ 19 Ⓐ Ⓑ Ⓒ Ⓓ Ⓔ 24 Ⓐ Ⓑ Ⓒ Ⓓ Ⓔ

5 Ⓐ Ⓑ Ⓒ Ⓓ Ⓔ 10 Ⓐ Ⓑ Ⓒ Ⓓ Ⓔ 15 Ⓐ Ⓑ Ⓒ Ⓓ Ⓔ 20 Ⓐ Ⓑ Ⓒ Ⓓ Ⓔ 25 Ⓐ Ⓑ Ⓒ Ⓓ Ⓔ

Section VII

1 Ⓐ Ⓑ Ⓒ Ⓓ Ⓔ 8 Ⓐ Ⓑ Ⓒ Ⓓ Ⓔ 15 Ⓐ Ⓑ Ⓒ Ⓓ Ⓔ 22 Ⓐ Ⓑ Ⓒ Ⓓ Ⓔ 29 Ⓐ Ⓑ Ⓒ Ⓓ Ⓔ 36 Ⓐ Ⓑ Ⓒ Ⓓ Ⓔ

2 Ⓐ Ⓑ Ⓒ Ⓓ Ⓔ 9 Ⓐ Ⓑ Ⓒ Ⓓ Ⓔ 16 Ⓐ Ⓑ Ⓒ Ⓓ Ⓔ 23 Ⓐ Ⓑ Ⓒ Ⓓ Ⓔ 30 Ⓐ Ⓑ Ⓒ Ⓓ Ⓔ 37 Ⓐ Ⓑ Ⓒ Ⓓ Ⓔ

3 Ⓐ Ⓑ Ⓒ Ⓓ Ⓔ 10 Ⓐ Ⓑ Ⓒ Ⓓ Ⓔ 17 Ⓐ Ⓑ Ⓒ Ⓓ Ⓔ 24 Ⓐ Ⓑ Ⓒ Ⓓ Ⓔ 31 Ⓐ Ⓑ Ⓒ Ⓓ Ⓔ 38 Ⓐ Ⓑ Ⓒ Ⓓ Ⓔ

4 Ⓐ Ⓑ Ⓒ Ⓓ Ⓔ 11 Ⓐ Ⓑ Ⓒ Ⓓ Ⓔ 18 Ⓐ Ⓑ Ⓒ Ⓓ Ⓔ 25 Ⓐ Ⓑ Ⓒ Ⓓ Ⓔ 32 Ⓐ Ⓑ Ⓒ Ⓓ Ⓔ

5 Ⓐ Ⓑ Ⓒ Ⓓ Ⓔ 12 Ⓐ Ⓑ Ⓒ Ⓓ Ⓔ 19 Ⓐ Ⓑ Ⓒ Ⓓ Ⓔ 26 Ⓐ Ⓑ Ⓒ Ⓓ Ⓔ 33 Ⓐ Ⓑ Ⓒ Ⓓ Ⓔ

6 Ⓐ Ⓑ Ⓒ Ⓓ Ⓔ 13 Ⓐ Ⓑ Ⓒ Ⓓ Ⓔ 20 Ⓐ Ⓑ Ⓒ Ⓓ Ⓔ 27 Ⓐ Ⓑ Ⓒ Ⓓ Ⓔ 34 Ⓐ Ⓑ Ⓒ Ⓓ Ⓔ

7 Ⓐ Ⓑ Ⓒ Ⓓ Ⓔ 14 Ⓐ Ⓑ Ⓒ Ⓓ Ⓔ 21 Ⓐ Ⓑ Ⓒ Ⓓ Ⓔ 28 Ⓐ Ⓑ Ⓒ Ⓓ Ⓔ 35 Ⓐ Ⓑ Ⓒ Ⓓ Ⓔ

PRACTICE EXAMINATION 1

SECTION I

30 minutes
38 questions

Directions: Each of the questions below contains one or more blank spaces, each blank indicating an omitted word. Each sentence is followed by five (5) lettered words or sets of words. Read and determine the general sense of each sentence. Then choose the word or set of words which, when inserted in the sentence, best fits the meaning of the sentence.

1. Even when his reputation was in _____, almost everyone was willing to admit that he had genius.
   - (A) ascendancy
   - (B) retaliation
   - (C) eclipse
   - (D) differentiation
   - (E) rebuttal

2. How many of the books published each year in the United States make a(n) _____ contribution toward improving men's _____ with each other?
   - (A) important—problems
   - (B) standardized—customs
   - (C) referential—rudeness
   - (D) squalid—generalities
   - (E) significant—relationships

3. No one can say for sure how _____ the awards have been.
   - (A) determined
   - (B) effective
   - (C) reducible
   - (D) effervescent
   - (E) inborn

4. The medieval church condemned man's partaking in _____ pleasures.
   - (A) educational
   - (B) ascetic
   - (C) ecclesiastical
   - (D) sensual
   - (E) hermetic

5. The fact that a business has _____ does not create an _____ for it to give away its wealth.
   - (A) prospered—imperative
   - (B) halted—impossibility
   - (C) incorporated—impulse
   - (D) supplemented—obligation
   - (E) accumulated—aspect

6. When I watch drivers routinely slam their cars to a halt, _____ take corners on two wheels, and blunder wildly over construction potholes and railroad crossings, I consider it a _____ to automotive design that cars don't shake apart far sooner.
   - (A) gradually—curiosity
   - (B) sensibly—blessing
   - (C) gracefully—misfortune
   - (D) habitually—tribute
   - (E) religiously—instruction

7. On the ground, liquid hydrogen must be stored in large stainless-steel tanks with double walls filled with _____ and evacuated to a high vacuum.
   - (A) stones
   - (B) air
   - (C) insulation
   - (D) aluminum
   - (E) water

201

Directions: In each of the following questions, you are given a related pair of words or phrases in capital letters. Each capitalized pair is followed by five (5) lettered pairs of words or phrases. Choose the pair which best expresses a relationship similar to that expressed by the original pair.

8. PLUTOCRAT : WEALTH ::
   (A) autocrat : individual
   (B) theocrat : religion
   (C) oligarch : ruler
   (D) democrat : popularity
   (E) republican : conservation

9. HANDCUFFS : PRISONER ::
   (A) manacles : penitentiary
   (B) shoes : feet
   (C) leash : dog
   (D) tail : kite
   (E) ring : finger

10. JAVELIN : CANNONBALL ::
    (A) discus : sling
    (B) throw : catch
    (C) spear : bullet
    (D) arrow : shotput
    (E) Greek : Spanish

11. IMP : CHERUB ::
    (A) low : high
    (B) nettle : irk
    (C) bad : good
    (D) devil : angel
    (E) fork : arrow

12. RADIO : PHONOGRAPH ::
    (A) letter : book
    (B) picture : painting
    (C) television : show
    (D) movie : photograph
    (E) brush : canvas

13. IMMIGRATE : COUNTRY ::
    (A) alien : port
    (B) emigrate : ship
    (C) move : placement
    (D) patriot : flag
    (E) enlist : army

13. URGE : INSIST ::
    (A) pursue : hound
    (B) refuse : deny

(C) expunge : purge
(D) request : demand
(E) impulse : push

15. GRAPNEL : ANCHOR ::
    (A) thong : pouch
    (B) hook : gaff
    (C) ship : steam
    (D) hold : cargo
    (E) single : serene

16. INDICTED : SENTENCED ::
    (A) impeached : removed
    (B) arraigned : tried
    (C) elected : served
    (D) guilty : punished
    (E) empaneled : closeted

Directions: Below each of the following passages, you will find questions or incomplete statements about the passage. Each statement or question is followed by lettered words or expressions. Select the word or expression that most satisfactorily completes each statement or answers each question in accordance with the meaning of the passage. After you have chosen the best answer, blacken the corresponding space on the answer sheet.

It has always been difficult for the philosopher or scientist to fit time into his view of the universe. Prior to Einsteinian physics, there was no truly adequate formulation of the relationship of time to the other forces in the universe, even though some empirical equations included time quantities. However, even the Einsteinian formulation is not perhaps totally adequate to the job of fitting time into the proper relationship with the other dimensions, as they are called, of space. The primary problem arises in relation to things which might be going faster than the speed of light, or have other strange properties.

Examination of the Lorentz-Fitzgerald formulas yields the interesting speculation that if something did actually exceed the speed of light it would have its mass expressed as an imaginary number and would seem to be going backwards in time. The barrier to exceeding the speed of light is the apparent need to have an infinite quantity of mass moved at exactly the speed of light. If this situation could be leaped over in a large quantum jump—which seems highly unlikely for masses that are large in normal circumstances—then the other side may be achieveable.

The idea of going backwards in time is derived from the existence of a time vector that is negative, although just what this might mean to our senses in the unlikely circumstance of our experiencing this state cannot be conjectured.

There have been, in fact, some observations of particle chambers which have led some scientists to speculate that a particle called the tachyon may exist with the trans-light properties we have just discussed.

The difficulties of imagining and coping with these potential implications of our mathematical models points out the importance of studying alternative methods of notation for advanced physics. Professor Zuckerkandl, in his book *Sound and Symbol*, hypothesizes that it might be better to express the relationships found in quantum mechanics through the use of a notation derived from musical notations. To oversimplify greatly, he argues that music has always given time a special relationship to other factors or parameters or dimensions. Therefore, it might be a more useful language in which to express the relationships in physics where time again has a special role to play, and cannot be treated as just another dimension.

The point of this, or any other alternative to the current methods of describing basic physical processes, is that time does not appear—either by common experience or sophisticated scientific understanding—to be the same sort of dimension or parameter as physical dimensions, and is deserving of completely special treatment, in a system of notation designed to accomplish that goal.

One approach would be to consider time to be a field effect governed by the application of energy to mass—that is to say, by the interaction of different forms of energy, if you wish to keep in mind the equivalence of mass and energy. The movement of any normal sort of mass is bound to produce a field effect that we call positive time. An imaginary mass would produce a negative time field effect. This is not at variance with Einstein's theories, since the "faster" a given mass moves the more energy was applied to it and the greater would be the field effect. The time effects predicted by Einstein and confirmed by

experience are, it seems, consonant with this concept.

17. The "sound" of Professor Zuckerkandl's book title probably refers to
    (A) the music of the spheres
    (B) music in the abstract
    (C) musical notation
    (D) the seemingly musical sounds produced by tachyons
    (E) quantum mechanics

18. The passage supports the inference that
    (A) Einstein's theory of relativity is wrong
    (B) the Lorentz-Fitzgerald formulas contradict Einstein's theories
    (C) time travel is clearly possible
    (D) tachyons do not have the same sort of mass as any other particles
    (E) it is impossible to travel at precisely the speed of light

19. The tone of the passage is
    (A) critical but hopeful
    (B) hopeful but suspicious
    (C) suspicious but speculative
    (D) speculative but hopeful
    (E) impossible to characterize

20. The central idea of the passage can be best described as being which of the following?
    (A) Anomalies in theoretical physics notation permit intriguing hypotheses and indicate the need for refined notation of the time dimension.
    (B) New observations require the development of new theories and new methods of describing the new theories.
    (C) Einsteinian physics can be much improved on in its treatment of tachyons.
    (D) Zuckerkandl's theories of tachyon formation are preferable to Einstein's.
    (E) Time requires a more imaginative approach than tachyons.

21. According to the author, it is too soon to
    (A) call Beethoven a physicist
    (B) adopt proposals such as Zuckerkandl's
    (C) plan for time travel
    (D) study particle chambers for tachyon traces
    (E) attempt to improve current notation

22. It can be inferred that the author sees Zuckerkandl as believing that mathematics is a(n)
    (A) necessary evil
    (B) language
    (C) musical notation
    (D) great hindrance to full understanding of physics
    (E) difficult field of study

23. In the first sentence, the author refers to "philosopher" as well as to "scientist" because
    (A) this is part of a larger work
    (B) philosophers study all things
    (C) physicists get Doctor of Philosophy degrees
    (D) the study of the methods of any field is a philosophical question
    (E) the nature of time is a basic question in philosophy as well as physics

24. When the passage says the "particle called the tachyon may exist," the reader may infer that
    (A) scientists often speak in riddles
    (B) the tachyon was named before it existed
    (C) tachyons are imaginary in existence as well as mass
    (D) the tachyon was probably named when its existence was predicted by theory, but its existence was not yet known
    (E) many scientific ideas may not exist in fact

A legendary island in the Atlantic Ocean beyond the Pillars of Hercules was first mentioned by Plato in the *Timaeus*. Atlantis was a fabulously beautiful and prosperous land, the seat of an empire nine thousand years before Solon. Its inhabitants overran part of Europe and Africa, Athens alone being able to defy them. Because of the impiety of its people, the island was destroyed by an earthquake and inundation. The legend may have existed before Plato and may have sprung from the concept of Homer's Elysium. The possibility that such an island once existed has caused much speculation, resulting in a theory that pre-Columbian civilizations in America were established by colonists from the lost island.

25. The title below that best expresses the ideas of this passage is
    (A) A Persistent Myth
    (B) Geography According to Plato
    (C) The First Discoverers of America
    (D) Buried Civilizations
    (E) A Labor of Hercules

26. According to the passage, we may safely conclude that the inhabitants of Atlantis
    (A) were known personally to Homer
    (B) were ruled by Plato
    (C) were a religious and superstitious people
    (D) used the name Columbus for America
    (E) left no recorded evidence of their civilization

27. According to the legend, Atlantis was destroyed because the inhabitants
    (A) failed to obtain an adequate food supply
    (B) failed to conquer Greece
    (C) failed to respect their gods
    (D) believed in Homer's Elysium
    (E) had become too prosperous

Directions: Each of the following questions consists of a word printed in capital letters, followed by five (5) lettered words or phrases. Select the word or phrase which is most nearly *opposite* to the capitalized word in meaning.

28. RETALIATE:
    (A) maintain serenity
    (B) stand tall
    (C) turn the other cheek
    (D) improve relations with
    (E) entertain the views of

29. ANALYSIS:
    (A) dialysis
    (B) electrolysis
    (C) parenthesis
    (D) synthesis
    (E) emphasis

30. PEREMPTORY:
    (A) humble
    (B) resistant
    (C) weak

(D) spontaneous
(E) deferential

31. SALACIOUS:
    (A) expensive
    (B) wholesome
    (C) empty
    (D) religious
    (E) private

32. INSOLVENT:
    (A) physically pure
    (B) financially stable
    (C) metaphysically correct
    (D) chemically active
    (E) emotionally strong

33. HOMOGENEOUS:
    (A) parsimonious
    (B) consciousness
    (C) variegated
    (D) loquacious
    (E) differential

34. AMALGAMATE:
    (A) recriminate
    (B) procrastinate
    (C) scintillate

(D) segregate
(E) enjoin

35. TEMERITY:
    (A) imbroglio
    (B) diffidence
    (C) cognomen
    (D) effervescence
    (E) composure

36. MUTATION:
    (A) constancy
    (B) decency
    (C) adolescent
    (D) clangorous
    (E) unamended

37. SYBARITIC:
    (A) foolish
    (B) obdurate
    (C) consistent
    (D) austere
    (E) conservative

38. PROSAIC:
    (A) fulsome
    (B) mundane
    (C) extraordinary
    (D) certain
    (E) gregarious

STOP

END OF SECTION. IF YOU HAVE ANY TIME LEFT, GO
OVER YOUR WORK IN THIS SECTION ONLY. DO NOT
WORK IN ANY OTHER SECTION OF THE TEST.

SECTION II

30 minutes
38 questions

Directions: Each of the questions below contains one or more blank spaces, each blank indicating an omitted word. Each sentence is followed by five (5) lettered words or sets of words. Read and determine the general sense of each sentence. Then choose the word or set of words which, when inserted in the sentence, best fits the meaning of the sentence.

1. The professor _____ contemporary journalism for being too _____.
   (A) berated—childish
   (B) lauded—voyeuristic
   (C) criticized—authentic
   (D) requited—responsible
   (E) attacked—important

2. Rattling his newspaper to show his _____, the husband made known his _____ of his wife's new breakfast table.
   (A) calm—disposition
   (B) irritation—approval
   (C) duplicity—ingenuousness
   (D) anger—disapproval
   (E) opinion—character

3. His remarks were _____ and _____, indicative of his keen and incisive mind.
   (A) unsentimental—deliberate
   (B) ingenuous—noteworthy
   (C) impartial—apolitical
   (D) trenchant—penetrating
   (E) apish—dramatic

4. The _____ of this poisonous algae has caused the _____ of many kinds of fish.
   (A) proliferation—exodus
   (B) genesis—genocide
   (C) vagrancy—death
   (D) affects—loss
   (E) morality—decline

5. The new machine failed to _____ the garbage; as a result, the kitchen was filled to bursting with smelly leftovers.

   (A) expand
   (B) compact
   (C) produce
   (D) criticize
   (E) procrastinate

6. According to legend, Daniel Webster made a _____ with Satan, but managed to talk his way out of it at the last moment.
   (A) economy
   (B) standard
   (C) trawler
   (D) van
   (E) compact

7. When her purse fell overboard, Sally lost her _____, keys, wallet, and cigarettes.
   (A) vehicle
   (B) piano
   (C) compact
   (D) compost
   (E) complexion

Directions: In each of the following questions, you are given a related pair of words or phrases in capital letters. Each capitalized pair is followed by five (5) lettered pairs of words or phrases. Choose the pair which best expresses a relationship similar to that expressed by the original pair.

8. MORALITY : LEGALITY ::
   (A) home : court
   (B) man : law
   (C) mayoralty : gubernatorial
   (D) priest : jury
   (E) sin : crime

9. ELLIPSE : CURVE ::
   (A) stutter : speech
   (B) triangle : base
   (C) revolution : distance
   (D) square : polygon
   (E) circumference : ball

10. SUGAR : SACCHARIN ::
    (A) candy : cake

(B)   hog : lard
(C)   cane : sugar
(D)   spice : pepper
(E)   butter : margarine

11.   REQUEST : ORDER ::
(A)   reply : respond
(B)   regard : reject
(C)   suggest : require
(D)   wish : crave
(E)   measure : ecstasy

12.   WATER : FAUCET ::
(A)   fuel : throttle
(B)   liquid : solid
(C)   kitchen : sink
(D)   steam : pipe
(E)   leak : lumber

13.   FLASK : BOTTLE ::
(A)   whiskey : milk
(B)   metal : glass
(C)   powder : liquid
(D)   quart : pint
(E)   brochure : tome

14.   CALIBER : RIFLE ::
(A)   quality : shoot
(B)   compass : bore
(C)   army : navy
(D)   gauge : rails
(E)   cavalry : infantry

15.   CHOP : MINCE ::
(A)   fry : bake
(B)   meat : cake
(C)   axe : mallet
(D)   cut : walk
(E)   stir : beat

16.   PECCADILLO : CRIME ::
(A)   district attorney : criminal
(B)   hesitate : procrastinate
(C)   armadillo : shield
(D)   bushel : peck
(E)   sheriff : jail

Directions: Below each of the following passages, you will find questions or incomplete statements about the passage. Each statement or question is followed by lettered words or expressions. Select the word or expression that most satisfactorily completes each statement or answers each question in accordance with the meaning of the passage. After you have chosen the best answer, blacken the corresponding space on the answer sheet.

The vegetative forms of most bacteria are killed by drying in air, although the different species exhibit pronounced differences in their resistance. The tubercle bacillus is one of the more resistant, and vibrio cholera is one of the more sensitive to drying. In general, the encapsulated organisms are more resistant than the non-encapsulated forms. Spores are quite resistant to drying; the spores of the anthrax bacillus, for example, will germinate after remaining in a dry condition for ten years or more. The resistance of the pathogenic forms causing disease of the upper respiratory tract is of particular interest in connection with airborne infection, for the length of time that a droplet remains infective is a result, primarily, of the resistance of the particular microorganism to drying.

17.   The passage uses the term "vegetative forms" to refer to
(A)   plants that infest human habitations
(B)   the growing stage of the bacteria as opposed to the dormant stage
(C)   the fact that bacteria are really vegetables
(D)   the similarities between some bacteria and most vegetables
(E)   the difficulty in classifying the types of bacteria

18.   According to the passage, the risk of infection from airborne microorganisms would likely be greater during a(n)
(A)   heat wave
(B)   ice storm
(C)   windless period
(D)   time of high humidity
(E)   shortage of fuel oil

19.   It may be inferred from the passage that
(A)   bacteria can be most easily killed by removal of moisture
(B)   drying out a house will eliminate the risk of airborne infection

    (C)   hot-air heating is better than steam heating because steam heating uses water

    (D)   spores are incapable of producing bacteria

    (E)   none of the above

20. Tuberculosis is highly infectious because

    (A)   an airborne disease of the upper respiratory tract is easily spread to those coming in contact with a patient

    (B)   droplets of sputum remain infective for a long time due to the resistance of the organisms to drying

    (C)   spores are resistant to drying

    (D)   the causative organism is encapsulated

    (E)   none of these

Foods are overwhelmingly the most advertised group of all consumer products in the United States. Food products lead in expenditures for network and spot television advertisements, discount coupons, trading stamps, contests, and other forms of premium advertising. In other media—newspapers, magazines, newspaper supplements, billboards, and radio—food advertising expenditures rank near the top. Food manufacturers spend more on advertising than any other manufacturing group, and the nation's grocery stores rank first among all retailers.

Throughout the 1970's, highly processed foods have accounted for the bulk of total advertising. Almost all coupons, electronic advertising, national printed media advertising, consumer premiums (other than trading stamps) as well as most push promotion come from processed and packaged food products. In 1978, breakfast cereals, soft drinks, candy and other desserts, oils and salad dressings, coffee, and prepared foods accounted for only an estimated 20 percent of the consumer food dollar. Yet these items accounted for about one-half of all media advertising.

By contrast, highly perishable foods such as unprocessed meats, poultry, fish and eggs, fruits and vegetables, and dairy products accounted for over half of the consumer food-at-home dollar. Yet these products accounted for less than 8 percent of national media advertising in 1978, and virtually no discount coupons. These products tend to be most heavily advertised by the retail sector in local newspapers, where they account for an estimated 40 percent of retail grocery newspaper ads.

When measured against total food-at-home expenditures, total measured food advertising accounts for between 3 to 3.7 cents out of every dollar spent on food in the nation's grocery stores. A little less than one cent of this amount is accounted for by electronic advertising (mostly television) while incentives account for 0.6 cents. The printed media accounts for 0.5 cents and about one-third of one cent is comprised of discount coupon redemptions. The estimate for the cost of push promotion ranges from 0.7 to 1.4 cents. This range is necessary because of the difficulty in separating nonpromotional aspects of direct selling—transportation, technical, and other related services.

Against this gross consumer cost must be weighed the joint products or services provided by advertising. In the case of electronic advertising, the consumer who views commercial television receives entertainment, while readers of magazines and newspapers receive reduced prices on these publications. The consumer pays directly for some premiums, but also receives nonfood merchandise as an incentive to purchase the product. The "benefits" must, therefore, be subtracted from the gross cost to the consumer to fully assess the net cost of advertising.

Also significant are the impacts of advertising on food demand, nutrition, and competition among food manufacturers. The bulk of manufacturers' advertising is concentrated on a small portion of consumer food products. Has advertising changed the consumption of these highly processed products relative to more perishable foods such as meats, produce, and dairy products? Has the nutritional content of U.S. food consumption been influenced by food advertising? Has competition among manufacturers and retailers been enhanced or weakened by advertising? These are important questions and warrant continued research.

21. The author's attitude toward advertising can be characterized as

    (A)   admiring

    (B)   condemning

    (C)   uncertain

    (D)   ambivalent

    (E)   inquisitive

22. As used in the passage, the term "push promotion" means

    (A)   coupon redemption

(B) retail advertising

(C) advertising in trade journals

(D) direct selling

(E) none of the above

23. The author implies that advertising costs

(A) are greater for restaurants than for at-home foods

(B) should be discounted by the benefits of advertising to the consumer

(C) are much higher in the United States than anywhere else in the world

(D) for prepared foods are considerably higher than for natural foods for all media

(E) cause highly processed foods to outsell unprocessed, fresh foods

24. The purpose of the article is to

(A) warn about rising food advertising costs

(B) let experts see how overextended food advertising has become

(C) describe the costs of food advertising and the issues yet to be understood about its effects

(D) congratulate the food industry on its effective advertising

(E) calculate the final balance sheet for food advertising

25. All of the following are stated or implied to be important topics for further research EXCEPT

(A) effects of advertising on food and nutrient consumption patterns

(B) effects of advertising on food manufacturer competitive patterns

(C) effects of advertising on meat consumption patterns

(D) effects of advertising on out-of-home eating patterns

(E) effects of advertising on "junk" food consumption patterns

26. According to the passage, all of the following are definitely false EXCEPT

(A) more food is advertised in newspapers than on television

(B) less money is spent advertising food than automobiles

(C) more of the food advertising budget is

spent on push promotion than on television ads

(D) less money is spent on food store advertising than on clothing store ads

(E) food advertising is the leading group in radio advertising

27. If it were discovered that the nutritional content of the U.S. food supply were degraded by the advertising of highly processed foods and such advertising was totally banned, which of the following possible result of the ban could be inferred from the passage?

(A) The subscription costs of publications might rise.

(B) The cost of cable television might rise.

(C) The cost of free television might rise.

(D) Fewer consumers would watch certain television shows.

(E) No possible effect can be forecast based on the passage.

Directions: Each of the following questions consists of a word printed in capital letters, followed by five (5) lettered words or phrases. Select the word or phrase that is most nearly *opposite* to the capitalized word in meaning.

28. INTRANSIGENT:

(A) impassable

(B) conciliatory

(C) harsh

(D) fly-by-night

(E) corroborative

29. INGENUOUS:

(A) granite-like

(B) slow-witted

(C) talented

(D) devious

(E) humanitarian

30. CANARD:

(A) rebuttal

(B) truth

(C) image

(D) flattery

(E) blasphemy

31. DISINTERESTED:

(A) opposed

(B) avid

(C) superficial
(D) related
(E) partial

32. PROPITIATE:
    (A) anger
    (B) depart
    (C) hurt
    (D) applaud
    (E) promote

33. ABSOLVE:
    (A) muddy
    (B) blame
    (C) free
    (D) repent
    (E) recant

34. HEDONIST:
    (A) female
    (B) martinet
    (C) scientist
    (D) intellectual
    (E) puritan

35. CRETIN:
    (A) moron

(B) seer
(C) genius
(D) scholar
(E) talent

36. DECANT:
    (A) level off
    (B) upset greatly
    (C) tap
    (D) slosh out
    (E) cork firmly

37. ARRANT:
    (A) humble
    (B) deceptive
    (C) partial
    (D) wise
    (E) intrepid

38. WASTREL:
    (A) conservator
    (B) prodigal
    (C) lutist
    (D) noble
    (E) phantasm

STOP

END OF SECTION. IF YOU HAVE ANY TIME LEFT, GO
OVER YOUR WORK IN THIS SECTION ONLY. DO NOT
WORK IN ANY OTHER SECTION OF THE TEST.

SECTION III

30 minutes
30 questions

Directions: For each of the following questions two quantities are given, one in Column A and one in Column B. Compare the two quantities and mark your answer sheet with the correct lettered conclusion. These are your options:
   A: If the quantity in column A is the greater;
   B: if the quantity in Column B is the greater;
   C: if the two quantities are equal;
   D: if the relationship cannot be determined from the information given.
Common Information: In any question, information applying to both columns is centered between the columns and above the quantities in columns A and B. The common information applies to both columns. Any symbol that appears in both columns represents the same idea or quantity in both columns.

Numbers: All numbers used are real numbers.
Figures: Assume that the position of points, angles, regions and so forth are in the order shown. Figures are assumed to lie in a plane unless otherwise indicated. Figures accompanying questions are intended to provide information you can use in answering the questions. However, unless a note states that a figure is drawn to scale, you should solve the problems by using your knowledge of mathematics and *not* by estimating sizes by sight or measurement.
Lines: Assume that lines shown as straight are indeed straight.

	COLUMN A	COLUMN B
1.	5% of 36	36% of 5
2.	$\sqrt{15}$	$\sqrt{5} + \sqrt{10}$

3.
$$(346 \times 23) + p = 34.731$$
$$(346 \times 23) + q = 35.124$$

	p	q

4.

$$x° < y°$$
PQRS is a rectangle

	PT	TQ

5.
$$x > 0$$

	x^2	2x

6.	$\dfrac{4}{5} - \dfrac{3}{4}$	$\dfrac{1}{20}$
7.	the ratio 3:13	the ratio 13:51

8.
Let S_n be defined by the equation:
$$S_n = 3n + 2$$

	$S_5 + S_4$	$S_9 + S_8$

9.	the cost of ten pounds of meat at $2.50 per pound.	the cost of five kilograms of meat at $5.00 per kilogram.
10.	$\dfrac{10}{10,000}$	$\dfrac{1000}{1,000,000}$

COLUMN A   COLUMN B

11.

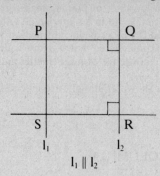

$l_1 \parallel l_2$

$\overline{PQ}$	$\overline{QR}$

12. | the number of pears in a cubical box with a side of 24 inches | the number of potatoes in a cubical box with a side of 36 inches |

13.
$$\frac{4x^2 + 3x + 2x^2 + 2x = 3x^2 + 2x + 3x^2 + 2x + 3}{x^2}$$
$$9$$

14. $n \cdot 1 \cdot 1$ $n + 1 + 1$

15.

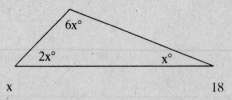

x 18

Directions: For each of the following questions, select the best of the answer choices and blacken the corresponding space on your answer sheet.

Numbers: All numbers used are real numbers.

Figures: The diagrams and figures that accompany these questions are for the purpose of providing information useful in answering the question. Unless it is stated that a specific figure is not drawn to scale, the diagrams and figures are drawn as accurately as possible. All figures are in a plane unless otherwise indicated.

16. From the time 6:15 P.M. to the time 7:45 P.M. of the same day, the minute hand of a standard clock describes an arc of
   (A) 30°
   (B) 90°
   (C) 180°

(D) 540°
(E) 910°

17. Which of the following fractions is the LEAST?
   (A) $\frac{7}{8}$
   (B) $\frac{7}{12}$
   (C) $\frac{8}{9}$
   (D) $\frac{1}{2}$
   (E) $\frac{6}{17}$

18. The length of each side of a square is $\frac{3x}{4} + 1$.
   What is the perimeter of the square?
   (A) $x + 1$
   (B) $3x + 1$

(C) 3x + 4

(D) $\frac{9}{16}x^2 + \frac{3}{2}x + 1$

(E) It cannot be determined from the information given.

19. A truck departed from Newton at 11:53 A.M. and arrived in Far City, 240 miles away, at 4:41 P.M. on the same day. What was the approximate average speed of the truck on this trip?

(A) $\frac{5640}{5}$ MPH

(B) $\frac{16}{1200}$ MPH

(C) 50 MPH

(D) $\frac{240}{288}$ MPH

(E) $\frac{1494}{240}$ MPH

20. If m, n, o and p are real numbers, each of the following expressions equals m(nop) EXCEPT

(A) (op)(mn)
(B) ponm
(C) p(onm)
(D) (mp)(no)
(E) (mn)(mo)(mp)

Questions 21–25 are based on the following graphs:

US PLANE CRASHES

(Total passenger-miles in billions)

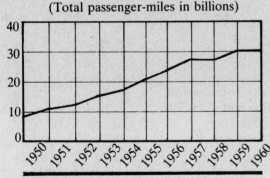

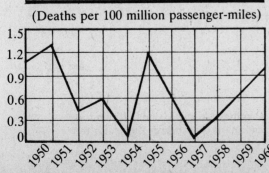

(Deaths per 100 million passenger-miles)

21. Which of the following conclusions may be inferred from the graphs?

  I. The highest rate of passenger deaths per mile travelled during the period covered by the graphs occured in 1951.

 II. The largest yearly increase in deaths per mile travelled occurred in the period 1954 to 1955.

III. The rate of passenger deaths per mile travelled was approximately the same in both 1954 and 1957.

(A) I only
(B) II only
(C) I and II only
(D) III only
(E) I, II, and III

22. In which year did the longest uninterrupted period of increase in the rate of passenger deaths per mile travelled finally end?
(A) 1951
(B) 1953
(C) 1955
(D) 1957
(E) 1960

23. How many fatalities were reported in the year 1955?
(A) 20 billion
(B) 1.2 million
(C) 240,000
(D) 2000
(E) 240

24. The greatest number of fatalities were recorded in which year?
(A) 1960
(B) 1957
(C) 1955
(D) 1953
(E) 1951

25. In which year did the greatest number of passengers travel by air?
(A) 1960
(B) 1955
(C) 1953
(D) 1951
(E) Cannot be determined from the information given.

ABCD is a square

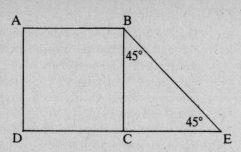

26. If the area of the triangle BCE is 8, what is the area of the square ABCD?
    (A) 16
    (B) 82
    (C) 8
    (D) 4
    (E) 22

27. The diagonal of the floor of a rectangular closet is $7\frac{1}{2}$ feet. The shorter side of the closet is $4\frac{1}{2}$ feet. What is the area of the closet in square feet?
    (A) 37
    (B) 27
    (C) $\frac{54}{4}$
    (D) $\frac{21}{4}$
    (E) 5

28. If the ratio of women to men in a meeting is 4 to 1, what percent of the persons in the meeting are men?
    (A) 20%
    (B) 25%
    (C) $33\frac{1}{3}$%
    (D) 80%
    (E) 100%

29. Which of the following fractions expressed in the form $\frac{p}{q}$ is most nearly approximated by the decimal .PQ, where P is the tenths' digit and Q is the hundredths' digit?
    (A) $\frac{1}{8}$
    (B) $\frac{2}{5}$
    (C) $\frac{3}{4}$
    (D) $\frac{4}{5}$
    (E) $\frac{8}{9}$

30. If b books can be purchased for d dollars, how many books can be purchased for m dollars?
    (A) $\dfrac{bm}{d}$
    (B) bdm
    (C) $\dfrac{d}{bm}$
    (D) $\dfrac{b + m}{d}$
    (E) $\dfrac{b - m}{d}$

STOP

END OF SECTION. IF YOU HAVE ANY TIME LEFT, GO OVER YOUR WORK IN THIS SECTION ONLY. DO NOT WORK IN ANY OTHER SECTION OF THE TEST.

SECTION IV

30 minutes
30 questions

Directions: For each of the following questions two quantities are given, one in Column A and one in Column B. Compare the two quantities and mark your answer sheet with the correct lettered conclusion. These are your options:

A: If the quantity in Column A is the greater;
B: if the quantity in Column B is the greater;
C: if the two quantities are equal;
D: if the relationship cannot be determined from the information given.

Common Information: In any question, information applying to both columns is centered between the columns and above the quantities in columns A and B. The common information applies to both columns. Any symbol that appears in both columns represents the same idea or quantity in both columns.

Numbers: All numbers used are real numbers.

Figures: Assume that the position of points, angles, regions and so forth are in the order shown. Figures are assumed to lie in a plane unless otherwise indicated. Figures accompanying questions are intended to provide information you can use in answering the questions. However, unless a note states that a figure is drawn to scale, you should solve the problems by using your knowledge of mathematics and *not* by estimating sizes by sight or measurement.

Lines: Assume that lines shown as straight are indeed straight.

	COLUMN A	COLUMN B
1.	the number of hours in 7 days	the number of days in 24 weeks

---

2.	35% of 60	60% of 35

3.

PLAYER	AGE
Tom	30
Juanita	35
Brooke	28
Glenda	40
Marcia	22
Dwight	24

	Tom's age	Average (arithmetic mean) age of the six players

4.

$$4 < m < 6$$
$$5 < n < 7$$

	m	n

---

5. A square region, P, and a rectangular region, Q, both have areas of 64.

	length of a side of P	length of Q if its width is 4

6.

$$x > 0$$

	$3x^3$	$(3x)^3$

7.

$$x \cdot y = 1$$
$$x \neq 0, y \neq 0$$

	x	y

	COLUMN A	COLUMN B

8. the number of primes of which 11 is an integer multiple | the number of primes of which 13 is an integer multiple

9. *x, y,* and *z* are consecutive positive integers, not necessarily in that order, and *x* and *z* are odd

xy | yz

AD is a transmitter tower held up by guy wires AB and AC

10. length of support wire AB | length of support wire AC

11. 2468 | $8 + 6 \cdot 10 + 4 \cdot 10^2 + 2 \cdot 10^3$

12. $a^2 = b$
$a > 0$

$\dfrac{2a}{b}$ | $a \cdot a$

13. x | 10

14. A family-size box of cereal contains 10 ounces more and costs 80¢ more than the regular size box of cereal.

cost per ounce of the cereal in the family-size box | 8¢

COLUMN A	COLUMN B

15. the number of different
duos which can be formed
from a group of 5 people

the number of different
trios which can be formed
from a group of 5 people

Directions: For each of the following questions, select the best of the answer choices and blacken the corresponding space on your answer sheet.
Numbers: All numbers used are real numbers.
Figures: The diagrams and figures that accompany these questions are for the purpose of providing information useful in answering the questions. Unless it is stated that a specific figure is not drawn to scale, the diagrams and figures are drawn as accurately as possible. All figures are in a plane unless otherwise indicated.

16. If $x = 3$ and $y = 2$, then $2x + 3y =$
    (A) 5
    (B) 10
    (C) 12
    (D) 14
    (E) 15

17. If the profit on an item is $4 and the sum of the cost and the profit is $20, what is the cost of the item.
    (A) $24
    (B) $20
    (C) $16
    (D) $12
    (E) Cannot be determined from the information given.

18. In 1950, the number of students enrolled at a college was 500. In 1970, the number of students enrolled at the college was $2\frac{1}{2}$ times as great as that in 1950. What was the number of students enrolled at the college in 1970?
    (A) 1250
    (B) 1000
    (C) 1750
    (D) 500
    (E) 250

19. If n is an integer between 0 and 100, then any of the following could be $3n + 3$ EXCEPT
    (A) 300
    (B) 297

(C) 208
(D) 63
(E) 6

20. A figure that can be folded over along a straight line so that the result is two equal halves which are then lying on top of one another with no overlap is said to have a line of symmetry. Which of the following figures has only one line of symmetry?
    (A) square
    (B) circle
    (C) equilateral triangle
    (D) isosceles triangle
    (E) rectangle

21. A laborer is paid $8 per hour for an 8-hour day and $1\frac{1}{2}$ times that rate for each hour in excess of 8 hours in a single day. If the laborer received $80 for a single day's work, how long did he work on that day?
    (A) 6 hr. 40 min.
    (B) 9 hr. 20 min
    (C) 9 hr. 30 min.
    (D) 9 hr. 40 min.
    (E) 10 hr.

Questions 22–25 are based on the graphs on page 218.

22. According to the graphs, approximately how much money belonging to the investment portfolio was invested in high-risk stocks?
    (A) $95,000
    (B) $89,000
    (C) $50,000
    (D) $42,000
    (E) $36,000

23. Approximately how much money belonging to the investment portfolio was invested in state-issued bonds?
    (A) $260,000
    (B) $125,000
    (C) $34,000

INVESTMENT PORTFOLIO

Total Investment Profile

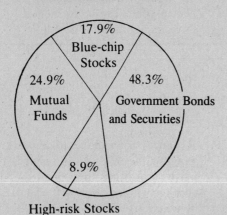

Government Bonds and Securities

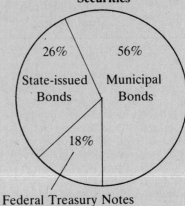

$1,080,192 = 100%

Municipal Bonds

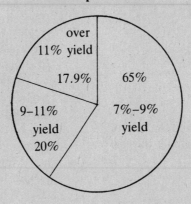

(D) $26,000
(E) $500

24.   Which of the following was the greatest?
   (A)   the amount of money invested in municipal bonds which yielded between 7% and 9%
   (B)   the amount of money invested in municipal bonds which yielded over 9%
   (C)   the amount of money invested in federal treasury notes
   (D)   the amount of money invested in state-issued bonds
   (E)   the amount of money invested in high-risk stocks

25.   Which of the following earned the least amount of money for the investment portfolio?
   (A)   municipal bonds
   (B)   state-issued bonds

(C)   government bonds and securities
(D)   mutual funds
(E)   Cannot be determined from the information given.

26.   A vertex of square MNOP is located at the center of circle O. If arc NP is 4π units long, then the perimeter of the square MNOP is
   (A)   32
   (B) 32π
   (C)   64
   (D) 64π

(E) Cannot be determined from the infor-
    mation given.

27. How many minutes will it take to completely
    fill a water tank with a capacity of 3750 cubic
    feet if the water is being pumped into the
    tank at the rate of 800 cubic feet per minute
    and is being drained out of the tank at the
    rate of 300 cubic feet per minute?
    (A) 3 min. 36 sec
    (B) 6 minutes
    (C) 7 min. 30 sec.
    (D) 8 minutes
    (E) 1875 minutes

28. Paul is standing 180 yards due north of point
    P. Franny is standing 240 yards due west of
    point P. What is the shortest distance
    between Franny and Paul?
    (A) 60 yards
    (B) 300 yards
    (C) 420 yards
    (D) 900 yards
    (E) 9000 yards

29. If a rectangle has an area of $81x^2$ and a
    length of 27x, then what is its width?
    (A) 3x
    (B) 9x
    (C) $3x^2$
    (D) $9x^2$
    (E) $2128x^3$

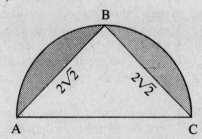

30. Triangle ABC is inscribed in a semicircle.
    What is the area of the shaded region
    above?
    (A) $2\pi - 2$
    (B) $2\pi - 4$
    (C) $4\pi - 4$
    (D) $8\pi - 4$
    (E) $8\pi - 8$

STOP

END OF SECTION. IF YOU HAVE ANY TIME LEFT, GO
OVER YOUR WORK IN THIS SECTION ONLY. DO NOT
WORK IN ANY OTHER SECTION OF THE TEST.

SECTION V

30 minutes
25 questions

Directions: Each of the following questions or groups
of questions is based on a short passage or a set of
propositions. In answering these questions it may
sometimes be helpful to draw a simple picture or chart.
When you have selected the best answer to each
question, darken the corresponding circle on your
answer sheet.

Questions 1–5

Asters are not as pretty as lilacs and don't smell
as nice as either lilacs or daffodils.

Daffodils are prettier than lilacs, but don't
smell as nice.

Irises are not as pretty as lilacs and don't smell as nice as daffodils or roses.

Lilacs are prettier than roses, but don't smell as nice.

1. Which of the following statements is neither definitely true nor definitely false?
   (A) Asters are not as pretty as lilacs.
   (B) Daffodils are prettier than asters.
   (C) Irises smell better than asters.
   (D) Lilacs do not smell as nice as daffodils.
   (E) Roses smell the best of all.

2. Which of the following is definitely true?
   (A) Roses are as pretty as daffodils.
   (B) Lilacs are as pretty as daffodils.
   (C) Irises are prettier than asters.
   (D) Daffodils do not smell as nice as irises.
   (E) Asters don't smell as nice as roses.

3. If irises are prettier than roses, then they are definitely prettier than which of the following?
   (A) asters only
   (B) daffodils only
   (C) lilacs only
   (D) asters and roses only
   (E) cannot be determined

4. Which of the following are both prettier and better smelling than asters?

   I. daffodils
   II. irises
   III. roses

   (A) I only
   (B) II only
   (C) III only
   (D) I and II only
   (E) I and III only

5. If dahlias are prettier than asters but do not smell as nice, then
   (A) dahlias might smell better than irises
   (B) dahlias might smell better than daffodils
   (C) dahlias might smell better than roses
   (D) dahlias cannot be prettier than lilacs
   (E) dahlias cannot be prettier than roses

Questions 6–8

PRO-ABORTION SPEAKER: Those who oppose abortion upon demand make the foundation of their arguments the sanctity of human life, but this seeming bedrock assumption is actually as weak as shifting sand. And it is not necessary to invoke the red herring that many anti-abortion speakers would allow that human life must sometimes be sacrificed for a greater good, as in the fighting of a just war. There are counter-examples to the principle of the sanctity of life which are even more embarrassing to pro-life advocates. It would be possible to reduce the annual number of traffic fatalities to virtually zero by passing federal legislation mandating a nationwide fifteen-mile-per-hour speed limit on *all* roads. You see, implicitly we have always been willing to trade off quantity of human life for quality.

ANTI-ABORTION SPEAKER: The analogy my opponent draws between abortion and traffic fatalities is weak. No one would propose such a speed limit. Imagine people trying to get to and from work under such a law, or imagine them trying to visit a friend or relatives outside their own neighborhoods, or taking in a sports event or a movie. Obviously such a law would be a disaster.

6. Which of the following best characterizes the anti-abortion speaker's response to the pro-abortion speaker?
   (A) His analysis of the traffic fatalities case actually supports the argument of the pro-abortion speaker.
   (B) His analysis of the traffic fatalities case is an effective rebuttal of the pro-abortion argument.
   (C) His response provides a strong affirmative statement of the anti-abortionist position.
   (D) His response is totally irrelevant to the issue raised by the pro-abortion speaker.
   (E) His counter-argument attacks the character of the pro-abortion speaker instead of the merits of his argument.

7. Which of the following represents the most logical continuation of the reasoning contained in the pro-abortion speaker's argument?
   (A) Therefore, we should not have any

laws on the books to protect human life.

(B) We can only conclude that the anti-abortionist is also in favor of strengthening enforcement of existing traffic regulations as a means to reducing the number of traffic fatalities each year.

(C) So the strongest attack on the anti-abortionist position is that he contradicts himself when he agrees that we should fight a just war even at the risk of considerable loss of human life.

(D) Even the laws against contraception are good examples of this tendency.

(E) The abortion question just makes explicit that which for long has remained hidden from view.

8. In his argument, the pro-abortionist makes which of the following assumptions?

   I. It is not a proper goal of a society to protect human life.

   II. The human fetus is not a human life.

   III. The trade-off between the number of human lives and the quality of those lives is appropriately decided by society.

(A) I only
(B) II only
(C) I and II only
(D) III only
(E) I, II, and III

Questions 9–12

The streets of Mainville are laid out regularly, with all roads and all drives parallel to each other. All the streets and all the avenues are also parallel to each other, and they are perpendicular to the roads and drives.

Magnolia Parkway runs from the intersection of Apple Street and Zinnia Drive to the intersection of Blueberry Avenue and Hyacinth Road.

Abbot Causeway is perpendicular to Magnolia Parkway.

9. Which of the following must be true?
(A) Magnolia Parkway is parallel to Maple Street.
(B) Magnolia Parkway is perpendicular to Maple Street.

(C) Magnolia Parkway intersects Maple Street.
(D) Magnolia Parkway does not intersect Maple Street.
(E) None of the above.

10. Which of the following must be false?
(A) Abbot Causeway is not parallel to Yellowstone Road.
(B) Abbot Causeway is not perpendicular to Oak Street.
(C) Melody Drive crosses Petunia Street.
(D) Melody Drive crosses Fanfare Road.
(E) Fanfare Road does not cross Petunia Street.

11. If all roads are laid out north to south and all of the streets are laid out east to west, which of the following is possible?

   I. Magnolia Parkway runs from northwest to southeast.

   II. Zinnia Drive runs east to west.

   III. Apple Street intersects Hyacinth Road.

(A) I only
(B) II only
(C) III only
(D) I and III only
(E) I, II, and III

12. If all of the blocks formed by roads, streets, avenues, and drives are one-quarter of a mile on a side, which of the following must be true?
(A) Magnolia Parkway is more than one-quarter of a mile in length.
(B) Apple Street is more than one-quarter of a mile in length.
(C) Hyacinth Road is less than one-quarter of a mile in length.
(D) All the streets and avenues are the same length.
(E) None of the roads and drives are the same length.

Questions 13–17

A construction company is building a pre-fabricated structure which requires specialized crane operators for five different parts of the job. Six operators are available: R, S, T, U, V, and W, and each phase will take one day and will be done by a single operator. Though an operator may do more than one phase of the job, no operator will work two days in a row.

Both R and S can handle any phase of the job.
T can work only on days immediately following days on which S has worked.
U can work only the days that T can.
V can only work on the third and fifth days of the job.
W can only work on the fourth day of the job.

13. Which of the following are true?

    I.   R could do up to three of the phases of the job.

    II.   S could do up to three of the phases of the job.

    III.   T could do no more than two of the phases of the job.

    (A) I only
    (B) II only
    (C) III only
    (D) II and III only
    (E) I, II, and III

14. If S works the first day of the job, which of the following is (are) true?

    I.   Only T or U can work the second day.
    II.   T, U, or R could work the second day.
    III.   R, S, or W could work the third day.

    (A) I only
    (B) II only
    (C) III only
    (D) I and III only
    (E) I, II, and III

15. If R works the first day, which of the following are true?

    I.   S must work the second day.
    II.   S cannot work the third day.
    III.   Only T, U, or V can work on the third day.

    (A) I only
    (B) II only
    (C) I and, II only
    (D) I and III only
    (E) I, II, and III

16. If R works on both the first and third days, which of the following most accurately describes the possibilities on the fourth day?

    (A) Only S is eligible to work.
    (B) Only R, S, T, or W are eligible to work.
    (C) Only S or W are eligible to work.
    (D) Only R, S, or W are eligible to work.
    (E) Only S, T, U, or W are eligible to work.

17. R, S, and V do not work on the third day; therefore,

    (A) R worked on the first day.
    (B) Only S can work on the fourth day.
    (C) Only R can work on the fourth day.
    (D) Only W can work on the fourth day.
    (E) Either T or U worked on the second day.

Questions 18–22

The parties to an important labor negotiation are two representatives of management, Morrison and Nelson; two representatives of labor, Richards and Smith; and the Federal Mediator, Jones. They are meeting at a round table with eight seats, and the order of seating has become a significant psychological part of the negotiations.

    I.   The two representatives of management always sit next to each other.

    II.   The two representatives of labor always sit with one seat between them.

    III.   Both sides like to make sure that they are as close to the mediator as the other side is, and no closer to the opposing side than necessary.

    IV.   The mediator prefers to have at least one seat between himself and any of the other negotiators.

18. If conditions I, II, and IV are met, which of the following is necessarily true?

    (A) Jones sits next to one of the management representatives.
    (B) Morrison sits next to one of the labor representatives.
    (C) One of the labor representatives will sit next to either Morrison or Nelson.
    (D) Either Richards or Smith sits next to Jones.
    (E) None of the above is necessarily true.

19. If conditions I, II, and III are met, which of the following is NOT a possible seating arrangement of the negotiators, starting with Jones and going clockwise around the table?
    (A) Jones, Morrison, Nelson, empty, empty, Richards, empty, Smith
    (B) Jones, Nelson, Morrison, empty, empty, Smith, empty, Richards
    (C) Jones, Richards, empty, Smith, empty, empty, Nelson, Morrison
    (D) Jones, Smith, Richards, empty, empty, empty, Morrison, Nelson
    (E) All of the above are possible seating arrangements.

20. The Secretary of Labor joins the negotiations and sits across the table from the mediator. If all of the conditions are still met as much as possible, which of the following is true?

    I.   A labor representative will sit next to the secretary.
    II. A management representative will sit next to the secretary.
    III. Both a labor representative and one from management will sit next to the mediator.

    (A) I only
    (B) II only
    (C) I and II only
    (D) I and III only
    (E) I, II, and III

21. If the two sides meet without the mediator and sit so that Morrison is seated directly opposite Smith, which of the following is possible?
    (A) Richards and Nelson will both be seated to Morrison's left and to Smith's right.
    (B) Richards will be as close to Morrison as he is to Smith.
    (C) Nelson will be separated from Richards by one seat.
    (D) Nelson will be separated from Smith by three seats.
    (E) Nelson and Richards will be seated directly across from each other.

22. If, under the original conditions, Morrison's aide joins the negotiations and sits next to Morrison, which of the following is not possible?
    (A) Richards sits directly opposite Morrison.
    (B) Richards sits directly opposite Morrison's aide.
    (C) Smith sits directly opposite Nelson.
    (D) Smith sits directly opposite Morrison's aide.
    (E) Morrison's aide sits next to the Jones.

---

23. All high-powered racing engines have stochastic fuel injection. Stochastic fuel injection is not a feature which is normally included in the engines of production-line vehicles.

    Passenger sedans are production-line vehicles.

    Which of the following conclusions can be drawn from these statements?
    (A) Passenger sedans do not usually have stochastic fuel injection.
    (B) Stochastic fuel injection is found only in high-powered racing cars.
    (C) Car manufacturers do not include stochastic fuel injection in passenger cars because they fear accidents.
    (D) Purchasers of passenger cars do not normally purchase stochastic fuel injection because it is expensive.
    (E) Some passenger sedans are high-powered racing vehicles.

24. CLARENCE: Mary is one of the most important executives at the Trendy Cola Company.
    PETER: How can that be? I know for a fact that Mary drinks only Hobart Cola.

    Peter's statement implies that he believes that
    (A) Hobart Cola is a subsidiary of Trendy Cola
    (B) Mary is an unimportant employee of Hobart Cola
    (C) all cola drinks taste pretty much alike
    (D) an executive uses only that company's products
    (E) Hobart is a better-tasting cola than Trendy

25. Current motion pictures give children a distorted view of the world. Animated features depict animals as loyal friends, compassionate creatures, and tender souls, while "spaghetti Westerns" portray men and women as deceitful and treacherous, cruel and wanton, hard and uncaring. Thus, children are taught to value animals more highly than other human beings.

Which of the following, if true, would weaken the author's conclusion?

I. Children are not allowed to watch "spaghetti Westerns."

II. The producers of animated features do not want children to regard animals as higher than human beings.

III. Ancient fables, such as *Androcles and the Lion*, tell stories of the cooperation between humans and animals, and they usually end with a moral about human virtue.

(A) I only
(B) II only
(C) I and II only
(D) III only
(E) I, II, and III

STOP

END OF SECTION. IF YOU HAVE ANY TIME LEFT, GO OVER YOUR WORK IN THIS SECTION ONLY. DO NOT WORK IN ANY OTHER SECTION OF THE TEST.

SECTION VI

30 minutes
25 questions

Directions: Each of the following questions or groups of questions is based on a short passage or a set of propositions. In answering these questions it may sometimes be helpful to draw a simple picture or chart. When you have selected the best answer to each question, darken the corresponding circle on your answer sheet.

Questions 1–4

The first three names in each set are names usually used for males.

The last two names in each set are names usually used for females.

Each name in a set begins with a different letter.

Each name in a set contains the same number of letters.

I.	Jack	Paul	Dave	June	Edna
II.	Pete	Mike	Henry	Emma	Mary
III.	Frank	James	Chuck	Nancy	Betty
IV.	Louis	Tommy	Greta	Linda	Annie
V.	Phil	Dick	Mona	Alma	Inga

1. Which name would correctly complete the following set?

Allen   Wally   _____   Eliza   Julia

(A) Ethel
(B) Mabel
(C) Waldo
(D) Harry
(E) Angus

2. All of the conditions established above are met by which of the sets?
   (A) I only
   (B) III only
   (C) I and V only
   (D) II and IV only
   (E) III and V only

3. Which set satisfies all of the conditions except the third?
   (A) I
   (B) II
   (C) III
   (D) IV
   (E) V

4. Which of the following substitutions would make its set meet the stated conditions?
   (A) "Mark" for "June" in set I
   (B) "Lila" for "Henry" in set II
   (C) "Boris" for "Frank" in set III
   (D) "Simon" for "Louis" in set IV
   (E) "Fred" for "Mona" in set V

Questions 5–6

A behavioral psychologist interested in animal behavior noticed that dogs who are never physically disciplined (e.g., with a blow from a rolled-up newspaper) never bark at strangers. He concluded that the best way to keep a dog from barking at strange visitors is to not punish the dog physically.

5. The psychologist's conclusion is based on which of the following assumptions?

   I. The dogs he studied never barked.
   II. Dogs should not be physically punished.
   III. There were no instances of an unpunished dog barking at a stranger which he had failed to observe.

   (A) I only
   (B) II only
   (C) III only
   (D) II and III only
   (E) I, II, and III

6. Suppose the psychologist decides to pursue his project further, and he studies twenty-five dogs which are known to bark at strangers. Which of the following possible findings would undermine his original conclusion?

   I. Some of the owners of the dogs studied did not physically punish the dog when it barked at a stranger.
   II. Some of the dogs studied were never physically punished.
   III. The owners of some of the dogs studied believe that a dog that barks at strangers is a good watchdog.

   (A) I only
   (B) II only
   (C) I and II only
   (D) II and III only
   (E) I, II, and III

7. Only White Bear gives you all-day deodorant protection and the unique White Bear scent.

   If this advertising claim is true, which of the following cannot also be true?

   I. Red Flag deodorant gives you all-day deodorant protection.
   II. Open Sea deodorant is a more popular deodorant than White Bear.
   III. White Bear after-shave lotion uses the White Bear scent.

   (A) I only
   (B) II only
   (C) I and III only
   (D) III only
   (E) All of the propositions could be true.

Questions 8–12

Paul, Quincy, Roger, and Sam are married to Tess, Ursula, Valerie, and Wilma, not necessarily in that order. Roger's wife is older than Ursula. Sam's wife is older than Wilma, who is Paul's sister. Tess is the youngest of the wives. Roger was the best man at Wilma's wedding.

8. If Quincy and his wife have a boy named Patrick, then
   (A) Tess will be Patrick's aunt
   (B) Valerie will be Patrick's aunt
   (C) Paul will be Patrick's cousin
   (D) Ursula will be Patrick's mother
   (E) none of the above

9. Which of the following is true?
   (A) Roger's wife is younger than Valerie.
   (B) Roger's wife is younger than Wilma.
   (C) Paul's wife is younger than Ursula.
   (D) Sam's wife is older than Valerie.
   (E) Quentin's wife is older than Ursula.

10. If each husband is exactly two years older than his wife, which of the following must be false?
    (A) Roger is older than Ursula.
    (B) Tess is younger than anyone.
    (C) Paul is younger than Sam.
    (D) Quincy is younger than Paul.
    (E) Valerie is younger than Paul.

11. If the wives were—from youngest to oldest—28, 30, 32, and 34 years old; and Paul, Quincy, Roger, and Sam were respectively 27, 29, 31, and 33 years old, which of the following must be false?
    (A) Tess is older than her husband.
    (B) Valerie is older than her husband.
    (C) Ursula is younger than Valerie's husband.
    (D) Wilma is younger than Ursula's husband.
    (E) Tess is younger than Wilma's husband.

12. If Tess and Valerie get divorced from their current husbands and marry each other's former husband, then
    (A) Sam's wife will be younger than Paul's wife
    (B) Sam's wife will be younger than Roger's wife
    (C) Roger's wife will be older than Quincy's wife
    (D) Roger's wife will be older than Paul's wife
    (E) Paul's wife will be younger than Quincy's wife

Questions 13–17

Six persons, J, K, L, M, N, and O, run a series of races with the following results.

O never finishes first or last.

L never finishes immediately behind either J or K.

L always finishes immediately ahead of M.

13. Which of the following, given in order from first to last, is an acceptable finishing sequence of the runners?
    (A) J, L, M, O, N, K
    (B) L, O, J, K, M, N
    (C) L, M, J, K, N, O
    (D) L, M, J, K, O, N
    (E) N, K, L, M, L, J

14. If, in an acceptable finishing sequence, J and K finish first and fifth respectively, which of the following must be true?
    (A) L finishes second.
    (B) O finishes third.
    (C) M finishes third.
    (D) N finishes third.
    (E) N finishes sixth.

15. If, in an acceptable finishing sequence, L finishes second, which of the following must be true?

    I. O must finish fourth.
    II. N must finish fifth.
    III. Either J or K must finish sixth.

    (A) I only
    (B) II only
    (C) III only
    (D) I and III only
    (E) I, II, and III

16. All of the following finishing sequences, given in order from 1 to 6, are acceptable EXCEPT
    (A) J, N, L, M, O, K
    (B) J, N, O, L, M, K
    (C) L, M, J, K, O, N
    (D) N, J, L, M, O, K
    (E) N, K, O, L, M, J

17. Only one acceptable finishing sequence is possible under which of the following conditions?

    I. Whenever J and K finish second and third respectively.
    II. Whenever J and K finish third and fourth respectively.
    III. Whenever J and K finish fourth and fifth respectively.

    (A) I only
    (B) II only
    (C) III only
    (D) I and II only
    (E) I, II, and III

Questions 18–22

Jack Caribe, the ocean explorer, is directing a study of the parrot fish, an important part of coral reef ecology. Each day he must schedule the diving teams. His crew consists of four professional scuba divers—Ken, Leon, Matel, and Nina—and four marine biologists—Peter, Quentin, Rosemary, and Sue.

No one can dive more than twice a day and a professional diver must always be on the boat as the dive-master. Jack is not assigned, but can do any task he wishes, including dive-master.

Each dive team must have at least one professional diver and one biologist.

Mabel and Peter have fought, and Jack won't put them together for now. Mabel, a strong swimmer, works very badly with slow-paced Quentin.

Sue and Ken are recently married and always dive together.

18. If Nina is dive-master supervising three diving teams, which of the following is NOT a possible dive team?
    (A) Ken, Sue, and Peter
    (B) Ken, Sue, and Quentin
    (C) Leon, Peter, and Quentin
    (D) Leon, Peter, and Rosemary
    (E) Mabel and Rosemary

19. If Jack is the dive-master with four teams diving, how many different possible two-diver teams are there?
    (A) 6
    (B) 7
    (C) 8
    (D) 9
    (E) 10

20. If Mabel is the dive-master, which of the following is NOT a possible dive team?
    I. Peter, Quentin, and Rosemary
    II. Leon and Nina
    III. Ken, Sue, and Quentin
    IV. Ken, Peter, and Rosemary

    (A) I and II only
    (B) I, II, and III only
    (C) I, II, and IV only
    (D) III only
    (E) I, II, III, and IV

21. If biologist Olga joins the expedition and Leon is away getting supplies, which of the following is a possible schedule for the morning dive teams?
    (A) Ken, Sue, and Peter; Mabel, Olga, and Rosemary; Nina, Jack, and Quentin
    (B) Ken, Mabel, and Sue; Nina, Rosemary, Peter, and Olga
    (C) Ken, Olga, and Quentin; Rosemary, Sue, and Mabel
    (D) Olga, Rosemary, and Peter; Ken and Sue; Nina and Peter
    (E) Mabel, Olga, and Peter; Ken, Sue, and Quentin; Nina, Jack, and Rosemary

22. If Peter and Mabel become friends again and Leon is the dive-master, which of the following is a possible diving team?
    (A) Peter, Mabel, and Ken
    (B) Peter, Mabel, and Sue
    (C) Peter, Quentin, and Rosemary
    (D) Peter, Mabel, Ken, and Sue
    (E) Mabel, Sue, and Rosemary

23. During New York City's fiscal crisis of the late 1970's, governmental leaders debated whether to offer federal assistance to New York City. One economist who opposed the suggestion asked, "Are we supposed to help out New York City every time it gets into financial problems?"

    The economist's question can be criticized because it
    (A) uses ambiguous terms
    (B) assumes everyone else agrees New York City should be helped
    (C) appeals to emotions rather than using logic
    (D) relies upon second-hand reports rather than first-hand accounts
    (E) completely ignores the issue at hand

24. It is a well-documented fact that for all teenaged couples who marry, the marriages of those who do not have children in the first year of their marriage survive more than twice as long as the marriages of those teenaged couples in which the wife does give birth within the first twelve months of marriage. Therefore, many divorces could be avoided if teenagers who marry were encouraged not to have children during the first year.

    The evidence regarding teenaged marriages supports the author's conclusion only if
    (A) in those couples in which a child was born within the first twelve months

there is not a significant number in which the wife was pregnant at the time of marriage

(B) the children born during the first year of marriage to those divorcing couples lived with the teenaged couple

(C) the child born into such a marriage did not die at birth

(D) society actually has an interest in determining whether or not people should get divorced if there are not children involved

(E) encouraging people to stay married when they do not plan to have any children is a good idea

25. There are no lower bus fares from Washington, D.C. to New York City than those of Flash Bus Line.

Which of the following is logically inconsistent with the above advertising claim?

I. Long Lines Airways has a Washington, D.C., to New York City fare which is only one-half that charged by Flash.

II. Rapid Transit Bus Company charges the same fare for a trip from Washington, D.C. to New York City as Flash charges.

III. Cherokee Bus Corporation has a lower fare from New York City to Boston than does Flash.

(A) I only
(B) II only
(C) I and II only
(D) I, II and III
(E) None of the statements is inconsistent.

STOP

END OF SECTION. IF YOU HAVE ANY TIME LEFT, GO OVER YOUR WORK IN THIS SECTION ONLY. DO NOT WORK IN ANY OTHER SECTION OF THE TEST.

SECTION VII

30 minutes
38 questions

Directions: Each of the questions below contains one or more blank spaces, each blank indicating an omitted word. Each sentence is followed by five (5) lettered words or sets of words. Read and determine the general sense of each sentence. Then choose the word, or set of words, which, when inserted in the sentence, best fits the meaning of the sentence.

1. He admitted the _____ of his actions, but he justified them on the grounds of _____.
   (A) validity—equity
   (B) probity—morality
   (C) iniquity—expedience
   (D) degeneracy—transcendentalism
   (E) lunacy—heredity

2. The novel, describing the experiences of a man who is brought back from the dead by a new scientific technique, is a _____ on doctors, research foundations, and many _____ of contemporary society.
   (A) treatise—interests
   (B) satire—foibles
   (C) dossier—infallibilities
   (D) criticism—nostalgias
   (E) capsule—infirmities

3. It is usually a good thing when a discussion is taken firmly by the hand and led down from the heights of _____ to the level ground of hard _____.
   (A) ridiculousness—sublimity

(B) mountaintops—meadowland
(C) audacity—sincerity
(D) fantasy—fact
(E) speculation—reality

4. These avant-garde thinkers believe that the major peace movements are ineffective because the thinking that underlies these movements is old-fashioned, confused, _____, and out of step with the findings of _____ science.
(A) stimulating—natural
(B) delusionary—behavioral
(C) loaded—true
(D) uncertain—physical
(E) blatant—scholastic

5. Today, we who read Latin return far more often to the exuberance of Apuleius than to the carefully molded _____ of Cicero.
(A) literature
(B) redundancies
(C) objects
(D) piracies
(E) platitudes

6. She defines science as whatever can be _____, and religion as that which is forever undefinable.
(A) measured
(B) counted
(C) ascertained
(D) insured
(E) sensed

7. The case for the dinosaurs' having been warm-blooded is based on _____ details that belie the creatures' superficial similarity to reptiles.
(A) unknown
(B) internal
(C) external
(D) precise
(E) important

Directions: In each of the following questions, you are given a related pair of words or phrases in capital letters. Each capitalized pair is followed by five (5) lettered pairs of words or phrases. Choose the pair which best expresses a relationship similar to that expressed by the original pair.

8. DISEMBARK : SHIP ::
(A) board : train
(B) dismount : horse
(C) intern : jail
(D) discharge : navy
(E) dismantle : clock

9. PROTEIN : MEAT ::
(A) calories : cream
(B) heat : sugar
(C) cyclamates: diet
(D) starch : potatoes
(E) fat : cholesterol

10. NECK : NAPE ::
(A) foot : heel
(B) head : forehead
(C) arm : wrist
(D) stomach : back
(E) eye : lid

11. GRIPPING: PLIERS ::
(A) chisel : gouging
(B) breaking : hammer
(C) elevating : jack
(D) killing : knife
(E) fastening : screwdriver

12. RADIUS : CIRCLE ::
(A) rubber : tire
(B) bisect : angle
(C) equator : earth
(D) cord : circumference
(E) spoke : wheel

13. MISDEMEANOR : FELONY ::
(A) mild : seriously
(B) thief : burglar
(C) murder: manslaughter
(D) cracked: smashed
(E) crime : degree

14. SYMPHONY : CODA ::
(A) drama : prologue
(B) letter : introduction
(C) music : note
(D) opera : aria
(E) novel : epilogue

15. HOMONYM : SOUND ::
    (A) synonym : meaning
    (B) antonym : opposite
    (C) acronym : letters
    (D) pseudonym : fake
    (E) synopsis : summary

16. QUASH : QUELL ::
    (A) melon : water
    (B) obviate : put down
    (C) motion : riot
    (D) motor : engine
    (E) current : voltage

Directions: Below each of the following passages you will find questions or incomplete statements about the passage. Each statement or question is followed by lettered words or expressions. Select the word or expression that most satisfactorily completes each statement, or answers each question in accordance with the meaning of the passage. After you have chosen the best answer, blacken the corresponding space on the answer sheet.

The forces that generate conditions conducive to crime and riots are stronger in urban communities than in rural areas. Urban living is more anonymous living. It often releases the individual from community restraints more common in tradition-oriented societies. But more freedom from constraints and controls also provides greater freedom to deviate. And living in the more impersonalized, formally controlled urban society means that regulatory orders of conduct are often directed by distant bureaucrats. The police are strangers executing these prescriptions on, at worst, an alien subcommunity and, at best, an anonymous set of subjects. Minor offenses in a small town or village are often handled without resort to official police action. As disputable as such action may seem to be, it nonetheless results in fewer recorded violations of the law compared to the city. Although perhaps causing some decision difficulties for the police in small towns, formal and objective law enforcement is not always acceptable to villagers.

Urban areas with mass populations, greater wealth, more commercial establishments, and more products of our technology also provide more frequent opportunities for theft. Victims are impersonalized, property is insured, consumer goods in more abundance are vividly displayed and are more portable.

17. The author of the above passage appears to feel that
    (A) the display of expensive consumer goods is the primary cause of crime
    (B) being known to your neighbors increases the force of normal community ethical rules
    (C) small communities have more minor crime than urban centers
    (D) there is no way to prevent urban crime
    (E) making the police more friendly will reduce crime in small towns

18. It can be inferred from the above passage that
    (A) urban crime can be controlled by greater emphasis on moral education
    (B) making urban family life more like that in smaller communities will reduce urban crime
    (C) the crime rate in small communities is more like that of urban centers than is generally supposed.
    (D) the greater concentration of transient individuals in urban centers includes a greater number of unstable individuals, which accounts for much of the difference in crime rates between urban and non-urban areas.
    (E) it is doubtful that much can be done to control crime

19. The author's view of traditional societies is best expressed by which of the following?
    (A) Many traditional societies provide inadequate freedom of personal movement and travel.
    (B) Traditional societies have lower crime rates because of the effects of moral teaching in school.
    (C) Traditional societies provide less freedom for the individual in many circumstances.
    (D) Inadequate technology has undermined many traditional societies.
    (E) A large number of traditions from earlier traditional societies survive in modern traditional conventions.

20. According to the passage, all of the following contribute to higher crime rates in urban areas EXCEPT
    (A) store window displays
    (B) higher standards of living
    (C) urban anonymity
    (D) population densities
    (E) inadequate staffing of the police departments

As befits a nation made up of immigrants from all over the Christian world, Americans have no distinctive Christmas symbols; but we have taken the symbols of all the nations and made them our own. The Christmas tree, the holly, and the ivy, the mistletoe, the exchange of gifts, the myth of Santa Claus, the carols of all nations, the plum pudding and the wassail bowl are all elements in the American Christmas of the mid-twentieth century. Though we have no Christmas symbols of our own, the American Christmas still has a distinctive aura by virtue of two characteristic elements.

The first of these is that, as might be expected in a nation as dedicated to the carrying on of business as the American nation, the dominant role of the Christmas festivities has become to serve as a stimulus to retail business. The themes of Christmas advertising begin to appear as early as September, and the open season on Christmas shopping begins in November. Fifty years ago, Thanksgiving Day was regarded as the opening day of the season for Christmas shopping; today, the season opens immediately after Halloween. Thus, virtually a whole month has been added to the Christmas season—for shopping purposes.

Second, the Christmas season of festivities has insensibly combined with the New Year's celebration into one lengthened period of Saturnalia. This starts with the "office parties" a few days before Christmas, continues on Christmas Eve, now the occasion in America of one of two large-scale revels that mark the season—save that the Christmas Eve revels are often punctuated by a visit to one of the larger churches for midnight Mass, which has increasingly tended to become blended into a part of the entertainment aspect of the season—and continues in spirited euphoria until New Year's Eve, the second of the large-scale revels. New Year's Day is spent resting, possibly regretting one's excesses, watching a football "bowl" game, and indulging in the

lenitive of one's choice. January 2 marks, for most, the return to temperance and decorum and business as usual.

21. The author's attitude toward the manner in which Christmas is celebrated in the United States is one of
    (A) great disapproval
    (B) humorous confusion
    (C) laudatory acclaim
    (D) objective analysis
    (E) great optimism

22. Which of the following would be most in accord with the main ideas of the passage?
    (A) In Puritan Massachusetts Bay Colony, it was a crime, punishable by the stocks, to fail to observe Christmas.
    (B) Christmas customs in Europe and America that are associated with the Feast of the Nativity were not originally Christian.
    (C) Rudolph the Red-nosed Reindeer has become a traditional aspect of Christmas, yet was created only a few years ago by commercial interests.
    (D) The custom of wassailing continued well into the nineteenth century.
    (E) In widely separated areas of the world, religious observances tend to cluster around striking natural phenomena.

23. According to the passage, the American celebration of the Christmas season has
    (A) demonstrated great symbolic originality
    (B) little justification for existing
    (C) departed completely from the example of early settlers
    (D) made little attempt to promote a variety of entertainment
    (E) borrowed extensively from the traditions of other countries

24. Which of the following does the author find to be distinctive to the American Christmas season?
    (A) the purchase and exchange of Christmas gifts
    (B) eating and drinking in celebration
    (C) going to midnight Mass on Christmas Eve

(D)   the timing of Christmas
(E)   the dedication to commerce

25.   What would the author of the passage likely say by way of analysis of the use of Christmas cards by Americans to celebrate Christmas?
   (A)   The sending of large numbers of expensive cards is largely an extension of the business aspect of the American Christmas celebration.
   (B)   The reaching out to many friends, both close and far, through the cards, is an extension of the festive spirit of the American Christmas celebration.
   (C)   The multiplicity of cards and forms is a reflection of the very heterogeneous views of Americans on the celebration of Christmas.
   (D)   The cards, once religious in meaning, have, like the Christmas Eve masses at churches, become part of the general Saturnalia with which the months-long Christmas season is crowned.
   (E)   The extension of the Christmas season has permitted more cards to be sent and handled by the overworked postal system.

26.   Which of the following would be the best counter to the author's argument that spurring retail trade is the major purpose of Christmas giving?
   (A)   Many other countries have similar, if smaller, traditions of gift-giving during the Christmas season.
   (B)   It is the natural joy of the citizens of a wealthy nation and their generous desire to share their wealth which leads to so many gifts being given.
   (C)   Many retail businesses do large volumes of business all year long.
   (D)   Many other celebrations are accompanied by business purposes.
   (E)   The author's argument cannot be countered in any way.

27.   Which of the following can best be inferred from the passage?
   (A)   The great waves of immigrants from many countries in the late 1800's and early 1900's had a significant effect on the American celebration of Christmas.
   (B)   Only the earliest settlers brought traditions on which the American Christmas celebration is based.
   (C)   Every year sees the start of a new Christmas "tradition."
   (D)   The Saturnalia of Christmas week is a release from the hard work of the Christmas shopping season.
   (E)   New Year's is indistinguishable from Christmas Eve at this point.

Directions: Each of the following questions consists of a word printed in capital letters, followed by five (5) lettered words or phrases. Select the word or phrase which is most nearly *opposite* to the capitalized word in meaning.

28.   TENDER:
   (A)   difficult
   (B)   leonine
   (C)   tepid
   (D)   saccharine
   (E)   hardened

29.   INADEQUATE:
   (A)   glossy
   (B)   rapid
   (C)   aspiring
   (D)   confining
   (E)   sufficient

30.   NONSTRIATED:
   (A)   marked
   (B)   striped
   (C)   plagued
   (D)   stippled
   (E)   stripped

31.   SCRUTINIZE:
   (A)   question
   (B)   leer
   (C)   sensitize
   (D)   pore over
   (E)   disregard

32.   LOFTY:
   (A)   assessed
   (B)   debased
   (C)   general

(D) intrusive
(E) kinky

33. COLORLESS:
(A) red
(B) black
(C) flamboyant
(D) vicious
(E) pretty

34. CELERITY:
(A) depression
(B) postponement
(C) slowness
(D) choler
(E) anonymity

35. FURIOUS:
(A) medium
(B) restrained
(C) ticklish
(D) disjointed
(E) witty

36. OVERPOWER:
(A) succumb
(B) twinge
(C) oust
(D) betray
(E) retrench

37. PALACE:
(A) manse
(B) dwelling
(C) skyscraper
(D) mansion
(E) hovel

38. SUSPEND:
(A) turn on
(B) resume
(C) switch
(D) pend
(E) disallow

STOP

END OF SECTION. IF YOU HAVE ANY TIME LEFT, GO
OVER YOUR WORK IN THIS SECTION ONLY. DO NOT
WORK IN ANY OTHER SECTION OF THE TEST.

PRACTICE EXAMINATION 1—ANSWER KEY

Section I

1.	C	10.	C	19.	D	28.	C	37.	D
2.	E	11.	D	20.	A	29.	D	38.	C
3.	B	12.	A	21.	C	30.	E		
4.	D	13.	E	22.	B	31.	B		
5.	A	14.	D	23.	E	32.	B		
6.	D	15.	B	24.	D	33.	C		
7.	C	16.	A	25.	A	34.	D		
8.	B	17.	B	26.	E	35.	B		
9.	C	18.	E	27.	C	36.	A		

Section II

1.	A	10.	E	19.	E	28.	B	37.	C
2.	D	11.	C	20.	B	29.	D	38.	A
3.	D	12.	A	21.	E	30.	B		
4.	A	13.	E	22.	D	31.	E		
5.	B	14.	D	23.	B	32.	A		
6.	E	15.	E	24.	C	33.	B		
7.	C	16.	B	25.	D	34.	E		
8.	E	17.	B	26.	C	35.	C		
9.	D	18.	D	27.	A	36.	D		

Section III

1.	C	7.	B	13.	C	19.	C	25.	E
2.	B	8.	B	14.	B	20.	E	26.	A
3.	B	9.	C	15.	A	21.	E	27.	B
4.	A	10.	C	16.	D	22.	E	28.	A
5.	D	11.	D	17.	E	23.	E	29.	E
6.	C	12.	D	18.	C	24.	A	30.	B

Section IV

1.	C	7.	D	13.	C	19.	C	25.	E
2.	C	8.	C	14.	D	20.	D	26.	A
3.	A	9.	D	15.	C	21.	B	27.	C
4.	D	10.	B	16.	C	22.	A	28.	B
5.	B	11.	C	17.	C	23.	B	29.	A
6.	B	12.	D	18.	A	24.	A	30.	A

Section V

1.	C	6.	A	11.	D	16.	C	21. B
2.	E	7.	E	12.	A	17.	A	22. A
3.	E	8.	D	13.	E	18.	C	23. A
4.	A	9.	E	14.	B	19.	D	24. D
5.	A	10.	D	15.	C	20.	D	25. A

Section VI

1.	D	6.	B	11.	C	16.	D	21. B
2.	B	7.	E	12.	A	17.	E	22. D
3.	A	8.	A	13.	D	18.	D	23. E
4.	E	9.	C	14.	E	19.	A	24. A
5.	C	10.	D	15.	C	20.	C	25. E

Section VII

1.	C	10.	A	19.	C	28.	E	37.	E
2.	B	11.	C	20.	E	29.	E	38.	B
3.	D	12.	E	21.	D	30.	B		
4.	B	13.	D	22.	C	31.	E		
5.	E	14.	E	23.	E	32.	B		
6.	C	15.	A	24.	E	33.	C		
7.	B	16.	B	25.	A	34.	C		
8.	B	17.	B	26.	B	35.	B		
9.	D	18.	C	27.	A	36.	A		

EXPLANATORY ANSWERS

SECTION I

1. **(C)** Even indicates that there is some opposite meaning between the first part of the sentence, with the blank, and the second part, which says that he had genius. Since the second part is positive, the blank must be negative and must be something that properly describes a reputation. (A) and (C) are the only answers that properly describe a reputation, but (C) is negative, and thus correct.

2. **(E)** The second blank asks for something that can be improved between and among men. (A) and (C) fail since one does not seek to improve problems or rudeness, but rather to improve the habits, customs or relationships that lead to problems or rudeness—one doesn't want better problems, but reduced ones. Generalities is also not something which is improved. Between (B) and (E), the first word must describe the kind of contribution which might make an improvement. A significant improvement is more likely to do so than a standardized one; hence (E) is the best answer.

3. **(B)** All the answer choices are adjectives, but only (B) is the sort of thing that one would wonder about concerning an award. (A) is attractive, but it would be used in a sentence saying ". . . how the awards have been determined," rather than the given order. Thus, (B) is the best answer.

4. **(D)** This question requires a little thought about what the pleasures the medieval church might be against. Education, while not very common, was certainly not forbidden. (B) and (C) describe the actual views of the church, since ascetic means being opposed to sensual pleasures, and ecclesiastical means being of the church. (D) and (E) present some difficulty since hermetic can mean of the occult as well as airtight. The church would probably be against the occult, but it would be occult practices that would be opposed, not occult pleasures alone. Sensual pleasures would definitely be opposed, so (D) is the best answer.

5. **(A)** The sentence structure shows that the first blank is the statement of having wealth the disposition of which is opposed in the second half of the sentence. Thus, only (A) is reasonable on the first blank since it is the only choice which describes a business that can give away wealth.

6. **(D)** The second part of the sentence is admiring of the ability of cars to last as long as they do under routine abuse, thus only (D) will fit with that spirit. In the first blank, we are carrying forward the idea of routine abuse. Gradual, sensible, religious and graceful do not fit. Habitually does. Again, (D) is the best answer.

7. **(C)** There is a little peculiarity to this sentence in that it speaks of filling the walls with something and then of evacuating them to a high vacuum. It seems as if it were doing contradictory things to the same space. Therefore, we must ask what could be put into something that is then made into a vacuum. Clearly, air and water fail. The second idea in the sentence is that we are dealing with the storage of liquid hydrogen, which is very cold. Thus the idea of a vacuum bottle which is filled with insulation becomes reasonable. Hence, (C) is the best answer.

8. **(B)** A plutocrat is a ruler distinguished by his wealth. A theocrat is a ruler distinguished by religion. An oligarch and an autocrat are also rulers, and a democrat is a believer in the rule of the people or majority. However, wealth is a distinguishing characteristic, which (C) does not replicate. (A) is slightly more difficult to dismiss since an autocrat is an individual, ruling as such; but he is not selected or distinguished—prior to rule—by the characteristic of being an individual. All rulers are individuals. (E) is attempting to confuse the issue by claiming that a republican is interested in conservation. First of all, a republican with a lower-case *r* is someone who believes in government having the form of a republic. Conservation is the preserving of something, usually the natural world or environment.

9. **(C)** Handcuffs are used to control and restrict the movements of a prisoner. A leash does the same for a dog. (A) can be eliminated for the very reason that makes it appealing initially. The excellent relationship between handcuffs and manacles is absolutely not replicated between prisoner (a person) and penitentiary (an institution). All four of the other answer choices fit the probable first cut at a relationship—seeing that the handcuffs somehow go on the prisoner. (B), (C), and (E) all relate in the sense of the first word physically surrounding some part of the second

word. The last step can be taken either on the basis of the idea of restriction, as elaborated above, or on the basis of a dog being an independent entity, like a prisoner. Or the idea that shoes are helpful to the feet, while a leash is not helpful to the dog. The ring is decorative, while handcuffs and leashes are generally not.

10. **(C)** The javelin and the cannonball have a shape relationship of elongated and rod-shaped to spherical, which is duplicated in spear and bullet. In addition, the original pair are both weapons, one propelled by muscle power and one by gunpowder, which also fits (C). None of the others has such a balanced relationship. However, several have partial relationships. In (A), a discus and a javelin are both used in track and field; a sling is a weapon, but a discus really is not. Also, a sling is the delivery system and a cannonball is the missile. (B) has a good start since a javelin is certainly thrown, but not many people willingly catch cannonballs. (E) is easy to eliminate since even if one considers a javelin to be a Greek item, a cannonball is not particularly Spanish. (D) is the second-best answer since it shares the shape relationship described above with (C). The differences are that an arrow is a weapon, like a javelin and a spear, but it is a missile, being shot from a bow. A shotput is like a cannonball in composition and shape, but is not, as far as its being a shotput is concerned, either a weapon or something shot from a weapon. When shape is an issue, it is sometimes not the only issue.

11. **(D)** An imp is a junior-grade devil and a cherub is a junior-grade angel, roughly speaking. A devil and an angle have the same oppositeness. (A) and (C) have a feeling of oppositeness, but lack the specific structure of (D). (A) is merely opposite. (C) has the moral element, but is not about beings. The low and high is unlikely when there are specific moral referents available. The others are not even real opposites.

12. **(A)** A radio and a phonograph are both electronic appliances, but none of the answer choices are two related appliances. A radio and a phonograph both deal with the same type of information system—sound. All of the answer choices also exhibit this relationship to one degree or another. This tells us that we are at least on the right track. What are the further refinements we can make to the idea of similar media? A radio gives an impermanent sound, while a phonograph gives the possibility of being used again and again, and is designed to do that. (E) fails here, even if it survived the same media requirement. In (C), both are impermanent. In the other three answer choices, it appears at first that they are all permanent. (B) is difficult to deal with since both sides of the analogy are so similar, certainly much more similar than in the original pair. A movie

and a photograph and a letter and a book are the last two possibilities. The major difference between a movie and a photograph is that a movie moves. In the original pair, either both move or neither moves, depending on how you view it— the movement is to be interpreted in terms of the media, not the mechanism, since the media is the issue. In (A) there is somewhat less permanence in a letter than in a book, particularly in the intention. A book is intended to be around for a time, but a letter is usually, and typically, a transitory medium. This is not a perfect analogy, but with a little patience, it can be solved.

13. **(E)** To immigrate is to enter a country, and to enlist is to enter the army. Since the original pair are a verb and a noun, it is likely that the correct answer will either be the same or an adverb and an adjective. Thus (A) and (D) do not appeal. (B) looks good since immigrate is so close to emigrate—the exact opposite. But a ship is not the exact opposite of a country. Many analogies have little vertical relationships, but in evaluating an answer choice that does have a vertical relationship in one part of the pairs, you should demand that there be a relationship in the other side of the pairs as well. (C) is a verb and a noun and while immigrate is a kind of moving, the country is not the placement, but the place.

14. **(D)** Urge is a somewhat weaker form of insist, so the analogy relationship is one of degree. (B) and (C) have no degree idea and are eliminated. (E) has only a mild one and is weak. (A) and (D) are both quite good. In choosing between them, we must refer to the meanings of the words and go beyond the simple idea of degree. Urge and request are ideas that leave their object a choice, while insist and demand do not permit as much choice. (A) cannot show a similar affinity.

15. **(B)** A grapnel is a hook-like object that is used to hook over edges to hold a rope for climbing up walls or cliffs, etc. A gaff is a nautical type of hook, usually used to take fish aboard. Thus we have similar hooking types of objects, with one side of the pair being generally a land object and the other a nautical object. None of the other answer choices has any hook idea in them. Since this is an unusual idea, it is likely to be very powerful if it is present in all four parts of an analogy. None of the other choices has a strong synonym idea either.

16. **(A)** An indictment is an early part of a legal proceeding in which the nature of the charges is laid out. Similarly, an impeachment is the early part of another legal process in which the charges are laid out. The second part of each pair is the part of the process in which the punishment is meted out. (C) has some strength since it consists of a designation process and an end process, but it

has no secondary similarity as between the two processes described in the original pair and (A). In (B), the first word, arraigned, is similar to indicted, though not really the same in all respects, but tried is not the final outcome. (D) has the second part right, punished, but guilty is not the same as sentenced, which follows the finding of guilty, overlooking the difficulties that the answer presents us with different parts of speech.

17. **(B)** (A) and (D) are simply not related to the passage at all.

 (B), (C), and (E) have some merit. (E) has the merit of being a topic in the book, but it is not clear that sound is a good reference to quantum mechanics. While quantum mechanics is mentioned by the book as a thing to be symbolized, the book also has to discuss the symbolization of music, and that seems to be much more related to sound than quantum mechanics.

 Both (B) and (C) have the merit of referring to the music, but with a title that refers to "sound" AND "symbol," it seems likely that the sound part refers to music and the symbol part to the notational system, rather than the other way around.

18. **(E)** (A) becomes unlikely when the first paragraph calls Einsteinian physics a "truly adequate" system, even though it may not be totally correct. Other keys to not choosing this otherwise appealing answer choice are the reference to the Theory of Relativity, which is not specifically mentioned at all, and the last paragraph's reiteration of the correctness of Einstein.

 (B) is referred to in the passage as a specification of the strangeness of Einsteinian physics, and thus is part of them rather than contradictory to them. (C) fails because of the several cautionary statements such as the "unlikely" event of our ever experiencing a reversed time flow.

 (D) refers to the imaginary mass of tachyons, but the passage says only that the tachyon "may" exist, not that it does.

 (E) has the flag word *precisely,* which tells you that the answer choice is not referring to going faster than light, but to attaining exactly the speed of light. The need to move an infinite quantity of mass to go exactly the speed of light is referred to as a barrier, and is intuitively unlikely.

19. **(D)** Speculative is certainly a fair characterization of the passage. (D) is preferable to (C) because the passage is hopeful that some of these speculative things may come to pass, rather than suspicious of anything. (E) is an unlikely choice for any question of this sort.

20. **(A)** As is usual with this sort of question, there are several good answers among which to choose. (D) is clearly wrong because Zuckerkandl is not stated to have any theories of tachyon formation.

(E) similarly fails for lack of reference to the passage. Its only appeal is its obscurity.

 (A), (B), and (C) require closer inspection. (C) seems to find that Einsteinian physics cannot treat tachyons, but actually it is predicted by the formulas associated with Einsteinian physics that such strange things as reverse time flow might occur, so (C) is out. The primary difference between (A) and (B) is the question of whether it is the notation and theories on the one hand or the observations on the other which indicates the need for improved notation. (B), while a good abstract statement of the progress of science, does not "cover the waterfront" on this passage. The only observations, cited in the passage support the theoretical speculations rather than disprove the theories. Hence, (A).

21. **(C)** It is certainly not too soon for (D), since that has happened. It seems likely that the time for (A) will never arrive, but it is not discussed in the passage. The author is clearly not satisfied with the current notational system, and thus (E) is definitely in order. While (B) has merit because the author does not endorse Zuckerkandl's ideas, (C) has more merit since (C) is definitely stated to be far from accomplishment, if indeed it is possible at all.

22. **(B)** In the author's admitted oversimplification of Zuckerkandl, he says that music might be a better language for physics. Better than what? Better than math, which is, thus, also seen as a language. (D) fails because of the word great, though even without that disqualifier it would be inferior to (B).

23. **(E)** Without attempting to probe the nature of philosophy, which is certainly not an issue on a test question, (E) best links the topic of the passage to philosophy. (A), (B), and (C) are flack and (D) should not seem very good. Perhaps the nature of any field is a philosophical question, but the methods must usually be just technical matters within the field.

24. **(D)** By citing the particular part of the passage, the question requires you to see what follows from that particular phraseology. The cited phrase has the interesting aspect that something is named by scientists which is not definitely in existence. The rest of the passage certainly spoke of the tachyon as being a theoretical object, so (D)'s statement about the timing of the naming of the tachyon is certainly a good bet. It is still not certainly known—in the passage's terms—but it does have a name. It is theoretically described and it therefore seems likely that no one would have named the object without some reason, though it was not yet actually discovered.

 (A) is flack and should be dismissed quickly.

Such an answer choice is rarely correct unless it reflects a specific statement in the passage.

(C) may well be true, in a witty but somewhat paradoxical statement. However, even if it turns out there is no such thing as a tachyon, that is not what can be inferred from the cited passage.

Both (E) and (B) have some appeal. (B)'s. dissolves on close inspection. The difference between (B) and (D) is the issue of whether the particle was named before it was known to exist or before it actually existed in the world. While it is possible that it is named and will only later come into existence, there is nothing in the passage about creating tachyons. Thus (D) is preferable to (B). (E) is a meritorious statement in that it is certainly true and we do know that it is true (definitely true that the ideas *may* not exist) but we have no information to support the qualifier many; so (E) fails.

25. **(A)** The passage stresses the endurance of the legend of Atlantis, an island first mentioned in Plato's *Timaeus*. Although (B) mentions Plato, geography is not relevant. Choice (C) also has some relation to the speculations about Atlantis, but only (A) covers the broadest possibilities.

26. **(E)** Since the main thrust of the passage indicates that Atlantis is a legendary island, no recorded evidence by its inhabitants could have been left. Thus, (E) is the only choice that could be derived.

27. **(C)** The passage states that the island was destroyed because of the "impiety of its people." There is no other cause mentioned.

28. **(C)** Retaliate means to return like for like, especially acting to revenge some wrong. To turn the other cheek means to not return like for like, but to return good for evil. As with many antonym problems, there seems little difficulty when the meaning of the word is read from the dictionary. In practice, you might have been attracted to (A) or (D) even if you had some idea of what retaliate meant. In order for (A) to be the correct opposite, retaliate would have to mean to lose serenity, or to become upset. While it is true that much retaliation is done while one is upset, the essence of retaliation is action, not merely the emotional state. (D)'s attraction stems from the understanding that retaliation will rarely improve relations with the object of the retaliation. Here, again, the failure of the wrong answer choice is not that it is without any merit, but that it is a different thing than the stem word, a result rather than an action. (E) suffers the same defect since it deals with broad-mindedness, while retaliation is not narrow-mindedness.

29. **(D)** Analysis is the breaking up of something into its parts. Synthesis is putting something together out of its parts. (C) might appeal to an over subtle thinker, since analysis is to some extent directed and productive thinking, while a parenthesis is an aside or tangent. However, a parenthesis is not necessarily unproductive, nor is analysis always to the point. Dialysis is a chemical process, such as kidney dialysis, which cleans the blood. Electrolysis is the use of electricity to change or, in the case of hair, to destroy something. Emphasis is the placing of stress or importance on something. Analysis has to do with structure, not importance.

30. **(E)** Peremptory means seizing the initiative and overriding other considerations. (B) and (D) are not very good, but (A) and (C) have some merit. Humble would be the opposite of arrogant, and a peremptory tone is often considered arrogant in the sense of taking over what should be the rights of others. However, peremptory specifically refers to the act of taking over control, and (E), deferential, refers specifically to the act of giving over control, which is even better. (C) has less merit than does (A), but reflects the understanding that it is an attempt of strength to preempt. It may be true that a weak person is not likely to be peremptory, but weak is a much broader term.

31. **(B)** Salacious means obscene; thus wholesome is the best opposite indicating a morally "good" quality in opposition to the morally "bad" quality of salacious. Also, wholesome has precisely the connotation of being sound of mind, while salacious implies the opposite. Religious is not a very good opposite since it refers to faithfulness to some system or religious beliefs, but does not imply any particular standard being followed. One man's religion may well be another's obscenity.

32. **(B)** Insolvent refers to the inability to raise so-called liquid assets such as cash, and thus to the condition of being unable to pay one's debts; hence (B). The other answer choices all echo other words unrelated in meaning to insolvent. (D), for instance, has some echo of the word solvent as a chemical, which is not the same as financially solvent. Insolvent refers only to financial matters.

33. **(C)** Homogenous comes from the prefix *homo-*, meaning same and the root *gen*, meaning kind; thus the word means all of the same kind. Both (C) and (E) have merit. (C) refers to the state of being diversified, which is a precise opposite of the state of being all the same. (E)'s merit is primarily the inclusion of the word different within the word differential. (E) actually refers to the size or scope of a difference, which is related to the idea of there being a difference. This is not itself the state of having differences, as (C) is. (A) means very thrifty, even stingy. (B) is the state of being conscious. (D) means talkative, from the root *loq-*, meaning talk or speech, as in eloquent.

34. **(D)** The root word amalgam is a combination of something. Thus combine is a very precise syno-

nym, leaving segregate, which means to separate, as a good opposite. (A) means to blame; (B), to delay; (C), to shine or glitter; and (E), to command or forbid.

35. **(B)** Temerity means boldness, even audacity. Diffidence, (B), is shyness or reluctance to advance or act. (A) is a difficult and embarrassing situation. (C) is a name, or nickname, from the root *nomen* meaning name, as in nomenclature; and *cog*, meaning known as, from the same root as cognition, thinking.

36. **(A)** Mutation means change. (A) is the noun form of constant. Mutation does not refer only to genetic mutation, but can mean any change from the original that is sudden and relatively permanent. (E) has some merit since it does at least refer to change. However, unamended means unchanged and would be a better opposite to mutated. Unamended does not refer to the thing or process itself.

37. **(D)** Sybaritic means loving luxury, or luxurious. (B), meaning stubborn, is no opposite. (D), the correct answer, means sparse and without luxury or ostentation. (E) has some association with being opposed to wild luxury, since a conservative in the original meaning of the word is someone who wishes to conserve things, and presumably not waste them. Similarly, a conservative party will not be sybaritic. However, conservative is much broader than austere or sybaritic, and is thus not as good an opposite as austere.

38. **(C)** Prosaic, meaning everyday or commonplace, derives from the word prose. Fulsome is so full that it is obnoxious. (B), mundane, is a synonym for prosaic, since it comes from the root *mundis,* meaning earth, and refers to typical earthly things, as opposed to glorious, heavenly things.

SECTION II

1. **(A)** Since the first word of each choice would acceptably complete the sentence up to "journalism," we cannot make any preliminary eliminations. As for the second word, it is logical to berate (chastise) for being childish. It is not logical to laud (praise) for being voyeuristic (unhealthily obsessed with sex), to criticize for being authentic (a positive expression), to requite (make amends) for being responsible, or to attack for being important.

2. **(D)** You can immediately eliminate (A), (C), and (E), because rattling a newspaper shows neither calm, duplicity, nor opinion. Looking more closely at (B), we now have: "Rattling his newspaper to show his irritation, the husband made known his approval of his wife's new breakfast table." Since showing irritation is certainly not a sign of approval, and since, according to (D), showing anger is a rational sign of disapproval, (D) is the only possible answer.

3. **(D)** You can eliminate (A), (B), (C), and (E) because in these cases either one or both of the words in each choice are adjectives describing qualities of remarks which are not necessarily indicative of a keen or incisive mind. Trenchant and penetrating, on the other hand, are synonyms; both are used specifically to describe keenness of mind.

4. **(A)** Choice (B) is unacceptable because genocide is used only in relation to people. Similarly, (C) and (E) are unacceptable because the terms vagrancy and morality are associated only with human beings. Choice (D) is unacceptable because it confuses affects (personal properties) with effects (results brought about). This leaves proliferation (growth and spreading out) of algae as the cause of the exodus (departure) of many kinds of fish.

5. **(B)** Because the new machine failed to make the garbage smaller, the garbage filled the kitchen. Compact is a transitive verb meaning make smaller.

6. **(E)** You can talk your way out of some sort of agreement, but not out of an economy, standard, trawler, or van. One of the lesser known meanings of compact is a brief agreement.

7. **(C)** What Sally lost were the contents of her purse. This would immediately preclude vehicle, piano, compost, or complexion. However, a compact is a small case containing powder, puff, and mirror, and is usually carried in a lady's purse.

8. **(E)** The original pair are two ways of judging the merit of actions. The two standards are based on different ideas. Both words in the original pair are abstractions, so it is likely that both of the parts of the correct answer will also be abstractions. (C) can be eliminated for not having any moral or legal play, while some of the others do. Both (D) and (E) have a first part that has some moral aspect and a second part that has some legal aspect. (A) has the first, perhaps, and (B) has the second, but neither has both. In choosing between (D) and (E), it is clear that sin and crime are both offenses against precisely the same standards, relatively, as in the original pair. The question then is how well (D) keeps the same relationship. A priest is concerned with morality, it is true, but he is also concerned with religion, which is not quite the same. A jury is concerned with legality, but actually is the trier of fact in most cases. Furthermore, the two are concrete and the origi-

nal pair are abstract. Since we have at least as good an abstract pair in (E), it is ahead on all counts.

9. **(D)** An ellipse is a kind of curve and a square is a kind of polygon. A polygon is a figure with many sides, each one of which is a straight line. None of the other answer choices have this relationship. (A) has a little appeal since a stutter is a kind of speech, but is in particular a defective kind of speech and an ellipse is not particularly defective. (E) has to do with geometry, as does (B), but in (E) we have a measurement and an object, which might have a shape related to the measurement. In (B) we have a potentially confusing relationship. A base is part of a triangle in the sense of being one of the constituent parts that go to make up a triangle. This is different from the idea of being part of a group, which is the relationship in the original pair.

10. **(E)** Sugar is the original substance and saccharin is the manufactured imitation. The same applies to butter and margarine. (B) and (C) have relationships of source to product or derivative. (D) is a general class and a member of the class. (A) is two types of the same thing. In (A) there is some appeal since both the stem words are sweeteners and both the words in (A) are sweet. However, since the stem pair are neither synonyms nor antonyms, there must be some other idea than merely general relationship.

11. **(C)** The relationship is one of strength and the freedom of the recipient to do as he wishes. (A) and (B) do not have the idea of degree at all. (C), (D), and (E) do have that idea, but (E) fails since (C) and (D) both have the additional concept of being words relating one person to another person or thing. (C) is superior in that it has not only the element of degree (require is stronger than suggest) but also the additional element of interaction between two people, an element not present in (D).

12. **(A)** Water and faucet relate in a few different ways. First of all a faucet carries a flow of water through it. But a more specific idea is that a faucet is a way of controlling the flow of water. The first idea would fit (D), but while steam and water both will flow, a pipe and a faucet should not jibe in your mind very well. A throttle, however, does control the flow of fuel just like a faucet controls the flow of water. (B) has only a rudimentary appeal since state of matter such as solid and liquid would most likely be something like water and ice, the liquid and solid forms of the same thing. (C)'s two parts relate to the original pair in a general way, but they do not relate to each other in any useful way. (E) has virtually no relationship in the choice at all.

13. **(E)** A flask is a small container; a bottle could be considered a larger one, perhaps. A brochure is a small type of publication, while a tome is definitely a larger one. This is not a perfect analogy and could be difficult since (A) presents a totally different idea. (C) and (D) do not relate to the original pair, except (D) might be backward. (B) is possible, but a flask need not be metal. (A) has the merit that one does think of whiskey being usually contained in a flask and milk in a bottle. However, that is a vertical relationship and (E) is a horizontal one, and the primary relationship is always preferred.

14. **(D)** Caliber is a way of measuring the size of rifles, since it refers to the size of the rifle barrel on the inside. Gauge is the way of measuring the width of the tracks or rails. The others have no measurement idea at all. Quality in (A) has some idea of connecting with caliber since one speaks of a high caliber as meaning high quality. Similarly (B)'s bore relates to rifle, but in each case the very strength of the secondary connection proves that there is no primary connection.

15. **(E)** This is a matter of degree. Mince is chopping very fine or very much. Beating is very vigorous stirring. Furthermore, both the original pair and (E) are cooking terms, which only (A) shares. (A) fails since there is no internal relationship.

16. **(B)** A peccadillo is a minor infraction; a crime is major. Hesitate is a small degree, while procrastinate is a high degree. Bushel and peck have some relationship of magnitude, but the verbs are preferable here since there is the idea of doing something very much.

17. **(B)** This answer can be approached two ways. The first that will occur to you is the elimination of answer choices. In an inference question, elimination must be done carefully until the proper answer appears. The second way is to go right to the issue of the usage of vegetative in the passage. This happens to reward a little "outside" knowledge of microbiology.

(A) is not mentioned anywhere, either in terms of plants or in terms of the disease possibilities of human habitations. (C) and (E) are also not mentioned. Any answer choice, like (C), that says something is a fact bears a heavy burden and must be examined carefully. Here it fails. (E) fails because the author does not seem to have any trouble classifying bacteria, since he throws around quite a few names. One point is to notice that bacillus is used to describe particular types of bacteria, as shown by the references in the first two sentences, which both discuss the same phenomenon, first as an aspect of bacteria and then in terms of bacillus characteristics exemplifying this process.

(D) has some merit, and in fact there are some similarities and the author is using that idea to describe the bacteria more concisely. However, the question stem is asking for the reason that the author is using the term as well as the significance of it—the burden of information it carries here. The vegetative stage is contrasted to the dormant stage such as with the anthrax bacillus, which will grow after being dry for ten years.

The direct way of approaching the answer is to see that the vegetative stage is a stage of vulnerability to the drying-out process, as contrasted to the spore stage, which is not as vulnerable. Since the spore stage is dormant, the vegetative phase is growth. The word germinate also helps, since a seed germinates and then grows into a plant.

18. **(D)** It is important to stick within the limits of the information that the passage gives you. The only item that is mentioned in this short passage in relation to the idea of increasing or decreasing the risk of infection is the susceptibility of various microorganisms to drying out. Therefore, the risk of infection will be great when the risk of drying out is least, that is, when it is humid. (B) will appeal to outside knowledge that getting chilled is supposed to increase the risk of infection. This may or may not be true, depending on which study you read, but it is definitely not in the passage.

19. **(E)** In order for a statement to be inferred, we must be convinced that there is a very good chance that the author will agree with the statement, given what he has already said.

(A) is not inferrable, because of the word best. It is stated in the passage that removing the moisture from a bacteria will kill it, but there is no comparison of methods made, and thus there can be no statement of relative merit or efficiency.

(B) cannot be inferred because the word eliminate is too strong. Certainly the passage permits the inference that drying out a house will reduce the chances of infection, but not that they will be eliminated entirely.

(C) is a little tricky since it plays on our idea that dry is good and wet is bad as far as infection is concerned. There are two objections to (C). First, it doesn't actually say anything about infection at all, which is a moderately serious objection since infection and bacteria are the sole topic of the passage. Second, and more important, steam heating does not mean that the air is any wetter than with any other form of heating. Steam heating is not the spraying of steam about the house, but the passage of steam through pipes, which become hot and radiate heat into the room. Although this requires a trifle of outside knowledge, the knowledge that steam heat does not mean steam in the air is within the reasonable bounds of common knowledge for GRE-takers.

20. **(B)** The passage makes it clear that infectiousness is a function of the resistance of the bacteria to drying, and also that the tubercle bacteria is one of the more resistant. There are two points to be made in addition to this citation to the passage. First, the tubercle bacillus' connection to tuberculosis is fair to ask about even though it is not common knowledge. The passage refers to tubercle and the question to tuberculosis. A knowledge of word parts might suffice to make the connection clear, but even if that failed, you should not choose (E) on the basis that the question is simply unrelated to the passage because the passage did not mention tuberculosis. That would indeed be unfair. Thus you can deduce the connection between tubercle and tuberculosis. Second, the question asks about infectiousness. All of the answers except (E) speak to aspects of the passage that might explain why something is infectious. However, the basic idea of the passage was the connection between drying out and dying on the part of microorganisms. Therefore, (B) and (C) are preferable in all likelihood, and a close examination of those two will likely lead you to the connection between the tubercle and tuberculosis as just described.

21. **(E)** The author is curious about the amount and effects of advertising, hence (E). No value judgments are made in the passage which could support (A), (B), or (D). (C) weakly reflects the author's desire to learn more about advertising.

22. **(D)** This term is not explicitly defined, but at the end of the fourth paragraph the range in costs of "push promotion" is explained by difficulties in separating out the elements of direct selling, hence (D). (A), (B), and (C) are unlikely from the second paragraph, which distinguishes them from "push promotion."

23. **(B)** (B) is stated in the next-to-last paragraph. (A) fails since restaurants are nowhere mentioned. (C), while true in the real world, is not stated in the passage. (D) has the difficulty that both prepared and natural are not in the passage and it is not entirely clear that these are identical to highly processed and highly perishable, respectively. Given the merit of (B), (D) can be eliminated. (E) is simply false, since highly processed foods are stated to account for only 20 percent of the food dollar.

24. **(C)** (C) describes the article perfectly. (A) and (D) fail for want of such value judgments in the passage. (E) is not done in any final way, though some discussion is given of the topic. (B) is not stated and may even go against the tenor of the passage since a statement that something is large does not imply that it is too large.

25. **(D)** (A), (B), and (C) are explicitly stated at the end of the last paragraph. (E) is implied because of the concern about highly processed versus less-processed foods. (D) is not there since no mention of restaurant versus home eating is made.

26. **(C)** This is a bit of a detail question, but general considerations can help. Food advertising is, overall, #1 in dollar volume, which eliminates (A) and (D), since we are looking for an exception to falseness. (E) speaks to radio ads only, and the first paragraph stated that, in radio, food is near the top.

The other two discuss the breakdown of the food advertising dollar among the different media. The fourth paragraph states that television is less than 1 cent, incentives 0.6 cents, print 0.5 cents, and push promotion 0.7 to 1.4 cents. This shows that (A) is false, and also that (C) is indeterminate, which is to say not definitely false and, thus the correct answer.

27. **(A)** (A) results from the author's attempt at a balance sheet, where he states that food ads subsidize publications. While it is true that free television is also subsidized by food ads, its cost will not rise since it is free. Cable television is not mentioned in the passage as having ads at all, so (B) is out, and the author does not claim that people watch programs for the ads, as (D) would have it. (E) fails when (A) succeeds.

28. **(B)** Intransigent means unwilling to compromise, while conciliatory means willing to compromise or reconcile when differences exist. (B) or (D) seem somewhat connected to the stem word because of the "trans" portion that is common to both intransigent and transportation. However, the real history of the word is that it comes from the same root as transact and means an unwillingness to have a transaction. This can serve as an example of being careful with word parts. The "trans" portion might have had some relation to (B) or (D), but the "sig" portion was not being taken into consideration, and thus an error could be made.

29. **(D)** One thing that you know about ingenuous is that it is NOT ingenious. Ingenuous means open and honest; thus devious is the best opposite.

30. **(B)** A canard is an untruth or a false report, hence (B). Canard is usually used to describe something that is unflattering as well as untrue ("a base canard"); thus (D) might appear to have some merit. Blasphemy is irreverence toward God or something sacred, which has some element of being (presumably) untrue, but it is a very specific word relating to sacred things, while canard is not limited in that way.

31. **(E)** DISinterested means not taking sides, being impartial—hence (E). UNinterested means having no desire to become involved in any way, which would be a good opposite to (B).

32. **(A)** Propitiate means to appease or make favorably inclined. Anger is a very good opposite to both shades of meaning. Hurt has some apparent merit, since hurting someone may well anger them, but it is the actual state of mind of being angry or unfavorably disposed which is the full opposite to propitiate. None of the other answers has any real opposite meaning to propitiate, though depart may seem acceptable if the stem word is unknown. The "pro" part of the stem word is not likely to be enough, by itself, to give a right answer.

33. **(B)** Absolve means to clear from blame, while blame means to assign guilt. Muddy might appeal if you thought that absolve meant simply to solve. While it is true that there are a few cases where the addition of a prefix changes the meaning very little, most words with prefixes have a significantly altered meaning. Repent also has to do with guilt, but it is a wish by the guilty person that he had not done his misdeeds. In some religious contexts, repentance may precede absolution, but they are not the same. Recant means to take back one's speech or change ones stated opinions, perhaps because of error. Free has no real connection to absolve.

34. **(E)** A hedonist is one who believes that pleasure or happiness is the highest good. This has often been used to mean specifically physical or sensual pleasure as being the highest good. A puritan is one who believes in a strict, even austere, religious life and frowns on physical pleasure. A martinet is a person who adheres strictly to the rules, but there is no connotation either for or against physical or sensual pleasures. As a person who appreciates the life of the mind and the value of ideas, an intellectual would be somewhat opposite to a hedonist, but need not be opposed to physical or sensual pleasure as is the puritan. A scientist may be seen as a subgroup of an intellectual in this problem.

35. **(C)** A cretin is a person of subnormal intellectual abilities. A genius has greater than normal intellectual capacity. A seer and a scholar are persons with intellectual achievements and wisdom, but these meanings are not referring to the capacity of the person so much as what has been done with that capacity. A talent need not be talented intellectually and thus is not necessarily an opposite of cretin. Moron is virtually a synonym for cretin.

36. **(D)** To decant means to pour off gently without disturbance. To slosh out would be to pour out roughly with great disturbance. Cork, meaning to seal in, also has some connection, but is not describing some movement of the liquid. The other answers have little connection as stated, though upset does oppose the gentleness of decant, and tap does refer to the process of opening up a barrel, as of beer. Level off appeals

because of the "cant" portion of decant, which originally meant to tilt, but now refers to pouring.

37. **(C)** Arrant means total or complete. Thus, partial is the best opposite. One of the most common usages is in the phrase arrant nonsense, meaning complete nonsense. This usage might lead to an association with foolishness and thus tempt you to choose wise. Arrant does NOT mean arrogant; thus, humble could be eliminated even if the exact meaning of arrant escaped you. Intrepid means brave and fearless, which is unconnected to arrant.

38. **(A)** A wastrel is a wasteful person, a spendthrift. A conservator is someone whose job, or nature, is to conserve or preserve things. A prodigal is very similar to a wastrel and thus not an opposite. A lutist plays a lute and a noble is highborn, of good breeding, but could be of whatever personality. A phantasm is a mirage or hallucination.

SECTION III

1. **(C)** "Of" in this case indicates multiplication. The product of 5 and 36 will be equal to the product of 36 and 5, and .05 and .36 will have the same number of decimal places; therefore, the two quantities must be equal. You do not need to actually do the multiplication in full.

2. **(B)** It is not possible to combine the two radicals of the right column. Although $\sqrt{5} \times \sqrt{10} = \sqrt{50}$, $\sqrt{5} + \sqrt{10} \neq \sqrt{15}$. The operation works only for multiplication. Since $\sqrt{15} < \sqrt{16}$, $\sqrt{15}$ must be less than 4. Since $\sqrt{5} > \sqrt{4}$, $\sqrt{5}$ must be greater than 2; and since $\sqrt{10}$ is greater than $\sqrt{9}$, $\sqrt{10}$ must be greater than 3. The two terms of the right column are slightly greater than 2 and 3 respectively, so their sum must be greater than 5. Column B is slightly greater than 5. Column A is less than 4.

3. **(B)** The (346×23) is only flack. It does not point to any difference between p and q. Since the first term of both equations is the same, we can assign it the constant value k. The given information can now be simplified:

$$k + p = 34,731$$
$$k + p = 35,124$$

Since 35,124 is greater than 34,731, q must be greater than p.

4. **(A)** Remember that the drawings in this subsection are not necessarily drawn to scale. Thus, you should not solve problems on the basis of a visual estimate of size or shape alone. However, manipulating the diagram in your mind—seeing what the possibilities are if some line is lengthened or shortened or some angle varied—can often help

you to see the answer to a quantitative comparison problem without computation, or at least will reduce your difficulties.

In this case, exploring what it means to say that x < y can start with seeing what it would mean if x = y. As the first diagram shows, x = y means that SRT has two equal legs, ST and TR. T will be in the middle of PQ, hence PT = QT. But as y gets larger, it will result in the line RT hitting the line PQ closer and closer to Q, thus making TQ smaller and PT larger. Therefore PT is always larger than TQ when y > x.

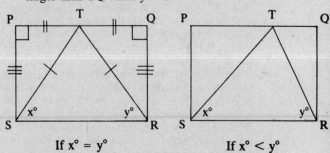

If $x° = y°$　　　　　If $x° < y°$

5. **(D)** Since x might be a fraction, it is not possible to determine which of the columns is greater. If x is $\frac{1}{2}$, then Column A is $\frac{1}{4}$ while Column B is 1, making Column B greater in that instance. But if x is 2, Column A is 4 and Column B is 4, making the two columns equal. Finally, if x is greater than 2, say 3, then Column A is 9 and Column B is 6, making A greater.

6. **(C)** Since the numbers here are relatively manageable, the easiest solution to this problem is to do the indicated arithmetic operation:

$$\frac{4}{5} - \frac{3}{4} = \frac{16 - 15}{20} = \frac{1}{20}$$

You might also notice that $\frac{4}{5} = 80\%$ and $\frac{3}{4} = 75\%$, with their difference being 5%, which is $\frac{1}{20}$.

7. **(B)** We can see that the fraction $\frac{3}{13} < \frac{3}{12}$, thus $\frac{3}{13} < \frac{1}{4}$; but $\frac{13}{51} > \frac{13}{52}$, thus $\frac{13}{51} > \frac{1}{4}$. Therefore, $\frac{3}{13} < \frac{1}{4} < \frac{13}{51}$, answer **(B)**. We look for reference points. For example, the 52 cards in a deck are in four suits of 13 cards each.

8. **(B)** This problem uses the term S_n to indicate that whatever n may be, the S_n value will be found by multiplying n by 3 and adding 2 to the result. One way of solving this problem would be to do the actual work indicated for 5, 4, 9 and 8, finding that S_n for 5 is $S_5 = 3(5) + 2 = 17$ and $S_4 = 14$, $S_9 = 29$, $S_8 = 26$, with 17 + 14 being smaller than 29 + 26.

But there is really no reason to do the actual work. Since the QC issue is which column is bigger, we always pay attention to how things get bigger or smaller. S_n will get bigger as n gets bigger because it is just multiplying n by 3. Since Column A has two smaller numbers, the sum is smaller.

9. **(C)** The problem does *not* presuppose that the student is familiar with the metric system. The cost of the meat in Column A is: 10 lbs. × $2.50/lb. = $25.00. The cost of the meat in Column B is: 5 kilos × $5.00/kilo = $25.00.

10. **(C)** The problem is most easily solved by cancelling the zeros in each fraction:

$$\frac{1\cancel{0}}{10,00\cancel{0}} = \frac{1}{1000} \qquad \frac{1\cancel{000}}{1,000,\cancel{000}} = \frac{1}{1000}$$

So Column A and Column B are both $\frac{1}{1000}$ and equal.

11. **(D)** Do not try to solve a quantitative comparison by visually estimating lengths of lines. In this case, there is not sufficient information to deduce that PQRS is or is not a square—even though it is drawn as one. The following group of drawings will show that no conclusion regarding the relative lengths of PQ and QS is possible. PQ could be equal to QR, but it doesn't have to be.

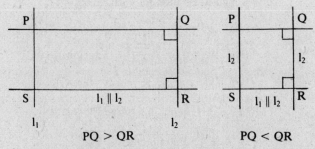

$$PQ > QR \qquad\qquad PQ < QR$$

12. **(D)** The information supplied in the two columns is sufficient only to allow us to compute the *capacities* or *volumes* of the boxes described. We have no information regarding the size of pears or the size of potatoes, and we are not even told what part of each box's capacity is being used.

13. **(C)** The problem is most easily solved by grouping like terms and simplifying. We want the x terms on one side, pure numbers on the other.

$$4x^2 + 2x^2 + 3x + 2x = 3x^2 + 3x^2 + 2x + 2x + 3$$
$$6x^2 + 5x = 6x^2 + 4x + 3$$
$$x = 3$$

Since x = 3, x^2 must be 9 and the two columns are equal.

14. **(B)** The most natural approach here is to perform the indicated operations:

$$n \cdot 1 \cdot 1 = n \qquad n + 1 + 1 = n + 2$$

While the comparison n to n + 2 is simple, let us carry through the process completely to review comparing across the columns. It is possible to simplify across the comparison, that is, we subtract an 'n from both columns. (*Note:* It is permissible to add or subtract like terms from columns because such operations do not interfere with the balance of an equality nor the direction of an inequality. It is also permissible to multiply or divide both columns by the same term, provided that the term is a positive one. One must not, however, multiply or divide both columns by a negative term, for such an operation would reverse the direction of an inequality; or by zero, for such an operation would destroy the inequality.) So we are left with zero in Column A and 2 in Column B. B is greater.

15. **(A)** The figure is a triangle, so the sum of the interior angles must be 180°:

$$6x + 2x + x = 180°$$
$$9x = 180°$$
$$x = 20°$$

So Column A is greater than Column B.

16. **(D)** The minute hand will make one complete circle of the dial by 7:15. Then it will complete another half circle by 7:45. Since there are 360° in a circle, the arc travelled by the minute hand will be one full 360° plus half of another full 360° yielding 360° + 180° = 540°.

17. **(E)** One way of solving this problem would be to convert each of the fractions to a decimal or find a common denominator so that a direct comparison can be made. This is too time-consuming. Instead, anytime the GRE asks a question similar to this one, the student can be confident that there is very likely some shortcut available. Here the shortcut is to recognize that every answer choice, except for (E), is either equal to or greater than $\frac{1}{2}$. $\frac{7}{8}$ and $\frac{8}{9}$ are clearly much larger than $\frac{1}{2}$. $\frac{7}{12}$ must be greater than $\frac{1}{2}$ since $\frac{6}{12}$ is equal to $\frac{1}{2}$. But $\frac{6}{17}$ is less than $\frac{1}{2}$—$\frac{6}{12}$ would be $\frac{1}{2}$. So (E) is the smallest of the fractions. Even if the shortcut had eliminated only two or three answers, it would have been worthwhile.

18. **(C)** Even though it is not absolutely necessary to draw a figure to solve this problem, anyone finding the solution elusive will likely profit from a "return to basics:"

$$\frac{3x}{4} + 1$$
$$\frac{3x}{4} + 1 \quad \boxed{} \quad \frac{3x}{4} + 1 \qquad P = 4\left(\frac{3x}{4} + 1\right)$$
$$\frac{3x}{4} + 1$$

Quickly sketching the figure may help you avoid the mistake of multiplying the side of the square by another side, giving the area, answer (D), not the perimeter. The perimeter will be 4s, not s^2: $4(\frac{3x}{4}+1) = \frac{12x}{4} + 4 = 3x + 4$.

19. **(C)** Average speed is nothing more than miles travelled over the time taken: rate (speed) =

$\dfrac{\text{distance}}{\text{time}}$. The elapsed time here is 4 hours and 48 minutes. 48 minutes is $\frac{4}{5}$ hours. Our formula then will be: $\dfrac{240 \text{ miles}}{4\frac{4}{5} \text{ hours}}$. We attack the problem by converting the denominator to a fraction: $4\frac{4}{5} = \frac{24}{5}$, and then we invert and multiply:

$$\frac{240 \text{ miles}}{4\frac{4}{5} \text{ hrs.}} = \frac{240}{\frac{24}{5}} = \frac{5}{24} \times 240 = 50 \text{ miles per hour.}$$

Notice that setting up the problem in this way avoids a lot of needless arithmetic. This is characteristic of the GRE. Most problems do not require a lengthy calculation. Usually the numbers used in constructing the questions are selected in a way that will allow for cancelling, factoring, or other shortcut devices. On the test, fractions are usually easier to work with than decimals.

20. **(E)** Multiplication is both associative and commutative. By associative, we mean that the grouping of the elements is not important—for example, $(5 \times 6) \times 7 = 5 \times (6 \times 7)$. By commutative we mean that the order of the elements is unimportant—for example, $5 \times 6 = 6 \times 5$. So (A), (B), (C), and (D) are all alternative forms for m(nop), but (E) is not: $(mn)(mo)(mp) = m^3nop$.

21. **(E)** Looking at the two charts, we see that the upper one, representing the total passenger miles, shows a smooth increase, generally speaking, while the lower one shows large changes. Since the lower one is deaths per passenger-mile, the sharp changes in the rate must be from sharp changes in the number of deaths.

Proposition I is inferable since the highest level reached by the line on the lower graph was approximately 1.3, in 1951. II is also inferable. The largest jump in the line on the lower graph, for a one-year period, occurred in the period 1954–1955. Finally, III is also inferable. The two low points on the line of the lower graph occurred in 1954 and 1957; both were approximately .1.

22. **(E)** The question stem asks about the *longest*, not the most severe or greatest increase. Although the *largest* increase ended in 1955, the *longest* increase lasted from 1956 until 1960. The word finally is also a clue.

23. **(E)** In 1955, total passenger-miles were 20 billion, and the fatality rate was 1.2 per 100 million miles. To compute the acutal number of fatalities, we must multiply the total miles by the rate of fatalities (just as one multiplies 5 gallons by 25 miles per gallon to compute the total miles travelled as 125 miles): $20,000,000,000 \times \dfrac{1.2}{100,000,000} =$ (to make matters easier, we cancel zeros) $20,\not0\not0\not0,\not0\not0\not0,000 \times \dfrac{1.2}{1\not0\not0,\not0\not0\not0,000} = 240$.

24. **(A)** Problem 23 shows us how the number of fatalities can be found. But it would be counterproductive to spend a lot of time computing the actual number of deaths for each of the five years mentioned. Instead, a rough estimate will suffice. At first glance, it appears that the only reasonable possibilities are 1951, 1955, and 1960, since the fatality rate (lower graph) is at least approximately equal in those years. Now, it is absolutely critical to realize that, though the fatality rate in 1951 was higher than the fatality rate in 1960 (1.3 compared with 1.0), there were three times as many miles travelled in 1960 than in 1951. Similarly, though the fatality rate was higher in 1955 than it was in 1960 (1.2 compared with 1.0), there were 50% more miles travelled in 1960 than in 1955. This reasoning shows that the largest numbers of fatalities occurred in 1960. Even though the fatality rate that year was not as high as those for 1955 and 1951, this was more than offset by the larger number of passenger-miles travelled. Of course, a longer method of attack is to actually do a rough calculation for each:

(A) 1951: $\dfrac{1.3}{100 \text{ million}} \times 10 \text{ billion} = 130$

(B) 1953: $\dfrac{.6}{100 \text{ million}} \times 15 \text{ billion} = 90$

(C) 1955: $\dfrac{1.2}{100 \text{ million}} \times 20 \text{ billion} = 240$

(D) 1957: $\dfrac{.1}{100 \text{ million}} \times 25 \text{ billion} = 25$

(E) 1960: $\dfrac{1}{100 \text{ million}} \times 30 \text{ billion} = 300$

25. **(E)** This problem is at once both easy and difficult. It is easily solved if the key word, passenger, is not overlooked. The lower graph records passenger miles travelled, but it tells us nothing about the number of different passengers who travelled those miles. The real-world likelihood that more passenger-miles *probably* means more passengers is only a probability and not a basis for a certain calculation.

26. **(A)** There is an easy and a more complicated way to handle this question. The more complex method is to begin with the formula for the area of a triangle: Area = $\frac{1}{2}$ (altitude)(base). Since angle CBE is equal to angle E, BC must be equal to CE, and it is possible to reduce the altitude to the base (or vice versa). So, Area = $\frac{1}{2}$ (side)^2. The area is 8, so $8 = \frac{1}{2}s^2$, and s = 4. Of course, s is also the side of the square, so the area of the square ABCD is s^2 or 16.

Now, an easier method of solving the problem is to recognize that BC and CE are equal to sides of the square ABCD, so the area of BCE is simply half that of the square. So the square must be double the triangle, or 16. A 45–45–90 right triangle is half of a square, and its hypotenuse is the diagonal of the square.

27. **(B)** Although some students will be able to solve this problem without the use of a diagram, for most drawing the floor plan of the closet is the logical starting point:

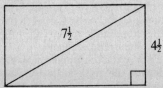

Now it becomes clear that the Pythagorean Theorem is the key to solving this problem. Once the dimensions are converted to fractions, the problem is simplified further: the triangle is a 3–4–5 right triangle ($\frac{9}{2}, \frac{12}{2}, \frac{15}{2}$). The two legs of the right triangle are simultaneously the width and length of the rectangle. So the area of the closet is: $\frac{9}{2} \times 6 = \frac{54}{2} = 27$.

28. **(A)** There are four times as many women as there are men, so if there are x men in the meeting, there are 4x women. This means that there is a total of 5x persons in the meeting (x + 4x). Since the men are x men out of a total of 5x, the men constitute one-fifth, or 20%. Choices (D) and (E) can be avoided by noting that there are more women than men in the room and men thus come to less than 50%.

29. **(E)** This is an unusual problem, one which requires careful reading rather than some clever mathematical insight. The question asks us to compare the fractions in the form $\frac{P}{Q}$ with the decimal .PQ. For example, we convert the fraction $\frac{1}{8}$ into the decimal .18 for purposes of comparison and ask how closely the second approximates the first. Since $\frac{1}{8}$ is .125, we see that the fit is not a very precise one. Similarly, with $\frac{2}{9}$, the corresponding decimal we are to compare is .29, but the actual decimal equivalent of $\frac{2}{9}$ is .22$\frac{2}{9}$. The equivalent for $\frac{3}{4}$ is .34, not even close to the actual decimal equivalent of .75. Similarly, for $\frac{4}{5}$, the artificially derived .45 is not very close to the actual decimal equivalent of .80; but for $\frac{8}{9}$ we use the decimal .89, and this is fairly close—the closest of all the fractions listed—to the actual decimal equivalent of $\frac{8}{9}$, which is .888.

If you have difficulties in finding the decimals for fractions, try to relate the fractions to percentages, which are in hundredths, or to other, more common decimal-fraction equivalencies. For example, one-third is probably known to you as approximately .33 or 33%. A ninth is one-third of a third; hence a ninth is approximately 33%/3 = 11% or .11. Eight-ninths is thus 8(11%) = 88%.

30. **(A)** If a problem seems a bit too abstract to handle using algebraic notation, a sometimes useful technique is to try to find a similar, more familiar situation. For example, virtually everyone could answer the following question: Books cost $5 each; how many books can be bought for $100? The calculation goes: $\frac{1 \text{ book}}{\$5} \times \$100 = 20$ books. So, too, here the number of books which can be purchased per d dollars must be multiplied by the number of dollars to be spent, m: $\frac{b}{d} \times m$, or $\frac{bm}{d}$. Pursuing this line of attack, it might be worthwhile to point out that substitution of real numbers in problems like this is often an effective way of solving the problem. Since the variables and the formulas are general—that is, they do not depend upon any given number of books or dollars—the correct answer choice must work for all possible values. Suppose we assume, therefore, 2(b) books can be purchased for $5(d), and that the amount to be spent is $50(m). Most people can fall back onto common sense to calculate the number of books that can be purchased with $50: 20 books. But of the five formulas offered as answer choices, only (A) gives the number 20 when the values are substituted: For b = 2, d = 5 and m = 50, (A) = $\frac{(2)(50)}{5} = 20$, (B) = (2)(5)(50) = 500, (C) = $\frac{5}{(2)(50)} = \frac{1}{20}$, (D) = $\frac{2 + 50}{5} = \frac{52}{5}$, (E) = $\frac{2 - 50}{5} = \frac{-48}{5}$. Substitution will take longer than a direct algebraic approach, but it is much better than simply guessing, if you have the time and can't get the algebra to work right.

SECTION IV

1. **(C)** It would be a mistake to start multiplying before setting the two quantities up:

24 hours/day × 7 days
7 days/week × 24 weeks

Both quantities are 24 × 7, and it is not necessary to multiply them out to see that they are equal.

2. **(C)** As in question 1, it is not necessary to actually carry out the indicated multiplication. Remembering that a % sign indicates that the number is the same as dividing by 100, each side becomes $\frac{(35)(60)}{100}$. Thus, (C). Always keep in mind that the % sign or a percentage is just a number like any other number. The % sign is equivalent to the fraction $\frac{1}{100}$.

3. **(A)** Although the most direct way to solve this problem is to add the column of ages and divide by 6 (average = 29.8), you may find it quicker to do a "running average." Assume that the average is 30 (Tom's age). If that is correct, then the sum of ages above 30 must balance exactly the sum of the ages below 30. Juanita makes the balance +5 (above 30). Brooks brings it down by 2, for a total

of +3. Glenda adds 10, for +13. Marcia brings it down by 8, for +5. Finally Dwight's age is 6 below 30, which brings the figure down to a −1. This shows that the average will be slightly below 30.

4. **(D)** Since m ranges between 4 and 6, and h ranges between 5 and 7, it is impossible to determine the relationship between m and n. For example, m and n might both be 5.5, or m might be 4.1 and n 6.9, or m might be 5.9 and n 5.1. Neither m nor n is restricted to integers.

5. **(B)** The side of the square must be 8, since $s^2 = 64$. The length of the rectangle Q must be 16, since $W \times L = 64$.

6. **(B)** The simplest way to solve this problem is first to perform the indicated operation for Column B: $(3x)^3 = 27x^3$. Now, since $x > 0$, x^3 must be positive, and it is permissible to divide both columns by x^3. The result is that Column A becomes 3 while column B becomes 9. $9 > 3$, so (B) is correct.

7. **(D)** Since it is not specified that x and y are equal to one another, the relationship is indeterminate. You can see this by visualizing x and y varying inversely with one another, e.g., when x is 2, y is $\frac{1}{2}$, when x is 3, y is $\frac{1}{3}$, etc. Also if you use substitution: if $x = 2$, then y must be $\frac{1}{2}$. On the other hand, x might be $\frac{1}{2}$, in which case y is 2.

8. **(C)** Since 11 is itself a prime number, it is factorable only by itself and 1, and that is one instance in which 11 is an integer multiple of a prime number. But it is also the only one. Any other number that is factorable by 11—say, 22—cannot, by definition, be a prime number (it would be factorable by 11 and some other number, as well as by itself and 1). Thirteen is also a prime number, which means that the only prime number of which it is an integer multiple is itself. So both 11 and 13 are each integer factors of only one prime number—themselves.

9. **(D).** Although we know that y is the even integer and that, of x and z, one is the next-largest and the other is the next-smallest integer from y, we do not know which is which. If x is the smaller and z the larger, then Column B may be greater, but if x is the larger and z the smaller, Column A may be greater. Consequently, the correct answer here must be (D).

10. **(B)** Of course, the problem is really about right triangles, not about transmitter towers, and the actual height of the tower is not important. The tower forms the common leg of two right triangles, so our triangles will have one leg of, say, length t. Then, the triangle on the left has a second leg which is shorter than the second leg of the triangle on the right (80 m vs. 100 m).

Consequently, the hypotenuse (the support wire) of the triangle on the left must be shorter than that of the triangle on the right.

11. **(C)** Notice that the number in Column A can be understood to be the sum of 2 times 1000 (the 2 is in the thousandths position), 4 times 100 (the 4 is in the hundredths decimal position), 6 times 10 (the 6 is in the tenths decimal position), and 8 (the eight is in the units position). This is equivalent to the expression in Column B. The only differences are that the ordering of the elements is reversed in Column B and the hundredths and thousandths are expressed in powers of ten.

12. **(D)** Since $a^2 = b$, we can substitute a^2 wherever b appears. Thus Column A can be rewritten as: $\frac{2a}{a^2}$, which is equal to $\frac{2}{a}$. Since a is positive, we can multiply both columns by a. Thus, Column A becomes 2, and Column B becomes (a)(a)(a), or a^3. Now it is easy to see that the relationship must be indeterminate. If a is a fraction, then Column A is greater. If a is a number like 2, then Column B is larger.

13. **(C)** Since vertical or opposite angles are equal, we know that $4x = x + 30$. Solving for x: $3x = 30$, $x = 10$; so the two columns are equal.

14. **(D)** To find the cost per ounce of the family-size box, we need to know both its size in ounces and its cost. While we know the relationship between the regular and family sizes for both of those items, we do not know the actual size or cost of the regular size and thus cannot use our knowledge of the relationship between the two sizes to any advantage. We wouldn't even know whether the family size or the regular size had the highest cost per ounce of cereal.

15. **(C)** One direct and simple way of solving this problem would be to count on your fingers the actual number of different duos and trios which could be formed from a group of five. The result is ten. A more elegant way of solving the problem is to recognize that $2 + 3 = 5$. In other words, each time a pair is selected to form a duo, three persons from the group have been left behind, and they form a trio. Or each time a different group of three is selected to form a duo, a pair of persons is left behind, and they constitute a duo. So even without calculating the actual number of different trios and duos that could be made, you can reach the conclusion that the number of possible combinations for each is the same.

16. **(C)** This problem simply requires finding the value of the expression $2x + 3y$, when $x = 3$ and $y = 2$: $2(3) + 3(2) = 12$.

17. **(C)** You do not need a course in business arithmetic to solve this problem, only the common-sense notion that profit is equal to gross revenue less cost. Expressed algebraically, we have P = GR − C; then, transposing the C term, we have C + P = GR, which is read: cost plus profit (or mark-up) is equal to gross revenue (or selling price). In this case, P = $4, GR = $20: C + 4 = 20, so C = 16.

18. **(A)** The information given says that the 1970 student population is $2\frac{1}{2}$ times as great as the 1950 student population. So: '70SP = '50SP × $2\frac{1}{2}$, or '70SP = 500 × $2\frac{1}{2}$ = 500 × $\frac{5}{2}$ = 1250.

19. **(C)** We must test each of the answer choices. The question asks for the one choice in which the answer is not equal to 3n + 3. In (A), for example, does 300 = 3n + 3? A quick manipulation will show that there is an integer, n, which solves the equation: 297 = 3n, so n = 99. For (C), however, no integral n exists: 3n + 3 = 208, 3n = 205, n = $68\frac{1}{3}$. So (C) is the answer we want. Another approach is to test each of the answer choices for being divisible by 3 since 3n + 3 is divisible by 3 when n is an integer. If the sum of all the single digits in a number add to a number divisible by 3, the number is itself divisible by 3; if not, not (208, for example: 2 + 0 + 8 = 10, is not divisible by 3). Being divisible by 3 does not mean an answer fits the conditions, but not being divisible by 3 means that it doesn't.

20. **(D)** The easiest approach to this problem is to draw the figures.

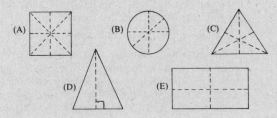

The dotted lines show possible lines of symmetry—that is, these are lines along which a paper cutout of the figure could be folded and the result will be that the two halves exactly match one another. (D) must be our answer, since it is the only figure with but one line of symmetry.

21. **(B)** This problem can, of course, be solved using an equation. We know that the laborer worked 8 hours @ $8 per hour, but what we need to know is how much overtime he worked. We let x be the number of overtime hours: (8 hrs. × $8/hr.) + (x hrs. × $12/hr) = $80. The $12/hr. is the laborer's overtime rate—that is, $8 × $1\frac{1}{2}$ = $12. Now it is a fairly simple matter to manipulate the equation:

$$64 + 12x = 80$$
$$12x = 16$$
$$x = \tfrac{16}{12}$$
$$x = 1\tfrac{1}{3}$$

Since $\frac{1}{3}$ of an hour is 20 minutes, the laborer worked 1 hour and 20 minutes of overtime, which, when added to the standard 8 hours, gives a total work day of 9 hours and 20 minutes.

Now, it is not absolutely necessary to use an equation. The equation is just a way of formalizing common sense reasoning, which might have gone like this: Well, I know he made $64 in a regular day. If he made $80 on a given day, $16 must have been overtime pay. His overtime rate is time-and-a-half, that is, $1\frac{1}{2}$ times $8/hr, or $12/hr. In the first hour of overtime he made $12, that leaves $4 more. Since $4 is one-third of $12, he has to work another one-third of an hour to make that, which is twenty minutes. So he works 8 hours at standard rates for $64, one full hour of overtime for another $12, and another $\frac{1}{3}$ of an overtime hour for $4. So $80 represents 9 hours and 20 minutes of work.

22. **(A)** This problem is both easy and difficult. Conceptually, the problem is easy to set up. High-risk stocks constitute 8.9% of the total investment of $1,080,192. To find the value of the high-risk stocks we just take 8.9% of $1,080,192. Then the problem becomes slightly difficult because it requires a tedious calculation—or at least it seems to. We say seems to because you do not actually have to do the arithmetic. The answer choices are spread fairly far apart, that is, they differ from one another by several thousands of dollars. Round 8.9% off to an even 9%, and $1,080,192 to 1,080,000. Then do the arithmetic in your head: 9% of one million is 90,000, then 9% of 80,000 is 7200, so you need an answer choice which is close to $97,000—slightly less since you rounded your percentage (8.9%) in an upward direction. With a bit of practice, you will find that this technique is more efficient than actually doing arithmetic.

23. **(B)** In this problem, the technique of rounding off and estimating is even more useful. The problem is easy enough to set up: Since state-issued bonds constituted 26% of all government bonds and securities, and since government bonds and securities constituted 48.3% of the total investment fund, state-issued bonds must constitute 26% of 48.3% of the total fund. To compute the dollar value of state-issued bonds, we need to find 26% of 48.3% of $1,080,192, but that will require substantial calculation. You can attack it in this way: 26% is close to one-fourth, and one-fourth of 48% would be 12%, so state-issued bonds are 12% of the total. Now, 10% of the total of $1,080,000 (rounded off), would be $108,000, and one-fifth of that (since 2% is one-fifth of 10%)

is approximately $20,000. So 12% must be approximately $128,000, answer (B).

24. **(A)** In this problem you can use the method of pairing. Make a rough comparison of answers (A) and (B). If you find that one of the two is clearly the larger, strike the smaller and proceed to compare answer (C) with the larger of (A) and (B). Again, this calculation will be a rough one, and if you find that one of the two is clearly larger, strike the smaller and proceed to compare the larger with (D). Follow this procedure until you have exhausted the list, and one answer remains as the largest. Now, if it turns out that any two answers are too close for a rough estimate to tell them apart, keep them both and compare them to the other answers before actually committing yourself to a detailed calculation, which is unlikely to be necessary. When there are two close answers, it is likely that a later one will supersede both of them.

In this problem we compare (A) and (B) first. Since both figures are shares of the same pie, we can compare their shares directly. Since the amount invested in municipal bonds with a 7–9% yield is 65%, (A) must be larger than (B) (the other two combined could account for only 35% of the pie), so we strike (B) and hold on to (A). Municipal bonds yielding 7–9% are 65% of all municipal bonds, and since municipal bonds account for 56% of all government bonds and securities, we can determine that the 7–9% yield municipal bonds account for roughly ⅔ of the 56% of all government bonds and securities, or slightly less than 40%. This shows that (B) must be larger than (C), since (C) accounts for only 18% of all government bonds and securities—nowhere near 40%. Similarly, we can eliminate (D) from consideration because state-issued bonds account for only 26% of all government bonds and securities—again, that is not even close to 40%. Finally, we compare (A) with (E). Since municipal bonds with a 7–9% yield constitute slightly less than 40% of all government bonds and securities, and since government bonds and securities account for approximately 48% of the entire investment fund, municipal bonds yielding 7–9% must account for 40% of that 48%, or approximately 19% of the total fund. High-risk stocks account for only 8.9% of the total fund, so (E) must be less than (A), and (A) is our answer.

25. **(E)** This question requires a careful reading of the stem. It asks which kind of investment *earned* the least amount of money, but this group of graphs shows the amount *invested* in types of investment. It cannot be assumed that each type of investment was equally profitable, so we have no way of determining which of the types of investment generated the most income.

26. **(A)** Since MNOP is a square, we know that angle O must be a right angle, that is, 90°. From that we can conclude that arc NP is one-fourth of the entire circle. If arc NP is 4π units long, then the circumference of the circle must be 4 times that long, or 16π units. We are now in a position to find the length of the radius of circle O, and once we have the radius, we will also know the length of the sides of square MNOP, since MN and OP are both radii. The formula for the circumference of a circle is $C = 2\pi r$, so:

$$2\pi r = 16\pi$$
$$2\cancel{\pi}r = 16\cancel{\pi}$$
$$r = 8$$

So the side of the square MNOP must be 8, and its perimeter must be $s + s + s + s$ or $4(8) = 32$.

27. **(C)** The most direct way of solving this problem is first to compute the rate at which the water is filling the tank. Water is flowing into the tank at 800 cu. ft. per minute, but it is also draining out at the rate of 300 cu. ft. per minute. The net gain each minute, then, is 500 cu. ft. We then divide 3750 cu. ft. by 500 cu. ft./min., which equals 7.5 minutes. We convert the .5 minutes to 30 seconds, so our answer is 7 min. 30 sec.

28. **(B)** A quick sketch of the information provided in the problem shows that we need to employ the Pythagorean Theorem:

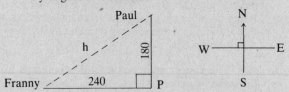

The shortest distance from Paul to Franny is the hypotenuse of this right triangle:

$$180^2 + 240^2 = h^2$$

It is extremely unlikely that the GRE would present a problem requiring such a lengthy calculation. So there must be a shortcut available. The key is to recognize that 180 and 240 are multiples of 60—3×60 and 4×60, respectively. This must be a 3,4,5 right triangle, so our hypotenuse must be $5 \times 60 = 300$.

29. **(A)** This problem requires a very simple insight: Area of rectangle = width × length. What makes it difficult is that many students—while they are able to compute the area of any rectangle in which the dimensions are given—"freak out" when dimensions are expressed in terms of a variable rather than real numbers. Those who keep a cool head will say, "Oh, the area is the width times the length." The area here is $81x^2$, the length is $27x$, therefore:

$$(W)(L) = \text{Area}$$
$$(W)(27x) = (81x^2)$$

Divide both sides by x:

$$(W)(27) = 81x$$
$$W = 3x$$

30. **(B)** To solve this problem, you must recognize that angle ABC is a right angle. That is because the triangle is *inscribed* in a semicircle (the vertex of the triangle is situated on the circumference of the circle), and an inscribed angle intercepts twice the arc. For example:

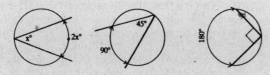

Once it is recognized that ABC is a right triangle, the shaded area can be computed by taking the area of the triangle from the area of the semicircle, or expressed in pictures:

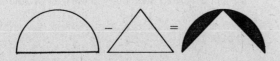

Line AC is the hypotenuse of ABC, so its length is:

$$AC^2 = (2\sqrt{2})^2 + (2\sqrt{2})^2$$
$$AC^2 = 8 + 8 = 16$$
$$AC = 4$$

AC is also the diameter of the circle, so the radius of the entire circle is 2 (radius is one-half diameter). We are now in a position to compute the area of the semicircle. Since the area of the entire circle would be πr^2, the area of the semicircle is $\dfrac{\pi r^2}{2}$: $\dfrac{\pi (2)^2}{2} = 2\pi$.

Then we compute the area of the triangle. The area of a triangle is $\frac{1}{2}ab$, and in any right triangle either of the two sides will serve as the altitude, the other serving as the base. For example:

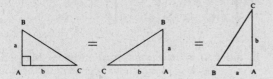

In this case, we have area $= \frac{1}{2}(2\sqrt{2})(2\sqrt{2}) = 4$. Referring to our pictorial representation of the problem:

$$\bigcirc - \triangle = 2\pi - 4.$$

SECTION V

Questions 1–5

Arranging the Information

This problem set concerns items arranged along two different and non-connected parameters; smell and prettiness. Since there is no connection between the two parameters (such as prettier flowers smell better, or whatever), the two can be analyzed separately:

←PRETTIER——less PRETTY→

A less pretty than L	L A
D prettier than L	D L A
I less pretty than L	D L A
	←I→
L prettier than R	D L A
	←I→
	←R→

Now for the smell ←BETTER—SMELL—WORSE→

A not as nice as L or D	L A
	←D→
D not as nice as L	L D A
I not as nice as D or R	L D A
	←R×I→
L not as nice as R	R L D A
	← I→

Answering the Questions

1. **(C)** We are looking for indeterminacies, and, as the diagram shows, the smell relationship between irises and asters is unknown. (A), (B), and (E) are all definitely true, while (D) is false.

2. **(E)** (A), (B), and (E) are false, with (C) being possible, but unknown. (E) is definitely true since roses smell the best of all.

3. **(E)** The bottom of the prettiness scale has irises, roses, and asters all being in one group, whose interrelationships are not known. Even knowing how irises and roses relate does not solve the problem of how asters fit into the scheme of things. Thus, it is not determinable just what, if anything, irises are prettier than.

4. **(A)** The diagrams make it clear that only daffodils qualify. As discussed in problem 3, the relationship between the prettiness of roses, irises, and asters is not known.

5. **(A)** Be careful, when you enter this new item, not to conclude too much. Even though the diagram happens to list irises and asters next to each other in the smell scale, putting dahlias

below the asters does not make it below the irises. The new diagram is:

←BETTER—SMELL—WORSE→
L not as nice as R   R   L   D   A←Dahlia→
                                        ←I→

Thus, dahlias overlap irises and (A) is correct. The other choices are false.

6. **(A)** The anti-abortion speaker unwittingly plays right into the hands of the pro-abortion speaker. The "pro" speaker tries to show that there are many decisions regarding human life in which we allow that an increase in the quality of life justifies an increase in the danger to human life. All that the "anti" speaker does is to help prove this point. He says the quality of life would suffer if we lowered the speed limit to protect human life. Given this analysis, (B) must be incorrect, for the "anti" speaker's position is completely ineffective as a rebuttal. Moreover, (C) must be incorrect, for his response is not a strong statement of an anti-abortion position. (D) is incorrect, for while his response is of no value to the position he seeks to defend, it cannot be said that it is irrelevant. In fact, as we have just shown, his position is very relevant to that of the "pro" speaker's because it supports that position. Finally, (E) is not an appropriate characterization of the "anti" speaker's position, for he tries, however inartfully, to attack the merits of the "pro" speaker's position, not the character of that speaker.

7. **(E)** The "pro" speaker uses the example of traffic fatalities to show that society has always traded the quality of life for the quantity of life. Of course, he says, we do not always acknowledge that that is what we are doing; but if we were honest, we would have to admit that we were making a trade-off. Thus, (E) is the best conclusion of the passage. The author's defense of abortion amounts to the claim that abortion is just another case in which we trade off one life (the fetus) to make the lives of others (the survivors) better. The only difference is that the life being sacrificed is specifiable and highly visible in the case of abortion, whereas in the case of highway fatalities, no one knows in advance on whom the axe will fall. (A) certainly goes far beyond what the author is advocating. If anything, he probably recognizes that sometimes the trade-off will be drawn in favor of protecting lives, and thus we need some such laws. (B) must be wrong, first because the "anti" speaker claims this is not his position, and second because the "pro" speaker would prefer to show that the logical consequence of the "anti" speaker's response is an argument in favor of abortion. (C) is not an appropriate continuation because the author has already said this is a weak counter-example and that he has even stronger points to make. Finally, the author might be willing to accept contraception (D) as yet

another example of the trade-off, but his conclusion can be much stronger than that. The author wants to defend abortion, so the conclusion of his speech ought to be that abortion is an acceptable practice—not that contraception is an acceptable practice.

8. **(D)** This is a very difficult question. That III is an assumption the author makes requires careful reading. The author's attitude about the just war tips us off. He implies that this is an appropriate function of government and, further, that there are even clearer cases. Implicit in his defense of abortion is that a trade-off must be made and that it is appropriately a collective decision. I is not an assumption of the argument. Indeed, the author seems to assume, as we have just maintained, that the trade-off is an appropriate goal of society. Finally, the author does not assume II; if anything, he almost states that he accepts that the fetus is a life, but it may be traded off in exchange for an increase in the quality in the lives of others.

Questions 9–12

Arranging the Information

This is a map problem. The map can be constructed by first putting down one each of an unnamed street, avenue, road, and drive in accordance with the first part of the information.

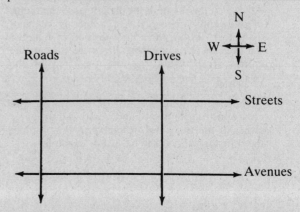

In order to insert the information about Magnolia Parkway, the two intersections named must be constructed and then the parkway inserted. Since the problem spends so much time describing angles between the various kinds of roadways, we can be sure that the angle between Magnolia Parkway and the other roadways will be of some interest. Since Magnolia Parkway is drawn between two points—the two intersections—its direction will depend on the relative placement of the points. There is nothing in the problem to prevent Hyacinth from being above or below, or for that matter even on the same level as, Zinnia. Therefore, Magnolia could have any angle whatsoever.

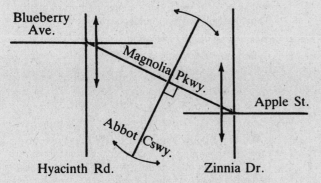

The last step is to put Abbot Causeway at right angles to Magnolia Parkway. Note that we do not know whether or not Magnolia Parkway and Abbot Causeway actually intersect, but only their relative angles. The floor in one room and the wall down the hall are perpendicular, but do not intersect.

Answering the Questions

9. **(E)** Since Magnolia Parkway could actually run in any direction at all, neither answer choice (A) nor (B) must be true, though they are both possible. Neither answer choice (C) nor (D) must be true, because there is no indication that Maple Street has anything to do with Magnolia Parkway, nor any that it doesn't. Hence, (E) is correct.

10. **(D)** Melody Drive and Fanfare Road are parallel, according to the given information, and therefore they cannot cross. If the question had used the word intersect, the answer would have still been the same, although some of the more subtle thinkers might have considered the possibility of the two running into each other end to end, as it were. This is not a subtle test and such refinements are out of place.

    (A) and (B) are not definitely false since Abbot's direction is determined by reference to Magnolia, and Magnolia can be any orientation at all, so these are both potentially true or false. (C) and (E) are also possibly true since a drive or road is perpendicular to a street.

11. **(D)** I is possible because Magnolia can be any direction. II is not possible because all drives are parallel to the roads and the roads are north/south. III is possible because streets are perpendicular to roads, so they might intersect. Hence, (D).

    This problem is noteworthy because the added

information was useful in evaluating only some of the statements and it turned out that the third statement was knowable and possible even though it did not have the same kinds of terms (direction versus intersection) as the information added in the question stem.

12. **(A)** Since both the distance between Zinnia and Hyacinth, and between Blueberry and Apple must be at least one-quarter of a mile, Magnolia must be at least as long as the diagonal of a square that is one-quarter mile on a side—that is, greater than one-quarter of a mile.

    (B) does not have to be true since it is possible for Apple Street to be just one block long. (C) is most reasonably interpreted as being false since a roadway would seem to have to be at least one block long. Though the real world does contain streets and alleys that are less than a regulation block long, this question stem specifically states that all of the blocks formed by these kinds of roadways are one-quarter mile long. Don't look for unfair tricks—they aren't there.

Questions 13–17

Arranging the Information

Since this is a flow or process situation where the interest is on who can go when, the information should be arranged to show that:
No two days in row
R, S anytime
T only after S (but not necessarily after S)
$U = T$
$V = 3$ or 5
$W = 4$

Answering the Questions

13. **(E)** All three statements could be true.
    I and II are possible since both R and S could do the first, third, and fifth days of the job.
    III is possible, but only when S does the first and third days of the job, since T must follow S.

14. **(B)** Only II is possible. We wish to chart possibilities for the first three days, but we are especially interested in the ones which permit T and U to work on the second day, since that affects I and II. S on the first day makes T and U possible on the third day:

	FIRST DAY	SECOND DAY	THIRD DAY
	S	T or U	R, S, or V
OR	S	R	S or V

    Thus, we see that T, U, or R are possible on the

second day, which eliminates I. I could also fail if R worked the first day and S worked the second day. II is OK because it has no only.

III fails because W can work only on the fourth day.

15. **(C)** Only I and II are true. If R works the first day, only S can work the second day because T and U can only follow S and V and W can only work the third and fourth days, respectively. If S works the second day, he cannot work the third.

III is not true, because R could follow S and work the third day.

16. **(C)** As we saw in problem 15, if R works the first day, S must work the second day, but here R works the third day. U and T cannot follow R, eliminating answer choices (B) and (E). R cannot follow himself, which eliminates (B) (again) and (D). Since W can work the fourth day, (A) fails to cover all of the possibilities and (C) is correct.

Note that it is more accurate to say only that so and so can work and have that describe the only persons who can work than it is to include all who can work plus some who can't.

17. **(A)** (B), (C), and (D) focus on the fourth day's possibilities. (B) and (C) fail because they ignore W, who can also work on the fourth day. (D) fails because S could also work the fourth day.

Thus, we must consider the previous days as (A) and (E) ask. If R, S, and V did not work the third day, who did? W couldn't, so it must have been either T or U, who worked the third day, not the second as (E) would have it. Thus, (E) is out and (A) in. If T or U worked the third day, then S must have worked the second day since those two can only follow S. Only R and S can work the first day and since they can't work two days in a row, R must have worked the first day.

Questions 18–22

Arranging the Information

Since all of the questions are "if" or conditional questions, we can expect that the original arrangement of information will not give a single, definite answer. Further, since question 18 uses only some of the information, we should start with that, adding the other conditions as we do the other problems.

Conditions I and II set up blocks which can then be moved. The management block is two seats and the labor three, with an empty one in the middle of the labor block. We do not know which of the two members of each side will occupy which of the seats in their block. IV sets up another block of three seats for the mediator, with him flanked by two empty seats.

Answering the Problems

18. **(C)** The three conditions used result in three blocks of 3, 3, and 2 seats, which add up to eight. Thus, we will have a definite arrangement:

We don't know who particularly is in the seats, only the grouping. (C) correctly notes that one labor person will sit next to one management person, whichever pair it might be.

(A) and (D) fail because IV specifically states that Jones will have empty seats on either side of him.

(B) fails only because we do not know which management representative will occupy the seat next to a labor representative.

(E) fails when (C) succeeds.

19. **(D)** In contrast to problem 18, IV is out and III is in. This means that the mediator will not have empty seats by him, but since III requires that the two parties be equally near the mediator, the nearer member of each side will be seated next to the mediator. Thus, the seating will be:

However, the labor and management parties could also switch sides to produce the following arrangement:

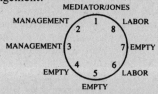

This is significant because the question asks specifically about the clockwise ordering of the negotiators. Since either labor negotiator could occupy either of the labor seats and either of the management negotiators could occupy either of the management seats, there are plenty of possibilities. The correct answer choice will be one which violates one of the basic rules I, II, or III.

(D) is correct because it has the two labor negotiators sitting next to each other in violation of condition II. All of the others satisfy the ideas of having management on one side of the mediator and labor on the other, management together, and labor seated with an empty seat between.

20. **(D)** The secretary sits opposite the mediator, and ALL the other conditions apply AS MUCH AS POSSIBLE. This means that some might be sacrificed. I and II say "always" while III and IV say "like" and "prefer." I and II take precedence. Here is the diagram with the secretary opposite the mediator and I and II satisfied:

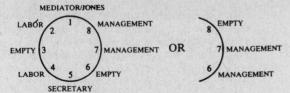

The diagram shows that conditions I and II could be met with the management negotiators either next to the mediator or next to the secretary. Condition III would have the management team sit next to the mediator. Condition IV cannot possibly be met without violating II, and since it is only a preference, it goes by the board. Thus, the final diagram is the preceding main one and the alternative listed on the right is eliminated by condition III.

Statements I and III in the problem are true, but II is false, as the diagram shows.

21. **(B)** Even though the mediator is absent, all of the applicable conditions are still in force, which are only I and II. III and IV do not apply since they refer to the mediator, who is not present. The only part of III that applies is keeping away from each other. Here is the diagram:

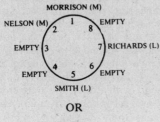

OR

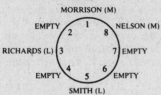

These are the only two possibilities because they want to be as far away from each other as possible so Richard and Nelson would not sit next to each other, eliminating (A). (B) is not only possible, but necessary.

(C) does not fit the diagram. (E) is not possible since these two sit in different relations to the two

negotiators who do sit opposite each other. (D) is unlikely in the first place, and amounts to sitting opposite Smith, which is where Morrison is.

22. **(A)** This problem puts us back to the situation with the mediator and all of the conditions operating. Since Morrison and Nelson always sit next to each other, the aide must be on the other side of Morrison making the management side a block of three seats in a row: Aide, Morrison, Nelson. But the aide and Nelson could flip-flop from one side of Morrison to the other. There are now six people, leaving only two empty chairs. Since one of those empty chairs must be between the two labor negotiators, there cannot be empty chairs on both sides of the mediator; thus, the mediator must be flanked by occupied seats. The middle management seat is Morrison. The diagram:

Since the two labor seats can also flip-flop between Smith and Richards, we must be careful.

(A) is not possible because the seat opposite Morrison must be empty. The aide and Nelson are opposite the two labor seats, so (B), (C), and (D) are possible. (E) is possible if that is where he happens to be.

23. **(A)** (C) and (D) are wrong because they extrapolate without sufficient information. (E) contradicts the last given statement and so cannot be a conclusion of it. That would be like trying to infer "all men are mortal" from the premise that "no men are mortal." (B) commits an error by moving from "all S are P" to "all P are S." Just because all racing engines have SFI does not mean that all SFI's are in racing engines. Some may be found in tractors and heavy-duty machinery.

24. **(D)** Peter's surprise is over the fact that an important executive of a company would use a competitor's product, hence (D). (B) is wrong because Peter's surprise is not that Mary is unimportant; rather, he knows Mary is important, and that is the reason for his surprise. (E) is irrelevant to the exchange, for Peter imagines that, regardless of taste, Mary ought to consume the product she is in part for producing. The same reasoning can be applied to (C). Finally, (A) is a distraction.

25. **(A)** The author's point depends upon the assumption that children see both animated features and "spaghetti Westerns." Obviously, if that assumption is untrue, he cannot claim that his conclusion follows. It may be true that children

get a distorted picture of the world from other causes, but the author has not claimed that. He claims only that it comes from their seeing animated features and "spaghetti Westerns." Presumably, the two different treatments cause the inversion of values. The intention of the producers in making the films is irrelevant since an action may have an effect not intended by the actor. Hence, II would not touch the author's point. Further, that there are other sources of information which present a proper view of the world does not prove that the problem cited by the author does not produce an inverted view of the world. So III would not weaken his point.

SECTION VI

Questions 1–4

Arranging the Information

This problem is one which presents a set of conditions and a group of situations to which the conditions are to be applied. The five sets do not necessarily meet all of the conditions. A preview of the question stems indicates that it is worthwhile to identify errors in the sets. It is probably more efficient to check all of them at once, condition by condition, since they are laid out so nicely.

In checking the first stated condition that the first three names in each set should be typically male names, you can just read down the columns of names. All of the names in columns one and two for all five sets are male names. In column three, however, you find that the last two, Greta and Mona from sets IV and V respectively, are female names and, thus, errors. You could circle or underline them to indicate the fact that they are errors.

Checking the second condition, that the names in the last two columns should be female names, produces no errors.

The requirement that each name in a set begin with a different letter does produce some errors. Remember that the duplication of first letters indicates that either of the two or more failing to meet the condition could be wrong. This sort of condition is somewhat different than the previous ones. With the first two conditions you could check each item individually and know for sure whether it was wrong. This condition is one of limitation where you cannot say whether it is Jack or June which is the problem in set I, Mike or Mary in II, or Louis or Linda in IV. Technically, it is not the names which are in error, but the sets.

A check of the last condition, that each of the names in a set be the same number of letters, shows Henry in II as the only problem. Again, technically it may not be Henry that is wrong, but the lack of agreement within the set. It could be that all four of the other names are wrong.

Answering the Questions

1. **(D)** The missing name must be a male name, in accordance with the first requirement, thus eliminating (A) and (B). The correct answer choice must also have a different first letter from any of the other names already in the set. Waldo (C) duplicates Wally, and Angus (E) duplicates Allen, which leaves only (D).

2. **(B)** Our general review of the conditions gives the answer to this problem. I is out because of the *J*'s. II is out because of the *M*'s and Henry. III is OK. IV and V are out for the female names in position three and the *L*'s in IV. Answer choice (B).

3. **(A)** The third condition is to have different first letters for all of the names. Set III satisfies all of the conditions without exception, so it cannot be the answer to this problem, which eliminates choice (C). Set I has only the error of the *J*'s, as described in the general discussion and in the discussion of problem 2; thus, choice (A) is correct. The other sets cited in answer choices (B), (D), and (E) have other forms of error, as previously described in the discussion of arranging the information.

4. **(E)** You have to be careful with a question like this, which seeks to correct some sort of error in the given information. Some of the suggested answers may correct one error only to make a new one. Answer choice (A), for example, corrects the problem of the *J*'s in set I, but puts a male name in the fourth position, which is a new error.

   (B) makes a similar error because, in the act of correcting the number-of-letters problem with Henry, a female name is placed where a male name should go.

   (C) makes a change in an already correct set, which means that it is not going to "make" set III correct. In addition, the Boris would duplicate a first letter with Betty, and thus create an error.

   (D) does accurately correct an error in set IV—the *L*'s—without making a new error, but this is not enough to make the set correct since it still has a female name in the third position.

   (E) is the correct answer because the substitution of Fred for Mona in set V solves the only problem that set had, without creating any new errors.

5. **(C)** III is an assumption of the psychologist. He observed the dogs for a certain period of time, and found that each time a stranger approached they kept silent. From those observed instances he concluded that the dogs never barked at strangers. Obviously his theory would be disproved (or at least it would have to be seriously qualified) if, when he was not watching, the dogs barked their

heads off at strangers. I is not assumed, however. The psychologist was concerned only with the dogs' reactions to strangers. As far as we know, he may have seen the dogs barking during a frolic in the park, or while they were being bathed, or at full moon. II is not an assumption the author makes. The author makes a factual claim: Dogs treated in this way do not bark at strangers. We have no basis for concluding that the author does or does not think that dogs ought or ought not to bark at strangers. In fact, it seems as likely that the author thinks a great way to train watch dogs is to hit them with rolled-up newspapers.

6. **(B)** II would undermine the psychologist's thesis that "only a beaten dog barks". It cites instances in which the dog was not beaten and still barked at strangers. This would force the psychologist to reconsider his conclusion about the connection between beating and barking. I is not like II. It does not state the dogs were never beaten; it states only that the dogs were not beaten when they barked at strangers. It is conceivable that they were beaten at other times. If they were, then even though they might bark at strangers (and not be beaten at that moment), they would not be counter-examples to the psychologist's theory. III is not an assumption of the psychologist, as we saw in the preceding question, so denying it does not affect the strength of his argument. The psychologist is concerned with the factual connection between beating a dog and its barking; information about the owners' feelings can hardly be relevant to that factual issue.

7. **(E)** Careful reading of the ad shows that all three propositions could be true even if the ad is correct. First, another deodorant might also give all-day protection. The ad claims that White Bear is the only deodorant which gives you *both* protection and scent—a vacuous enough claim since White Bear is probably the only deodorant with the White Bear scent. Of course, III is not affected by this point, since the White Bear Company may put its unique scent into many of its products. Finally, II is also not inconsistent with the ad—that another product is more popular does not say that it has the features the ad claims for the White Bear deodorant.

Questions 8–12

Arranging the Information

This is a situation with so few items in it that it looks likely to be completely determined once everything is fitted in. It is probably going to be helpful to keep track of the cross-references in a separate chart.

Entering the first item: Roger's wife is older than Ursula, and hence not Ursula.

PAUL	QUINCY	ROGER	SAM
		not U	
		older than U	

TESS	URSULA	VAL	WILMA
	not R		

	P	Q	R	S
T				
U		N		
V				
W				

"N" MEANS NOT SPOUSE OF
"Y" MEANS IS SPOUSE OF

Sam's wife is older than Wilma (and hence not Wilma), who is Paul's sister (and hence not Paul's wife).

Roger's wife, is the oldest.
Sam's wife is older than Wilma; hence, Wilma is not Roger's wife.
Wilma is not P's, R's, or S's wife, so must be Q's wife.

	P	Q	R	S
T		N		
U		N	N	
V		N		
W	N	Y	N	N

"N" MEANS NOT SPOUSE OF
"Y" MEANS IS SPOUSE OF

Tess is the youngest, and hence not S's or R's but P's wife.

	P	Q	R	S
T	Y	N	N	N
U	N	N	N	
V		N	N	
W	N	Y	N	N

"N" MEANS NOT SPOUSE OF
"Y" MEANS IS SPOUSE OF

This leads to the further deduction that U can only go with S, leaving R and V to go with each other.

	P	Q	R	S
T	Y	N	N	N
U	N	N	N	Y
V	N	N	Y	N
W	N	Y	N	N

"N" MEANS NOT SPOUSE OF
"Y" MEANS IS SPOUSE OF

We have the miscellaneous information that the ages of the wives are also in order. V, as R's wife, is the oldest, with T the youngest, and U is older than W, yielding, in age, V>U>W>T.

Paul is Wilma's sister.

We did not actually need the last item of information to find out the marriages.

Answering the Problems

8. **(A)** Quincy's wife's (Wilma) brother's (Paul) wife, Tess, will be Patrick's aunt, (A). You must look to Paul since that is the only brother/sister relationship, which is the only thing that could yield an aunt relationship.

9. **(C)** This is just a matter of checking on who is married to whom and using the age relationships,

previously developed. Paul's wife is Tess, who is youngest of all.

10. **(D)** The main idea here is to use the age relationships of the wives to help sort out the husbands. Since Wilma is older than Tess, their husbands Quincy and Paul must have the same relationship, thus, (D) is false.

(A) is true since Roger, older than the oldest wife, must be the oldest of the group, and (B) is true since Tess must be the youngest of all. The husbands are older than the wives and she is the youngest wife. (C) is true since the wives of these two have just that relationship.

(E) might or might not be true, but it is certainly not definitely false. The wives might be one day older than each other, or decades.

11. **(C)** Since the answer choices are all in terms of the marriages, let us arrange the information that way:

PAUL	27	QUINCY	29
TESS	28	WILMA	30
ROGER	31	SAM	33
VAL.	34	URS.	32

Note that since the husband's ages are generally younger, it is not surprising that in three of the couples the wife is older.

Reading from this chart we see that (C) is false.

12. **(A)** This goes back to the original information and does not use the information from the previous problem. We simply have to sort out who is married to whom, and use the age relationships developed previously.

The couples are P/V, Q/W, R/T, S/U and the ages are V>U>W>T. Sam's wife is still Ursula, and she is younger than only Valerie, who is now Paul's wife, choice (A), eliminating (B). (C) and (D) would be correct before the switch in spouses, when Valerie, the oldest wife, was married to Roger. Now, however, Tess, the youngest wife, is married to Roger, so they are false. (E) similarly would have been true before the divorces and remarriages, but not now.

Questions 13–17

This is a linear ordering set. We begin by summarizing the information for easy reference:

O ≠ 1st or 6th
L ≠ J ⎱
L ≠ K ⎰ (We know that L > M, so this means L cannot be next to J or K in the line.)
L→M

13. **(D)** For this question, we simply check each choice against the initial conditions. On the

ground that O does not finish first or last, we eliminate (C). On the ground that L cannot be next in line to either J or K, we eliminate (A) and (E). Finally, since L must finish immediately ahead of M, we eliminate (B). Only (D) satisfies all of the restrictions.

14. **(E)** We begin by processing the additional information:

1	2	3	4	5	6
J				K	

This places the L-M combination in positions 3 and 4, respectively (to avoid the J-K conflict). And O must be in position 2, with N in position 6:

1	2	3	4	5	6
J	O	L	M	K	N

This shows that only (E) is true.

15. **(C)** We begin by processing the additional information:

1	2	3	4	5	6
N	L	M			

We put N in first because J, K, and O cannot be there. We know further that either J or K must be sixth, since O cannot finish last. But there are four possible arrangements using these restrictions:

1	2	3	4	5	6
N	L	M	O	J	K
N	L	M	O	K	J
N	L	M	K	O	J
N	L	M	J	O	K

Testing the statements, we see that I is merely possible but not necessary. II is definitely not possible. Finally, III is true under the assumptions given, so III alone is the correct choice.

16. **(D)** For this question, we test each arrangement against the initial conditions. We know that four of the five will be acceptable and that only one will not be acceptable. The exception is the correct choice. (D) is not acceptable since we have the impermissible arrangement of J in second place and L in third place.

17. **(E)** For this question, we must treat each statement as providing additional information. As for statement I, we get

1	2	3	4	5	6
N	J	K	O	L	M

With J and K in 2 and 3 respectively, we must put L in 5, and therefore M in 6. But O must then be in 4, with N in 1. So there is only one possible arrangement using this information. As for II, we have

1	2	3	4	5	6
L	M	J	K	O	N

With K in 4, we must put the L-M combination in 1 and 2. This means that N finishes last with O in position 5. So, again, the statement guarantees only one arrangement. Finally, III:

$$\begin{array}{cccccc} 1 & 2 & 3 & 4 & 5 & 6 \\ L & M & O & J & K & N \end{array}$$

With J and K in 4 and 5, L and M must be in 1 and 2 or 2 and 3. But they cannot be in 2 and 3 for this would require O to be first or last. So L and M must be in 1 and 2; N must be in 6; and O must be in 3.

Questions 18–22

Arranging the Information

Previewing these problems and the information makes it clear that all we have is a partial description of what might be the diving arrangements. We can classify this either algebraically, by writing equations such as "M not P or Q," "K with S," or we can make a diagram showing the connections which are stated:

DIVERS   BIOLOGISTS

AT LEAST ONE PER TEAM OF EACH CATEGORY
ALWAYS WITH

KEN ←——————————→ SUE
NEVER WITH

MABEL ←——————————→ PETER
                                              QUENTIN

LEON   ROSEMARY
NINA
DIVE-MASTER FROM
THIS GROUP

Answering the Questions

18. **(D)** You must note the condition that there are three dive teams. Since there are seven people, not counting Jack or Nina, to be divided into 3 teams (one could stay aboard ship, but it doesn't matter), the teams must be 2, 2, and 2 or 3 persons. Ken and Sue are on one team. Mabel can't be with either Peter or Quentin so she must be with Rosemary; hence (D) is not possible, yielding (D) as the correct answer.

   That leaves Leon to be with either Peter or Quentin and the other of that pair to go with either Ken or Leon's team or stay on ship.

   If you wished to choose (A) or (B), you may have thought the newlyweds wouldn't dive with anyone, but all that was said was that they dive together. (C) and (E) are valid possibilities, as previously explained, which leaves (D).

19. **(A)** Ken and Sue are one team. Since Mabel won't dive with the two male biologists, she must dive with Rosemary as a two-diver team. Nina and Ken on the one hand, and Peter and Quentin on the other, can trade freely and they can team up four ways (M & P, M & Q, N & P, and N & Q) for a grand total of six.

20. **(C)** Mabel's being the dive-master opens things up a little, but the basic restrictions still hold. I is not possible because they are all biologists. II is not possible because they are both professional divers with no biologist. III is possible in a way similar to that discussed in problem 18. IV is not possible because it involves splitting Ken and Sue. Hence, (C).

21. **(B)** (C) is out because it parts Ken and Sue. (D) has a team composed only of biologists or only of professional divers, and thus fails. (A) and (E) both fail to keep anyone on board as a dive-master. (B) is, thus, the answer. There is no limit to the size of the teams.

22. **(D)** (A), (B), and (E) all split Ken and Sue and thus are not possible. (C) fails for having only biologists. (D) is possible and the answer.

23. **(E)** This is a very sticky question, but it is similar to ones which have been on the GRE. The key here is to keep in mind that you are to pick the BEST answer, and sometimes you will not be very satisifed with any of them. Here (E) is correct by default of the others. (A) has some merit. After all, the real economist isn't very careful in his statement of his claim. He says "here we go again" when there is no evidence that we have ever been there before. But there is no particular term he uses which we could call ambiguous. (B) is wrong because although the economist assumes some people take that position (otherwise, against whom would he be arguing?), he does not imply that he alone thinks differently. (C) is like (A), a possible answer, but this interpretation requires additional information. You would have to have said to yourself, "Oh, I see that he is against it. He is probably saying this in an exasperated tone and in the context of a diatribe." If there were such additional information, you would be right, and (C) would be a good answer. But there isn't. (E) does not require this additional speculation and so is truer to the given information. (D) would also require speculation. (E) is not perfect, just BEST by comparison.

24. **(A)** The main point of the passage is that pregnancy and a child put strain on a young marriage, and that such marriages would have a higher survival rate without the strain of children. It would seem, then, that encouraging such couples not to have children would help them stay married; but that will be possible only if they have not already committed themselves, so to speak, to having a child. If the wife is already pregnant at

the time of marriage, the commitment has already been made, so the advice is too late. (B) and (C) are wrong for similar reasons. It is not only the continued presence of the child in the marriage which causes the stress, but the very pregnancy and birth. So (B) and (C) do not address themselves to the *birth* of the child, and that is the factor to which the author attributes the dissolution of the marriage. (D) is wide of the mark. Whether society does or does not have such an interest, the author has shown us a causal linkage, that is, a mere fact of the matter. He states: If this, then fewer divorces. He may or may not believe there should be fewer divorces. (E) is wrong for this reason also, and for the further reason that it says "do not *plan*" to have children. The author's concern is with children during the early part of the marriage. He does not suggest that couples should never have children.

25. **(E)** This question is primarily a matter of careful reading. The phrase "no lower bus fares" must not be read to mean that Flash uniquely has the lowest fare; it means only that no one else has a fare lower than that of Flash. It is conceivable that several companies share the lowest fare. So II is not inconsistent with the claim made in the advertisement. III is not inconsistent since it mentions the New York City to Boston route, and it is the Washington, D.C., to New York City route which is the subject of the ad's claim. Finally, I is not inconsistent since it speaks of an *air* fare and the ad's language carefully restricts the claim to *bus* fares.

SECTION VII

1. **(C)** The first blank is something that is admitted, and therefore not something positive. This eliminates (A) and (B). The second blank is a basis for justifying an action that is not positive or admirable in itself. (D) fails totally here since transcendentalism does not justify degeneracy. (E) has a little more merit in that heredity might in some circumstances explain lunatic actions, but it does not justify them. On the other hand, expedience might justify an iniquitous action. Thus, (C) is the best answer choice.

2. **(B)** The sentence is about a novel, which is a piece of fiction, so (A) and (C) are not inherently strong choices for the first blank. A satire, however, is a well-known style of fiction and has considerable merit for the first blank. For the second blank, (D) is particularly poor usage and (C) is not much better. Working the two blanks together, we see that (A) is not terrible in that a treatise could be on the interests of society, though there is really nothing in the sentence to

justify either word. (B) works very well since satires often show up the foibles, or weaknesses, of their subjects. (E) has only the slight merit that infirmities is a medical-sounding term and the topic and other nouns mentioned are medically related. This is inadequate to overcome the strength of (B), so (B) is the best answer choice.

3. **(D)** There are three clues in the sentence. First of all, the two blanks are opposites since one is high and the other low. Secondly, the progression from the first to the second is a good thing. The third clue is that the second blank is described as hard. (B) is eliminated since the idea of high and low is a figurative or metaphorical usage rather than a literal one. (C) fails since there is no clear advantage to go from audacity to sincerity, and sincerity is not hard. (A) has merit since it is good to go from the ridiculous to the sublime, although it is not really a strict progression. However, sublimity is not particularly referred to as being hard, so (A) fails.

   In distinguishing between (D) and (E), the most helpful idea is the phrase the heights of fantasy, since speculation is not usually referred to as achieving heights. Also, fact is more often called hard than is reality, though both might work. Thus, (D) is narrowly, but clearly, better than (E), and (D) is the best answer.

4. **(B)** The first blank is part of a list and thus will be something that belongs in a list with old-fashioned, confused, and out of step. (B) fits the best since it is the strongest negative, and all of those are negative. (D) is barely acceptable. (C) and (E) do not convey any meaning in that context, and (A) is positive and therefore incorrect here. The second blank describes the kind of science appropriate for discussing and analyzing peace and war. These are not physical-science issues, but issues in behavioral science since war is a human behavior. Thus, (B) is the best answer for both parts of the question.

5. **(E)** The sentence sets up a contrast between the exuberance of Apuleius' work and the writings of Cicero, which are carefully molded. (C) and (D) are nonsensical since Cicero was a writer and not a pirate, and to call his writings objects is beside the point. We know that the writings are the issue even if we have never heard of the authors, since the introductory part of the sentence said that this behavior applied to those who read Latin; thus, writings are implied. We need something that is opposite to exuberance. Platitudes is the closest we can get. Literature does not distinguish the two since both are literature. Redundancies are boring since they are repetitions, but there is nothing that is likely to be carefully molded about a redundancy since that error is usually the result of carelessness.

6. **(C)** The sentence sets up a contrast between the blank and undefinable. (A), (B), and (E) are common ideas about the nature of science, but they are not relevant to this sentence. Ascertained, in (C), means things which can be known and found to be true; thus it is the best opposite to undefinable. Insured in its proper meaning has no relevance, but might trap the unwary into thinking of assured, which means guaranteed, certain, and thus has some merit.

7. **(B)** Belie means give the lie to. Thus the blank details are opposite in meaning to the superficial similarity to reptiles. One good opposite to superficial is internal. (A) fails since a case cannot be based on unknown details. (D) and (E) have some merit since they are the sort of details which might be useful, but they do not oppose superficial as well as internal does, and thus (B) is the best answer.

8. **(B)** Disembark is the term that describes the act of leaving a ship. Dismount is the term that describes the act of getting off (leaving) a horse. (A) and (C) are working in the wrong direction and speak of joining with the train or jail. (E) has the prefix dis-, but in this case the meaning is to take the clock apart, and not to leave as with disembark. (D) is the second-best answer, but leaving the navy is a less physical and more abstract idea than leaving a ship or a horse. Thus (B) is the best answer.

9. **(D)** Protein is the major nutrient available from meat, and starch the one available from potatoes. (E) and (C) have different ideas about food relationship than what the constituent nutrients are. (B) has some surface plausibility since the calories from sugar are used to heat the body, along with calories from other sources. However, this is not the relationship that meat and protein have. (A) is the second-best answer since cream certainly has calories. However, calories are a measure of the food energy of a food and not an actual constituent as such. It is as if one spoke of the weight of a piece of firewood as a measure of its heating capacity. In any case, protein and starch are specific types of nutrients while calories are only a measure. Thus, (D) is the best answer.

10. **(A)** The nape is the back part of the neck. The heel is the back part of the foot. All of the answer choices are anatomical; all except (D) are very closely related, and (D) has the idea of front and back. Only (A) has both ideas, thus it is the best answer.

11. **(C)** Gripping is the special task of pliers. Elevating is the special task of a jack. (A) has merit, but is backward. (B), (D) and (E) are all possible uses of the tool mentioned, but they are not the principal or typical uses. Thus, (C) is the best answer.

12. **(E)** The radius of a circle runs from the center of the circle to the outside of the circle. The same can be said of a spoke and wheel. (A) merely states a component material, and thus fails. (B) has a process as the first term, while the original pair has a part of the circle, so (B) fails. (C) and (D) speak about geometrical relationships, but ones that are different from that described in the original pair. A chord might be a diameter, but it is, specifically, a line from one side of the circle to another, and not a radius. An equator of a sphere, or the Earth, goes all the way around the outside and not from the middle to the outside. Thus, (E) is the best answer.

13. **(D)** The relationship is one of degree. A misdemeanor is a minor crime, while a felony is more serious. However, both are also negative, and thus the correct answer will probably have two negative words differing only in degree. The terms in (A) differ in degree, but both are not negative. (B) does not have any difference in degree. A burglar is a type of thief. (C) has a difference in degree, but is backward. (E) has different ideas in the two terms. So (D), which has two negatives that differ in degree, is the best answer.

14. **(E)** A coda is a somewhat separate section that may end a symphony. An epilogue is a somewhat separate section that may be used to end a novel. (C) and (D) deal with parts of artistic creations, but not specifically endings. An aria may be a climax, but it is not the ending. (A) and (B) concern beginnings and are not therefore as good an analogy as another ending. Thus (E) is the best answer.

15. **(A)** A homonym is a word that is similar to another word in sound. A synonym is a word that is similar to another word in meaning. (B) has a little merit; it speaks of opposition and does not describe the basis of the opposition in the way that the stem pair describes the basis of the similarity. An acronym is composed of letters, but that is not the same as giving the basis for a similarity. (D) and (E) also have a proper characterization of the first word by the second word, but more is needed. Thus, (A) is the best answer.

16. **(B)** The two stem words mean pretty much the same thing. To quash something is to stop it, as is to quell something. (B) has the same meaning as the original pair and in a similar way. Quashing a motion at law means that the motion is dead and void. To quell a rebellion does mean the rebellion is over, but it is not as absolute as quashing. Only (D) has a pair of similar words, but they are not as close in meaning as (B).

17. **(B)** The passage describes the urban setting as impersonal and, thus, with less forceful social constraints. Whether this is true or not is not the

issue. Since the passage holds this view, the lack of personal contact is the key idea. Therefore, where personal contact is greater, the force of social constraints is greater.

(A) fails because of the word primary. No single primary cause is ascribed by the passage. (C) is not stated in the passage. What small communities have more of is *unreported* minor crime. (E) has some merit since the thrust of the passage is that the nature of the urban experience creates the conditions for crime. However, many of the individual aspects described could be ameliorated. Shops could use different displays, opportunities for crime could be reduced, impersonality could be negated, etc. Thus, (D) is not a necessary corollary of the passage. (E) is something that might work in large urban areas, if it could be accomplished, but, as stated, it applies only to small towns, which already have this happy situation. Thus, (B) is the best answer.

18. **(C)** The passage notes that there is crime in small towns that is not reported or dealt with officially, but which would be dealt with officially and thus reported in urban centers. This leads to the conclusion that crime in small towns is underreported; hence, (C).

(A) may or may not be true, but nothing in the passage supports the idea that moral education as a specific activity will have any deterrent effect on crime. (B) is another common prescription for crime that is not addressed by the passage. (D) is also not an issue in the passage. (E) fails for the same reason that 17 (D) does. Thus, (C) is the best answer.

19. **(C)** The author does not say much about traditional societies, nor is it entirely clear to which societies he may be referring. However, he does contrast modern society to the traditional society in a way that lets you answer the question. The author states that there is greater freedom in the current society; therefore it can be concluded that there is less freedom in a traditional society. The question of less than what is a fair one, but the context of the passage is the comparison between current industrialized, urbanized society and the traditional one.

(A) is too strong a conclusion since it makes a judgment of adequacy which the passage cannot support, and also refers to personal movement and travel, which is not what the passage is discussing. (B) is one of those answer choices that is fine until it says too much. The implication that traditional societies have a lower crime rate is a good one, but the reason is not stated to be the effects of moral teaching in school and, according to the passage, is more likely to be the day-to-day operation of the society than the schools. So, (B) fails. (D) and (E) are simply irrelevant and not mentioned in the passage. Thus, (C) is the best answer.

20. **(E)** This is a straightforward matter of checking the passage and noting that only (E) is not referred to. (A) is specifically mentioned in the discussion of vivid displays. (B) is another way of saying the greater abundance of goods. (C) is one of the key ideas in the first part of the passage. (D) is an element of the anononymity and also the opportunity for crime. (E) is potentially mentioned in the sense that a greater number of police might mean that there would be fewer opportunities for crime, but this is further removed from the passage than any of the others, which address the actual impulse to crime or the physical opportunity for crime and are mentioned directly in the passage. Thus, (E) is the best answer.

21. **(D)** The author maintains a tone devoid of judgmental words; thus, (A) and (C) fail. There may be some humor in the passage, but the author does not feel confused about anything, eliminating (B). There is no projection of the future, and thus no basis for either optimism or pessimism, which causes (E) to fail and leaves (D).

22. **(C)** Commercialization of Christmas in America in the past half-century is the theme of the passage. (C) is an example of that and also of the eclecticism of American traditions. None of the other answer choices strikes either of these chords.

23. **(E)** (E) is stated in the first paragraph, which eliminates (A). (B) is a judgment that could perhaps be made, but is not present in the passage. (D) seems false, given the revelling and Saturnalia aspect of the season, though the clinging to the Christmas Eve Mass as entertainment may give a shred of support to this choice. (C) has some merit since the passage does cite the changes in the past fifty years and we certainly know of our own knowledge that the early settlers did not have large department stores in which to shop. However, (C) is not supported in the passage nearly as well as (E).

24. **(E)** (A) is very attractive for two reasons. First, the gift-giving is a part of the commercialism noted by the author as the first distinctive part of the American Christmas celebration. Second, only the exchange of gifts is cited as being borrowed from other lands in the first paragraph. However, (E) much more clearly conveys the passage's idea than (A), since it is the stimulus to retail business (commerce) which is cited by the author. (B) and (C) are clearly not exclusively American and it is the length of the eating and drinking celebration, not the fact of it, that is the second distinction found by the author. (D) is flack.

25. **(A)** In a question asking you to extend the author's analysis to another situation or time, you must always give preference to anything which

carries forward the precise ideas of the passage. (A) focuses on commercialism, and thus precisely continues the ideas of the passage. (B) and (D) try to reach the Saturnalia distinction, but the question stem cited "large numbers of expensive cards," so money is the issue. (C) and (E) are nice, but unconnected to the passage.

26. **(B)** This is similar to a "weakening the argument" question in Logical Reasoning. The author's argument is essentially based on the size of the gift-giving enterprise, and concludes that so much buying and selling must be its own purpose. (B) proposes a somewhat plausible alternative. (C) also has some merit, but still leaves the Christmas gifting as a commercial enterprise. (A) and (D) actually support, or at least are consistent with, the author's argument. (E) fails when (B) succeeds.

27. **(A)** (C) and (D) have no basis in the passage. (E) is inconsistent with the passage since Christmas Eve has the Mass. We are, thus, left with the choice of (A) or (B). It is true that we cannot know exactly where the traditions noted in the passage came from, nor when, but the passage does call attention to the role of immigrants in enriching the American Christmas symbology, and thus (A) is better than (B).

28. **(E)** Something tender is soft and pliable. Something hardened is just the opposite. Tenderized would be an even better match. Tender has other meanings, such as being emotionally sensitive, but these are not used in this particular problem. Difficult has some opposite feel, but tender and hard, or hardened, have both the physical and metaphorical relationship: Leonine means lion-like, often used for describing hair or the way someone stands or moves. Saccharine means extremely sweet. Tepid is lukewarm.

29. **(E)** Inadequate means not enough of. Sufficient means, precisely, to have enough of. Glossy, meaning shiny, rapid, and aspiring, meaning hoping for something good or high, are not at all related in meaning. Confining has the meaning of being limited to, but its connection is more of a similarity than an oppositeness.

30. **(B)** Striated means striped, so this is a pure vocabulary question. The appearance of (B) and (E) means you must be careful to be sure which is which. Marked and stippled have some merit since non-striated means not striped and thus not marked in a way. However, it is better to have an opposite that is precisely the same sort of thing in the opposite way, when that is available.

31. **(E)** To scrutinize is to examine very carefully. To disregard is to fail to examine at all. (D) is nearly a synonym of the stem word. (B) and (C) are

unrelated. (A) has some merit since it has a meaning of examining or probing, but has no idea of strength or examination.

32. **(B)** Lofty means high, particularly in a moral sense, such as lofty ideals. Debased means greatly reduced in value, especially morally, though money can be debased, too. None of the other answers have any idea of high or low. Kinky means unusual and perhaps perverted, and thus has some oppositeness, but debased specifically means made low.

33. **(C)** Flamboyant means flashy, colorful, striking the attention. Colorless is just the opposite. (A) and (B) have some appeal since they are colors, but the opposite of colorless is not a single color, but the abstract concept of full of color. (D) is unrelated. (E) has some feel of oppositeness since it would be hard to see something as pretty if it were colorless, but this is a derived and associated relationship at best.

34. **(C)** Celerity means quickness, from the same root as acceleration. Hence, slowness is a fine opposite. Depression has some merit since a rate or speed could be depressed and thus made lower. But this is a general idea of reduction, while slowness is the specific idea of reduction in speed. Similarly, a postponement could slow things down, but it only works through the idea of slowness, and thus slowness is better. Choler means anger. Anonymity is there to confuse you into believing that the stem word is celebrity instead of celerity.

35. **(B)** Furious means with fury, hence strong and unrestrained; (B) is thus a good opposite. Furious can also refer to a degree of anger, but there is no better opposite to that meaning than restrained. Medium has an idea of moderation, but this is shared by restrained, and medium lacks the reference to control and behavior that restrained can have. (E) reflects a mental attribute, but not one that is opposite. (C) and (D) are simply unrelated. Disjointed means unconnected, or walking as if one's limbs were improperly connected.

36. **(A)** Overpower is to use superior force to vanquish another party. Succumb means to give way to superior force. This is an example of an antonym of a giver/receiver type. A twinge is a little flash of pain. Oust has a power meaning, but is more of a synonym than antonym. Retrench means to retreat, but not to be overpowered.

37. **(E)** A palace is a grand place to live. A hovel is the lowest, meanest place to live. (D) is more like a palace than a hovel. (B) is simply a general term. When the stem word is a particular kind of something, we should look for an opposite kind of

the same thing. A manse is an estate. A skyscraper is just another kind of building.

38. **(B)** To suspend is to stop temporarily. Resume is to end the suspension. (E) is slightly synonymous since it is the stoppage of something, perhaps. (D) has the same sort of meaning as suspend, but is intransitive. (A) has a similar meaning to (B) in that it means that the process will be actively proceeding. However, turn on has no idea of turning on after a stoppage or suspension, which resume does. Thus, resume is better.

ANSWER SHEET—PRACTICE EXAMINATION 2

Section I

1 Ⓐ Ⓑ Ⓒ Ⓓ Ⓔ   8 Ⓐ Ⓑ Ⓒ Ⓓ Ⓔ   15 Ⓐ Ⓑ Ⓒ Ⓓ Ⓔ   22 Ⓐ Ⓑ Ⓒ Ⓓ Ⓔ   29 Ⓐ Ⓑ Ⓒ Ⓓ Ⓔ   36 Ⓐ Ⓑ Ⓒ Ⓓ Ⓔ

2 Ⓐ Ⓑ Ⓒ Ⓓ Ⓔ   9 Ⓐ Ⓑ Ⓒ Ⓓ Ⓔ   16 Ⓐ Ⓑ Ⓒ Ⓓ Ⓔ   23 Ⓐ Ⓑ Ⓒ Ⓓ Ⓔ   30 Ⓐ Ⓑ Ⓒ Ⓓ Ⓔ   37 Ⓐ Ⓑ Ⓒ Ⓓ Ⓔ

3 Ⓐ Ⓑ Ⓒ Ⓓ Ⓔ   10 Ⓐ Ⓑ Ⓒ Ⓓ Ⓔ   17 Ⓐ Ⓑ Ⓒ Ⓓ Ⓔ   24 Ⓐ Ⓑ Ⓒ Ⓓ Ⓔ   31 Ⓐ Ⓑ Ⓒ Ⓓ Ⓔ   38 Ⓐ Ⓑ Ⓒ Ⓓ Ⓔ

4 Ⓐ Ⓑ Ⓒ Ⓓ Ⓔ   11 Ⓐ Ⓑ Ⓒ Ⓓ Ⓔ   18 Ⓐ Ⓑ Ⓒ Ⓓ Ⓔ   25 Ⓐ Ⓑ Ⓒ Ⓓ Ⓔ   32 Ⓐ Ⓑ Ⓒ Ⓓ Ⓔ

5 Ⓐ Ⓑ Ⓒ Ⓓ Ⓔ   12 Ⓐ Ⓑ Ⓒ Ⓓ Ⓔ   19 Ⓐ Ⓑ Ⓒ Ⓓ Ⓔ   26 Ⓐ Ⓑ Ⓒ Ⓓ Ⓔ   33 Ⓐ Ⓑ Ⓒ Ⓓ Ⓔ

6 Ⓐ Ⓑ Ⓒ Ⓓ Ⓔ   13 Ⓐ Ⓑ Ⓒ Ⓓ Ⓔ   20 Ⓐ Ⓑ Ⓒ Ⓓ Ⓔ   27 Ⓐ Ⓑ Ⓒ Ⓓ Ⓔ   34 Ⓐ Ⓑ Ⓒ Ⓓ Ⓔ

7 Ⓐ Ⓑ Ⓒ Ⓓ Ⓔ   14 Ⓐ Ⓑ Ⓒ Ⓓ Ⓔ   21 Ⓐ Ⓑ Ⓒ Ⓓ Ⓔ   28 Ⓐ Ⓑ Ⓒ Ⓓ Ⓔ   35 Ⓐ Ⓑ Ⓒ Ⓓ Ⓔ

Section II

1 Ⓐ Ⓑ Ⓒ Ⓓ Ⓔ   8 Ⓐ Ⓑ Ⓒ Ⓓ Ⓔ   15 Ⓐ Ⓑ Ⓒ Ⓓ Ⓔ   22 Ⓐ Ⓑ Ⓒ Ⓓ Ⓔ   29 Ⓐ Ⓑ Ⓒ Ⓓ Ⓔ   36 Ⓐ Ⓑ Ⓒ Ⓓ Ⓔ

2 Ⓐ Ⓑ Ⓒ Ⓓ Ⓔ   9 Ⓐ Ⓑ Ⓒ Ⓓ Ⓔ   16 Ⓐ Ⓑ Ⓒ Ⓓ Ⓔ   23 Ⓐ Ⓑ Ⓒ Ⓓ Ⓔ   30 Ⓐ Ⓑ Ⓒ Ⓓ Ⓔ   37 Ⓐ Ⓑ Ⓒ Ⓓ Ⓔ

3 Ⓐ Ⓑ Ⓒ Ⓓ Ⓔ   10 Ⓐ Ⓑ Ⓒ Ⓓ Ⓔ   17 Ⓐ Ⓑ Ⓒ Ⓓ Ⓔ   24 Ⓐ Ⓑ Ⓒ Ⓓ Ⓔ   31 Ⓐ Ⓑ Ⓒ Ⓓ Ⓔ   38 Ⓐ Ⓑ Ⓒ Ⓓ Ⓔ

4 Ⓐ Ⓑ Ⓒ Ⓓ Ⓔ   11 Ⓐ Ⓑ Ⓒ Ⓓ Ⓔ   18 Ⓐ Ⓑ Ⓒ Ⓓ Ⓔ   25 Ⓐ Ⓑ Ⓒ Ⓓ Ⓔ   32 Ⓐ Ⓑ Ⓒ Ⓓ Ⓔ

5 Ⓐ Ⓑ Ⓒ Ⓓ Ⓔ   12 Ⓐ Ⓑ Ⓒ Ⓓ Ⓔ   19 Ⓐ Ⓑ Ⓒ Ⓓ Ⓔ   26 Ⓐ Ⓑ Ⓒ Ⓓ Ⓔ   33 Ⓐ Ⓑ Ⓒ Ⓓ Ⓔ

6 Ⓐ Ⓑ Ⓒ Ⓓ Ⓔ   13 Ⓐ Ⓑ Ⓒ Ⓓ Ⓔ   20 Ⓐ Ⓑ Ⓒ Ⓓ Ⓔ   27 Ⓐ Ⓑ Ⓒ Ⓓ Ⓔ   34 Ⓐ Ⓑ Ⓒ Ⓓ Ⓔ

7 Ⓐ Ⓑ Ⓒ Ⓓ Ⓔ   14 Ⓐ Ⓑ Ⓒ Ⓓ Ⓔ   21 Ⓐ Ⓑ Ⓒ Ⓓ Ⓔ   28 Ⓐ Ⓑ Ⓒ Ⓓ Ⓔ   35 Ⓐ Ⓑ Ⓒ Ⓓ Ⓔ

Section III

1 Ⓐ Ⓑ Ⓒ Ⓓ Ⓔ   6 Ⓐ Ⓑ Ⓒ Ⓓ Ⓔ   11 Ⓐ Ⓑ Ⓒ Ⓓ Ⓔ   16 Ⓐ Ⓑ Ⓒ Ⓓ Ⓔ   21 Ⓐ Ⓑ Ⓒ Ⓓ Ⓔ   26 Ⓐ Ⓑ Ⓒ Ⓓ Ⓔ

2 Ⓐ Ⓑ Ⓒ Ⓓ Ⓔ   7 Ⓐ Ⓑ Ⓒ Ⓓ Ⓔ   12 Ⓐ Ⓑ Ⓒ Ⓓ Ⓔ   17 Ⓐ Ⓑ Ⓒ Ⓓ Ⓔ   22 Ⓐ Ⓑ Ⓒ Ⓓ Ⓔ   27 Ⓐ Ⓑ Ⓒ Ⓓ Ⓔ

3 Ⓐ Ⓑ Ⓒ Ⓓ Ⓔ   8 Ⓐ Ⓑ Ⓒ Ⓓ Ⓔ   13 Ⓐ Ⓑ Ⓒ Ⓓ Ⓔ   18 Ⓐ Ⓑ Ⓒ Ⓓ Ⓔ   23 Ⓐ Ⓑ Ⓒ Ⓓ Ⓔ   28 Ⓐ Ⓑ Ⓒ Ⓓ Ⓔ

4 Ⓐ Ⓑ Ⓒ Ⓓ Ⓔ   9 Ⓐ Ⓑ Ⓒ Ⓓ Ⓔ   14 Ⓐ Ⓑ Ⓒ Ⓓ Ⓔ   19 Ⓐ Ⓑ Ⓒ Ⓓ Ⓔ   24 Ⓐ Ⓑ Ⓒ Ⓓ Ⓔ   29 Ⓐ Ⓑ Ⓒ Ⓓ Ⓔ

5 Ⓐ Ⓑ Ⓒ Ⓓ Ⓔ   10 Ⓐ Ⓑ Ⓒ Ⓓ Ⓔ   15 Ⓐ Ⓑ Ⓒ Ⓓ Ⓔ   20 Ⓐ Ⓑ Ⓒ Ⓓ Ⓔ   25 Ⓐ Ⓑ Ⓒ Ⓓ Ⓔ   30 Ⓐ Ⓑ Ⓒ Ⓓ Ⓔ

Section IV

1 Ⓐ Ⓑ Ⓒ Ⓓ Ⓔ 6 Ⓐ Ⓑ Ⓒ Ⓓ Ⓔ 11 Ⓐ Ⓑ Ⓒ Ⓓ Ⓔ 16 Ⓐ Ⓑ Ⓒ Ⓓ Ⓔ 21 Ⓐ Ⓑ Ⓒ Ⓓ Ⓔ 26 Ⓐ Ⓑ Ⓒ Ⓓ Ⓔ

2 Ⓐ Ⓑ Ⓒ Ⓓ Ⓔ 7 Ⓐ Ⓑ Ⓒ Ⓓ Ⓔ 12 Ⓐ Ⓑ Ⓒ Ⓓ Ⓔ 17 Ⓐ Ⓑ Ⓒ Ⓓ Ⓔ 22 Ⓐ Ⓑ Ⓒ Ⓓ Ⓔ 27 Ⓐ Ⓑ Ⓒ Ⓓ Ⓔ

3 Ⓐ Ⓑ Ⓒ Ⓓ Ⓔ 8 Ⓐ Ⓑ Ⓒ Ⓓ Ⓔ 13 Ⓐ Ⓑ Ⓒ Ⓓ Ⓔ 18 Ⓐ Ⓑ Ⓒ Ⓓ Ⓔ 23 Ⓐ Ⓑ Ⓒ Ⓓ Ⓔ 28 Ⓐ Ⓑ Ⓒ Ⓓ Ⓔ

4 Ⓐ Ⓑ Ⓒ Ⓓ Ⓔ 9 Ⓐ Ⓑ Ⓒ Ⓓ Ⓔ 14 Ⓐ Ⓑ Ⓒ Ⓓ Ⓔ 19 Ⓐ Ⓑ Ⓒ Ⓓ Ⓔ 24 Ⓐ Ⓑ Ⓒ Ⓓ Ⓔ 29 Ⓐ Ⓑ Ⓒ Ⓓ Ⓔ

5 Ⓐ Ⓑ Ⓒ Ⓓ Ⓔ 10 Ⓐ Ⓑ Ⓒ Ⓓ Ⓔ 15 Ⓐ Ⓑ Ⓒ Ⓓ Ⓔ 20 Ⓐ Ⓑ Ⓒ Ⓓ Ⓔ 25 Ⓐ Ⓑ Ⓒ Ⓓ Ⓔ 30 Ⓐ Ⓑ Ⓒ Ⓓ Ⓔ

Section V

1 Ⓐ Ⓑ Ⓒ Ⓓ Ⓔ 6 Ⓐ Ⓑ Ⓒ Ⓓ Ⓔ 11 Ⓐ Ⓑ Ⓒ Ⓓ Ⓔ 16 Ⓐ Ⓑ Ⓒ Ⓓ Ⓔ 21 Ⓐ Ⓑ Ⓒ Ⓓ Ⓔ

2 Ⓐ Ⓑ Ⓒ Ⓓ Ⓔ 7 Ⓐ Ⓑ Ⓒ Ⓓ Ⓔ 12 Ⓐ Ⓑ Ⓒ Ⓓ Ⓔ 17 Ⓐ Ⓑ Ⓒ Ⓓ Ⓔ 22 Ⓐ Ⓑ Ⓒ Ⓓ Ⓔ

3 Ⓐ Ⓑ Ⓒ Ⓓ Ⓔ 8 Ⓐ Ⓑ Ⓒ Ⓓ Ⓔ 13 Ⓐ Ⓑ Ⓒ Ⓓ Ⓔ 18 Ⓐ Ⓑ Ⓒ Ⓓ Ⓔ 23 Ⓐ Ⓑ Ⓒ Ⓓ Ⓔ

4 Ⓐ Ⓑ Ⓒ Ⓓ Ⓔ 9 Ⓐ Ⓑ Ⓒ Ⓓ Ⓔ 14 Ⓐ Ⓑ Ⓒ Ⓓ Ⓔ 19 Ⓐ Ⓑ Ⓒ Ⓓ Ⓔ 24 Ⓐ Ⓑ Ⓒ Ⓓ Ⓔ

5 Ⓐ Ⓑ Ⓒ Ⓓ Ⓔ 10 Ⓐ Ⓑ Ⓒ Ⓓ Ⓔ 15 Ⓐ Ⓑ Ⓒ Ⓓ Ⓔ 20 Ⓐ Ⓑ Ⓒ Ⓓ Ⓔ 25 Ⓐ Ⓑ Ⓒ Ⓓ Ⓔ

Section VI

1 Ⓐ Ⓑ Ⓒ Ⓓ Ⓔ 6 Ⓐ Ⓑ Ⓒ Ⓓ Ⓔ 11 Ⓐ Ⓑ Ⓒ Ⓓ Ⓔ 16 Ⓐ Ⓑ Ⓒ Ⓓ Ⓔ 21 Ⓐ Ⓑ Ⓒ Ⓓ Ⓔ

2 Ⓐ Ⓑ Ⓒ Ⓓ Ⓔ 7 Ⓐ Ⓑ Ⓒ Ⓓ Ⓔ 12 Ⓐ Ⓑ Ⓒ Ⓓ Ⓔ 17 Ⓐ Ⓑ Ⓒ Ⓓ Ⓔ 22 Ⓐ Ⓑ Ⓒ Ⓓ Ⓔ

3 Ⓐ Ⓑ Ⓒ Ⓓ Ⓔ 8 Ⓐ Ⓑ Ⓒ Ⓓ Ⓔ 13 Ⓐ Ⓑ Ⓒ Ⓓ Ⓔ 18 Ⓐ Ⓑ Ⓒ Ⓓ Ⓔ 23 Ⓐ Ⓑ Ⓒ Ⓓ Ⓔ

4 Ⓐ Ⓑ Ⓒ Ⓓ Ⓔ 9 Ⓐ Ⓑ Ⓒ Ⓓ Ⓔ 14 Ⓐ Ⓑ Ⓒ Ⓓ Ⓔ 19 Ⓐ Ⓑ Ⓒ Ⓓ Ⓔ 24 Ⓐ Ⓑ Ⓒ Ⓓ Ⓔ

5 Ⓐ Ⓑ Ⓒ Ⓓ Ⓔ 10 Ⓐ Ⓑ Ⓒ Ⓓ Ⓔ 15 Ⓐ Ⓑ Ⓒ Ⓓ Ⓔ 20 Ⓐ Ⓑ Ⓒ Ⓓ Ⓔ 25 Ⓐ Ⓑ Ⓒ Ⓓ Ⓔ

Section VII

1 Ⓐ Ⓑ Ⓒ Ⓓ Ⓔ 8 Ⓐ Ⓑ Ⓒ Ⓓ Ⓔ 15 Ⓐ Ⓑ Ⓒ Ⓓ Ⓔ 22 Ⓐ Ⓑ Ⓒ Ⓓ Ⓔ 29 Ⓐ Ⓑ Ⓒ Ⓓ Ⓔ 36 Ⓐ Ⓑ Ⓒ Ⓓ Ⓔ

2 Ⓐ Ⓑ Ⓒ Ⓓ Ⓔ 9 Ⓐ Ⓑ Ⓒ Ⓓ Ⓔ 16 Ⓐ Ⓑ Ⓒ Ⓓ Ⓔ 23 Ⓐ Ⓑ Ⓒ Ⓓ Ⓔ 30 Ⓐ Ⓑ Ⓒ Ⓓ Ⓔ 37 Ⓐ Ⓑ Ⓒ Ⓓ Ⓔ

3 Ⓐ Ⓑ Ⓒ Ⓓ Ⓔ 10 Ⓐ Ⓑ Ⓒ Ⓓ Ⓔ 17 Ⓐ Ⓑ Ⓒ Ⓓ Ⓔ 24 Ⓐ Ⓑ Ⓒ Ⓓ Ⓔ 31 Ⓐ Ⓑ Ⓒ Ⓓ Ⓔ 38 Ⓐ Ⓑ Ⓒ Ⓓ Ⓔ

4 Ⓐ Ⓑ Ⓒ Ⓓ Ⓔ 11 Ⓐ Ⓑ Ⓒ Ⓓ Ⓔ 18 Ⓐ Ⓑ Ⓒ Ⓓ Ⓔ 25 Ⓐ Ⓑ Ⓒ Ⓓ Ⓔ 32 Ⓐ Ⓑ Ⓒ Ⓓ Ⓔ

5 Ⓐ Ⓑ Ⓒ Ⓓ Ⓔ 12 Ⓐ Ⓑ Ⓒ Ⓓ Ⓔ 19 Ⓐ Ⓑ Ⓒ Ⓓ Ⓔ 26 Ⓐ Ⓑ Ⓒ Ⓓ Ⓔ 33 Ⓐ Ⓑ Ⓒ Ⓓ Ⓔ

6 Ⓐ Ⓑ Ⓒ Ⓓ Ⓔ 13 Ⓐ Ⓑ Ⓒ Ⓓ Ⓔ 20 Ⓐ Ⓑ Ⓒ Ⓓ Ⓔ 27 Ⓐ Ⓑ Ⓒ Ⓓ Ⓔ 34 Ⓐ Ⓑ Ⓒ Ⓓ Ⓔ

7 Ⓐ Ⓑ Ⓒ Ⓓ Ⓔ 14 Ⓐ Ⓑ Ⓒ Ⓓ Ⓔ 21 Ⓐ Ⓑ Ⓒ Ⓓ Ⓔ 28 Ⓐ Ⓑ Ⓒ Ⓓ Ⓔ 35 Ⓐ Ⓑ Ⓒ Ⓓ Ⓔ

PRACTICE EXAMINATION 2

SECTION I

30 minutes
38 questions

Directions: Each of the questions below contains one or more blank spaces, each blank indicating an omitted word. Each sentence is followed by five (5) lettered words or sets of words. Read and determine the general sense of each sentence. Then choose the word or set of words which, when inserted in the sentence, best fits the meaning of the sentence.

1. She was easily intimidated by her employer, who made a practice of _____ his authority over her.
   - (A) relinquishing
   - (B) compounding
   - (C) dismissing
   - (D) abusing
   - (E) denying

2. The children marveled at the strange foliage; it was their _____ to the tropics.
   - (A) voyage
   - (B) devotion
   - (C) introduction
   - (D) responsibility
   - (E) conduit

3. _____ and _____, she left many to mourn her generous heart when she died.
   - (A) Selfless—altruistic
   - (B) Thoughtful—rarefied
   - (C) Beloved—dogmatic
   - (D) Kind—ruthless
   - (E) Political—gentle

4. A wave of self-_____ convulsed her as she realized the _____ she had caused others.
   - (A) pity—suffering
   - (B) doubt—happiness
   - (C) contempt—pain
   - (D) esteem—service
   - (E) concern—inconvenience

5. The late-summer waters of the northern shore were _____ chilly for the vacationers who liked to swim.
   - (A) wonderfully
   - (B) disappointingly
   - (C) hopefully
   - (D) seasonally
   - (E) realistically

6. The innovations of the _____ Age have had _____ effects on people in all walks of life.
   - (A) Atomic—irrelevant
   - (B) Electronic—universal
   - (C) Bronze—pretentious
   - (D) Nuclear—profane
   - (E) Computer—marked

7. The _____ spectacle drew a(n) _____ shudder from the assembled guests.
   - (A) elaborate—credible
   - (B) grisly—horrified
   - (C) understated—appreciative
   - (D) glittering—approving
   - (E) grotesque—pleased

Directions: In each of the following questions, you are given a related pair of words or phrases in capital letters. Each capitalized pair is followed by five (5) lettered pairs of words or phrases. Choose the pair which best expresses a relationship similar to that expressed by the original pair.

267

8. ISLAND : OCEAN ::
   - (A) hill : stream
   - (B) forest : valley
   - (C) oasis : desert
   - (D) tree : field
   - (E) peninsula : pier

9. MATHEMATICS : NUMEROLOGY ::
   - (A) biology : botany
   - (B) psychology : physiology
   - (C) anatomy : medicine
   - (D) astronomy : astrology
   - (E) philosophy : science

10. DISLIKABLE : ABHORRENT ::
   - (A) trustworthy : helpful
   - (B) ominous : loving
   - (C) silly : young
   - (D) tender: hard
   - (E) difficult : arduous

11. MINARET : MOSQUE ::
   - (A) Christian : Moslem
   - (B) steeple : church
   - (C) dainty : grotesque
   - (D) modern : classic
   - (E) romantic : Gothic

12. WHEAT : CHAFF ::
   - (A) wine : dregs
   - (B) bread: crumbs
   - (C) laughter : raillery
   - (D) oat : oatmeal
   - (E) crop : bird

13. DRAMA : DIRECTOR ::
   - (A) class : principal
   - (B) movie : scenario
   - (C) actor : playwright
   - (D) tragedy : Sophocles
   - (E) magazine : editor

14. IMPLACABLE : GOAL ::
   - (A) officious : procedure
   - (B) zealous : method
   - (C) infectious : disease
   - (D) placid : mirror
   - (E) inferable : conclusion

15. CARTOON : DRAWING ::
   - (A) comic : painting
   - (B) laughter : tears
   - (C) crayon : brush
   - (D) ditty : aria
   - (E) caricature : portrait

16. INSOUCIANT : LIGHTHEARTED ::
   - (A) merry : laughter
   - (B) thieving : light-fingered
   - (C) calm : unworried
   - (D) grin : ecstatic
   - (E) convalescent : illness

Directions: Below each of the following passages, you will find questions or incomplete statements about the passage. Each statement or question is followed by lettered words or expressions. Select the word or expression that most satisfactorily completes each statement or answers each question in accordance with the meaning of the passage. After you have chosen the best answer, blacken the corresponding space on the answer sheet.

However important we may regard school life to be, there is no gainsaying the fact that children spend more time at home than in the classroom. Therefore, the great influence of parents cannot be ignored or discounted by the teacher. They can become strong allies of the school personnel or they can consciously or unconsciously hinder and thwart curricular objectives.

Administrators have been aware of the need to keep parents apprised of the newer methods used in schools. Many principals have conducted workshops explaining such matters as the reading readiness program, manuscript writing, and developmental mathematics.

Moreover, the classroom teacher, with the permission of the supervisors, can also play an important role in enlightening parents. The many interviews carried on during the year as well as new ways of reporting pupils' progress, can significantly aid in achieving a harmonious interplay between school and home.

To illustrate, suppose that a father has been drilling Junior in arithmetic processes night after night. In a friendly interview, the teacher can help the parent sublimate his natural paternal interest into productive channels. He might be persuaded to let Junior participate in discussing the family budget, buying the food, using a yardstick or measuring cup at home, setting the clock, calculating mileage on a trip, and engaging in scores of other activities that have a mathematical basis.

If the father follows the advice, it is reasonable to assume that he will soon realize his son is making satisfactory progress in mathematics and, at the same time, enjoying the work.

Too often, however, teachers' conferences with parents are devoted to petty accounts of children's misdemeanors, complaints about laziness and poor work habits, and suggestion for penalties and rewards at home.

What is needed is a more creative approach in which the teacher, as a professional adviser, plants ideas in parents' minds for the best utilization of the many hours that the child spends out of the classroom.

In this way, the school and the home join forces in fostering the fullest development of youngsters' capacities.

17. The central idea conveyed in the above passage is that
    (A) home training is more important than school training because a child spends so many hours with his parents
    (B) teachers can and should help parents to understand and further the objectives of the school
    (C) parents unwittingly have hindered and thwarted curricular objectives
    (D) there are many ways in which the mathematics program can be implemented at home
    (E) parents have a responsibility to help students to do their homework

18. The author directly discusses the fact that
    (A) parents drill their children too much in arithmetic
    (B) principals have explained the new art programs to parents
    (C) a father can have his son help him construct articles at home
    (D) a parent's misguided efforts can be redirected to proper channels
    (E) there is not sufficient individual instruction in the classroom

19. It can reasonably be inferred that the author
    (A) is satisfied with present relationships between home and school

    (B) feels that the traditional program in mathematics is slightly superior to the developmental program
    (C) believes that schools are lacking in guidance personnel
    (D) feels that parent-teacher interviews can be made much more constructive than they are at present
    (E) is of the opinion that teachers of this generation are inferior to those of the last generation

20. A method of parent-teacher communication NOT mentioned or referred to by the author is
    (A) classes for parents
    (B) new progress report forms
    (C) parent-teacher interviews
    (D) informal teas
    (E) demonstration lesson

21. The author implies that
    (A) participation in interesting activities relating to a school subject improves one's achievement in that area
    (B) too many children are lazy and have poor work habits
    (C) school principals do more than their share in interpreting the curriculum to the parents
    (D) only a small part of the school day should be set apart for drilling in arithmetic
    (E) teachers should occasionally make home visits to parents

22. The author's primary purpose in writing this passage is to
    (A) tell parents to pay more attention to the guidance of teachers in the matter of educational activities in the home
    (B) help ensure that every child's capacities are fully developed when he leaves school
    (C) urge teachers and school administrators to make use of a much underused resource—the parent
    (D) improve the teaching of mathematics
    (E) brainwash parents into doing the best thing for their child's education

23. It is most reasonable to infer that the author is a(n)
    (A) elementary-school teacher
    (B) parent
    (C) student
    (D) college teacher
    (E) professor of education

24. The author would most approve of which of the following parental activities to assist in the learning of composition and writing skills?
    (A) one hour of supervised writing exercises nightly
    (B) encouraging the child to write letters to relatives
    (C) spelling words out loud with the child while washing the dishes
    (D) reviewing all the child's written schoolwork
    (E) giving the child money for good grades on written work

A philosophy of mutual deterrence is developing in CB warfare comparable to that in nuclear warfare. In fact, much of the literature on the subject repeats that the stalemate in the latter opens up the need for capability in the former. As an arms race, CBW does not present the spiraling costs of the ICBM–ABM systems, hence a movement to CB weapons (especially chemical) among some smaller nations. So far as the major powers are concerned, the elements in CBW which are in common with the nuclear arms race include the now accepted approach to that race. Thus in discussing control of CB warfare, an editorial in the British journal, *Nature,* concluded:

"The balance of terror between the great power blocs may not be to everybody's taste, but it is probably still the best way of avoiding war."

25. The writer in the British journal might feel that the research and development of CB systems should be
    (A) encouraged and expanded
    (B) conducted only by the major powers
    (C) immediately halted
    (D) maintained as it is now
    (E) considered necessary and desirable

26. The justification for the United States' participation in CB warfare programs is mainly due to the
    (A) need for undetectable weaponry
    (B) still untapped knowledge in the field
    (C) costliness of the nuclear programs
    (D) Soviet Union's having such a program
    (E) ability of modern research to develop them

27. The main purpose of this article is to
    (A) show the difficulties involved in stopping CB warfare programs
    (B) explain the cost of CB warfare
    (C) discuss alternatives to CB warfare
    (D) chronicle the history of CB warfare
    (E) make the reader aware of the dangers of CB warfare

Directions: Each of the following questions consists of a word printed in capital letters, followed by five (5) lettered words or phrases. Select the word or phrase which is most nearly *opposite* to the capitalized word in meaning.

28. MANSION:
    (A) hovel
    (B) hotel
    (C) motel
    (D) castle
    (E) house

29. ENDEMIC:
    (A) permanent
    (B) frustrating
    (C) terrorizing
    (D) democratic
    (E) pandemic

30. COMPENDIOUS:
    (A) profound
    (B) verbose
    (C) simple
    (D) ambiguous
    (E) miscellaneous

31. ASSUAGE:
    (A) cleanse
    (B) steady
    (C) aggravate
    (D) bless
    (E) advance

32. PRATE:
    (A) remark casually
    (B) laugh raucously
    (C) talk meaningfully
    (D) weep copiously
    (E) whisper fearfully

33. ARROGATE:
    (A) speak uncivilly
    (B) act rashly
    (C) play enthusiastically
    (D) take justifiedly
    (E) judge harshly

34. PROLIX:
    (A) terse
    (B) arid
    (C) speechless
    (D) upperclass
    (E) masterful

35. TYRO:
    (A) alert
    (B) democrat

(C) fury
(D) expert
(E) collapse

36. SEDITION:
    (A) flotation
    (B) patriotism
    (C) conservation
    (D) merit
    (E) approval

37. TOUSLE:
    (A) shovel
    (B) groom
    (C) catch
    (D) caress
    (E) clean

38. TRANSIENT:
    (A) final
    (B) preserved
    (C) movable
    (D) agreeable
    (E) persistent

STOP

END OF SECTION. IF YOU HAVE ANY TIME LEFT, GO
OVER YOUR WORK IN THIS SECTION ONLY. DO NOT
WORK IN ANY OTHER SECTION OF THE TEST.

SECTION II

30 minutes
38 questions

Directions: Each of the questions below contains one or more blank spaces, each blank indicating an omitted word. Each sentence is followed by five (5) lettered words or sets of words. Read and determine the general sense of each sentence. Then choose the word or set of words which, when inserted in the sentence, best fits the meaning of the sentence.

1. Being more _____ to artistic activities, Miriam had difficulty _____ to secretarial work.
    (A) oriented—reacting

(B) attuned—conforming
(C) aligned—adapting
(D) inured—turning
(E) inclined—adjusting

2. Naturally _____ from birth, Arnold practiced hard to _____ his talents.
    (A) adept—perfect
    (B) handicapped—overcome
    (C) agile—supercede
    (D) gifted—limit
    (E) inept—develop

3. The teacher's pride was hurt when he discovered that half his class had _____ the exam.
   - (A) enjoyed
   - (B) reassessed
   - (C) flunked
   - (D) redeemed
   - (E) interpreted

4. The reporter's _____ probings finally brought results in the case.
   - (A) scattered
   - (B) severe
   - (C) obsessive
   - (D) relentles
   - (E) earnest

5. _____ mob began to form, full of angry men _____ incoherent threats.
   - (A) An excited—whispering
   - (B) A listless—shouting
   - (C) An ugly—gesturing
   - (D) A lynch—muttering
   - (E) A huge—waving

6. As a staunch _____ of our right to leisure time, Ken had few _____.
   - (A) proponent—friends
   - (B) advocate—defenders
   - (C) disciple—rivals
   - (D) defenders—equals
   - (E) opponent—duties

7. In the _____ downpour, the girls managed to _____ us and disappear.
   - (A) ensuing—evade
   - (B) incessant—pervade
   - (C) uncouth—escape
   - (D) torrential—provoke
   - (E) insipid—avoid

Directions: In each of the following questions, you are given a related pair of words or phrases in capital letters. Each capitalized pair is followed by five (5) lettered pairs of words or phrases. Choose the pair which best expresses a relationship similar to that expressed by the original pair.

8. TELEPHONE : LETTER ::
   - (A) loudspeaker : microphone
   - (B) phonograph : manuscript
   - (C) telegraph : mail
   - (D) sound : sight
   - (E) brush : canvas

9. IMMIGRATION : ENTRANCE ::
   - (A) native : foreigner
   - (B) emigration : departure
   - (C) arrival : door
   - (D) travel : alien
   - (E) refuge : gate

10. HOTEL : SHELTER ::
    - (A) bed : pillow
    - (B) boat : transportation
    - (C) train : ride
    - (D) restaurant : drink
    - (E) home : recuperation

11. MOON : PLANET ::
    - (A) planet : star
    - (B) comet : asteroid
    - (C) Mercury : Jupiter
    - (D) star : nova
    - (E) crater : volcano

12. ASCETIC : LUXURY ::
    - (A) misogynist : women
    - (B) philosopher : knowledge
    - (C) capitalist : industry
    - (D) gourmet : hunger
    - (E) teacher : blackboard

13. SPASM : MUSCLE ::
    - (A) flash : light
    - (B) respite : thought
    - (C) tender : touch
    - (D) pinch : taste
    - (E) sound : noise

14. CORRUGATED : STRIPED ::
    - (A) cardboard : zebra
    - (B) dimpled : speckled
    - (C) rough : solid
    - (D) smooth : dotted
    - (E) bumpy : flashing

15. OXYGEN : GASEOUS ::
    - (A) feather : light
    - (B) mercury : fluid
    - (C) iron : heavy
    - (D) sand : grainy
    - (E) mountain : high

16. AGILE : ACROBAT ::
    (A) greasy : mechanic
    (B) peanuts : vendor
    (C) plant : fruit
    (D) eloquent : orator
    (E) fast : car

Directions: Below each of the following passages, you will find questions or incomplete statements about the passage. Each statement or question is followed by lettered words or expressions. Select the word or expression that most satisfactorily completes each statement or answers each question in accordance with the meaning of the passage. After you have chosen the best answer, blacken the corresponding space on the answer sheet.

Vacations were once the prerogative of the privileged few, even as late as the 19th century. Now they are considered the right of all, except for such unfortunate masses as, for example, the bulk of China's and India's population, for whom life, save for sleep and brief periods of rest, is uninterrupted toil.

Vacations are more necessary now than before because today the average life is less well-rounded and has become increasingly compartmentalized. I suppose the idea of vacations, as we conceive it, must be incomprehensible to primitive peoples. Rest of some kind has of course always been a part of the rhythm of human life, but earlier ages did not find it necessary to organize it in the way that modern man has done. Holidays and feast days were sufficient.

With modern man's increasing tensions, with the stultifying quality of so much of his work, this break in the year's routine became steadily more necessary. Vacations became mandatory for the purpose of renewal and repair. And so it came about that in the United States, the most self-indulgent of nations, the most tense and compartmentalized, vacations have come to take a predominant place in domestic conversation.

17. The title below that best expresses the ideas of this passage is:
    (A) Vacation Preferences
    (B) Vacations: The Topic of Conversation
    (C) Vacations in Perspective
    (D) The Well-Organized Vacation
    (E) Renewal, Refreshment and Repair

18. We need vacations now more than ever before because we have
    (A) a more carefree nature
    (B) much more free time
    (C) little diversity in our work
    (D) no emotional stability
    (E) a higher standard of living

19. It is implied in the passage that the lives of Americans are very
    (A) habitual
    (B) ennobling
    (C) patriotic
    (D) varied
    (E) independent

In my early childhood I received no formal religious education. I did, of course, receive the ethical and moral training that moral and conscientious parents give their children. When I was about ten years old, my parents decided that it would be good for me to receive some formal religious instruction and to study the Bible, if for no other reason than that a knowledge of both is essential to the understanding of literature and culture.

As lapsed Catholics, they sought a group which had as little doctrine and dogma as possible, but what they considered good moral and ethical values. After some searching, they joined the local Meeting of the Religious Society of Friends. Although my parents did not attend Meetings for Worship very often, I went to First Day School there regularly, eventually completing the course and receiving an inscribed Bible.

At the Quaker school, I learned about the concept of the "inner light" and it has stayed with me. I was, however, unable to accept the idea of Jesus Christ being any more divine than, say, Buddha. As a result, I became estranged from the Quakers who, though believing in substantially the same moral and ethical values as I do, and even the same religious concept of the inner light, had arrived at these conclusions from a premise which I could not accept. I admit that my religion is the poorer for having no revealed word and no supreme prophet, but my inherited aversion to dogmatism limits my faith to a Supreme Being and the goodness of man.

Later, at another Meeting for Worship, I found that some Quakers had similar though not so strong reservations about the Christian aspects of their belief. I made some attempt to rejoin a Meeting for Worship, but found that, though they remained far closer to me than any other organized religious group, I did not wish to become one again. I do attend Meeting for Worship on occasion, but it is for the help in deep contemplation which it brings rather than any lingering desire to rejoin the fold.

I do believe in a "Supreme Being" (or ground of our Being, as Tillich would call it). This Being is ineffable and not to be fully understood by humans. He is not cut off from the world and we can know him somewhat through the knowledge which we are limited to—the world. He is interested and concerned for humankind, but on man himself falls the burden of his own life. To me the message of the great prophets, especially Jesus, is that good is its own reward, and indeed the *only* possible rewards are intrinsic in the actions themselves. The relationship between each human and the Supreme Being is an entirely personal one.

It is my faith that each person has this unique relationship with the Supreme Being. To me that is the meaning of the inner light. The purpose of life, insofar as a human can grasp it, is to understand and increase this lifeline to the Supreme Being, this piece of divinity that *every* human has. Thus, the taking of any life by choice is the closing of some connection to God, and unconscionable. Killing anyone not only denies them their purpose, but corrupts the purpose of all men.

20. The author of the preceding passage is most probably writing in order to
    (A) persuade a friend to convert to Quakerism
    (B) reassure a friend that he has not become immoral
    (C) explain the roots of his pacifism
    (D) analyze the meaning of the "inner light"
    (E) recall his parents' religious teachings

21. If offered a reward for doing a good deed, the author would
    (A) spurn the reward indignantly
    (B) accept it only as a token of the other person's feelings of gratitude

    (C) neither take nor refuse the reward
    (D) explain to the offerer that rewards are blasphemous
    (E) make any excuse at all to avoid taking the reward

22. According to the passage, the Quakers
    (A) are the group he wishes to become a member of again
    (B) have historically been pacifists
    (C) are Christians, but only in a weak sense
    (D) share basic religious thought with the author
    (E) are relatively dogmatic and doctrinaire

23. Which of the following would the author likely see as most divine?
    (A) Jesus Christ
    (B) Buddha
    (C) Mohammed
    (D) Moses
    (E) They would be seen as equally divine.

24. It can be inferred that
    (A) the author views the inner light as uniquely an attribute of Quakers
    (B) Quakers treat all men the same, whether they have inner light or not
    (C) the Catholics are not concerned with killing
    (D) the author's parents found Catholic religious views unsuitable or inadequate
    (E) Buddhist belief is as congenial to the author as Quaker belief

25. The author argues that
    (A) we must seek greater comprehension of our own inner lights
    (B) humans must always seek to increase the number of inner lights, hence, population increase is desirable
    (C) the unique relationship between each person and his inner light makes him more divine than those without an inner light
    (D) only a person without an inner light could kill
    (E) faith is essential to life, especially faith based on those most divine persons who are often called prophets

26. If the author were faced with a situation where the killing of another human would occur both by his action and his inaction, then
    (A) he could not act because it would kill someone
    (B) he could not fail to act because it would kill someone
    (C) he would have to kill himself to avoid the situation
    (D) he would have to abandon his beliefs
    (E) he would have to choose to act or not act on some basis other than whether a human would die

27. The author rejected which of the following aspects of religious thought?
    (A) the existence of God
    (B) the need to follow moral rules such as those in the Christian Bible
    (C) the divine nature of human beings
    (D) the revealed word of God
    (E) the value of sharing religious experiences

Directions: Each of the following questions consists of a word printed in captial letters, followed by five (5) lettered words or phrases. Select the word or phrase which is most nearly *opposite* to the capitalized word in meaning.

28. CONSONANT :
    (A) insuperable
    (B) incongruous
    (C) nonexistent
    (D) sounded
    (E) abundant

29. CONCISE :
    (A) wordy
    (B) mundane
    (C) ignorant
    (D) muddy
    (E) wrong

30. FECUND :
    (A) sinister
    (B) premier
    (C) young
    (D) barren
    (E) beneficial

31. FORTUITOUS :
    (A) unfortunate
    (B) unintelligent
    (C) discontent
    (D) fearful
    (E) pious

32. SATURNINE :
    (A) earthy
    (B) cheerful
    (C) complicated
    (D) maudlin
    (E) straight

33. FRANGIBLE :
    (A) argumentative
    (B) docile
    (C) insincere
    (D) sturdy
    (E) inedible

34. LETHARGY :
    (A) acidity
    (B) prodigy
    (C) rigidity
    (D) alertness
    (E) corpulence

35. CUPIDITY :
    (A) lovelessness
    (B) generosity
    (C) smartness
    (D) wastefulness
    (E) prodigality

36. PROTEAN :
    (A) depriving
    (B) flowering
    (C) uniform
    (D) universal
    (E) separate

37. COGENT :
    (A) repetitive
    (B) urgent
    (C) complicated
    (D) confined
    (E) fatuous

38. HIRSUTE :
    (A) naked
    (B) plain
    (C) melted
    (D) bald
    (E) clear

STOP

END OF SECTION. IF YOU HAVE ANY TIME LEFT, GO
OVER YOUR WORK IN THIS SECTION ONLY. DO NOT
WORK IN ANY OTHER SECTION OF THE TEST.

SECTION III

30 minutes
30 questions

Directions: For each of the following questions two quantities are given, one in Column A and one in Column B. Compare the two quantities and mark your answer sheet with the correct lettered conclusion. These are your options:
  A: If the quantity in Column A is the greater;
  B: If the quantity in Column B is the greater;
  C: if the two quantities are equal;
  D: if the relationship cannot be determined from the information given.

Common Information: In any question, information applying to both columns is centered between the columns and above the quantities in columns A and B. The common information applies to both columns. Any symbol that appears in both columns represents the same idea or quantity in both columns.

Numbers: All numbers used are real numbers.

Figures: Assume that the position of points, angles, regions and so forth are in the order shown. Figures are assumed to lie in a plane unless otherwise indicated. Figures accompanying questions are intended to provide information you can use in answering the questions. However, unless a note states that a figure is drawn to scale, you should solve the problems by using your knowledge of mathematics and *not* by estimating sizes by sight or measurement.

Lines: Assume that lines shown as straight are indeed straight.

COLUMN A	COLUMN B

1.

$$x = -y$$

COLUMN A	COLUMN B
x	y

2.

COLUMN A	COLUMN B
$\dfrac{1}{100}$	.01%

3.

The price of paper increased from
$1.23 per ream to $1.48 per ream.

COLUMN A	COLUMN B
the percent increase in the price of paper	20%

4.

M is the average (arithmetic mean) of
x and y.

COLUMN A	COLUMN B
$\dfrac{M + x + y}{3}$	$\dfrac{x + y}{2}$

5.

COLUMN A	COLUMN B
$(a + 2)(b + 3)$	$(a + 3)(b + 2)$

	COLUMN A	COLUMN B

6.   Q is the midpoint of line segment PR.

       length of PQ   length of QR

___

7. $x - y \neq 0$

       $\dfrac{x^2 - y^2}{x - y}$ $x + y$

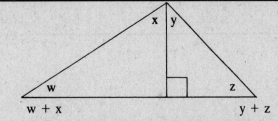

8. $w + x$ $y + z$

___

9. Planes X and Y are 300 miles apart and flying toward each other on a direct course and at constant speeds. X is flying at 150 miles per hour. After 40 minutes, they pass one another.

       speed of plane Y   150 miles per hour

___

10.   66.6% $\frac{2}{3}$

___

11. the average (arithmetic mean) of the number of degrees in the angles of a pentagon   the average (arithmetic mean) of the number of degrees in the angles of a hexagon

___

12. A bookshelf contains 16 books written in French and 8 books written in Italian and no other books. 75% of the books written in French and 50% of the books written in Italian are removed from the bookshelf.

the proportion of the original number of books remaining on the shelf $\frac{2}{3}$

___

13.

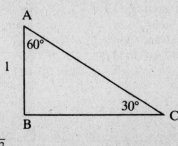

       $\sqrt{3}$ BC

___

	COLUMN A	COLUMN B

14. $x^2 - 1 = 0$

                 x   1

---

15. Tickets to a concert cost $25 and $13. An agent sells 11 tickets for a total price of $227.

     the number of $25-   the number of $13-
        tickets sold   tickets sold

Directions: For each of the following questions, select the best of the answer choices and blacken the corresponding space on your answer sheet.

Numbers: All numbers used are real numbers.

Figures: The diagrams and figures that accompany these questions are for the purpose of providing information useful in answering the questions. Unless it is stated that a specific figure is not drawn to scale, the diagrams and figures are drawn as accurately as possible. All figures are in a plane unless otherwise indicated.

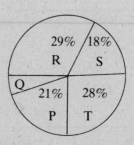

16. $\frac{3}{4} + \frac{4}{5} =$
  (A) $\frac{3}{5}$
  (B) $\frac{7}{20}$
  (C) $\frac{7}{9}$
  (D) $\frac{12}{9}$
  (E) $\frac{31}{20}$

17. If $x + 6 = 3$, then $x + 3 =$
  (A) -9
  (B) -3
  (C) 0
  (D) 3
  (E) 9

18. A person is standing on a staircase. He walks down 4 steps, up 3 steps, down 6 steps, up 2 steps, up 9 steps, and down 2 steps. Where is he standing in relation to the step on which he started?
  (A) 2 steps above
  (B) 1 step above
  (C) the same place
  (D) 1 step below
  (E) 2 steps below

19. What portion of the circle graph above belongs to sector Q?
  (A) 4%
  (B) 5%
  (C) 6%
  (D) 75%
  (E) 96%

20. $326(31) - 326(19)$ is
  (A) 3912
  (B) 704
  (C) 100
  (D) 32.6
  (E) 10

21. A professor begins his class at 1:21 PM and ends it at 3:36 PM the same afternoon. How many minutes long was the class?
  (A) 457
  (B) 215
  (C) 150
  (D) 135
  (E) 75

22. A sales representative will receive a 15% commission on a sale of $2800. If she has

already received an advance of $150 on that commission, how much more is she due on the commission?
(A) $120
(B) $270
(C) $320
(D) $420
(E) $570

23. If a circle has an area of $9\pi x^2$ units, what is its radius?
(A) 3
(B) 3x
(C) $3\pi x$
(D) 9x
(E) $81x^4$

24. Hans is taller than Gertrude, but he is shorter than Wilhelm. If Hans, Gertrude, and Wilhelm are heights x, y, and z, respectively, which of the following accurately expresses the relationships of their heights?
(A) $x > y > z$
(B) $x < y < z$
(C) $y > x > z$
(D) $z < x < y$
(E) $z > x > y$

25. For which of the following figures can the perimeter of the figure be determined if the area is known?

   I.   a trapezoid
   II. a square
  III. an equilateral triangle
  IV. a parallelogram

(A) I only
(B) II only
(C) III only
(D) II and III only
(E) I, II, III, and IV

26. A child withdraws from his piggy bank 10% of the original sum in the bank. If he must add 90¢ to bring the amount in the bank back up to the original sum, what was the original sum in the bank?

(A) $1.00
(B) $1.90
(C) $8.10
(D) $9.00
(E) $9.90

27. If cylinder P has a height twice that of cylinder Q and a radius half that of cylinder Q, what is the ratio between the volume of cylinder P and the volume of cylinder Q?
(A) 1:8
(B) 1:4
(C) 1:2
(D) 1
(E) 2:1

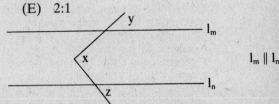

28. In the figure above, which of the following is true?
(A) $y + z = x$
(B) $y = 90°$
(C) $x + y + z = 180$
(D) $y = x + z$
(E) $z = x + y$

29. If the width of a rectangle is increased by 25% while the length remains constant, the resulting area is what percent of the original area?
(A) 25%
(B) 75%
(C) 125%
(D) 225%
(E) Cannot be determined from the information given.

30. The average of four consecutive odd positive integers is always
(A) an odd number
(B) divisible by 4
(C) the sum of two prime numbers
(D) a multiple of 3
(E) greater than 4

STOP

END OF SECTION. IF YOU HAVE ANY TIME LEFT, GO
OVER YOUR WORK IN THIS SECTION ONLY. DO NOT
WORK IN ANY OTHER SECTION OF THE TEST.

SECTION IV

30 minutes
30 questions

Directions: For each of the following questions two quantities are given, one in Column A and one in Column B. Compare the two quantities and mark your answer sheet with the correct lettered conclusion. These are your options:

  A: If the quantity in Column A is the greater;
  B: if the quantity in Column B is the greater;
  C: if the two quantities are equal;
  D: if the relationship cannot be determined from the information given.

Common Information: In any question, information applying to both columns is centered between the columns and above the quantities in columns A and B. The common information applies to both columns. Any symbol that appears in both columns represents the same idea or quantity in both columns.

Numbers: All numbers used are real numbers.

Figures: Assume that the position of points, angles, regions and so forth are in the order shown. Figures are assumed to lie in a plane unless otherwise indicated. Figures accompanying questions are intended to provide information you can use in answering the questions. However, unless a note states that a figure is drawn to scale, you should solve the problems by using your knowledge of mathematics and *not* by estimating sizes by sight or measurement.

Lines: Assume that lines shown as straight are indeed straight.

	COLUMN A	COLUMN B

1.

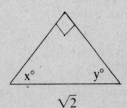

$\sqrt{2}$

	COLUMN A	COLUMN B
	x	y
2.	$x > 0$ $y > 0$	
	x% of y% of 100	y% of x% of 100
3.	0.3	$\sqrt{0.9}$
4.	$(x + y)^2$	$x(x + y) + y(x + y)$
5.	$\dfrac{17}{8786}$	$\dfrac{17}{8787}$
6.	$-(3^6)$	$(-3)^6$

COLUMN A   COLUMN B

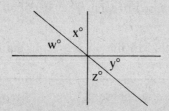

7.

    90 − (w + x)   90 − (y + z)

8.

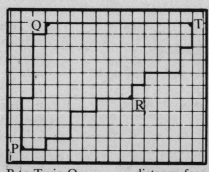

All angles
are right angles

distance from P to T via Q   distance from P to T via R

9. the length of side of any equilat- the length of the diameter of
eral polygon inscribed in circle 0   circle 0

10.   Peter's grade was higher than that of
Victor, and Victor's grade was less
than that of Georgette.

    Georgette's grade   Peter's grade

11.

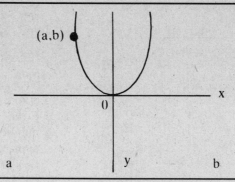

    a   y   b

12.   3x + 5   2x + 3

13.   x < 0

    $(x^3)^5$ $x^3 \cdot x^5$

14.   A man buys 16 shirts. Some of them
cost $13 each, while the remainder

COLUMN A	COLUMN B

cost $10 each. The cost of all 16 shirts
was $187.

the number of $13 shirts purchased	the number of $10 shirts purchased

15.	the volume of a sphere with radius of 5	the volume of a cube with a side of 10

Directions: For each of the following questions, select the best of the answer choices and blacken the corresponding space on your answer sheet.
Numbers: All numbers used are real numbers.
Figures: The diagrams and figures that accompany these questions are for the purpose of providing information useful in answering the questions. Unless it is stated that a specific figure is not drawn to scale, the diagrams and figures are drawn as accurately as possible. All figures are in a plane unless otherwise indicated.

16. If $(x-y)^2 = 12$ and $xy = 1$, then $x^2 + y^2 =$
   (A) 14
   (B) 13
   (C) 12
   (D) 11
   (E) 10

17.

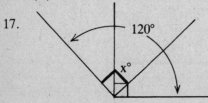

(*Note:* Figure not drawn to scale.)

What is the measure of angle x?
   (A) 30°
   (B) 45°
   (C) 60°
   (D) 90°
   (E) 240°

18. If n is a positive integer and 95 and 135 are divided by n, and the remainders are 5 and 3 respectively, then n =
   (A) 6
   (B) 8
   (C) 10
   (D) 15
   (E) 21

19. A student conducts an experiment in biology lab and discovers that the ratio of the number of insects in a given population having characteristic X to the number of insects in the population not having characteristic X is 5:3, and that $\frac{3}{8}$ of the insects having characteristic X are male insects. What proportion of the total insect population are male insects having the characteristic X?
   (A) 1
   (B) $\frac{5}{8}$
   (C) $\frac{6}{13}$
   (D) $\frac{15}{64}$
   (E) $\frac{1}{5}$

20. If the following were arranged in order of magnitude, which term would be the middle number in the series?
   (A) $\frac{3^8}{3^6}$
   (B) $3^3 - 1$
   (C) 3^0
   (D) 3^{27}
   (E) $3(3^2)$

Questions 21–25 refer to the graph on the next page.

21. From 1972 to 1977, inclusive, the total number of fares collected for subways was approximately how many million?
   (A) 1900
   (B) 1700
   (C) 1500
   (D) 1300
   (E) 1100

22. From 1975 to 1977, the number of fares collected for subways dropped by approximately what percent?
   (A) 90

PUBLIC TRANSPORTATION IN METROPOLITAN AREA P

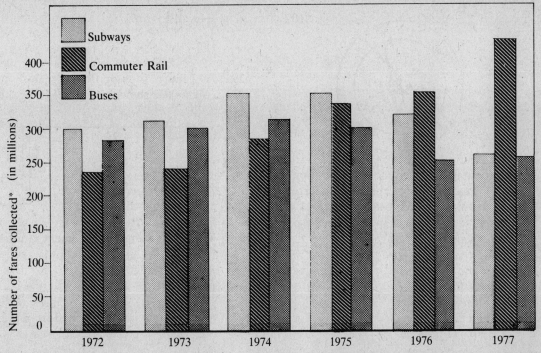

*One passenger paying one fare for one trip

(B) 33
(C) 25
(D) 15
(E) 9

23. If in 1974 the average subway fare collected was 50¢ and the average bus fare collected was 30¢, then the ratio of the total dollar amount of subway fares collected to the total dollar amount of bus fares was approximately
(A) $\frac{1}{4}$
(B) $\frac{1}{3}$
(C) $\frac{3}{5}$
(D) 1
(E) $\frac{7}{4}$

24. The number of commuter rail fares collected in 1977 accounted for approximately what percent of all fares collected on subways, buses, and commuter rail in that year?
(A) 200%
(B) 100%
(C) 50%
(D) 28%
(E) 12%

25. Approximately how many more commuter rail fares were collected in 1977 than were collected in 1972?
(A) 50 million
(B) 80 million
(C) 100 million
(D) 125 million
(E) 195 million

26. Lines l_m and l_n lie in the plane x and intersect one another on the perpendicular at point P. Which of the following statements must be true?

I. A line which lies in plane x and intersects line l_m on the perpendicular at a point other than P does not intersect l_n.

II. Line segment MN, which does not intersect l_m, does not intersect l_n.

III. If line l_o lies in plane y and intersects l_m and point P, plane y is perpendicular to plane x.

(A) I only
(B) II only
(C) I and II only

(D) I and III only
(E) I, II, and III

(C) $\dfrac{9x}{10}$

(D) $\dfrac{10x}{9}$

(E) 9x

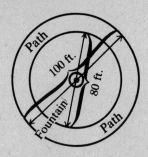

27. The fountain in the above illustration is located exactly at the center of the circular path. How many cubic feet of gravel are required to cover the circular garden path six inches deep with gravel?
(A) 5400π cu. ft.
(B) 4500π cu. ft.
(C) 1250π cu. ft.
(D) 450π cu. ft.
(E) 5π cu. ft.

28. A business firm reduces the number of hours its employees work from 40 hours per week to 36 hours per week while continuing to pay the same amount of money. If an employee earned x dollars per hour before the reduction in hours, how much does he earn per hour under the new system?

(A) $\dfrac{1}{10}$

(B) $\dfrac{x}{9}$

29. A ceiling is supported by two parallel columns as shown in the following drawing:

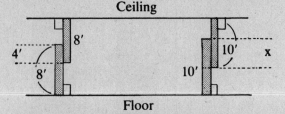

What is the length of segment x in feet?
(A) 10
(B) 8
(C) 6
(D) 4
(E) Cannot be determined from the information given.

30. A painter has painted one-third of a rectangular wall which is ten feet high. When she has painted another 75 square feet of wall, she will be three-quarters finished with the job. What is the length (the horizontal dimension) of the wall?
(A) 18 feet
(B) 12 feet
(C) 10 feet
(D) 9 feet
(E) 6 feet

STOP

END OF SECTION. IF YOU HAVE ANY TIME LEFT, GO OVER YOUR WORK IN THIS SECTION ONLY. DO NOT WORK IN ANY OTHER SECTION OF THE TEST.

SECTION V

30 minutes
25 questions

Directions: Each of the following questions or groups of questions is based on a short passage or a set of propositions. In answering these questions it may sometimes be helpful to draw a simple picture or chart. When you have selected the best answer to each question, darken the corresponding circle on your answer sheet.

Questions 1–4

P drank more at the Murchison's party than W and left later than V.

T drank more than P and less than V and left later than P and earlier than S.

U drank less than Q and more than V and left later than S.

W drank more than R and left earlier than V.

1. Which of the following left earliest?
   (A) P
   (B) S
   (C) T
   (D) U
   (E) W

2. Which of the following drank the least?
   (A) P
   (B) R
   (C) T
   (D) U
   (E) V

3. Based on the above information, which of the following is true?
   (A) V was the second to leave and drank the most.
   (B) U was the last to leave and drank the most.
   (C) T was the third-to-last to leave and drank more than at least three other partygoers.
   (D) S was the second-to-last to leave and drank the most.
   (E) None of the above is true.

4. If S drank more than W, which of the following drank more than S?
   (A) P and R

(B) P, Q, U, and V
(C) P, R, and Q
(D) everyone except R and W
(E) Cannot be determined from the information given.

Questions 5–6

During the 1970's the number of clandestine CIA agents posted to foreign countries increased 25 percent and the number of CIA employees not assigned to field work increased by 21 percent. In the same period, the number of FBI agents assigned to case investigation rose by 18 percent, but the number of non-case-working agents rose by only 3 percent.

5. The statistics best support which of the following claims?
   (A) More agents are needed to administer the CIA than are needed for the FBI.
   (B) The CIA needs more people to accomplish its mission than does the FBI.
   (C) The number of field agents tends to increase more rapidly than the number of non-field agents in both the CIA and the FBI.
   (D) The rate of change in the number of supervisory agents in an intelligence-gathering agency or a law-enforcement agency is proportional to the percentage change in the results produced by the agency.
   (E) At the end of the 1960's, the CIA was more efficiently administered than was the FBI.

6. In response to the allegation that it was more overstaffed with support and supervisory personnel than the FBI, the CIA could best argue:
   (A) The FBI is less useful than the CIA in gathering intelligence against foreign powers.
   (B) The rate of pay for a CIA non-field agent is less than the rate of pay for a non-investigating FBI agent.

(C) The number of FBI agents should not rise so rapidly as the number of CIA agents, given the longer tenure of an FBI agent.

(D) A CIA field agent working in a foreign country requires more back-up support than does an FBI investigator working domestically.

(E) The number of CIA agents is determined by the Congress each year when they appropriate funds for the agency, and the Congress is very sensitive to changes in the international political climate.

7. All effective administrators are concerned about the welfare of their employees, and all administrators who are concerned about the welfare of their employees are liberal in granting time off for personal needs; therefore, all administrators who are not liberal in granting time off for their employees' personal needs are not effective administrators.

If the argument above is valid, then it must be true that

(A) no ineffective administrators are liberal in granting time off for their employees' personal needs

(B) no ineffective administrators are concerned about the welfare of their employees

(C) some effective administrators are not liberal in granting time off for their employees' personal needs

(D) all effective administrators are liberal in granting time off for their employees' personal needs

(E) all time off for personal needs is granted by effective administrators

Questions 8–12

Lois wants to take four courses this semester. There are only seven courses in which she is interested and that do not conflict with her job: three science courses—biology, chemistry, and physics—and four humanities courses—English, French, music, and writing. To meet college requirements she must take two science courses this semester. There are some scheduling problems, however: English overlaps both chemistry and music, which are sequential; biology is given at the same time as French.

8. If Lois decides she will take English, what will her other three courses be?

(A) biology, physics, and chemistry
(B) biology, physics, and writing
(C) biology, physics, and French
(D) physics, chemistry, and writing
(E) physics, writing, and French

9. If the chemistry course is changed to a time which Lois cannot make, and she decides to take music, which of the following would be her schedule?

(A) biology, physics, English, and music
(B) biology, physics, French, and music
(C) biology, physics, writing, and music
(D) physics, English, French, and music
(E) physics, writing, English, and music

10. If Lois takes four courses this semester she cannot

I. take French and not take chemistry
II. take music and not take chemistry
III. take English and not take physics

(A) I only
(B) II only
(C) III only
(D) I and II only
(E) I and III only

11. Which of the following must always be true?

I. Lois must take physics if she takes music.
II. Lois must take chemistry if she takes French.
III. Lois must take French if she takes chemistry.

(A) I, II, and III
(B) II and III only
(C) I and II only
(D) III only
(E) II only

12. If the physics course is moved to the same time as English, and Lois takes physics, what further problem(s) does she face?

(A) She won't be able to take two science classes.
(B) She won't be able to take biology.
(C) She won't be able to take writing.

(D) She won't be able to take either biology or French.

(E) She won't be able to take four courses which interest her.

Questions 13–17

The coach of the Malibu University swimming team is planning his strategy for the rest of his team's meet with the State University swim team. Each event is scored on the basis of five points to the winner, three points for second place, and one point for third place. The score is currently tied, but the coach thinks his team can win because they have greater depth than the other team. The State University team has only enough good swimmers to just fill out their two entries for each of the last three events with one strong entry and one weak one. The last events are the individual medley, the medley relay, and the freestyle relay. Each relay team has four members. The coach considers these facts: State's top individual medley racer is sure to win, but their second entry can only manage a time of four minutes even.

13. What is the minimum number of points that Malibu has to score in the last three races in order to win the meet?
    (A) 14
    (B) 13
    (C) 12
    (D) 11
    (E) 10

14. If State's swimmers take first and third in the individual medley race, which of the following results for the last two races would still let Malibu win?
    (A) first place only in both races
    (B) first place in one race and second and third in the other
    (C) second and third in both races
    (D) first in one race and at least first and third in the other
    (E) There is no way for Malibu to win the meet.

15. Malibu swimmer George can only swim in one more race. He and Jim are the only Malibu swimmers who can beat four minutes in the individual medley. Under which of the following conditions would it be advanta-

geous for George NOT to swim in the individual medley race?
    (A) if adding George will move the medley relay team from fourth to third
    (B) if adding George to the freestyle relay team will move it from third to second
    (C) if adding George to one medley relay team allows shifting of swimmers so that they finish first and fourth instead of second and third
    (D) if adding George to the medley team allows shifting swimmers so that the results are a first and third in one race, and a second and third in the other rather than just two firsts
    (E) There are no conditions under which it is advantageous to hold George out of the individual medley race.

16. If Malibu places second and third in the individual medley race, at least how many of its entries must score points in order to guarantee that Malibu will win the meet?
    (A) 2
    (B) 3
    (C) 4
    (D) 5
    (E) Cannot be determined from the information given.

17. State's top individual medley swimmer is disqualified. If Malibu's two swimmers in that race finish in 3 minutes 57 seconds and 3 minutes 58 seconds respectively, which of the following is false?
    (A) If State places first and fourth in the other two races, they will still win the meet.
    (B) If Malibu places first and third in one relay, they do not even have to swim in the other in order to win the meet.
    (C) If three of Malibu's remaining swimmers score points, Malibu could still lose the meet.
    (D) If all four of State's relay teams score points, State could still lose the meet.
    (E) Even if only three of State's relay teams score points, State could still win the meet.

Questions 18–22

A collie, poodle, retriever, setter, and sheepdog live in separate houses on a five-house block with the Joneses, Kings, Lanes, Murrays, and Neffs—not necessarily in that order.

The sheepdog lives next door to the Lanes, as does the collie.

The Joneses have the heaviest dog and live next to the sheepdog.

The retriever weighs more than the setter or the poodle.

The Lanes live two houses away from the Joneses and from the Kings.

The Kings do not own the setter.

The sheepdog lives with the Murrays.

18. Which of the following is definitely false?
    (A) The poodle lives next to the collie.
    (B) The poodle does not live next to the sheepdog.
    (C) The sheepdog lives next to the collie.
    (D) The setter lives next to the sheepdog.
    (E) The retriever lives two houses from the setter.

19. Which of the following is definitely true?
    (A) The Joneses live next to the Neffs.
    (B) The Joneses live next to the collie.
    (C) The Joneses live at the opposite end of the block from the Lanes.
    (D) The Kings live next to the sheepdog.
    (E) The Kings live next to the collie.

20. If a cat named Kitzen goes to live with the second-heaviest dog, which of the following must be true?
    (A) Kitzen lives with the Kings.
    (B) Kitzen lives with the Lanes.
    (C) Kitzen lives with the Murrays.
    (D) Kitzen lives with the Neffs.
    (E) The answer cannot be determined from the information given.

21. If the Neffs and the Joneses trade houses, but the dogs living in the houses stay with the houses, which of the following now becomes true?
    (A) The poodle lives next to the Joneses.
    (B) The sheepdog lives next to the Joneses.
    (C) The setter lives next to the Neffs.
    (D) The collie lives with the Lanes.
    (E) The retriever lives with the Murrays.

22. If the Murrays move away and give their dog to the Lanes, which of the following would be true?
    (A) The sheepdog now lives with the collie.
    (B) The sheepdog does not now live with the poodle.
    (C) The sheepdog lives next to the Joneses.
    (D) The sheepdog lives next to the Kings.
    (E) The sheepdog lives next to the setter.

---

23. Clark must have known that his sister Janet and not the governess pulled the trigger, but he silently stood by while the jury convicted the governess. Any person of clear conscience would have felt terrible for not having come forward with the information about his sister, and Clark lived with that information until his death thirty years later. Since he was an extremely happy man, however, I conclude that he must have helped Janet commit the crime.

Which of the following assumptions must underlie the author's conclusion of the last sentence?
    (A) Loyalty to members of one's family is conducive to contentment.
    (B) Servants are not be treated with the same respect as members of the peerage.
    (C) Clark never had a bad conscience over his silence because he was also guilty of the crime.
    (D) It is better to be a virtuous man than a happy one.
    (E) It is actually better to be content in life than to behave morally towards one's fellow humans.

24. "Whom did you pass on the road?" the King went on, holding his hand out to the messenger for some hay.

"Nobody," said the messenger.

"Quite right," said the King. "This young lady saw him, too. So, of course, Nobody walks slower than you."

The King's response shows that he believes
    (A) the messenger is a very good messenger

(B) "Nobody" is a person who might be seen

(C) the young lady's eyesight is better than the messenger's

(D) the messenger is not telling him the truth

(E) there was a person actually seen by the messenger on the road

25. New Evergreen Gum has twice as much flavor for your money as Spring Mint Gum, and we can prove it. You see, a stick of Evergreen Gum is twice as large as a stick of Spring Mint Gum, and the more gum, the more flavor.

Which of the following, if true, would undermine the persuasive appeal of the above advertisement?

I. A package of Spring Mint Gum contains twice as many sticks as a package of Evergreen Gum at the same price.

II. Spring Mint Gum has more concentrated flavor than Evergreen Gum.

III. Although a stick of Evergreen Gum is twice as large in volume as a stick of Spring Mint Gum, it weighs only 50% as much.

(A) I only
(B) II only
(C) I and II only
(D) II and III only
(E) I, II, and III

STOP

END OF SECTION. IF YOU HAVE ANY TIME LEFT, GO OVER YOUR WORK IN THIS SECTION ONLY. DO NOT WORK IN ANY OTHER SECTION OF THE TEST.

SECTION VI

30 minutes
25 questions

Directions: Each of the following questions or groups of questions is based on a short passage or a set of propositions. In answering these questions it may sometimes be helpful to draw a simple picture or chart. When you have selected the best answer to each question, darken the corresponding circle on your answer sheet.

Questions 1–5

The letters S, T, U, V, W, X, Y, and Z represent eight consecutive whole numbers, not necessarily in that order.

W is four more than Z and three less than X.

S is more than T and less than X.

U is the average of V and X.

1. If the lowest number of the series is 8, what is the value of W?
(A) 10
(B) 11
(C) 12
(D) 13
(E) 14

2. Which of the following is (are) true?

I. W is not the greatest number in the series.

II. Z is not the greatest number in the series.

III. X is not the greatest number in the series.

(A) I only
(B) II only
(C) I and II only
(D) I and III only
(E) I, II, and III

3. If V is less than W, which one of the following is a possible order of the numbers, starting with the highest number on the left?
(A) X, S, U, W, V, T, Y, Z
(B) X, S, T, W, V, U, Y, Z
(C) Z, S, T, W, U, V, Y, X
(D) X, T, S, V, W, U, Z, Y
(E) X, U, S, T, W, V, Y, Z

4. If U did not have to be greater than V, which of the following is a new possibility?
(A) X is one greater than U.
(B) U is one greater than Z.
(C) U is four less than W.
(D) Z is two greater than U.
(E) U is equal to W.

5. If Y is three greater than Z, which of the following is (are) true?

I. W is greater than U.
II. S is greater than W.
III. Y is greater than V.
IV. V is two less than Y.

(A) I and II only
(B) I and III only
(C) I, II, and IV only
(D) II, III, and IV only
(E) none of the above

Questions 6–7

New Weight Loss Salons invites all of you who are dissatisfied with your present build to join our Exercise for Lunch Bunch. Instead of putting on even more weight by eating lunch, you actually cut down on your daily caloric intake by exercising rather than eating. Every single one of us has potential to be thin, so take the initiative and begin losing excess pounds today. Don't eat! Exercise! You'll lose weight and be healthier, happier, and more attractive.

6. Which of the following, if true, would weaken the logic of the argument made by the advertisement?

I. Most people will experience increased desire for food as a result of the exercise and will lose little weight as a result of enrolling in the program.
II. Nutritionists agree that skipping lunch is not a healthy practice.
III. In our society, obesity is regarded as unattractive.
IV. A person who is too thin is probably not in good health.

(A) I only
(B) I and II only
(C) II and III only
(D) III and IV only
(D) I, II, and III

7. A person hearing this advertisement countered, "I know some people who are not overweight and are still unhappy and unattractive." The author of the advertisement could logically and consistently reply to this objection by pointing out that he never claimed that
(A) being overweight is always caused by unhappiness
(B) being overweight is the only cause of unhappiness and unattractiveness
(C) unhappiness and unattractiveness can cause someone to be overweight
(D) unhappiness necessarily leads to being overweight
(E) unhappiness and unattractiveness are always found together

8. Clara prefers English Literature to Introductory Physics. She likes English Literature, however, less than she likes Basic Economics. She actually finds Basic Economics preferable to any other college course, and she dislikes Physical Education more than she dislikes Introductory Physics.

All of the following statements can be inferred from the information given above EXCEPT
(A) Clara prefers Basic Economics to English Literature
(B) Clara likes English Literature better than she likes Physical Education
(C) Clara prefers Basic Economics to Advanced Calculus

(D) Clara likes World History better than she likes Introductory Physics

(E) Clara likes Physical Education less than she likes English literature

Questions 9–12

John is trying to figure out the best arrangement of spices in the spice rack of his small efficiency kitchen. The rack has two shelves with three spaces on each shelf. He decides that the six spices he uses most often, and thus wishes to put in the rack, are: basil, cumin, fennel, pepper, salt, and thyme. Since the thyme and the basil look similar and come in similar containers, the chances of confusion will be reduced if they are not placed next to each other either horizontally or vertically. Since the pepper and salt are usually both used at the same time, they should be next to each other on the same shelf.

9. Given the above information, which of the following arrangements is (are) unacceptable?

    I. Thyme and basil can be on the same shelf.

    II. Thyme and cumin can be on the same shelf.

    III. Thyme and salt can be on the same shelf.

    (A) Any of the above are acceptable.
    (B) I only
    (C) II only
    (D) II and III only
    (E) All cannot be true.

10. If the two left-hand spices on the upper shelf are thyme and cumin, respectively, which of the following is an acceptable arrangement of the lower shelf, reading from left to right?
    (A) fennel, salt, basil
    (B) fennel, pepper, basil
    (C) basil, salt, pepper
    (D) salt, pepper, basil
    (E) salt, fennel, pepper

11. If the lower shelf has salt, pepper, and basil from left to right, how many possible arrangements are there for the upper shelf?
    (A) 2
    (B) 3

(C) 4
(D) 5
(E) 6

12. John buys a new brand of thyme and basil because it has more flavor. If the new containers are very similar to one another, and also are too tall to fit on the lower shelf, which of the following must be true?
    (A) Either salt or pepper will be next to or below fennel.
    (B) Salt will be below thyme.
    (C) Pepper will be next to either fennel or cumin.
    (D) Thyme will be above either salt or pepper.
    (E) Basil will be above either salt or pepper.

Questions 13–17

Williams is the director of investments for a major pension fund. He believes that blue-chip common stocks and government securities will generally not do as well as corporate bonds in the coming year, but government regulations require that at least one-third of the fund's capital be in blue-chip common stocks and another third in government securities.

13. Under current regulations, what seems to be the best way for Williams to invest the pension fund?
    (A) two-thirds government securities, one-third blue-chip stock
    (B) two-thirds government securities, one-third corporate bonds
    (C) one-third government securities, two-thirds corporate bonds
    (D) one-third each government securities, blue-chip stocks, and corporate bonds
    (E) half government securities and half blue-chip stocks

14. If the pension fund has $6 billion in assets, what is the maximum that Williams could invest in blue-chip stocks?
    (A) $2 billion
    (B) $3 billion
    (C) $4 billion
    (D) $5 billion
    (E) $6 billion

15. If the government regulations are changed to require only one-quarter where one-third was previously required, Williams will probably
   (A) increase the fund's holdings of government securities
   (B) increase the fund's holdings of corporate bonds
   (C) increase the fund's holdings of blue-chip stock
   (D) hold less cash
   (E) hold more cash

16. If the return on government securities suddenly goes up five percentage points, Williams will probably
   (A) sell blue chip stock to buy government securities
   (B) sell corporate bonds to buy government securities
   (C) sell both corporate bonds and blue-chip stocks to buy government securities
   (D) keep the fund the way it was
   (E) His action cannot be predicted.

17. In the middle of the year, the fund is invested equally in corporate bonds, blue-chip stock, and government securities. The sudden merger of one of the main employers serviced by the fund results in the early retirement of thousands of workers, creating in turn a cash shortage for the fund. To generate the needed cash, Williams might do any one of the following EXCEPT
   (A) sell two times more corporate bonds than blue-chip stocks
   (B) sell two times more corporate bonds than government securities
   (C) sell only corporate bonds and blue-chip stocks
   (D) sell only government securities and blue-ship stock
   (E) sell only government securities and corporate bonds

Questions 18–22

Max is planning his sales calls for the next day. He is judged and paid by his company both on the basis of the number of calls he makes and the amount of sales he generates.

Acme Co. will take only one hour and will probably result in an order of 5 boxes.

Bell Corp. will take three hours and will either result in an order of 20 boxes or nothing.

Camera Shops, Inc., will take one hour and yield an order of 10 boxes.

Deland Bros. will take from one to three hours and probably result in an order of 10–30 boxes.

18. Under these conditions, what is the greatest number of boxes Max can reasonably hope to sell in a seven-hour working day?
   (A) 65
   (B) 60
   (C) 45
   (D) 40
   (E) 35

19. Under these conditions, what is the minimum number of boxes that Max can reasonably expect to sell in eight working hours?
   (A) none
   (B) 15
   (C) 20
   (D) 25
   (E) 35

20. If Max has sold 20 boxes to Deland Bros. and then his car breaks down and is not fixed until 2:00 P.M., what is the maximum sales figure for the day he can reasonably hope to achieve by 5:00 P.M.?
   (A) 20 boxes
   (B) 35 boxes
   (C) 40 boxes
   (D) 45 boxes
   (E) 55 boxes

21. If Max has an unbreakable thirty-minute luncheon appointment at 1:30 P.M., what is his best schedule for a 9:00 A.M. to 5:00 P.M. day?
   (A) Acme and Camera, then Bell and Deland
   (B) Bell and Acme, then Camera and, if time permits, Deland
   (C) Bell and Camera, then Deland and, if time permits, Acme
   (D) Camera and Bell, and Acme and Deland
   (E) Deland and Acme, then Camera and Bell

22. If Max is sick and has to carry all his calls over to the next day, when he must be at Edwards & Co. from 10:30 A.M. to 1:30

P.M., what would be his best schedule for the day from 9:00 A.M. to 5:00 P.M.?

(A) Deland, Edwards, Camera, and Bell
(B) Camera, Edwards, Deland and, if time permits, Acme
(C) Camera, Edwards, Acme and, if time permits, Deland
(D) Acme, Edwards, Deland and, if time permits, Camera
(E) Bell, Edwards, Deland and, if time permits, Camera

23. There is something irrational about our system of laws. The criminal law punishes a person more severely for having successfully committed a crime than it does a person who fails in his attempt to commit the same crime—even though the same evil intention is present in both cases. But under the civil law a person who attempts to defraud his victim but is unsuccessful is not required to pay damages.

Which of the following, if true, would most weaken the author's argument?

(A) Most persons who are imprisoned for crimes will commit another crime if they are ever released from prison.
(B) A person is morally culpable for his evil thoughts as well as for his evil deeds.
(C) There are more criminal laws on the books than there are civil laws on the books.
(D) A criminal trial is considerably more costly to the state than a civil trial.
(E) The goal of the criminal law is to punish the criminal, but the goal of the civil law is to compensate the victim.

24. An independent medical research team recently did a survey at a mountain retreat founded to help heavy smokers quit or cut down on their cigarette smoking. Eighty percent of those persons smoking three packs a day or more were able to cut down to one pack a day after they began to take End-Smoke with its patented desire suppressant. Try End-Smoke to help you cut down significantly on your smoking.

Which of the following could be offered as valid criticism of the above advertisement?

I. Heavy smokers may be physically as well as psychologically addicted to tobacco.
II. A medicine which is effective for very heavy smokers may not be effective for the population of smokers generally.
III. A survey conducted at a mountain retreat to aid smokers may yield different results than one would expect under other circumstances.

(A) I only
(B) II only
(C) III only
(D) II and III only
(E) I, II, and III

25. In his most recent speech, my opponent Governor Smith, accused me of having distorted the facts, misrepresenting his position, suppressing information, and deliberately lying to the people.

Which of the following possible responses by this speaker would be LEAST relevant to his dispute with Governor Smith?

(A) Governor Smith would not have begun to smear me if he did not sense that his own campaign was in serious trouble.
(B) Governor Smith apparently misunderstood my characterization of his position, so I will attempt to state more clearly my understanding of it.
(C) At the time I made those remarks, certain key facts were not available, but new information uncovered by my staff does support the position I took at that time.
(D) I can only wish Governor Smith had specified those points he considered to be lies so that I could have responded to them now.
(E) With regard to the allegedly distorted facts, the source of my information is a Department of Transportation publication entitled "Safe Driving."

STOP

END OF SECTION. IF YOU HAVE ANY TIME LEFT, GO
OVER YOUR WORK IN THIS SECTION ONLY. DO NOT
WORK IN ANY OTHER SECTION OF THE TEST.

SECTION VII

30 minutes
38 questions

Directions: Each of the questions below contains one or more blank spaces, each blank indicating an omitted word. Each sentence is followed by five (5) lettered words or sets of words. Read and determine the general sense of each sentence. Then choose the word or set of words which, when inserted in the sentence, best fits the meaning of the sentence.

1. The long waiting list for the overworked psychiatrists and psychologists, and the twentieth-century _____ for lying on the couch and talking about oneself and one's neuroses have resulted from a too intense _____ with oneself.
   (A) wish—inspection
   (B) process—tirade
   (C) plan—understanding
   (D) fad—preoccupation
   (E) garb—implication

2. Electronic eavesdropping technology has become so _____ that the comparatively little law on the subject has become as _____ as the horse and buggy.
   (A) repulsive—fictitious
   (B) omnivorous—ridiculous
   (C) sophisticated—outmoded
   (D) clandestine—entangled
   (E) popular—homey

3. The human intelligence that created industrial civilization now has the assignment of making that civilization _____ man's basic needs.
   (A) compatible with
   (B) reducible to
   (C) assignable to
   (D) warrantable for
   (E) characteristic of

4. One felt a little shiver of _____ at the thought of venturing out into that world where our footsteps _____ as we walked.
   (A) condescension—talked
   (B) indecision—squeaked
   (C) compunction—disappeared

(D) apprehension—echoed
(E) remorse—retraced

5. Although the _____ of running has greatly increased over the years, its basic _____ has not changed very much.
   (A) popularity—isolation
   (B) recognition—reward
   (C) equipment—feel
   (D) speed—technique
   (E) acceptability—foolhardiness

6. Water sports such as sailing and scuba diving are almost as critical to the island's economy as is (are) _____.
   (A) manufacturing
   (B) private enterprise
   (C) public works
   (D) recreational activities
   (E) snorkeling

7. Basic research provides the _____ fund of scientific knowledge on which the applied researchers draw to give society a rich rate of interest.
   (A) depleted
   (B) endowed
   (C) capital
   (D) deterred
   (E) realistic

Directions: In each of the following questions, you are given a related pair of words or phrases in capital letters. Each capitalized pair is followed by five (5) lettered pairs of words or phrases. Choose the pair which best expresses a relationship similar to that expressed by the original pair.

8. COTTON : SOFT ::
   (A) wool : warm
   (B) iron : hard
   (C) nylon : strong
   (D) wood : burn
   (E) silk : expensive

9. CHICKEN : ROOSTER ::
   (A) deer : doe
   (B) duck : drake
   (C) flock : hen
   (D) ewe : ram
   (E) pig : piglet

10. CONDUCTOR : ORCHESTRA ::
    (A) captain : sports
    (B) employer : employee
    (C) coach : team
    (D) director : playing
    (E) teacher : music

11. DESTROY : DEMOLISH ::
    (A) cry : wail
    (B) break : mar
    (C) slack : looseness
    (D) strict : lax
    (E) plan : action

12. FUNNEL : LIQUID ::
    (A) hose : water
    (B) speaker : sound
    (C) window : air
    (D) vent : smoke
    (E) chimney : fumes

13. OSCILLATE : PENDULUM ::
    (A) obligate : promise
    (B) swim : fish
    (C) turn : car
    (D) spin : gyroscope
    (E) learn : student

14. PREMIERE : MOVIE ::
    (A) unveiling : statue
    (B) rookie : football
    (C) debutante : teenager
    (D) ruler : subject
    (E) best : better

15. ROOF : PITCH ::
    (A) triangle : side
    (B) basement : cement
    (C) mountain : grade
    (D) tree : sap
    (E) ceiling : rafter

16. LIST : CAPSIZE ::
    (A) delete : fat
    (B) lean : turn over

(C) straighten : float
(D) shore : land
(E) print : dietetic

Directions: Below each of the following passages you will find questions or incomplete statements about the passage. Each statement or question is followed by lettered words or expressions. Select the word or expression that most satisfactorily completes each statement or answers each question in accordance with the meaning of the passage. After you have chosen the best answer, blacken the corresponding space on the answer sheet.

Although vocal cords are lacking in cetaceans, phonation is undoubtedly centered in the larynx.

The toothed whales, or odontocetes (sperm whale and porpoises), are much more vociferous than the whalebone whales, or mysticetes. In this country, observers have recorded only occasional sounds from two species of mysticetes (the humpback and right whale). A Russian cetologist reports hearing sounds from at least five species of whalebone whales, but gives no details of the circumstances or descriptions of the sounds themselves. Although comparison of the sound-producing apparatus in the two whale groups cannot yet be made, it is interesting to note that the auditory centers of the brain are much more highly developed in the odontocetes than in the mysticetes—in fact, to a degree unsurpassed by any other mammalian group.

17. The correspondence between Russian and American findings on the sounding of whalebone whales is
    (A) to be inferred from examination of the data
    (B) in complete agreement with English cetologists
    (C) compatible with pre-existing knowledge
    (D) a common set of vocal cords for porpoises and whales
    (E) not discussed in this passage

18. Which of the following animals has the most highly developed auditory center in the brain?
    (A) elephants
    (B) humpback whales

(C)   raccoons
(D)   sperm whales
(E)   right whales

19.   The noises produced by whales
   (A)   are produced in the upper part of the windpipe
   (B)   are louder than those of other sea animals
   (C)   are used to locate their mates
   (D)   can be heard only by other whales
   (E)   are used to locate feeding grounds

20.   According to the information given,
   (A)   porpoises have vocal cords but right whales do not
   (B)   Russians report vocal cords in five species of whales
   (C)   there is a correlation between vocal cords and auditory areas of the brain
   (D)   whales have several sets of vocal cords
   (E)   whales do not have vocal cords

Davis, California, like many other American cities, has been threatened by unchecked growth, swarming automobiles, and steeply rising energy costs. But unlike towns and cities which leave energy policy to the federal government or energy corporations, the citizens of Davis have acted on their own.

After lengthy debate, Davis' City Council moved to curb growth. It turned against the automobile and embraced the bicycle as a means of transport. It sponsored an inquiry into energy uses and endorsed a series of measures aimed at reducing energy consumption by as much as one half. It cut back the use of petroleum-derived pesticides on the thousands of trees and shrubs that shade the city's streets, adopting instead a policy of biological control for insects. The city's own cars and trucks have been transformed into a fleet of compact vehicles. When a Davis employee has to get around town, he borrows a bike from the city rack. Davis even passed a law formally and solemnly sanctioning the clothesline.

The citizens of Davis have been involved in progressive city planning and energy conservation since 1968, when they persuaded the City Council to facilitate bicycle transporation by developing a system of bikeways. The city's general plan for development, drawn up in 1972, was based on questionnaires distributed to residents. When a survey of residents showed that automobiles represented 50 percent of energy consumption and space heating and cooling accounted for 25 percent, transporation and building construction became important focal points in the Davis plan.

Armed with survey information revealing that a building's east-west orientation on a lot, as well as its insulation, window area, roof and wall colors, overhang shading, and other factors greatly influenced space heating and cooling needs, the City Council drew up a building construction code which greatly reduces the cost of winter heating and eliminates the need for air conditioning even on Davis' hottest (114°) days. To demonstrate to local builders and developers methods for complying with the new code, Davis built two model solar homes, a single-family dwelling which takes advantage of natural southern exposure sunlight and a duplex adaptable to difficult siting situations where direct sunlight is blocked. Many of Davis' measures simply facilitate natural solar heating or sun-shading. Where most communities require that fences be built close to houses, Davis realized that that practice meant blocking winter sunlight. New fences in Davis must be placed closer to the street, giving residents the benefit of natural solar heat in winter. Reducing required street widths provided more shade and saves asphalt to boot.

Davis' other energy-conserving moves run the gamut—from a city ordinance encouraging cottage industry (to cut down on commuting and the need for new office building construction) to planting evergreens on city streets to reduce leaf pickup in the fall, from a ban on non-solar swimming pool heaters to a recycling center that supports itself by selling $3,000 worth of recyclables a month.

21.   It can be inferred from the passage that Davis' City Council felt that
   (A)   bicycles are healthful because they promote physical fitness
   (B)   control of automobile traffic is an essential part of energy management
   (C)   Davis citizens are always ready to do the most modern, up-to-date thing
   (D)   clotheslines are an important part of energy management for everyone
   (E)   survey results should always determine legislative actions

22. Why did Davis build two model solar homes instead of just one?
    (A) To show what they could do when they put their minds to it.
    (B) To show that even the hottest days could be mastered without airconditioning.
    (C) To demonstrate that even multiple dwellings in difficult locations could be solar powered.
    (D) To indicate that other cities were inadequate to the job.
    (E) To prove that winter sunlight could be used for heating.

23. The purpose of this article is probably to
    (A) congratulate Davis on their fine work
    (B) help Davis to spread their message
    (C) chide the federal government for not doing enough to help cities like Davis
    (D) poke fun at Davis' "clothesline law"
    (E) hold up Davis as an example to other cities

24. We may infer from the article all of the following EXCEPT
    (A) air conditioning need not be as important in new houses as many people make it
    (B) the City Council had grave doubts about the accuraccy of the energy survey.
    (C) the City Council realized that they were making major decisions when they enacted their energy and growth laws
    (D) more people will generally use more energy
    (E) lighting and sun direction influence house energy efficiency

25. It appears that Davis is
    (A) a "good old American town"
    (B) committed to social justice
    (C) a medium to small-size city
    (D) governed by a Council-Manager form of municipal government
    (E) blessed by a strong radical element in the population

26. The passage supports the conclusion that
    (A) Davis does not have much industry

    (B) Davis cannot go any farther than it already has toward being energy efficient
    (C) Davis' example will work for any city
    (D) the days of the automobile are numbered
    (E) planning can solve all our problems

27. If, after continuing its programs, Davis did another energy survey in 1992 and found that its total energy use had gone up from 1972, all of the following could help to explain this finding EXCEPT
    (A) population growth might have been substantial because Davis became such a nice place to live
    (B) builders were unable to comply with the stringent and complex building code
    (C) new facilities were constructed that used considerable energy even with advanced design
    (D) as the population got older they could no longer use bicycles as much and had to use cars more
    (E) the 1972 energy survey seriously underestimated the energy used at that time

Directions: Each of the following questions consists of a word printed in capital letters, followed by five (5) lettered words or phrases. Select the word or phrase which is most nearly *opposite* to the capitalized word in meaning.

28. INFIRM:
    (A) ghastly
    (B) glassy
    (C) weird
    (D) healthy
    (E) stable

29. LAMENTATION:
    (A) jubilation
    (B) erosion
    (C) evolution
    (D) plan
    (E) decision

30. LECHERY:
    (A) karma
    (B) apathy
    (C) largess
    (D) gratitude
    (E) chastity

31. SCOTCH:
    (A) foster
    (B) quail
    (C) sully
    (D) teetotal
    (E) transplant

32. QUERULOUS:
    (A) joking
    (B) not curious
    (C) dreamy
    (D) sated
    (E) satisfied

33. DESUETUDE:
    (A) kindliness
    (B) intrigue
    (C) prominent
    (D) use
    (E) upset

34. DELECTABLE:
    (A) awkward
    (B) unpleasant
    (C) manifold
    (D) colossal
    (E) imperious

35. OBDURATE:
    (A) stirring
    (B) curable
    (C) durable
    (D) easily swayed
    (E) navigable

36. BLANDISHMENT:
    (A) colorfulness
    (B) independence
    (C) criticism
    (D) spiciness
    (E) piquancy

37. NIGGARDLY:
    (A) lavish
    (B) destitute
    (C) peccant
    (D) cloyed
    (E) palliative

38. VACUOUS:
    (A) precognitive
    (B) precocious
    (C) insightful
    (D) plentiful
    (E) slight

STOP

END OF SECTION. IF YOU HAVE ANY TIME LEFT, GO
OVER YOUR WORK IN THIS SECTION ONLY. DO NOT
WORK IN ANY OTHER SECTION OF THE TEST.

PRACTICE EXAMINATION 2—ANSWER KEY

Section I

1.	D	10.	E	19.	D	28.	A	37.	B
2.	C	11.	B	20.	E	29.	E	38.	E
3.	A	12.	A	21.	A	30.	B		
4.	C	13.	E	22.	C	31.	C		
5.	B	14.	A	23.	E	32.	C		
6.	E	15.	E	24.	B	33.	D		
7.	B	16.	C	25.	B	34.	A		
8.	C	17.	B	26.	D	35.	D		
9.	D	18.	D	27.	A	36.	B		

Section II

1.	E	10.	B	19.	A	28.	B	37.	E
2.	A	11.	A	20.	C	29.	A	38.	D
3.	C	12.	A	21.	B	30.	D		
4.	D	13.	A	22.	D	31.	A		
5.	D	14.	B	23.	E	32.	B		
6.	D	15.	B	24.	D	33.	D		
7.	A	16.	D	25.	A	34.	D		
8.	B	17.	C	26.	E	35.	B		
9.	B	18.	C	27.	D	36.	C		

Section III

1.	D	7.	C	13.	C	19.	A	25.	D
2.	A	8.	C	14.	D	20.	A	26.	D
3.	A	9.	A	15.	A	21.	D	27.	C
4.	C	10.	B	16.	E	22.	B	28.	A
5.	D	11.	B	17.	C	23.	B	29.	C
6.	C	12.	B	18.	A	24.	E	30.	B

Section IV

1.	D	7.	C	13.	B	19.	D	25.	E
2.	C	8.	C	14.	A	20.	B	26.	A
3.	B	9.	B	15.	B	21.	A	27.	D
4.	C	10.	D	16.	A	22.	C	28.	D
5.	A	11.	B	17.	C	23.	E	29.	B
6.	B	12.	D	18.	A	24.	C	30.	A

Section V

1.	E	6.	D	11.	E	16.	A	21.	A
2.	B	7.	D	12.	E	17.	A	22.	B
3.	C	8.	B	13.	A	18.	C	23.	C
4.	E	9.	C	14.	D	19.	E	24.	B
5.	C	10.	E	15.	B	20.	E	25.	E

Section VI

1.	C	6.	B	11.	C	16.	E	21.	C
2.	C	7.	B	12.	A	17.	D	22.	B
3.	A	8.	D	13.	D	18.	A	23.	E
4.	B	9.	A	14.	C	19.	D	24.	D
5.	E	10.	D	15.	B	20.	C	25.	A

Section VII

1.	D	10.	C	19.	A	28.	D	37.	A
2.	C	11.	A	20.	E	29.	A	38.	C
3.	A	12.	E	21.	B	30.	E		
4.	D	13.	D	22.	C	31.	A		
5.	D	14.	A	23.	E	32.	E		
6.	A	15.	C	24.	B	33.	D		
7.	C	16.	B	25.	C	34.	B		
8.	B	17.	E	26.	A	35.	D		
9.	B	18.	D	27.	B	36.	C		

EXPLANATORY ANSWERS

SECTION I

1. **(D)** One who intimidates his employees does so by improper use of his authority. Abusing is the obvious answer. The other choices clearly have no connection with use or abuse.

2. **(C)** If the foliage of the tropics seemed strange to the children, this would indicate that it was new or unusual to them. The missing space calls for an idea of newness or the first time. Only introduction conveys this sense.

3. **(A)** This question calls for a pair of synonyms descriptive of a "generous heart." Selfless ("never thinking of oneself") and altruistic ("thinking always of others first") fit this requirement. Of the other four choices, one is a pair of antonyms (kind and ruthless), and the remaining three are unrelated pairs.

4. **(C)** Choices (A), (D), and (E) are eliminated because neither self-pity nor self-esteem nor self-concern can convulse ("cause to writhe in suffering") anybody. Choice (B) is out because causing happiness to others rarely brings any self-doubt to a person.

5. **(B)** The shore is associated in the sentence with "vacationers who liked to swim." But "chilly" describes temperatures usually disliked by swimmers. Therefore, the chilliness of "late-summer waters" would cause the swimmers to become unhappy or displeased. Disappointed is a good synonym for displeased or unhappy; disappointingly is the best adverb to fill the gap. None of the other choices has anything to do with disappointment.

6. **(E)** Choice (A) is out because the Atomic Age has had relevant, not irrelevant, effects on people. Choice (B) is out because it would lead to a redundance (i.e., universal effects on people in all walks of life). Choices (C) and (D) are eliminated because pretentious and profane make no sense with effects. Only (E) makes sense.

7. **(B)** A "shudder" is never described as credible, appreciative, approving, or pleased. Therefore, (A), (C), (D), and (E) are eliminated. Only grisly makes good sense.

8. **(C)** An island can be thought of as a small spot of contrast in the ocean, as is the oasis in the desert. Another way of seeing the relationship is as an opposite one, but that is not as accurate or strong. (D) has some appeal since a single tree might stand in the middle of a field, but it is not part of the definition of tree for it to be alone in a field, while an island and an oasis are typically defined by their isolation.

9. **(D)** Mathematics is the serious and scientific approach to the relations between numbers, while numerology is a mystical and non-scientific approach to the same topic. Astronomy is similarly the scientific approach to relationships among the stars and planets, while astrology is the mystical and non-scientific approach to the same topic. All of the other pairs are either of various scientific disciplines, or of philosophy, which is not like the first part of the stem pair.

10. **(E)** The relationship is one of degree, with the first part of the pair being the lesser degree. (E) has this. Trustworthy and helpful may have some connection, but it is not one of degree. (D) is a relationship of opposites, and the others are more complex, if they are there at all.

11. **(B)** A minaret is the typical roofing design of a mosque, while a steeple is the typical roofing design of a church. This should be an easy question since the stem relates a part of a building to the whole building, and there is only one answer choice that duplicates this.

12. **(A)** Chaff is the waste or leftovers from sorting out wheat. Dregs are the same for wine. (C)'s only connection is that another meaning of chaff is to tease, and raillery is a type of joking. This is not enough. (D) and (E) are unconnected to the original ideas. (B) has some merit since crumbs are the leftovers of bread. However, chaff is a part of the wheat that never had any value, being the stems and such; similarly for dregs. Crumbs, however, were presumably the same as the bread and could have been eaten.

13. **(E)** The director is the person in charge of the content and presentation of a drama. Similarly, the editor is in charge of the content and presentation of a magazine. (D) does not work since there is no name in the original, and Sophocles was a playwright and a specific personage. Also, the first

part of (D) is an abstraction and the second isn't which distinguishes it from the stem. (C) has two persons, which does not correlate with a person and an abstraction. (B) has a little merit since the scenario in some sense controls the movie, but we must look for a person who controls something, if possible. (A) is the second-best answer since the principal is certainly supposed to be in charge of the class, though teacher would be a better answer. However, the magazine and the drama are both artistic and creative endeavors, while the class is not, particularly for a principal.

14. **(A)** A goal is the object of someone who is implacable; an implacable person sticks to his goal, no matter what. An officious person is one who will stick to the rules and procedures, no matter what. (D) has the relationship that something which is placid, like a pond, might make a mirror. But this is a little farfetched for an analogy question and certainly is not the relationship of the stem pair. (C) is a situation of causation, since an infectious thing might cause a disease, but that is also wrong. (B) and (E) have some merit: A conclusion is a type of goal of a process of inference, or it is something that is presumably inferable. However, the goal is the object of a person who is implacable and a conclusion is not the object of a person who is inferable—if indeed a person can be inferable in the first place. (B) turns on the idea of a zealous person being strong on something, but it is not necessarily the method; but an officious person is definitely concerned with the procedures.

15. **(E)** A cartoon is a common and simplified type of drawing. A caricature is a simplified and usually, common, type of portrait. A ditty is a common or simplified sort of song, but it is stretching it a little to call it a simplified aria. (C) fails since a crayon need not be a common or vulgar type of implement relative to a brush. (A) and (B) try only to play with the humorous aspect of a cartoon.

16. **(C)** The relationship in the stem pair nearly is one of synonyms. Insouciant means literally carefree and is exactly lighthearted. A calm person is unworried. (A), (D), and (E) all have noun to noun or adjective relationships which are more difficult to fit into the original model of two adjectives. (B) and (C) fit that all right, and (B) could also be described as fitting the form that someone who is thieving is light-fingered, but it is no longer an emotion. Also, the stem pair are positive in tone.

17. **(B)** The number of hours at home is seen by the author as an opportunity to extend the work of the school, but not as being more important. The author says it is a great influence, but not that it is the greatest; thus, (A) fails. (C) and (D) are both stated in the passage, but they are used as examples of (B)'s more general idea. (E) is, if anything, opposed, since the example of the parent helping with the homework was largely negative. If the more general mathematics usage ideas are considered helping with homework, then this is like (C) and (D): only an example of (B).

18. **(D)** (A) is incorrect since no generalization is made, only an example used. (B) and (E) are absent from the passage altogether. (C) is attractive, but not actually in the passage. It sounds like one of the things which might be done to help math, perhaps using the yardstick that is mentioned, but this is not, in fact, mentioned. (D) is the subject of the entire passage, and of the last several paragraphs in particular.

19. **(D)** (B), (C), and (E) are without foundation, and (A) is false. (D) is precisely what is urged by the author.

20. **(E)** This is a detail question. (E), a demonstration lesson, is not necessarily included in classes for parents since the classes for the parents would focus on what the parents should do at home, rather than reviewing, as such, what the children do at school. New progress report methods are mentioned, (B), as are (D) and (C).

21. **(A)** The passage made its point by giving an example in which interesting related activities led to improvement. Although the example was abstract to some extent, the author's use of it as a piece of evidence implies that he believes it to be true; thus, (A) is implied.

(D) picks up on the passage's negative evaluation of drill in the home and the types of non-drill reinforcements recommended by the author; however, since the focus of the passage is exclusively on home activities, only the weakest of inferences can be made about the author's views on activities at school. (D) is probably the second-best answer.

None of the other choices is much connected with the passage. (B) alleges laziness, but only inadequate support is seen as the student's problem in the passage. The only mention of a principal, (C), is in reference to his approval being sought for innovative or unusual teacher initiatives. (E) refers to visits by teachers to the parents at home, but the only parent-teacher communication urged in the passage is the reference to informal interviews, which need not be conducted at the parent's home.

22. **(C)** All of the answers touch upon the substance of the passage, and it is the differences among them which give the answer choice. The passage is aimed at teachers and specifies actions to be taken by teachers in order to influence the parents' future actions. Thus, (A) errs in claiming the passage speaks directly to the parent, as does (E).

(E) also suffers from the perjorative word brain-wash, since the author believes that many parents are willing and eager to help their children and lack only proper guidance.

(D) takes the example of mathematics as the point, when all subjects are at issue.

(B) and (C) have the most merit. There can be no doubt that the author hopes to serve the purpose outlined in (B), to some small extent, by writing his passage, BUT the goal of having the child's capacities totally developed is most general and abstract, while the passage has a closer, clearer purpose as expressed by (C). (C) fits the passage much more closely than does (B), which could describe the ultimate purpose of hundreds of articles.

23. **(E)** Since the tone is one of instructing the teacher, (E) is very attractive, but the others must be eliminated. (B) and (C) fail because of the passage's instructions-to-the-teacher tone. (D) is not supported in the passage since no reference to college is needed nor present. (A) has the merit of focusing on the right sort of person since the passage refers to elementary school subjects such as arithmetic. However, while an elementary school teacher could be instructing his fellow teachers, it is precisely the job of the professor of education to do so; hence (E) is preferable.

24. **(B)** The passage states that mere drill work or rewarding schoolwork is not what the author has in mind; thus, (A), (C), and (E) are eliminated. (D) is not quite the same as the others, but it focuses on the parent working with the child rather than trying to incorporate learning experiences into the child's everyday life at home, which the author wishes to see done more. Thus (B), which encourages the child to write more outside of school, is precisely the sort of thing which the author has in mind.

25. **(B)** The quotation from the journal must be taken in the context of the entire passage. The passage states that the editorial was discussing the control of CB warfare, but that does not mean that the editorial approved of control. However, in speaking of a balance of terror as being a possible protection against war, the article is certainly not asking for more terror, but only that it be balanced. Thus (A) and (E) are weak. (C) fails since the editorial clearly feels that the balance is working. To be sure, one might have a balance of terror without CB warfare, but nothing in the quote from the editorial implies that the author of the editorial wishes to see CB warfare preparations stopped.

(B) and (D) both have merit. The editorial writer is plainly accepting, if not approving, of the way things are now. The major distinction to be drawn between the two answer choices is that (B) is restricted to the great powers and D is not.

Since the quotation refers only to the great power blocs, (B) is the better answer because it stays within the scope of the quotation.

26. **(D)** Although the passage does not explicitly state the reasons for the United States' participation in CB warfare programs, there is evidence to support (D). The quotation from the editorial serves to point out how the same ideas have been taken from the nuclear arms situation and applied to the CB warfare situation. The key concept that has been borrowed is the balance of terror. A balance means that what one side has, the other must have. The only difficulty is the word mainly. The most important idea of the passage is the one stated in the first sentence and echoed in the final quotation—mutual deterrence and mutual balance of terror. Thus, the idea of mutuality and response to the other power bloc is paramount. This means that the major reason for one group having the weapons is that the other group has them or will have them. Thus, (D) is preferable because it fits in better with the major ideas of the passage.

27. **(A)** As discussed above, the major concept of the passage is to show the use of CB warfare as another element of the balance of terror and mutual deterrence. The passage does not *explain* the cost of CB warfare, though it refers to the cost as being low; thus, (B) fails. Nor are alternatives or history discussed, eliminating (C) and (D). (E) has a little merit in that the reader is made forcefully aware that CB warfare is regarded as powerful enough to take its place beside nuclear weapons as a part of the balance of terror in the world. Still, there is little discussion of the dangers of CB warfare as such. The inclusion of the CB warfare in the balance of terror, the very thing that preserves the precarious peace, is a strong indication that it will be difficult indeed to stop CB warfare programs.

It could be argued that this is not the main idea and that the first sentence is the main idea. However, of the answer choices available, (A) seems served best by the main idea and thrust of the passage.

28. **(A)** A mansion is a grand home, while a hovel is a very mean and poor one. Hotel and motel refer to transient accommodations that can be rented, but so could a mansion. A castle is grander than a mansion, while a house is a standard living accommodation. Hovel is the best opposite because it is poor, while the mansion is grand.

29. **(E)** This is a hard question because the word endemic is both uncommon and often misused. Endemic means peculiar to some locality or region, while pandemic means widespread, or among all peoples (*demos*). Both pandemic and endemic could be either permanent or temporary and might

well be frustrating or terrorizing, or the opposite, depending on the characteristic that was pandemic. Democratic merely shares the root word *demos*.

30. **(B)** Compendious means terse, briefly stated. It is an exposition which contains the whole matter in a brief way. Thus verbose, referring to the use of more words than necessary, is the best opposite. Ambiguous has some flavor of oppositeness. A compendious statement would be very clear and probably not ambiguous, but that is a byproduct of its including the entire subject in a brief statement. A subject that was ambiguous might, on the other hand, produce a compendious yet similarly ambiguous summary. Terse, however, does not mean simple.

31. **(C)** Assuage means to ease or make milder. Aggravate is a very precise opposite. None of the others has any real connection to the proper meaning of assuage.

32. **(C)** To prate is to talk foolishly or without meaning; hence (C) is the best opposite. Again, the other answers do not connect.

33. **(D)** Arrogate means to take without justification or right. (D) is a very precise opposite. This is mainly a matter of knowing the word, though the connection of arrogate with arrogant might lead you to guess the correct answer.

34. **(A)** This difficult word, prolix, means verbose or wordy. Terse means just the opposite. Speechless is not a good opposite. Since prolix means speaking in a particular way, the best opposite will be speaking in the opposite way. Upper class might look good at first, but the connection is to prole or proletarian, meaning working, or lower, class, which is incorrect. If you can pin down the basis for such an impulse and specify just what it is that draws you to an answer, you can often avoid an incorrect answer.

35. **(D)** A tyro is a rank beginner; thus, expert is the best opposite. Democrat appeals to tyrant, but that is a different word entirely. Alert, if it has any appeal at all, is reaching for the sound of tired.

36. **(B)** Sedition is working to undermine the established government or social order. Patriotism, while not a precise opposite, does speak to a love of the established country and political system. Flotation appeals to the echo of the word sediment, which does come from the same root as sedition, but means the material that is precipitated out of a liquid and settles on the bottom of the container, whereas sedition means the unsettling of the bottom, or roots, of a society. The other choices have only the appeal of being positive characteristics, while sedition would be generally viewed as negative.

37. **(B)** Tousle means to disarrange or roughen up, particularly hair. Groom is to arrange one's appearance and hair. Catch connects to toss, but you should avoid that since toss is not tousle. Caress is more of a synonym than an antonym, since tousling may often be a gesture of affection.

38. **(E)** Transient means something that lasts only for a short time. Thus persistent, meaning something that endures, is a very good opposite. Final also has real merit since the final decision is something that will not change and thus seems to endure in some sort of way. However, final is really opposite to preliminary, not transient. There is a tendency to think of passing things as leading up to some final, permanent resolution. Between final and persistent, the most salient difference is that a persistent thing will continue to exist, while many final things will pass away, such as final editions of a newspaper, for example.

SECTION II

1. **(E)** Choice (D) is eliminated because being inured to one kind of activity has nothing to do with functioning in another kind of activity. According to the context of this sentence, adjusting to work is more accurate than adapting, conforming, or reacting. Both (B)'s and (C)'s second words are inappropriate.

2. **(A)** Choices (B), (C), and (D) are eliminated immediately because nobody practices to overcome, supercede, or limit his talents. Choice (E) is out because a naturally inept person has no talents to develop. An adept person has talents that he can perfect.

3. **(C)** A teacher's pride is directly affected by his class's performance on an exam. Since the missing word must express that which will hurt the teacher's pride, we can fill in the gap with any suggestion of doing poorly or getting low grades on the exam. Flunked leaves no room for doubt, especially when the other four choices are relatively positive terms.

4. **(D)** A reporter's probings (investigations) will get results, provided that those probings are persistent. Choices (A), (B) and (C) have nothing to do with persistence. This leaves (D) and (E) as possibilities. However, finally implies that the probings were done over a long period of time without interruption. Relentless means without slowing down or stopping, and completes the thought perfectly. Earnest (serious) does not necessarily have anything to do with slowing down or stopping work in any way.

5. **(D)** In this item, the final two words are the key. It is impossible to shout, gesture, or wave incoherent threats. An excited mob wouldn't whisper.

6. **(D)** This sentence assumes that most people support having leisure time, ruling out (A) and (B). A staunch disciple is bad usage. That an opponent of leisure would have few duties is illogical.

7. **(A)** The first blank describes a downpour. (C), meaning ill-mannered, and (E), meaning without distinctive or attractive qualities, are not descriptive of a rainstorm and are thus incorrect. For the second blank we have a verb that is related to and immediately preceding the act of disappearing. (A), (C), and (E) do describe an action that might precede disappearance since the girls would need to get away from "us" first and then disappear, unless they could teleport. Thus, (B) and (D) are eliminated on the second blank, leaving (A) as the best answer. (D), provoke, is possible, but not as good as evade, since provoke is not particularly related to the disappearing.

8. **(B)** A telephone and a letter are both methods of communication. The difference between them is that a telephone is electronic and communicates through the medium of speech, while a letter is paper, or non-electronic, and communicates through the medium of writing. (A) is two electronic items, both of which work with sound, so that is not apt. (C) has the idea of electronic versus non-electronic, but both telegraph and mail involve writing. Sound and sight has some merit since speech relates to sound, and writing to sight, but there is no flavor of the relationship between types of appliances. (E) is two parts of the same medium. (B) has both analogous relationships and is best.

9. **(B)** Immigration is migration into, or entering, a place, while emigration is migration out of, or departing from, a place. (C) has real merit since immigration is an arrival of sorts and a door is an entrance of sorts; but notice the beginnings of an imbalance in the analogy if we use (C). The first parts of the analogy have the stem pair use the more specific term and the second parts have the answer choice use the more specific term. In comparing with (B), we see that although (B) has an opposite idea—leaving—the relationship WITHIN the analogy pairs is the same. The first term in each pair is a type of migration, which is not true of (C). Thus, (B) is an example of a more specific relationship in the secondary, or vertical, way, but it is one that is carried through properly in the rest of the pair and thus is a strengthening idea. If we had emigration and the second part of the pair did not work as well as immigration/emigration, then the emigration answer choice would have been weak.

(A) is an antonym relationship, which is not the same as the original. (E) might have a little appeal since immigration is sometimes the search for a refuge and a gate can be an entrance, but this is weak and derivative and not nearly as strong as either (B) or (C).

10. **(B)** A hotel is a kind of shelter. A boat is a kind of transportation. (A) has the relationship of two things that are typically associated—the pillow is typically found on a bed. That does not work here. (D) and (E) have somewhat more appeal. A restaurant provides drink and a hotel provides shelter. Similarly, though with less force, a home provides recuperation. Note that (B) and (C) also fit this mold. The fact that the idea works for most of the answer choices tells us it is probably right, but needs refinement. The refinement here is how the provision takes place and how is the provision related to the institution or article in the front of the pair? The major purpose of a hotel is to provide shelter, and it is itself a form of shelter. This is not true of either (D) or (E). In distinguishing (B) from (C), we see that one difference is the difference between transportation and ride. Transportation is more general, and shelter is a very general idea and more like transportation than ride. A train is not really thought of as a type of ride, while a boat is defined as a type of transportation.

11. **(A)** A moon is associated with a planet in that it circles or orbits a planet. A planet similarly orbits a star. A planet is larger than a moon, and (C) has some idea of size difference, but so does (A). The additional idea of orbiting is very powerful because it is quite intrinsic to the idea of astronomy, from which field all of these terms come. Further, in (D) a nova is larger than a star, but is derived from a star, since a nova is an exploding star.

12. **(A)** An ascetic dislikes and avoids luxury, as a misogynist dislikes and avoids women. (B) fails since a philosopher seeks truth and likes it. (C) and (E) have internal relationships that are positive and typical; in each case the person is associated with the idea or object. (D) has some merit since a gourmet would certainly not like to be hungry. However, the idea of a gourmet is not that he eats to satisfy his hunger, but rather that he eats to satisfy his taste or palate. The stem *gyn-* in misogynist means woman, and *mis-* would mean against or opposed.

13. **(A)** A spasm is a brief, intense movement of a muscle, and by extension is any brief, intense action. A flash is a brief intense activity of light. (C) and (D) each contain half of a good analogy, pinch and touch, which, if combined as an answer choice, might be even better than flash and light. Respite is a restful break from something difficult—not the same at all. Sound and noise are nearly synonyms, but a spasm is not a muscle.

14. **(B)** Corrugated is having ridges, and striped is a two-dimensional equivalent. One might, for in-

stance, indicate in a painting that something was corrugated by making stripes. This idea of having the same shape but being two- and then three-dimensional is carried through very well by (B), dimpled and speckled. (A) is appealing, but the connection is a secondary one between corrugated and cardboard and between zebra and striped. (E) is the only other answer choice with any merit. Bumpy and flashing both have the idea of being intermittent, as do both of the original pair. However, (B) also has this idea as well as the further connection of the two- and three-dimensionality.

15. **(B)** Oxygen, under normal conditions, is gaseous; that is its typical state of matter. All of the answer choices have some of the idea that the adjective in the second position is a typical descriptor of the noun in the first position. This means that refinement is needed. One refinement would be to ask what sort of typical description is being given. All of the descriptions are physical, again confirming that we are on the right track. But gaseous describes a state of matter and only (B) has a similar adjective. (D)'s grainy is second best since it is a form idea, but grainy is a subdivision of solid, while fluid and gaseous are non-solids. It is a slight detraction from the merit of (B) that fluid is a term that includes gaseous, while there is no possibly similar link between oxygen and mercury.

16. **(D)** An acrobat must be agile as part of his trade. Similarly, an orator must be able to speak well or be eloquent, if he is to do his job right. (C)'s relationship is class to member of the class, which is incorrect. (B) does not describe a characteristic of the vendor, but rather what he sells. (E) describes a characteristic that a car might have, but it is not the only characteristic or even a necessary one for a car to have to be a good car. If the analogy had been speed : racecar, it would have been much stronger. (A) has some merit in that greasy is a typical characteristic of a mechanic. However, it is not something that helps him to do his job well, as agility and eloquence help, respectively, the acrobat and orator. Thus, (D) is best.

17. **(C)** The question is asking us for a summary statement of the passage to be the title of the passage. This must be correct in what it says and not make any mistakes. (A) fails because the passage is discussing the need for vacations, not the preferences for different kinds of vacations. (B) has the appeal of referring to the last sentence and the idea that vacations are a topic of conversation. However, the purpose of that statement is to show how important vacations are, not to say anything about conversational habits as such. (C) certainly has real merit since the effect of the passage is to give some context for and reasons

behind vacation practices. Thus, (C) has nothing particularly wrong with it, although it might have been even better if it had said something about the application of the author's ideas to the modern, industrialized world. (D) fails for similar reasons as (A): There is nothing in the passage about the content of the vacations, or their organization on an individual basis. There is some idea that the taking of vacations is well organized in the U.S. (E) has the merit of referring to the underlying need that vacations serve, but actually fails to mention the idea of vacations at all. Thus, (E) is inferior to (C), and (C) is the best answer. Note that a combination of several answers might have given an even stronger one. For instance, Vacations in Perspective: The Increasing Need for Renewal, Refreshment, and Repair in the Industrialized World. This is almost perfect, though much too long.

18. **(C)** This question asks for a specific piece of the author's argument. In this case the reason why "we" in the industrialized world need vacations more is the "stultifying" quality of our work, the need for a "break in the routine." Both these references should have indicated to you, when you read the passage, that the work is too unvaried day after day. Thus, (C) goes right to the heart of the matter. (A) and (D) are ideas not mentioned in the passage. (B) and (E) are also unmentioned and fall into that class of wrong answers that we might fall for from our general knowledge rather than from the passage. These answers might have great merit in the real world, but they are not based on the passage, so they are wrong on the test.

19. **(A)** This is really the same basic idea as the previous question, but in a different guise. We must, however, evaluate each answer choice. (A) is implied, as discussed above. (B) and (C) are simply nice things to say about ourselves that have no basis in the passage. (D) is the opposite of (A), and thus you could probably settle the both of them with the same line of reasoning. You might ask yourself whether there is anything in the passage to indicate that the lives of Americans are either varied or habitual. There might be nothing, but in this case there is and (D) is wrong and (A) is right. The only possible support for (D) in the passage is the fact that we do go on vacations, which are presumably somewhat varied, but the bulk of our lives is filled with habitual behavior. (E) fails since the whole tone of the passage is that people are not independent and do not have control over their lives, which is one of the reasons they need vacations.

20. **(C)** The form of this essay is to recount a number of formative historical aspects of the author's personal religious and moral development. The last paragraph states the author's current faith,

which has resulted from these influences. Thus, (C) is a good description of the passage's workings and purpose.

(A) catches the tone of the passage as being explanatory and directed, but the author does not consider himself a Quaker and thus it is improbable that (A) is correct. (B) has the word Friend with a capital letter, thus indicating that a Quaker is addressed. However, while the passage might serve the purpose stated in (B), it would only do so through the idea of (C), and, indeed, the significant differences which the author does find between himself and Quakers might upset (B)'s purpose.

(D) is only relevant to a very small portion of the passage and the analysis of the inner light that does occur primarily sets the stage for the pacifism of the last paragraph, which still leaves (C) preferable to (D). (E) is not really in the passage, since it is only the parents' attitudes toward religious dogmatism that are discussed, rather than any explicit teachings.

21. **(B)** Two types of reward are played with in this question and in the passage. In the passage, the idea of a good deed being its own reward refers to inner feelings generated by the knowledge of having done a good deed. In the question, the connotation is one of a financial or material reward. While these are different, there is no reason to believe that the author would refuse a financial reward—he has sworn no vow of poverty—but at the same time he would not want it to seem that the financial reward was the reason for the good deed.

(C) is impossible or unnecessarily complicated. You may have thought that this answer choice was a way of referring to the possibility of having the financial reward given to a charity or some such, but it does not say that and if you choose it you are reading too much into the answer choice.

(D) fails since there is no basis in the passage for having any idea as to what, if anything, the author might consider blasphemous. The financial reward does not necessarily obviate the spiritual one.

(A) and (E) both suppose that the author is totally opposed to receiving a financial reward, which is more than we know from the passage. We would only entertain an answer of this sort if all others were totally impossible—and even then you should be unhappy with so weak an answer.

In contrast to the other answer choices, (B) has the virtue of being considerate of the other person's feelings, which seems to be implied in the author's respect for the divinity of all other persons.

22. **(D)** The author states that the idea of "inner light" is basic to his views and he uses it in that way. He got this idea from the Quakers and restates that it is a shared thought.

(B) is something that some people may know to be true of many—though not all—Quakers in the real world. In this passage, however, the author makes absolutely no reference to the pacifism of the Quakers, and indeed only discusses his own pacifism after he has dissociated himself from the Quakers. If one were forced to choose between the Quakers being pacifists and preachers of holy crusades, the passage would support the former over the latter, but nothing is said about the historical nature of Quakerism in the passage.

(A) and (E) are specifically rejected in the passage and (C) is known to be true only of some Quakers at one Meeting for Worship.

23. **(E)** The author sees no reason for Jesus being more divine "than, say, Buddha." Thus, he likely sees all major religious leaders as being equally divine.

24. **(D)** The position taken by the author's parents can be inferred from the first sentence of the second paragraph, where the parents' dislike of doctrine and dogma is traced to their lapsed Catholicism, and thus a probable reason for the lapse.

(A) is false both because the author has an inner light and sees himself as a non-Quaker and because the last paragraph refers to "this piece of divinity that every human has."

(B) if false because the inner-light views of the author and the Quakers are stated to be the same, so the Quakers view all men as having an inner light.

(C) has no basis in the passage since the author's parents' dissatisfaction with Catholic views is not said to be in the matter of killing.

(E) is incorrect since the author states that he is closer to the Quakers than to any other organized religious group. While the organization of Buddhism is not the same as many Christian religions, it could not be called unorganized.

25. **(A)** (A) is stated in the last paragraph. (B) plays on the statement that we must "increase this lifeline" ("the inner light"). The increase is linked with understanding, and better refers to increased strength rather than numbers. (C) and (D) fail for the same reasons as 24 (A) and (B). (E) is either unsupported or, better, rejected in the passage since the author has a faith without help of prophets and which appears to be adequate for him, even though he says that it is poorer for lacking a prophet, etc. The extra divinity of prophets is also a questionable inference to base on this passage.

26. **(E)** This is a logical reasoning question. If both action and inaction will cause death, then death is no longer a difference between the options available and cannot be used to make the decision as to which option should be taken. (C) does not avoid the situation because it would simply be a method

of choosing inaction. (D) fails because beliefs should not be abandoned because of the existence of situations to which they do not apply. Note that when the author argues against "the taking of any life by choice," this does not mean only by action. Inaction is a choice, too.

27. **(D)** Choice (D) is explicitly rejected by the author when he says that his personal religion might be the poorer for having no revealed word. The difficulties in this problem stem more from the attractiveness of several of the other answer choices.

    (A) is explicitly agreed to by the author when he says that he limits his faith to a Supreme Being and the goodness of man. This statement of belief in the goodness of man is not the reason that the author can be said to believe in the divine nature of human beings. The concept of inner light is a piece of divinity in each man, according to the author, and will suffice to validate (C). (C) does not require that every piece of man be divine.

    (B) is agreeable to the author for two reasons. First, that is why his parents sent him to First Day School, and he is approving of their conduct. Second, and even more important, (B) is known from the author's approval of the general precepts of Jesus and from his own insistence on goodness for its own sake.

    (E) is deducible from the fact that the author found the entire experience of sharing religious experiences with the Quakers valuable as a child, and continues to find it valuable as an adult.

28. **(B)** Consonant means harmonious in sound and, by extension, harmonious and consistent in general. Incongruous means inconsistent, out of place, or inharmonious, and is a perfect opposite. An insuperable objection is one that cannot be overcome. Sounded has some relation to consonant, coming from the same *son* stem, meaning sound. However, that is not enough to create an antonym relationship.

29. **(A)** A concise piece of writing says a great deal in a few words. Both wordy and muddy have some opposite feeling, but the essential meaning of concise has to do with length, so wordy, meaning too long and with too many words, is a better opposite. Saying a great deal in a few words is likely to be clear, but that is a further association and not the main meaning. A concise statement might certainly be wrong, and even ignorant or mundane, which means commonplace or everyday.

30. **(D)** Fecund means very fertile and productive, which is precisely the opposite of barren. Premier is a play on the rhyme between fecund and second, which is, of course, misleading.

31. **(A)** A fortuitous event is both fortunate and unlooked for. Here, the only opposite available is unfortunate, which, while not perfect, is the best. The *fortu-* stem might have been a hint to help you. Pious means full of piety for, or revering, God or some "superior" such as parents.

32. **(B)** A saturnine person has a gloomy disposition; thus, cheerful is a perfect opposite. Earthy has several meanings, the most common being coarse, unrefined, and unaffected. The fact that saturnine refers to the planet Saturn does not mean that earthy is at all opposite. Maudlin is tearfully or weakly sentimental, or even silly, when referring to a drunk.

33. **(D)** Frangible means breakable, even fragile. Sturdy is again the only opposite. Docile means easily managed or taught. Inedible appeals to some students, though the reasons are not clear. Perhaps frangible reminds them of some tropical fruit.

34. **(D)** Lethargy is a state of drowsy apathy, mental dullness, and lack of initiative. Alertness is pretty close to a perfect opposite. Acidity is the degree of acidness. A prodigy is someone with extraordinary gifts or talents in some field. Corpulence is fatness or fleshiness.

35. **(B)** Cupidity is greediness, wanting everything for oneself. Generosity is a willingness or desire to give things to others. While Cupid is the god of love, cupidity has come to mean unusually strong love of money. Lovelessness is not the opposite. Prodigality has some oppositeness to cupidity since prodigality means wanton wastefulness.

36. **(C)** Protean means changeable, particularly in shape or form. Uniform means to have one shape, or to be constant in some way. This is a nearly perfect opposite. Universal has some oppositeness in the sense of applying everywhere, and thus implying consistency or even constancy: A universal principle is uniformly applicable, perhaps. However, this is not as good an opposite as uniform, which directly addresses the issue of changeability of form and shape.

37. **(E)** A cogent argument is convincing and forceful. A fatuous statement is unreal, foolish, or illusory, and thus hardly convincing. This is not a perfect opposite. A cogent statement is often taken to be short and to the point, but it is only the "to the point" part which is correct. Cogency need not be related to length; thus (A) and (D) are inadequate. Similarly, cogent need not be simple, so there is no oppositeness in (C). Urgent connects to an idea of importance and time pressure, while cogency is about persuasiveness. One could be cogent about both urgent and non-urgent matters; thus (B) is not correct.

38. **(D)** Hirsute means hairy. Both naked and bald have direct merit, and plain and clear have a little

appeal, though no merit. Since hirsute means having hair, the perfect opposite would be not having hair, which is bald. Naked is not bad, but not as good as bald because it is a more general word, meaning without covering, while bald means without a covering of hair.

SECTION III

1. **(D)** Since no information is given directly about x or y, we cannot determine the relationship. Do not assume that since x = −y, y will be greater than −y and thus greater than x. It is possible that y is a negative number, in which case x is a positive number and greater than y. Also, x and y could both be equal to zero.

2. **(A)** $\frac{1}{100}$ is equal to 1%, so Column A is greater. .01% is expressed as a fraction is $\frac{1}{10,000}$.

3. **(A)** To compute a percentage increase, it is necessary to create a fraction: $\frac{\text{difference}}{\text{starting amount}}$. In this problem, the price of paper increased from $1.23 to $1.48, for a difference of $0.25. Thus, our fraction is $\frac{.25}{1.23}$. If we actually needed to calculate the percentage increase, we would then divide 1.23 into .25 and multiply that quotient by 100 (to convert the decimal to a percent). For purposes of answering the quantitative comparison question, however, a rough estimate will be sufficient. The percentage increase in the price is more than 25 ÷ 125, and that would be a $\frac{1}{5}$, or 20% increase. Thus Column A is slightly greater than 20%, so Column A must be greater.

4. **(C)** The intuitive way of solving this problem is to reason that $\frac{M + x + y}{3}$ is the *average* of M, x, and y, and that $\frac{x + y}{2}$ is the average of x and y. Since the average of any number and itself is *itself*—that is, the average of x and x is x— Column A must be equal to Column B. The same conclusion can be more rigorously demonstrated by substituting $\frac{x + y}{2}$ for M in column A:

$$\frac{\frac{x + y}{2} + x + y}{3} = \frac{\frac{x + y + 2(x + y)}{2}}{3} = \frac{3x + 3y}{6} = \frac{x + y}{2}$$

5. **(D)** The natural starting point for solving this problem is to perform the indicated operations— that is, to multiply the expressions:

$$(a + 2)(b + 3) \qquad (a + 3)(b + 2)$$
$$ab + 3a + 2b + 6 \qquad ab + 2a + 3b + 6$$

Of course, since ab and 6 are common to both expressions, the multiplication cannot make any difference in the comparison of the two columns.

After we strip away the ab terms and 6, we are left with 3a + 2b in Column A and 2a + 3b in Column B. Since no information is given about the relative magnitudes of a and b, the answer must be (D).

6. **(C)** The easiest way to get a handle on this question is to draw the line.

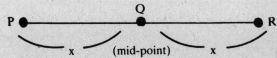

Since Q is the midpoint, we know that PQ is equal to QR.

7. **(C)** This problem requires that the expression in Column A be factored. From basic algebra you will recall that (x + y)(x −y) = x² − y². So the denominator of Column A can be factored into (x + y)(x − y). Then the x − y can be cancelled, leaving x + y for both columns.

8. **(C)** To make the explanation easier to grasp, we add the following notation:

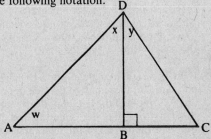

Since BD is perpendicular to AC, both triangle ABD and triangle CBD are right triangles. Consequently:

w + x + 90°= 180° and y + z + 90° = 180°
so: w + x = 90° and y + z = 90°

9. **(A)** The two planes converge on each other at the rate of 300 miles/40 minutes, or 300 miles/$\frac{2}{3}$ hr. That is a rate of 450 miles per hour—the *sum* of their speeds. Since plane X is flying at 150 MPH, plane Y must be flying at 300 MPH. Another way of solving the problem would be to reason that *if* plane Y were flying at 150 MPH, the two planes would be converging at the rate of 300 MPH and it would take a full hour, not 40 minutes, for them to pass. This shows that plane Y must be flying at a speed faster than 150 MPH.

10. **(B)** $\frac{2}{3}$ = 66.666 . . .%. That is a repeating decimal which never ends. But even though it cannot be expressed in regular decimal form, that decimal must be larger than 66.6%, which is 66.60%.

11. **(B)** The sum of the interior angles of a pentagon is 540°, and that of a hexagon is 720°. If you did not recall this, you could have computed the sum in the following way:

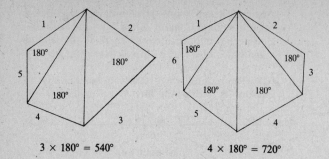

$3 \times 180° = 540°$ $4 \times 180° = 720°$

(Notice that the sum of the interior angles is unrelated to the relative lengths of the sides.)

The average size of the angles of the pentagon, then, is 540 divided by 5, or 108°. And the average size of the angles of the hexagon is 720° divided by 6, or 120°. The general rule is: The average size of the angle grows as the number of sides in the polygon increases.

12. **(B)** The shelf originally contains 24 books. We remove 75% of the 16 French books, or 12, which leaves 4 French books remaining on the shelf. Then we remove 50% of the 8 Italian books, leaving 4 Italian books. Only 8 books remain on the shelf—that is, $\frac{1}{3}$ of the total.

13. **(C)** In a right triangle in which the angles are 90°, 60°, and 30°, the length of the side opposite the 30° angle is one-half the length of the hypotenuse, and the length of the side opposite the 60° angle is one-half the length of the hypotenuse times $\sqrt{3}$. Since two of the angles of this triangle total 90°, and there are 180° in a triangle, angle B must equal 90°, and this is a right triangle. Side AB is opposite the 30° angle, and so must be one-half the hypotenuse. AB is 1; therefore, AC must be 2. BC, then, will be one-half the length of the hypotenuse times $\sqrt{3}$. So BC will be $\sqrt{3}$.

14. **(D)** There are several ways of solving this problem. One way is to manipulate the centered equation so that $x^2 = 1$. Then it should be clear that $x = \pm 1$, and so x might be +1 or −1. Similarly, one might factor $x^2 − 1$ to get $(x + 1)(x − 1) = 0$, showing that there are two values for x, only one of which is +1.

15. **(A)** This problem can be solved using simultaneous equations. Let x be the number of $13 tickets and y the number of $25 tickets.

THEN: $x + y = 11$
AND: $13x + 25y = 227$
By the first equation: $x = 11 − y$
Substituting in $13(11 − y) + 25y = 227$
the second equation:
Then manipu- $143 − 13y + 25y = 227$
lating:

$$12y = 84$$
$$y = 7$$

And if the number of $25 tickets is equal to 7, the number of $13 tickets is only 4, so Column A is greater. An easier and therefore a *better* way of solving the problem is to recognize that the *average* value of the tickets must be approximately $20. If an equal number of tickets had been sold (impossible, of course, since an odd number of tickets was sold), the average would have been midway between $13 and $25, or $19. Since the average is *above* $19, more of the expensive tickets must have been sold.

16. **(E)** A simple method for adding any two fractions is:

STEP A: Find the new denominator by multiplying the old ones.
STEP B: Multiply the numerator of the first fraction by the denominator of the second.
STEP C: Multiply the denominator of the first fraction by the numerator of the second.
STEP D: Add the result of B and C.
STEP E: Reduce, if necessary.

The process is more easily comprehended when presented in the following way:

$$\frac{a}{b} + \frac{c}{d} = \frac{ad + bc}{bd}$$

Here, we have:

$$\frac{3}{4} + \frac{4}{5} = \frac{15 + 16}{20} = \frac{31}{20}$$

17. **(C)** Since $x + 6 = 3$, $x = −3$. Then, substituting −3 for x in the second expression, $x + 3$ is $−3 + 3 = 0$.

18. **(A)** Probably the easiest way to solve this problem is just to count the steps on your fingers, but the same process can be expressed mathematically. Let those steps he walks down be assigned negative values, and those steps he walks up be positive. We then have: $−4 + 3 − 6 + 2 + 9 − 2 = +2$. So the person comes to rest two steps above where he started.

19. **(A)** In a circle graph such as this, the sectors must total 100%. The sectors P, R, S, and T account for 21%, 29%, 18%, and 28%, respectively, for a total of 96%. So Q must be 4%.

20. **(A)** The easiest way to solve this problem is to factor the 326 from both terms of the expression:

$$326(31 − 19) = 326(12) = 3912$$

Of course, you might actually do the arithmetic by multiplying first 326 by 31 and then 326 by 19 and then subtracting the smaller total from the larger. That takes quite a bit longer! But if you did not see the first way (factoring) and can manage the arithmetic in thirty or forty seconds, you should proceed with the *one* way you know to get the correct answer. However, the better approach by far is to find a way of avoiding the calculation.

21. **(D)** This is a problem which is most easily solved by literally counting on your fingers. From 1:21 to 2:21 is 60 minutes. From 2:21 to 3:21 is 60 minutes. So far we have a total of 120 minutes. Then, from 3:21 to 3:36 is 15 minutes, for a total of 135 minutes.

22. **(B)** First, we must compute the total commission that will be owed: 15% of $3200 = $420. Then we must take into account the fact that the sales representative has already received $150 of that sum. So she is now owed: $420 − $150 = $270.

23. **(B)** The area of a circle is pi times radius squared, or $A = \pi r^2$. Here the area is $9\pi x^2$. So we write: $9\pi x^2 = \pi r^2$. Notice that the π terms cancel out, leaving: $9x^2 = r^2$. Taking the square root of both sides of the equation: $\sqrt{9x^2} = \sqrt{r^2}$, so $r = 3x$.

24. **(E)** Since this problem deals with the heights of the individuals, a quite natural starting point would be to draw a picture:

Hans is taller than Gertrude: H
G

Hans is shorter than Wilhelm: W (z)
H (x)
G (y)

Given the picture, it is easily determined that W is taller than H who is taller than G, so z is greater than x is greater than y, or $z > x > y$.

25. **(D)** First, we can show that the area of the square and the area of the equilateral triangle are determinable from their respective perimeters. The square is more easily handled. Since the perimeter of the square is 4 times the length of one side, given the perimeter of the square it is possible to determine the side of the square. Then, once the side of the square is known, the area can be computed as side times side. The equilateral triangle is a bit trickier:

$$P = 3x \qquad A = \tfrac{1}{2}\left(\frac{\sqrt{3}x}{2}\right)\left(\frac{x}{2}\right)$$

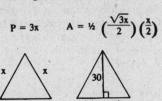

Given the perimeter, it is possible to determine the length of each leg of the triangle (leg = $P/3$, since each leg is equal). Now, since we know that an equilateral triangle has angles of 60°, and that a

perpendicular in this triangle drawn to the opposite base bisects the angle, we can set up a 90° − 30° = 60° triangle. It will be possible to compute the length of each leg of such a triangle, given the length of the hypotenuse. Therefore, we can determine the altitude, and we know the base; so, given the perimeter, we can compute the area. Then, the easiest way to demonstrate that it is not possible to compute the area of a trapezoid or of a parallelogram on the basis of perimeter alone is to draw some pictures:

PARALLELOGRAM:

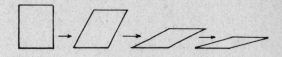

TRAPEZOID:

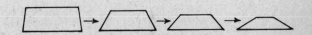

To prove this algebraically would require too much detailed work, but the student should be able to see intuitively that the area of the figures from left to right decreases, and that when the angles eventually become sharp enough, the area will be nearly zero.

26. **(D)** In simple English, the 90¢ the child must replace to bring the amount back up to its original amount is 10% of the original amount. Expressed in notation, that is:

$$90¢ = .10 \text{ of } x$$
$$\$9.00 = x$$

27. **(C)** Let us begin by assigning letters to the height and radius of each cylinder. Since most people find it easier to deal with whole numbers instead of fractions, let us say that cylinder Q has a radius of 2r, so that cylinder P can have a radius of r. Then, we assign cylinder Q a height of h so that P can have a height of 2h. Now, the formula for the volume of a cylinder is $\pi r^2 \times h$. So P and Q have volumes:

Volume P = $\pi(r)^2 \times 2h$ Volume Q = $(2\pi r)^2 \times h$
P = $2\pi r^2 h$ Q = $4\pi r^2 h$

Thus, the ratio of P:Q is $\dfrac{2\pi r^2 h}{4\pi r^2 h} = 2/4 = 1/2$.

28. **(A)** We begin by extending the lines to give this picture:

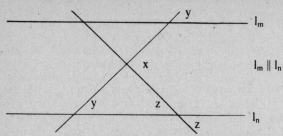

Then we add another angle y (lines l_m and l_n are parallel, so alternate interior angles are equal) and another z (opposite angles are equal). We know that x + w = 180°, and we know that y + z + w = 180°. So, x + w = y + z + w, and x = y + z.

29. **(C)** Let us begin by drawing the rectangle:

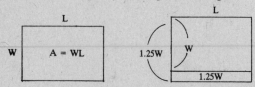

$$A = 1.25W \times L = 1.25WL$$

The original area is WL. The width of the new rectangle is W + .25%W or 1.25 W. So the new area is 1.25WL. It then follows that the new area is $\dfrac{1.25WL}{WL}$, or 125% of the old area.

30. **(B)** Let us take any odd integer, m. The next consecutive odd integer will be two more than m, or m + 2. The third integer in the series will be m + 4, and the fourth integer in the series will be m + 6. The sum of the four is: (m) + (m + 2) + (m + 4) + (m + 6) = 4m + 12. And when (4m + 12) is divided by 4, the result is: $\dfrac{4m + 12}{4} = m + 3$. So the sum of the four consecutive odd integers (4m + 12) is always evenly divisible by 4.

SECTION IV

1. **(D)** Although this is a right triangle, and though the hypotenuse has length $\sqrt{2}$, the triangle need not be a 45°–45°–90° triangle. The easiest way to show this is with a drawing:

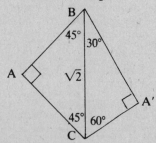

2. **(C)** Since it makes no difference in which order the elements are multiplied, Column A is equivalent to Column B.

3. **(B)** It is important to remember that the square root of a number between 0 and 1, whether expressed as a decimal or as a fraction, is *larger* than the number itself. For example, $\sqrt{\frac{1}{4}} = \frac{1}{2}$ but $\frac{1}{2} > \frac{1}{4}$. So, too, here $\sqrt{0.9}$ is actually greater than 0.9. Another method for solving the problem is to square both sides of the comparison. If the two quantities were originally equal, then squaring both sides will not upset the balance. Further, if either of the two quantities is greater than the other, squaring both sides will not interfere with the *direction* of the inequality. (It will interfere with the *magnitude* of the inequality, but the quantitative comparison question is a "yes or no"; exercise: which is larger, *not* how much larger.) Squaring both sides:

$$\begin{array}{cc} (0.3)^2 & (\sqrt{0.9})^2 \\ .09 & 0.9 \end{array}$$

Clearly, Column B is larger.

4. **(C)** Performing the multiplication in each column is the simplest approach to the question:

$$\begin{array}{cc} (x + y)^2 & x(x + y) + y(x + y) \\ (x + y)(x + y) & x^2 + xy + xy + y^2 \\ x^2 + xy + xy + y^2 & x^2 + 2xy + y^2 \\ x^2 + 2xy + y^2 & \end{array}$$

5. **(A)** One property of positive fractions is that, given the same denominator, the larger numerator makes the larger fraction and, conversely, given the same numerator, the larger denominator makes the *smaller* fraction. In this question, the numerators are equal. The fraction in Column B has the larger denominator, so it is actually smaller than the fraction in Column A.

6. **(B)** A quick glance at the two expressions shows that Column A must be negative and Column B positive. Whatever the absolute value of the number 3^6, in Column A it will be negative since it is prefixed with the minus sign. Column B, however, will be positive. The minus sign is enclosed within the parentheses. This indicates that we are raising *minus* three to the sixth power. Since six is an even number, the final result will be positive (negative times negative times negative times negative times negative times negative yields a positive).

7. **(C)** We should notice first that we are definitely not in a position to say that the magnitude of the unlabeled angles is 90°. But we need not make the assumption! We know that w = y and x = z because vertical angles are equal. Therefore, w + x = y + z. We can drop these expressions from both sides of our comparison. In effect, we are

subtracting equals from both sides of the comparison, a maneuver which, as we have already seen, will neither upset the balance of the original equality nor interfere with the direction of the inequality. This leaves us with 90 on both sides of the comparison, so we conclude that the original comparison must have been an equality.

8. **(C)** At first glance, the problem appears to be a difficult one. A closer look, however, shows that it is actually quite simple. Both paths cover the same vertical distance of 10 units and the same horizontal distance of 14 units. Since it makes no difference whether one moves vertically or horizontally first, the two paths are equal. Notice further that each path covers a distance of 24 units. That is equal to the length of one width and one length of a rectangle with dimension 10 and 14 which could be constructed using P and T as vertices.

9. **(B)** Let us begin by inscribing an equilateral triangle in a circle:

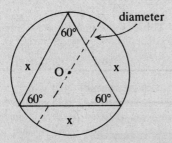

Since the longest chord of any circle is the chord drawn through the center of the circle (that is, the diameter of the circle), and since no side of the triangle can pass through the center, the side of the equilateral triangle must be shorter than the diameter of the circle in which it is inscribed. Having determined that, we then proceed to ask whether the length of the side of a square inscribed in the same circle is longer or shorter than that of the side of the equilateral triangle.

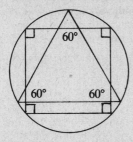

The side of the square is shorter, and we can see that the greater the number of sides, the shorter will be the length of those sides. From this we can conclude that for all equilateral polygons inscribed in circles, the side of the polygon will be shorter than the diameter of the circle.

10. **(D)** Using P, V, and G to represent Peter's, Victor's and Georgette's grades, respectively, the centered information tells us: $P > V$ and $G > V$. But we have no information regarding the relationship between P and G.

11. **(B)** The parabola drawn on the graph actually adds no information needed for solving the problem. Regardless of what figure is drawn through point (a,b), and there are of course an infinite number of different ones, point (a,b) is in the second quadrant—that is, the upper left-hand section of the coordinate system. In that quadrant all x-values are negative and all y-values are positive, so a must be negative and b must be positive. Therefore, b is greater than a.

12. **(D)** We simplify the comparison as much as possible. First we subtract 3 from both sides and then we subtract 2x from both sides. This reduces Column A to $x + 2$ and Column B to 0. We can now ask the simpler question: which is greater, $x + 2$ or 0? This is simpler because we can immediately see that the answer will depend on the value of x, information we lack.

13. **(B)** First, let us perform the indicated operations. In Column A we find a power raised to a power, and that calls for the multiplication of the two exponents: $(x^3)^5 = x^{3 \cdot 5} = x^{15}$. In Column B we find multiplication of like bases, so we add the exponents: $x^3 \cdot x^5 = x^{3+5} = x^8$. The centered information states that x is negative. Since a negative number raised to a power which is odd yields a negative number (negative times negative times negative . . . yields a negative number), Column A is negative. Column B, however, must be positive since it is raised to an even power. Consequently, whatever x might be, Column A is negative, Column B is positive; therefore, Column B must be greater than Column A.

14. **(A)** The problem can be worked out using simultaneous equations, but that is not the most efficient way of solving it. For that reason we will set up the equations (for the "afficionados"), but we will not actually solve for x and y. Let x be the number of shirts costing $13 and y the number costing $10:

$$x + y = 16$$
$$13x + 10y = 187$$
Final solution: $x = 9$ and $y = 7$.

We have omitted the detailed calculations because there is a simpler method. Let us assume, for the sake of argument, that the two columns are equal—that is, that the man bought equal numbers of both types of shirts. If we are correct in assuming that he bought eight $13 shirts and eight $10 shirts, then $(8 \times 13) + (8 \times 10)$ ought to equal $187. When we do the multiplication, we get the result $184. That tells us our original assumption of equal numbers was incorrect and, further, that the answer to the question is not (C). We should then make a second assumption, but should we assume that he bought more expensive shirts than we first guessed, or fewer? A moment of reflection will show that we should adjust our initial assumption to include a greater number of expensive shirts, for only by increasing that number will we add to the $184 which was the result of our original assumption. So we would next assume—again for the purposes of argument—that the man bought nine $13 shirts and only seven $10 shirts. But at this point we have already solved the problem! We do not need to know the precise ratio, e.g., whether 9:7, 10:6, 11:5, 12:4, 13:3, 14:2, or 15:1; we have already determined that the ratio is one of those listed, and so it must be the case that Column A is larger.

15. **(B)** This problem, too, can be solved with a little gimmick. It is not necessary to actually calculate the volumes in question. You need only recognize that the sphere will have a diameter of 10 and that this is equal to the side of the cube. This means that the sphere can be placed within the cube, so the cube must have a greater volume.

16. **(A)** We begin by multiplying $(x - y)^2$:

$$(x - y)(x - y) = x^2 - 2xy + y^2 = 12$$

Then we substitute 1 for xy:

$$x^2 - 2(1) + y^2 = 12$$
$$x^2 + y^2 = 14$$

17. **(C)** Let us begin by adding the following notation:

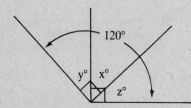

Since the entire angle is 120°, $y + 90 = 120$, so $y = 30$. Similarly, $z + 90 = 120$, so $z = 30$. Since $x + y + z = 120$, $x + 30 + 30 = 120$, so $x = 60$.

18. **(A)** Certainly the easiest and most direct way to solve this problem is to test each of the integers. There is no reason to try and find some fancy mathematical equation to describe the problem when a simple substitution of answer choices will do. When 95 is divided by 6, 10, and 15—answers (A), (C), and (D)—the remainder in each case is 5. And when 135 is divided by 10, the remainder is 5, not 8; and when 135 is divided by 15 there is a remainder of 0. When 135 is divided by 6, the

remainder is 3. So only 6 fits both the conditions for n.

19. **(D)** Since the ratio of insects with X to those without X is 5:3, we know that $\frac{5}{8}$ of the population has X. (There are 8 equal units—5 + 3—5 of which are insects with X.) Then, of those $\frac{5}{8}$, $\frac{3}{8}$ are male. So we take $\frac{3}{8}$ of the $\frac{5}{8}$ ($\frac{3}{8} \times \frac{5}{8}$), and that tells us that $\frac{15}{64}$ of the total population are male insects with X.

20. **(B)** We can order the elements by clarifying the exponents:

(A) $\frac{3^8}{3^6} = 3^{8-6} = 3^2 = 9$

(B) $3^3 - 1 = 27 - 1 = 26$

(C) $3^0 = 1$

(D) 3^{27} is too large to compute here, but is obviously the greatest quantity in the group.

(E) $3(3^2) = 3^3 = 27$

The order is (C), (A), (B), (D), (E); so (B) is the middle term.

21. **(A)** This is just a matter of adding up the total fares collected for subways in the six years:

1972:	300 million
1973:	325 million
1974:	350 million
1975:	350 million
1976:	320 million
1977:	260 million
	1925

22. **(C)** The number of fares collected in 1975 was 350 million, and the number of fares collected in 1977 was 260 million. The number of fares dropped by 90 million, but we are looking for the rate, or percentage, of decrease. So we set our fraction up, starting amount, $\frac{90}{350}$, which is approximately 25%.

23. **(E)** The number of subway fares collected in 1974 was 350 million; the number of bus fares collected in that year was 315 million. Our ratio then is $\frac{50 \times 350}{30 \times 315}$, which we then reduce by a factor of 10, $\frac{5 \times 350}{3 \times 315}$, and again by a factor of 5, $\frac{5 \times 70}{3 \times 63}$; then we can do the arithmetic a little more easily: $\frac{350}{189}$. If we round 189 off to 190 and reduce again by a factor of 10, we get $\frac{35}{20}$, or $\frac{7}{4}$ as a good approximation of the ratio. Actually, we need not do all of this arithmetic. We can see at a glance that more subway fares were collected than bus fares; so, given that the subway fares are more

expensive, we can conclude that the revenues derived from subway fares were greater than those for bus fares, and that means our ratio must be greater than 1. Only (E) is possible.

24. **(C)** In 1977, the total number of fares collected was 260 (subways) + 425 (commuter rail) + 255 (bus) = 940 total. Of the 940 million fares collected, 425 were commuter rail fares, so the commuter rail fares accounted for about $\frac{1}{2}$, or 50%, of all the fares collected in that year.

25. **(E)** 425 million commuter rail fares were collected in 1977, and 230 million were collected in 1972. The difference is 195 million.

26. **(A)** Proposition I is necessarily true. Since lines l_m and l_n are perpendicular to one another, a line that intersects l_m on the perpendicular must be parallel to line l_n.

Proposition II is not necessarily true. Line segment MN may fail to intersect l_m simply because it is too short—that is, if extended, for all we know MN will intersect l_n.

Proposition III is not necessarily true. Line l_o may intersect l_m at point P without plane y's being perpendicular to plane x.

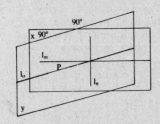 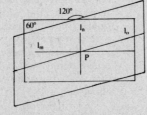

27. **(D)** The proper way to "visualize" this problem is to imagine that the gravel-covered walk will be a very squat-shaped cylinder with a donut hole removed (the circular region inside the walk). Expressed more abstractly, we need to compute the volume of a cylinder with a radius of 50 feet ($\frac{1}{2}$ of 100 = 50) and a height of 6 inches, or $\frac{1}{2}$ foot. Then we compute the volume of a cylinder with a radius of 40 feet ($\frac{1}{2}$ of 80 = 40) and a height of 6 inches, or $\frac{1}{2}$ foot. Then we subtract the second from the first and what is left is the volume we seek. Now, since both cylinders have the same height, it will be easier to compute the areas of the bases first and subtract before multiplying by $\frac{1}{2}$ foot.

Area of larger circle: Area = $\pi r^2 = \pi(50)^2 = 2500\,\pi$.
Area of smaller circle: Area = $\pi r^2 = \pi(40)^2 = 1600\pi$.

By subtracting 1600π from 2500π, we determine that the area of the garden path is 900π square

feet. To determine the volume of gravel we need, we then multiply that figure by $\frac{1}{2}$ foot (the depth of the gravel), and arrive at our answer 450π cu. ft.

28. **(D)** Let d stand for the hourly rate under the new system. Since the employee is to make the same amount per week under both systems, it must be the case that:

$$\frac{\$x}{\text{hr. times 40 hrs.}} = \frac{\$d}{\text{hr. times 36 hrs.}}$$

Now we must solve for d:

$$40\,x = 36d, \quad d = \frac{10x}{9}.$$

The problem can also be solved in an intuitive way. Since the employee is working less time yet making the same weekly total, he must be earning slightly more per hour under the new system than under the old. Answer (A) is just the naked fraction $\frac{1}{10}$, without making reference to monetary units. Answer (B) implies that the employee is making $\frac{1}{9}$ as much per hour under the new system as under the old—that would be a decrease in the hourly rate. Similarly, (C) says that the employee is making only 90% of his old hourly rate and that, too, is a decrease. Finally, (E) says that the employee is making *9 times* the hourly rate he made under the old system, a figure which is obviously out of line. The only reasonable choice is (D). The moral is: Even if you cannot set up the math in a technically correct way, use a little common sense.

29. **(B)** Since the columns are perpendicular to both ceiling and floor, we know that they are parallel. The left-hand column must be 12 feet long: If the two 8-foot pieces were laid end to end, they would total 16 feet, but there is a 4-foot overlap, so the length of the column is 16 feet minus 4 feet, or 12 feet. The right-hand column must also be 12 feet long. But the two 10-foot pieces, if laid end to end, would form a column 20 feet long. Therefore, the overlap, x, must be 8 feet (20 − x = 12).

30. **(A)** This problem must be solved in two stages. First, we need to calculate the total area of the wall. The information given in the problem states that $\frac{1}{3}$ of the job plus another 75 square feet equals $\frac{3}{4}$ of the job. In algebraic notation, this is:

$$\frac{1}{3}x + 75 = \frac{3}{4}x$$
$$75 = \frac{3}{4}x - \frac{1}{3}x$$
$$75 = \frac{5}{12}x$$
$$x = 180$$

So the entire wall is 180 square feet—that is, W × L = 180. We know that the height of the wall is 10 feet; so 10 × L = 180, and L = 18.

SECTION V

Questions 1–4

Arranging the Information

This set of questions presents two separate ideas for ordering the information. Previewing the question stems, especially numbers 1 and 2, indicates that at least a fair degree of certainty should be obtainable. Since the ideas of time of departure and relative amount drunk are separate, two diagrams must be constructed, one at a time. Starting with drinking:

←DRANK MORE——DRANK LESS→

P drank more than W				P	W
T drank more than P			T	P	W
T drank less than V		V	T	P	W
U drank less than Q can't do now					
U drank more than V	U	V	T	P	W
U drank less than Q OK now	Q	U	V	T	P	W
W drank more than R	Q	U	V	T	P	W	R

Now for departure times:

←LATER——EARLIER→

P later than V				P	V
T later than P			T	P	V
T earlier than S		S	T	P	V
U later than S	U	S	T	P	V
W earlier than V	U	S	T	P	V	W

Answering the Questions

With such complete diagrams, answering the questions is primarily a matter of reading the diagrams carefully. In this set of questions, there is no uncertainty at all.

1. **(E)** W left earlier than anyone else, so (E) must be the answer. Sometimes you may have a question where the very earliest (latest, greenest, whatever-est) is not listed as a possible answer choice and you have to check out the other answers more closely. It is usually a good idea to look for the most—earliest in this case—and see if that is an answer choice, because if it is available to be chosen, it must be the right answer.

2. **(B)** R drank less than anybody else, so (B) must be the answer. The same approach described for 1 would work here.

3. **(C)** The diagrams show that T was the third-to-last to leave and drank more than P, W, and R; hence, answer choice (C) is correct. Note that whenever you have such referential terms as most or third, they are to be interpreted within the context of the information given. Most, therefore, means "most—out of those about whom information was given or who were mentioned anyway."

   (A) fails because although the first part of it is true, U and Q both drank more than V. (B) is also partly true, but the answer we are looking for, and find in (C), must be completely true. U was "outdrunk" by Q. (D) also has the first part true and the last part false—or at least not known to be true. S's drinking was not characterized in any way in the information given. (E) fails because (C) succeeds.

4. **(E)** Simply knowing that S drank more than W—who drank the second-least of anyone mentioned—does not give any information about how S relates to any of the other partygoers. If you wanted to choose answer choice (D), you were not remembering that merely because S was greater than W did not put S into the first available slot above W.

5. **(C)** You should remember that there is a very important distinction to be drawn between numbers and percentages. For example, an increase from one murder per year to two murders per year can be described as a "whopping big 100% increase." The argument speaks only of percentages, so we would not want to conclude anything about the numbers underlying those percentages. Therefore, both (A) and (B) are incorrect. They speak of "more agents," and "more people," and those are numbers rather than percentages. Furthermore, if we would not want to draw a conclusion about numbers from data given in percentage terms, we surely would not want to base a conclusion about efficiency or work accomplished on percentages. Thus, (D) and (E) are incorrect. What makes (C) the best answer of the five is the possibility of making percentage comparisons *within* each agency. Within both agencies, the number of field agents increased by a greater *percentage* than the number of non-field agents.

6. **(D)** Keeping in mind our comments about (D) and (E) in the preceding question, (A) must be

wrong. We do not want to conclude from sheer number of employees anything about the actual work accomplished. (B) and (E) are incorrect for pretty much the same reason. The question stem asks us to give an argument defending the CIA against the claim that it is overstaffed. Neither rate of pay nor appropriations has anything to do with whether or not there are too many people on the payroll. (C) is the second-best answer, but it fails because it does not keep in mind the ratio of non-field to field agents. Our concern is not with the number of agents generally, but the number of support and supervisory workers (reread the question stem). (D) focues on this nicely by explaining why the CIA should experience a faster increase (which is to say, a greater percentage increase) in the number.

7. **(D)** Let us use letters to represent the categories. "All effective administrators" will be A. "Concerned about welfare" will be C. "Are liberal" will be L. The three propositions can now be represented as:

1. All A are W.
2. All W are L.
3. All non-L are not A.

Proposition 3 is equivalent to "all A are not non-L," and that is in turn equivalent to "all A are L." Thus, (D) follows fairly directly as a matter of logic. (A) is incorrect, for while we know that "all A are L," we would not want to conclude that "no L are A"—there might be some ineffective administrators who grant time off. They could be ineffective for other reasons. (B) is incorrect for the same reason. Even though all effective administrators are concerned about their employees' welfare, this does not mean that an ineffective administrator could not be concerned. He might be concerned, but ineffective for another reason. (C) is clearly false, given our propositions; we know that all effective administrators are liberal. Finally, (E) is not inferable. Just because all effective administrators grant time off does not mean that all the time off granted is granted by effective administrators.

Questions 8–12

Arranging the Information

In arranging this sort of information, where there are subgroups and the major conditions appear to be the cross connections between their members—as here with the two types of courses—the information may be arranged with an algebraic notation which here would give rise to the equations C NOT = E, B NOT = F, and E NOT = M, with the added notation that there must be two of B, C, or P chosen. To this must be added new deductions as they are made for each problem.

Another way of diagramming this information—which works well for situations of this particular sort, though it is not as general as the algebraic approach—is to list the two groups and connect different items with an annotated line indicating what sort of connection is being made: must go with, cannot go with, etc. Here this would look like this:

SCIENCES   OTHER COURSES

(must = 2)

           NOT WITH   NOT WITH

CHEMISTRY←————→ENGLISH←————————→MUSIC

          NOT WITH

BIOLOGY ←————→FRENCH

PHYSICS   WRITING

Arrows are helpful in case the relationship is just a one-way situation, though that is not too common.

A further deduction would be that English and French cannot go together since either one of them forbids one of the sciences, and if they were both scheduled there would only be one science—which is not permitted.

Answering the Questions

8. **(B)** A step-by-step approach is the key. If Lois takes English, then chemistry and music are out. If chemistry is out, then physics and biology are the two sciences she must take. If biology is scheduled, then French is out. This leaves choice (B). The other answers all include some subject not possible. (A) is not wrong because it has three sciences. That is possible. (A) is wrong because chemistry can't be scheduled with English.

9. **(C)** If chemistry is out, then once again biology and physics are required. Biology precludes French and music displaces English, leaving answer choice (C).

   In any case, choices (A) and (E) are impossible because they have both English and music. Choice (B) is out because French cannot be with biology. Choice (D) cannot be scheduled since it has both French and English which cannot be combined, as previously explained.

10. **(E)** I and III work by the same logic. In each case the taking of one of the non-science courses eliminates one of the science courses from consideration, thus requiring the other two science courses. II is trying to trap you into saying that since neither music nor chemistry can combine with English, they must combine with each other. This is not true. It is possible to have a curriculum of music, physics, biology, and writing.

11. **(E)** I here is trying the same trick as II in problem 10; it does not always have to be true. II must be true since French eliminates biology, and requires the other two sciences. III need not be true since a curriculum of chemistry, biology, writing, and music is but one counter-example.

12. **(E)** With Lois taking physics, now scheduled at the same time as English, she cannot take English, chemistry, or music because they overlap with the new physics time. Only French or biology may be taken, plus writing. This means that only three courses can be taken, **(E)**, though two science courses can still be taken—eliminating (A). (B), (C), and (D) are eliminated by the schedule just discussed.

Questions 13–17

Arranging the Information

Previewing the questions indicates that the total points and the breakdown of points are the key issues. Nine points are awarded for each race ($5 + 3 + 1$), times three races yields 27 points at issue. Since the teams are tied now, 14 points in the last three races will win the meet. Since there are two entries from each team in each race, the most that a team could win in a single race is 8 points ($5 + 3$). For keeping track of the results for each alternative raised by the problems a simple chart will be enough:

	Ind Med	Med Relay	Free Relay
FIRST (5)			
SECOND (3)			
THIRD (1)			
TOTAL (9)			

Answering the Questions

13. **(A)** This was answered in the preceding discussion.

14. **(D)** You don't need to keep track of both teams' points once you know that 14 is the magic number. If State won first and third in the individual medley, then Malibu won second and three points. Therefore, Malibu needs eleven more points to win the meet. (D) provides exactly eleven ($5 + 5 + 1$). (A) yields only 10 ($5 + 5$), (B) only 9 ($5 + 3 + 1$), (C) only 8 ($3 + 1 + 3 + 1$). The incorrectness of (E) is proved by the validity of (D).

15. **(B)** The individual medley is set up with the idea that State's top swimmer is sure to win, with only second and third being at issue. If George swims, Malibu will get four points ($3 + 1$), but if George

doesn't, then State's second swimmer will get the point for third place and Malibu will get only three points for second place. Thus, the loss to Malibu if George does not swim in the individual medley is one point.

There are two ways of computing the point value of the various coaching moves being contemplated. Both are correct and either one will work, but you have to use one or the other consistently. In this discussion, we are counting only the effect of the coaching move on Malibu's score. One could have said that taking George out of the individual medley will take away one point from Malibu AND give one to State, thus causing a difference of two points.

In order for it to be advantageous for Malibu for George to swim in another race, the net increase in the other race will have to be at least two points. If it is only one point, there is no advantage.

(A) will add only one point for third ($1-0$)—no advantage.

(B) will add two points ($3-1$), so it is an advantage.

(C) will add one point ($5 - (3 + 1)$), no advantage.

(D) will add nothing; Malibu scores ten points either way.

(E) is, of course, not true, given (B), but would not be an advantage anyway.

16. **(A)** This is a two-step problem. First, you must calculate how many points are needed; second, how many swimmers are needed to win those points. Fourteen is the magic number and Malibu has scored four in the individual medley, leaving ten. Two firsts will do the trick.

17. **(A)** The situation posited is that Malibu wins first and second in the individual medley, since State's other swimmer cannot beat four minutes even. This means that the score is 8 to 1 in favor of Malibu.

(A) is false because this would only earn State 10 more points for a total of 11 when 14 was needed.

(B) is true since that would add 8 more points to the Malibu total, making 16—enough for victory.

(C) is true because those three swimmers might be two thirds and a second, totalling only 5 points ($3 + 1 + 1$), which, when added to the 8 won in the individual medley, is only 13—not enough to guarantee victory.

(D) is possible since the minimum that four scoring teams could win is 8 points for second and third in each race. Eight plus the one point earned in the individual medley totals only nine.

(E) is possible since the three might be two firsts and a second, which would be 13 points to add to the one from the individual medley—yielding the magic total of 14.

Questions 18–22

Arranging the Information

There are three kinds of information—house order on the block, family name, and type of dog—and there are five items of each sort. Thus, we will have a grid that is 5 by 3.

HOUSE ORDER	1	2	3	4	5
DOG*					
FAMILY					

*Note that two of the dogs begin with the letter "s," so more than initials must be used.

Since the preview of the questions reveals no questions about subsets of the information set nor any questions about contradictions or redundancies, we can safely start with any statement and pick the third-from-last, which gives order of house information.

Setting up the preceding diagram is the most efficient way to approach the problem. Note that much of the other information does concern house order even though it does not directly number houses.

If the Lanes live two houses from both the other families, then the Lanes must live in the middle and the others at the ends. We will put the others in as 1 and 5, but remember that they might flip-flop.

HOUSE ORDER	1	2	3	4	5
DOG					
FAMILY	KINGS		LANES		JONESES

Now we can link in the next-to-last statement and the second statement's items.

HOUSE ORDER	1	2	3	4	5
DOG	NOT SETTER				
	NOT SHEEP	SHEEP?	NOT SHEEP	SHEEP?	NOT SHEEP
	NOT COLLIE	COLLIE?	NOT COLLIE	COLLIE?	NOT COLLIE
FAMILY	KINGS		LANES		JONESES

Entering the third item, we find that the Kings can't have the sheepdog (since it is next to the Joneses) or any dog other than the poodle, and thus must have the poodle. Since the sheepdog lives next to the Joneses, it must be in position 4 (always remembering that the order could be left-to-right or right-to-left). This in turn means that the only slot available for the collie is at house 2.

HOUSE ORDER	1	2	3	4	5
DOG	POODLE	COLLIE	NOT SHEEP NOT COLLIE NOT POODLE	SHEEP	NOT SHEEP NOT COLLIE NOT POODLE HEAVIEST DOG
FAMILY	KINGS		LANES		JONESES

The next statement, that the retriever weighs more than the setter or poodle, means that the Joneses don't have either of the lighter dogs, which makes four dogs eliminated for them, and they must have the retriever. If the Joneses have the retriever than the only dog left for the Lanes is the setter.

HOUSE	1	2	3	4	5
DOG	POODLE	COLLIE	SETTER	SHEEPDOG	RETRIEVER
FAMILY	KINGS		LANES		JONESES

The last statement now fills in the last two families as being:

HOUSE	1	2	3	4	5
DOG	POODLE	COLLIE	SETTER	SHEEPDOG	RETRIEVER HEAVIEST DOG
FAMILY	KINGS	NEFFS	LANES	MURRAYS	JONESES

Answering the Questions

Almost all of these questions are largely a matter of reading from the diagram.

18. **(C)** The second statement also shows the falseness of (C) by itself.

19. **(E)** This can only be gotten quickly from the diagram.

20. **(E)** Although the heaviest dog is known (retriever), the rank-order of the other dogs by weight is not known, thus the answer to this question is not determinable.

21. **(A)** The Neffs now live with the collie and the Joneses with the retriever, in houses 2 and 5 respectively. When swapped, the Joneses in house 2 are next to the Kings and the poodle. Note that since we are looking for something which now becomes true, it must be something to do with the Joneses or the Neffs. Thus, (D) and (E) are improbable.

22. **(B)** The sheepdog will now be in house 3 with the Lanes and the setter; thus, (B) is correct and (A) false. (B) is the most general statement available, and thus deserving of a thorough review early in your work on the problem.

23. **(C)** Clark was unhappy if he had a clear conscience but knew, or Clark was happy if he knew but had an unclear conscience. It is not the case that Clark was unhappy, so he must have been happy. Since he knew, however, his happiness must stem from an unclear conscience. (A), (D), and (E) are incorrect because they make irrelevant value judgments. As was just shown, the author's point can be analyzed as a purely logical one. (B) is just distraction, playing on the connection between "governess" and "servant," which, of course, are not the same thing.

24. **(B)** The key here is that the word nobody is used in a cleverly ambiguous way—and, as many of you probably know, the "young lady" in the story is Lewis Carroll's Alice. This is fairly representative of his word play. (E) must be incorrect since it misses completely the little play on words: "I saw Nobody," encouraging a response such as "Oh, is he a handsome man?" (D) is beside the point, for the King is not interested in the messenger's veracity. He may be interested in his reliability (A); but, if anything, we should conclude the King finds the messenger unreliable since "nobody walks slower" than the messenger. (C) is wrong because the question is not a matter of eyesight. The King does not say, "If you had better eyes, you might have seen Nobody."

25. **(E)** The advertisement employs the term more in an ambiguous manner. In the context, one might expect the phrase more flavor to mean more highly concentrated flavor, that is, more flavor per unit weight. What the ad actually says, however, is that the sticks of Evergreen are *larger*, so if they are larger, there must be more *total* flavor. All three propositions, if they are true (as we are asked to assume they are), are good attacks on the ad. First, I, it is possible to beat the ad at its own game. If flavor is just a matter of chewing enough sticks, then Spring Mint is as good a deal because, flavor unit for flavor unit, it is no more expenseive than Evergreen. Second, II would also undermine the ad by focusing on the ambiguity we have just discussed. Finally, III also uncovers another potential ambiguity. If the ad is comparing volume rather than weight, Spring Mint may be a better value. After all, who wants to buy a lot of air?

SECTION VI

Questions 1–5

Arranging the Information

The eight numbers are arranged, like all numbers, along a single line. The original information tells us that they are consecutive, so the diagram will be of eight slots, each right next to the other. Enter the information one item at a time.

This is the diagram:

←GREATER——SMALLER→

__ __ __ __ __ __ __ __

W is four more than Z and three less than X—this defines the end points and W.

←GREATER——SMALLER→

X __ __ W __ __ __ Z

S greater than T—cannot do now.
S less than X—redundant since X is largest, but these establish the relationship: X > S > T.
U is the average of V and X—this means that U is greater than V because the average is between two numbers and X is the largest number in the group. Furthermore, for every step that U is below X, V is the same number of steps below U. This establishes some possibilities:

←GREATER——SMALLER→

possibility #1　X　U?　V?　W　__　__　__　Z
possibility #2　X　__　U?　W　V?　__　__　Z

These are the only possibilities because U cannot take W's place, and if U is below W, then V will be below Z, which is not possible within the context of eight consecutive numbers. The final diagram shows the two possibilities and the notation that S is greater than T. Nothing is known about Y at all.

Answering the Questions

1. **(C)** Z is the lowest number in the series and W is four greater, and thus equal to 8 + 4 = 12.

2. **(C)** I: As previously discussed, W cannot be the greatest number because it is less than X. As for II, Z cannot be the greatest number because it is less than W. Thus, I and II are true.

    III is false because X, being 7 greater than Z in a series of eight consecutive numbers, must be the greatest number.

3. **(A)** The question asks for a possible arrangement, so elimination of impossibilities is the proper approach. X is the greatest number, not Z, which eliminates answer choice (C). Z is the lowest number, which eliminates answer choices (C) (again) and (D). W is three less than X, and thus must be the fourth number from the left, which again eliminates answer choice (D) as well as (E). U, being the average of X and V, must lie exactly between them, which it does not in

4. **(B)** Under the original conditions, U could not have been immediately above Z since there had to be room for V below U. With the removal of that requirement, (B) is now possible. (A) was a possibility anyway, so it is not the newly created possibility for which the problem asks. (C) is not possible because the eight numbers are consecutive numbers, and thus not equal to each other. (E) is wrong for the same reason. (D) violates the limitation that the numbers be a string of eight consecutive numbers. By placing U below Z, the difference between the highest and lowest numbers in the string becomes too great.

5. **(E)** If Y is three greater than Z, it goes just below W. This eliminates possibility 2, shown previously, and gives the following diagram. Once U and V and Y are tied down, so are S and T.

←GREATER——SMALLER→

X U V W Y S T Z

Inspection of the diagram indicates that none of the four statements is true, hence, answer choice (E) is correct.

6. **(B)** I would undermine the advertisement considerably. Since the point of the ad is that you will lose weight, any unforeseen effects which would make it impossible to lose weight would defeat the purposes of the program. II is less obvious, but it does weaken the ad somewhat. Although the ad does not specifically say you will be healthier for having enrolled in the program, surely the advantages of the program are less significant if you have to pay an additional, hidden cost, i.e., health. III, if anything, supports the advertisement. IV is irrelevant since the ad does not claim you will become too thin.

7. **(B)** This question is like one of those simple conversation questions: "X: All bats are mammals. Y: Not true, whales are mammals too." In this little exchange, B misunderstands A to have said that "All mammals are bats." In 7, the objection must be based on a misunderstanding. The objector must think that the ad has claimed that the only cause of unhappiness, etc., is being overweight, otherwise he would not have offered his counter-example. (A) is wrong because the ad never takes a stand on the *causes* of overweight conditions—only on a possible cure. This reasoning invalidates (C) and (D) as well. (E) makes a similar error, but about effects not about causes. The ad does not say everyone who is unhappy is unattractive, or vice versa.

8. **(D)** The easiest way to set this problem up is to draw a relational line:

PE   IP   EL   BE

Dislikes————————→Likes

We note that Clara likes Basic Economics better than anything else, which means she must like it better than Advanced Calculus. So even though Advanced Calculus does not appear on our line, since we know that Basic Economics is the maximum, Clara must like Advanced Calculus less than Basic Economics. So (C) can be inferred. But we do not know where World History ranks on the preference line, and since Introductory Physics is not a maximal or a minimal value, we can make no judgment regarding it and an unplaced course. Quick reference to the line will show that (A), (B), and (E) are inferrable.

Questions 9–12

Arranging the Information

Since three of the four questions are conditional questions introducing different variations or new information, you know that you will not get a definite result from the original set of information. This means that you should quickly sketch out the limitations and requirements in the original information, and spend most of your time in the answering of the questions.

In addition to the basic setup of there being two shelves with three spaces on each, there are only three relationships which are specified.

Thyme and basil are not next to each other.

Thyme and basil are not above or below each other.

Salt and pepper must be next to each other on the same shelf.

Answering the Questions

In answering the sort of question where there are many possibilities, it is often most efficient to focus on the limiting factors since there are fewer of them.

9. **(A)** All that the question asks is whether the three arrangements are unacceptable. Thus, all you have to do for each arrangement is to find one possibility of its being acceptable in order to eliminate the arrangement from consideration.

I. Thyme and basil on same   T ___ B
    shelf but not next to each
    other.   ___ ___ ___

    Salt and pepper must be on
    the other shelf to be
    together.   T C B

Others fit in without problem.   S   P   F
(This is only one possible arrangement.)

Thus, I is possible.

II is shown to be possibly acceptable by the same arrangement as given above for I. If you happened to have made a different arrangement for I, you would need to start with T and C on the same shelf, and see if you could fill it all in without violating any of the restrictions of the problem.

III: For T and S to be on the same shelf requires that one shelf be T, S, P (or any arrangement of the three which has S and P together). For example:

T	S	P
C	F	B

B can be added without being under T.
So III is acceptable also.

Since all of the arrangements are acceptable, the correct answer is (A).

10. **(D)**   The wording of the problem means that your job is to find the four answer choices which are not acceptable. The correct answer choice is not necessarily the only way to meet the conditions, but merely a possibility.

One general rule is that salt and pepper have to be next to each other. Therefore, any shelf arrangement which does not have them next to each other is wrong. This eliminates (A), (B), and (E).

The difference between the remaining answer choices—(C) and (D)—is whether the basil is on the left or on the right. If the basil is on the left, it will be immediately below the thyme, which is forbidden. Hence, (D) is the only acceptable arrangement.

11. **(C)**   The problem sets up this starting point:

—	—	—
S	P	B

This means that thyme cannot be in the upper right-hand slot; but there are no restrictions on cumin or fennel. The possibilities are these:

T	C	F		T	F	C
S	P	B		S	P	B
C	T	F		F	T	C
S	P	B		S	P	B

Since thyme is the limiting item, you should start your work with it. First place thyme in the left-hand slot and flip-flop the other two, then put thyme in the middle slot and flip-flop the other two again = 4 ways.

12. **(A)**   This is a problem where a condition is added. Even though new containers are bought, they are similar, and thus still must not be placed next to each other. The new condition is that they must both be in the top shelf. This means that the top shelf must have basil at one end and thyme at the other. Since salt and pepper still must be next to each other and there is only one empty space on the upper shelf, salt and pepper must be on the bottom shelf, though they can slide from side to side and could be placed with pepper on the left or on the right of the salt.

There are two ways of approaching this problem. Either you can focus on elimination of answer choices that are not acceptable by constructing counter-examples, or you can focus on trying to find an acceptable arrangement that meets the new conditions. Since it is a fairly loosely constrained situation, the former is more efficient, especially since it will at least provide the elimination of some answer choices.

If you try the elimination route, it is best to start with the simplest and most definite arrangements, since their unacceptability will likely be easier to demonstrate.

That (B), (C), and (D) are not necessarily true is shown by the acceptable arrangement:

B	F/C	T
P	S	F/C

(E) is shown to be false by interchanging B and T in the diagram. (A), however, must be true. In either position, F must be above or next to one of the pair S or P.

Questions 13–17

Arranging the Information

This is a problem where most of the action occurs in the questions rather than in the arranging of the given information. It is important, however, to get a grasp of what conditions there are.

There are three types of investments: corporate bonds, blue-chip common stocks, and government securities. That is all there is, unless something new is introduced in one of the questions. There is one regulation: one-third each in blue chips and government securities, which means that only the last third is discretionary for Williams. His other idea is that for the next year he would like bonds.

Answering the Questions

13. **(D)** Since Williams thinks that bonds are the best investment, but he can only put one-third of the fund's assets into them because of the regulations, one-third to each type of investment is the best he can do, choice (D).

    (B) and (C) violate the regulation. (A) and (E) violate Williams' sense of what is the best investment at this time.

14. **(C)** Although we noted in the previous problem that the best investment strategy, according to Williams' view of things, is one-third to each type of investment, he COULD invest two-thirds in blue-chip stocks. The regulation only says that there is to be a minimum of the two categories, not a maximum. Two-thirds of $6 billion is $4 billion.

15. **(B)** This is a matter of what his preferences are. He likes bonds, so if the opportunity presents itself, he will buy them. (D) and (E) are entirely outside the scope of the problem set.

16. **(E)** Although the increase in the return of government securities sounds very large, this is not a question that depends on how closely you follow the investment markets. Within the scope of the problem, we cannot tell what this increase will mean. (A), (B), and (C) would only be good ideas if the new rate for government securities were higher than the rates for the other investments, which we simply do not know. If the rates were higher, he might well wish to change his investments. Hence, (D) is not adequate. (E) is the only possible answer.

17. **(D)** The key here is that he has invested one-third each in the three types of investments. This means that he has the minimum possible amount of government securities and blue chip stocks. If he sells off, he must take care to maintain at least one-third of each of the required investments. Selling only government securities and blue chip stocks will definitely lead him to an illegal situation, so (D) is not possible.

    The others are all acceptable since he can have more than one-third of the fund invested in a required security if he wants. Let us work (A) in detail as an example: Suppose he starts with 30 units of each type of investment:

    BONDS 30   STOCKS 30   GOV'T. SEC. 30

    If he sells twice as many bonds as stocks, say 20 and 10, he will still be legal since the stocks will still be one-third.

    BONDS 10   STOCKS 20   GOV'T. SEC. 30

Similar arguments apply to (B) and, in a more general way, to (C) and (E).

Questions 18–22

Arranging the Information

In a problem set of this sort, the major purpose of arranging the information in the beginning is to make it clear and easy to use. The points to note are that *both* calls and sales are used to judge Max's performance, so we cannot concentrate on just one of those factors. The statements that are phrased as "probably" should be construed as basically definite, especially in comparison to the even less certain other statements.

CUSTOMER	HOURS NEEDED	SALES IN BOXES
A	1	5
B	3	0 OR 20
C	1	10
D	1 TO 3	10 TO 30

Note that for Bell the sale will be either 0 or 20—not anything in between. Also, for Deland there is no connection between the number of hours he is there and the size of the order he lands. It will take as long as it takes, and he will make the sale that he makes.

Answering the Questions

18. **(A)** The reasonable maximum will be what happens if everything goes as well as it possibly can. If Deland takes two hours or less, Max can see all four customers. If he gets the maximum order from each, he will sell 5 + 20 + 10 + 30 = 65 boxes.

19. **(D)** Again the word reasonably implies that nothing really unexpected will happen. (A), none, is not at all expected. There is no real question about what the minimum for each customer is from the preceding chart. The real question is whether he sees them all or not. The problem answers this by noting that he will work eight hours, which is long enough for him to see all four customers. The minimum is, thus, 5 + 0 + 10 + 10 = 25 boxes.

20. **(C)** Max has 20 boxes sold, so the question is how many additional boxes can he sell from 2:00 P.M. to 5:00 P.M. If he sees Acme and Camera, he will probably sell 15 boxes, but if he spends those three hours at Bell, he might sell 20 boxes.

Thus, the maximum is 20 boxes to Deland and possibly 20 more to Camera, for a total of 40.

If you wanted to say (A), you probably were just saying how many he could sell in the afternoon, while the problem requested the "daily" sales figure.

21. **(C)** If Max schedules Deland after 2:00 P.M., that is improper. He could not know that he will have enough time since he must allow three hours for Deland if it happens to take that long. In addition, he would not want to omit Deland since they might give him his biggest order of the day and have the largest minimum order (tie with Camera).

For these reasons, (A), (B), and (D) are poor schedules.

(E) is defective because it schedules four hours of work starting at 2:00 P.M., which runs past the 5:00 P.M. deadline set by the problem.

Under schedule (C), Max will certainly see his best possibilities and still has a chance of seeing the fourth customer if things move quickly at Deland.

22. **(B)** In this situation, there is a 1½-hour slot before Edwards and 3½ hours afterward. (A) and (E) try to fit a three-hour customer into the 1½-hour slot, which is wrong. (C) claims to provide for seeing Deland if time permits, but the only flexibility is the Deland appointment itself, which cannot be forecast. Thus, (C) fails.

The difference between (D) and (B) is whether to be sure of Acme or Camera. Since Camera is a larger sale, it should get the guaranteed spot in the morning, eliminating (D).

A consideration not used much here, but of theoretical interest, is the choice between seeing Bell or Deland. He cannot see both of the three-hour customers. Deland is preferable to Bell for three reasons: (1) the minimum expected sale is higher, (2) the maximum expected sale is higher, and (3) there is the possibility of finishing early enough to also get to another customer.

23. **(E)** The point of the passage is that there is a seeming contradiction in our body of laws. Sometimes a person pays for his attempted misdeeds, and other times he does not pay for them. If there could be found a good reason for this difference, then the contradiction could be explained away. This is just what (E) does. It points out that the law treats the situations differently because it has different goals: Sometimes we drive fast because we are in a hurry, other times we drive slowly because we want to enjoy the scenery. (B) would not weaken the argument for it only intensifies the contradiction. (D) makes an attempt to reconcile the seemingly conflicting positions by hinting at a possible goal of one action that is not a goal of the other. But, if anything, it intensifies the contradiction because one might infer that we should not try persons for attempted crimes because criminal trials are expensive, but we should allow compensation for attempted frauds because civil trials are less expensive. (C) and (A) are just distractions. Whether there are more of one kind of law than another on the books has nothing to do with the seeming contradiction. And whether persons are more likely to commit a second crime after they are released from prison does not speak to the issue of whether an unsuccessful attempt to commit a crime should be a crime in the first place.

24. **(D)** The ad is weak for two reasons. First, although it is addressed to smokers in general, the evidence it cites is restricted to heavy (three-packs-a-day) smokers. Second, the success achieved by the product was restricted to a highly specific and unusual location—the mountain retreat of a clinic with a population trying hard to quit smoking. Thus, II will undermine the appeal of the advertisement because it cites the first of the weaknesses. III also will tell against the ad since it mentions the second of these weaknesses. I, however, is irrelevant to the ad's appeal since the cause of a smoker's addiction plays no role in the claim of this ad to assist smokers in quitting or cutting down.

25. **(A)** The question stem asks us to focus on the "dispute" between the two opponents. What will be relevant to it will be those items which affect the merits of the issues, or perhaps those which affect the credibility of the parties. (C) and (E) both mention items—facts and their source—which would be relevant to the substantive issues. (B) and (D) are legitimate attempts to clarify the issues and so are relevant. (A) is not relevant to the issues nor is it relevant to the credibility (e.g., where did the facts come from) of the debaters. (A) is the least relevant because it is an *ad hominem* attack of the illegitimate sort.

SECTION VII

1. **(D)** The first blank is parallel to the waiting list. Thus, garb is not very good for the first blank, since clothing is not very connected to psychologists. The aspect that is connected with psychologists is the act of lying on the couch. All the

choices except (E) are possibilities for the first blank, though (B) fails on usage grounds since one does not speak of the process *for* something, but the process *of* something in this context. Thus (A), (C), and (D) are still possible, though (D) is the best since it concerns the fact of lying on the couch rather than the plan or wish for it.

For the second blank, only (D) has real merit since the whole concept of psychological action is to have some sort of focus on oneself. Thus, overdoing it would be a preoccupation with oneself. Understanding is also a goal of psychological work, but not understanding *with,* since that usage means to have an agreement with someone. The appropriateness of prepositions, as we have discussed twice in this problem, is often a great help in solving sentence-completion problems.

2. **(C)** There is a contrast between the electronic technology and the law. The law is little and is like a horse and buggy; thus (C), outmoded, is an excellent choice for the second blank. The technology has become so much of what it is that it presents a problem. We speak of advanced technology as sophisticated. Only (D) and (C) have any merit for the first blank, and (C) is superior since the clandestine aspect of the technology does not relate well to the horse and buggy. Thus, (C) is the best answer choice.

3. **(A)** The flavor of the sentence is: "You did it, now you make it work." Thus, (A) is preferable. One might make a small case for (B) in the sense that the civilization should be meeting only Man's needs. But the word basic makes that a difficult interpretation to support, since there is nothing in the sentence to say that the author wishes to limit civilization only to Man's basic needs and leave out any other needs. Thus, (A) is preferable. (C), (D), and (E) fail to give any meaning at all without reading extra words into the sentence. (D), for example, might appeal a little if one read it as warrantable for meeting Man's basic needs, but it does not really say that.

4. **(D)** There is no need to claim that the author of the sentence is guilty of anything; thus, (E) fails. Or that he is about to be guilty of anything, so (C) fails. (A) is weak for both blanks. The idea of condescension usually requires another person and is, in any case, not a shivery feeling. A shivery feeling is fear, or apprehension, which means the same thing in this context. The echoing of the footsteps is also a shivery thing, so (D) is the best answer choice. (B), the second-best, fails because one would not normally speak of a shiver of indecision, and squeaky footsteps are neither indecisive nor fearsome.

5. **(D)** This is a difficult question in which all of the answers have some merit. The structure of the sentence is that the first blank has increased and, nevertheless, the second blank has not changed. Thus the two must have some sort of relationship between them in which one would have expected that the increase in the first would result in some sort of change in the second. (A) is slightly plausible since an increase in the popularity of running might make the runner less isolated, but a basic isolation is not a very clear idea. (B) is a little less meritorious since the increase in recognition does not mean that there will be an increase in reward, whether one means financial or psychological. (C) has more merit than either of the previous two in what it alludes to. However, (C) fails because equipment would not really increase. The number of pieces of equipment might increase, but not the equipment itself. Also, this use of feel is poor. (E) has the merit of saying that even though it is a more acceptable activity, it is still foolhardy. However, foolhardy refers to a human characteristic that runners might have, but running in the abstract would not. (D) is better than the others since speed and athletic technique would be expected to change together, but they have not. Speed is precisely the sort of thing about running that increases, and basic technique is a standard phrase. Thus, (D) is the best answer.

6. **(A)** There are two types of activities in the sentence: water sports and the blank. (D) fails because it includes water sports and it cannot be contrasted to itself. Similarly, snorkeling cannot be contrasted to water sports because it is part of water sports. (B) and (C) fail since they are not defined in the same way as water sports, which is a particular economic activity, while (B) and (C) are distinctions based on the auspices of an activity rather than its actual function. (A) is the only answer choice which gives an activity expected to be critical to the economy and which is a different kind of activity than water sports. Thus, (A) is the best answer.

7. **(C)** The idea of the sentence, its image, is of a bank account. Science is like a bank account and the basic research is the deposits that earn interest. Capital funds earn interest and none of the other answer choices do, except possibly (B), but there is nothing in the sentence to support the additional idea of endowment, so capital is preferable.

8. **(B)** The relationship between cotton and soft is clear: cotton is soft and is typically used as an example of softness. (D) is eliminated since the fact that wood will burn is not quite the same as the fact that cotton is soft. Even if the word in the

choice were flammable, it would still not be good enough. Silk's cost, nylon's strength, and wool's warmth are all true characteristics. However, silk would be used as an example of smoothness, not expense, and the original is talking about a physical characteristic, soft, and expense is not quite the same; thus, (E) fails. The warmth of wool is a characteristic which comes in use, but the same could be said of softness. The best way to contrast (A), (B), and (C) is to see how they relate to the original pair. Wool relates well to cotton, as does nylon. On the other hand, hard relates best to soft. In a case like this, the proper choice will depend on the internal relationship within each pair of words. Softness of a material is more akin to the hardness of a material than it is to warmth or strength. Even though the material is quite a different material, it is the relationship that is important, and where a characteristic is being given, the type of relationship is more dependent on the nature of the characteristic than it is on the nature of the material. Thus, (B) is the best answer.

9. **(B)** A chicken is the general name for the species. A rooster is the name for the male of the species. The same is true of duck and drake. (A) and (C) have female species names in the second position and are thus likely to be wrong. (E) has adult and child of the same species, which is not the significance of drake and duck. (D) is the second-best answer, but it has a distinctly female name first and then the male. Thus, (B) is the best answer.

10. **(C)** The conductor of an orchestra is in charge of directing the orchestra's playing and trying to get them to do their job as well as possible. The same could be said of the coach of a team. Neither the coach nor the conductor actually play, but they have an impact on the performance because they decide what shall be played and how it shall be played. (D) is a little off because of the use of the word playing as the second term. If the word cast had been used, or players, then it would have been an excellent answer since the original pair cited the actual performers, the orchestra, rather than the act itself as (D) does. Thus, (D) is inadequate. (B) and (E) have elements that may be in the original relationship, but they do not cover the entire situation. Only (C) does that, and thus is the best answer choice.

11. **(A)** Destroy and demolish are very similar words and both are negative. The same can be said of cry and wail. If there is any difference in degree or intensity, then the second term in each case may be slightly stronger. (D) has an opposite pair and thus is eliminated. (B) is not really a good match.

To break is not the same as to mar, which refers to destroying the beauty of something. (E) is unrelated and (C) is the second-best answer choice, but not negative. Thus, (A) is preferable.

12. **(E)** A funnel is used to collect liquid and get it into another container. A chimney has the same idea of providing a passage from one area to another, with a physical shape that is also similar if you include the entire chimney structure and not just the portion that sticks out of the roof. (B) is poor since the speaker creates the sound and the funnel does not create the liquid. (A) is moderately good, but since water is a kind of liquid, creating a strong secondary relationship, we would need to have a strong continuation of that between funnel and hose, which there is not. They are differently shaped and work differently. (C) and (D) do provide a means of passing a substance through a wall or other obstacle, but their physical shape has no relation to a funnel. The physical shape is particularly relevant here since the shape of the funnel is closely related to its function. Thus, (E) is the best answer.

13. **(D)** As a pendulum moves, it typically oscillates. As a gyroscope moves, it typically spins. Thus we have a balanced and repetitive motion that is the typical motion of a device in each case. None of the other answer choices share any of these characteristics.

14. **(A)** The premiere of a movie is its first public and official showing. Similarly the unveiling of a statue is its first public and official showing. A rookie in football is a player who is just starting his career, but there is no mention of his actual debut. Thus, (B) fails. (C) plays on the idea that a debutante is a teenager who is having her first social "season." However, the equivalent to the original pair would be something like DEBUTANTE : COMING-OUT BALL, or some such. (D) plays on the idea of a premier as a ruler, and (E) plays on the idea of premier as the best of something. These are both without merit as analogies here and are not even carried through very well in the choices themselves. Thus, (A) is the best answer.

15. **(C)** Pitch is a term used to describe the slope of a roof. Grade is a term used to describe the slope of a mountain. None of the other answer choices has any idea of measurement, much less this special type of measurement.

16. **(B)** The terms list and capsize are nautical ones. When a boat is listing, it is leaning over to one side or the other. When a boat capsizes, it turns over.

This is primarily a vocabulary question, and the other answers are not even close when the proper meanings of the stem words are known.

17. **(E)** This can be an easy problem if you let yourself take the easy road, which is that there is nothing on which to hook the answer to such a question. In practice, such questions are extremely rare, but this is good exercise in being certain of your understanding of the structure of the passage. Although Russian findings are reported, no American findings are mentioned; hence, (E).

18. **(D)** This question is simply a matter of not letting the technical jargon throw you. We are asked about the auditory center. The passage says that auditory centers of the odontocetes (just call them the O's) are the highest. What do we know about the O's? Well, they are the sperm whales and the porpoises, hence (D).

19. **(A)** Although (B), (C), (D), and (E) are all reasonable and even probably true characteristics of whale vocalization, they are not mentioned in the passage. The structure of (A) alerts you to consider the question of whether you are told the place in which the whales produce their sounds. You have been, and the larynx is somewhere in the throat. Since this is not particularly a vocabulary section, the odds are good that the issue is not whether you know exactly which portion of the throat is called the larynx; thus, (A) is the best answer.

20. **(E)** If you happen to know that cetaceans means whales, then the question is trivial and can be answered directly from the first sentence. However, the question is answerable, even if you do not know what cetaceans means before reading the passage. The first sentence says that cetaceans do not have vocal cords but make sounds. The rest of the passage discusses different kinds of sounds made by different whales. The implication is inescapable that the cetaceans are the whales. The passages on the test will not have one sentence that is totally unrelated to the rest of the passage.

21. **(B)** The council acted on the basis of a study that showed that automobiles were the major users of energy in the city. Further, the encouragement of bicycles and other automobile-use-reducing measures indicated that (B) is correct. (A), while perhaps true and an ancillary benefit of the bikeways, is not mentioned in the passage. (D) is false since the strong terms important and everyone are unsupported by the passage's almost

humorous reference to this action of the council. (E) is similarly too strong because of always. (C) has some superficial merit, but the passage does not really say that the measures undertaken by Davis are all modern or up to date. Some might well be viewed as old-fashioned, though excellent for saving energy. The standard applied to the actions was whether they save energy, not whether they are fashionable.

22. **(C)** The purpose of the demonstration homes was to show the local contractors that the new regulations could be met with ease. (B) and (E), thus, have some appeal, but the question asks why two instead of just one, which (C) addresses. (A) has a little merit in that it is certainly true that a demonstration project shows what you can do, but that was not why two houses instead of one were built. (D) has no basis.

23. **(E)** Here we must look to the reasons for writing an article about Davis. The first paragraph provides the best support for (E), though both (A) and (B) have some appeal. (C) is not an implication of the passage and (D) is trivial. (B) fails since the passage does not state that Davis wishes or needs to "spread" its message, since its actions were intended to be suited to its own particular circumstances. (A) is part of (E) and if (E) stands up, as it does, then it is preferable to (A) since it covers more of the passage.

24. **(B)** (A) and (E) are implied by the fact that codes take these positions. (D) is implied by the statement that the codes are to curb growth in order to limit energy use. (C) is implied by the lengthy debate held by the council. (B) is probably false since the council acted on the basis of the survey and would likely have delayed action, or refused it, if the survey was of doubtful accuracy. Thus, (B) is a better answer than (C).

25. **(C)** The fact that Davis has thousands of trees and a fleet of cars indicates that it is not a tiny town, yet the utility of bikeways for general transportation even by city employees indicates that Davis is not too large either. The limitation of the model homes to single- and two-family dwellings also indicates less than major urban concentration, as does the recycling center's sales volume.

(A) is a meaningless term not defined in the passage. (B) has to do with social issues not dealt with in the passage at all. The citizens of Davis could be all kinds of horrible things and still be concerned enough to save energy. (D) has the tempting half-truth that it is known that the city has a council, but nothing is said of a manager, mayor, or whatever else there might be. The lack of reference to a mayor is some small argument against it, but not for a manager. (E) is unsupported by the passage in any way.

26. **(A)** The analysis of energy-use patterns in Davis does not even mention industry, and thus supports (A). (B) has some merit, but is stated in terms— "any further"—too strong to be supported. If (C) means that the same actions will work in any city, this is clearly false since Davis' actions are based on a close analysis of its own situation. The passage does support the idea that other cities should do something about their energy use, but it is perhaps too strong to say "any" city. (E) is good and bad in the same ways as (C). Yes, planning helps, but not necessarily to solve all problems. Also, the passage only speaks to energy management, not to crime, etc. (D) has no support. Even in Davis, the automobile was only restricted, not eliminated, and nothing in the passage would support that conclusion.

27. **(B)** (B) is known to be false since the feasibility of meeting the new code was demonstrated by the two model houses. The answer choice does not address the question of whether the builders will meet the code, only that they can.

    (A) will mean more energy even if each person uses less. (C) clearly means more energy, and (E) explains the discrepancy very easily. (D) shows that more cars were used, but has the weakness that we are unsure of the breakdown between cars and bicycles before the energy survey. However, the passage noted that the town had been involved in building bikeways in 1968, four years before the 1972 survey. This means that reduced bicycle use will reflect on the 1972 results.

28. **(D)** Infirm means sickly and unhealthy, thus healthy is a good opposite. (E) might appeal since firm by itself can mean stable, as in a firm foundation, and infirm does mean unstable, but it refers particularly to health and thus healthy is better. The other choices are unrelated.

29. **(A)** Lamentation is to grieve for something, thus a state of deep sadness. Jubilation is a state of exhilarated happiness. (B) might possibly appeal if you based your answer on some sort of similarity between cement and lament—the sort of grasping at straws which is the hallmark of a poor guess. The tiny similarity in a sea of differences is more likely to yield a poor answer than a good one.

30. **(E)** Lechery means indulgence of lust and, as usually used, has a negative sexual connotation. Chastity also has a sexual connotation and means precisely a lack of indulgence in lust. Karma means fate and is not even the same word as used in the title of the *Kama Sutra,* the famous Hindu text that is well known for its sexual commentaries.

31. **(A)** To scotch something is to stop it. To foster it is to help it along and promote it. To quail means to lose heart; sully means to dirty; a teetotaler is opposed to drinking alcohol, but that does not make teetotal the opposite word to scotch.

32. **(E)** Querulous means full of complaints. Thus, (E) is a good opposite since a satisfied person will not have any complaints. (D), sated, also has merit since it means to satisfy an appetite or desire to the full. This is a close decision and the nod can be given to satisfied either because it is more general or because querulous often refers to a tone of voice, as does satisifed, while sated would not usually do that. They are close, however, and you will not see anything closer on the test. (B) might appeal if you had little idea of the meaning of querulous, since to query is to ask and asking might be opposite to not curious. It would not have been a bad guess, but it would have been wrong.

33. **(D)** Desuetude is the state of no longer being in use or practice. Use is the opposite. It would be hard to guess the meaning of desuetude since it looks rather different from use.

34. **(B)** Delectable means delightful and enjoyable. Unpleasant is a very good opposite. Manifold may refer to a part of a car as a noun. As an adjective it means many and various. Colossal means gigantic, particularly in physical size, after the Colossus of Rhodes. Imperious, deriving from imperial, means domineering or overbearing.

35. **(D)** Obdurate means extremely stubborn; hence (D) is a perfect opposite. Durable shares the root *dur-,* meaning hard, but does not mean the opposite. This is pretty much a question of knowing the word, though if you were guessing, you might marginally eliminate (C) since it is not clearly opposite and shares a root.

36. **(C)** Blandishment is flattery, so criticism is its opposite. (A) would appeal on the basis of color being the opposite of bland. However, bland does not originally mean without flavor, as it is sometimes used, but rather gentle and agreeable or non-stimulating. The agreeable idea has led to blandishment, which is agreeable speech or flattery. Spiciness and piquancy, both of which means sharp-flavoredness, are opposites to the idea of bland, perhaps, but not to blandishment. The

test-makers would call this a precision question that tests your precise knowledge of the word.

37. **(A)** Niggardly means parsimonious or stingy; hence lavish, meaning openhanded or generous, is a fairly good opposite. The term lavish is not often used to describe a person's character, but rather the scope of some event or the preparation for an event, such as lavish catering. Destitute means without any money. Peccant means sinning or faulty, and is related to peccadillo, meaning a small sin. Something cloys when there is too much of it and the senses can no longer appreciate it. Too many sweets are particularly cloying. There is an idea of much here, but not enough to be an opposite to niggardly. A palliative is something that improves a bad condition.

38. **(C)** Vacuous means without meaning. Insightful means having great meaning. Both words are used to describe the quality and merit of comments, but with opposite significance. Precognition is the ability to tell the future; precocious means to be advanced beyond one's years.

ANSWER SHEET—PRACTICE EXAMINATION 3

Section I

1 Ⓐ Ⓑ Ⓒ Ⓓ Ⓔ   8 Ⓐ Ⓑ Ⓒ Ⓓ Ⓔ   15 Ⓐ Ⓑ Ⓒ Ⓓ Ⓔ   22 Ⓐ Ⓑ Ⓒ Ⓓ Ⓔ   29 Ⓐ Ⓑ Ⓒ Ⓓ Ⓔ   36 Ⓐ Ⓑ Ⓒ Ⓓ Ⓔ

2 Ⓐ Ⓑ Ⓒ Ⓓ Ⓔ   9 Ⓐ Ⓑ Ⓒ Ⓓ Ⓔ   16 Ⓐ Ⓑ Ⓒ Ⓓ Ⓔ   23 Ⓐ Ⓑ Ⓒ Ⓓ Ⓔ   30 Ⓐ Ⓑ Ⓒ Ⓓ Ⓔ   37 Ⓐ Ⓑ Ⓒ Ⓓ Ⓔ

3 Ⓐ Ⓑ Ⓒ Ⓓ Ⓔ   10 Ⓐ Ⓑ Ⓒ Ⓓ Ⓔ   17 Ⓐ Ⓑ Ⓒ Ⓓ Ⓔ   24 Ⓐ Ⓑ Ⓒ Ⓓ Ⓔ   31 Ⓐ Ⓑ Ⓒ Ⓓ Ⓔ   38 Ⓐ Ⓑ Ⓒ Ⓓ Ⓔ

4 Ⓐ Ⓑ Ⓒ Ⓓ Ⓔ   11 Ⓐ Ⓑ Ⓒ Ⓓ Ⓔ   18 Ⓐ Ⓑ Ⓒ Ⓓ Ⓔ   25 Ⓐ Ⓑ Ⓒ Ⓓ Ⓔ   32 Ⓐ Ⓑ Ⓒ Ⓓ Ⓔ

5 Ⓐ Ⓑ Ⓒ Ⓓ Ⓔ   12 Ⓐ Ⓑ Ⓒ Ⓓ Ⓔ   19 Ⓐ Ⓑ Ⓒ Ⓓ Ⓔ   26 Ⓐ Ⓑ Ⓒ Ⓓ Ⓔ   33 Ⓐ Ⓑ Ⓒ Ⓓ Ⓔ

6 Ⓐ Ⓑ Ⓒ Ⓓ Ⓔ   13 Ⓐ Ⓑ Ⓒ Ⓓ Ⓔ   20 Ⓐ Ⓑ Ⓒ Ⓓ Ⓔ   27 Ⓐ Ⓑ Ⓒ Ⓓ Ⓔ   34 Ⓐ Ⓑ Ⓒ Ⓓ Ⓔ

7 Ⓐ Ⓑ Ⓒ Ⓓ Ⓔ   14 Ⓐ Ⓑ Ⓒ Ⓓ Ⓔ   21 Ⓐ Ⓑ Ⓒ Ⓓ Ⓔ   28 Ⓐ Ⓑ Ⓒ Ⓓ Ⓔ   35 Ⓐ Ⓑ Ⓒ Ⓓ Ⓔ

Section II

1 Ⓐ Ⓑ Ⓒ Ⓓ Ⓔ   8 Ⓐ Ⓑ Ⓒ Ⓓ Ⓔ   15 Ⓐ Ⓑ Ⓒ Ⓓ Ⓔ   22 Ⓐ Ⓑ Ⓒ Ⓓ Ⓔ   29 Ⓐ Ⓑ Ⓒ Ⓓ Ⓔ   36 Ⓐ Ⓑ Ⓒ Ⓓ Ⓔ

2 Ⓐ Ⓑ Ⓒ Ⓓ Ⓔ   9 Ⓐ Ⓑ Ⓒ Ⓓ Ⓔ   16 Ⓐ Ⓑ Ⓒ Ⓓ Ⓔ   23 Ⓐ Ⓑ Ⓒ Ⓓ Ⓔ   30 Ⓐ Ⓑ Ⓒ Ⓓ Ⓔ   37 Ⓐ Ⓑ Ⓒ Ⓓ Ⓔ

3 Ⓐ Ⓑ Ⓒ Ⓓ Ⓔ   10 Ⓐ Ⓑ Ⓒ Ⓓ Ⓔ   17 Ⓐ Ⓑ Ⓒ Ⓓ Ⓔ   24 Ⓐ Ⓑ Ⓒ Ⓓ Ⓔ   31 Ⓐ Ⓑ Ⓒ Ⓓ Ⓔ   38 Ⓐ Ⓑ Ⓒ Ⓓ Ⓔ

4 Ⓐ Ⓑ Ⓒ Ⓓ Ⓔ   11 Ⓐ Ⓑ Ⓒ Ⓓ Ⓔ   18 Ⓐ Ⓑ Ⓒ Ⓓ Ⓔ   25 Ⓐ Ⓑ Ⓒ Ⓓ Ⓔ   32 Ⓐ Ⓑ Ⓒ Ⓓ Ⓔ

5 Ⓐ Ⓑ Ⓒ Ⓓ Ⓔ   12 Ⓐ Ⓑ Ⓒ Ⓓ Ⓔ   19 Ⓐ Ⓑ Ⓒ Ⓓ Ⓔ   26 Ⓐ Ⓑ Ⓒ Ⓓ Ⓔ   33 Ⓐ Ⓑ Ⓒ Ⓓ Ⓔ

6 Ⓐ Ⓑ Ⓒ Ⓓ Ⓔ   13 Ⓐ Ⓑ Ⓒ Ⓓ Ⓔ   20 Ⓐ Ⓑ Ⓒ Ⓓ Ⓔ   27 Ⓐ Ⓑ Ⓒ Ⓓ Ⓔ   34 Ⓐ Ⓑ Ⓒ Ⓓ Ⓔ

7 Ⓐ Ⓑ Ⓒ Ⓓ Ⓔ   14 Ⓐ Ⓑ Ⓒ Ⓓ Ⓔ   21 Ⓐ Ⓑ Ⓒ Ⓓ Ⓔ   28 Ⓐ Ⓑ Ⓒ Ⓓ Ⓔ   35 Ⓐ Ⓑ Ⓒ Ⓓ Ⓔ

Section III

1 Ⓐ Ⓑ Ⓒ Ⓓ Ⓔ   6 Ⓐ Ⓑ Ⓒ Ⓓ Ⓔ   11 Ⓐ Ⓑ Ⓒ Ⓓ Ⓔ   16 Ⓐ Ⓑ Ⓒ Ⓓ Ⓔ   21 Ⓐ Ⓑ Ⓒ Ⓓ Ⓔ   26 Ⓐ Ⓑ Ⓒ Ⓓ Ⓔ

2 Ⓐ Ⓑ Ⓒ Ⓓ Ⓔ   7 Ⓐ Ⓑ Ⓒ Ⓓ Ⓔ   12 Ⓐ Ⓑ Ⓒ Ⓓ Ⓔ   17 Ⓐ Ⓑ Ⓒ Ⓓ Ⓔ   22 Ⓐ Ⓑ Ⓒ Ⓓ Ⓔ   27 Ⓐ Ⓑ Ⓒ Ⓓ Ⓔ

3 Ⓐ Ⓑ Ⓒ Ⓓ Ⓔ   8 Ⓐ Ⓑ Ⓒ Ⓓ Ⓔ   13 Ⓐ Ⓑ Ⓒ Ⓓ Ⓔ   18 Ⓐ Ⓑ Ⓒ Ⓓ Ⓔ   23 Ⓐ Ⓑ Ⓒ Ⓓ Ⓔ   28 Ⓐ Ⓑ Ⓒ Ⓓ Ⓔ

4 Ⓐ Ⓑ Ⓒ Ⓓ Ⓔ   9 Ⓐ Ⓑ Ⓒ Ⓓ Ⓔ   14 Ⓐ Ⓑ Ⓒ Ⓓ Ⓔ   19 Ⓐ Ⓑ Ⓒ Ⓓ Ⓔ   24 Ⓐ Ⓑ Ⓒ Ⓓ Ⓔ   29 Ⓐ Ⓑ Ⓒ Ⓓ Ⓔ

5 Ⓐ Ⓑ Ⓒ Ⓓ Ⓔ   10 Ⓐ Ⓑ Ⓒ Ⓓ Ⓔ   15 Ⓐ Ⓑ Ⓒ Ⓓ Ⓔ   20 Ⓐ Ⓑ Ⓒ Ⓓ Ⓔ   25 Ⓐ Ⓑ Ⓒ Ⓓ Ⓔ   30 Ⓐ Ⓑ Ⓒ Ⓓ Ⓔ

Section IV

1 Ⓐ Ⓑ Ⓒ Ⓓ Ⓔ   6 Ⓐ Ⓑ Ⓒ Ⓓ Ⓔ   11 Ⓐ Ⓑ Ⓒ Ⓓ Ⓔ   16 Ⓐ Ⓑ Ⓒ Ⓓ Ⓔ   21 Ⓐ Ⓑ Ⓒ Ⓓ Ⓔ   26 Ⓐ Ⓑ Ⓒ Ⓓ Ⓔ

2 Ⓐ Ⓑ Ⓒ Ⓓ Ⓔ   7 Ⓐ Ⓑ Ⓒ Ⓓ Ⓔ   12 Ⓐ Ⓑ Ⓒ Ⓓ Ⓔ   17 Ⓐ Ⓑ Ⓒ Ⓓ Ⓔ   22 Ⓐ Ⓑ Ⓒ Ⓓ Ⓔ   27 Ⓐ Ⓑ Ⓒ Ⓓ Ⓔ

3 Ⓐ Ⓑ Ⓒ Ⓓ Ⓔ   8 Ⓐ Ⓑ Ⓒ Ⓓ Ⓔ   13 Ⓐ Ⓑ Ⓒ Ⓓ Ⓔ   18 Ⓐ Ⓑ Ⓒ Ⓓ Ⓔ   23 Ⓐ Ⓑ Ⓒ Ⓓ Ⓔ   28 Ⓐ Ⓑ Ⓒ Ⓓ Ⓔ

4 Ⓐ Ⓑ Ⓒ Ⓓ Ⓔ   9 Ⓐ Ⓑ Ⓒ Ⓓ Ⓔ   14 Ⓐ Ⓑ Ⓒ Ⓓ Ⓔ   19 Ⓐ Ⓑ Ⓒ Ⓓ Ⓔ   24 Ⓐ Ⓑ Ⓒ Ⓓ Ⓔ   29 Ⓐ Ⓑ Ⓒ Ⓓ Ⓔ

5 Ⓐ Ⓑ Ⓒ Ⓓ Ⓔ   10 Ⓐ Ⓑ Ⓒ Ⓓ Ⓔ   15 Ⓐ Ⓑ Ⓒ Ⓓ Ⓔ   20 Ⓐ Ⓑ Ⓒ Ⓓ Ⓔ   25 Ⓐ Ⓑ Ⓒ Ⓓ Ⓔ   30 Ⓐ Ⓑ Ⓒ Ⓓ Ⓔ

Section V

1 Ⓐ Ⓑ Ⓒ Ⓓ Ⓔ   6 Ⓐ Ⓑ Ⓒ Ⓓ Ⓔ   11 Ⓐ Ⓑ Ⓒ Ⓓ Ⓔ   16 Ⓐ Ⓑ Ⓒ Ⓓ Ⓔ   21 Ⓐ Ⓑ Ⓒ Ⓓ Ⓔ

2 Ⓐ Ⓑ Ⓒ Ⓓ Ⓔ   7 Ⓐ Ⓑ Ⓒ Ⓓ Ⓔ   12 Ⓐ Ⓑ Ⓒ Ⓓ Ⓔ   17 Ⓐ Ⓑ Ⓒ Ⓓ Ⓔ   22 Ⓐ Ⓑ Ⓒ Ⓓ Ⓔ

3 Ⓐ Ⓑ Ⓒ Ⓓ Ⓔ   8 Ⓐ Ⓑ Ⓒ Ⓓ Ⓔ   13 Ⓐ Ⓑ Ⓒ Ⓓ Ⓔ   18 Ⓐ Ⓑ Ⓒ Ⓓ Ⓔ   23 Ⓐ Ⓑ Ⓒ Ⓓ Ⓔ

4 Ⓐ Ⓑ Ⓒ Ⓓ Ⓔ   9 Ⓐ Ⓑ Ⓒ Ⓓ Ⓔ   14 Ⓐ Ⓑ Ⓒ Ⓓ Ⓔ   19 Ⓐ Ⓑ Ⓒ Ⓓ Ⓔ   24 Ⓐ Ⓑ Ⓒ Ⓓ Ⓔ

5 Ⓐ Ⓑ Ⓒ Ⓓ Ⓔ   10 Ⓐ Ⓑ Ⓒ Ⓓ Ⓔ   15 Ⓐ Ⓑ Ⓒ Ⓓ Ⓔ   20 Ⓐ Ⓑ Ⓒ Ⓓ Ⓔ   25 Ⓐ Ⓑ Ⓒ Ⓓ Ⓔ

Section VI

1 Ⓐ Ⓑ Ⓒ Ⓓ Ⓔ   6 Ⓐ Ⓑ Ⓒ Ⓓ Ⓔ   11 Ⓐ Ⓑ Ⓒ Ⓓ Ⓔ   16 Ⓐ Ⓑ Ⓒ Ⓓ Ⓔ   21 Ⓐ Ⓑ Ⓒ Ⓓ Ⓔ

2 Ⓐ Ⓑ Ⓒ Ⓓ Ⓔ   7 Ⓐ Ⓑ Ⓒ Ⓓ Ⓔ   12 Ⓐ Ⓑ Ⓒ Ⓓ Ⓔ   17 Ⓐ Ⓑ Ⓒ Ⓓ Ⓔ   22 Ⓐ Ⓑ Ⓒ Ⓓ Ⓔ

3 Ⓐ Ⓑ Ⓒ Ⓓ Ⓔ   8 Ⓐ Ⓑ Ⓒ Ⓓ Ⓔ   13 Ⓐ Ⓑ Ⓒ Ⓓ Ⓔ   18 Ⓐ Ⓑ Ⓒ Ⓓ Ⓔ   23 Ⓐ Ⓑ Ⓒ Ⓓ Ⓔ

4 Ⓐ Ⓑ Ⓒ Ⓓ Ⓔ   9 Ⓐ Ⓑ Ⓒ Ⓓ Ⓔ   14 Ⓐ Ⓑ Ⓒ Ⓓ Ⓔ   19 Ⓐ Ⓑ Ⓒ Ⓓ Ⓔ   24 Ⓐ Ⓑ Ⓒ Ⓓ Ⓔ

5 Ⓐ Ⓑ Ⓒ Ⓓ Ⓔ   10 Ⓐ Ⓑ Ⓒ Ⓓ Ⓔ   15 Ⓐ Ⓑ Ⓒ Ⓓ Ⓔ   20 Ⓐ Ⓑ Ⓒ Ⓓ Ⓔ   25 Ⓐ Ⓑ Ⓒ Ⓓ Ⓔ

Section VII

1 Ⓐ Ⓑ Ⓒ Ⓓ Ⓔ   6 Ⓐ Ⓑ Ⓒ Ⓓ Ⓔ   11 Ⓐ Ⓑ Ⓒ Ⓓ Ⓔ   16 Ⓐ Ⓑ Ⓒ Ⓓ Ⓔ   21 Ⓐ Ⓑ Ⓒ Ⓓ Ⓔ

2 Ⓐ Ⓑ Ⓒ Ⓓ Ⓔ   7 Ⓐ Ⓑ Ⓒ Ⓓ Ⓔ   12 Ⓐ Ⓑ Ⓒ Ⓓ Ⓔ   17 Ⓐ Ⓑ Ⓒ Ⓓ Ⓔ   22 Ⓐ Ⓑ Ⓒ Ⓓ Ⓔ

3 Ⓐ Ⓑ Ⓒ Ⓓ Ⓔ   8 Ⓐ Ⓑ Ⓒ Ⓓ Ⓔ   13 Ⓐ Ⓑ Ⓒ Ⓓ Ⓔ   18 Ⓐ Ⓑ Ⓒ Ⓓ Ⓔ   23 Ⓐ Ⓑ Ⓒ Ⓓ Ⓔ

4 Ⓐ Ⓑ Ⓒ Ⓓ Ⓔ   9 Ⓐ Ⓑ Ⓒ Ⓓ Ⓔ   14 Ⓐ Ⓑ Ⓒ Ⓓ Ⓔ   19 Ⓐ Ⓑ Ⓒ Ⓓ Ⓔ   24 Ⓐ Ⓑ Ⓒ Ⓓ Ⓔ

5 Ⓐ Ⓑ Ⓒ Ⓓ Ⓔ   10 Ⓐ Ⓑ Ⓒ Ⓓ Ⓔ   15 Ⓐ Ⓑ Ⓒ Ⓓ Ⓔ   20 Ⓐ Ⓑ Ⓒ Ⓓ Ⓔ   25 Ⓐ Ⓑ Ⓒ Ⓓ Ⓔ

PRACTICE EXAMINATION 3

SECTION I

30 minutes
38 questions

Directions: Each of the questions below contains one or more blank spaces, each blank indicating an omitted word. Each sentence is followed by five (5) lettered words or sets of words. Read and determine the general sense of each sentence. Then choose the word or set of words which, when inserted in the sentence, best fits the meaning of the sentence.

1. We should have _____ trouble ahead when the road _____ into a gravel path.
   (A) interrogated—shrank
   (B) anticipated—dwindled
   (C) expected—grew
   (D) enjoyed—transformed
   (E) seen—collapsed

2. The _____ of the waiter, fresh lobster, was all gone, so we _____ ourselves with crab.
   (A) suggestion—resolved
   (B) embarrassment—consoled
   (C) recommendation—contented
   (D) specialty—pelted
   (E) regrets—relieved

3. The _____ workroom had not been used in years.
   (A) derelict
   (B) bustling
   (C) bereft
   (D) bereaved
   (E) stricken

4. Tempers ran hot among the old-timers, who _____ the young mayor and his _____ city council.

(A) despised—attractive
(B) admired—elite
(C) resented—reform
(D) forgave—activist
(E) feared—apathetic

5. With the discovery of _____ alternative fuel source, oil prices dropped significantly.
   (A) a potential
   (B) a feasible
   (C) a possible
   (D) a variant
   (E) an inexpensive

6. The masters of the world are the bacteria and viruses. They _____ all other life and all other life lives and reproduces merely to provide them with _____.
   (A) dominate—companionship
   (B) outnumber—room and board
   (C) infest—opportunity
   (D) serve—shelter
   (E) are symbiotic with—partners

7. He could understand that his prisoners would _____ him at first, but he had hoped that after all this time his fairness would inspire _____ rather than trepidation at his arrival.
   (A) misunderstand—love
   (B) escape—cordiality
   (C) abhor—loyalty
   (D) dislike—camaraderie
   (E) fear—trust

Directions: In each of the following questions, you are given a related pair of words or phrases in capital letters. Each capitalized pair is followed by five (5) lettered pairs of words or phrases. Choose the pair which best expresses a relationship similar to that expressed by the original pair.

8. CAT : MOUSE ::
   (A) bird : worm
   (B) dog : tail
   (C) trap : cheese
   (D) hide : seek
   (E) lion : snake

9. VANILLA : BEAN ::
   (A) tabasco : stem
   (B) chili : seed
   (C) mint : flower
   (D) ginger : root
   (E) sage : berry

10. ENERGY : DISSIPATE ::
    (A) battery : recharge
    (B) atom : split
    (C) food : eat
    (D) money : squander
    (E) gas : generate

11. NOSE : FACE ::
    (A) ring : finger
    (B) stem : root
    (C) knob : door
    (D) shoe : foot
    (E) vine : building

12. RIFLE : SOLDIER ::
    (A) bow : arrow
    (B) sword : knight
    (C) horse : cowboy
    (D) marine: tank
    (E) lock : robber

13. DEER : VENISON ::
    (A) pig : hog
    (B) sheep : mutton
    (C) lamb : veal
    (D) steer : stew
    (E) beef : stew

14. INEFFABLE : KNOWLEDGE ::
    (A) genial : interesting
    (B) puzzling : trick
    (C) frustrating : release
    (D) baffling : solution
    (E) controllable : rage

15. ICING : CAKE ::
    (A) veneer : table
    (B) ice : pond
    (C) pastry : bake
    (D) apple : pie
    (E) printing : page

16. CHALK : BLACKBOARD ::
    (A) door : handle
    (B) table : chair
    (C) ink : paper
    (D) pencil : writing
    (E) paint : wall

Directions: Below each of the following passages, you will find questions or incomplete statements about the passage. Each statement or question is followed by lettered words or expressions. Select the word or expression that most satisfactorily completes each statement or answers each question in accordance with the meaning of the passage. After you choose the best answer, blacken the corresponding space on the answer sheet.

There is a confused notion in the minds of many persons, that the gathering of the property of the poor into the hands of the rich does no ultimate harm, since in whosesoever hands it may be, it must be spent at last, and thus, they think, return to the poor again. This fallacy has been again and again exposed; but granting the plea true, the same apology may, of course, be made for blackmail, or any other form of robbery. It might be (though practically it never is) as advantageous for the nation that the robber should have the spending of the money he extorts, as that the person robbed should have spent it. But this is no excuse for the theft. If I were to put a turnpike on the road where it passes my own gate, and endeavor to exact a shilling from every passenger, the public would soon do away with my gate, without listening to any pleas on my part that it was as advantageous to them, in the end, that I should spend their shillings, as that they themselves should. But if, instead of outfacing them with a turnpike, I can only persuade them to come in and buy stones, or old iron, or any other useless thing, out of my ground, I may rob them to the same extent, and be moreover, thanked as a public benefactor and promoter of commercial prosperity. And this main question for the poor of England—for the poor of all countries—is wholly omitted in every treatise on the subject of wealth. Even by the laborers themselves, the operation of capital is regarded only in its effect on their immediate interests, never in the far more terrific power of its appointment of the kind and the object of labor. It matters little, ultimately, how much a laborer is paid for making anything; but it matters fearfully what the thing is, which he is compelled to make. If his labor is so ordered as to produce food, fresh air, and fresh water, no matter that his wages are low;—the food and the fresh air and water will be at last there, and he will at last get them. But if he is paid to destroy food and fresh air, or to produce iron bars instead of them,—the food and air will finally *not* be there, and he will *not* get them, to his great and final inconvenience. So that, conclusively, in political as in household economy, the great question is, not so much what money you have in your pocket, as what you will buy with it and do with it.

17. We may infer that the author probably lived in the
    (A) 1960's in the United States
    (B) early days of British industrialization
    (C) 18th-century France
    (D) Golden Age of Greece
    (E) England of King Arthur

18. It can be inferred that the author probably favors
    (A) capitalism
    (B) totalitarianism
    (C) socialism
    (D) anarchism
    (E) theocracy

19. According to the passage, the individual should be particularly concerned with
    (A) how much wealth he can accumulate
    (B) the acquisition of land property rather than money
    (C) charging the customer a fair price
    (D) the quality of goods which he purchases with his funds
    (E) working as hard as possible

20. The passage implies that
    (A) "A stitch in time saves nine."
    (B) "It is better late than never."
    (C) "He who steals my purse steals trash."
    (D) "None but the brave deserve the fair"
    (E) "All's well that ends well."

21. It can be inferred that in regard to the accumulation of wealth the author
    (A) equates the rich with the thief
    (B) indicates that there are few honest businessmen
    (C) condones some dishonesty in business dealings
    (D) believes destruction of property is good because it creates consumer demand
    (E) says that the robber is a benefactor

22. What is the "main question for the poor" referred to by the author in the passages?
    (A) the use to which the laborer can put his money
    (B) the methods by which capital may be accumulated
    (C) the results of their work and their lack of authority to determine to what ends their work shall be put
    (D) whether full measure of recompense shall be accorded to the laboring person for the investment of his time in worthy work
    (E) the extent to which a man can call his life his own

23. According to the views expressed in the passage, people should be happiest doing which of the following?
    (A) mining ore for the manufacture of weapons
    (B) cleaning sewage ponds at a treatment plant
    (C) waiting tables for a rich man
    (D) helping a poor man do his job
    (E) studying economic theory

24. The author of the above passage would probably react to an energy shortage by
    (A) blaming the rich for the problem
    (B) urging that energy be used more efficiently and effectively
    (C) supporting the search for more oil,

coal, and other energy-producing mineral deposits
(D) denying that there is really any shortage at all
(E) fomenting revolution by the poor

Man, said Aristotle, is a social animal. This sociability requires peaceful congregation, and the history of mankind is mainly a movement through time of human collectivities that range from migrant tribal bands to large and complex civilizations. Survival has been due to the ability to create the means by which men in groups retain their unity and allegiance to one another.

Order was caused by the need and desire to survive the challenge of the environment. This orderly condition came to be called the "state," and the rules that maintained it, the "law." With time the partner to this tranquillity, man marched across the centuries of his evolution to the brink of exploring the boundaries of his own galaxy. Of all living organisms, only man has the capacity to interpret his own evolution as progress. As social life changed, the worth and rights of each member in the larger group, of which he was a part, increased. As the groups grew from clans to civilizations, the value of the individual did not diminish, but became instead a guide to the rules that govern all men.

25. The best expression of the main idea of this article is
(A) oppression and society
(B) the evolution of man
(C) man's animal instincts
(D) the basis for social order
(E) a history of violence and strife

26. The author would expect the greatest attention to individual rights and values to be found in
(A) farming communities
(B) small villages
(C) prehistoric families
(D) nomadic tribes
(E) modern cities

27. According to the article, man's uniqueness is attributed to the fact that he is
(A) evolving from a simpler to a more complex being

(B) a social animal
(C) capable of noting his own progress
(D) capable of inflicting injury and causing violence
(E) able to survive by forming groups with allegiance to one another

Directions: Each of the following questions consists of a word printed in capital letters, followed by five (5) lettered words or phrases. Select the word or phrase which is most nearly *opposite* to the capitalized word in meaning.

28. REFRACTORY:
(A) refreshing
(B) burdensome
(C) privileged
(D) manageable
(E) upright

29. ADROIT:
(A) deterred
(B) skillful
(C) foolish
(D) sinister
(E) awkward

30. PALLIATE:
(A) apologize
(B) hesitate
(C) wait impatiently
(D) decide finally
(E) worsen

31. VILIFY:
(A) sing the praises of
(B) show satisfaction with
(C) regard with distrust
(D) welcome with glee
(E) accept halfheartedly

32. IRASCIBLE:
(A) placid
(B) fortuitous
(C) shameless
(D) entrancing
(E) yielding

33. GELID:
(A) chilly

(B) solid
(C) mature
(D) pallid
(E) boiling

34. CONDIGN:
(A) unavoidable
(B) unsatisfactory
(C) unguarded
(D) undeserved
(E) uninitiated

35. PUNCTILIOUS:
(A) tardy
(B) correct
(C) careless
(D) apathetic
(E) repulsive

36. FECKLESS:
(A) spotted
(B) fatuous
(C) fawning
(D) strong
(E) calm

37. INSOLENT:
(A) sullen
(B) rich
(C) determined
(D) kind
(E) affable

38. SERENDIPITOUS:
(A) calm
(B) planned
(C) flat
(D) evil
(E) regulated

STOP

END OF SECTION. IF YOU HAVE ANY TIME LEFT, GO
OVER YOUR WORK IN THIS SECTION ONLY. DO NOT
WORK IN ANY OTHER SECTION OF THE TEST.

SECTION II

30 minutes
38 questions

Directions: Each of the questions below contains one or more blank spaces, each blank indicating an omitted word. Each sentence is followed by five (5) lettered words or sets of words. Read and determine the general sense of the sentence. Then choose the word or set of words which, when inserted in the sentence, best fits the meaning of the sentence.

1. The product of a _____ religious home, he often found _____ in prayer.
(A) zealously—distraction
(B) devoutly—solace
(C) vigorously—comfort

(D) fanatically—misgivings
(E) pious—answers

2. Our _____ objections finally got us thrown out of the stadium.
(A) hurled
(B) modest
(C) wary
(D) vocal
(E) pliant

3. Only a single wall still stood in mute _____ to Nature's force.
(A) evidence

(B) tribute
(C) remainder
(D) memory
(E) testimony

4. After completing her usual morning chores, Linda found herself _____ tired.
    (A) surprisingly
    (B) erratically
    (C) buoyantly
    (D) forcibly
    (E) unceasingly

5. The current spirit of _____ among the various departments of the university have led to a number of _____ publications which might not otherwise have been written.
    (A) competition—angry
    (B) futility—significant
    (C) cooperation—interdisciplinary
    (D) patriotism—American
    (E) machoism—pugilistic

6. Human senses are designed to ____ specific stimuli, and after a focus is achieved, other sensory data is _____.
    (A) look for—heightened
    (B) respond to—insulated
    (C) concentrate on—discounted
    (D) favor—added up
    (E) create—born

7. Immigrants arriving in a new country have the special problem of _____ their established behaviors and learning new habits whose results are _____.
    (A) abandoning—uncertain
    (B) strengthening—different
    (C) controlling—guaranteed
    (D) loosening—definite
    (E) maintaining—simpler

Directions: In each of the following questions, you are given a related pair of words or phrases in capital letters. Each capitalized pair is followed by five (5) lettered pairs of words or phrases. Choose the pair which best expresses a relationship similar to that expressed by the original pair.

8. MONEY : EMBEZZLEMENT ::
    (A) bank : cashier
    (B) writing : plagiarism
    (C) remarks : insult
    (D) radiation : bomb
    (E) death : murder

9. FOIL : FENCE ::
    (A) pencil : mark
    (B) road : run
    (C) gloves : box
    (D) train : travel
    (E) bow : bend

10. CLIMB : TREE ::
    (A) row : canoe
    (B) ascend : cliff
    (C) throw : balloon
    (D) file : nail
    (E) float : loan

11. LION : CUB ::
    (A) duck : drake
    (B) rooster : chicken
    (C) human : child
    (D) mother : daughter
    (E) fox : vixen

12. ROOM : HOUSE ::
    (A) refrigerator : kitchen
    (B) chair : room
    (C) cabin : ship
    (D) wheel : car
    (E) cockpit : plane

13. ACORN : OAK ::
    (A) fig : bush
    (B) flower : stalk
    (C) nut : plant
    (D) bulb : tulip
    (E) branch : leaf

14. SORROW : DEATH ::
    (A) laugh : cry
    (B) plum : peach
    (C) happiness : birth
    (D) fear : hate
    (E) confusion : anger

15. EXPLOSION : DEBRIS ::
    (A) fire : ashes
    (B) flood : water
    (C) famine : war
    (D) disease : germ
    (E) heat : burn

16. SOLECISM : GRAMMAR ::
    (A) divorce : marriage
    (B) foul : rules
    (C) incest : family
    (D) stumble : running
    (E) apostasy : dogma

Directions: Below each of the following passages, you will find questions or incomplete statements about the passage. Each statement or question is followed by lettered words or expressions. Select the word or expression that most satisfactorily completes each statement, or answers each question in accordance with the meaning of the passage. After you have chosen the best answer, blacken the corresponding space on the answer sheet.

The deliberate violation of constituted law (civil disobedience) is never morally justified if the law being violated is not the prime target or focal point of the protest. While our government maintains the principle of the Constitution by providing methods for and protection of those engaged in individual or group dissent, the violation of law simply as a technique of demonstration constitutes rebellion.

Civil disobedience is by definition a violation of the law. The theory of civil disobedience recognizes that its actions, regardless of their justification, must be punished. However, disobedience of laws not the subject of dissent, but merely used to dramatize dissent, is regarded as morally as well as legally unacceptable. It is only with respect to those laws which offend the fundamental values of human life that moral defense of civil disobedience can be rationally supported.

For a just society to exist, the principle of tolerance must be accepted, both by the government in regard to properly expressed individual dissent and by the individual toward legally established majority verdicts. No individual has a monopoly on freedom and all must tolerate opposition. Dissenters must accept dissent from their dissent, giving it all the respect they claim for themselves. To disregard this principle is to make civil disobedience not only legally wrong but morally unjustifiable.

17. The author's attitude toward civil disobedience is one of
    (A) indifference
    (B) admiration
    (C) hostility
    (D) respect
    (E) contempt

18. What would the author most likely feel about a demonstration against apartheid which resulted in the disruption of businesses not associated with the problem in any way?
    (A) profound antipathy toward the goal of the demonstration
    (B) severe condemnation of the location of the businesses
    (C) tolerant acceptance of the demonstration's results
    (D) amused indifference toward the demonstrator's goals
    (E) regretful disapproval of the methods of protest

19. It can be inferred from the passage that
    (A) a just society cannot accept illegal civil disobedience
    (B) a just society cannot accept immoral actions of any sort
    (C) dissenters who use civil disobedience cannot use it merely to dramatize their cause
    (D) civil disobedience is sometimes the right thing to do
    (E) many authorities respect dissent as necessary to the functioning of a free society

The Planning Commission asserts that the needed reduction in acute care hospital beds can best be accomplished by closing the smaller hospitals, mainly voluntary and proprietary. This strategy follows from the argument that closing entire institutions saves more money than closing the equivalent number of beds scattered throughout the health system.

The issue is not that simple. Larger hospitals generally are designed to provide more complex care. Routine care at large hospitals costs more than the same care given at smaller hospitals. Therefore, closure of all the small hospitals would commit the city to paying considerably more for inpatient care delivered at acute care hospitals than would be the case with a mixture of large and small institutions. Since reimbursement rates at the large hospitals are now based on total costs, paying the large institutions a lower rate for routine care would simply raise the rates for complex care by a comparable amount. Such a reimbursement rate adjustment might make the charges for each individual case more accurately reflect the actual costs, but there would be no reduction in total costs.

There is some evidence that giant hospitals are not the most efficient. Service organizations—and medical care remains largely a service industry—frequently find that savings of scale have an upper limit. Similarly, the quality of routine care in the very largest hospitals appears to be less than optimum. Also, the concentration of all hospital beds in a few locations may affect the access to care.

Thus, simply closing the smaller hospitals will not necessarily save money or improve the quality of care.

Since the fact remains that there are too many acute care hospital beds in the city, the problem is to devise a proper strategy for selecting and urging the closure of the excess beds, however many it may turn out to be.

The closing of whole buildings within large medical centers has many of the cost advantages of closing the whole of smaller institutions, because the fixed costs can also be reduced in such cases. Unfortunately, many of the separate buildings at medical centers are special use facilities, the relocation of which is extremely costly. Still, a search should be made for such opportunities.

The current lack of adequate ambulatory care facilities raises another possibility. Some floors or other large compact areas of hospitals could be transferred from inpatient to ambulatory uses. Reimbursement of ambulatory services is chaotic, but the problem is being addressed. The overhead associated with the entire hospital should not be charged even *pro rata* to the ambulatory facilities. Even if it were, the total cost would probably be less than that of building a new facility. Many other issues would also need study, especially the potential overcentralization of ambulatory services.

The Planning Commission language seems to imply that one reason for closing smaller hospitals is that they are "mainly voluntary and proprietary," thus, preserving the public hospital system by making the rest of the hospital system absorb the needed cuts. It is important to preserve the public hospital system for many reasons, but the issue should be faced directly and not hidden behind arguments about hosptial size. If indeed that was the meaning.

20. The best title for the passage would be
   (A) Maintaining Adequate Hospital Facilities
   (B) Defending the Public Hospitals
   (C) Methods of Selecting Hospital Beds to be Closed
   (D) Protecting the Proprietary and Voluntary Hospitals
   (E) Economic Efficiency in Hospital Bed Closings

21. The Planning Commission is accused by the author of being
   (A) unfair
   (B) racist
   (C) foolish
   (D) shortsighted
   (E) ignorant

22. On the subject of the number of hospital beds the author
   (A) is in complete agreement with the Planning Commission
   (B) wishes to see large numbers of beds closed
   (C) wishes to forestall the closing of any more hospital beds
   (D) is unsure of the number of excess beds there really are
   (E) wishes to avoid exchanging quantity for quality

23. All of the following are reasons the author opposes the Planning Commision's Recommendation EXCEPT
   (A) service industries have an upper limit for savings of scale
   (B) single buildings of large centers may be closable instead of smaller hospitals

(C) public hospitals have a unique contribution to make and should not be closed

(D) the smaller hospitals recommended for closure provide services more cheaply than larger hospitals

(E) hospitals are service organizations

24. With which of the following would the author probably NOT agree?

(A) Large medical centers provide better and more complex care than do smaller hospitals.

(B) Reimbursement rates do not necessarily reflect the actual costs of providing medical care to a given patient.

(C) Patients needing only routine medical care can often be distinguished from those requiring complex care prior to hospitalization.

(D) Too much centralization of ambulatory care is possible.

(E) Access to medical care is an important issue.

25. The author's purpose in discussing ambulatory care is to

(A) discuss alternatives to closing hospital beds

(B) present a method of reducing the fiscal disadvantages of closing only parts of larger hospitals

(C) show another opportunity for saving money

(D) help preserve the public hospital system

(E) attack the inefficient use of space in larger hospitals

26. With which of the following is the author LEAST likely to agree?

(A) a proposal to save costs in a prison system by building only very large prison complexes

(B) a plan to stop the closing of any beds whatsoever in the city, until the costs of various alternatives can be fully considered

(C) an order by the Planning Commission mandating that no public hospitals be closed

(D) a proposal by an architecture firm that

new hospital buildings have centralized record systems

(E) a mayoral commission being formed to study the plight of the elderly

27. How does the author feel that his suggestions for closing inpatient beds could impact on the ambulatory care system?

(A) Ambulatory care costs will probably be reduced.

(B) A reduction of hospital beds will increase the demand for ambulatory services.

(C) Smaller hospitals will have to cut back ambulatory services to stay fiscally viable.

(D) The Planning Commission would order the opening of new ambulatory services.

(E) The use as ambulatory facilities of the space made available in large hospitals by bed closings might result in having too many ambulatory services based in large hospitals.

Directions: Each of the following questions consists of a word printed in capital letters, followed by five (5) lettered words or phrases. Select the word or phrase which is most nearly *opposite* to the capitalized word in meaning.

28. FETID:

(A) in an embryonic state

(B) easily enraged

(C) acclaimed by peers

(D) reduced to skin and bones

(E) having a pleasant odor

29. ILLUSORY:

(A) nimble

(B) realistic

(C) powerful

(D) underrated

(E) remarkable

30. DOUR:

(A) gay

(B) sweet

(C) wealthy

(D) responsive
(E) noiseless

31. MENDACIOUS:
    (A) broken
    (B) efficacious
    (C) truthful
    (D) destructive
    (E) brilliant

32. ENERVATE:
    (A) debilitate
    (B) fortify
    (C) introduce
    (D) conclude
    (E) escalate

33. DISCRETE:
    (A) loud
    (B) combined
    (C) loose
    (D) circle
    (E) major

34. PRIMITIVE:
    (A) polite
    (B) naive
    (C) weak
    (D) sophisticated
    (E) knowledgeable

35. PARTITION:
    (A) solidify
    (B) unify
    (C) parse
    (D) enjoin
    (E) maintain

36. CLANDESTINE:
    (A) aboveground
    (B) public
    (C) outside
    (D) burnt out
    (E) physical

37. PHLEGMATIC:
    (A) hoarse
    (B) voluntary
    (C) oral
    (D) effusive
    (E) impulsive

38. MANUMIT:
    (A) throw
    (B) lock
    (C) promise
    (D) uncountable
    (E) enslave

STOP

END OF SECTION. IF YOU HAVE ANY TIME LEFT, GO
OVER YOUR WORK IN THIS SECTION ONLY. DO NOT
WORK IN ANY OTHER SECTION OF THE TEST.

SECTION III

30 minutes
30 questions

Directions: For each of the following questions two quantities are given, one in Column A and one in Column B. Compare the two quantities and mark your answer sheet with the correct lettered conclusion. These are your options:

A: If the quantity in Column A is the greater;

B: if the quantity in Column B is the greater;
C: if the two quantities are equal;
D: if the relationship cannot be determined from the information given.

Common Information: In any question, information applying to both columns is centered between the columns and above the quantities in columns A and B. The common information applies to both columns. Any symbol that appears in both columns represents the same idea or quantity in both columns.

Numbers: All numbers used are real numbers.

Figures: Assume that the position of points, angles, regions and so forth are in the order shown. Figures are assumed to lie in a plane unless otherwise indicated. Figures accompanying questions are intended to provide information you can use in answering the questions. However, unless a note states that a figure is drawn to scale, you should solve the problems by using your knowledge of mathematics and *not* by estimating sizes by sight or measurement.

Lines: Assume that lines shown as straight are indeed straight.

	COLUMN A	COLUMN B
1.	the distance travelled by a car with an average speed of 30 miles per hour	the distance travelled by a car with an average speed of 40 miles per hour
2.	The number of tens in 46	The number of thousands in 3612
3.	7.6351123	7.636

4.

	AD	DC
5.	$\dfrac{12}{10 - 8}$	$\dfrac{12}{10 - 6}$

6.

	$z° + y°$	$x°$

7.	the area of a square with side 30 inches	the area of a square with side two feet six inches

	COLUMN A	COLUMN B

8.

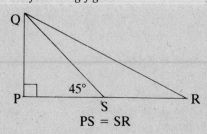

	x + y + z	a + b + c

Questions 9 and 10 refer to the following figure:

$$PS = SR$$

9.	PS	QP
10.	the area of PQS	the area of SQR
11.	The fraction of a day represented by 16 hours	The fraction of an hour represented by 45 minutes
12.	The sum of the 3 greatest odd integers less than 20	The sum of the 3 greatest even integers less than 20

13. Roberta can run a mile in 7.2 minutes, and Debbie can run 7.2 miles in an hour.

Roberta's average rate per hour	Debbie's average rate per hour

14. The relationships among the grades of 5 students are as follows:
   A's grade is higher than that of B.
   E's grade is less than that of D.
   D's grade is less than that of C.
   B's grade is higher than that of C.

E's grade	A's grade

15.
$$x = \frac{1}{4}(3x + \frac{8}{x^2})$$

x	2

Directions: For each of the following questions, select the best of the answer choices and blacken the corresponding space on your answer sheet.
Numbers: All numbers used are real numbers.
Figures: The diagrams and figures that accompany these questions are for the purpose of providing information useful in answering the questions. Unless it is stated that a specific figure is not drawn to scale, the diagrams and figures are drawn as accurately as possible. All figures are in a plane unless otherwise indicated.

16. Of the following which is LEAST?
    (A) $\frac{3}{5}$
    (B) $\frac{2}{3}$
    (C) $\frac{17}{29}$
    (D) $\frac{3}{7}$
    (E) $\frac{4}{5}$

17. If a square MNOP has an area of 16, then its perimeter is
    (A) 4
    (B) 8
    (C) 16
    (D) 32
    (E) 64

18. John has more money than Mary but less than Bill. If the amounts held by John, Mary and Bill are x, y, and z, respectively, which of the following is true?
    (A) $z < x < y$
    (B) $x < z < y$
    (C) $y < x < z$
    (D) $y < z < x$
    (E) $x < y < z$

19. If $x = 3$ and $(x - y)^2 = 4$, then y could be
    (A) −5
    (B) −1
    (C) 0
    (D) 5
    (E) 9

20. 10% of 360 is how much more than 5% of 360?
    (A) 5
    (B) 9
    (C) 18
    (D) 36
    (E) 48

21. If $x^2 + 3x + 10 = 1 + x^2$, then $x^2 =$
    (A) 0
    (B) 1
    (C) 4
    (D) 7
    (E) 9

Questions 22–25 refer to the information in the graph on page 346:

22. In the year 1971, approximately how many vehicles that were purchased were imported?
    (A) 2.25 million
    (B) 6 million
    (C) 8.25 million
    (D) 14.25 million
    (E) 21 million

23. The percent increase in the average purchase price of a vehicle from 1950 to 1970 was approximately
    (A) 75%
    (B) 150%
    (C) 225%
    (D) 275%
    (E) 340%

24. In which of the following time periods was there the greatest increase in the total number of family-owned vehicles purchased?
    (A) 1950–1951
    (B) 1959–1960
    (C) 1960–1962
    (D) 1964–1966
    (E) 1971–1974

25. Between 1950 and 1974, the average number of vehicles owned per household increased by approximately what percent?
    (A) 1.1%
    (B) 2.2%
    (C) 50%
    (D) 100%
    (E) 220%

26. Which of the following must be true?

    I. Any two lines which are parallel to a third line are also parallel to each other.

PURCHASES OF FAMILY-OWNED VEHICLES IN COUNTRY X
(in millions of units)

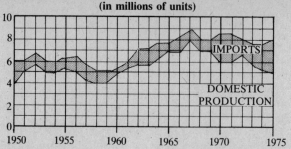

FINANCIAL FACTORS OF
FAMILY-OWNED VEHICLE PURCHASE

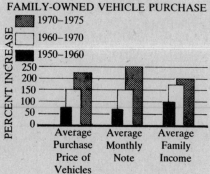

AVERAGE NUMBER OF VEHICLES
OWNED PER HOUSEHOLD

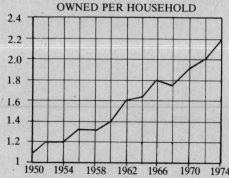

II. Any two planes which are parallel to a third plane are parallel to each other.

III. Any two lines which are parallel to the same plane are parallel to each other.

(A) I only
(B) II only
(C) I and II only
(D) II and III only
(E) I, II, and III

27. An item costs 90% of its original price. If 90¢ is added to the discount price, the cost of the item will be equal to its original price. What is the original price of the item?
(A) $.09
(B) $.90
(C) $9.00
(D) $9.90
(E) $9.99

28. In the figure below, the coordinates of the vertices A and B are (2,0) and (0,2), respectively. What is the area of the square ABCD?
(A) 2
(B) 4
(C) $4\sqrt{2}$
(D) 8
(E) $8\sqrt{2}$

29. If $mx + ny = 12my$, and $my \neq 0$, then $\frac{x}{y} + \frac{n}{m} =$
(A) 12
(B) 12mn
(C) 12m + 12y
(D) 0
(E) mx + ny

30. In circle O shown to the right, MN > NO.
    All of the following must be true EXCEPT
    (A) MN < 2MO
    (B) x > y

    (C) z = y
    (D) x = y + z
    (E) x > 60°

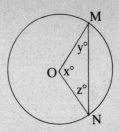

STOP

END OF SECTION. IF YOU HAVE ANY TIME LEFT, GO
OVER YOUR WORK IN THIS SECTION ONLY. DO NOT
WORK IN ANY OTHER SECTION OF THE TEST.

SECTION IV

30 minutes
30 questions

Directions: For each of the following questions two quantities are given, one in Column A
and one in Column B. Compare the two quantities and mark your answer sheet with the
correct lettered conclusion. These are your options:
    A: If the quantity in Column A is the greater;
    B: if the quantity in Column B is the greater;
    C: if the two quantities are equal;
    D: if the relationship cannot be determined from the information given.
Common Information: In any question, information applying to both columns is centered
between the columns and above the quantities in columns A and B. The common information applies to both columns. Any symbol that appears in both columns represents the
same idea or quantity in both columns.
Numbers: All numbers used are real numbers.
Figures: Assume that the position of points, angles, regions and so forth are in the order
shown. Figures are assumed to lie in a plane unless otherwise indicated. Figures accompanying questions are intended to provide information you can use in answering the questions. However, unless a note states that a figure is drawn to scale, you should solve the
problems by using your knowledge of mathematics and *not* by estimating sizes by sight or
measurement.
Lines: Assume that lines shown as straight are indeed straight.

COLUMN A	COLUMN B

1. 10 $\dfrac{1}{0.1} + \dfrac{0.1}{10}$

2. l_1 l_2 $l_1 \parallel l_2$

    $x°$ $y°$

    x   y

COLUMN A	COLUMN B

3. $3 \times \frac{1}{3} \times 6 \times \frac{1}{6}$ $4 \times \frac{1}{4} \times 7 \times \frac{1}{7}$

---

4. $3x + 2 = 11$

x   2

---

5. $x > 0$ and $y > 0$

5% of x   5% of y

6.

x°   y° + z°

7.
$$\frac{x}{3} - 16 = 32$$
$$\frac{y}{4} + 12 = 24$$

x   y

---

8. $x > 0$

$x(x + 3) + 2(x + 3)$ $(x + 3)^2$

---

9. AB and CD are diameters of the same circle.

AC   BD

---

10. $1^{x - y} = 1$

x   y

11.

PQ   RP

---

12. Tickets to a concert cost $5 for adults and $2.50 for children. 29 more adult tickets were sold than children's tickets, and the total receipts from ticket sales were $302.50.

the number of adult tickets sold   50

COLUMN A	COLUMN B

13. the number of integer multiples of 4 between 281 and 301 | the number of integer multiples of 5 between 2401 and 2419

14.

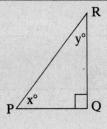

$$\frac{x°}{y°} = \frac{2}{1}$$

$\dfrac{PQ}{PR}$ | $\dfrac{1}{2}$

15.

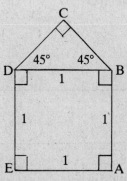

the area enclosed by polygon ABCDE | 1.25

Directions: For each of the following questions, select the best of the answer choices and blacken the corresponding space on your answer sheet.
Numbers: All numbers used are real numbers.
Figures: The diagrams and figures that accompany these questions are for the purpose of providing information useful in answering the questions. Unless it is stated that a specific figure is not drawn to scale, the diagrams and figures are drawn as accurately as possible. All figures are in a plane unless otherwise indicated.

16. $\frac{4}{5} - \frac{3}{4} =$
  (A) $-\frac{7}{9}$
  (B) $-\frac{3}{5}$
  (C) $-\frac{1}{20}$
  (D) $\frac{1}{20}$
  (E) $\frac{3}{5}$

17. Into how many line segments, each 2 inches long, can a line segment one and one-half yards long be divided?
  (A) 9
  (B) 18
  (C) 27
  (D) 36
  (E) 48

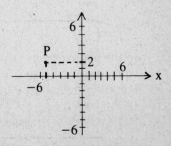

18. In the figure on the preceding page, the coordinates of point P are
    (A) (−5,−2)
    (B) (−5,2)
    (C) (−2,5)
    (D) (2,−5)
    (E) (5,2)

19. If circle O has a radius of 4, and if P and Q are points on circle O, then the maximum length of arc which could separate P and Q is
    (A) 8π
    (B) 4π
    (C) 4
    (D) 2π
    (E) 2

20. All of the following are prime numbers EXCEPT
    (A) 13
    (B) 17
    (C) 41
    (D) 79
    (E) 91

21. A girl at point X walks 1 mile east, then 2 miles north, then 1 mile east, then 1 mile north, than 1 mile east, then 1 mile north to arrive at point Y. From point Y, what is the shortest distance to point X?
    (A) 7 miles
    (B) 6 miles
    (C) 5 miles
    (D) 2.5 miles
    (E) 1 mile

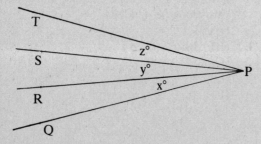

22. In the figure above, the measure of ∠QPS is equal to the measure of ∠TPR. Which of the following must be true?
    (A) x = y
    (B) y = z
    (C) x = z

    (D) x = y = z
    (E) none of the above

Questions 23–27 refer to the following graph:

QUARTERLY ANNUAL PROFIT RATES* FOR DEPARTMENT STORE X

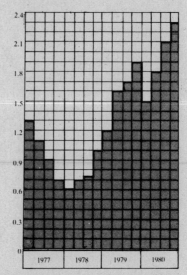

*ANNUAL PROFIT RATE = 4× THE ACTUAL PROFITS MADE IN THAT QUARTER

23. Approximately what was the actual profit made by Department Store X in the second quarter of 1979?
    (A) $6.4 million
    (B) $1.6 million
    (C) $1.2 million
    (D) $0.4 million
    (E) $0.3 million

24. For the time period shown on the graph, in which of the following quarters did Department Store X make the least amount of profits?
    (A) third quarter of 1980
    (B) second quarter of 1979
    (C) first quarter of 1979
    (D) third quarter of 1978
    (E) second quarter of 1977

25. During the period 1978–1980, inclusive, how many quarters exceeded an annual profit rate of $1.5 million?
    (A) 6
    (B) 5

(C) 4
(D) 3
(E) 2

26. In the year 1980, total profit made by Department Store X was approximately
(A) $30.2 million
(B) $7.6 million
(C) $1.9 million
(D) $1.2 million
(E) $.75 million

27. The total annual profit made by Department Store X increased by approximately what percent from 1977 to 1980 inclusive?
(A) 40%
(B) 50%
(C) 90%
(D) 120%
(E) 150%

28. $4 - 3(2 + 1(3 - (2 + 3) + 2) + 2) + 4 =$
(A) −4
(B) 0
(C) 2
(D) 8
(E) 12

29. Newtown is due north of Oscarville. Highway L runs 31° south of east from Newtown and Highway M runs 44° north of east from Oscarville. If L and M are straight, what is the measure of the acute angle they form at their intersection?
(A) 105°
(B) 89°
(C) 75°
(D) 59°
(E) 46°

30. If a sum of money is divided equally among n children, each child will receive $60. If another child is added to the group, then when the sum is divided equally among all the children, each child will receive a $50 share. What is the sum of money?
(A) $3000
(B) $300
(C) $110
(D) $10
(E) Cannot be determined from the information given.

STOP

END OF SECTION. IF YOU HAVE ANY TIME LEFT, GO OVER YOUR WORK IN THIS SECTION ONLY. DO NOT WORK IN ANY OTHER SECTION OF THE TEST.

SECTION V

30 minutes
25 questions

Directions: Each of the following questions or groups of questions is based on a short passage or a set of propositions. In answering these questions it may sometimes be helpful to draw a simple picture or chart. When you have selected the best answer to each question, darken the corresponding circle on your answer sheet.

Questions 1–4

To apply for a Dark Days Fellowship, a student must see the Dean of Students, fill out a financial statement, and obtain a thesis approval from either Professor Fansler or Professor Cross.

A student must see the Dean of Students before filling out the financial statement in order to make sure that it is filled out correctly.

The Dean of Students has office hours for students only on Thursday and Friday mornings, and Monday and Tuesday afternoons.

The Financial Aid Office, where the financial statement has to be filed in person, is open only Monday and Tuesday mornings, Wednesday afternoons, and Friday mornings.

Professor Fansler is in her office only on Monday and Tuesday mornings.

Professor Cross is in his office only on Tuesday and Friday mornings.

1. A student has already seen the Dean of Students and wishes to complete the rest of the application process in one day. If he must obtain his approval from Professor Fansler, when should he come to the campus?
   (A) Monday morning only
   (B) Tuesday morning only
   (C) Friday morning only
   (D) either Monday or Tuesday morning
   (E) either Monday, Tuesday, or Friday morning

2. If a student completed her application process in one visit, which of the following must be false?
   I. She got her thesis approved by Professor Cross.
   II. She got her thesis approved by Professor Fansler.
   III. She completed everything in the afternoon.

   (A) I only
   (B) II only
   (C) III only
   (D) I and III only
   (E) II and III only

3. If a student wanting to apply for a Dark Days Fellowship has classes only on Tuesdays and Thursdays and doesn't want to make an extra trip to the campus, which of the following is true?
   I. The thesis approval must be obtained from Professor Fansler.

II. The thesis approval must be obtained from Professor Cross.
III. The entire application process can be completed in one day.
IV. The entire application process can be completed within the same school week.

   (A) I and II only
   (C) II and III only
   (C) I, II, and III only
   (D) None of the statements are true.
   (E) All of the statements are true.

4. A student has already obtained thesis approval from Professor Fansler. She wishes to complete the application process in only one more visit. When can she do this?
   (A) Monday or Tuesday only
   (B) Monday, Tuesday, or Friday only
   (C) Friday morning only
   (D) any morning except Wednesday
   (E) any morning except Wednesday or Thursday.

5. PROFESSOR: Under the rule of primogeniture, the first male child born to a man's first wife is always first in line to inherit the family estate.
   STUDENT: That can't be true; the Duchess of Warburton was her father's only surviving child by his only wife and she inherited his entire estate.

   The student has misinterpreted the professor's remark to mean which of the following
   (A) Only men can father male children.
   (B) A daughter cannot be a first-born child.
   (C) Only sons can inherit the family estate.
   (D) Illegitimate children cannot inherit their fathers' property.
   (E) A woman cannot inherit her mother's property.

6. As dietician for this 300-person school I am concerned about the sudden shortage of beef. It seems that we will have to begin to serve fish as our main source of protein. Even though beef costs more per pound

than fish, I expect that the cost I pay for protein will rise if I continue to serve the same amount of protein using fish as I did with beef.

The speaker makes which of the following assumptions?
(A) Fish is more expensive per pound than beef.
(B) Students will soon be paying more for their meals.
(C) Cattle ranchers make greater profits than fishermen.
(D) Per measure of protein, fish is more expensive than beef.
(E) Cattle are more costly to raise than fish.

Questions 7–9

The detective is following a subject who goes into a new seven-story office building. The detective doesn't want to risk sharing the elevator with the subject. Fortunately the building has a modern elevator panel which shows the location of the elevator and exactly to which up and down calls it is responding.

The subject got on the elevator with two other persons.

Each floor of the building has only one office, and it is not possible to use the stairway to go from floor to floor.

The elevator stopped on the third, fourth, fifth, and seventh floors. There were no calls for the elevator at those floors.

The elevator returned directly to the lobby from the seventh floor and was empty when it arrived.

7. If the detective assumes that the subject did not push more than one floor button or do anything suspicious in front of any witnesses, which of the following is the detective's safest conclusion?
(A) The subject got off at either the fifth or the seventh floor.
(B) The subject got off at the fourth, fifth, or seventh floor.
(C) The subject got off at the fifth floor.
(D) The subject got off at the fourth or fifth floor.
(E) The subject got off at the third or fourth floor.

8. If, on the next trip, the elevator stops at the second, third, and seventh floors going up, and the sixth floor coming down, on how many different floors must the detective consider checking for the subject?
(A) 6
(B) 5
(C) 4
(D) 3
(E) 2

9. The detective learns that one of the persons riding the elevator with the subject got out on the fourth floor, and someone else got in on that floor. On which floor(s) is(are) the subject(s) most likely to have gotten out?
I. the third floor
II. the fourth floor
III. the fifth floor
IV. the seventh floor

(A) I and II only
(B) I, II and III only
(C) I, II, and IV only
(D) III and IV only
(E) I, II, III, and IV

Questions 10–11
I. All wheeled conveyances which travel on the highway are polluters.
II. Bicycles are not polluters.
III. Whenever I drive my car on the highway, it rains.
IV. It is raining.

10. If the above statements are all true, which of the following statements must also be true?
(A) Bicycles do not travel on the highway.
(B) Bicycles travel on the highway only if it is raining.
(C) If my car is not polluting, then it is not raining.
(D) I am now driving my car on the highway.
(E) My car is not a polluter.

11. The conclusion "my car is not polluting" could be logically deduced from statements I–IV if statement
(A) II were changed to: "Bicycles are polluters."

(B) II were changed to: "My car is a polluter."

(C) III were changed to: "If bicycles were polluters, I would be driving my car on the highway."

(D) IV were changed to: "Rainwater is polluted."

(E) IV were changed to: "It is not raining."

Questions 12–16

    I. Some Z are not Y.
   II. Some Y are not X.
  III. Some X are not Z.
  IV. All X are not Y.

12. Which of the following can be deduced from conditions I, II, and III?
(A) There are no X that are both Y and Z.
(B) Some X are not Y.
(C) Some Z are not X.
(D) Some Y are not Z.
(E) None of the above.

13. Which of the following must be false, given conditions I, II, III, and IV?
(A) There are no X that are neither Y nor Z.
(B) There are no Z that are not X.
(C) There are no X that are Z.
(D) There are no Y that are Z.
(E) None of the above.

14. Given the above conditions, which of the following conditions adds no new information?

    I. No Z are both X and Y.
   II. Some X are neither Z nor Y.
  III. Some Y are neither X nor Z.

(A) I only
(B) II only
(C) III only
(D) I and II only
(E) I and III only

15. Which of the following are inconsistent with the given information?
(A) Some Z are not X.
(B) Some Y are not Z.
(C) No X are not Z.

(D) No Y are not Z.
(E) All of the above are inconsistent with the given information.

16. If no Z are Y and no X are Z, which of the following must be false?
(A) Some Z are neither X nor Y.
(B) Some Y are neither X nor Z.
(C) Some X are neither Y nor Z.
(D) No Z are never X.
(E) No Z are never non-Y.

Questions 17–22

The National Zoo has a very active panda bear colony. One day six of the pandas broke out of their compound and visited the seals. After they were returned to their compound, they were examined by the Panda-keeper. The following facts were recorded.

Bin-bin is fatter than Ging-ging and drier than Eena.

Col-col is slimmer than Fan-fan and wetter than Ging-ging.

Dan-dan is fatter than Bin-bin and wetter than Ging-ging.

Eena is slimmer than Ging-ging and drier than Col-col.

Fan-fan is slimmer than Eena and drier than Bin-bin.

Ging-ging is fatter than Fan-fan and wetter than Bin-bin.

17. Which of the pandas is (are) fatter than Eena and drier than Ging-ging?
(A) Dan-dan only
(B) Fan-fan only
(C) Bin-bin only
(D) both Fan-fan and Col-col
(E) both Dan-dan and Bin-bin

18. Which of the pandas is both slimmer and wetter than Eena?
(A) Ging-ging
(B) Fan-fan
(C) Dan-dan
(D) Col-col
(E) Bin-bin

19. Which of the following is (are) both fatter and wetter than Ging-ging?
(A) Fan-fan

(B) Dan-dan
(C) Col-col
(D) Fan-fan and Col-col
(E) Eena and Dan-dan

20. Which of the following is the driest?
(A) Col-col
(B) Dan-dan
(C) Eena
(D) Fan-fan
(E) Ging-ging

21. Which of the following statements must be false?

   I. Dan-dan is drier than Col-col.
   II. Fan-fan is wetter than Dan-dan.
   III. Dan-dan is three inches fatter than Ging-ging.

(A) I only
(B) II only
(C) III only
(D) I and II only
(E) II and III only

22. A new panda, Yin-yin, is purchased from the Peking Zoo. If dominance in panda bears is determined by fatness, then what will Yin-yin's rank be if he is fatter than Fan-fan and slimmer than Bin-bin?
(A) second from the top
(B) third from the top
(C) fourth from the top
(D) next to the bottom
(E) Cannot be determined from the information given.

23. In *The Adventure of the Bruce-Partington Plans,* Sherlock Holmes explained to Dr. Watson that the body had been placed on top of the train while the train paused at a signal.

   "It seems most improbable," remarked Watson.

   "We must fall back upon the old axiom," continued Holmes, "that when all other contingencies fail, whatever remains, however improbable, must be the truth."

Which of the following is the most effective criticism of the logic contained in Holmes' response to Watson?

(A) You will never be able to obtain a conviction in a court of law.
(B) You can never be sure you have accounted for all other contingencies.
(C) You will need further evidence to satisfy the police.
(D) The very idea of putting a dead body on top of a train seems preposterous.
(E) You still have to find the person responsible for putting the body on top of the train.

24. Rousseau assumed that human beings in the state of nature are characterized by a feeling of sympathy toward their fellow humans and other living creatures. In order to explain the existence of social ills, such as the exploitation of man by man, Rousseau maintained that our natural feelings are crushed under the weight of unsympathetic social institutions.

Rousseau's argument described above would be most strengthened if it could be explained how
(A) creatures naturally characterized by feelings of sympathy for all living creatures could create unsympathetic social institutions
(B) we can restructure our social institutions so that they will foster our natural sympathies for one another
(C) modern reformers might lead the way to a life which is not inconsistent with the ideals of the state of nature
(D) non-exploitative conduct could arise in conditions of the state of nature
(E) a return to the state of nature from modern society might be accomplished

25. Judging by the architecture, I would say that the chapel dates from the early eighteenth century. Furthermore, the marble threshold to the refectory is worn to a depth of one and three-eighths inches at the middle. Since the facilities were designed to accommodate approximately forty monks, I estimate that the monastery was occupied for approximately seventy-five years before it was abandoned, and that date would coincide with the violent civil and religious wars of the first decade of the 1800's.

Which of the following is NOT an assumption made by the author in describing the dates of the buildings?

(A) The marble threshold he studied is the same one originally included in the building.

(B) Architectural features can be associated with certain historical periods.

(C) The monastery he is investigating was nearly fully occupied during the time span in question.

(D) There is a correlation between usage and wear of marble flooring.

(E) Religious organizations have often abandoned outlying monasteries during times of political strife.

STOP

END OF SECTION. IF YOU HAVE ANY TIME LEFT, GO OVER YOUR WORK IN THIS SECTION ONLY. DO NOT WORK IN ANY OTHER SECTION OF THE TEST.

SECTION VI

30 minutes
25 questions

Directions: Each of the following questions or groups of questions is based on a short passage or a set of propositions. In answering these questions it may sometimes be helpful to draw a simple picture or chart. When you have selected the best answer to each question, darken the corresponding circle on your answer sheet.

Questions 1–3:

Five cats, F, G, H, J, and K, are being tested for three parts in a cat-food commercial. The on-camera cats must eat heartily and avoid fighting with each other. F is the best eater, but the most likely to fight. G and H eat best only when they are together, but fight with K.

1. If J is sick and cannot perform, which of the following can be inferred about an attempt to film the commercial?

   I. F, G, and H will do the commercial.
  II. G and H will fight with each other.
 III. The cats will likely fight during the filming.

  (A) I only
  (B) II only
  (C) III only
  (D) I and III only
  (E) I, II, and III

2. If G and J go home, how many additional peaceful cats will be needed to fill out the cast?

  (A) 0
  (B) 1
  (C) 2
  (D) 3
  (E) The commercial cannot be successfully filmed.

3. If F calms down and will no longer fight, how many different casts of cats are available?

  (A) 1
  (B) 2
  (C) 3
  (D) 4
  (E) 5

4. Which of the following activities would depend upon an assumption which is inconsistent with the judgment that you cannot argue with taste?

  (A) a special exhibition at a museum

(B) a beauty contest
(C) a system of garbage collection and disposal
(D) a cookbook filled with old New England recipes
(E) a movie festival

Questions 5–6

Stock market analysts always attribute a sudden drop in the market to some domestic or international political crisis. I maintain, however, that these declines are attributable to the phases of the moon, which also cause periodic political upheavals and increases in tension in world affairs.

5. Which of the following best describes the author's method of questioning the claim of market analysts?
(A) He presents a counter-example.
(B) He presents statistical evidence.
(C) He suggests an alternative causal linkage.
(D) He appeals to generally accepted beliefs.
(E) He demonstrates that market analysts' reports are unreliable.

6. It can be inferred that the author is critical of the stock analysts because he
(A) believes that they have oversimplified the connection between political crisis and fluctuations of the market
(B) knows that the stock market generally shows more gains than losses
(C) suspects that stock analysts have a vested interest in the stock market, and are therefore likely to distort their explanations
(D) anticipates making large profits in the market himself
(E) is worried that if the connection between political events and stock market prices becomes well known, unscrupulous investors will take advantage of the information.

Questions 7–11

Farmer Brown has a large square field divided into nine smaller squares, all equal, arranged in three rows of three fields each. One side of the field runs exactly east-west.

The middle square must be planted with rice because it is wet.
The wheat and barley should be contiguous so that they can be harvested all at once by the mechanical harvester.
Two of the fields should be planted with soybeans.
The northwesternmost field should be planted with peanuts, and the southern third of the field is suitable only for vegetables.

Questions 7–9 refer to the following squares:
(A) the square immediately north of the rice
(B) the square immediately east of the rice
(C) the square immediately west of the rice
(D) the square immediately east of the peanuts
(E) the square immediate northeast of the rice

7. Which square cannot be planted with soybeans?

8. Which square cannot be planted with wheat?

9. If Farmer Brown decides to plant the wheat next to the peanuts, in which square will the barley be?

10. If the three southern squares are planted, from west to east, with squash, tomatoes, and potatoes, which vegetables could be planted next to soybeans?

   I. Squash
  II. Tomatoes
 III. Potatoes

(A) I only
(B) II only
(C) III only
(D) I and III only
(E) I, II, and III

11. If Farmer Brown decides not to plant any peanuts or wheat, what is the maximum number of fields of vegetables that he could plant?
(A) 3

(B) 5
(C) 6
(D) 7
(E) 8

Questions 12–15

  I.   L, M, Z, and P are all possible.
 II.   All M are L.
III.   All L are Z.
IV.   No M are Z.
 V.   Some Z are L.
VI.   No P are both M and L but not Z.

12. Which of the above statements contradicts previous ones?
(A) III
(B) IV
(C) V
(D) VI
(E) None of the statements contradicts previous statements.

13. If statements II and III are true, which of the other statements must also be true?
(A) IV only
(B) V only
(C) VI only
(D) IV and V only
(E) V and VI only

14. If X is an L, it must also be a(n)
(A) M only
(B) P only
(C) Z only
(D) L and Z only
(E) L, P, and Z

15. Given the above statements, which of the following must be false?
(A) There are some L's.
(B) Some Z are not L.
(C) There are some P's which are Z's but not M or L.
(D) There cannot be any Z's that are not L or M.
(E) None of the above are necessarily false.

Questions 16–22

Captain Mulhouse is choosing the last part of his crew for the sailboat *Fearsome,* with which he hopes to earn the right to defend the America's Cup. He needs four more crew members, of whom at least two must be grinders for the winches, with the others being sail trimmers.

The candidates for grinder are David, Erica, and Francis.
The candidates for trimmer are Larry, Mary, Nancy, and Paul.
Nancy will not crew with Paul.
Erica will not crew with Larry.
David will not crew with Nancy.

16. If Nancy is chosen, which of the following must be other members of the crew?
(A) David, Erica, and Mary
(B) Erica, Francis, and Larry
(C) Erica, Francis, and Mary
(D) Erica, Francis, and Paul
(E) Francis, Larry, and Mary

17. If Paul is chosen, which candidates will NOT be chosen to be on the crew?
(A) David, Erica, and Francis
(B) David, Erica, and Mary
(C) David, Francis, and Larry
(D) David, Francis, and Mary
(E) Erica, Francis, and Larry

18. Given the above statements about the relationships among the potential crew members, which of the following must be true?

  I.   If David is rejected, then Mary must be chosen.
 II.   If David is rejected, then Francis must be chosen.
III.   If David is chosen, then Paul must also be chosen.

(A) II only
(B) III only
(C) I and II only
(D) I and III only
(E) II and III only

19. If Larry is chosen as a trimmer, which of the following could be the other members of crew?

  I.   David, Francis, and Mary
 II.   David, Francis, and Nancy
III.   David, Francis, and Paul

(A) I only
(B) II only
(C) III only
(D) I and II only
(E) I and III only

20. Which of the following statements must be true?

    I. If Captain Mulhouse chooses Larry, then Francis must also be chosen.
    II. If Captain Mulhouse chooses Mary, then Nancy must also be chosen.
    III. If Larry is chosen, Nancy cannot be chosen.

    (A) I only
    (B) I and II only
    (C) I and III only
    (D) II and III only
    (E) I, II, and III

21. If Paul is chosen to be part of the *Fearsome's* crew and David is not, who must be the other members of the crew?
    (A) Erica, Francis, and Larry
    (B) Erica, Francis, and Mary
    (C) Erica, Francis, and Nancy
    (D) Erica, Mary, and Nancy
    (E) Francis, Larry, and Mary

22. If Erica makes the crew and Francis does not, which of the following statements must be true?

    I. Paul will be a member of the crew.
    II. Mary will be a member of the crew.

    (A) both I and II
    (B) neither I nor II
    (C) I only
    (D) II only
    (E) either I or II, but not both

23. Since Ronnie's range is so narrow, he will never be an outstanding vocalist.

    The statement above is based on which of the following assumptions?

    I. A person's range is an important indicator of his probable success or failure as a professional musician.

II. Vocalizing requires a range of at least two and one-half octaves.
III. Physical characteristics can affect how well one sings.

(A) I only
(B) II only
(B) I and III
(D) III only
(E) I, II, and III

24. MARY: All of the graduates from Midland High School go to State College.
    ANN: I don't know. Some of the students at State College come from North Hills High School.

Ann's response shows that she has interpreted Mary's remark to mean that
(A) most of the students from North Hills High School attend State College
(B) none of the students at State College are from Midland High School
(C) only students from Midland High School attend State College
(D) Midland High School is a better school than North Hills High School
(E) some Midland High School graduates do not attend college

25. All Burrahobbits are Trollbeaters, and some Burrahobbits are Greeblegrabbers.

If these statements are true, which of the following must also be true?

    I. If something is neither a Trollbeater nor a Greeblegrabber, it cannot be a Burrahobbit.
    II. It is not possible not to be a Trollbeater without being a Greeblegrabber.
    III. Any given thing either is a Trollbeater or it is not a Burrahobbit.

    (A) I only
    (B) II only
    (C) I and II only
    (D) III only
    (E) I, II, and III

STOP

END OF SECTION. IF YOU HAVE ANY TIME LEFT, GO
OVER YOUR WORK IN THIS SECTION ONLY. DO NOT
WORK IN ANY OTHER SECTION OF THE TEST.

SECTION VII

30 minutes
25 questions

Directions: For each of the following questions, select the best of the answer chioces and blacken the corresponding space on your answer sheet.
Numbers: All numbers used are real numbers.
Figures: The diagrams and figures that accompany these questions are for the purpose of providing information useful in answering the questions. Unless it is stated that a specific figure is not drawn to scale, the diagrams and figures are drawn as accurately as possible. All figures are in a plane unless otherwise indicated.

1. What is 40% of $\frac{10}{7}$?
    (A) $\frac{2}{7}$
    (B) $\frac{4}{7}$
    (C) $\frac{10}{28}$
    (D) $\frac{1}{28}$
    (E) $\frac{28}{10}$

2. A prime number is one with 2 divisors and which is divisible only by itself and 1. Which of the following are prime numbers?

    I. 17
    II. 27
    III. 51
    IV. 59

    (A) I only
    (B) I and II only
    (C) I, III, and IV only
    (D) I and IV only
    (E) III and IV only

3. As shown in the diagram in the preceding column, AB is a straight line and angle BOC = 20°. If the number of degrees in angle DOC is 6 more than the number of degrees in angle x, find the number of degrees in angle x.
    (A) 77
    (B) 75
    (C) 78
    (D) $22\frac{6}{7}$
    (E) 87

4. As shown in the figure, a cylindrical oil tank is $\frac{1}{3}$ full. If 3 more gallons are added, the tank will be half-full. What is the capacity, in gallons, of the tank?
    (A) 15
    (B) 16
    (C) 17
    (D) 18
    (E) 19

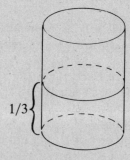

1/3

5. A boy receives grades of 91, 88, 86, and 78 in four of his major subjects. What must he receive in his fifth major subject in order to average 85?
    (A) 86
    (B) 85
    (C) 84
    (D) 83
    (E) 82

D

C

x   20°

A   O   B

6. If a steel bar is 0.39 feet long, its length in *inches* is
   (A) less than 4
   (B) between 4 and $4\frac{1}{2}$
   (C) between $4\frac{1}{2}$ and 5
   (D) between 5 and 6
   (E) more than 6

7. In the figure, PS is perpendicular to QR. If PQ = PR = 26 and PS = 24, then QR =
   (A) 14
   (B) 16
   (C) 18
   (D) 20
   (E) 22

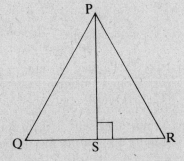

8. If x = 0, for what value of y is the following equation valid? $5x^3 + 7x^2 - (4y + 13)x - 7y + 15 = 0$
   (A) $-2\frac{1}{7}$
   (B) 0
   (C) $+2\frac{1}{7}$
   (D) $\frac{15}{11}$
   (E) $3\frac{1}{7}$

9. A man buys some shirts and some ties. The shirts cost $7 each and the ties cost $3 each. If the man spends exactly $81 and buys the maximum number of shirts possible under these conditions, what is the ratio of shirts to ties?
   (A) 5:3
   (B) 4:3
   (C) 5:2
   (D) 4:1
   (E) 3:2

10. If a man walks $\frac{2}{3}$ mile in 5 minutes, what is his average rate of walking in miles per hour?
    (A) 4
    (B) $4\frac{1}{2}$
    (C) $4\frac{4}{5}$

    (D) $5\frac{1}{5}$
    (E) $5\frac{3}{4}$

11. One end of a dam has the shape of a trapezoid with the dimensions indicated. What is the dam's area in square feet?

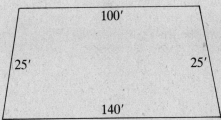

    (A) 1000
    (B) 1200
    (C) 1500
    (D) 1800
    (E) Cannot be determined from the information given.

12. If $1 + \frac{1}{t} = \frac{t+1}{t}$, what does t equal?
    (A) +2 only
    (B) +2 or −2 only
    (C) +2 or −1 only
    (D) −2 or +1 only
    (E) t is any number except 0

13. Point A is 3 inches from line b as shown in the diagram. In the plane that contains point A and line b, what is the total number of points which are 6 inches from A and also 1 inch from b?
    (A) 0
    (B) 1
    (C) 2
    (D) 3
    (E) 4

14. If R and S are different integers, both divisible by 5, then which of the following is *not necessarily* true?
    (A) R − S is divisible by 5
    (B) RS is divisible by 25
    (C) R + S is divisible by 5
    (D) $R^2 + S^2$ is divisible by 5
    (E) R + S is divisible by 10

15. If a triangle of base 7 is equal in area to a circle of radius 7, what is the altitude of the triangle?
    (A) 8π

(B) 10π

(C) 12π

(D) 14π

(E) Cannot be determined from the information given.

16. If the following numbers are arranged in order from the smallest to the largest, what will be their correct order?

I. $\dfrac{9}{13}$

II. $\dfrac{13}{9}$

III. 70%

IV. $\dfrac{1}{.70}$

(A) II, I, III, IV

(B) III, II, I, IV

(C) III, IV, I, II

(D) II, IV, III, I

(E) I, III, IV, II

17. The coordinates of the vertices of quadrilateral PQRS are P(0, 0), Q(9, 0), R(10, 3) and S(1, 3), respectively. The area of PQRS is

(A) $9\sqrt{10}$

(B) $\frac{9}{2}\sqrt{10}$

(C) $\frac{27}{2}$

(D) 27

(E) not determinable from the information given

18. In the circle shown, AB is a diameter. If secant AP = 8 and tangent CP = 4, find the number of units in the diameter of the circle.

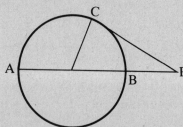

(A) 6

(B) $6\frac{1}{2}$

(C) 8

(D) $3\sqrt{2}$

(E) Cannot be determined from the information given.

19. A certain type of siding for a house costs $10.50 per square yard. What does it cost for the siding for a wall 4 yards wide and 60 feet long?

(A) $800

(B) $840

(C) $2520

(D) $3240

(E) $5040

20. A circle whose radius is 7 has its center at the origin. Which of the following points are outside the circle?

I. (4, 4)

II. (5, 5)

III. (4, 5)

IV. (4, 6)

(A) I and II only

(B) II and III only

(C) II, III, and IV only

(D) II and IV only

(E) III and IV only

21. A merchant sells a radio for $80, thereby making a profit of 25% of the cost. What is the ratio of cost to selling price?

(A) $\frac{4}{5}$

(B) $\frac{3}{4}$

(C) $\frac{5}{6}$

(D) $\frac{2}{3}$

(E) $\frac{3}{5}$

22. How many degrees are between the hands of a clock at 3:40?

(A) 150°

(B) 140°

(C) 130°

(D) 125°

(E) 120°

23. Two fences in a field meet at 120°. A cow is tethered at their intersection with a 15-foot rope, as shown in the figure. Over how many square feet may the cow graze?

(A) 50π

(B) 75π

(C) 80π

(D) 85π

(E) 90π

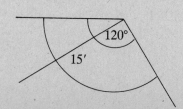

24. If $\frac{17}{10}y = 0.51$, then y =
    (A) 3
    (B) 1.3
    (C) 1.2
    (D) .3
    (E) .03

25. A junior class of 50 girls and 70 boys sponsored a dance. If 40% of the girls and 50% of the boys attended the dance, approximately what percent attended?
    (A) 40
    (B) 42
    (C) 44
    (D) 46
    (E) 48

STOP

END OF SECTION. IF YOU HAVE ANY TIME LEFT, GO OVER YOUR WORK IN THIS SECTION ONLY. DO NOT WORK IN ANY OTHER SECTION OF THE TEST.

PRACTICE EXAMINATION 3—ANSWER KEY

Section I

1.	B	10.	D	19.	D	28.	D	37.	E
2.	C	11.	C	20.	E	29.	E	38.	B
3.	A	12.	B	21.	A	30.	E		
4.	C	13.	B	22.	C	31.	A		
5.	E	14.	D	23.	B	32.	A		
6.	B	15.	A	24.	B	33.	E		
7.	E	16.	C	25.	D	34.	D		
8.	A	17.	B	26.	E	35.	C		
9.	D	18.	C	27.	C	36.	D		

Section II

1.	B	10.	B	19.	D	28.	E	37.	D
2.	D	11.	C	20.	E	29.	B	38.	E
3.	E	12.	C	21.	D	30.	A		
4.	A	13.	D	22.	D	31.	C		
5.	C	14.	C	23.	C	32.	B		
6.	C	15.	A	24.	A	33.	B		
7.	A	16.	B	25.	B	34.	D		
8.	B	17.	D	26.	A	35.	B		
9.	C	18.	E	27.	E	36.	B		

Section III

1.	D	7.	C	13.	A	19.	D	25.	D
2.	A	8.	C	14.	B	20.	C	26.	C
3.	B	9.	C	15.	C	21.	E	27.	C
4.	D	10.	C	16.	D	22.	A	28.	D
5.	A	11.	B	17.	C	23.	E	29.	A
6.	C	12.	A	18.	C	24.	C	30.	D

Section IV

1.	B	7.	A	13.	A	19.	B	25.	A
2.	C	8.	B	14.	C	20.	E	26.	C
3.	C	9.	C	15.	C	21.	C	27.	C
4.	A	10.	D	16.	D	22.	C	28.	A
5.	D	11.	A	17.	C	23.	D	29.	C
6.	A	12.	C	18.	B	24.	D	30.	B

Section V

1. D	6. D	11. E	16. D	21. B
2. E	7. B	12. E	17. C	22. E
3. D	8. B	13. A	18. D	23. B
4. C	9. E	14. D	19. B	24. A
5. C	10. A	15. C	20. D	25. E

Section VI

1. C	6. A	11. B	16. C	21. B
2. C	7. E	12. B	17. E	22. A
3. C	8. C	13. C	18. C	23. D
4. B	9. E	14. D	19. E	24. C
5. C	10. D	15. D	20. A	25. A

Section VII

1. B	6. C	11. D	16. E	21. A
2. D	7. D	12. E	17. D	22. C
3. A	8. C	13. E	18. A	23. B
4. D	9. E	14. E	19. B	24. D
5. E	10. C	15. D	20. D	25. D

EXPLANATORY ANSWERS

SECTION I

1. **(B)** As most people do not enjoy trouble, and as you can't interrogate it, we may logically conclude that they foresaw, or anticipated, trouble. A road doesn't grow into a path, nor does it collapse into one.

2. **(C)** The word waiter makes it clear that it is a dining situation that is being described. Thus, the crab will not be used to pelt, throw at, or resolve ourselves. This eliminates (A) and (D). (E) would also be a rather peculiar usage and should be eliminated. Between (B) and (C), the decision can be made by noting the structure of the sentence. The lobster is clearly the result of some act of the waiter. It is possible that the lobster is the embarrassment of the waiter, but more reasonable that it was his recommendation, especially since its being gone resulted in the eating of crab. Thus, (C) is the best choice.

3. **(A)** Derelict in this sense means empty, abandoned. Only people are bereaved or bereft. Bustling means busy and is thus incompatible with disuse.

4. **(C)** This sentence implies discord between the old-timers and the young mayor. Old-timers are likely to resent those officials who are trying to change, or reform, things.

5. **(E)** There may be many possible alternative fuel sources, but unless they are inexpensive, they won't affect the price of gas.

6. **(B)** Since the burden of the sentence is that the bacteria and viruses are the masters, (D) and (E) do not work because they do not describe a situation of virus mastery in the first blank. For the second blank, the idea that viruses and bacteria live off all other life, (B), is a good carrying through of the idea of mastery. (A) fails since companionship is not required by bacteria or provided them by humans or birds. (C) is second-best, but opportunity is rather general, and (B) describes just which opportunity is being offered and taken, thus (B) is the best answer choice.

7. **(E)** Since the author of the sentence is clearly a guard or something like that of the prisoners, he would expect some negative reaction from them. The word trepidation after the second blank is a contrast to the second blank and also describes the kind of feeling which was expected at first, but which the author finds disappointing now. Trepidation is alarm, or mild fear or unease; thus (E), fear, is best for the first blank. The second blank can be approached as either being the opposite of trepidation, which could be trust, again (E), or by asking what would best describe the result of a guard treating his prisoners with fairness. It is unlikely that a prisoner would ever love his guard or be loyal to him, though (B), (D), and (E) are all acceptable.

8. **(A)** The relationship between cat and mouse is predator to prey. (A) shows this same relationship between bird and worm. A dog may chase its tail, but not as a predator. A lion may on occasion kill a snake, but it is not its typical prey. (D) has the merit of evoking the idea of a cat-and-mouse game being hide and seek. Of course, it is the mouse (second element) which hides and the cat which seeks. A purely verbal relationship such as would be needed to justify cat and mouse is absent from the GRE. Trap and cheese has no merit aside from the alleged fact that mice like cheese.

9. **(D)** A vanilla bean is the source of the flavoring vanilla. We thus have a product and a source, or original form. Ginger is a root. None of the other choices correctly state the source or form of the flavoring cited. Tabasco comes from peppers, as does chili. Mint and sage are leaves.

10. **(D)** Energy is something that is dissipated. Money is squandered. The linkage is strengthened by noting that dissipated has the idea that there was no beneficial result from the expenditure of energy. The same holds true for squander. (A) has no merit since recharging a battery is just the opposite of dissipating energy; it is collecting it and making it useful. (B) has some merit in that the result of splitting an atom is certainly the release and dissipation of a great deal of energy, but it is a process of splitting, which itself is not dissipating. (C) has a little real merit since eating food certainly results in the food being broken down and changed, but it is not intrinsically wasteful or lacking in purpose. (E)'s only merit is that a gas will likely dissipate after it is generated. This is totally inadequate.

11. **(C)** A nose is a part of a face that sticks out. A knob is a part of a door that also sticks out. The first guess at an analogy might say that a nose goes

on the face. This would fit all five of the answer choices and thus be good, but would need refinement. The next thing would be to look at the answer choices and see the different ways that the first item goes onto the second item. (A) and (D) have the first item go over and around the second item. (B) merely has the first item as an extension of the second. (E) has the first item as something that is on the surface of the second item, but does not particularly stick out, but rather clings closely to the surfaces. (C) is the relationship that relates to the original pair in the best way.

12. **(B)** A rifle is the typical weapon of a soldier, at least as a soldier would be understood today. A sword is a typical weapon of a knight. In approaching this problem it is clear that weapons are an issue, or at least tools. (E) is not a tool of the robber, but rather a tool against him, so that's out. (A) has a weapon in the first slot, but instead of the user of the weapon in the second slot, we find another weapon. This fails. (C) has a tool of the cowboy, but it is not the same as a rifle. It may be true that a horse is the cowboy's best friend and the rifle is the soldier's best friend, but that is no basis for an analogy question on the GRE. Marine and tank in (D) would be very nice, except that it is backward. This does not happen often, but it happens.

13. **(B)** Venison is the name for meat from a deer. Mutton is the name for meat from a sheep. (C) is simply wrong since veal is meat from a young cow, not a lamb, which is a young sheep. (E) is very weak since a stew can be made with any meat. (A) fails because both of the words are names for the same group of animals and not the name for the meat from those animals, which is pork. (D) is the second-best answer, since when you order a steak in a restaurant, you will get the meat of a steer. However, that is not the name of the meat of a steer, but of a particular cut of meat. Steer meat also comes in many other cuts. Thus, steak is not the name of a type of meat from a particular animal, and (B) is correct.

14. **(D)** Something that is ineffable cannot be known. Something that is baffling cannot be solved. (C) has some merit since one might say of a certain situation that it is frustrating because there is no release from it, but that is an awkward way of putting it and not really what frustrating means. In (B), one finds that a trick is puzzling, but that is positive in its connection, while the original analogy is negative. (E) has no real connection since the essence of a rage is not whether or not it is controllable. Similarly for genial and interesting. Thus, (D) is the answer.

15. **(A)** The first idea of the analogy between icing and cake would be either that the icing goes on the cake or that it is a part of the cake. All of the answer choices meet one of these criteria or both. (C) and (D) do not have any special merit because they are baking terms. On the contrary, if they were to work, they would have to be even tighter than some other, non-overlapping answer choice. (C) fails because baking is the process of making pastry, and cake is not a process here. Ice might cake up on some exposed part of a house or plane or something, but what is meant here is plain old icing on the cake. (D) fails because the apple is only in the pie and not on it. (E) would fail with the additional idea that the icing is a significant layer on top of the cake and the thickness of the print on the page is not something that is significant enough to come to our attention. No other answer choice but (A) has the idea of decoration and beauty that is implicit in the stem pair. One speaks of the icing on the cake as the last touch to making something just right. A veneer is a thin layer of beautiful wood that is laid over another material to make a beautiful finish or outside appearance. Unlike the ice in the pond, it is applied by people for a particular purpose. Thus, (A) is the best answer.

16. **(C)** Chalk is used to make marks on a blackboard. They are associated through the process of writing. (A) can be eliminated since a door and a handle are separate parts of the same operation or mechanism, but there is nothing that has one of them making a mark on the other. (C), (D), and (E) do have that marking idea. (B), like (A), is only a physical relationship and no process is invoked. (D) can be eliminated since its second item is the name of the process rather than the thing that is written upon. In contrasting (C) and (E), the major difference is the typical use of ink and paper for writing. While it is true that paper and ink are used for things other than writing, and paint can be used to write on a wall, these are not the typical uses which first come to mind. Thus, (C) is better than (E). One slight difficulty is that chalk is solid and thus is both the material deposited on the surface and the implement that is held. Pen and brush might do as well as ink and paint.

17. **(B)** The passage makes only one geographic reference, and that is to England, with the use of "this is the question" for England. Thus, (A), (C), and (D) are out. Since the author is doing a fairly modern analysis of the problems of distributing wealth, it is not likely that he lived in King Arthur's time. Hence, (B) rather than (E).

18. **(C)** (B), (D), and (E) are eliminated on the simple grounds that there is nothing in the passage on which to base them. The preference for (C) over (A) is not great, but can be arrived at by considering that what the author is advocating is paying less attention to the wages and the money part of the economy and more towards its ultimate ends. The denial of the virtue of money and the

implication that the rich are robbers (by analogy) also tend away from capitalism at least, if not toward socialism.

19. **(D)** (D) is included in the concluding sentence of the passage. (A) and (E) are specifically disputed in the passage, since it is the entire process that matters and not merely the pay rate or effort. (C) is not disputed, but is not emphasized either, while (B) is simply absent.

20. **(E)** The passage emphasizes that it is the ends of the productive process that are critical, thus, giving some support to (E). (C) has some appeal since money as such is not too important to the author, but its uses are important. (A), (B), and (D) derive any attractiveness they may have solely from the relative obscurity of (E).

21. **(A)** While the author stops short of outright accusation of the rich as robbers, they are treated in much the same manner in the passage, which creates the analogy desired.

    (E) is untrue. The author says that one might as well say the robber is a benefactor, or at least does no harm, but this is a way of disputing a statement, not agreeing with it.

    (D) fails since the passage is generally opposed to waste, while (B) and (C) are incorrect because only dishonesty is mentioned in relation to business.

22. **(C)** The choice is between (A) and (C). (B) is of no interest to the author, while (D) is only acceptable for the last three words. (E) is relevant but far too general.

    (A) refers to the last sentence and (C) refers to the sentences immediately after the posing of the great question. The distinction here is that (A) describes the great question for ALL members of society, while (C) describes the plight of the poor specifically.

23. **(B)** (B) is preferable because it is something that helps to provide the necessities of life—clean air and water, etc. (D) fails since it does not specify the job. (A) is not strong since weapons are generally destructive, though this is not impossible. (C) is less attractive than (B) since it has no stated positive value. The dislike of the rich would also enter into it. (E) is attractive since it is clear that this is something of which the author has done a great deed. It is clearly the second-best choice, but is not as good as (B) since there is no clear message in the passage as to the value of studying theory. If (E) specifically were the arousal of the laborer to his best interests, that might be even better than (B) since it would mean all would do good work and not just the one.

24. **(B)** (A) is attractive since the author certainly is not in favor of the rich or most of their works. However, his main point—the "main question for the poor"—is the use to which the resources of society are to be put. He will definitely see that it is waste and poor use of resources which lead to such problems as an energy shortage, since he has claimed that there will be enough of the good things if only everyone would work at the right things in the right way.

    While (C) has the advantage of being a very simple and direct response to an energy shortage, we are looking for something in the passage to link to our answer, and there is really nothing to support the idea that the author wishes to see more mineral exploitation. On the contrary, he denigrates such activities.

    (D) has no basis in the passage, but might appear to have the connection that the author does believe that there are enough resources to go around. Thus it might be mistakenly inferred that he would deny the shortage altogether. This is mistaken because the author says in the passage that all sorts of shortages and a despoiling of the environment are perfectly possible—even likely— if nothing is changed.

    (E), like (A), is something the author might well like to do on general principles, but there is no immediate link to the question, especially not in preference to (B).

25. **(D)** Choices (A) and (E) are incorrect because neither oppression nor violence are mentioned or implied in the passage. Choices (B) and (C) are also incorrect; evolution and instinct are mentioned in the passage, but as supporting ideas rather than as the central theme. We are left with choice (D), which does relate the main idea—the concept of social order—which is mentioned or at least implied in almost every sentence.

26. **(E)** The author states in the second paragraph that "as social life changed, the worth and rights of each member in the larger group, of which he was a part, increased." Since the social groups grew from clans to civilizations, the largest social group mentioned in the choices was "modern cities." It can therefore be assumed that the greatest attention to rights and values will be found there.

27. **(C)** It is stated very clearly that "of all living creatures, only man has the capacity to interpret his own evolution as progress." Choices (A), (B), (D), and (E) are all characteristics of many living organisms and therefore would not be unique to man.

28. **(D)** Refractory means stubborn or unmanageable. (D) is a perfect opposite to that meaning of refractory. None of the other answer choices connects to this meaning.

29. **(E)** Adroit means expert in something, particularly manual or mental tasks. Awkward is a good

opposite to the manual dexterity meaning of adroit. Skillful is close to being a synonym. Sinister comes from the Latin root meaning left, and although adroit comes from the Latin root meaning right, they are not opposites in English.

30. **(E)** Palliate means to make less severe or bad. Worsen is a perfect opposite.

31. **(A)** Vilify means to heap insults on. (A), (B), and (D) all have some merit. (A) is better since insult and praise are perfect opposites. The use of the word sing might be somewhat confusing since it is an idiomatic usage and one would not sing insults, but one does sing praises. Presumably one would not do (B) or (D) if one was vilifying someone, but they are not direct opposites. (E) would be opposite something that meant accept totally, not vilify.

32. **(A)** Irascible means irritable, and sounds like it, too. Placid is a very good opposite since a placid person is not easily disturbed. Fortuitous means fortunate; entrancing means able to put one into a trance, presumably a trance of delight. Shameless is the only word, other than placid, which is a personality characteristic, but it is not the same sort of thing at all.

33. **(E)** Gelid means frozen. Boiling is a good opposite since these are the two normal extremes of water. Chilly means mildly cold and has a connection to gelid, but a good antonym will be the same thing in an opposite way and mildly cold (chilly) is not as good an opposite to very cold (gelid) as is very hot (boiling).

34. **(D)** Condign means deserved or fitting, particularly of a punishment. Undeserved is a rather precise opposite. Unguarded might echo the use of condign with punishments, but it is not correct.

35. **(C)** A punctilious person takes extreme care over all aspects of his duties. Careless is taking no care or even extremely poor care. Tardy, meaning late, tries to reach for the word punctual, but that means on the dot (punct-) in terms of time, while punctilious means up to the dot or mark in terms of care and completeness. Correct has no merit since it describes something that is done conscienciously or scrupulously, and thus is not opposite at all.

36. **(D)** Feckless means weak, ineffective, feeble, or worthless. Strong is opposite to one of the meanings (feeble). Fatuous means foolish and ineffective; fawning is to seek favor by servile behavior. Calm might have some appeal, but the connection is to the word reckless, not feckless.

37. **(E)** Insolent means boldly rude. Affable means polite. This is a good opposite, though a word

meaning extremely polite would be even better. Sullen is more of a synonym than an antonym. Kind is a positive personality trait and insolence is a negative one, but that is never enough for an antonym. More precision is required.

38. **(B)** A serendipitous discovery is a desirable but unsought result. The degree of desirability is not the issue so much as the unplanned nature of the discovery. Thus, planned is an acceptable opposite, while evil is not. There is no moral connotation to serendipity. Regulated is probably the second-best answer choice and has real merit. However, regulated applies more to control than specifically to planning, and thus is not quite to the point.

SECTION II

1. **(B)** To say a pious religious home is redundant. Only (B) completes the thought and intent of the sentence.

2. **(D)** The objections mentioned must have been vocal to get them thrown out.

3. **(E)** A single wall implies that, formerly, there were other walls. That only one wall still stood is testimony, not tribute, to Nature's power. Evidence to is poor diction.

4. **(A)** Assuming that routine activity is not exhausting, it would be surprising to find yourself exhausted by it one day.

5. **(C)** (E) fails since pugilistic, in the second blank, is not the way to describe articles unless they are about boxing. (D) is also poor since we have no particular indication that the university is in the United States or the Americas. In considering the first blank, we might discount (B) on the grounds that among is hinting at a relationship between the various departments and futility is not a relationship word, while cooperation and competition are precisely that. In choosing between (A) and (C), we would have to ask whether competition would be more likely to breed angry articles or if cooperation would lead to interdisciplinary ones. Since we are talking about the departments of a university, interdisciplinary is very apt, while competition in a university need not yield angry articles. Thus, (C) is the best answer choice.

6. **(C)** The first blank is something that leads up to having a focus on specific stimuli. (E) is rather a poor lead-in to focus, but the others are all possible. For the second blank, (B) and (D) are inadequate since the other data would not be insulated without some statement of what they were insulated from, if indeed sensory data being

insulated makes any sense at all. Isolated would have worked, perhaps, but that is not present. Added up is also inadequate, though added might have been acceptable. In choosing between (A) and (C), we have to take the workings of the pair of words into account. In (A) the situation would be that the focus starts in one place and then other things are somehow increased by the focus being in one place. This is a little strange, but (C) is a perfectly reasonable situation. If the senses are designed for specific stimuli, then it would be most reasonable that other stimuli would fade. Hence, (C) is the best answer.

7. **(A)** If new behaviors are learned, then the likelihood is that the old behaviors are changed. Also, the situation of being in a new country would mean changes are needed. Thus, (A) and (D) are the best ways of filling in the first blank. The difference between (A) and (D) for the second blank could not be sharper. (A) says uncertain and (D) says definite. If one is learning new habits in a new country, it is more reasonable to speak of uncertainties presenting a problem than of definite results presenting a problem. Thus, (A) is the better answer choice.

8. **(B)** Embezzlement is the unlawful taking of money. Plagiarism is the unlawful taking of a writing. The idea of lawful and unlawful uses of things can create a number of special words, which make interesting analogy problems. (E) is the only other choice to have an unlawful idea, and murder is certainly unlawful death, but it is the giving of death, if you will, rather than the taking of it and thus does not conform to the original pair as well as (B). (A) links only to the idea of money and does not replicate any relationship from the original. (C) and (D) have no idea of unlawfulness. Thus, (B) is the best answer.

9. **(C)** A foil is a type of sword used in fencing. Gloves are a type of equipment used in boxing. (A) has merit since a pencil is used to mark, but (C) is just as good on that level and also carries the idea of sporting equipment. Likewise, (B) and (D) have some idea of the first word being a way of performing the second, but it is not as good as (C). (E) does have an idea of sporting equipment, but the activity referred to in the second word, bending, is done to the bow and not with it and is not the sport itself.

10. **(B)** Climb is what one does to a tree in order to get to the top of it. Ascend is the word that is used to describe the climbing of a cliff. Scale could also be used, but it isn't here. The other answer choices, except (C), are also fairly typical actions performed with or to the objects mentioned in the second position. However, they lack the additional idea of being a way of getting to the top of

the item mentioned. (C) lacks even that and hence fails totally. Thus, (B) is the best answer.

11. **(C)** Cub is the name given to a young lion. Child is the name given to a young human. A drake is a male duck, and a vixen is a female fox. Rooster is a male chicken. Mother and daughter are only different in age, but have the similarity of belonging to the same family, which a lion and cub do not necessarily do.

12. **(C)** A room is a part of a house and in particular it is usually a living unit of the house. A cabin is a living unit of a ship. (A), (B), and (D) all have the idea of the first item being in the second one, but they are not constituent parts in the way a house is made up of a number of rooms. (C) and (E) both have the idea of the first item's being spaces inside the second item. However, a cabin is a living space and a cockpit is not; thus, (C) is the best answer.

13. **(D)** "Great oaks from little acorns grow," and tulips grow from bulbs. (A) and (C), while relationships between living things, are not the seed to the final plant. (B) and (E) also lack the idea of the seed, though they do have the merit of having the leaf or flower grow out of the stalk or branch. (B) and (E) would make a reasonable analogy with each other, but not with the given stem pair. Thus, (D) is the best answer.

14. **(C)** Sorrow is the appropriate and typical feeling accompanying a death. Happiness is the appropriate and typical feeling accompanying birth. In each case the feeling is felt by others than the dead or new-born person, of course. None of the other answer choices has a feeling and an event appropriate to the feeling. Indeed, none of the others has any event at all.

15. **(A)** The leftovers after an explosion is debris. The leftovers after a fire are ashes. As a first approximation, one might have tried the idea of the first item leading to or causing the second item. (C) does not fit this concept and is eliminated. (D) does but is backward. The leftovers from a flood, (B), are more properly the flotsam and jetsam deposited about the landscape rather than the water itself, which *is* the flood. In distinguishing (A) from (E), the decisive issue is that in the original pair and in (A), the second item is a waste product, while in (E) the burn is a resulting hurt. One would throw out debris and ashes, but one would not throw out the burn.

16. **(B)** A solecism is a violation of the rules of good speech, including the rules of grammar. A foul is a violation of the rules of a game. (A) refers to the end of a marriage, not a mistake or a violation of the rules, and so is not adequate. In (E), apostasy is the total desertion of some dogma, but not an error under the rules of the dogma; or if it is an

error, it is so severe as to be in a different class than solecism. In (C), incest is certainly a violation of the normal rules of how a family should operate, but the word family does not refer to the *rules* of family life. Mores might have worked, but it is not present. (B) and (D) are both clearly errors. However, the difference between them is that the stumble is an error in doing the act of running, while a foul is an error in following the rules of something. Since a solecism can be an error in following the rules of grammar, (B) is the better answer.

17. **(D)** As the author states that the principle of tolerance must be accepted by both parties, his attitude toward civil disobedience is not one of hostility or contempt. Answers (C) and (E), then, are wrong. Choice (A) is also incorrect, as is choice (B), since the author does not totally admire civil disobedience. (D) is the best answer.

18. **(E)** The use of the word apartheid, which refers to the principles of racial separation practiced in South Africa, is not particularly relevant to answering the question. The focus of the passage is that civil disobedience is only proper when the laws broken are themselves the main focus of dissent. The incidental breaking of laws is not proper since there should be actions that spill over from the dissent into other areas of improper action. While the situation posed in the question stem does not specifically relate to the breaking of a law, the procedural concerns of the author are the ones that must be carried forward into the new situation. Therefore (E), which projects that the author would disapprove of the harm to innocent bystanders, is quite in accord with the focus in the passage on making sure that the actions of dissent are sharply focused on their object.

(A) and (D) are certainly not correct since the author has not indicated anything which would indicate to us his views about the issue at hand. Indeed, the issue being protested is not relevant to the author. It is true that he believes that only affronts to fundamental human values are the proper subject of civil disobedience, but we are not being asked to make such judgments, only to judge the procedural issues raised in the passage. Thus, (A) and (D) fail.

(B) is wrong since there is no basis on which to say that the author has or would have any opinion about the location of any business. On the contrary, the businesses are portrayed as the innocent bystanders (if the question says they are innocent bystanders, then they are innocent bystanders).

(C) is the converse of (E) and fails for all the reasons that (E) succeeds. The only merit of (C) is that it uses the word tolerant, which is certainly dear to the heart of the author. But the mere appearance of a word is not enough to make an answer correct.

19. **(D)** On structural grounds, (D) should be the answer choice to which you give first attention, quite apart from any matter of content. All four of the other answer choices are very strong statements with cannot or necessary. (D), on the other hand, only says "sometimes," which is much weaker.

(A) fails on grounds of meaning, since all civil disobedience is, by definition, illegal, and yet it is sometimes acceptable when it is done for the proper purposes and in the proper way.

(C) fails on careful reading since it is stating that the dissenters cannot use civil disobedience in a particular way, and the fact of the matter is that they can use it in any way they wish, but the author disapproves of their using it in this way.

(B) and (E) are the sort of statements that are hard to quarrel with, but they are not particularly relevant to this passage. The only requirement that the author imposes on the just society is that it be tolerant. This may not mean that it does or can accept immoral actions, whatever accept might amount to, but it certainly does not mean that the just society cannot accept these actions. (E) has problems with the idea of many authorities, since this is unclear from the passage, and, even more importantly, has the word free. There is absolutely nothing of any kind in the passage about a free society, but only about a just one. There may be a connection between the two ideas, but it is not made in the passage and thus we should not make it unless it is inescapable, which it isn't.

20. **(E)** (D) is of no interest to the author. (A), (B), and (C) are topics mentioned in the passage, but only as serving the general analysis of the Planning Commission's proposal. Thus, (E) is more descriptive of the actual passage.

21. **(D)** The author's argument essentially states that the commission may be right as far as it goes, but it is not that simple. This implies that the commission has been shortsighted. It is true that because of the shortsightedness, the author views the plan as foolish, and perhaps somewhat ignorant, but these derive from the shortsightedness, and the tone is respectful rather than condemnatory. (A) and (B) have no basis.

22. **(D)** (A) is attractive, but the word complete kills it. The author is clearly unsure of the number of beds that should be closed and sees that as a future issue. (B) and (C) fail for the same reason. (E) sounds good, but is not really mentioned.

23. **(C)** All of the statements are agreeable to the author, but (C) is specifically stated by the passage not to be properly addressed in the context of the commission's proposal. Because of (A) and (E), large hospitals may not be more efficient. (B) and (D) are both reasons why small hospitals should not be closed.

24. **(A)** (A) is only half agreeable. The author states the larger centers provide more complex care, and if the larger hospitals do not provide the most efficient care—as the author claims they don't—then it is certainly probable that they do not definitely provide the better care than smaller hospitals of the sort that can be received at both kinds of facilities.

    (B) is inferable from the statement that only overall costs are used to set rates. (C) is inferable from the author's support of the existence of institutions that can only provide that sort of care, while also supporting quality. (D) is stated to be a possible problem. (E) is inferable from the concern shown for greater or lesser access in the third and fifth paragraphs.

25. **(B)** The author knows that he cannot simply say to the commission that they shouldn't close the smaller hospitals. He must present evidence that it is not the best approach to the agreed-upon goal of saving money and closing unneeded beds—hence, (B). (A) is false since closing beds is agreed to by the author. (C) is true, but not as precise as (B); also the word another is troublesome since it is actually an alternative which is proposed. (D) is not currently at issue. (E) is appealing, but the inefficiencies of larger hospitals are not stated to be in the use of space.

26. **(A)** Prisons are, in a manner of speaking, service organizations (like hospitals), and thus very large ones may not be more efficient, according to the author; thus, (A). (B) is probably just what the author wants, since he is unsure of the number of beds that should be closed anyway. (C) is stated to be agreeable to the author in the last paragraph. (D) and (E) are indeterminable. There is no basis for agreement or disagreement given in the passage.

27. **(E)** The concern about possible *over-centralization* of ambulatory services is raised in the context of the proposal to close portions of the larger hospitals rather than the entirety of smaller hospitals. This juxtaposition of the two means that the author believes that closing parts of the larger hospitals might have the poor result of turning over so much space in those locations to ambulatory care that a disproportionate part of the ambulatory care system would reside at the larger hospitals. His use of the prefix over- indicates disapproval.

    The only references to the costs of ambulatory care are to its chaos and to some needs to keep it down. This implies a concern by the author that ambulatory care costs might increase, not that they might be decreased. Hence, (A) fails.

    (B) and (C) refer to connections that are not in the passage. The author refers to increasing the facilities for ambulatory services, but not to increasing the demand, which he seems to think is there already. If you answered (C), you are answering from current events and not from the passage.

    (D) has the appeal of being something that the author would probably like to have happen, but it is not implicit in the passage that the Planning Commission has the power to bring it about, and he certainly does not ask it. Rather, the force of the argument about the use of the space left by the closed portions of larger medical centers is that this space would certainly not go to waste.

28. **(E)** Fetid means having a bad or offensive odor; thus, (E) is a very good opposite. Embryonic means not yet born or fully developed.

29. **(B)** Illusory means based on an illusion, thus not realistic. Nimble means agile and physically well coordinated.

30. **(A)** Dour means gloomy or sullen, and gay is an excellent opposite. Sweet plays on the idea of sour, which does have some real merit since a dour disposition can also be referred to as sour. However, since we are speaking of personalities, gay is a better opposite to dour/sour than is sweet, since a sweet disposition is not so much cheerful as amiable or gracious. They are fairly close, however.

31. **(C)** Mendacious means lying and untruthful, so (C) is a perfect opposite. Broken plays on the mend- part of the word, as does destructive. Efficacious means efficient and effective.

32. **(B)** Enervate means to weaken significantly. Fortify means to strengthen. Debilitate means to weaken and is essentially a synonym, rare on the GRE as an answer choice.

33. **(B)** Discrete means separate, as in three discrete parts. One thing that you know about the word is that it is NOT discreet, which means tactful and quiet, thus (A) and (C) are incorrect. Combined is a good opposite, if not perfect.

34. **(D)** Primitive means basic, undeveloped, but not necessarily strong; thus, (C) is incorrect. Similarly, (A) is not connected. The other three answer choices are all referring to various levels of development of different ideas. The contrast between the answer choices shows that naive is a low level of development of understanding of the way things work, and is thus more of a synonym than an opposite. Sophisticated has to do with a highly developed understanding of something, while knowledgeable has to do with having a great deal of knowledge about something. Thus, sophisticated has the connotation of great development, which corresponds to the sense of primitive as having very little development.

35. **(B)** Partition means to divide into parts. Both (A) and (B) have some meaning of joining together, which is opposite to partition. In distinguishing solidify from unify, you might ask what the opposite of solid is. Since the opposite of solid is liquid, and partition refers to dividing into parts rather than liquefying, solidify is not correct. Parse means to separate into parts grammatically and is thus either the same as the stem word, or unrelated. Maintain is also unrelated. Enjoin is a word that has a superficial appeal since joining is what is wanted in an answer. However, enjoin means to legally forbid something from happening.

36. **(B)** Clandestine means secret, private, or concealed, usually on purpose. (A), (B), and (C) all have some merit. Outside, by itself, is not the opposite of hidden. Aboveground and public are therefore the two best answers, and both have a real oppositeness to clandestine. In choosing between them, the key factor is the very specific way in which aboveground works versus the more general meaning of public. The perfect opposite to aboveground is underground, which certainly means hidden, but public specifically means that it is revealed. Underground/aboveground refers more to the legitimacy of the activity—can it stand the light of day?—than to whether it is hidden or not. While it is true that clandestine activities by certain groups have, in recent years, been characterized as illicit, that is not part of the original meaning of the word clandestine. The shady flavor comes from the idea that a clandestine activity may be kept hidden by deception.

37. **(D)** Phlegmatic means cooly self-possessed and undemonstrative. Effusive means to make a great demonstration of feeling. Hoarse connects to the idea of phlegm in the throat, which might make one hoarse, but that is not helpful here.

38. **(E)** Manumit means to free a slave; hence enslave is a perfect opposite.

SECTION III

1. **(D)** Since we do not know for how long either car travelled, we cannot draw any conclusion about how far the cars travelled. For example, if both travelled for an equal amount of time, then car B will have travelled farther. But if car B travelled for one hour while car A travelled for two hours, then car A would have travelled farther (60 miles versus 40 miles).

2. **(A)** The number 46 is equal to 4(10) plus 6. The number 3612 is equal to 3(1000) plus 6(100) plus 1(10) plus 2. So there are four tens in 46, and there are three thousands in 3612, so our answer must be (A).

3. **(B)** Since 7.636 is greater than 7.635, the numbers following the third-place digit (5) are irrelevant to the comparison. No matter how far the decimal on the left is extended, it will never reach 7.636.

4. **(D)** Although BD is perpendicular to AC, we should not conclude that it bisects AC:

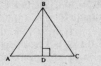

These configurations are consistent with the information given in the problem and show that no conclusion about AD and DC is possible.

5. **(A)** Probably the easiest way to solve this problem is to perform the indicated operations:

$$\frac{12}{2} = 6 \qquad \frac{12}{4} = 3$$

So Column A is greater than Column B.

6. **(C)** Since the dimensions of this triangle are 3, 4, and 5, it must be a right triangle: $5^2 = 4^2 + 3^2$. The converse of the Pythagorean Theorem (the square of the hypotenuse of a right triangle is equal to the sum of the squares of the two other sides) is that any triangle in which the square of the longest side is equal to the sum of the squares of the two remaining sides is a right triangle. Since this is a right triangle and 5 is the longest side, 5 must be opposite a 90° angle. The two remaining angles must total 90° since there are 180° in any triangle. Since x is 90° and $z + y = 90°$, the two columns are equal.

7. **(C)** Rather than actually doing the calculation (that is, multiplying 30 by 30 and then converting the measurements in Column B to inches and multiplying them), the problem is more easily solved by recognizing that the sides of the two squares are equal in length. 2 feet 6 inches is equal to 30 inches. Since both have equal sides, and since the area of a square is solely a function of the length of its side (s × s = area), our two squares must be equal in area.

8. **(C)** Since vertical angles are equal, we know that a = z, b = y, and c = x. Therefore, a + b + c must be equal to x + y + z.

9. **(C)** The proper way of approaching this question is to fill in the blanks in the figure:

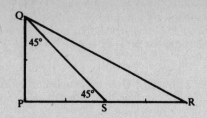

We know that x = 45°, since 90° + 45° + x = 180°. That allows us to conclude that QP = PS, since both are opposite equal angles.

10. **(C)** At first glance this result is surprising since the two triangles have such different shapes. However, the formula for area is the guide. Area is equal to height times base divided by 2. If the height and base are equal, then the area will be equal. PS = SR, so the bases are equal. The heights are equal since the line PQ is a measure of the height of both triangles since it is the perpendicular distance from Q to the base of both triangles.

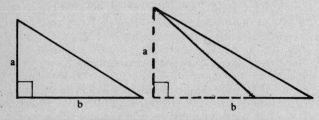

Since the triangles have bases *and* altitudes of equal length, their areas too must be equal—despite the fact that they have different shapes.

11. **(B)** Since there are 24 hours in a day, 16 hours represents $\frac{16}{24}$ of a day, or $\frac{2}{3}$. Then, since there are 60 minutes in an hour, 45 minutes represents $\frac{45}{60}$ of an hour, or $\frac{3}{4}$. Since $\frac{3}{4}$ is larger than $\frac{2}{3}$, our answer choice is (B).

12. **(A)** The three greatest odd integers less than 20 are 19, 17, 15; the even ones less than 20 are 18, 16, 14. You could add them up to get 51 in Column A and 48 in Column B. But why bother? 19 > 18, 17 > 16, and 15 > 14, so the odds have it.

13. **(A)** We already know Debbie's average rate per hour; that is given in the centered information as 7.2 miles/hour. How, then, are we to compute the rate for Roberta? One way, among many others, of doing this is to set up a direct proportion:

$$\frac{1 \text{ mile}}{7.2 \text{ minutes}} = \frac{x \text{ miles}}{60 \text{ minutes}}$$

This is the mathematical way of writing "If Roberta runs 1 mile every 7.2 minutes, then she can run x miles in 60 minutes." Arithmetically, we then cross-multiply to solve for x:

7.2x = 60
x = 8.33

So Roberta's speed is greater than Debbie's, and (A) must be the answer.

14. **(B)** The best approach to this problem may be to set up a number line.

A's grade is higher than that of B.
B's grade is higher than that of C.
D's grade is less than that of C.
E's grade is less than that of D.

This shows us that A's grade is the greatest and E's is the least. So Column B must be greater than Column A.

15. **(C)** This is a rather difficult problem. But the difficulty is not in the starting—it lies between the starting and the finishing. There is really only one starting point, and that is to manipulate the centered equation to find x, since x is what we are asked about:

$$x = \frac{1}{4}\left(3x + \frac{8}{x^2}\right)$$

Multiplying by 4: $4x = 3x + \frac{8}{x^2}$

Subtracting 3x: $x = \frac{8}{x^2}$

Multiplying by x^2: $x^3 = 8$
So: $x = 2$

Since x = 2, the two columns must be equal. There is yet another note to be made. Since this was a difficult problem, it might have been wise to skip it in order to get on to the remaining fifteen problems in the section. It would have been a mistake to spend 4 or 5 minutes trying to solve this item, when the questions which follow are much easier.

16. **(D)** Of course, one sure method for comparing the fractions is to convert each to its decimal equivalent and then to compare the equivalents directly. That process, however, will surely be too time-consuming, and is, in any event, totally unnecessary. The "test-wise" approach to a problem of this sort is to find a benchmark by which each of the fractions can be measured. In this case, it appears that $\frac{1}{2}$ will do nicely. We can then see that $\frac{2}{3}$, $\frac{3}{5}$, $\frac{17}{29}$, and $\frac{4}{5}$ are all greater than $\frac{1}{2}$, while $\frac{3}{7}$ is less than $\frac{1}{2}$. So $\frac{3}{7}$ must be the smallest of the group.

17. **(C)** The formula for the area of a square is *side times side*. Since the square has an area of 16, we know s × s = 16, $s^2 = 16$, so side = 4. Then we compute the perimeter of the square as the sum of the lengths of its four sides: 4 + 4 + 4 + 4 = 16.

18. **(C)** Since John has more money than Mary, we note that x is greater than y. Then, John has less money than Bill has, so x is less than z. This gives us x > y or y < x and x < z. Thus (C), y < x < z.

19. **(D)** One way to attack this question is to multiply the expression $(x - y)^2$ and then substitute the value 3 for x. $(x - y)^2 = 4$, so $x^2 - 2xy + y^2 = 4$. Then, if x = 3, we have $(3)^2 - 2(3)y + y^2 = 4$, or 9 − 6y + y^2 = 4. Now we rewrite that in standard form (grouping like terms and arranging terms in descending order of exponents): $y^2 - 6y + 5 = 0$. At this juncture, the mathematicians will factor the expression on the left: (y − 5)(y − 1) = 0. Thus, the two roots of the equation are 5 and 1. So, 5 is a possible value.

   Of course, a non-mathematical attack is also possible. We know that one of the five answers must be correct. So, we can simply try each one until we find one that will fit in the equation. For this we begin by putting 3 in for x: $(3 - y)^2 = 4$. We then test (A): $(3 - -5)^2 = (8)^2 = 64$ and 64 ≠ 4, so we know that −5 is not a possible value for y. On the other hand, if we try (D): $(3 - 5)^2 = (-2)^2 = 4$, and 4 does equal 4. We have taken a shortcut here by not working each of the answer choices.

20. **(C)** There are several ways of running the calculation for this problem. One way is to reason: 10% of 360 is 36. Since 5% is one half of 10%, 5% of 360 is one half of 36, or 18. Since 10% of 360 is 36, and since 5% of 360 is 18, the difference between the two is 36 − 18 = 18.

21. **(E)** Again, perhaps the most natural starting point for a solution is working on the expression, rearranging by grouping like terms. $x^2 + 3x + 10 = 1 + x^2$. By transposing (subtracting from both sides) the x^2 term, we see that the x^2 is eliminated:

   3x + 10 = 1, so 3x = −9, and x = −3

   Although the x^2 terms was eliminated from our initial expression, we know the value of x. It is now a simple matter to substitute −3 for x in the expression x^2, and we learn $x^2 = 9$.

22. **(A)** The question tests whether you understand how to read the chart. This chart is cumulative. By that we mean that the number of imports is added to the number of domestic vehicles. In 1971, 6 million domestic vehicles were purchased. Then, the number of imports is the *difference* between 6 million (the top of the domestic-production part of

the chart) and 8.25 million (the top of the import-production part of the chart). 8.25 − 6 = 2.25 million. The number 8.25 million is the *combined total* of import and domestic cars.

23. **(E)** For the information necessary to answer this question, we consult the Financial Factors graph. The left-hand grouping of bars shows us the *Percent Increase* in the average purchase price. From 1950 to 1960, the average purchase price rose by 75%. Then, from 1960 to 1970, it rose by another 150%. Given this, we can compute the total percent increase. Now, it would be an error simply to add these two numbers together. The 150% increase starts from a larger *base* than does the 75% increase. Suppose that the average purchase price in 1950 is x (or, for the non-mathematicians, we might just assume a nice round number such as $100). Then, from 1950 to 1960, that number increased by 75%. Since 75% of x is .75x, the increase was .75x (or 75% of $100 or $75), bringing the average price up to 1.75x (or $100 + $75 = $175). Then we have another 150% increase on top of the 1.75x. 150% of 1.75x is 2.625x (or $262.50), which must then be added to the 1.75x (or $175). This brings the average price to approximately 4.40x (or $440). We started with an average purchase price of x ($100); we ended with an average purchase price of 4.40x ($440). So we can now compute the percentage increase. Percentage increase is found by taking the difference between the two values and forming a fraction, placing the difference over the earlier total: $\dfrac{4.40x - x}{x} = \dfrac{3.40x}{x} = 3.40$. Then the 3.40 is converted from a decimal to a percentage by multiplying by 100, so the total percentage increase is 340%.

24. **(C)** For this question we use the method of compare and eliminate. From 1950 to 1951, purchases increase by slightly less than 1 million. Then, from 1959 to 1960, purchases also grew by slightly less than 1 million. But instead of trying to refine our comparison at this point, let us place both (A) and (B) on the back burner, and then we can check the remaining choices to see whether one of them is larger than both (A) and (B). We move to (C), and the increase in vehicles purchased was about $1\frac{1}{2}$ million. So we can eliminate both (A) and (B), and we did that without trying to be very precise about the value for (A) and (B). Then we move to (D). From 1964 to 1966 purchases appear to have risen by just about one million, so we eliminate (D) from consideration, preserving (C) as our best choice thus far. Finally, we check (E). From 1971 to 1974 the total actually declined, so (C) must be our answer.

25. **(D)** We explained the method for computing percentage increase when we examined question 23 of this series. We create a fraction using the

difference between the two totals as the numerator and the earlier total as the denominator. Here the average number of vehicles owned increases from about 1.1 in 1950—notice the chart does not begin at zero—to 2.2 in 1974. The difference between 2.2 and 1.1. is 1.1, and the earlier total is 1.1, so our fraction is $\frac{1.1}{1.1} = 1$. Then we multiply that decimal number by 100 to convert to a percentage: $1 \times 100 = 100\%$.

26. **(C)** Proposition I is true. It is the geometry theorem that two lines parallel to a third must be parallel to each other.

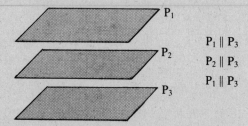

Proposition II is also necessarily true. Just as with lines, if two planes are parallel to a third plane, they must likewise be parallel to each other.

$$P_1 \parallel P_3$$
$$P_2 \parallel P_3$$
$$P_1 \parallel P_3$$

Proposition III, however, is not necessarily true. Two lines might be drawn in a plane parallel to another plane and yet intersect with one another:

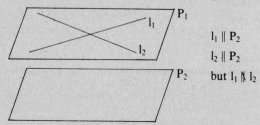

$$l_1 \parallel P_2$$
$$l_2 \parallel P_2$$
$$\text{but } l_1 \nparallel l_2$$

27. **(C)** We all know the simple formula that price minus discount equals discounted price—that much is just common-sense arithmetic. What we sometimes overlook, however, is the fact that the discounted price can be expressed either in monetary terms, e.g., $5.00 or 37¢, or in percentage terms, e.g., 50% of the original price. In this case, the discount is given as a percentage of the original price. So we have, original price − 90¢ = 90% of original price; or, using x for the original price: $x - \$.90 = .9x$. This is an equation with only one variable, so we proceed to solve for x: $.1x = \$.90$, so $x = \$9.00$.

28. **(D)** We begin by computing the length of the side of the square ABCD. Since the x and y axes meet on the perpendicular, we have a right triangle formed by the origin (the point of intersection of x and y) and points A and B. Since point A has the coordinates (2,0), we know that OA is two units long—the x coordinate is 2. Similarly, point B is two units removed from O, so OB is also two units long. Thus, the two legs of our right triangle are 2 and 2. Using the Pythagorean Theorem:

$$2^2 + 2^2 = s^2, \text{ so } s = \sqrt{8} = 2\sqrt{2}$$

Now that we have the length of the side, we compute the area of ABCD by side × side: $(2\sqrt{2})(2\sqrt{2}) = 8$.

29. **(A)** This problem is particularly elusive since there is no really clear starting point. One way of getting a handle on it is to manipulate the expression $\frac{x}{y} + \frac{n}{m}$. If we add the two terms together using the common denominator of my, we have $\frac{mx + ny}{my}$. We can see that this bears a striking similarity to the first equation given in the problem: mx + ny = 12 my. If we manipulate that equation by dividing both sides by my, we have $\frac{mx + ny}{my} = 12$. But since $\frac{x}{y} + \frac{n}{m}$ is equivalent to $\frac{mx + ny}{my}$, we are entitled to conclude that $\frac{x}{y} + \frac{n}{m}$ is also equal to 12.

30. **(D)** This problem, too, is fairly difficult. The difficulty stems from the fact that its solution requires several different formulas. For example, we can conclude that (A) is necessarily true. MN is not a diameter. We know this since a diameter passes through the center of the circle. So whatever the length of MN, it is less than that of the diameter (the diameter is the longest chord which can be drawn in a circle). Since 2MO would be equal to a diameter (twice the radius is the diameter), and since MN is less than a diameter, we can conclude that MN is less than 2MO. We also know that z = y. Since MO and NO are both radii of circle O, they must be equal. So we know that in triangle MNO, MO = NO; and since angles opposite equal sides are equal, we conclude that z = y. (B) requires still another line of reasoning. Since MN is greater than NO, the angle opposite MN, which is x, must be greater than the angle opposite NO, which is y. So x is greater than y. Finally, (E) requires yet another line of reasoning. If MN were equal to NO, it would also be equal to MO, since MO and NO are both radii. In that case, we would have an equilateral triangle and all angles would be 60°. Since MN is greater than MO and NO, the angle opposite MN, which is x, must be greater than 60°. So (D) must be the correct answer. A moment's reflection will show that it is not necessarily true that x = y + z. This would be true only in the event that MNO is a right triangle, but there is no information given in the problem from which we are entitled to conclude that x° = 90°.

SECTION IV

1. **(B)** One sure approach to this problem is to perform the addition indicated in the right-hand column: $\frac{1}{0.1} + \frac{0.1}{10} = \frac{100 + 1}{10} = \frac{101}{10} = 10.1$. This shows that Column B is larger. A quicker way of finding the correct answer is to divide .1 into 1, which yields 10. Then, no matter what the second term of Column B turns out to be, when it is added to the first term, the sum must be greater than 10.

2. **(C)** Since l_1 and l_2 are parallel, the third line creates a whole set of angle relationships, e.g., alternate interior angles are equal, and so on. For this problem, all we really need to see is that x and y must be equal since the transverse cuts the parallel lines on the perpendicular (all angles created must be equal to 90°). Because x and y are both 90°, our answer must be (C).

3. **(C)** The first line of attack on a problem like this is to cancel, thereby simplifying the comparison:
$$\frac{\cancel{3}}{\cancel{1}} \times \frac{\cancel{1}}{\cancel{2}} \times \frac{\cancel{6}}{\cancel{1}} \times \frac{\cancel{1}}{\cancel{6}} = 1$$
$$\frac{\cancel{4}}{\cancel{1}} \times \frac{\cancel{1}}{\cancel{4}} \times \frac{\cancel{7}}{\cancel{1}} \times \frac{\cancel{1}}{\cancel{7}} = 1$$

It is clear that 1 is equal to 1, so our answer must be (C).

4. **(A)** Since we are asked about x, the first line of attack here must be to solve for x in the centered equation:
$$3x + 2 = 11$$
$$3x = 9$$
$$x = 3$$

Since x is 3, and 3 is greater than 2, our answer must be (A). Merely substituting 2 for x would only eliminate (C).

5. **(D)** One approach is to recognize that no comparison of 5% of an unspecified number and 5% of a different unspecified number is possible. For those who had any difficulty with this insight, however, a good attack on the problem would be to divide both sides of the comparison by 5%. This effectively removes the 5%, reducing the comparison to x versus y. Now it is even easier to see that the answer must be (D) since no information is provided about x and y except the fact that each is greater than zero.

6. **(A)** This is a relatively difficult problem. To solve it, the student needs to recognize that if the triangle had dimensions of 3, 4, and 5 it would be a right triangle: $3^2 + 4^2 = 5^2$. That is to say, all triangles which have dimensions that satisfy the Pythagorean Theorem must have a 90° angle. If we knew that x was 90°, we would know that the remaining two angles would have to total to 90° because there are 180° in a triangle. But this is not a case of a 3–4–5 triangle, and 3, 4, and 5.1 will not satisfy the Pythagorean Theorem, so this is *not* a right triangle. Given that it is not a right triangle, then, we need to ask in what way does it differ from a right triangle. The answer is that the side 5.1 is slightly larger than 5, which would have given us a right triangle. So, too, angle x must be slightly larger than 90°. Now if x is slightly larger than 90°, the sum of the remaining two angles must be slightly less than 90° because, again, there are only 180° in a triangle. So x° must be greater than y° + z°.

7. **(A)** We begin our attack on this problem by solving for x and y in the equations given:
$$\frac{x}{3} - 16 = 32 \qquad \frac{y}{4} + 12 = 24$$
$$\frac{x}{3} = 48 \qquad \frac{y}{4} = 12$$
$$x = 144 \qquad y = 48$$

Since x is larger than y, our answer must be (A).

Another method would be to see that $\frac{x}{3}$ with 16 subtracted is larger than $\frac{y}{4}$ with 12 added. Thus $\frac{x}{3}$ is much larger, relatively speaking, than $\frac{y}{4}$ and, even though the 4 versus 3 in the denominator is a reason for $\frac{y}{4}$ to be smaller than $\frac{x}{3}$, it might seem clear that x must be larger. There is no problem with negative numbers since both $\frac{x}{3}$ and $\frac{y}{4}$ are positive, which means that both x and y are positive.

8. **(B)** Performing the indicated operations:

Column A	Column B
$x(x + 3) + 2(x + 3)$	$(x + 3)^2$
$x^2 + 3x + 2x + 6$	$(x + 3)(x + 3)$
$x^2 + 5x + 6$	$x^2 + 6x + 9$

Subtracting x^2, 5x, and 6 from both columns:

$$0 \qquad x + 3$$

Since $x > 0$, Column B is greater than 3, and therefore larger than Column A.

9. **(C)** Let us first draw the picture:

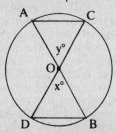

Now, most students will intuitively see that AB must be equal to CD no matter what the magnitudes of x° and y are. (Note: We mean by 'intuitively' not measurement or reliance on eye-estimation, but merely the sort of thing where one says, "I can't prove it, but I know it must be correct.") A simple proof can also be given. Since x and y are equal (vertical angles are equal), they intercept equal arcs (cut off equal parts of the circle). The chords (AB and CD) subtend (join) equal arcs of the same circle and so must be equal.

Another way of proving that AC = BC is to point out that AO and CO are radii and are equal to CO and BO, which are also radii. Then we know that x and y are equal, so AOC and COB are congruent triangles. Consequently, the third sides must also be equal.

10. **(D)** At first glance, it might appear that x and y must be equal. After all, any number raised to the zero power is equal to 1. And this reasoning would be sound if the base were anything except 1. For 1 raised to any power is equal to 1:

$$1^{7-1} = 1^6 = 1$$
$$1^{7-5} = 1^2 = 1$$

So the values of x and y are not important: 1 raised to any power is still just 1.

11. **(A)** We begin by filling in more details:

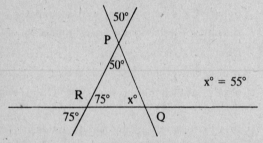

This is because vertical angles are equal. Then we can compute the remaining angle as 55° (50° + 75° + x = 180°, x = 55°). Now, in any given triangle, the larger the angle the longer the side. Since PQ is opposite a 75° angle while RP is opposite a 55° angle, PQ must be larger than RP.

12. **(C)** It is possible to solve this comparison using simultaneous equations or substitution: Let x be the number of adult tickets, and let y be the number of children's tickets. Then x − y = 29, and 5x + 2.5y = 302.50. But there is an easier way. Let us assume, for the purposes of analysis, that the number of adult tickets sold was exactly 50. On that assumption, the receipts derived from adult tickets was $250. We know further, on that assumption, that 21 tickets were sold for $2.50, and total receipts from children's tickets would be $52.50. Combining our two totals, we come up with gross sales of $302.50. And since that is the total receipts specified in the centered information, we have proved that the number of adult tickets is 50.

If the resulting total dollars had not equalled what the problem told us it should, then (C) would be eliminated as a possible answer choice. If the total based on the assumption of the columns being equal was high, then fewer tickets were sold than assumed.

13. **(A)** This problem is solved by merely counting on one's fingers. The first multiple of 4 greater than 281 is 284 (284 divided by 4 = 71), the second is 288, the third is 292, the fourth is 296, and the fifth is 300. So there are five multiples of 4 between 281 and 301. The first multiple of 5 greater than 2401 is 2405, the second is 2410, the third is 2415 and that is the last one that is less than 2419. So there are only three multiples of 5 between 2401 and 2419. Since 5 is greater than 3, our answer choice must be (A).

Another method would be to notice that there are more numbers from 281 to 301 than from 2401 to 2419 and that you cover more ground with a multiple of 5 than a multiple of 4, so Column A would be a longer distance on the number line in smaller pieces, while Column B would be a smaller distance and larger pieces. The specification of multiples might work against that since we are not addressing the length, but the number of multiples, but Column A starts with a multiple of 4 while Column B starts just after a multiple of 5.

14. **(C)** This is a fairly difficult problem. The first thing to realize is that x = 60° and y = 30°. We learn this by a calculation. Since x is twice as large as y, we know that x = 26. Then we also know that x + y = 90. By substitution, we have y + 2y = 90, so y = 30 and x = 60. We can now see that we have the special case of the right, or 30:60:90, triangle. In such a triangle, the side opposite the 30° angle is equal to one-half the hypotenuse, and the side opposite the 60° angle is equal to one-half the hypotenuse times the square root of three:

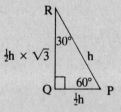

Since PR is the hypotenuse, PQ is the side opposite the 30°angle, and PQ = ½PR. So we can substitute ½PR for PQ in the right column: $\frac{\frac{1}{2}PR}{PR} = \frac{1}{2}$; so our two columns are equal.

15. **(C)** It is possible to go through an entire computation here. By the Pythagorean Theorem, DC and CB must be:

$$s^2 + s^2 = 1^2$$
$$2s^2 = 1$$
$$s = \sqrt{\tfrac{1}{2}}$$
$$s = \frac{1}{\sqrt{2}} = \frac{\sqrt{2}}{2}$$

Then DC and CB can function as altitude and base of DCB, and we use the formula for the area of a triangle: $\frac{1}{2}ab = \frac{1}{2}(\sqrt{2}/2)(\sqrt{2}/2) = \frac{1}{4}$. The area of the square is easily gotten as $1 \times 1 = 1$. So the area of the entire figure is $1 + \frac{1}{4}$ or 1.25. But there is an easier way to solve the problem:

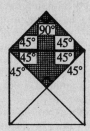

We can see intuitively that DCB is $\frac{1}{4}$ the area of the square. Since the area of the square is 1, the area of DCB must be $\frac{1}{4}$, and the combined areas are 1.25, the area of the entire polygon ABCDE.

16. **(D)** This is a relatively easy problem. It can be solved by doing the subtraction: $\frac{4}{5} - \frac{3}{4} = \frac{16 - 15}{20} = \frac{1}{20}$. In this case, a substitution of percentages for fractions might be useful if you are knowledgeable about the equivalencies: $\frac{4}{5} = 80\%$ and $\frac{3}{4} = 75\%$. $80\% - 75\% = 5\% = \frac{1}{20}$.

17. **(C)** First we must convert one and one-half yards into inches. There are 36 inches in a yard, so one and one-half yards must contain $36 + 18$ or 54 inches. Now, to determine how many two-inch segments there are in 54 inches, we just divide 54 by 2, which equals 27. So there must be 27 two-inch segments in a segment which is one and one-half yards long.

18. **(B)** It is important to remember that the positive x values are to the right of the origin (the intersection between the x and y axes), and that the negative values on the x axis are to the left of the origin. Also, the positive y values are above the origin, while the negative y values are below the x axis.

	y	
(−,+)		(+,+)
II		I
		x
III		IV
(−,−)		(+,−)

When reading an ordered pair such as (x,y) (called ordered because the first place is always the x-coordinate and the second place is always the y-coordinate), we know the first element is the movement on the horizontal or x axis, while the second element of the pair gives us the vertical distance. In this case, we are five units to the left of the origin, so that gives us an x value of negative 5. We are 2 units above the horizontal axis, so that gives us the second value (y) of +2. Thus our ordered pair is (−5,2), answer (B).

19. **(B)** The formula for computing the circumference of a circle is $2\pi r$. In this case our radius is 4, so the circumference of the circle is 8π. Now, P and Q will be as far apart as they can possibly be when they are directly opposite one another:

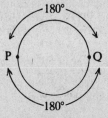

Or a half circle away from each other. So the maximum distance by which P and Q could be separated—measured by the circumference of the circle and not as the crow flies—is one-half the circumference, or 4π.

20. **(E)** Remember that a prime number is an integer which has only itself and 1 as integral factors. Thus, 13, 17, 41, and 79 are all prime numbers because their only factors are 13 and 1, 17 and 1, 41 and 1, and 79 and 1, respectively. 91, however, is not a prime number since it can be factored by 7 and 13 as well as by 1 and 91.

21. **(C)** The natural starting point here would be to draw the picture:

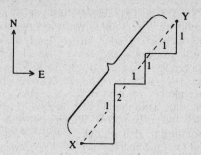

Since directions are perpendicular, we can perform the needed calculation with the Pythagorean Theorem. To simplify things, we can show that the above picture is equivalent to this:

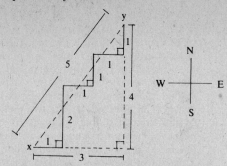

Now we can solve for the distance between X and Y with one use of the Pythagorean Theorem. Since the two legs of the right triangle are 3 and 4, we know that the hypotenuse must be 5. (Remember that 3, 4, and 5, or any multiples thereof such as 6, 8, and 10, always make a right triangle.)

22. **(C)** Let us begin by substituting x, y, and z for ∠QPS and ∠TPR. Since ∠QPS and ∠TPR are equal, we know x + y = z + y, and since y = y, we know that x = z. As for (A) and (B), we do not know whether y is equal to x and z; it could be larger or smaller or equal:

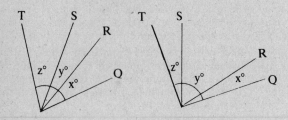

We can also eliminate (D) since we have no information that would lead us to conclude that all three are of equal measure.

23. **(D)** The footnote at the bottom of the chart tells us that the annual rate, that is shown in the table, is computed by taking the actual profits made in the quarter and multiplying by 4. An annual rate for a quarter shows how the store would do in a year if the quarter's activity were maintained for a whole year (over four quarters). So, to compute the actual profit for that quarter we need to divide by 4:

$$\frac{\$1.6 \text{ million}}{4} = \$.4 \text{ million}$$

24. **(D)** There are two interesting points to be made about this question. First, in dealing with a problem like this, you must start from the answer choices. In essence, the question asks "of the following five choices . . . ." It is often a waste of time to go first to the chart to find the quarter in which profits were actually the lowest for all quarters shown on the chart. That is, in fact, the first quarter of 1978, but that does not appear as an answer choice. Second, although the number recorded by the graph is actually four times that of actual profits (see question 23 above), there is no need to divide each of these by four. Obviously, the greater the annual profit rate, the larger the actual profit made in the quarter. In this case, the smallest annual rate of the five listed in the problem occurred in the third quarter of 1978, about $0.75 million, so the actual profits must have been smallest in that quarter.

25. **(A)** This is a fairly simple problem. We need only consult the graph for that period to see that in six quarters, the annual profit rate exceeded $1.5 million: 2nd quarter of 1979 ($1.6 million), 3rd quarter of 1979 ($1.7 million), 4th quarter of 1979 ($1.9 million), 2nd quarter of 1980 ($1.8 million), 3rd quarter of 1980 ($2.1 million), and 4th quarter of 1980 ($2.3 million).

26. **(C)** Remember that the amount reported on the graph is four times the actual profits made in the quarter. So, if we take the annual profit rate for each quarter and divide it by four, we will have the actual profits for each quarter. We can then add those numbers up to get the annual profits (actual). It is a bit simpler, however, just to add the four annual rates and then divide the whole thing by 4:

1st	1.4 million
2nd	1.8 million
3rd	2.1 million
4th	2.3 million
Total	7.6 million

$7.6 million divided by four = $1.9 million. So the actual profit in that year was $1.9 million.

In practice, however, an estimate rather than a complete calculation will suffice since the answer choices are fairly far apart, though (C) and (D) are somewhat similar. The four quarters of 1980 go up, with the balance point or average somewhere around 1.8. Since that was the annualized figure, (C) would be good choice. (D) and (E) are impossible since each of the four quarters had rates above those choices, while (A) and (B) are figures beyond the highest reach of the chart.

27. **(C)** Again, we can simply use annual rates. There is no reason to divide everything by 4 for each quarter. The annual rates for 1977 are:

1st	1.3 million
2nd	1.1 million
3rd	0.9 million
4th	0.7 million
Total	4.0 million

We can retrieve the total for 1980 from question 26 above, and work the percentage change formula: $\frac{7.6 - 4.0}{4.0} = \frac{3.6}{4.0} = \frac{9}{10}$ which is 90%. Again, estimation can save work. The four quarters of

1977 are in orderly progression, with the midpoint being 0.9. As noted for problem 26, the 1980 profits can be estimated at 1.8 or slightly less (1st quarter is farther below 1.8 than other quarters are above 1.8). An increase from 0.9 to 1.8 would be a 100% increase, which is closest to (C).

28. **(A)** This problem is rather tedious, though it is not conceptually difficult. Let us start working in the interior:

$$4 - 3(2 + 1(3 - (2 + 3) + 2) + 2) + 4$$
$$4 - 3(2 + 1(3 - \quad 5 \quad + 2) + 2) + 4$$
$$4 - 3(2 + 1(\quad 0 \quad) + 2) + 4$$
$$4 - 3(2 + \quad 0 \quad + 2) + 4$$
$$4 - 3(\quad 4 \quad) + 4$$
$$4 \quad -12 \quad + 4$$
$$- 4$$

29. **(C)** By this juncture the drill should be well known. We must begin by drawing a picture:

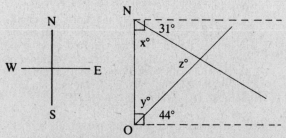

Now, since the angles at N and O are 90°, we can compute the magnitude of x and y: $x = 90° - 31° = 59°$, and $y = 90° - 44° = 46°$. Then, since x, y, and z are the interior angles of a triangle, we know $x + y + z = 180°$. Substituting for x and y, we have $59° + 46° + z = 180°$, and we solve for z: $z = 75°$. Since z is the angle of intersection between the two highways, our answer must be (C).

30. **(B)** Let us use x to represent the sum of money. Then we know that when x is divided equally by n, the result is $60; or, expressed in formal notation: $\frac{x}{n} = 60$. We then know that when x is divided by n + 1 (that is, the original number plus another child), the result is $50, or $\frac{x}{n + 1} = 50$. Now, let us manipulate these equations so that we isolate n:

$$\frac{x}{n} = 60 \qquad \frac{x}{n + 1} = 50$$
$$\frac{x}{60} = n \qquad \frac{x}{50} = n + 1$$
$$\frac{x}{60} = n \qquad \left(\frac{x}{50}\right) - 1 = n$$

Since n = n, we know that $x/60 = x/50 - 1$, and we have an equation with only one variable: $x/60 - x/50 = -1$, so:

$$\frac{5x - 6x}{300} = -1$$

AND: $\quad -x = -300$

SO: $\quad x = 300$

The sum of money is $300 and our answer is (B). (Note that you could also solve for n; in this case n = 5, and 5 × $60 = $300.)

SECTION V

Questions 1–4

Arranging the Information

This problem has two aspects, the order in which items have to be done and the times during the week when the various offices and individuals are available. Note that although the first statement in the information set does seem to give some feeling that thesis approval by the professors must come after the filling out of the application, this would be reading too much into the problem. In fact, the additional statements about the required order of events indicate, by silence about the timing of thesis approval, that the approval can come after the visit to the dean. Question 4 supports this by putting the approval process ahead of the other items. The filing at the Financial Aid Office must be last.

Since the information is given to us in terms of mornings and afternoons, that is the way to arrange it. There are no immediate interactions between the items of information (such as might have been the case if Professor Fansler's office hours were always three days after Professor Cross's, or if the Dean's hours were described in terms of those of the Financial Aid Office). Therefore, a straight listing of the information on hours is all that is required.

	MON.	TUES.	WED.	THUR.	FRI.
AM	Fin. Aid	Fin. Aid		Dean	Dean
	Fansler	Fansler			Fin. Aid
		Cross			Cross
PM	Dean	Dean			
			Fin. Aid		

DEAN MUST PRECEDE FIN. AID; FIN. AID LAST; PROF'S PRE/POST DEAN.

Answering the Questions

1. **(D)** Since the thesis must be approved by Fansler only and not by Cross, only Monday and Tuesday mornings are possibilities, which eliminates (C) and (E). The student also has to go to the Financial Aid Office after seeing the professor.

Since the Financial Aid Office is open on both Monday and Tuesday mornings, both of those times are good; hence, (D) rather than (A) or (B).

2. **(E)** This problem is, of course, separate from the preceding one, so we must consider that the student is starting out fresh and needs to see the Dean, a professor, and the Financial Aid Office. They are asking for what must be false, so we seek elimination by seeing possibilities.

   I is not necessarily false, because it is possible to have thesis approval from Professor Cross and complete the job in one day. On Friday morning all three of the required parties are open for business and, ignoring waiting time (which you do because if they didn't bring it up, you shouldn't), there would be no problem. This eliminates answer choices (A) and (D).

   II is false because Professor Fansler's approval can only be obtained on Monday or Tuesday morning. While it is true that both the Financial Aid Office and the Dean are open on Mondays and Tuesdays, the order is wrong. By the time the Dean is open for business the Financial Aid Office is closed, so the application cannot be filed that day. This eliminates answer (C).

   III is also false because neither of the professors is available in the afternoon. Hence, (B) is out and (E) is correct.

3. **(D)** This problem does not require that the process be completed in any particular time, but only that all the action take place on Tuesdays and Thursdays. Since both professors have office hours on Tuesdays, statements I and II are not necessarily true. As it happens, this is enough to give you the answer since all of the answer choices except (D) allege that either I or II or both are true.

   III is false because on Thursdays only the Dean is open, and because on Tuesdays the Financial Aid Office closes before the Dean opens, as was previously discussed.

   IV requires you to interpret what a school week might be. If a mere seven-day period was intended (start on Thursday and complete on the following Tuesday), that would not be called a "school" week. A school week is Monday through Friday, and the application cannot be done on a consecutive Tuesday and Thursday. Thus, all four of the statements are false.

4. **(C)** On Wednesday and Thursday only one of the proper offices is open, so they are not possible one-visit days, but this only eliminates (D). Friday morning is a possible one-visit time, which eliminates answer choice (A). Monday and Tuesday mornings, while blessed with open offices for the professors and the Financial Aid Office, do not have the Dean, so (E) is eliminated (as is (D) for the second time).

   Monday and Tuesday have the problem of order of office openings previously referred to, and thus are not one-visit days—which eliminates (B), leaving (C) as the answer.

5. **(C)** Notice that the student responds to the professor's comment by saying, "That can't be true," and then uses the Duchess of Warburton as a counter-example. The Duchess would only be a counter-example to the professor's statement had the professor said that women cannot inherit the estates of their families. Thus, (C) must capture the student's misinterpretation of the professor's statement. What has misled the student is that he has attributed too much to the professor. The professor has cited the general rule of primogeniture—the eldest male child inherits—but he has not discussed the special problems which arise when no male child is born. In those cases, presumably a non-male child will have to inherit. (E) incorrectly refers to inheriting from a mother, but the student is discussing a case in which the woman inherited her father's estate. (D) is wrong for the student specifically mentions the conditions which make a child legitimate: born to the wife of her father. (A) was inserted as a bit of levity: Of course, only men can *father* children of either sex. Finally, first-born or not, a daughter cannot inherit as long as there is any male child to inherit, so (B) must be incorrect.

6. **(D)** The key phrase in this paragraph is "beef costs more per pound than fish." A careful reading would show that (A) is in direct contradiction to the explicit wording of the passage. (B) cannot be inferred since the dietician merely says, "I pay." Perhaps he intends to keep the price of a meal stable by cutting back in other areas. In any event, this is an example of not going beyond a mere factual analysis to generate policy recommendations, unless the question stem specifically invites such an extension, e.g., which of the following courses of action would the author recommend? (C) makes an unwarranted inference. From the fact that beef is more costly one would not want to conclude that it is more profitable. (E) is wrong for this reason also. (D) is correct because it focuses upon the per measure cost of protein, which explains why a fish meal will cost the dietician more than a beef meal, even though fish is less expensive per pound.

Questions 7–9

Arranging the Information

The question stems and the original information indicate that the items of interest will be what projections can be made on the basis of the given information. This means that there will be less time spent on arranging and more spent on working out the problems.

The starting information boils down to the conclusion that the subject got off at the third, fourth, fifth, or seventh floor. Since there were only three people on the elevator, this should immediately raise in your mind the possibility of subterfuge.

Answering the Questions

7. **(B)** The question stem adds a condition that builds on the fact that someone obviously pressed buttons for more than one floor, since the elevator carrying only three people, stopped four times and no one got on the elevator. There is no reason to assume on the test that either of the other two riders pushed two buttons, though in real life it is certainly a possibility. Rather, the limitation is that the subject, who is the likeliest to have pressed two buttons, would not have pressed two buttons so long as there were others in the elevator. Therefore, the second button pressed by the subject must have been after the other two riders got off the elevator. The earliest stop at which both could have gotten off the elevator is the third floor.

If we assume, as we must for the problem, that at most three buttons were pressed when the elevator started (one for each rider), then the subject could have pressed the extra button either after the third floor (if both other riders got off there) or after the fourth floor (if one rider got off at each of the third and fourth floors). Therefore, the subject did not get off at the third floor but may have gotten off at any one of the other floors. Thus, answer choice (E) is eliminated for saying that the subject may have gotten off at the third floor. Each of the other answers is possible, but we are looking for the safest conclusion, which is the one which has the least chance of being wrong. (B) is the safest conclusion because it is definitely correct within the parameters of the question. (A) omits the possibility that the subject got off at the fourth floor, (C) the fourth and seventh, and (D) the seventh.

8. **(B)** The preceding discussion in 7 indicates that there are only three possible floors on the way up the building. However, that deduction is based on the detective's assumption as stated in the question stem. This assumption does NOT carry over into the problem. If we do not have the limitation on the actions of the subject posited in 7, then the first upward ride of the elevator yields four possible floors on which the subject may have left the elevator. The downward empty return from seven limits nothing.

The second up-and-down trip described in this question stem mentions two additional floors, two and six, but only six is a possible location of the subject. The elevator stopped at two on the way up, and therefore could not have brought the

subject to two. The stairs are closed. If the subject got off on seven the first trip, then he may have gone down to six on the second trip, thus three, four, five, six, and seven are all possibilities, hence, answer (B).

9. **(E)** This seems a peculiar result, but we must be certain that we do not assume more than the problem gives us. The problem does not tell us that the subject was on the elevator when it reached the fourth floor. He may have exited on the third floor. Also, he may have exited on the fourth floor since we only know what is explicitly stated. The detective might have learned this piece of information indirectly, rather than from the people getting on and off the elevator. In any case, he knows only what they say.

The original reason for putting the subject on the top two floors was the fact that there were more stops than people, but this proves to be false for this problem. Thus, the person getting on at four may have been going to the fifth or seventh floor, leaving the other as well as three and four as possible exits for the subject. Thus, (E).

10. **(A)** Statements I and II combine to give us (A). If all wheeled conveyances which travel on the highway are polluters, and a bicycle does not travel on the highway, then a bicycle cannot be a polluter. If (A) is correct, (B) must be incorrect because bicycles do not travel on the highways at all. (C) and (D) make the same mistake. III must be read to say "if I am driving, it is raining," not "if it is raining, I am driving." (E) is clearly false since my car is driven on the highway. Don't make the problem harder than it is.

11. **(E)** Picking up on our discussion of (C) and (D) in the previous question, III must read "if I am driving, then it is raining." Let that be: "If P, then Q." If we then had not-Q, we could deduce not-P. (E) gives us not-Q by changing IV to "it is not raining." Changing I or II or even both is not going to do the trick, for they don't touch the relationship between my driving my car and rain—they deal only with pollution and we need the car to be connected. Similarly, if we change III to make it deal with pollution, we have not adjusted the connection between my driving and rain, so (C) must be wrong. (D) is the worst of all the answers. Whether rainwater is polluted or not has nothing to do with the connection between my driving and rain. Granted, there is the unstated assumption that my car only pollutes when I drive it, but this is O.K.

Questions 12–16

Arranging the Information

If we indicate the idea of "some" by putting the number of the proposition with a question mark over the two areas of a Venn diagram, we will get the following for propositions I, II, and III:

Diagram 1:

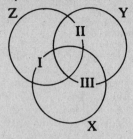

Adding the information from proposition IV, we get:

Diagram 2:

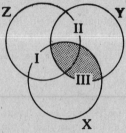

Answering the Questions

12. **(E)** Refer to Diagram 1. The three statements we are dealing with here are simply indications as to where some things are and say nothing about where things aren't. Thus, (A) cannot be known to be true from I, II, and III, and is eliminated.

The same general argument eliminates answer choices (B), (C), and (D). Since the "some" statements covered areas divided into two parts in the diagram, we cannot know which of the two areas is the actual inhabited location, or perhaps both are. The areas pointed to in the three answer choices are indicated here:

Diagram 3:

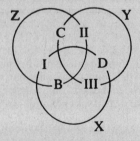

13. **(A)** Referring to Diagram 2, we see that one of the areas at first thought to be possibly inhabited in accordance with statement III is rendered impossible by statement IV's obliteration of the overlap between X and Y. This, in turn, means that only the area of X has something in it. Hence, (A) is impossible and the answer sought.

(B) and (C) refer to the two areas governed by statement I, and we do not know whether one or both of these has members. Similar reasoning applies to answer choice (D).

14. **(D)** I is already known since statement IV of the original information forbids X to be also Y. II is known for the same reasons that (A) in 13 is false. III is uncertain since II of the original information says only that there is either some member of Y + Z, or both, Hence, (D).

15. **(C)** (A) is possibly true since the Z-things which are not also Y-things might not have characteristic X. (B) is possibly true since the pure Y region is left open (logically possible). For the same reason (D) is possible: the open pure Y region does not assert there are pure Y-things—only that they are possible. (E) is incorrect since (A), (B), and (D) are possibly true. (C), however, is equivalent to "All X are Z" and that is inconsistent with the diagram.

16. **(D)** Coding in the additional information gives us this diagram:

Diagram 4:

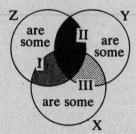

From this diagram we see that there are some individual items which are only X, others only Y, and others only Z. No overlap of any sort is permitted. (D) falsely states that Z must be X. (E) states that you cannot find a Z except for those Z that are not Y, which is correct.

Questions 17–22

Arranging the Information

Previewing the question stems for this set of questions shows that there is only one conditional question and it is based on a new individual. This leads you to suppose that you should be able to completely describe this situation. In addition, a preview of the general information at the start of the problem set indicates that there are only two ways in which the pandas are to be related to each other and that the two ways—wet/dry and fat/slim—are both separate.

Let us first arrange the information into a usable format, starting with the fat/slim idea. Each piece of information must fit in with some previously arranged piece of information in order to create a complete and valid arrangement. Since each panda's name begins with a different letter, we can use single letters to indicate each panda.

←FATTER————SLIMMER→

B fatter
than G   B   G

C slimmer than F—
can't do now

D fatter than B	D	B	G			
E slimmer than G	D	B	G	E		
F slimmer than E	D	B	G	E	F	

C slimmer than F—
can do now

	D	B	G	E	F	C

G fatter than F—
redundant

Now we can do the dry/wet idea.

←DRIER————————WETTER→

B drier than E		B	E	

C wetter than G—
can't do now

D wetter than G—
can't do now

E drier than C		B	E	C

C wetter than G—
can do now

B   E   C

← G

D wetter than G—
can do now

B   E   C

————G D→

F drier than B	F	B	E	C

————G D→

G wetter than B	F	B	E	C

————G D→

Answering the Questions

17. **(C)** Only B is on the fatter (left) side of E and also on the drier (left) side of G.

18. **(D)** Only C is both slimmer (right) and wetter (right) than E.

19. **(B)** Only D is both fatter (left) and wetter (right) than G. Even though the exact wetness position of D is not known, it is wetter than G.

20. **(D)** F is the driest (left-most) in the final diagram.

21. **(B)** I is not false for sure because the exact wetness relationship between D and C is not known. D might be wetter or drier than C. II is definitely false since F is drier than D. III is not knowable from the given information since the exact amounts by which the various pandas are fatter or slimmer is not stated. D is fatter than G, but not necessarily by three inches. However, the statement is not false because it might be true. Thus, only II is definitely false.

22. **(E)** The exact rank cannot be determined because the new panda Y's being slimmer than B and fatter than F leaves unclear the relationship between Y and pandas G and F.

23. **(B)** We have seen examples of the form of argument Holmes has in mind before: "P or Q; not-P; therefore, Q." Here, however, the first premise of Holmes' argument is more complex: "P or Q or R . . . S," with as many possibilities as he can conceive. He eliminates them one by one until no single possibility is left. The logic of the argument is perfect, but the weakness in the form is that it is impossible to guarantee that all contingencies have been taken into account. Maybe one was overlooked. Thus, (B) is the correct answer. (A), (C), and (E) are wrong for the same reason. Holmes' method is designed to answer a particular question—in this case, "Where did the body come from?" Perhaps the next step is to apply the method to the question of the identity of the murderer as (E) suggests, but at this juncture he is concerned with the preliminary matter of how the murder was committed. In any event, it would be wrong to assail the logic of Holmes' deduction by complaining that it does not prove enough. Since (A) and (C) are even more removed from the particular question raised, they, too, must be wrong. Finally, (D) is nothing more than a reiteration of Watson's original comment, and Holmes has already responded to it.

24. **(A)** Although we do not want to argue theology, perhaps a point taken from that discipline will make this question more accessible: "If God is only good, from where does evil come?" Rousseau, at least as far as his argument is characterized here, faces a similar problem. If man is by his very nature sympathetic, what is the source of his non-sympathetic social institutions? (A) poses this critical question. The remaining choices each commit the same fundamental error. Rousseau *describes* a situation. The paragraph never suggests that he proposed a *solution*. Perhaps Rousseau considered the problem of modern society irremediable.

25. **(E)** Here we are looking for the unstated or hidden assumptions of the author. (A) is one because the author dates the building by measuring the wear and tear on the threshold, but if that were a replacement threshold installed, say, 50 years after the building was first built, the author's calculations would be thrown off completely. So, to reach the conclusion he does, he must have assumed that he was dealing with the original threshold. (C) is very similar. The calculations work—based as they are on the estimated capacity of the monastery—only if the author is right about the number of people walking across the door sill. So it also follows that (D) is something he assumes. After all, if marble tended

to wear out spontaneously instead of under use— if sometimes it just evaporates—then the whole process of calculating time as a function of wear would be ill-founded. (E) is correct. The author uses the wars he cites to help him date *this particular group* of buildings. He never suggests that this has occurred often.

SECTION VI

Questions 1–3:

Arranging the Information

Previewing the questions indicates that the complex issue is the fighting. Thus, the diagram must keep track of combinations.

F ←not with any→ G with H J
                  |___|
                   not
                   with
                    ↓
                    K

Answering the Questions

1. **(C)** I is not inferable since there is no reason to prefer F to K as an addition to G and H. We are not given any reason to prefer eating to non-fighting and thus cannot judge the relative problems with F and K. II is not inferable since there is nothing that tells us that G and H will fight with each other, only with K. III is inferable since the only combinations available have to include fighters. If F is included, there is likely to be fighting. If F is not included, then G, H, and K will fight.

2. **(C)** If G and J go home, then only H, K, and F are left. All of these cats will fight with each other for reasons similar to those outlined for question 1. Therefore, two new cats are needed to combine with either H or K.

3. **(C)** Since the purposes of a cat cast are established in the situation description, we know that an available cast means one that will have a good chance of succeeding. With F calmed down, the only remaining problem is the fighting between G, H, and K. However, G and H should be together since we are told that they eat well together, and that is the goal of the commercial filming. Thus, we have G and H, who can be with J or with F, and we have F with K and J. Although we do not know how well K and J eat, they will at least not

fight and that is sufficient for them to qualify as available. Thus, there are three possible casts available.

4. **(B)** The proposition that you cannot argue with taste says that taste is relative. Since we are looking for an answer choice inconsistent with that proposition, we seek an answer choice that argues that taste, or aesthetic value, is absolute, or at least not relative—that there are standards of taste. (B) is precisely that.

(C) and (D) are just distractions, playing on the notion of taste in the physical sense and the further idea of the distasteful; but these superficial connections are not strong enough.

(A), (B), and (E) are all activities in which there is some element of aesthetic judgment or appreciation. In (A), the holding of an exhibition, while implying some selection principle and, thus, some idea of a standard of taste, does not purport to truly judge aesthetics in the way that (B), precisely a beauty *contest*, does. The exhibition may be of historical or biographical interest, for example. (E) also stresses more of the exhibition aspect than the judging aspect. You should not infer that all movie festivals are contests, since the word festival does not require this interpretation and, in fact, there are festivals at which the judging aspect is minimal or non-existent. The Cannes Film Festival, while perhaps the best-known, is not the only type of movie festival there is. The questions are not tests of your knowledge of the movie industry.

5. **(C)** Take careful note of the exact position the author ascribes to the analysts: They *always* attribute a sudden drop to a crisis. The author then attacks this simple causal explanation by explaining that, though a crisis is followed by a market drop, the reason is not that the crisis causes the drop but that both are the effects of some common cause, the changing of the moon. Of course, the argument seems implausible, but our task is not to grade the argument, only to describe its structure. (A) is not a proper characterization of that structure since the author never provides a specific example. (B), too, is inapplicable since no statistics are produced. (D) can be rejected since the author is attacking generally accepted beliefs rather than appealing to them to support his position. Finally, though the author concedes the reliability of the reports, (E), in question, he wants to draw a different conclusion from the data.

6. **(A)** Given the implausibility of the author's alternative explanation, he is probably speaking tongue-in-cheek, that is, he is ridiculing the analysts for *always* attributing a drop in the market to a political crisis. But whether you took the argument in this way or as a serious attempt to explain the fluctuations of the stock market, (A)

will be the correct answer. (E) surely goes beyond the mere factual description at which the author is aiming, as does (D) as well. The author is concerned with the *causes* of fluctuations; nothing suggests that he or anyone else is in a position to exploit those fluctuations. (C) finds no support in the paragraph, for nothing suggests that he wishes to attack the credibility of the source rather than the argument itself. Finally, (B) is inappropriate to the main point of the passage. Whether the market ultimately evens itself out has nothing to do with the causes of the fluctuations.

Questions 7–11

Arranging the Information

This problem set describes a layout or map situation. One clue is its being a set of regular shapes and the other is the use of compass directions. You have to distinguish between conditions which lead to definite squares being definite crops and ones which simply describe relationships between crops.

If two sides of the field run east-west, the other sides run north-south, and the field is aligned with the compass.

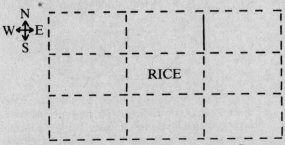

The information about wheat and barley cannot be coded into the diagram now, nor can the information about the soybeans, but peanuts can.

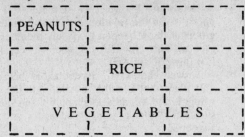

Answering the Questions

Questions 7, 8, and 9 refer to five squares. Let us locate them on the map:

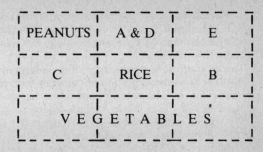

If the four unallocated fields are to be planted with one field of wheat, one of barley, and two of soybeans, the wheat and barley have to be two of the upper right-hand fields in order to be next to each other.

7. **(E)** If field (E) is planted with soybeans, then the wheat and barley cannot be next to each other.

8. **(C)** If (C) is planted with wheat, the barley cannot be next to it.

9. **(E)** Although there are two fields next to the peanuts, we have already eliminated (C) from consideration as a wheat field. Thus, the wheat must be in the field just north of the rice (A)/(D), and the barley must be in field (E) to be next to the wheat.

10. **(D)** The rice is in the middle, so the tomatoes cannot be next to the soybeans, eliminating II— AND answer choices (B) and (E). Either of the fields to the east or west of the rice field could be planted with the soybeans, as previously discussed; thus, I and III are possible, and (D) is correct.

   Note that the squash actually must be next to the soybeans, but that also means it is possible.

11. **(B)** It is a fair assumption that the other crops mentioned are to be planted and only the ones specifically omitted are not planted (to do otherwise would be mere nitpicking). This means that there will be one field of rice and barley, and two of soybeans—leaving five for vegetables.

Questions 12–15

Arranging the Information

This is a problem in which the main issue is the overlapping of different sets of groups, which means that Venn diagrams are a good method of arranging the information. This type of problem usually requires that the majority of your time be spent in arranging the information and somewhat less in answering the questions. However, a preview of the questions indicates that some of the statements might contradict some of the other statements. Question 13 indicates that statements I, II, and III are to be taken as true, and question

12, which asks about contradiction, only asks about possible contradiction after I, II, and III. Thus, it would seem that I, II, and III could be arranged without any problems.

The most efficient arrangement of the information of I and II is in a three-circle (Venn) diagram with circles standing for L, M, and Z. Remember that a Venn diagram is only good for up to three categories.

We will now draw a three-circle diagram for L, M, and Z. Statement I only indicates that there is some possibility of there being each of the four categories. It does not mean, for instance, that there will be an L by itself that is not any of the others, etc. This does not affect the diagram.

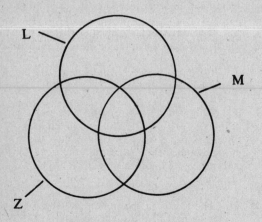

Statement II is coded into the diagram by marking out the parts of the diagram where M is not L.

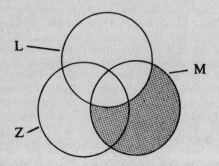

Statement III is coded into the diagram by eliminating the parts of the diagram where L is not Z, leaving us with this:

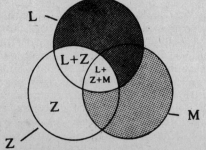

Thus, what remains possible is L with Z, L with M and Z, and Z by itself.

Answering the Questions

12. **(B)** Statement III was successfully integrated with the previous statements without encountering any problem, so answer choice (A) is eliminated. Statement IV, however, does present a problem. If no M are Z, this means that there can be no M found inside the Z circle. However, the only place where M can be found, after coding the first three statements, is inside the Z circle. The elimination of the possibility of having L, M, and Z together will eliminate the possibility of having M altogether, which is forbidden by statement I. Thus, answer choice (B) is correct. Note that one must proceed in order in this particular problem because the question asks about contradictions with all previous statements, which means that the first one with a contradiction must be the answer sought. Both statements V and VI are fully compatible with the following diagrams:

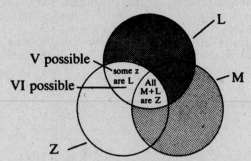

13. **(C)** In the previous question we saw that statement IV was contradictory to the previous statements, which excludes it from being deducible from statements II and III, eliminating answer choices (A) and (D). Statement V is not deducible from the others because it states that there are actually some Z. The existence of any Z is definitely not known since statements II and III only discuss the relationships that pertain to the groups if there happen to be any members of the groups. This eliminates answer choices (B) and (D) (again), and (E).

Answer choice (C) is deducible because the only place that L and M overlap is in the location where L and M and also Z apply. Thus, anything, such as P, which is going to be both L and M must also be Z.

14. **(D)** From the diagram we can see that there are two possible locations within the L area. One location is the LMZ area and the other is the LZ area. Thus, all L are Z, as statement III has said. The only reason that you would use the diagram instead of just relying on the original statement is

to make sure that there was no further limitation that had snuck in, as happened with M, all of which are also Z (ignoring the contradiction problem). You cannot make any statement about the overlap between P and X because statement VI only states where P will not be found and makes no promises that there are P's that actually are M and L, etc.

15. **(D)** The diagram shows that there is a definite possible area of Z which does not overlap any part of the L or M areas; therefore, it is still possible for Z to be by itself. It would be wrong to say that there definitely was some Z by itself, but it is also wrong to say that there cannot be any Z by itself.

(A) is not false since statement I states that L is possible. (B) is not known to be true or false. The statement that some Z are L does not make it false or true to say some Z are not L. As discussed in the previous problem, the actual occurrence of P's other than under M and L is still an open question, and (C) is, thus, not false. (E) is eliminated with the discovery that (D) is false.

Questions 16–22

Arranging the Information

Previewing the questions shows that most of them are conditional questions, and the setup of the situation is of that nature, too. This means that most of the work will be in answering the questions rather than in determining the arrangement of the information.

At least 2 of D E F

Either 1 or 2 from L M N P

Total of 4

N not=P

E not=L

D not=N, thus, if N, neither P or D

Answering the Questions

16. **(C)** If Nancy is chosen, then both David and Paul are out. Since at least two out of the trio of David, Erica, and Francis must be chosen, the elimination of David results in the forced selection of Erica and Francis, which eliminates answer choices (A) and (E). Since Nancy will not work with Paul, he cannot be a member of the crew, and answer choice (D) is eliminated. Since Erica is selected, as previously noted, and Erica will not work with Larry, answer choice (B) is eliminated, and we find that the crew will be David, Erica, Mary, and Nancy.

17. **(E)** If Paul is chosen, the only direct restriction is that Nancy is eliminated from the crew. This leaves only the restriction of the grinders versus the sail trimmers. If you wanted to select answer choice (A) because you thought there could only be two grinders, you missed the fact that the only restriction on the numbers of grinders versus sail trimmers was that AT LEAST two of the crew additions had to be grinders, which leaves open the possibility of all three of the grinder candidates being accepted. Thus, answer choice (A) is possible.

Answer choice (E), however, is not possible because Erica will not work with Larry as the answer choice requires. The other answer choices, (B), (C), and (D), do not violate any of the restrictions laid down by the problem.

18. **(C)** I must be true because if David is rejected, then the only two remaining grinder candidates—Erica and Francis—must be chosen. The selection of Erica means the elimination of Larry, leaving Mary, Nancy, and Paul. However, since Nancy will not work with Paul, only one of those two may be chosen, which gives Mary a definite berth on the boat.

II follows from the first sentence of the discussion of I.

III does not have to be true. The selection of David permits the selection of a crew such as David, Francis, Mary, and Paul or the selection of a crew without Paul—such as David, Francis, Mary, and Larry.

Thus, the answer is that I and II must be true and III is a maybe.

19. **(E)** As hinted at by the structure of the three Roman-numeral propositions, the acceptance of Larry as a crew member eliminates Erica from consideration, and thus requires the selection of David and Francis. The selection of David means that Nancy cannot be chosen, which leaves either Mary or Paul as acceptable candidates to fill the last sail trimmer slot with Larry. I and III are, thus, possible and II is not.

20. **(C)** I must be true since the choice of Larry eliminates Erica and requires the choice of David and Francis, as noted in question 19.

II is not necessarily true since the choice of Mary imposes no further restrictions on the choice of crew, so Mary and Nancy may or may not crew together.

III is also necessarily true. If Larry is chosen, Erica cannot be chosen; and this means David and Francis must be picked to meet the minimum number of two grinders. With David on the crew, Nancy cannot be on the crew.

21. **(B)** The choice of Paul eliminates Nancy, and, thus, answer choices (C) and (D). The omission of David forces the choice of Erica and Francis, which in turn eliminates Larry, and, thus, answer choices (A) and (E), leaving only Mary to fill out the crew, as stated in answer choice (B).

22. **(A)** If Erica makes the crew and Francis does not, this leaves David to fill in the second grinder slot. Erica's presence eliminates Larry, and David's eliminates Nancy, leaving a crew of David, Erica, Mary, and Paul. Thus, both I and II must be true.

23. **(D)** It is important not to attribute more to an author than he actually says or implies. Here the author states only that Ronnie's range is narrow so he will not be an outstanding vocalist. Vocalizing is only one kind of music career, so I, which speaks of professional musicians, takes us far beyond the claim the author actually makes. II also goes beyond what the author says. He never specifies what range an outstanding vocalist needs, much less what range is required to vocalize without being outstanding. Finally, III is an assumption since the author moves from a physical characteristic to a conclusion regarding ability.

24. **(C)** Ann's response would be appropriate only if Mary had said, "All of the students at State College come from Midland High." That is why (C) is correct. (D) is wrong because they are talking about the background of the students, not the reputations of the schools. (E) is wrong, for the question is from where the students at State College come. (B) is superficially relevant to the exchange, but it, too, is incorrect. Ann would not reply to this statement, had Mary made it, in the way she did reply. Rather, she would have said, "No, there are some Midland students at State College." Finally, Ann would correctly have said (A) only if Mary had said, "None of the students from North Hills attends State College," or, "Most of the students from North Hills do not attend State College." But Ann makes neither of these responses, so we know that (A) cannot have been what she thought she heard Mary say.

25. **(A)** Perhaps a small diagram is the easiest way to show this problem.

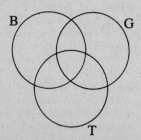

We will show that "all B are T" by eliminating that portion of the diagram where some area of B is not also inside T:

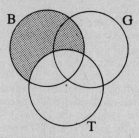

Now, let us put an x to show the existence of those B's which are G's:

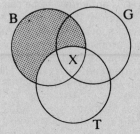

The diagram shows us that I is true. Since the only areas left for B's are within the T circle, the G condition is unimportant. II is not inferable. Although there is some overlap of the G and T circles, there is also some non-overlap. This shows that it may be possible to be a T without also being a G. III is not inferable since our diagrams are restricted to the three categories B, G, and T and say nothing about things outside of those categories.

SECTION VII

1. **(B)** $40\% = \frac{2}{5}$
   $\frac{2}{5} \times \frac{10}{7} = \frac{4}{7}$

2. **(D)** 27 and 51 are each divisible by 3. 17 and 59 are prime numbers. Hence, I and IV only.

3. **(A)** Angle DOC = 6 + x
   Angle AOC = (6 + x) + x = 180 − 20
   $$6 + 2x = 160$$
   $$2x = 154$$
   $$x = 77$$

4. **(D)** Let C = the capacity in gallons. Then $\frac{1}{3}C + 3 = \frac{1}{2}C$. Multiplying through by 6, we obtain $2C + 18 = 3C$, or $C = 18$.

5. **(E)** $\frac{91 + 88 + 86 + 78 + x}{5} = 85$
   $$343 + x = 425$$
   $$x = 82$$

6. **(C)** $12 \times .39 = 4.68$ inches; that is, between $4\frac{1}{2}$ and 5.

7. **(D)**

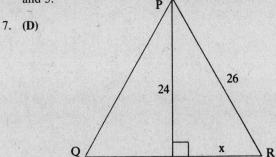

In the figure above, PS $\perp$ QR. Then, in right triangle PSR:

$$x^2 + 24^2 = 26^2$$
$$x^2 = 26^2 - 24^2$$
$$x = \sqrt{100} = 10$$

So QR = 20.

You might also have noticed that 24 and 26 are twice 12 and 13, respectively. 5, 12, and 13 are Pythagorean numbers (like 3, 4, and 5), so the missing length, x, must be twice 5, or 10.

8. **(C)** All terms involving x are 0. Hence, the equation reduces to:

$$0 - 7y + 15 = 0$$
$$\text{or } 7y = 15$$
$$y = 2\frac{1}{7}$$

9. **(E)** Let s = number of shirts t = number of ties, where s and t are integers:

$$\text{Then } 7s + 3t = 81$$
$$7s = 81 - 3t$$
$$s = \frac{81 - 3t}{7}$$

Since s is an integer, t must have an integral value such that $81 - 3t$ is divisible by 7. Trial shows that t = 6 is the smallest such number, making s = $\frac{81 - 18}{7} = \frac{63}{7} = 9$. Hence, s:t = 9:6 = 3:2

10. **(C)** Rate = $\dfrac{\text{distance}}{\text{time}} = \dfrac{\frac{2}{5}\text{ mile}}{\frac{5}{60}\text{ hour}} = \dfrac{\frac{2}{5}}{\frac{1}{12}}$ rate = $\frac{2}{5} \cdot \frac{12}{1}$

$\frac{24}{5} = 4\frac{4}{5}$ miles per hour.

11. **(D)** Draw the altitudes indicated. A rectangle and two right triangles are produced. From the figure, the base of each triangle is 20 feet. By the Pythagorean Theorem, the altitude is 15 feet. Hence, the area:

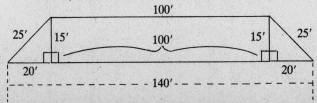

Area = Triangle + Rectangle + Triangle
 = $(\frac{1}{2} \cdot 15 \cdot 20)$ + $(100 \cdot 15)$ + $(\frac{1}{2} \cdot 15 \cdot 20)$
 = 150   + 1500   + 150
 = 1800 square feet

12. **(E)** If $1 + \frac{1}{t} = \frac{t+1}{t}$, then the right-hand fraction can also be reduced to $1 + \frac{1}{t}$, and we have an identity, which is true for all values of t except 0.

13. **(E)** All points 6 inches from A are on a circle of radius 6 with center at A. All points 1 inch from b are on 2 straight lines parallel to b and 1 inch from it on each side. These two parallel lines intersect the circle in 4 points.

14. **(E)** Let R = 5P and S = 5Q where P and Q are integers. Then $R - S = 5P - 5Q = 5(P - Q)$ is divisible by 5. $RS = 5P \cdot 5Q = 25PG$ is divisible by 25. $R + S = 5P + 5Q = 5(P + Q)$ is divisible by 5. $R^2 + S^2 = 25P^2 + 25Q^2 = 25(P^2 + Q^2)$ is divisible by 5. $R + S = 5P + 5Q = 5(P + Q)$, which is not necessarily divisible by 10.

15. **(D)** $\frac{1}{2} \cdot 7 \cdot h = \pi \cdot 7^2$. Dividing both sides by 7, we get $\frac{1}{2}h = 7\pi$, or $h = 14\pi$.

16. **(E)**

$$\frac{9}{13} = \begin{array}{r} .69 \\ \overline{)9.00} \\ \underline{78} \\ 120 \\ \underline{117} \end{array} \qquad \frac{13}{9} = \begin{array}{r} 1.44 \\ \overline{)13.00} \\ \underline{9} \\ 40 \\ \underline{36} \\ 40 \\ \underline{36} \end{array} \qquad 70\% = .7$$

$$\frac{1}{.70} = \frac{1}{7} \quad 10$$

$$= \begin{array}{r} 1.42 \\ 7)\overline{10.00} \\ 7 \\ \overline{30} \\ \underline{28} \\ \overline{20} \end{array}$$

Correct order is $\frac{9}{13}$, 70%, $\frac{1}{.70}$, $\frac{13}{9}$; or I, III, IV, II.

17. **(D)**

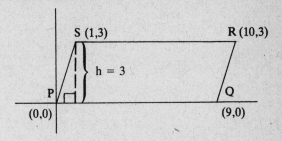

Since PQ and RS are parallel and equal, the figure is a parallelogram of base = 9 and height = 3. Hence, area = $9 \cdot 3 = 27$.

18. **(A)**

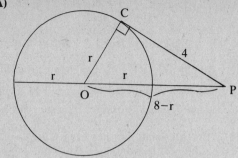

From the figure, in right $\triangle PCO$:

$$PO^2 = r^2 + 4^2$$
$$(8 - r)^2 = r^2 + 16$$
$$64 - 16r + r^2 = r^2 + 16$$
$$48 = 16r$$
$$r = 3$$

Hence, diameter = 6.

19. **(B)** Area of wall = $4 \cdot \frac{60}{3} = 4 \cdot 20 = 80$ sq. yd.
Cost = $80 \times \$10.50 = \$840.00$.

20. **(D)** Using the distance formula, derived from the Pythagorean Theorem, that the distance from (a,b) to (c,d) is $\sqrt{(a-c)^2 + (b-d)^2}$:
Distance of (4,4) from origin = $\sqrt{16 + 16} = \sqrt{32} < 7$
Distance of (5,5) from origin = $\sqrt{25 + 25} = \sqrt{50} > 7$
Distance of (4,5) from origin = $\sqrt{16 + 25} = \sqrt{41} < 7$
Distance of (4,6) from origin = $\sqrt{16 + 36} = \sqrt{52} > 7$
Hence, only II and IV are outside circle.

21. **(A)** Let x = the cost.

Then $x + \frac{1}{4}x = 80$
Multiplying by 4: $4x + x = 320$
Adding like terms: $5x = 320$
Dividing by 5: $= \$64$ (cost)

$$\frac{\text{Cost}}{\text{S.P.}} = \frac{64}{80}$$
$$= \frac{4}{5}$$

22. **(C)**

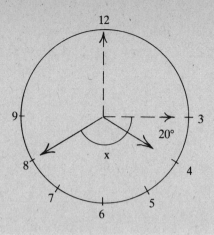

At 3:00, large hand is at 12 and small hand is at 3. During the next 40 minutes, large hand moves to 8 and small hand moves $\frac{40}{60} = \frac{2}{3}$ of the distance between 3 and 4; $\frac{2}{3} \times 30° = 20°$. Since there is a 30° arc between two numbers on a clock $\angle x = 5(30°) - 20° = 150° - 20° = 130°$.

23. **(B)** Area of sector = $\frac{120}{360} \cdot \pi \cdot 15^2$
$$= \frac{1}{3} \cdot \pi \cdot 15 \cdot 15$$
$$= 75\pi$$

24. **(D)** $\frac{17}{10}y = 0.51$
Multiplying both sides by 10, we get $17y = 5.1$, or $y = .3$.

25. **(D)** $40\% = \frac{2}{5} \times 50 = 20$ girls attended
$50\% = \frac{1}{2} \times 70 = 35$ boys attended

$$\frac{55}{50 + 70} = \frac{55}{120} = \frac{11}{24}$$

$$\begin{array}{r} .458 = 45.8\% \\ 24 \overline{)11.000} \\ \underline{96} \\ 140 \\ \underline{120} \\ 200 \\ \underline{192} \end{array}$$

Approx. 46%

ANSWER SHEET—PRACTICE EXAMINATION 4

Section I

1 Ⓐ Ⓑ Ⓒ Ⓓ Ⓔ   8 Ⓐ Ⓑ Ⓒ Ⓓ Ⓔ   15 Ⓐ Ⓑ Ⓒ Ⓓ Ⓔ   22 Ⓐ Ⓑ Ⓒ Ⓓ Ⓔ   29 Ⓐ Ⓑ Ⓒ Ⓓ Ⓔ   36 Ⓐ Ⓑ Ⓒ Ⓓ Ⓔ
2 Ⓐ Ⓑ Ⓒ Ⓓ Ⓔ   9 Ⓐ Ⓑ Ⓒ Ⓓ Ⓔ   16 Ⓐ Ⓑ Ⓒ Ⓓ Ⓔ   23 Ⓐ Ⓑ Ⓒ Ⓓ Ⓔ   30 Ⓐ Ⓑ Ⓒ Ⓓ Ⓔ   37 Ⓐ Ⓑ Ⓒ Ⓓ Ⓔ
3 Ⓐ Ⓑ Ⓒ Ⓓ Ⓔ   10 Ⓐ Ⓑ Ⓒ Ⓓ Ⓔ   17 Ⓐ Ⓑ Ⓒ Ⓓ Ⓔ   24 Ⓐ Ⓑ Ⓒ Ⓓ Ⓔ   31 Ⓐ Ⓑ Ⓒ Ⓓ Ⓔ   38 Ⓐ Ⓑ Ⓒ Ⓓ Ⓔ
4 Ⓐ Ⓑ Ⓒ Ⓓ Ⓔ   11 Ⓐ Ⓑ Ⓒ Ⓓ Ⓔ   18 Ⓐ Ⓑ Ⓒ Ⓓ Ⓔ   25 Ⓐ Ⓑ Ⓒ Ⓓ Ⓔ   32 Ⓐ Ⓑ Ⓒ Ⓓ Ⓔ
5 Ⓐ Ⓑ Ⓒ Ⓓ Ⓔ   12 Ⓐ Ⓑ Ⓒ Ⓓ Ⓔ   19 Ⓐ Ⓑ Ⓒ Ⓓ Ⓔ   26 Ⓐ Ⓑ Ⓒ Ⓓ Ⓔ   33 Ⓐ Ⓑ Ⓒ Ⓓ Ⓔ
6 Ⓐ Ⓑ Ⓒ Ⓓ Ⓔ   13 Ⓐ Ⓑ Ⓒ Ⓓ Ⓔ   20 Ⓐ Ⓑ Ⓒ Ⓓ Ⓔ   27 Ⓐ Ⓑ Ⓒ Ⓓ Ⓔ   34 Ⓐ Ⓑ Ⓒ Ⓓ Ⓔ
7 Ⓐ Ⓑ Ⓒ Ⓓ Ⓔ   14 Ⓐ Ⓑ Ⓒ Ⓓ Ⓔ   21 Ⓐ Ⓑ Ⓒ Ⓓ Ⓔ   28 Ⓐ Ⓑ Ⓒ Ⓓ Ⓔ   35 Ⓐ Ⓑ Ⓒ Ⓓ Ⓔ

Section II

1 Ⓐ Ⓑ Ⓒ Ⓓ Ⓔ   8 Ⓐ Ⓑ Ⓒ Ⓓ Ⓔ   15 Ⓐ Ⓑ Ⓒ Ⓓ Ⓔ   22 Ⓐ Ⓑ Ⓒ Ⓓ Ⓔ   29 Ⓐ Ⓑ Ⓒ Ⓓ Ⓔ   36 Ⓐ Ⓑ Ⓒ Ⓓ Ⓔ
2 Ⓐ Ⓑ Ⓒ Ⓓ Ⓔ   9 Ⓐ Ⓑ Ⓒ Ⓓ Ⓔ   16 Ⓐ Ⓑ Ⓒ Ⓓ Ⓔ   23 Ⓐ Ⓑ Ⓒ Ⓓ Ⓔ   30 Ⓐ Ⓑ Ⓒ Ⓓ Ⓔ   37 Ⓐ Ⓑ Ⓒ Ⓓ Ⓔ
3 Ⓐ Ⓑ Ⓒ Ⓓ Ⓔ   10 Ⓐ Ⓑ Ⓒ Ⓓ Ⓔ   17 Ⓐ Ⓑ Ⓒ Ⓓ Ⓔ   24 Ⓐ Ⓑ Ⓒ Ⓓ Ⓔ   31 Ⓐ Ⓑ Ⓒ Ⓓ Ⓔ   38 Ⓐ Ⓑ Ⓒ Ⓓ Ⓔ
4 Ⓐ Ⓑ Ⓒ Ⓓ Ⓔ   11 Ⓐ Ⓑ Ⓒ Ⓓ Ⓔ   18 Ⓐ Ⓑ Ⓒ Ⓓ Ⓔ   25 Ⓐ Ⓑ Ⓒ Ⓓ Ⓔ   32 Ⓐ Ⓑ Ⓒ Ⓓ Ⓔ
5 Ⓐ Ⓑ Ⓒ Ⓓ Ⓔ   12 Ⓐ Ⓑ Ⓒ Ⓓ Ⓔ   19 Ⓐ Ⓑ Ⓒ Ⓓ Ⓔ   26 Ⓐ Ⓑ Ⓒ Ⓓ Ⓔ   33 Ⓐ Ⓑ Ⓒ Ⓓ Ⓔ
6 Ⓐ Ⓑ Ⓒ Ⓓ Ⓔ   13 Ⓐ Ⓑ Ⓒ Ⓓ Ⓔ   20 Ⓐ Ⓑ Ⓒ Ⓓ Ⓔ   27 Ⓐ Ⓑ Ⓒ Ⓓ Ⓔ   34 Ⓐ Ⓑ Ⓒ Ⓓ Ⓔ
7 Ⓐ Ⓑ Ⓒ Ⓓ Ⓔ   14 Ⓐ Ⓑ Ⓒ Ⓓ Ⓔ   21 Ⓐ Ⓑ Ⓒ Ⓓ Ⓔ   28 Ⓐ Ⓑ Ⓒ Ⓓ Ⓔ   35 Ⓐ Ⓑ Ⓒ Ⓓ Ⓔ

Section III

1 Ⓐ Ⓑ Ⓒ Ⓓ Ⓔ   6 Ⓐ Ⓑ Ⓒ Ⓓ Ⓔ   11 Ⓐ Ⓑ Ⓒ Ⓓ Ⓔ   16 Ⓐ Ⓑ Ⓒ Ⓓ Ⓔ   21 Ⓐ Ⓑ Ⓒ Ⓓ Ⓔ   26 Ⓐ Ⓑ Ⓒ Ⓓ Ⓔ
2 Ⓐ Ⓑ Ⓒ Ⓓ Ⓔ   7 Ⓐ Ⓑ Ⓒ Ⓓ Ⓔ   12 Ⓐ Ⓑ Ⓒ Ⓓ Ⓔ   17 Ⓐ Ⓑ Ⓒ Ⓓ Ⓔ   22 Ⓐ Ⓑ Ⓒ Ⓓ Ⓔ   27 Ⓐ Ⓑ Ⓒ Ⓓ Ⓔ
3 Ⓐ Ⓑ Ⓒ Ⓓ Ⓔ   8 Ⓐ Ⓑ Ⓒ Ⓓ Ⓔ   13 Ⓐ Ⓑ Ⓒ Ⓓ Ⓔ   18 Ⓐ Ⓑ Ⓒ Ⓓ Ⓔ   23 Ⓐ Ⓑ Ⓒ Ⓓ Ⓔ   28 Ⓐ Ⓑ Ⓒ Ⓓ Ⓔ
4 Ⓐ Ⓑ Ⓒ Ⓓ Ⓔ   9 Ⓐ Ⓑ Ⓒ Ⓓ Ⓔ   14 Ⓐ Ⓑ Ⓒ Ⓓ Ⓔ   19 Ⓐ Ⓑ Ⓒ Ⓓ Ⓔ   24 Ⓐ Ⓑ Ⓒ Ⓓ Ⓔ   29 Ⓐ Ⓑ Ⓒ Ⓓ Ⓔ
5 Ⓐ Ⓑ Ⓒ Ⓓ Ⓔ   10 Ⓐ Ⓑ Ⓒ Ⓓ Ⓔ   15 Ⓐ Ⓑ Ⓒ Ⓓ Ⓔ   20 Ⓐ Ⓑ Ⓒ Ⓓ Ⓔ   25 Ⓐ Ⓑ Ⓒ Ⓓ Ⓔ   30 Ⓐ Ⓑ Ⓒ Ⓓ Ⓔ

Section IV

1 Ⓐ Ⓑ Ⓒ Ⓓ Ⓔ	6 Ⓐ Ⓑ Ⓒ Ⓓ Ⓔ	11 Ⓐ Ⓑ Ⓒ Ⓓ Ⓔ	16 Ⓐ Ⓑ Ⓒ Ⓓ Ⓔ	21 Ⓐ Ⓑ Ⓒ Ⓓ Ⓔ	26 Ⓐ Ⓑ Ⓒ Ⓓ Ⓔ
2 Ⓐ Ⓑ Ⓒ Ⓓ Ⓔ	7 Ⓐ Ⓑ Ⓒ Ⓓ Ⓔ	12 Ⓐ Ⓑ Ⓒ Ⓓ Ⓔ	17 Ⓐ Ⓑ Ⓒ Ⓓ Ⓔ	22 Ⓐ Ⓑ Ⓒ Ⓓ Ⓔ	27 Ⓐ Ⓑ Ⓒ Ⓓ Ⓔ
3 Ⓐ Ⓑ Ⓒ Ⓓ Ⓔ	8 Ⓐ Ⓑ Ⓒ Ⓓ Ⓔ	13 Ⓐ Ⓑ Ⓒ Ⓓ Ⓔ	18 Ⓐ Ⓑ Ⓒ Ⓓ Ⓔ	23 Ⓐ Ⓑ Ⓒ Ⓓ Ⓔ	28 Ⓐ Ⓑ Ⓒ Ⓓ Ⓔ
4 Ⓐ Ⓑ Ⓒ Ⓓ Ⓔ	9 Ⓐ Ⓑ Ⓒ Ⓓ Ⓔ	14 Ⓐ Ⓑ Ⓒ Ⓓ Ⓔ	19 Ⓐ Ⓑ Ⓒ Ⓓ Ⓔ	24 Ⓐ Ⓑ Ⓒ Ⓓ Ⓔ	29 Ⓐ Ⓑ Ⓒ Ⓓ Ⓔ
5 Ⓐ Ⓑ Ⓒ Ⓓ Ⓔ	10 Ⓐ Ⓑ Ⓒ Ⓓ Ⓔ	15 Ⓐ Ⓑ Ⓒ Ⓓ Ⓔ	20 Ⓐ Ⓑ Ⓒ Ⓓ Ⓔ	25 Ⓐ Ⓑ Ⓒ Ⓓ Ⓔ	30 Ⓐ Ⓑ Ⓒ Ⓓ Ⓔ

Section V

1 Ⓐ Ⓑ Ⓒ Ⓓ Ⓔ	6 Ⓐ Ⓑ Ⓒ Ⓓ Ⓔ	11 Ⓐ Ⓑ Ⓒ Ⓓ Ⓔ	16 Ⓐ Ⓑ Ⓒ Ⓓ Ⓔ	21 Ⓐ Ⓑ Ⓒ Ⓓ Ⓔ
2 Ⓐ Ⓑ Ⓒ Ⓓ Ⓔ	7 Ⓐ Ⓑ Ⓒ Ⓓ Ⓔ	12 Ⓐ Ⓑ Ⓒ Ⓓ Ⓔ	17 Ⓐ Ⓑ Ⓒ Ⓓ Ⓔ	22 Ⓐ Ⓑ Ⓒ Ⓓ Ⓔ
3 Ⓐ Ⓑ Ⓒ Ⓓ Ⓔ	8 Ⓐ Ⓑ Ⓒ Ⓓ Ⓔ	13 Ⓐ Ⓑ Ⓒ Ⓓ Ⓔ	18 Ⓐ Ⓑ Ⓒ Ⓓ Ⓔ	23 Ⓐ Ⓑ Ⓒ Ⓓ Ⓔ
4 Ⓐ Ⓑ Ⓒ Ⓓ Ⓔ	9 Ⓐ Ⓑ Ⓒ Ⓓ Ⓔ	14 Ⓐ Ⓑ Ⓒ Ⓓ Ⓔ	19 Ⓐ Ⓑ Ⓒ Ⓓ Ⓔ	24 Ⓐ Ⓑ Ⓒ Ⓓ Ⓔ
5 Ⓐ Ⓑ Ⓒ Ⓓ Ⓔ	10 Ⓐ Ⓑ Ⓒ Ⓓ Ⓔ	15 Ⓐ Ⓑ Ⓒ Ⓓ Ⓔ	20 Ⓐ Ⓑ Ⓒ Ⓓ Ⓔ	25 Ⓐ Ⓑ Ⓒ Ⓓ Ⓔ

Section VI

1 Ⓐ Ⓑ Ⓒ Ⓓ Ⓔ	6 Ⓐ Ⓑ Ⓒ Ⓓ Ⓔ	11 Ⓐ Ⓑ Ⓒ Ⓓ Ⓔ	16 Ⓐ Ⓑ Ⓒ Ⓓ Ⓔ	21 Ⓐ Ⓑ Ⓒ Ⓓ Ⓔ
2 Ⓐ Ⓑ Ⓒ Ⓓ Ⓔ	7 Ⓐ Ⓑ Ⓒ Ⓓ Ⓔ	12 Ⓐ Ⓑ Ⓒ Ⓓ Ⓔ	17 Ⓐ Ⓑ Ⓒ Ⓓ Ⓔ	22 Ⓐ Ⓑ Ⓒ Ⓓ Ⓔ
3 Ⓐ Ⓑ Ⓒ Ⓓ Ⓔ	8 Ⓐ Ⓑ Ⓒ Ⓓ Ⓔ	13 Ⓐ Ⓑ Ⓒ Ⓓ Ⓔ	18 Ⓐ Ⓑ Ⓒ Ⓓ Ⓔ	23 Ⓐ Ⓑ Ⓒ Ⓓ Ⓔ
4 Ⓐ Ⓑ Ⓒ Ⓓ Ⓔ	9 Ⓐ Ⓑ Ⓒ Ⓓ Ⓔ	14 Ⓐ Ⓑ Ⓒ Ⓓ Ⓔ	19 Ⓐ Ⓑ Ⓒ Ⓓ Ⓔ	24 Ⓐ Ⓑ Ⓒ Ⓓ Ⓔ
5 Ⓐ Ⓑ Ⓒ Ⓓ Ⓔ	10 Ⓐ Ⓑ Ⓒ Ⓓ Ⓔ	15 Ⓐ Ⓑ Ⓒ Ⓓ Ⓔ	20 Ⓐ Ⓑ Ⓒ Ⓓ Ⓔ	25 Ⓐ Ⓑ Ⓒ Ⓓ Ⓔ

Section VII

1 Ⓐ Ⓑ Ⓒ Ⓓ Ⓔ	8 Ⓐ Ⓑ Ⓒ Ⓓ Ⓔ	15 Ⓐ Ⓑ Ⓒ Ⓓ Ⓔ	22 Ⓐ Ⓑ Ⓒ Ⓓ Ⓔ	29 Ⓐ Ⓑ Ⓒ Ⓓ Ⓔ	36 Ⓐ Ⓑ Ⓒ Ⓓ Ⓔ
2 Ⓐ Ⓑ Ⓒ Ⓓ Ⓔ	9 Ⓐ Ⓑ Ⓒ Ⓓ Ⓔ	16 Ⓐ Ⓑ Ⓒ Ⓓ Ⓔ	23 Ⓐ Ⓑ Ⓒ Ⓓ Ⓔ	30 Ⓐ Ⓑ Ⓒ Ⓓ Ⓔ	37 Ⓐ Ⓑ Ⓒ Ⓓ Ⓔ
3 Ⓐ Ⓑ Ⓒ Ⓓ Ⓔ	10 Ⓐ Ⓑ Ⓒ Ⓓ Ⓔ	17 Ⓐ Ⓑ Ⓒ Ⓓ Ⓔ	24 Ⓐ Ⓑ Ⓒ Ⓓ Ⓔ	31 Ⓐ Ⓑ Ⓒ Ⓓ Ⓔ	38 Ⓐ Ⓑ Ⓒ Ⓓ Ⓔ
4 Ⓐ Ⓑ Ⓒ Ⓓ Ⓔ	11 Ⓐ Ⓑ Ⓒ Ⓓ Ⓔ	18 Ⓐ Ⓑ Ⓒ Ⓓ Ⓔ	25 Ⓐ Ⓑ Ⓒ Ⓓ Ⓔ	32 Ⓐ Ⓑ Ⓒ Ⓓ Ⓔ	
5 Ⓐ Ⓑ Ⓒ Ⓓ Ⓔ	12 Ⓐ Ⓑ Ⓒ Ⓓ Ⓔ	19 Ⓐ Ⓑ Ⓒ Ⓓ Ⓔ	26 Ⓐ Ⓑ Ⓒ Ⓓ Ⓔ	33 Ⓐ Ⓑ Ⓒ Ⓓ Ⓔ	
6 Ⓐ Ⓑ Ⓒ Ⓓ Ⓔ	13 Ⓐ Ⓑ Ⓒ Ⓓ Ⓔ	20 Ⓐ Ⓑ Ⓒ Ⓓ Ⓔ	27 Ⓐ Ⓑ Ⓒ Ⓓ Ⓔ	34 Ⓐ Ⓑ Ⓒ Ⓓ Ⓔ	
7 Ⓐ Ⓑ Ⓒ Ⓓ Ⓔ	14 Ⓐ Ⓑ Ⓒ Ⓓ Ⓔ	21 Ⓐ Ⓑ Ⓒ Ⓓ Ⓔ	28 Ⓐ Ⓑ Ⓒ Ⓓ Ⓔ	35 Ⓐ Ⓑ Ⓒ Ⓓ Ⓔ	

PRACTICE EXAMINATION 4

SECTION I

30 minutes
38 questions

Directions: Each of the questions below contains one or more blank spaces, each blank indicating an omitted word. Each sentence is followed by five (5) lettered words or sets of words. Read and determine the general sense of each sentence. Then choose the word or set of words which, when inserted in the sentence, best fits the meaning of the sentence.

1. Over the _____ of the sirens, you could still hear the hoarse _____ of his voice.
   (A) babble—roar
   (B) drone—power
   (C) gibbering—cries
   (D) wail—sound
   (E) groaning—whisper

2. Working _____ under the pressure of time, Edmond didn't notice his _____ mistake.
   (A) leisurely—stupid
   (B) frantically—inevitable
   (C) rapidly—careless
   (D) sporadically—simple
   (E) continually—redundant

3. Held up only by a _____ steel cable, the chairlift was _____ to carry only two people.
   (A) slender—instructed
   (B) single—intended
   (C) sturdy—obliged
   (D) massive—designed
   (E) narrow—appointed

4. Since he is a teacher of English, we would not expect him to be guilty of a _____ .
   (A) solecism
   (B) schism
   (C) misdemeanor
   (D) crime
   (E) strike

5. The servant's attitude was so _____ that it would have been _____ to anyone with an appreciation of sincerity.
   (A) natal—clear
   (B) hybrid—available
   (C) sycophantic—obnoxious
   (D) doleful—responsible
   (E) refulgent—candid

6. The theory of our justice system seems to be that incarcerating _____ in the company of their fellows will somehow teach them ethical standards, but experience shows that people tend to become _____ those with whom they most closely associate.
   (A) felons—angry with
   (B) malefactors—interested in
   (C) unfortunates—friendly with
   (D) defendants—marked by
   (E) criminals—more like

7. The trial was conducted in _____ manner, full of _____ .
   (A) an incredible—proper procedures
   (B) a negligent—sworn testimony
   (C) a judicial—spectacular denouements
   (D) a theatrical—extravagant histrionics
   (E) an outrageous—erudite citations

Directions: In each of the following questions, you are given a related pair of words or phrases in capital letters. Each capitalized pair is followed by five (5) lettered pairs of words or phrases. Choose the pair which best expresses a relationship similar to that expressed by the original pair.

8. BLOW : HORN ::
   (A) switch : tracks
   (B) light : lamp
   (C) go over : map
   (D) accelerate : engine
   (E) tune : radio

9. FEATHERS : PLUCK ::
   (A) goose : down
   (B) garment : weave
   (C) car : drive
   (D) wool : shear
   (E) leg : pull

10. MODESTY : ARROGANCE ::
    (A) debility : strength
    (B) cause : purpose
    (C) passion : emotion
    (D) finance : pauper
    (E) practice : perfection

11. BAY : OCEAN ::
    (A) mountain : valley
    (B) plain : forest
    (C) peninsula : continent
    (D) cape : reef
    (E) island : sound

12. SPINDLE : SPOOL ::
    (A) thread : needle
    (B) rod : reel
    (C) straight : curved
    (D) spoke : rim
    (E) axle : wheel

13. SETTING : GEM ::
    (A) stage : play
    (B) socket : bulb
    (C) hole : plug
    (D) margin : text
    (E) frame : painting

14. FRANGIBLE : BROKEN ::
    (A) smelly : offensive

(B) candid : unwelcome
(C) brittle : destroyed
(D) fluid : liquefied
(E) pliable : bent

15. INTERRUPT : HECKLE ::
    (A) disrupt : intrude
    (B) tease : hector
    (C) maintain : uphold
    (D) condemn : implore
    (E) speech : performance

16. MERCHANDISE : SHOPLIFTER ::
    (A) men : kidnapper
    (B) pride : insult
    (C) bank : peculator
    (D) cattle : rustler
    (E) mansion : burglar

Directions: Below each of the following passages, you will find questions or incomplete statements about the passage. Each statement or question is followed by lettered words or expressions. Select the word or expression that most satisfactorily completes each statement, or answers each question in accordance with the meaning of the passage. After you have chosen the best answer, blacken the corresponding space on the answer sheet.

The enemy, also, reaped some benefit of his eagerness for honor. For when Ptolemy, after he had entered Pelusium, in his rage and spite against the Egyptians, designed to put them to the sword, Antony withstood him, and hindered the execution. In all the great and frequent skirmishes and battles, he gave continual proofs of his personal valor and military conduct; and once in particular, by wheeling about and attacking the rear of the enemy, he gave the victory to the assailants in the front, and received for this service signal marks of distinction. Nor was his humanity towards the deceased Archelaus less taken notice of. He had been formerly his guest and acquaintance, and, as he was now compelled, he fought him bravely while alive, but, on his death, sought out his body and buried it with royal honors. The consequence was that he left behind him a great name among the Alexandrians, and all who were serving in the Roman army looked upon him as a most gallant soldier.

17. According to this passage, Antony graciously provided Archelaus with
    (A) friendship
    (B) statesmanship
    (C) burial
    (D) hospitality
    (E) military prowess

18. Which of the following can be inferred from the passage?
    (A) There was great friendship between Romans and Egyptians.
    (B) Antony was a great ally of Ptolemy's.
    (C) Archelaus was the greatest general of the Egyptians.
    (D) Antony was a great soldier.
    (E) Archelaus and Antony were great friends.

19. The author's attitude toward Antony is best described as
    (A) adulatory
    (B) appraising
    (C) admiring
    (D) inquisitive
    (E) intelligent

Every profession or trade, every art, and every science has its technical vocabulary, the function of which is partly to designate things or processes which have no names in ordinary English, and partly to secure greater exactness in nomenclature. Such special dialects, or jargons, are necessary in technical discussion of any kind. Being universally understood by the devotees of the particular science or art, they have the precision of a mathematical formula. Besides, they save time, for it is much more economical to name a process than to describe it. Thousands of these technical terms are very properly included in every large dictionary, yet, as a whole, they are rather on the outskirts of the English language than actually within its borders.

Different occupations, however, differ widely in the character of their special vocabularies. In trades and handicrafts and other vocations, such as farming and fishing, that have occupied great numbers of men from remote times, the technical vocabulary is very old. It consists largely of native words, or of borrowed words that have worked themselves into the very fiber of our language. Hence, though highly technical in many particu-

lars, these vocabularies are more familiar in sound, and more generally understood, than most other technicalities. The special dialects of law, medicine, divinity, and philosophy have also, in their older strata, become pretty familiar to cultivated persons, and have contributed much to the popular vocabulary. Yet, every vocation still possesses a large body of technical terms that remain essentially foreign, even to educated speech. And the proportion has been much increased in the last fifty years, particularly in the various departments of natural and political science and in the mechanic arts. Here new terms are coined with the greatest freedom, and abandoned with indifference when they have served their turn. Most of the new coinages are confined to special discussions and seldom get into general literature or conversation. Yet, no profession is nowadays, as all professions once were, a closed guild. The lawyer, the physician, the man of science, and the cleric associates freely with his fellow creatures, and does not meet them in a merely professional way. Furthermore, what is called popular science makes everybody acquainted with modern views and recent discoveries. Any important experiment, though made in a remote or provincial laboratory, is at once reported in the newspapers, and everybody is soon talking about it—as in the case of the Roentgen rays and wireless telegraphy. Thus, our common speech is always taking up new technical terms and making them commonplace.

20. Which of the following words is least likely to have started its life as jargon?
    (A) sun
    (B) calf
    (C) plow
    (D) loom
    (E) hammer

21. The author's main purpose in the passage is to
    (A) describe a phenomenon
    (B) argue a belief
    (C) propose a solution
    (D) stimulate action
    (E) be entertaining

22. When the author refers to professions as no longer being "closed guilds," he means that
    (A) it is much easier to become a professional today than it was in the past

(B) there is more social intercourse between professionals and others

(C) popular science has told their secrets
to the world

(D) anyone can now understand anything
in a profession

(E) apprenticeships are no longer required

23. If the author of the passage wished to study
a new field, he would probably
(A) call in a dictionary expert
(B) become easily discouraged
(C) look to the histories of the words in the
new field
(D) pay careful attention to the new field's
technical vocabulary
(E) learn how to coin new jargon in the
field

24. The writer of this article was probably a(n)
(A) linguist
(B) attorney
(C) scientist
(D) politician
(E) physician

25. The author of the passage probably lived in
(A) 1904 in India
(B) 1914 in the United States
(C) 1944 in Russia
(D) 1964 in England
(E) 1974 in France

26. It seems that the passage implies
(A) the English language is always becoming larger and larger
(B) the words of the English language are
always changing
(C) one can never be sure of what a word
means without consulting an expert
(D) technical terms in most non-scientific
fields have little chance of becoming
part of the main body of the language
in these scientific days
(E) such old-time farming words as harrow
and farrow are not really technical
terms at all.

27. Which of the following is (are) NOT advantages of jargon?

I. Jargon permits experts to make short
explanations of technical matters to
other experts.

II. Jargon saves money.

III. Jargon is mathematical.

IV. Jargon is more precise than ordinary
language for describing special topics.

(A) I only
(B) II and III only
(C) I and IV only
(D) I, III, and IV only
(E) I, II, III, and IV

Directions: Each of the following questions consists of a
word printed in capital letters, followed by five (5)
lettered words or phrases. Select the word or phrase
which is most nearly *opposite* to the capitalized word in
the meaning.

28. PIQUANT:
(A) factitious
(B) vain
(C) insipid
(D) slow
(E) colorful

29. OPPORTUNE:
(A) suprisingly agreeable
(B) closely berthed
(C) sharply edged
(D) badly shaped
(E) poorly timed

30. PETULANT:
(A) pliable
(B) equable
(C) uncouth
(D) abnormal
(E) untouchable

31. SAVORY:
(A) sad
(B) hidden
(C) lost
(D) unpalatable
(E) light

32. FULFILLED:
(A) satirical
(B) dry
(C) gorgeous
(D) delectable
(E) needy

33. RECLUSIVE:
    (A) joined
    (B) obscure
    (C) gregarious
    (D) urban
    (E) repetitive

34. COURTEOUS:
    (A) flaccid
    (B) emollient
    (C) insolent
    (D) scrupulous
    (E) flinching

35. USURP:
    (A) rise rapidly
    (B) use fully
    (C) produce quickly
    (D) hold carefully
    (E) own rightfully

36. ACRIMONIOUS:
    (A) legal
    (B) severe
    (C) cursive
    (D) harmonious
    (E) flippant

37. SKEPTIC:
    (A) cryptic
    (B) believer
    (C) support
    (D) eminent
    (E) caricature

38. INDUBITABLE:
    (A) wavering
    (B) aesthetic
    (C) unmitigated
    (D) questionable
    (E) belabored

STOP

END OF SECTION. IF YOU HAVE ANY TIME LEFT, GO
OVER YOUR WORK IN THIS SECTION ONLY. DO NOT
WORK IN ANY OTHER SECTION OF THE TEST.

SECTION II

30 minutes
38 questions

Directions: Each of the questions below contains one or more blank spaces, each blank indicating an omitted word. Each sentence is followed by five (5) lettered words or sets of words. Read and determine the general sense of each sentence. Then choose the word or set of words which, when inserted in the sentence, best fits the meaning of the sentence.

1. The _____ of the early morning light _____ the room, making it larger and cozier at once.
    (A) brilliance—shattered
    (B) softness—transformed
    (C) harshness—transfigured
    (D) warmth—disfigured
    (E) glare—annihilated

2. As _____ of the original team, Mickey had free _____ to all their games.
    (A) a survivor—advice
    (B) a scholar—passage
    (C) an institution—admission
    (D) an organizer—submission
    (E) a member—entrance

3. The presence of armed guards _____ us from doing anything disruptive.
    (A) defeated

(B) excited
(C) irritated
(D) prevented
(E) encouraged

4. A careful _____ of the house re-
vealed no clues.
   (A) dissemination
   (B) incineration
   (C) autopsy
   (D) dereliction
   (E) examination

5. For his diligent work in astronomy, Profes-
sor Wilson was _____ at the banquet
as _____ of the Year.
   (A) taunted—Teacher
   (B) praised—Lobotomist
   (C) lauded—Scientist
   (D) honored—Astrologer
   (E) welcomed—Administrator

6. The attorney is _____ debater; he
_____ the cross-questioning of the
Supreme Court Judge.
   (A) a forceful—anticipates
   (B) an intelligent—enjoys
   (C) an inept—dreads
   (D) a fatigued—ignores
   (E) a foolish—interrupts

7. Although there have been _____
delightful tunes, recent popular music can
hardly be called _____.
   (A) successful—aesthetic
   (B) individually—significant
   (C) some—new
   (D) increasingly—strong
   (E) many—debased

Directions: In each of the following questions, you are
given a related pair of words or phrases in capital
letters. Each capitalized pair is followed by five (5)
lettered pairs or words or phrases. Choose the pair
which best expresses a relationship similar to that
expressed by the original pair.

8. TEPID : HOT ::
   (A) pat : slap

(B) winter : summer
(C) topple : tumble
(D) cool : gel
(E) rain : storm

9. RIB : UMBRELLA ::
   (A) column : ceiling
   (B) hub : wheel
   (C) crank : engine
   (D) trunk : tree
   (E) rafter : roof

10. TADPOLE : FROG ::
    (A) gander : goose
    (B) caterpillar : butterfly
    (C) cub : lioness
    (D) frog : fish
    (E) chick : hen

11. WOOL : SHEEP ::
    (A) quill : porcupine
    (B) mohair : goat
    (C) scale : fish
    (D) shell : lobster
    (E) feather : bird

12. CAT : FELINE ::
    (A) horse : equine
    (B) tiger : carnivorous
    (C) bird : vulpine
    (D) chair : furniture
    (E) sit : recline

13. RUSTICITY : URBANITY ::
    (A) silk : wool
    (B) rust : steel
    (C) caution : daring
    (D) private : public
    (E) verbose : windy

14. CLOTHES : CLOSET ::
    (A) feet : rug
    (B) actor : script
    (C) ink : pen
    (D) beetle : insect
    (E) book : literature

15. PEPPER : BERRY ::
    (A) nutmeg : mace
    (B) persimmon : fruit
    (C) fennel : vegetable
    (D) basil : leaf
    (E) salt : rock

16. TOURNIQUET : BLEEDING ::
    (A) mint : breath
    (B) phenol : digestion
    (C) metronome : time
    (D) pressure : release
    (E) anodyne : pain

Directions: Below each of the following passages, you will find questions or incomplete statements about the passage. Each statement or question is followed by lettered words or expressions. Select the word or expression that most satisfactorily completes each statement, or answers each question in accordance with the meaning of the passage. After you have chosen the best answer, blacken the corresponding space on the answer sheet.

Whenever two or more unusual traits or situations are found in the same place, it is tempting to look for more than a coincidental relationship between them. The high Himalayas and the Tibetan plateau certainly have extraordinary physical characteristics, and the cultures which are found there are also unusual, though not unique. However, there is no intention of adopting Montesquieu's view of climate and soil as cultural determinants. The ecology of a region merely poses some of the problems faced by the inhabitants of the region, and while the problems facing a culture are important to its development, they do not determine it.

The appearance of the Himalayas during the late Tertiary Period and the accompanying further raising of the previously established ranges had a marked effect on the climate of the region. Primarily, of course, it blocked the Indian monsoon from reaching Central Asia at all. Secondarily, air and moisture from other directions were also reduced.

Prior to the raising of the Himalayas, the land now forming the Tibetan uplands had a dry continental climate with vegetation and animal life similar to that of much of the rest of the region on the same parallel, but somewhat different than that of the areas farther north, which were already drier. With the coming of the Himalayas and the relatively sudden drying out of the region, there was a severe thinning out of the animal and plant populations. The ensuing incomplete Pleistocene glaciation had a further thinning effect, but significantly did not wipe out life in the area. Thus, after the end of the glaciation there were only a few varieties of life extant from the original continental species. Isolated by the Kunlun range from the Tarim basin and Turfan depression, species which had already adapted to the dry steppe climate, and would otherwise have been expected to flourish in Tibet, the remaining native fauna and flora multiplied. Armand describes the Tibetan fauna as not having great variety, but being "striking" in the abundance of the particular species that are present. The plant life is similarly limited in variety, with some observers finding no more than seventy varieties of plants in even the relatively fertile Eastern Tibetan valleys, with fewer than ten food crops. Tibetan "tea" is a major staple, perhaps replacing the unavailable vegetables.

The difficulties of living in an environment at once dry and cold, and populated with species more usually found in more hospitable climes, are great. These difficulties may well have influenced the unusual polyandrous societies typical of the region. Lattimore sees the maintenance of multiple-husband households as being preserved from earlier forms by the harsh conditions of the Tibetan uplands, which permitted no experimentation and "froze" the cultures which came there. Kawakita, on the other hand, sees the polyandry as a way of easily permitting the best householder to become the head husband regardless of age. His detailed studies of the Bhotea village of Tsumje do seem to support this idea of polyandry as a method of talent mobility in a situation where even the best talent is barely enough for survival.

In sum, though arguments can be made that a pre-existing polyandrous system was strengthened and preserved (insofar as it has been) by the rigors of the land, it would certainly be an overstatement to lay causative factors of any stronger nature to the ecological influences in this case.

17. What are the "unusual situations and traits" referred to in the first sentence?

I. patterns of animal and plant growth
II. food and food preparation patterns of the upland Tibetans
III. social and familial organization of typical Tibetan society

(A) I only
(B) II only
(C) III only
(D) I and III only
(E) I, II, and III

18. What was the significance of the fact that the Pleistocene glaciation did not wipe out life entirely in the area?
(A) Without life, man could not flourish either.
(B) The drying out was too sudden for most plants to adapt to the climate.
(C) If the region had been devoid of life, some of the other species from nearby arid areas might possibly have taken over the area.
(D) The variety of Tibetan life was decreased.
(E) None of the above.

19. Which of the following most likely best describes Tibetan "tea"?
(A) a pale brown, clear, broth-like drink
(B) a dark brown tea drink, carefully strained
(C) a nutritious mixture of tea leaves and rancid yak butter
(D) a high caffeine drink
(E) a green tinted drink similar to Chinese basket-fried green tea

20. The purpose of the passage is to
(A) describe Tibetan fauna and flora
(B) describe the social organization of typical Tibetan villages
(C) analyze the causes of Tibet's unusual animal and plant populations
(D) analyze the possible causal links between Tibetan ecology and society
(E) probe the mysteries of the sudden appearance of the Himalayas

21. The author's knowledge of Tibet is probably
(A) based on firsthand experience
(B) the result of lifelong study
(C) derived only from books
(D) derived from Chinese sources
(E) limited to geological history

22. In which ways are the ideas of Lattimore and Kawakita totally opposed?
(A) Lattimore forbids change and Kawakita requires it.
(B) Kawakita opposes change and Lattimore favors it.
(C) Lattimore sees polyandry as primitive and Kawakita views it as modern.
(D) Lattimore criticizes polyandry as inefficient, but Kawakita finds it highly efficient.
(E) Their ideas are not totally opposed on any point.

23. According to the passage, which of the following would probably be the most agreeable to Montesquieu?
(A) All regions have different soils and, thus, different cultures.
(B) Some regions with similar climates will have similar cultures.
(C) Cultures in the same area, sharing soil and climate, will be essentially identical.
(D) European cultures are liberated to some degree from determinism.
(E) The plants of a country, by being the food of its people, cause the people to have similar views to one another.

24. The species of fauna and flora remaining in Tibet after the Pleistocene glaciation can properly be called continental because they
(A) are originally found in continental climates
(B) are the only life forms in Tibet, which is as big as a continent
(C) have been found in other parts of the Asian continent
(D) are found in a land mass that used to be a separate continent
(E) cannot be found on islands

The modern biographer's task is often seen as one of presenting the "dynamics" of the personality he is studying rather than giving the reader documents from which to deduce the personality. The biographer hopes to achieve a reasonable likeness so that the unearthing of more material will not alter the picture he has drawn. He hopes that new revelations will add dimension to his study but not change its lineaments appreciably. After all, he usually has had enough material to permit him to reach conclusions and to paint his portrait. With this abundance of material he can select moments of high drama and find episodes to illustrate character and make for vividness. In any event, biographers, I think, must recognize that the writing of a life may not be as "scientific" or as "definitive" as we have pretended. Biography partakes of a large part of the subjective side of man, and we must remember that those who walked abroad in our time may have one appearance for us—but will seem quite different to posterity.

25. The title below that best expresses the ideas of this passage is
    (A) The Dynamic Personality
    (B) The Growing Popularity of Biography
    (C) The Scientific Biography
    (D) A Verdict of Posterity
    (E) An Approach to Biography

26. According to the author, which is the real task of the modern biographer?
    (A) Interpreting the character revealed to him by the study of the presently available data.
    (B) Viewing the life of the subject in the biographer's own image.
    (C) Leaving to the reader the task of interpreting the character from contradictory evidence.
    (D) Collecting facts and setting them down in chronological order.
    (E) Being willing to wait until all the facts on the subject have been uncovered.

27. Which of the following would be the strongest criticism of the work of modern biographers as defined by the above passage?
    (A) Writing about modern figures will often fail to properly appreciate their place in history because insufficient time has passed for accurate historical judgment.
    (B) By presenting only, or primarily, his

conclusions about the character of his subject rather than the evidence upon which those conclusions are based, the modern biographer reduces the reader's ability to judge the worth of those judgments.
    (C) Illustrating a life with vivid pictures detracts from the reader's understanding of the prose itself.
    (D) By changing the style and content of biographies to suit modern tastes, it becomes impossible to compare old and modern biographical information.
    (E) Many authorities find that scientific judgments of character are impossible and, thus, only pretentious nonsense to attempt.

Directions: Each of the following questions consists of a word printed in capital letters, followed by five (5) lettered words or phrases. Select the word or phrase which is most nearly *opposite* to the capitalized word in meaning.

28. DELETERIOUS:
    (A) impulsive
    (B) salubrious
    (C) pathetic
    (D) inclusive
    (E) antipathetic

29. PUISSANCE:
    (A) ignorance
    (B) approbation
    (C) impotence
    (D) repudiation
    (E) malaise

30. SYCOPHANCY:
    (A) speak harmoniously
    (B) shout harshly
    (C) push forcefully
    (D) advise candidly
    (E) grasp greedily

31. ABERRATION:
    (A) typical behavior
    (B) correct manners
    (C) straight aim
    (D) full truthfulness
    (E) major improvement

32. ANOMALOUS:
    (A) capacious
    (B) vicious
    (C) connected
    (D) meaningful
    (E) usual

33. COGNIZANCE:
    (A) idiom
    (B) ignorance
    (C) abeyance
    (D) anecdote
    (E) fetish

34. QUIESCENT:
    (A) restless
    (B) exempt
    (C) malignant
    (D) mendicant
    (E) farcical

35. ESCHEW:
    (A) traduce
    (B) invite

(C) use
(D) emanate
(E) strengthen

36. TACITURN:
    (A) dubious
    (B) garrulous
    (C) strategic
    (D) pleasant
    (E) gullible

37. RECONDITE:
    (A) miniature
    (B) philosopher
    (C) arable
    (D) peasant
    (E) obvious

38. REDUNDANT:
    (A) dilatory
    (B) apocryphal
    (C) astute
    (D) necessary
    (E) bare

STOP

END OF SECTION. IF YOU HAVE ANY TIME LEFT, GO
OVER YOUR WORK IN THIS SECTION ONLY. DO NOT
WORK IN ANY OTHER SECTION OF THE TEST.

SECTION III

30 minutes
30 questions

Directions: For each of the following questions two quantities are given, one in Column A and one in Column B. Compare the two quantities and mark your answer sheet with the correct lettered conclusion. These are your options:

A: If the quantity in Column A is the greater;
B: if the quantity in Column B is the greater;
C: if the two quantitices are equal;
D: if the relationship cannot be determined from the information given.

Common Information: In any question, information applying to both columns is centered between the columns and above the quantities in columns A and B. The common information applies to both columns. Any symbol that appears in both columns represents the same idea or quantity in both columns.

Numbers: All numbers used are real numbers.

Figures: Assume that the position of points, angles, regions, and so forth are in the order shown. Figures are assumed to lie in a plane unless otherwise indicated. Figures accompanying questions are intended to provide information you can use in answering the questions. However, unless a note states that a figure is drawn to scale, you should solve the problems by using your knowledge of mathematics and *not* by estimating sizes by sight or measurement.

Lines: Assume that lines shown as straight are indeed straight.

	COLUMN A	COLUMN B
1.	$\sqrt{9}$	$\sqrt{5} + \sqrt{4}$
2.	$\frac{1}{6}$	16%

3.	$x^2 - 4 = 0$	
	x	2

4.	the cost of three pounds of grapes	the cost of four pounds of bananas
5.	0.17 + 6.01 + 5.27832	12

6.

area of sector P / area of sector Q	area of sector R / area of sector S

7.

x	30

8.	x > 0 and y < 0	
	$x^2 + y^2$	$(x + y)^2$

9.	x is 150% of y and y > 0	
	x	y

	COLUMN A	COLUMN B

10.

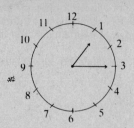

The number the minute hand points to after turning 480° clockwise.	The number the minute hand points to after turning 720° clockwise.

11.

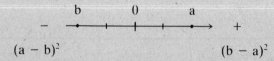

$(a - b)^2$	$(b - a)^2$

12.

$$2^m = 64$$
$$3^n = 81$$

m	n

13.

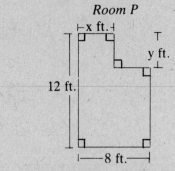 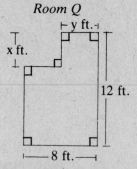

perimeter of room P	perimeter of room Q

14.

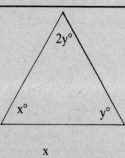

x	$2y$

15. | Total weight of x cartons each weighing y pounds | Total weight of y cartons each weighing x pounds |
|---|---|

Directions: For each of the following questions, select the best of the answer choices and blacken the corresponding space on your answer sheet.
Numbers: All numbers used are real numbers.
Figures: The diagrams and figures that accompany these questions are for the purpose of providing information useful in answering the questions. Unless it is stated that a specific figure is not drawn to scale, the diagrams and figures are drawn as accurately as possible. All figures are in a plane unless otherwise indicated.

16. If w, x, y, and z are real numbers, each of the following equals w(x + y + z) EXCEPT
    (A) wx + wy + wz
    (B) (x + y + z)w
    (C) wx + w(y + z)
    (D) 3w + x + y + z
    (E) w(x + y) + wz

17. .1% of 10 =
    (A) 1
    (B) .1
    (C) .01
    (D) .001
    (E) .0001

18. If x = +4, then (x − 7)(x + 2) =
    (A) −66
    (B) −18
    (C) 0
    (D) 3
    (E) 17

19. If 2x + y = 7 and x − y = 2, then x + y =
    (A) 6
    (B) 4
    (C) $\frac{3}{2}$
    (D) 0
    (E) −5

20. A girl rode her bicycle from home to school, a distance of 15 miles, at an average speed of 15 miles per hour. She returned home from school by walking at an average speed of 5 miles per hour. What was her average speed for the round trip if she took the same route in both directions?
    (A) 7.5 miles per hour
    (B) 10 miles per hour
    (C) 12.5 miles per hour
    (D) 13 miles per hour
    (E) 25 miles per hour

21. In the square below with side 4, the ratio $\dfrac{\text{area of shaded region}}{\text{area of unshaded region}} =$
    (A) $\dfrac{2 + x}{4}$
    (B) $\dfrac{4 - x}{8}$
    (C) 2
    (D) $\dfrac{4 + x}{4 - x}$
    (E) 2x

    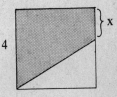

22. Ned is two years older than Mike, who is twice as old as Linda. If the ages of the three total 27 years, how old is Mike?
    (A) 5 years
    (B) 8 years
    (C) 9 years
    (D) 10 years
    (E) 12 years

23. A taxicab charges $1.00 for the first one-fifth mile of a trip and 20¢ for each following one-fifth mile or part thereof. If a trip is $2\frac{1}{2}$ miles long, what will be the fare?
    (A) $2.60
    (B) $3.10
    (C) $3.20
    (D) $3.40
    (E) $3.60

24. What is the side of a square if its area is $36x^2$?
    (A) 9
    (B) 9x
    (C) $6x^2$
    (D) 6
    (E) 6x

25. If Susan has $5 more than Tom, and if Tom has $2 more than Ed, which of the following exchanges will ensure that each of the three has an equal amount of money?
    (A) Susan must give Ed $3 and Tom $1.
    (B) Tom must give Susan $4 and Susan must give Ed $5.
    (C) Ed must give Susan $1 and Susan must give Tom $1.
    (D) Susan must give Ed $4 and Tom must give Ed $5.
    (E) Either Susan or Ed must give Tom $7.

26. A perfect number is one which is equal to the sum of all its positive factors that are less than the number itself. Which of the following is a perfect number?
    (A) 1
    (B) 4
    (C) 6
    (D) 8
    (E) 10

27.

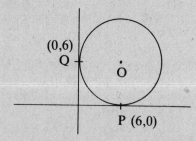

In the figure above, the coordinates of points P and Q are (6,0) and (0,6), respectively. What is the area of the circle O?
    (A) 36π
    (B) 12π
    (C) 9π
    (D) 6π
    (E) 3π

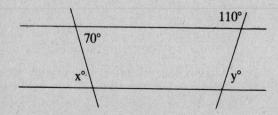

28. In the figure shown (bottom left), x + y =
    (A) 50
    (B) 140
    (C) 180
    (D) 220
    (E) 240

29. A cylinder has a radius of 2 ft. and a height of 5 ft. If it is already 40% filled with a liquid, how many more cubic feet of liquid must be added to fill it to capacity?
    (A) 6π
    (B) 8π
    (C) 10π
    (D) 12π
    (E) 16π

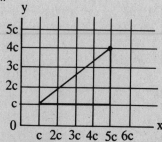

30. In the figure above, a triangle is superimposed on a grid in which all angles are right angles. If the area of the above triangle is 54, then c =
    (A) 3
    (B) 6
    (C) 10
    (D) 12
    (E) Cannot be determined from the information given.

STOP

END OF SECTION. IF YOU HAVE ANY TIME LEFT, GO OVER YOUR WORK IN THIS SECTION ONLY. DO NOT WORK IN ANY OTHER SECTION OF THE TEST.

SECTION IV

30 minutes
30 questions

Directions: For each of the following questions two quantities are given, one in Column A and one in Column B. Compare the two quantities and mark your answer sheet with the correct lettered conclusion. These are your options:

  A: If the quantity in Column A is the greater;
  B: if the quantity in Column B is the greater;
  C: if the two quantitices are equal;
  D: if the relationship cannot be determined from the information given.

Common Information: In any question, information applying to both columns is centered between the columns and above the quantities in columns A and B. The common information applies to both columns. Any symbol that appears in both columns represents the same idea or quantity in both columns.

Numbers: All numbers used are real numbers.

Figures: Assume that the position of points, angles, regions, and so forth are in the order shown. Figures are assumed to lie in a plane unless otherwise indicated. Figures accompanying questions are intended to provide information you can use in answering the questions. However, unless a note states that a figure is drawn to scale, you should solve the problems by using your knowledge of mathematics and *not* by estimating sizes by sight or measurement.

Lines: Assume that lines shown as straight are indeed straight.

	COLUMN A	COLUMN B
1.	$343 - \dfrac{343}{2}$	$\dfrac{343}{2}$

2. $$6x = 6$$

	$\dfrac{x}{6}$	$\dfrac{6}{x}$

3. On the real number line, n is between p and m and $m < n$.

	n	p

4.	$\dfrac{1}{63} - \dfrac{1}{69}$	$\dfrac{1}{65} - \dfrac{1}{67}$
5.	.06% of 1.34	1.34% of .06
6.	$3x^2 + 5$	$2x^2 + 4$

7. The digit 2 in the numeral 423,978 indicates $2 \cdot 10^b$.

	b	5

COLUMN A   COLUMN B

8. $x = -3$
                           $y = -5$

     $(x - y)^2$ $(x + y)^2$

9.

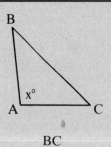
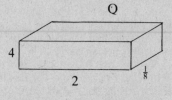

$x° < y°$

     BC   QR

10.

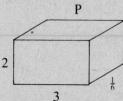
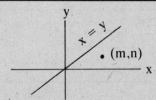

The volume of rectangular solid P   The volume of rectangular solid Q

---

11.   The greatest prime factor of 208   13

---

12. $x + 2.3 = 2y + 1.6$

     x   y

13.

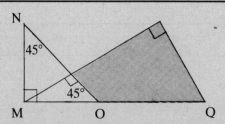

     m   n

---

14. $x*y = \dfrac{x + y}{xy}$ for all real numbers such
               that $xy \neq 0$.

     $1*2$ $2*1$

15.

Area of triangle MNO   Area of shaded portion

Directions: For each of the following questions, select the best of the answer choices and blacken the corresponding space on your answer sheet.

Numbers: All numbers used are real numbers.

Figures: The diagrams and figures that accompany these questions are for the purpose of providing information useful in answering the questions. Unless it is stated that a specific figure is not drawn to scale, the diagrams and figures are drawn as accurately as possible. All figures are in a plane unless otherwise indicated.

16. $(1.50)(2) =$
    (A) $\frac{1}{2}$
    (B) 1
    (C) $\frac{3}{2}$
    (D) $\frac{5}{2}$
    (E) 3

17. If $x = -2$, then $(x - 5)(x + 5) =$
    (A) -49
    (B) -21
    (C) 0
    (D) 9
    (E) 35

18. If an item which ordinarily costs $90 is discounted by 25%, what is the new selling price?
    (A) $22.50
    (B) $25.00
    (C) $45.00
    (D) $67.50
    (E) $112.50

19. During the time period covered by the chart, in how many years was the attrition rate for Sophomores greater than that for Freshmen?
    (A) 6
    (B) 10
    (C) 18
    (D) 21
    (E) 24

20. Between 1965 and 1970, the attrition rate for Juniors
    (A) increased by 100%
    (B) increased by 50%
    (C) increased by 20%
    (D) remained virtually unchanged
    (E) declined by 5%

21. In 1970 the ratio of the number of Freshmen who left College X to the number of Juniors who left College X was
    (A) 3:1
    (B) 3:2
    (C) 1
    (D) 2:3
    (E) Cannot be determined from the information given.

22. Which of the following propositions can be inferred from the graph?

    I. Between 1970 and 1975, the number of Freshmen leaving College X dropped by 20%.

Questions 19–23 refer to the following graph.

ATTRITION RATE AT COLLEGE X*

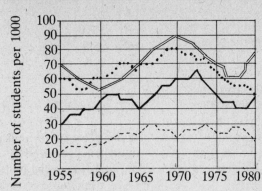

*Includes all students who voluntarily dropped out, took a leave of absence, were expelled for academic or disciplinary reasons, or left college for any other reasons

━━━━━ Freshmen   ·········· Sophomores   ──────── Juniors   ----- Seniors

II. In 1970, twenty more Juniors left College X than left College X in 1965.

III. During the period 1966 to 1969, only the rate of attrition for Seniors was decreasing.

(A) I only
(B) II only
(C) I and II only
(D) III only
(E) I, II, and III

23. For which of the four classes was the attrition rate in 1980 approximately 25% less than it had been in 1970?

    I. Freshmen
    II. Sophomore
    III. Juniors
    IV. Seniors

    (A) I only
    (B) I and II only
    (C) III only
    (D) II and III only
    (E) I, II, III, and IV

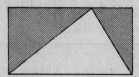

24. In the rectangle above, what is the ratio of
    $\dfrac{\text{area of shaded region}}{\text{area of unshaded region}}$?
    (A) $\frac{1}{4}$
    (B) $\frac{1}{2}$
    (C) 1
    (D) $\frac{2}{1}$
    (E) Cannot be determined from the information given.

25. Earl can stuff advertising circulars into envelopes at the rate of 45 envelopes per minute and Ellen requires a minute and a half to stuff the same number of envelopes. Working together, how long will it take Earl and Ellen to stuff 300 envelopes?
    (A) 15 minutes
    (B) 4 minutes
    (C) 3 minutes 30 seconds
    (D) 3 minutes 20 seconds
    (E) 2 minutes

DISTRIBUTION	NUMBER IN POPULATION
Having X Having Y	25
Having X Lacking Y	10
Lacking X Having Y	25
Lacking X Lacking Y	40

26. The table above gives the distribution of two genetic characteristics, X and Y, in a population of 100 subjects. What is the ratio of $\dfrac{\text{number of subjects having X}}{\text{number of subjects having Y}}$?
    (A) $\frac{7}{5}$
    (B) 1
    (C) $\frac{5}{7}$
    (D) $\frac{7}{10}$
    (E) $\frac{1}{4}$

27. If the ratio of the number of passenger vehicles to all other vehicles passing a checkpoint on a highway is 4 to 1, what percent of the vehicles passing the checkpoint are passenger vehicles?
    (A) 20%
    (B) 25%
    (C) 75%
    (D) 80%
    (E) 400%

28. If the price of an item is increased by 10% and then decreased by 10%, the net effect on the price of the item is
    (A) an increase of 99%
    (B) an increase of 1%
    (C) no change
    (D) a decrease of 1%
    (E) a decrease of 11%

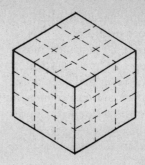

29. The graph above shows the yearly prices (in dollars) for a certain commodity. For which one-year period was the percentage decrease in price the greatest?
    (A) 1973–1974
    (B) 1974–1975
    (C) 1975–1976
    (D) 1976–1977
    (E) 1977–1978

30. The figure above represents a wooden block 3 inches on an edge, all of whose faces are painted black. If the block is cut up along the dotted lines, 27 blocks result, each 1 cubic inch in volume. Of these, how many will have no painted faces?
    (A) 1
    (B) 3
    (C) 4
    (D) 5
    (E) 7

STOP

END OF SECTION. IF YOU HAVE ANY TIME LEFT, GO OVER YOUR WORK IN THIS SECTION ONLY. DO NOT WORK IN ANY OTHER SECTION OF THE TEST.

SECTION V

30 minutes
25 questions

Directions: Each of the following questions or groups of questions is based on a short passage or a set of propositions. In answering these questions it may sometimes be helpful to draw a simple picture or chart. When you have selected the best answer to each question, darken the corresponding circle on your answer sheet.

Questions 1–3

Mr. and Mrs. N and Mr. and Mrs. P each have different tastes in music. One prefers classical, one jazz, one rock, and the last country music. Of the four, only two have blond hair and one of these likes jazz best. The wife with blond hair likes country music and her husband likes classical music best. Mrs. P has brown hair.

1. What is Mrs. P's preferred music?
   (A) classical
   (B) jazz
   (C) rock
   (D) country
   (E) Cannot be determined from the information given.

2. What color hair does Mr. P have and what music does he prefer?
   (A) blond hair and jazz music
   (B) blond hair and classical music
   (C) blond hair and rock music
   (D) brown hair and country music
   (E) brown hair and jazz music

3. Who prefers classical music?
   (A) Mrs. P
   (B) Mr. P
   (C) Mrs. N
   (D) Mr. N
   (E) Cannot be determined from the information given.

4. When this proposal to reduce welfare benefits is brought up for debate, we are sure to hear claims by the liberal congressmen that the bill will be detrimental to poor people. These politicians fail to understand, however, that budget reductions are accompanied by tax cuts—so everyone will have more money to spend, not less.

   Which of the following, if true, would undermine the author's position?

   I. Poor people tend to vote for liberal congressmen who promise to raise welfare benefits.
   II. Poor people pay little or no taxes so that a tax cut would be of little advantage to them.
   III. Any tax advantage which the poor will receive will be more than offset by cuts in the government services they now receive.

   (A) I only
   (B) II only
   (C) II and III only
   (D) III only
   (E) I, II, and III

5. Many people ask, "How effective is Painaway?" So, to find out we have been checking the medicine cabinets of the apartments in this typical building. As it turns out, eight out of ten contain a bottle of Painaway. Doesn't it stand to reason that you, too, should have the most effective pain-reliever on the market?

The appeal of this advertisement would be most weakened by which of the following pieces of evidence?
(A) Painaway distributed complimentary bottles of medicine to most apartments in the building two days before the advertisement was made.
(B) The actor who made the advertisement takes a pain-reliever manufactured by a competitor of Painaway.
(C) Most people want a fast, effective pain-reliever.
(D) Many people take the advice of their neighborhood druggists about pain-relievers.
(E) A government survey shows that many people take a pain-reliever before it is really needed.

6. CLYDE: You shouldn't drink so much wine. Alcohol really isn't good for you.
   GERRY: You're wrong about that. I have been drinking the same amount of wine for fifteen years, and I never get drunk.

Which of the following responses would best strengthen and explain Clyde's argument?
(A) Many people who drink as much white wine as Gerry does get very drunk.
(B) Alcohol does not always make a person drunk.
(C) Getting drunk is not the only reason alcohol is not good for a person.
(D) If you keep drinking white wine, you may find in the future that you are drinking more and more.
(E) White wine is not the only drink that contains alcohol.

Questions 7–12

Six compounds are being tested for possible use in a new ant poison, "Sweet 'N' Deadly."

   I. U is sweeter than V and more deadly than Z.
   II. V is sweeter than Y and less deadly than Z.
   III. W is less sweet than X and less deadly than U.

IV. X is less sweet and more deadly than Y.

V. Y is less sweet and more deadly than U.

VI. Z is sweeter than U and less deadly than W.

7. Which of the following is the sweetest?
   (A) V
   (B) W
   (C) X
   (D) Y
   (E) Z

8. Which of the following is (are) both sweeter and more deadly than V?
   (A) U only
   (B) W only
   (C) Z only
   (D) U and Z only
   (E) U and W only

9. Which of the following adds no new information about sweetness to the statements which preceeded it?
   (A) II
   (B) III
   (C) IV
   (D) V
   (E) VI

10. Which of the following is (are) sweeter than Y and more deadly than W?
    (A) U only
    (B) V only
    (C) Z only
    (D) U and V only
    (E) Z and V only

11. Which of the following is the least deadly?
    (A) U
    (B) V
    (C) W
    (D) Y
    (E) Z

12. Which of the following is the most deadly?
    (A) Z
    (B) W
    (C) U
    (D) Y
    (E) X

Questions 13–17

I. There are five pieces of lost luggage lined up in a row by themselves for customs inspection; the items weigh variously 5, 10, 15, 20, and 25 pounds. The items to be identified are a trunk, a box, a crate, a suitcase, and a hatbox; and the nationalities of the owners are American, Belgian, German, Swedish, and Turkish, not necessarily in that order.

II. The fifth item weighs 10 pounds.

III. The Swedish traveller's luggage has luggage on both sides of it.

IV. The Turkish traveller owns the item weighing 15 pounds.

V. The traveller who owns the 5-pound second item has lost a box.

VI. The American owns the item in the middle, which weighs 20 pounds.

VII. The German does not own the hatbox, which weighs less than all but one of the other items.

VIII. The item on the left is the heaviest and is a trunk.

13. Which of the following can be derived from statements I, III, and VI?
    (A) The Swede owns the first or second item.
    (B) The Swede owns the first or fourth item.
    (C) The Swede owns the second or fourth item.
    (D) The Swede owns the third or fourth item.
    (E) The Swede owns a 10-pound box.

14. What does the German own?
    (A) a 25-pound trunk
    (B) a 25-pound box
    (C) a 25-pound crate
    (D) a 10-pound hatbox
    (E) a 5-pound hatbox

15. Which of the following statements is false?
    (A) The Turk's missing luggage is heavier than the Belgian's.
    (B) The 5-pound item plus the American's item weighs the same as the German's item.
    (C) The Turk's missing luggage weighs more than the Swede's.

(D) The American's missing luggage weighs more than the German's.

(E) The crate is not next to the 25-pound item.

16. Which of the following is true?
    (A) The first item is owned by the Swede.
    (B) The 10-pound item is owned by the Belgian.
    (C) The suitcase is owned by the Turk.
    (D) The crate is owned by the American.
    (E) The box is owned by the German.

17. Which of the following additional pieces of information would, if true, allow the determination of the types of luggage that weigh 15 and 20 pounds?

    I. The crate weighs more than the suitcase.
    II. The crate is twice as heavy as the hatbox.
    III. The combined weight of the box and hatbox equals the weight of the suitcase.

    (A) I only
    (B) I and II only
    (C) I and III only
    (D) II and III only
    (E) I, II, and III

Questions 18–22

There are four grades of milk cows in the Bellman herd: AA, AAA, AAAA, and AAAAA. These are sometimes called 2A, 3A, 4A and 5A. These classifications are based on the amount and quality of the milk produced by a cow, or in the case of a bull, the qualities of the bull's mother. AA cows produce less milk of lesser quality and AAAAA cows produce the greatest quantity and the highest quality. The Bellmans have an extensive breeding program. The primary goal of the breeding program is to produce better grades of cattle, but sometimes other factors such as resistance to disease, fertility, and even temperament are considered in making the breeding decisions.

The milk-producing abilities of a cow are inherited primarily from its mother; but if the father is two or more grades different from the mother, then the offspring's grade will be one grade different from the mother's grade in the direction of the father's grade.

18. If a calf is grade 3A, which of the following pairs could have been its parents?
    (A) A father who was grade AAAAA and a mother who was grade AA.
    (B) A father who was grade AA and a mother who was grade AAAAA.
    (C) A father who was grade AAA and a mother was was grade AA.
    (D) A father who was grade AAAA and a mother who was grade AAAAA.
    (E) A father who was grade AAAAA and a mother who was grade AAAA.

19. If it is found that resistance to hoof and mouth disease is associated with having had grade 2A or 3A fathers, which of the following grades of cows will probably be least resistant?
    (A) AA
    (B) AAA
    (C) AAAA
    (D) AAAAA
    (E) All grades will have the same resistance.

20. If the Bellmans notice that the offspring of grade 4A cattle are the gentlest and easiest to handle, which of the following is the best method of quickly introducing the trait of gentleness into the largest part of the heard while getting the best milk results?
    (A) Breeding AAAA bulls to all the cows.
    (B) Breeding AAAA bulls to the AAAAA cows and AAAA cows to all the other bulls.
    (C) Breeding AAAA cows to all the bulls.
    (D) Breeding AAAAA cows to all the bulls.
    (E) Instituting a random breeding program.

21. Which of the following must be true?

    I. AA and AAAAA cannot be interbred.
    II. A 2A bull and a 4A cow produce a higher-grade calf than a 4A bull and a 3A cow.

III. The father of a 4A bull must have been grade 3A, 4A, or 5A.

(A) None of the statements must be true.
(B) I only
(C) II only
(D) I and III only
(E) II and III only

22. A certain hide color is found to breed true; that is, if either parent has the hide color, the calf will have the hide color. If the hide color is first noticed in grade AA cattle, at least how many generations, not including the first 2A cow or bull with the hide color, will it take to have a grade AAAAA cow with the hide color?
(A) two
(B) three
(C) four
(D) five
(E) six

23. We must do something about the rising cost of our state prisons. It now costs an average of $132 per day to maintain a prisoner in a double-occupancy cell in a state prison. Yet, in the most expensive cities in the world, one can find rooms in the finest hotels which rent for less than $125 per night.

The argument above might be criticized in all of the following ways EXCEPT
(A) it introduces an inappropriate analogy
(B) it relies on an unwarranted appeal to authority
(C) it fails to take account of costs which prisons have but hotels do not have
(D) it misuses numerical data
(E) it draws a faulty comparison

24. Doctors, in seeking a cure for *aphroditis melancholias*, are guided by their research into the causes of *metaeritocas polymanias* because the symptoms of the two diseases occur in populations of similar ages, manifesting symptoms in both cases of high fever, swollen glands, and lack of appetite. Moreover, the incubation period of both diseases is virtually identical, so these medical researchers are convinced that the virus responsible for *aphroditis melancholias* is very similar to that responsible for *metaeritocas polymanias*.

The conclusion of the author rests on the presupposition that
(A) *metaeritocas polymanias* is a more serious public health hazard than *aphroditis melancholias*
(B) for every disease, modern medical science will eventually find a cure
(C) saving human life is the single most important goal of modern technology
(D) *aphroditis melancholias* is a disease which occurs only in human beings
(E) diseases with similar symptoms will have similar causes

25. I. Everyone who has not read the report either has no opinion in the matter or holds a wrong opinion about it.
   II. Everyone who holds no opinion in the matter has not read the report.

Which of the following best describes the relationship between the two above propositions?
(A) If II is true, I may be either false or true.
(B) If II is true, I must also be true.
(C) If II is true, I is likely to be true.
(D) If I is true, II must also be true.
(E) If I is false, II must also be false.

STOP

END OF SECTION. IF YOU HAVE ANY TIME LEFT, GO
OVER YOUR WORK IN THIS SECTION ONLY. DO NOT
WORK IN ANY OTHER SECTION OF THE TEST.

SECTION VI

30 minutes
25 questions

Directions: Each of the following questions or groups of questions is based on a short passage or a set of propositions. In answering these questions it may sometimes be helpful to draw a simple picture or chart. When you have selected the best answer to each question, darken the corresponding circle on your answer sheet.

Questions 1–4

Seven children, J, K, L, M, N, O, and P, are students at a certain grammar school with grades 1 through 7.

One of these children is in each of the seven grades.

N is in the first grade, and P is in the seventh grade.

L is in a higher grade than K.

J is in a higher grade than M.

O is in a grade somewhere between K and M.

1. If there are exactly two grades between J and O, which of the following must be true?
   (A) K is in the second grade.
   (B) J is in the sixth grade.
   (C) M is in a higher grade than K.
   (D) L is in a grade between M and O.
   (E) K and L are separated by exactly one grade.

2. If J is in the third grade, which of the following must be true?
   (A) K is in grade 4 and L is in grade 5.
   (B) K is in grade 5 and L is in grade 6.
   (C) L is in grade 4 and M is in grade 6.
   (D) M is in grade 2 and K is in grade 4.
   (E) O is in grade 4 and L is in grade 5.

3. If K is in the second grade, in which of the following grades, respectively, could J and M be?

   I.   3 and 4
   II. 4 and 5
   III. 4 and 6

   (A) I, but not II and not III
   (B) II, but not I and not III
   (C) I or III, but not II

   (D) II or III, but not I
   (E) I, II, or III

4. If J and N are separated by exactly two grades, which of the following must be true?
   (A) M is in grade 2.
   (B) L is in grade 3.
   (C) K is in a lower grade than J.
   (D) K is in a lower grade than O.
   (E) O is in a grade between J and N.

5. JOCKEY: Horses are the most noble of all animals. They are both loyal and brave. I knew of a farm horse which died of a broken heart shortly after its owner died.

   VETERINARIAN: You're wrong. Dogs can be just as loyal and brave. I had a dog who would wait every day on the front steps for me to come home, and if I did not arrive until midnight, he would still be there.

   All of the following are true of the claims of the jockey and the veterinarian EXCEPT:
   (A) Both claims assume that loyalty and bravery are characteristics that are desirable in animals.
   (B) Both claims are, in principle, untestable, so neither can be empirically confirmed or denied.
   (C) Both claims assume that human qualities can be attributed to animals.
   (D) Both claims are supported by only a single example of animal behavior.
   (E) Neither claim is supported by evidence other than the opinion and observations of the speakers.

6. If George graduated from the University after 1974, he was required to take Introductory World History.

   The statement above can be logically deduced from which of the following?
   (A) Before 1974, Introductory World His-

tory was not a required course in the University.

(B) Every student who took Introductory World History at the University graduated after 1974.

(C) No student who graduated from the University before 1974 took Introductory World History.

(D) All students graduating from the University after 1974 were required to take Introductory World History.

(E) Before 1974, no student was not permitted to graduate from the University without having taken Introductory World History.

7. Children in the first three grades who attend private schools spend time each day working with a computerized reading program. Public schools have very few such programs. Tests prove, however, that public-school children are much weaker in reading skills when compared to their private-school counterparts. We conclude, therefore, that public-school children can be good readers only if they participate in a computerized reading program.

The author's initial statements logically support his conclusion only if which of the following is also true?

(A) All children can learn to be good readers if they are taught by a computerized reading program.

(B) All children can learn to read at the same rate if they participate in a computerized reading program.

(C) Better reading skills produce better students.

(D) Computerized reading programs are the critical factor in the better reading skills of private-school students.

(E) Public-school children can be taught better math skills.

Questions 8–12

In Dullsville, streets and roads run east–west and alternate with each other at $\frac{1}{4}$-mile intervals.

Easy Street is 1 mile north of Main Street.

Main Street is $\frac{3}{4}$ mile south of Abbey Road.

Tobacco Road is $\frac{3}{4}$ mile south of Main Street.

Mean Street is $\frac{1}{2}$ mile south of Main Street.

8. Which of these roads or streets is farthest from Main Street?

(A) Easy Street

(B) Tobacco Road

(C) Abbey Road

(D) Tobacco Road and Abbey Road are equally far.

(E) Tobacco Road and Easy Street are equally far.

9. An additional road, Royal, could be in any of the following locations except:

(A) $\frac{1}{4}$ mile north of Easy Street

(B) $\frac{1}{4}$ mile north of Mean Street

(C) $\frac{1}{2}$ mile south of Abbey Road

(D) 1 mile north of Mean Street

(E) 1 mile north of Tobacco Road

10. What is the distance between Abbey Road and Mean Street?

(A) $\frac{3}{4}$ mile

(B) 1 mile

(C) $1\frac{1}{4}$ miles

(D) $1\frac{1}{2}$ miles

(E) 2 miles

11. Sunrise Strip runs directly North-South across Dullsville's streets and roads. If a car starts going down Sunrise Strip at Abbey Road, then makes a U-turn at Tobacco Road and goes back to Main Street, about how far does it travel?

(A) $3\frac{1}{4}$ miles

(B) 3 miles

(C) $2\frac{1}{2}$ miles

(D) $2\frac{1}{4}$ miles

(E) 2 miles

12. What is the greatest distance between any two of the streets named?

(A) 1 mile

(B) $1\frac{1}{2}$ miles

(C) $1\frac{3}{4}$ miles

(D) 2 miles

(E) $2\frac{1}{4}$ miles

Questions 13–17

City College is selcting a four-person debate team. There are seven candidates of equal ability: X, Y, and Z, who attend the West campus, and L, M, N, and P, who attend the East campus. The team must have two members from each campus. Also, the members must be able to work well with all the other members of the team.

Debaters Y and L, Z and N, and L and M are incompatible pairs.

13. If debater Y is rejected and M is selected, the team will consist of
    (A) L, M, X, and Z
    (B) M, N, X, and Z
    (C) M, N, P, and X
    (D) M, N, P, and Z
    (E) M, P, X, and Z

14. If debater L is on the team, what other debaters must be on the team as well?
    (A) M, X, and Z
    (B) N, X, and Z
    (C) P, N, and Z
    (D) P, X, and Y
    (E) P, X, and Z

15. If both Y and Z are selected, which of the other debaters are thereby assured of a place on the team?
    (A) both L and M
    (B) both M and P
    (C) only N
    (D) both N and P
    (E) only P

16. Which of the following must be false?
    I.   Debaters M and Z cannot be selected together.
    II. Debaters N and Y cannot be selected together.
    III. Debaters P and Z cannot be selected together.

    (A) I only
    (B) II only
    (C) III only
    (D) I and III
    (E) I, II, and III

17. Which of the following statements is true of debater X?

    I.   Debater X must be selected as one of the West campus members of the team.
    II. Debater X must be selected if debater N is selected.
    III. Debater X cannot be selected if both L and N are rejected.

    (A) I only
    (B) II only
    (C) III only
    (D) I and II
    (E) I, II, and III

Questions 18–22

Jon is decorating his apartment and is trying to arrange his six Pop Art paintings on the east and west walls of his living room. The paintings are each multicolor representations of one of the letters of the alphabet: E, H, M, O, R, T.

Jon does not want the three letters on each wall to make any common English words. Also, the colors of the O and E do not look good next to each other, nor do the T and O go together well.

18. If Jon puts the M, O, and T on the west wall, which of the following is true?

    I.   O will be on one end of the west wall.
    II. H and R will not be, respectively, the left and right paintings on the east wall.
    III. E cannot be in the middle of the east wall.

    (A) I only
    (B) II only
    (C) I and II only
    (D) I and III only
    (E) I, II, and III

19. If Jon puts the E, H, and M on the east wall, which of the following must be true?
    (A) The E cannot be in the center of the east wall.
    (B) The O cannot be in the center of the west wall.
    (C) The R and M cannot face each other.
    (D) The T and M cannot face each other.
    (E) The H and R cannot face each other.

20. If Jon's mother is coming to visit and Jon decides to celebrate the visit by having his paintings spell "mother" starting with the leftmost painting on the east wall and going on around the room, which of the following must be false?
    (A) T is next to O.
    (B) H is next to E.
    (C) O is opposite E.

(D) T is opposite R.
(E) None of the above is false.

(D) responses
(E) composite

21. Which of the following is not possible?
(A) H, M, and R to be on the same wall
(B) T, H, and E to be on the same wall
(C) T and O to be opposite each other
(D) M and O to be opposite each other
(E) E and O to be opposite each other

22. If Jon trades his M painting for another O painting just like the one he has now, which of the following must be false?
(A) Either R or H will be next to either T or E.
(B) Either R or H will be next to an O.
(C) The O's can be on opposite walls in the middle.
(D) The T will be opposite either O or E.
(E) All of the above are possible.

23. The new car to buy this year is the Goblin. We had 100 randomly selected motorists drive the Goblin and the other two leading sub-compact cars. Seventy-five drivers ranked the Goblin first in handling. Sixty-nine rated the Goblin first in styling. From the responses of these 100 drivers, we can show you that they ranked Goblin first overall in our composite category of style, performance, comfort, and drivability.

The persuasive appeal of the advertisement's claim is most weakened by its use of the undefined word
(A) randomly
(B) handling
(C) first

24. I maintain that the best way to solve our company's present financial crisis is to bring out a new line of goods. I challenge anyone who disagrees with this proposed course of action to show that it will not work.

A flaw in the preceding argument is that it
(A) employs group classifications without regard to individuals
(B) introduces an analogy that is weak
(C) attempts to shift the burden of proof to those who would object to the plan
(D) it fails to provide statistical evidence to show that the plan will actually succeed
(E) it relies upon a discredited economic theory

25. I.   No student who commutes from home to university dates a student who resides at a university.
II. Every student who lives at home commutes to his university, and no commuter student ever dates a resident student.

Which of the following best describes the relationship between the two sentences above?
(A) If II is true, I must also be true.
(B) If II is true, I must be false.
(C) If II is true, I may be either true or false.
(D) If I is true, II is unlikely to be false.
(E) If II is false, I must also be false.

STOP

END OF SECTION. IF YOU HAVE ANY TIME LEFT, GO
OVER YOUR WORK IN THIS SECTION ONLY. DO NOT
WORK IN ANY OTHER SECTION OF THE TEST.

SECTION VII

30 minutes
38 questions

Directions: Each of the questions below contains one or more blank spaces, each blank indicating an omitted word. Each sentence is followed by five (5) lettered words or sets of words. Read and determine the general sense of each sentence. Then choose the word or sets of words which, when inserted in the sentence, best fits the meaning of the sentence.

1. The admiration the Senator earns is _____ by his _____ instinct for getting onto the front pages.
   (A) concocted—proverbial
   (B) evolved—haughty
   (C) undermined—aggressive
   (D) engendered—unerring
   (E) transcended—dogged

2. The accelerated growth of public employment _____ the dramatic expansion of budgets and programs.
   (A) parallels
   (B) contains
   (C) revolves
   (D) escapes
   (E) populates

3. You might _____ fairy tales and myths if you _____ them.
   (A) esteem—reject
   (B) uphold—read
   (C) reject—follow
   (D) understand—study
   (E) denounce—believe

4. Many diseases formerly considered _____ are now treated successfully.
   (A) incurable
   (B) rectifiable
   (C) mysterious
   (D) retrogressive
   (E) incorrigible

5. The consequences of the establishment of the colonies were a rapid and careless _____ of natural resources, and _____ human suffering.
   (A) depletion—appalling
   (B) cancellation—remarkable
   (C) disappearance—planned
   (D) development—unfailing
   (E) disintegration—compelled

6. Americans tend to equate business success with competence in public affairs, even though it is patent that business _____ are properly only slighty _____ government practices.
   (A) affairs—superior to
   (B) morals—inferior to
   (C) intellects—brighter than
   (D) leaders—sager than
   (E) procedures—related to

7. The many faults of the President's economic policies do not include _____; statements of the need to improve business conditions are followed by proposals that cause the _____ of dozens of firms daily.
   (A) weakness—demise
   (B) overintelligence—distress
   (C) consistency—bankruptcy
   (D) socialism—opening
   (E) clarity—confusion

Directions: In each of the following questions, you are given a related pair of words or phrases in capital letters. Each capitalized pair is followed by five (5) lettered pairs of words or phrases. Choose the pair which best expresses a relationship similar to that expressed by the original pair.

8. CABOOSE : BRAKEMAN ::
   (A) tower : bird
   (B) cabinet : president
   (C) bunkhouse : wrangler
   (D) castle : footman
   (E) cave : bear

9. SCRAWNY : LEAN ::
   (A) brawny : strong
   (B) tawny : thin
   (C) brainy : fat
   (D) chicken : bull
   (E) massive : thick

10. OBTUSE : BLUNT ::
    (A) thick : thin
    (B) acute : sharp
    (C) razor : butter knife
    (D) stupid : moronic
    (E) astute : dangerous

11. IGLOO : ICE ::
    (A) house : brick
    (B) tent : canvas
    (C) tepee : skins
    (D) boat : wood
    (E) plane : aluminum

12. LANGUOR : VIGOR ::
    (A) villain : hero
    (B) visible : audible
    (C) expert : tyro
    (D) lassitude : zeal
    (E) instruct : certify

13. MOLLUSK : CLAM ::
    (A) crustacean : whale
    (B) cetacean : lobster
    (C) canine : wolf
    (D) predator : lion
    (E) bird : bat

14. FERAL : TAME ::
    (A) carnivorous : herbivorous
    (B) frenzied : controlled
    (C) heightened : lessened
    (D) dangerous : staid
    (E) infections : vaccinated

15. STRATUM : STRATA ::
    (A) moral : mores
    (B) phratry : phyla
    (C) specie : species
    (D) criterion : criteria
    (E) platter : platoon

16. FECKLESS : HEEDLESS ::
    (A) cowardly : careless
    (B) dauntless : daring

(C) energetic : effortless
(D) grandiose : guiless
(E) feeble : fearful

Directions: Below each of the following passages, you will find questions or incomplete statements about the passage. Each statement or question is followed by lettered words or expressions. Select the word or expression that most satisfactorily completes each statement or answers each question in accordance with the meaning of the passage. After you choose the best answer, blacken the corresponding space on the answer sheet.

It is a measure of how far the Keynesian revolution has proceeded that the central thesis of "The General Theory" now sounds rather commonplace. Until it appeared, economists, in the classical (or non-socialist) tradition, had assumed that the economy, if left to itself, would find its equilibrium at full employment. Increases or decreases in wages and in interest rates would occur as necessary to bring about this pleasant result. If men were unemployed, their wages would fall in relation to prices. With lower wages and wider margins, it would be profitable to employ those from whose toil an adequate return could not previously have been made. It followed that steps to keep wages at artificially high levels, such as might result from the ill-considered efforts by unions, would cause unemployment. Such efforts were deemed to be the principal cause of unemployment.

Movements in interest rates played a complementary role by insuring that all income would ultimately be spent. Thus, were people to decide for some reason to increase their savings, the interest rates on the now more abundant supply of loanable funds would fall. This, in turn, would lead to increased investment. The added outlays for investment goods would offset the diminished outlays by the more frugal consumers. In this fashion, changes in consumer spending or in investment decisions were kept from causing any change in total spending that would lead to unemployment.

Keynes argued that neither wage movements nor changes in the rate of interest had, necessarily, any such agreeable effect. He focused attention on the total of purchasing power in the economy—what freshmen are now taught to call aggregate demand. Wage reductions might not increase employment; in conjunction with other changes, they might merely reduce this aggregate demand. And he held that interest was not the price that was paid to people to save but the price they got for exchanging holdings of cash, or its equivalent, their normal preference in assets, for less liquid forms of investment. And it was difficult to reduce interest beyond a certain level. Accordingly, if people sought to save more, this wouldn't necessarily mean lower interest rates and a resulting increase in investment. Instead, the total demand for goods might fall, along with employment and also investment, until savings were brought back into line with investment by the pressure of hardship which had reduced saving in favor of consumption. The economy would find its equilibrium not at full employment but with an unspecified amount of unemployment.

Out of this diagnosis came the remedy. It was to bring aggregate demand back up to the level where all willing workers were employed, and this could be accomplished by supplementing private expenditure with public expenditure. This should be the policy wherever intentions to save exceeded intentions to invest. Since public spending would not perform this offsetting role if there were compensating taxation (which is a form of saving), the public spending should be financed by borrowing—by incurring a deficit. So far as Keynes can be condensed into a few paragraphs, this is it. "The General Theory" is more difficult. There are nearly 400 pages, some of them of fascinating obscurity.

17. According to the passage, "The General Theory" advances which of the following ideas?

   I.   Government intervention is necessary to curtail excessive unemployment.
   II. Sometimes public spending must be financed by borrowing.
   III. Steps to increase wages create unemployment.

   (A) I only
   (B) II only
   (C) I and II only
   (D) II and III only
   (E) I, II, and III

18. Keynes emphasized that
   (A) unemployment was largely caused by high wages
   (B) interest rate fluctuations were desirable
   (C) lowering salaries would eventually create more jobs
   (D) the government should go into debt, if necessary, to provide jobs
   (E) an internal laissez faire policy is advantageous

19. The writer's attitude toward the Keynesian economic philosophy seems to be generally
   (A) antagonistic
   (B) questioning
   (C) favorable
   (D) mocking
   (E) bombastic

20. It my be inferred from the passage that Keynes would
   (A) favor the full employment of only those who wished to be employed
   (B) favor full employment at the cost of forcing unwilling workers to work
   (C) oppose government spending in conjunction with private spending
   (D) oppose a government deficit
   (E) force people to work

21. The "central thesis" referred to in the first sentence of the passage is the theory that
   (A) unemployment can only be reduced by government spending
   (B) unemployment is a function of the willingness of workers to work
   (C) interest in employment will decline with lowered wages
   (D) the equilibrium point of an economy will include some amount of unemployment
   (E) savings by consumers will increase government spending

22. It can be inferred from the passage that Keynes
   (A) was widely admired in his day
   (B) was not a socialist
   (C) had no idea of what his theories would mean

(D) could not agree on the role of interest rates in developing economies

(E) thought widely and deeply on many topics besides economics

23. According to Keynes, people prefer which of the following?
    (A) blue-chip stocks
    (B) government securities
    (C) savings accounts
    (D) corporate bonds
    (E) cash

In the seventeenth century, people believed that maggots came from decaying things. But Francesco Redi, a scientist, could not believe this. "How could living things come from dead things?" he asked. Redi began to believe that all worms found in the meat were derived from the droppings of flies, and not from the decaying meat. This, of course, was a guess and not a conclusion. Scientists call a good guess like this a "working hypothesis" because it gives the scientist an idea of how and where to start his work.

Then Redi began to gather and record facts to find out if his hypothesis was correct. He did this by carrying out many experiments, which were designed to help him get the facts he needed.

Redi prepared three jars with a piece of meat in each. He left one open; another was covered with cheesecloth; and the third was airtight. He observed not once, but many times, that the flies flew to the open jar and laid their eggs on the meat.

These eggs hatched into maggots. Flies also flew to the jar covered with cheesecloth, although they could not get into the jar to lay their eggs on the meat. Flies rarely flew to the airtight jar. From many such observations, Redi concluded that maggots came from flies' eggs and not from the meat.

Redi was not satisfied with doing just one experiment. Rather, he performed this experiment many times before arriving at his conclusion. In this manner he eliminated the possibility that his results were due to chance (luck).

24. In his experiment Redi left one jar open
    (A) because he had run out of lids and cheesecloth
    (B) so that the flies would have access to the meat

(C) accidentally
(D) only once
(E) none of the above

25. According to the passage, an essential part of proper scientific experimental procedure is to
    (A) leave part of the experiment open to the air
    (B) ensure that many varieties of a substance are used
    (C) vary the experimental conditions to guarantee good results
    (D) perform numerous trials to reduce the intrusion of random effects
    (E) watch everything that happens to living creatures

26. What would scientist Redi probably comment on the theory that life on Earth evolved from basic chemicals present in the Earth's primitive atmosphere and seas?
    (A) The theory was very reasonable.
    (B) The theory was certainly true.
    (C) Other theories of creation were possible.
    (D) Such developments are highly unlikely.
    (E) More data is needed to test the truth of this hypothesis.

27. According to the passage, the significance of a "working hypothesis" is that it
    (A) gives the scientist something to play with in his mind
    (B) provides a model of the true universe
    (C) allows useful structuring of experiments
    (D) provides employment for scientists
    (E) is a road to the truth

Directions: Each of the following questions consists of a word printed in capital letters, followed by five (5) lettered words or phrases. Select the word or phrase which is most nearly *opposite* to the capitalized word in meaning.

28. SCHISM:
    (A) amalgamation
    (B) paradox

(C) sanity
(D) doctrine
(E) faith

29. DILETTANTE:
(A) adept
(B) primary
(C) straight
(D) professional
(E) clasp

30. PROCRASTINATE:
(A) eulogize
(B) invest
(C) expedite
(D) insinuate
(E) mediate

31. VENERATE:
(A) abominate
(B) involve
(C) adapt
(D) instigate
(E) correlate

32. EMBELLISH:
(A) suffice
(B) disfigure
(C) trim
(D) demolish
(E) derogate

33. DISCIPLE:
(A) artisan
(B) craven
(C) renegade

(D) criminal
(E) devil

34. TERMINUS:
(A) roadway
(B) marina
(C) spontaneity
(D) beginning
(E) replica

35. STOIC:
(A) anemic
(B) passionate
(C) wasted
(D) pliable
(E) gossamer

36. BUCOLIC:
(A) circumspect
(B) urban
(C) abortive
(D) laconic
(E) punctilious

37. LUGUBRIOUS:
(A) cheerful
(B) hungry
(C) skillful
(D) jealous
(E) wise

38. INEXORABLE:
(A) erudite
(B) impregnable
(C) resistible
(D) perspicacious
(E) quixotic

STOP

END OF SECTION. IF YOU HAVE ANY TIME LEFT, GO
OVER YOUR WORK IN THIS SECTION ONLY. DO NOT
WORK IN ANY OTHER SECTION OF THE TEST.

PRACTICE EXAMINATION 4—ANSWER KEY

Section I

1.	D	10.	A	19.	C	28.	C	37.	B
2.	C	11.	C	20.	A	29.	E	38.	D
3.	B	12.	E	21.	A	30.	B		
4.	A	13.	E	22.	B	31.	D		
5.	C	14.	E	23.	D	32.	E		
6.	E	15.	B	24.	A	33.	C		
7.	D	16.	D	25.	B	34.	C		
8.	B	17.	C	26.	B	35.	E		
9.	D	18.	D	27.	C	36.	D		

Section II

1.	B	10.	B	19.	C	28.	B	37.	E
2.	E	11.	B	20.	D	29.	C	38.	D
3.	D	12.	A	21.	C	30.	D		
4.	E	13.	C	22.	E	31.	A		
5.	C	14.	C	23.	C	32.	E		
6.	C	15.	D	24.	A	33.	B		
7.	B	16.	E	25.	E	34.	A		
8.	A	17.	E	26.	A	35.	C		
9.	E	18.	C	27.	B	36.	B		

Section III

1.	B	7.	C	13.	C	19.	B	25.	A
2.	A	8.	A	14.	B	20.	A	26.	C
3.	D	9.	A	15.	C	21.	D	27.	A
4.	D	10.	A	16.	D	22.	D	28.	B
5.	B	11.	C	17.	C	23.	D	29.	D
6.	A	12.	A	18.	B	24.	E	30.	A

Section IV

1.	C	7.	B	13.	A	19.	A	25.	B
2.	B	8.	B	14.	C	20.	B	26.	D
3.	B	9.	D	15.	D	21.	E	27.	D
4.	A	10.	C	16.	E	22.	D	28.	D
5.	C	11.	C	17.	B	23.	C	29.	D
6.	A	12.	D	18.	D	24.	C	30.	A

Section V

1.	C	6.	C	11.	B	16.	B	21.	A
2.	A	7.	E	12.	E	17.	E	22.	A
3.	D	8.	D	13.	C	18.	A	23.	B
4.	C	9.	D	14.	A	19.	D	24.	E
5.	A	10.	A	15.	D	20.	B	25.	A

Section VI

1.	B	6.	D	11.	D	16.	E	21.	A
2.	B	7.	D	12.	C	17.	B	22.	C
3.	D	8.	A	13.	E	18.	C	23.	E
4.	A	9.	D	14.	E	19.	B	24.	C
5.	B	10.	C	15.	B	20.	D	25.	A

Section VII

1.	C	10.	B	19.	C	28.	A	37.	A
2.	A	11.	C	20.	A	29.	D	38.	C
3.	D	12.	D	21.	D	30.	C		
4.	A	13.	C	22.	B	31.	A		
5.	A	14.	B	23.	E	32.	B		
6.	E	15.	D	24.	B	33.	C		
7.	C	16.	A	25.	D	34.	D		
8.	C	17.	C	26.	D	35.	B		
9.	E	18.	D	27.	C	36.	B		

EXPLANATORY ANSWERS

SECTION I

1. **(D)** Sirens may drone or wail, but they don't babble, gibber, or groan. Hoarse sound is a better choice than hoarse power.

2. **(C)** "The pressure of time" indicates a need to work quickly. Assuming that mistakes are not inevitable or redundant, answer (C) is the only logical choice. The first blank is best filled by either frantically or rapidly.

3. **(B)** This sentence is concerned with the design of the lift. As it says "held up only by," we may assume that the cable is not large, which eliminates (C) and (D). Of the three remaining options, only intended (B) completes the sentence logically.

4. **(A)** The only thing known about the person described is that he is an English teacher. A solecism is a mistake in grammar and thus is a violation of the type of expertise expected of an English teacher. A schism, meaning a split of some sort, is as likely in English teachers as in anyone else, presumably. Similar comments can be made about the other answer choices.

5. **(C)** The word sincerity gives us a reference point from which to work. Thus, the second blank describes the reaction of someone valuing sincerity to an action described in the first blank. Therefore, the first blank must have something to do with sincerity. Only (C) does that, and a sycophant who is insincere would be obnoxious to someone who valued sincerity. Natal means of birth, hybrid is a mixed breed, doleful is sad, and refulgent is shining.

6. **(E)** Let us read the sentence closely. It speaks of incarcerating, which means jailing, some type of person with his fellows, that is, with others like him. Further, this companionship is theoretically supposed to teach ethical standards, BUT (the author disagrees with the theory) somehow experience shows that the theory does not work.

   First of all, since the theory described is one of teaching ethics, the objects of the teaching will not be defendants, who are not yet judged guilty, nor probably unfortunates who are simply unlucky. A much better answer is criminals deserving of jailing. When we eliminate (C) and (D), we see that one sort of criminal or another, (A), (B), or (E), is thrown in with other criminals and that this does not improve his ethical standards because of the second blank.

   (B) fails for the second blank since being interested in one's fellow criminals does not explain the failure to learn ethical standards. One might be interested in them and see how terrible they were. (A) is a little better since anger might be opposed to learning ethical standards, but (E)'s "more like" explains the whole problem. Putting someone in with criminals will make them more criminal, not less. Thus (E) is the best answer.

7. **(D)** The second blank is the evidence justifying the characterization stated in the first blank. (A) fails since proper procedures are not incredible, that is, difficult to believe. (B) fails since being full of sworn testimony is not negligent for a trial. (C) fails since a judicial manner means a measured and reasonable manner, which does not match with spectacular revelations. (E) fails since erudite citations are learned and knowledgeable, and that would not be outrageous in a trial. (D) fits well since histrionics refers to dramatics and theatricality.

8. **(B)** Blow is the verb that describes the activation of a horn. Light is the verb that describes the activation of a lamp. The other answer choices are all verbs that are typical actions to do with the nouns that are the second parts of the pair. However, none of them activate the noun. (D), accelerate has some connotation of activating an engine, but it is really only the speeding up, not the starting that is at issue. Thus, it is not the same.

9. **(D)** Pluck is the particular verb that is used to indicate the removal of feathers. Shear is the particular word that is used to indicate the removal of hair in general and wool in particular. (A) connects only in the sense that down is feathers. However there is no similarity in the relationship within the respective pairs. All the other answer choices do have words that relate the first item as a noun to which the second item, a verb, can be done. However, only (D) has the idea of removal. Thus (D) is the best answer.

10. **(A)** Modesty and arrogance are personality traits and antonyms. The only answer choice which concerns anything like a personality trait is (C), but these two terms are synonyms, so (C) is

430 / *Preparation for the GRE*

incorrect. Of the other answer choices, only (A) has any sort of specific oppositeness since debility means weakness; thus, it is the best answer. In (D), finance is the field and does not denote a rich person.

11. **(C)** A bay is a somewhat cut-off arm of the ocean. A peninsula is a somewhat cut-off arm of the land. (A) fails since the relationship is an opposition. (B) has some idea of opposition as well since a plain is basically treeless. (E) straddles the fence, as it were, but the relationship is between two small parts of larger ideas, which is not the relationship in the original pair. (D) has a similar weakness since both a cape and a reef are pieces of land partly and totally in the sea. This is an interesting relationship, but not the same as the original pair. This leaves (C) as the best answer.

12. **(E)** A spindle is the axle on which a spool turns. Wheel and axle have the same relationship. (A) has the idea of the first term going through the second, but lacks the special concept of an axle or spindle. (C) has some merit, but straight versus round would have been much stronger. (E) contains the idea of shape plus the idea of function and would be better. (D) has a straight item and a round item, but the straight item is part of the round item rather than the thing about which the round item revolves, as in the original and in (E). (B) is the second-best answer, but fails since a rod is not necessarily the thing about which the reel revolves. In addition, the idiomatic connection of a rod and reel is a fishing rod and reel. The reel is attached to the rod and does not revolve around it at all, but revolves on its own spindle. Thus, (E) is the best answer choice.

13. **(E)** A setting surrounds a gem and is designed to show the gem off to the best advantage. A frame is supposed to do the same thing for a painting. (B) and (C) both have the idea of the second term being in the first term, but have no additional idea of setting it off or enhancing it. (D) has a little idea, particularly if one were thinking of an illustrated margin, but that is not really mentioned here. (A) is the second-best answer since a stage is where the play occurs. However, it is the stage setting which is designed to show the play off to best advantage, not the stage as such. Thus, (E) is the best answer.

14. **(E)** Frangible means breakable, thus the original pair have the relationship of a potentiality and the realization of that potentiality. Pliable is bendable, and the realization of the potentiality is to be bent. (A), (B), and (C) do not have the idea of a realization of the specific potential of the first word. To be smelly is not specifically to have the potential of offending, but rather to have the potential of being smelled. In (D), a fluid can be either a liquid or a gas, and thus the potentiality for being liquefied is not really inherent in the fact

that something is a fluid any more than in something being any other state of matter. Thus, (E) is the only answer choice to show a potentiality and the strict achievement of that specific potentiality.

15. **(B)** Heckling is forceful and unpleasant interrupting. Hectoring is forceful and unpleasant teasing, though teasing has a playful feel to it which is entirely absent from hectoring. (D) has no similarity between the two elements and is eliminated. (A) has only a very slight similarity and the first item is more intense than the second, so it is in the wrong order and fails. (C) has a similarity, but not a great deal of difference in degree or intensity. (E) presents a situation which could possibly be construed as having some difference of intensity in that a performance might not be merely a speech but a complete performance. However, since a performance is a much more general term than a speech, this answer also fails and leaves (B) as the best answer choice.

16. **(D)** A shoplifter is a stealer of merchandise, specifically items that are for sale. A rustler is specifically a stealer of cattle. (B) fails since there is no illegality in it. (C) and (E) show the site of the crime, but not the item taken. (A) is the second best answer choice since a kidnapper could be thought of as a stealer of men. However, if someone said that a person was a thief, you would be surprised to find that the person was actually a kidnapper since that is a different sort of crime. We normally distinguish crimes against property from crimes against persons. Thus, (A) is a different sort of crime, as we normally classify these things, and (D) is the best answer.

17. **(C)** The only thing that Antony did for Archelaus was to make sure that he received a proper burial. This was out of Antony's own sense of honor, since the author states in the first sentence that Antony was eager for honor. (A) fails since there is no statement that the two were friends, but only acquaintances. (D) likewise fails since it states in the passage that Antony was Archelaus' guest, not the other way around. (E) and (B) both are qualities that Antony possessed, but they were not extended to Archelaus graciously since the two were on opposing sides. Thus, (C) is the best answer.

18. **(D)** All of the answer choices use the word great. When a word is repeated like this, which occasionally occurs for three or four answers, your attention is naturally directed to that word. Great is an extreme word and we must therefore look for something which was great. (A) certainly fails since the two countries were at war. We know this because Ptolemy is against the Egyptians, Antony is on Ptolemy's side, and the Roman army admires Antony, which is a fair implication that it was the Romans and Egyptians who were fighting.

(B) has some merit, but, at the same time, Antony does oppose some of Ptolemy's policies. (C) is not clear. Although Archelaus was definitely a soldier, since Antony fought him bravely, we do not know for sure that he was a general, much less how he might rank compared to the other Egyptian officers. (E) is not true since the passage is careful to say that they were merely acquaintances. (D) is certainly true since his military prowess is much in evidence and admired by all. Thus (D) is preferable to (B) since (D) is certain, while (B) is only possible.

19. **(C)** The author clearly approves of Antony, but he is not adulatory since he does point out how some of Antony's actions were of benefit to the enemy. Furthermore, the phrase "eagerness for honor" has a less than blindly approving tone. Admiring is a better choice than adulatory. Inquisitive and appraising both have some merit since the author is definitely looking into what Antony has done. However, appraising has the connotation of being somewhat skeptical, trying to find the true worth, as opposed to the apparent worth. There is no distinction of this sort being made, and thus admiring remains the best. Inquisitive is not really an attitude toward a person unless you are merely curious. Similarly, it is not clear that one's attitude toward a person would be intelligent. Remember that the question stem asked for the author's attitude toward Antony, not his evaluation of what characteristics Antony had.

20. **(A)** Jargon is stated to be a technical term, though the passage notes that in farming and other old and widespread occupations, the words will often be generally familiar. (A), sun, is not a technical term in any field, while the other four are technical terms for, respectively, husbandry, farming, weaving, and carpentry.

21. **(A)** None of the answer choices has any statement of the topic of the passage, but only a general form. The passage is descriptive only; hence (A). (C) and (D) are not done, (E) seems unlikely in this rather dry passage. (B) has the slight merit of the fact that the description given is a sort of argument that the phenomenon described does exist, but that is not so well described as a belief. Hence (A), not (B).

22. **(B)** It is important not to let outside knowledge interfere with understanding how THIS author is using a term. Although guilds in the Middle Ages were hard to get into, (A), and often required apprenticeships, (E), this is not in the passage since it is modern times that are under discussion.

(D) is too strong and (C)'s references to secrets is a little strange since it is only the reports not the secrets that are broadcast; but the strength of (B) is that it is one of the two specific statements following the phrase at issue. (C), the second-best answer, is not precisely what is stated about popular science in the passage.

23. **(D)** Since the author chose vocabulary to write an article about, he most likely studied it since it reflects the best way to discuss things in the field, as the passage states. (A), (B), and (E) have little to do with the passage. (D) is preferable to (C) because (D) includes (C) and also refers to actually learning knowledge in the new field.

24. **(A)** Since the passage primarily concerns words and their use, meanings, and history, (A) is the best answer. There is no specific support for any of the other answers.

25. **(B)** The last two sentences give us our best evidence for time and place. Roentgen rays and wireless telegraphy are key terms. They are obsolete terms for X-rays and radio, respectively, and certainly have an old-fashioned feel about them. The sentence with provincial in it tells us that the country of the author probably has knowledge of advanced science and many newspapers. The omission of radio and television from the list of media is also significant. (D) and (E) fail because of the date, since television and radio would surely be mentioned in those years. (A) fails since India was not a science center (nor a media center) in 1904. (B) is preferable to (C) since 1944 had radio and 1914 didn't.

26. **(B)** Since technical words come and go, (B) is very strong. (A) would only be true if words never left the language, which the passage does not say and common sense forbids. (C) fails since it refers to all words. (D) is shown to be false by the last sentence, if not the whole passage. (E) overlooks the author's position that such words as these are still technical words, even though common.

27. **(C)** These issues are discussed in the early part of the passage. The correct analysis of these four propositions depends largely on being sensitive to some restricted meanings of the words used in the passage. II is not true even though the passage says that the use of jargon is "economical," the commodity saved is time, not money. III fails for a similar reason. While the use of jargon permits "the precision of a mathematical formula," that does not mean that the jargon need be mathematical.

I is an advantage of jargon that is directly stated and is the real point of the comment on the economical nature of jargon. IV is also stated in the passage, deriving from the mathematically precise nature of jargon that that passage lauds. The qualifying phrase "for describing special topics" makes this proposition much easier to support since ordinary language can be perfectly precise for ordinary topics.

Your everyday perception that much jargon may not work as wonderfully as this author believes is, of course, irrelevant.

28. **(C)** Piquant means spicy or sharp, particularly in flavor, though one might speak of a piquant memory or other sensation. It usually is a positive idea. It comes from the same root as pique (as in to pique one's interest). Insipid means exactly to be without sufficient flavor or taste to be interesting. Factitious means false or artificial.

   If they do not know what insipid meant, some students might choose slow on the grounds that to pique interest is to sharpen or quicken interest, but that is a special use of the word quicken and is not opposite to slow. Furthermore, a vague opposite of a word only related to the stem word is not more than a stab at an answer and one should not be surprised if it is wrong.

29. **(E)** Opportune means something that is well timed, such as the arrival of a hero to rescue the heroine from the railroad tracks just as the train is about to crush her.

30. **(B)** A petulant person is given to showing sudden irritation over small things. An equable person is even-tempered and always behaves calmly and reasonably. Pliable means flexible or easy to shape or control. Uncouth means rude and vulgar. The others are unconnected to temperament.

31. **(D)** Savory means tasty, delicious. Unpalatable literally means that something is not pleasing to the palate. The other answers have nothing to do with taste.

32. **(E)** Fulfilled means to have been completed. A fulfilled person is one who has completed or done what he needed to do for his own happiness, in contrast to a fulfilled order, which is merely completed, or done satisfactorily. The latter is perhaps the major meaning of the word, but there is no answer choice to connect to it. Thus, needy, while not a perfect opposite, is the best answer available. Dry plays on the idea of filling, but this is too far removed to work. Fulfilled does come from some idea of being filled fully, but now has only the metaphorical usage of completion of a task or duty or need and not the original physical meaning.

33. **(C)** A reclusive person is one who does not like to meet other people and keeps to himself as much as possible. Gregarious describes a person who seeks out companionship and likes it. This is essentially a perfect opposite. Joined has some feeling of oppositeness since a reclusive person is separate from other persons, but gregarious is more precise. Similarly, urban has a trace of oppositeness since a reclusive person might be thought to be someone who is out in a faraway place, but actually a word such as anchorite or hermit would fit better for that sort of meaning. Obscure also has some feeling of being unusual and difficult to find and not quite in the midst of other things, but this is not nearly so good as gregarious.

34. **(C)** Courteous means observing good manners and being very polite. Being insolent is just the opposite—rude and insulting. The others have little connection to modes of behavior. Flaccid means limp; an emollient softens up things, especially living tissues; and scrupulous is conscientious and taking great care.

35. **(E)** To usurp something is to take and possess it when you have no right to it. Own rightfully is a good opposite. Use fully tries to play on the *usu-* in usurp. Hold carefully has the idea of holding or possessing something, but has no connotation as to the rightfulness of the possession.

36. **(D)** Acrimonious means to be sharp-tongued, and an acrimonious argument is bitter and hurtful. Harmonious discussion is when all the parties are in harmony. Severe is more of a synonym than an antonym, meaning extreme or harsh. Flippant has some oppositeness in that a flippant comment is a lighthearted one, certainly not meant to hurt; however, harmonious is better since it is positive in just the way that acrimonious is negative. Cursive is a style of handwriting or refers to something that runs together.

37. **(B)** A skeptic is one who is questioning and probing, usually about some belief. A believer is one who believes. The phrase true believer would be a better opposite since it means accepting a belief without question. But believer is the best available answer. Cryptic means encoded or difficult to decipher. Eminent is well known or highly regarded in some field. A caricature is a portrait of someone which grossly distorts and emphasizes one or two features of the subject.

38. **(D)** Indubitable means doubtless or undoubtable, or the connection is clear. A questionable item is precisely something about which one has doubts. Aesthetic refers to the appreciation of beauty. Unmitigated means without any redeeming features; and a belabored point in an argument is one which is worked over at great and excessive length.

SECTION II

1. **(B)** For the light to make the room cozier, it must be soft, not harsh. This implies that the light enhanced the room, rather than disfigured it.

2. **(E)** A person may be an institution, but not an institution of a team. It is more likely that a member of the original team, rather than a scholar, would have a free pass.

3. **(D)** Armed guards are intended to prevent any kind of disruption. Answer (D) is the only logical and grammatical choice.

4. **(E)** The sentence implies that the house was being searched, and since you don't perform an autopsy on a house, (E) is the best choice.

5. **(C)** An astronomer would not be honored as an astrologer, much less as an administrator. An astronomer is a scientist and banquets are honors.

6. **(C)** The first blank gives a characteristic of the debater that leads to his taking the action described in the second blank. (A) and (B) fail since the fact that someone is a forceful debater would not mean that they anticipate questions. Being an intelligent debater would not necessarily indicate enjoyment. An intelligent debater might anticipate, but that combination is not available. An inept debater would certainly dread questioning. A fatigued debater might miss, or fail to hear, the questions, but he would not ignore them by choice, which is what ignore implies. An attorney who interrupts a judge is probably foolish as an attorney, but his debating skills would not be described as foolish, which is not a good way of describing skills in any case. Thus, (C) is the best answer.

7. **(B)** The although tells you that there is some contrast between the first part of the sentence and the second. (A) fails since the fact that there have been successful, delightful tunes does not contrast to the idea of the music's being aesthetic or relating to beauty. Aesthetic is not very well used here in any case; aesthetically pleasing would be better. (B) does have a contrast between individual tunes, which have been delightful, and the whole of the music production, which has not been significant. (C) has some appeal, but there is not much contrast between delightful and new, making it a weaker sentence. (D) is the second best answer, though strong is a rather unspecific term and is only somewhat contrasted to increasingly delightful. (E) fails since the existence of many delightful tunes does not contrast with the idea of debased, or lowered in standards.

8. **(A)** Tepid is a mild or moderate temperature and hot is an extreme of the same sort of thing. A pat is a mild touching and a slap is an extreme one of the same sort. (B) fails since it has antonyms. (C) and (E) fail since they essentially have synonyms with no clear difference in the intensity of the words cited. (D) appeals since cool is slightly on the cool side, while tepid is slightly on the warm side. However, the very strength of this relation-

ship means that if (D) is to be the correct answer, there must be a similar strength between the second parts of the original and the answer choice. Gel does not mean icy. Gelid has that meaning. Gel merely means something that is gelatinous, like Jello. Thus, (A) is the best answer choice.

9. **(E)** At first, there might seem no relationship between rib and umbrella, but the little spokes that run from the center of the umbrella outwards and hold the umbrella up are called ribs. A rafter performs a similar function for a roof. (B), (C), and (D) all contain first items that are at the center of the second items and which, in (B) and (C), do not hold anything up. The trunk of the tree is more like a column, but (A) is preferable.

   (A) and (E) are the two best choices. The difference between them is that a rafter is part of the roof that it supports, while the column is not part of the ceiling that it supports. This is also shown by the fact that a rafter runs parallel to the roof, while a column is perpendicular to the ceiling.

10. **(B)** A good first cut at this problem would be to see that a tadpole is a young frog. (A) and (D) are eliminated by this idea and the fact that the other three agree indicates that we are probably on the right track. A gander is a male goose, not a young one. What difference is there between the three remaining answer choices? Well, (B) is about an insect, (C), a mammal, and (E), a bird. None of those help much since the original is about an amphibian. Using the idea of refinement, we might ask ourselves what is the relationship between this sort of young and this sort of adult. At this point we might see that a tadpole undergoes drastic changes before it becomes a frog, as does a caterpillar before it becomes a butterfly. The other two have no similar developmental changes. Thus, (B) is the best answer. It is a slight weakness of (B) that only some caterpillars become butterflies and others become moths.

11. **(B)** Wool is the special name of the shorn hair of the sheep when it is used in making cloth. Mohair is the special name for the shorn hair of the goat when used in making cloth. All of the answer choices concern the outer coverings of a particular animal. However, only wool and mohair are hairs.

12. **(A)** Feline means catlike; thus the correct answer will have an animal and an adjective derived from that animal. Equine means horselike, and thus (A) is the best answer. Vulpine in (C) means wolflike. (D) and (E) are not serious contenders once (A)'s merits are disclosed. (B) has some appeal since it is certainly true that a tiger is carnivorous. However, this is a characteristic of tigers rather than an adjective meaning tigerlike.

13. **(C)** The stem pair are opposites. Rusticity means

being like the country, or rural and unsophisticated, while urbanity means being sophisticated. The stem pair are thus both personality characteristics. If there is an answer choice that uses personality characteristics, I will certainly give it a good look. (C) does, and the characteristics are clearly opposite to each other. (E) has characteristics, but they are synonyms. (D) has two adjectives that are opposites, but they are not personality characteristics and there is no special connection that they have to the stem pair that might make us choose (D) over (C). (A) and (B) are not even clear opposites.

14. **(C)** That clothes go in a closet will likely be the first relationship that comes to mind. Only (C) continues that idea with ink going into a pen. In addition, both clothes and ink are stored in the appointed place until they are used. In (A), feet might be in a rug, but that is not a typical place and feet are certainly not stored in a rug.

15. **(D)** There is some knowledge required for this problem. It helps to know that pepper comes from berries that are dried. Peppercorns are dried berries. Basil is (usually) a dried leaf. All of the answer choices have as the first element a spice or flavoring of some sort, except for (B), which merely has a fruit. Salt is not a rock, nor does nutmeg come from mace, though both are from the same plant. (C) is, perhaps, the second-best answer choice since fennel is a vegetable. There are two ways of going beyond that to distinguish (C) and (D). First, fennel is not actually the seasoning, but fennel seeds are. Secondly, a berry and a leaf are parts of a plant, while vegetable is a type of plant.

16. **(E)** A tourniquet is a specific mechanism for the purpose of stopping bleeding. This suggests (C) since a metronome is a mechanism. However, the metronome does not do to time what a tourniquet does to bleeding, so the analogy fails. The only workable answer choice is (E). An anodyne is a painkiller and thus acts to stop pain. A phenol is a chemical, but has nothing in particular to do with digestion. Mint stops bad breath, but not breath.

17. **(E)** I and III are clearly indicated by the phrase physical characteristics and cultures. II is a combination of the two. Food is a physical characteristic in terms of what is available, and the preparation is a cultural aspect. Hence, all three are referred to in the passage, (E).

18. **(C)** (B) is the result primarily of the Himalaya's sudden appearance, rather than the glaciation, and (D) is of both. What we need is the idea of what would have been different if the existing plants had been entirely wiped out. (A) and (C) both speak to that, and (A) has some merit, though it is weakened by the word flourish, which

seems extreme. Though the use of life without any adjective seems odd, this is done in both (A) and (C). In (A), however, there is no sense of development or implication. (C) tells us what would have been different to the concern of the passage at that point—the diversity and type of fauna and flora. Note that the word possibly in (C) protects it from the criticism that the Kunlun range cut off other life from coming in, as does the non-specific reference to nearby arid areas. (E) would only be chosen if all of the others were definitely bad.

19. **(C)** We know only two things about the Tibetan tea. First, it is in written quotes, which means it is not just regular tea. Second, it is a possible replacement for vegetables. These both fit (C) better than any of the other answer choices. If you were reluctant to choose (C) because it sounded unlikely, you are wrong for two reasons. First, and the most important, it is almost exclusively the relationship to the passage that matters. Second, that is what Tibetan tea really is.

20. **(D)** (A), (B), and (C) are all in the passage, but they serve the purpose stated in (D). (E) is not mentioned as mysterious.

21. **(C)** The passage is full of references to the findings of others, which supports (B) and (C). (A) is unsupported by the few statements made in the passage without references. None of the statements refers to any firsthand experience by the author, eliminating (A). There is no special emphasis on China to support (D), and there is much in the passage other than geology, (E). Between (B) and (C), one must choose between the strong items in each choice—"lifelong" and "only." While the passage displays some erudition, it is not clear that a lifelong study is indicated, but all of the information can come from books and almost all of it certainly does, hence, (C).

22. **(E)** Although Lattimore and Kawakita have different emphases as to the source of the polyandry, it is not stated nor required that polyandry must be either preserved from earlier forms or an efficient way of selecting the householder. The other answers reflect differences which are not required.

23. **(C)** Montesquieu is stated to believe that climate and soil are cultural determinants, that is, they determine what the culture of the inhabitants of an area will be. (D) is unrelated to this idea, and (E) focuses on the food, not the soil and climate as such. (A) and (B) mention only one of the two factors said to be important to Montesquieu. (C) clearly states the idea of soil and climate being determinative of culture.

24. **(A)** The term continental climate is used in the passage with only a partial explication of what it might mean. However, the passage stresses the fact that the fauna and flora which were found in pre-glacial Tibet were typical of the entire region, though reduced in variety. Thus, the continental species are those found in a continental climate, the details of which you do not need to know.

(B) and (D) refer to events which are totally outside the scope of the passage and are therefore highly unlikely to be correct. (E) has the merit of referring to the location of the species and the idea that species are restricted to certain locations because of the environmental attributes of the locations. However, there is no mention of islands in the passage and, even more importantly, the fact that some species are not found on islands is not enough to classify it as continental in the way that term is used in the passage. Also, the idea of never being on any island of any sort is a little bizarre since there are doubtless islands in Tibet which have some of the species found in Tibet.

(C) has the merit of referring to the species' location in Asia, but it is not enough to just say "other parts" of Asia; Asia is very big. Also, the answer choice is not limited in any way and really means that these species are found all over Asia, which the passage makes clear is not the case.

25. **(E)** In a simple sense, (E) is the best answer because the other answers do not relate to the passage. (A) fails because the reference to "dynamic" in the passage is to the dynamics of personality and not as a characterization of a particular personality. (B) is simply not mentioned. (C) is not presented except to say that scientific biography may not be as easy as had been thought, but the modern biographer, not the scientific one, is the topic, and it is not even clear from the passage that these two types of biographers are the same, though they may overlap. (D) connects to the last sentence, in which the author allows that the future ideas about a biography subject are likely to be different than ours. But that is not the main idea. The last idea is often important, but need not be the most important. (E) is correct because the point of the passage is to describe and discuss the approach to biography that the author calls modern biography. And that is just what it does.

26. **(A)** The qualifying word in (A) is presently, and that is just fine with the author. Even though he knows that the future may come to a different conclusion, the modern biographer must do what he can with the materials available. (B) is inadequate since the author makes no such claim. It may be true that there are limitations of this sort, but it is not the modern biographer's real task. (C) is precisely what the modern biographer does not do, so it is wrong. (D), like (C), ignores the whole thrust of the passage that the modern biographer

interprets rather than merely setting down the facts in chronological order. (E) is clearly opposite to the thrust of the last sentence, which indicates that one must do the best one can even though there will be reinterpretations later. Thus, (A) is the best answer.

27. **(B)** The question asks us to do two things. First, we must be clear as to the definition of modern biographers that is given in the passage, and, second, we must see what criticisms are presented and how they agree with the passage. It is most likely that the answer choice is a criticism implied by the very definition of the modern biographer that is given in the passage. (B) meets that criterion since the passage specifically states that the original documents are not presented, except for a few illustrations, and thus the reader does not have the opportunity to make his own judgments. This clearly is a deficit and it is necessary to the kinds of biography that the author is describing.

(A) is certainly a criticism, but it is not as strong as (B) for two reasons. If this criticism were to be accepted, then no contemporary biography could ever be done and the author does not seem to be that critical. Also, the last sentence does not actually say that the views of future historians will be more accurate than those of current historians, only that they will be different. Secondly, this is an idea that is fully discussed in the passage and thus less likely to be the proper answer for a question that is clearly seeking something a little outside the scope of the passage as presented.

(C) fails since it uses the other meaning of illustration—a picture or drawing—rather than the actual meaning given in the text, of an example. In addition, it just doesn't make much sense. (D) is certainly an interesting criticism, but there is nothing in the passage that either supports the allegation that this change in technique was done to suit modern tastes or that it is therefore difficult to compare information. If there is any difficulty in comparing information, it will be because of the lack of direct documentation as described in (B). (E) is much too strong and there is no citation for "many" authorities. Equally important, the passage merely says that making a scientific judgment in these matters may not be as easy as was imagined, not that it is impossible.

28. **(B)** Deleterious means harmful, particularly to health or welfare. Salubrious means healthful, which makes it nearly a perfect opposite to one of the meanings of deleterious.

Inclusive tries to play on the root *delete-* in the word deleterious. However, delete comes from a Latin root and deleterious from a similar-looking Greek root. The other words have no real connection either. Pathetic means deserving of pity, but antipathetic means having a negative feeling towards something.

29. **(C)** Puissance means power, and impotence means lack of power. Approbation is strong approval; repudiation means disavowal. Malaise is sickness, particularly a general weakness without apparent cause.

30. **(D)** Sycophancy is servile, self-serving flattery and a sycophant is a "yes-man." The answer choices are all verbs, which is somewhat unusual, and you should have noticed the difficulty. However, since ALL of the answer choices are verbs, the part of speech does not tell you which answer choice to choose. Advising candidly is precisely the opposite of what a sycophant would do since a sycophant always agrees.

31. **(A)** An aberration is untypical behavior, particularly untypical bad behavior. Typical behavior is thus a perfect opposite. Major improvement has some oppositeness in that an aberration is likely a worse action than is typical, but there is nothing in (E) that connects to the "typical" portion of the meaning of aberration. (D) and (B) have some of the same difficulty except that they do not connect to any part of aberration as well as (E) does.

32. **(E)** Anomalous means something unusual, irregular, or abnormal. Usual is a perfect opposite since it includes the idea of relating to the general run of events. Anomalous things are often difficult to explain, but that is a derived meaning. Meaningful has some merit in the sense that abnormal items might lack meaning in the usual ways, but it is a bare echo of the real meaning of the word. Similarly, connected might appeal in the sense that an anomalous event is not connected to the usual rules or circumstances. Vicious would appeal only if one thought of the stem word as referring to animalistic. Capacious, meaning having a large capacity, usually in a physical way, is simply unrelated.

33. **(B)** Cognizance means the range or scope of knowledge, from a Latin root meaning to come to know. Ignorance is not, perhaps, a perfect opposite, but is clearly better than any of the others since it refers to the scope of lack of knowledge and none of the others refer to knowledge or learning in any way.

34. **(A)** Quiescent means being at rest or quiet. Restless refers to not being at rest, having a need for unceasing movement, such as the restless sea. This is not a perfect opposite, but the other answer choices have nothing to do with the idea of being quiet. Malignant means evil or harmful; a mendicant is a beggar; and farcical means being farcelike, a sham.

35. **(C)** To eschew means to avoid something in the sense of abstaining from it. One would eschew coarse language by not using it. Use is then a bit of a single partial opposite. Invite has some opposite flavor since it means to ask something into your area, but contrasted with use, it is the action in relation to the thing that is the issue. Traduce means to slander or falsely speak ill of someone. Emanate means to radiate out from, such as heat or light emanating from a source.

36. **(B)** Taciturn describes someone who speaks very little. This relates to the word tacit, which means unspoken, as in a tacit understanding. Garrulous, meaning talkative, is a good opposite, though it does have the additional flavor of talking about unimportant things. Dubious, meaning doubtful, and gullible, meaning one too easily deceived, are not connected to tacitturn. Pleasant has some feeling of oppositeness because a silent person may be thought of as unpleasant, even sullen, but it is an associated meaning and not a definition of taciturn.

37. **(E)** Recondite means obscure, especially referring to a little-known item of knowledge. There is some flavor of recondite knowledge being profound as well. Obvious, a good opposite to the idea of obscure, means easy to see, while recondite refers somewhat more to the number of people who know the item rather than the ease with which it can be learned or found out. Philosopher and peasant are nouns that play on the -ite ending, which sometimes signifies a noun rather than an adjective, though such nouns as anchorite derive from adjectival roots. Arable means useful for farming, and miniature means very small.

38. **(D)** Redundant means excess, surplus, and duplicative. Necessary is a good opposite to the idea of surplus. None of the other words relate to this idea. Dilatory means late or tardy; an apocryphal story is one that is probably not true; astute means clever or smart. Bare, in the sense of the cupboard being bare or empty, has some trace of oppositeness but is not right because it has no connotation of non-redundancy, only that it has no redundant contents.

SECTION III

1. **(B)** In treating radicals (square roots), it is important to keep in mind that the numbers under the radicals may be combined only when the two radicals are being multipled, not when the radicals are being added. Thus $\sqrt{5}\sqrt{4}$ is the standard notation for $\sqrt{5} \times \sqrt{4}$; the symbol for multiplication is omitted just as it is in algebraic notation (e.g., a times b is written ab). In this problem, the indicated operation is addition, not multiplication. While $\sqrt{5}\sqrt{4} = \sqrt{20}$, $\sqrt{5} + \sqrt{4} \neq \sqrt{9}$. Having established that, the problem is now easily solved. We know that $\sqrt{9} = 3$. (Note: $\sqrt{9} = 3$ not $\sqrt{9} =$

+ or − 3.) The printed radical is by convention a *non-negative* number. Only when we have $x^2 = 9$, do we have x = ±3, and that is because we are taking the square root of both sides of the equation:

$$x^2 = 9$$
$$x = ±\sqrt{9}$$
$$x = ±3$$

Notice that the ± symbol was inserted in front of the radical *before* taking the square root of 9.

As for Column B, $\sqrt{4} = 2$. And we also know that $\sqrt{5} > \sqrt{4}$, so $\sqrt{5} > 2$. This means that Column B is 2 plus something greater than 2, and thus totals something greater than 4, so B must be greater than A.

2. **(A)** Knowing the common fraction-percent equivalents would make this problem a cinch: $\frac{1}{6} = 16\frac{2}{3}\%$. But even if one does not remember that, the problem is easily solved by dividing 6 into 1: $6\overline{)1.00}^{.16\frac{2}{3}}$. So, Column A is greater than Column B.

3. **(D)** Here we can use the information about positive and negative roots discussed in question 1 above. The direct attack here is to solve for x:

$$x^2 − 4 = 0$$
$$x^2 = 4$$
$$x = ±\sqrt{4}$$
$$x = ±2$$

This shows that x might be either + or −2. To be sure, if x = +2, Column A is equal to Column B; but if x = −2, Column B is greater. This shows that our answer must be (D).

4. **(D)** Without knowing how much fruit costs per pound, we have no way of determining which costs more, three pounds of grapes or four pounds of bananas. We cannot assume that B is greater just because the bananas weigh more.

5. **(B)** You can solve this problem by performing the addition in Column A, but we have seen some problems in previous exercises in which the arithmetic would be too time-consuming. This problem borders on being one of those. If your first reaction was to add, and you then added the three numbers in less than 20 seconds, your're on firm ground. However, if you took 30 to 45 seconds to complete the addition, you should look for a shortcut. In this case, it is easy to see that the second and third terms are roughly 6 and 5. That will add up to 11. It remains only to ask whether the additional decimals in all three terms will total 1 (11 + 1 = 12). A quick glance shows that they do not add up to as much as 1, so Column B must be greater than Column A.

6. **(A)** Q and S are approximately equal, while P is much larger than R, thus making Column A

larger. Since this is a chart, it is likely that the scale is true. Even if you calculated S as 20%, you would then be left with the comparison $\frac{45\%}{20\%}$ to $\frac{15\%}{20\%}$, which need not be computed since the fractions can be compared on the basis of the denominators (bottoms) being equal and the numerators (tops) being different. The computation would show Column A as $\frac{9}{4}$ and Column B as $\frac{3}{4}$.

7. **(C)** We get started by filling in missing details. We are looking to connect our x's with a known shape.

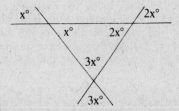

We complete the interior of the triangle using the principle that opposite angles are equal. Then, we know that the sum of the interior angles of a triangle is 180°, so:

$$x + 2x + 3x = 180°$$
$$6x = 180°$$
$$x = 30°$$

This shows that Column A and Column B are equal.

8. **(A)** Since the left expression is not factorable, the best way to begin is to multiply the right-hand expression and then strip everything from the comparison which will not make a difference: $(x + y)^2 = (x + y)(x + y) = x^2 + 2xy + y^2$. Now we see that we have an x^2 and a y^2 term on both sides of the comparison, so we strip them away (by subtracting x^2 and y^2 from both sides). This leaves 0 in Column A and +2xy in Column B. But the centered information states that x is positive and y is negative. So 2xy must be *negative*, which makes it less than 0. Column B is less than Column A so the answer is (A).

9. **(A)** This is one of those cases where the algebraic statement is probably easier to grasp than the English equivalent: "x is 150% of y" means x = 1.5y. We can see from this that since y > 0, 1.5y must be larger than y.

10. **(A)** A complete revolution of the minute hand will cover 360° (there are 360° around the center of a circle). So if the minute hand covers 480°, it will make one full turn coming back to the 3, then it will continue for another 120°, which is a third of the circle. Since there are 12 numbers on the face

of the clock, one-third of that is four numbers, so we add four numbers to the 3, arriving at 7. As for Column B, 720° is just two full turns, so the minute hand will go around twice, coming to rest again on the 3. So Column A is 7 while Column B is only 3.

11. **(C)** There are a couple of ways of approaching this problem. One is to do the indicated multiplication. The result in each case will be $a^2 - 2ab + b^2$, which shows that no matter what the values for a and b are, the expressions must be equal. Another approach is to notice that $a - b$ and $b - a$ both measure the distance from a to b. One of them does so by moving from positive to negative, the other does so by moving from negative to positive, but the absolute value is the same in both cases (the numerical value) though the signs are different. But when these values are squared, they both come out positive and therefore equal.

12. **(A)** 2 raised to the 6th power is 64, so m must be 6. 3 raised to the 4th power is 81, so n must be 4. 6 is greater than 4, so Column A is greater than Column B.

13. **(C)** We are looking to compare the perimeters, or the length of the walls, of the rooms. First we note that we are given information that all the angles are right angles. This is one point of similarity. Another point of similarity is that the two rooms are both 12 ft. by 8 ft. with a notch taken out. Since all the walls are at right angles, we know that the length of the right to left walls in each room must total 8 feet, plus the other two, which total 8 feet also, even though we do not know what x or y are. The two cross segments in room P, for instance, are x and $8 - x$ feet respectively. For Room Q they are y and $8 - y$ feet.

Similarly, the walls in the 12-foot direction must be 12 feet on each side of the room, even though broken up. Thus the total perimeter will be the same for both rooms. It is exactly 40 feet in both instances, though you do not need to compute it. For P it would be $12 + y + (12 - y) + x + (8 - x) + 8 = 40$, and similarly for Q. Note that you cannot make a comparison of the areas.

14. **(B)** Since x is an angle of an equilateral triangle $(6 = 6 = 6)$, we know that $x° = 60°$. Substituting 60° for x in the left-hand figure, we see that $60° + y° + 2y° = 180°$. So $3y = 120°$, and $y = 40°$. Now we know that $x = 60°$ and that $2y = 80°$, so Column B is greater than Column A.

15. **(C)** To compute the weight of the left-hand column, we must multiply x cartons by y pounds/cartons and get xy pounds. To compute the weight of the right-hand column we multiply y cartons by x pound/carton and get yx pounds. But since $xy = yx$, the columns must be equal.

16. **(D)** By multiplying out the given expression, we learn $w(x + y + z) = wx + wy + wz$, which shows that (A) is an equivalent expression. Second, given that it does not matter in multiplication in which order the elements are listed (i.e., $2 \times 3 = 3 \times 3$), we can see that (B) is also an equivalent expression. From $wx + wy + wz$, we can factor the w's out of the first two terms: $w(x + y) + wz$, which shows that (E) is an equivalent expression. Finally, we could also factor the w's from the last two terms: $wx + w(y + z)$, which shows that (C) is an equivalent expression. (D) is not, however, equivalent: $w + w + w + x + y + z$. The 3 would make you suspicious of (D).

17. **(C)** The answers tell you that the issue is the decimal point. The percent sign signifies that the number has been multipled by 100. To convert a percentage to a decimal, we divide by 100 and drop the percent sign, and this is equivalent to moving the decimal point two places to the left and dropping the percent sign. Thus, $.1\% = .001$. Then when we multiply by ten, we move the decimal point one place to the right: $.001 \times 10 = .01$. So our answer is (C).

18. **(B)** The most direct solution to this problem is to substitute the value $+4$ for x: $(+4 - 7)(+4 + 2) = (-3)(6) = -18$. Substitute before multiplying to keep it simple.

19. **(B)** Here we need to solve the simultaneous equations. Though there are different methods, one way to find the values of x and y is first to redefine y in terms of x. Since $x + y = 2$, $x = 2 + y$. We can now use $2 + y$ as the equivalent of x and substitute $2 + y$ for x in the other equation:

$$2(2 + y) + y = 7$$
$$4 + 2y + y = 7$$
$$3y = 3$$
$$y = 1$$

Once we have a value of y, we substitute that value into either of the equations. Since the second is a bit simpler, we may prefer to use it: $x - 1 = 2$, so $x = 3$. Now we can determine that $x + y$ is $3 + 1$, or 4.

Another approach would be to add the two equations together so that the y term will cancel itself out:

$$\begin{array}{r} 2x + y = 7 \\ + (\underline{x - y = 2)} \\ 3x = 9 \end{array}, \text{thus } x = 3.$$

20. **(A)** Average speed requires total distance divided by total time. Therefore it is incorrect to average the two speeds together for, after all, the girl moved at the slower rate for three times as long as she moved at the faster rate, so they cannot be weighted equally. The correct way to solve the problem is to reason that the girl covered

the 15 miles by bicycle in 1 hour. She covered the 15 miles by walking in 3 hours. Therefore, she travelled a total of 30 miles in a total of 4 hours. 30 miles/4 hours = 7.5 miles per hour.

21. **(D)** While we know by inspection that the shaded area is larger—the diagonal of a rectangle divides the rectangle in half—the answer choices tell us more is needed though (C) is eliminated. We begin by noting that the area which is left unshaded is a triangle with a 90° angle. This means that we have an altitude and a base at our disposal. Then we note that the shaded area is the area of the square minus the area of the triangle. So we are in a position to compute the area of the square, the triangle, and the shaded part of the figure. In the first place, the base of the triangle—which is the unshaded area of the figure—is equal to the side of the square, 4. The altitude of that triangle is four units long less the unknown distance x, or 4 − x. So the area of the triangle, $\frac{1}{2}ab$, is $\frac{1}{2}(4 − x)(4)$. The area of the square is $4 × 4$, or 16, so the shaded area is 16 minus the triangle, which we have just determined is $\frac{1}{2}(4 − x)(4)$. Let us first pursue the area of the triangle:

$$\tfrac{1}{2}(4 − x)(4) = (4 − x)(2) = 8 − 2x$$

Substituting in the shaded portion:

$$16 − (8 − 2x) = 8 + 2x$$

Now we complete the ratio. $8 + 2x$ goes on the top, since that is the shaded area, and $8 − 2x$ goes on the bottom, since that is the unshaded area: $\frac{8 + 2x}{8 − 2x}$. And we reduce by 2 to yield $\frac{4 + x}{4 − x}$.

22. **(D)** Since Linda is the youngest and the other ages are derived from hers, let us assign the value x for Linda's age. In that case Mike will be 2x years old, since he is twice as old as Linda. Finally, Ned will be 2x + 2 since he is two years older than Mike. Our three ages are: Linda, x; Mike, 2x; and Ned, 2x + 2. We know that these three ages total 27. Hence, x + 2x + 2x + 2 = 27. And now we solve for x:

$$5x + 2 = 27$$
$$5x = 25$$
$$x = 5$$

So Linda is 5 years old. Then, if Linda is 5, Mike must be 10 years old.

23. **(D)** Since our rates are by fifths of a mile, let us begin the solution by figuring out how many fifths of a mile (or parts thereof) there are in this trip. In $2\frac{2}{5}$ miles there are 12 fifths. Then we add another fifth for the additional bit of distance between $2\frac{2}{5}$ and $2\frac{1}{2}$ miles. So the whole trip can be broken down into 13 segments of one-fifth (or part of one-fifth). For the first, the charge is $1.00. That leaves 12 more segments, the charge for each of which is 20¢, giving a total charge for those 12

segments of $2.40. Now, the total charge for the trip is $1.00 for the first one-fifth of a mile and $2.40 for the remaining segments, or $3.40.

24. **(E)** We know that the formula for the area of a square is s^2 = area. So $s^2 = 36x^2$, and, taking the square root of both sides we learn s = 6x. (Note: there is no question here of a negative solution since geometrical distances are always positive.)

25. **(A)** Since we do not know how much money Ed has, we must assign that amount the value of x. We now establish that Tom has x + $2 since he has $2 more than Ed; and we know that Susan has (x + $2) + $5, which is x + $7, since she has $5 more than Tom. We want to divide this money equally. The natural thing to do, then, is to add up all the money and divide it by 3. The total held by all three individuals is: x + x + 2 + x + 2 + 5 = 3x + 9. Dividing that by 3, we want everyone to have x + 3. Ed has x so he needs to receive 3. Tom has x + 2 so he needs to receive 1. Susan has x + 7 so she needs to rid herself of 4. Susan gets rid of this 4 by giving 1 to Tom and 3 to Ed, giving us answer choice (A).

Some shortcutting is possible by considering that Susan has the most money, and then Tom and then Ed. Therefore, any answer which has Ed give up money cannot result in equal shares, eliminating (C) and (E). Furthermore, since Susan has the most, she must give up the most. In (D) Tom gives more than Susan, so this is eliminated. In (B), Susan gives out more than Tom, but she also receives from Tom, so her net giving out is only $1, compared to Tom's $4, so this is also wrong, which leaves (A).

26. **(C)** Do not let the term perfect number throw you. Accept the definition of any such oddball term and apply it to the problem. Since the factors of 6 less than 6 itself are 1, 2, and 3, 6 is the perfect number (1 + 2 + 3 = 6). 1 is not a perfect number since there are no factors of 1 less than itself. 4 is not a perfect number since the factors of 4 less than 4 are 1 and 2 and 1 + 2 ≠ 4. Nor is 8 a perfect number since the factors of 8 which are less than 8 itself are 1, 2, and 4, and those total 7, not 8. Finally, 10 is not a perfect number since the key factors here are 1, 2, and 5, which total 8, not 10.

27. **(A)** By connecting Q and O or P and O, it can be seen that the radius of circle O is 6 units. (Remember, when a circle is named after a point, that point is the center of the circle.) The formula for the area of a circle is πr^2, so the area of circle O is: $\pi(6)^2 = 36\pi$.

28. **(B)** We are given information about angles in the top of the figure and asked about angles in the bottom. The task, then, is to connect these items. We do not know that the horizontal lines are parallel, nor can we prove it. We do, however,

have a quadrilateral figure and several straight lines to work with. Considering the figure with a, b, and c as the three angles of the quadrilateral other than the 70°, we see:

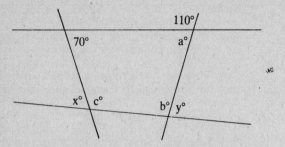

Angle a is on a straight line with 110° and thus equals 70°. We are looking only for x + y, so we need not have each individually. Working our way down through the quadrilateral, we see that the total degrees in the quadrilateral, as for all such figures, is 360°. Thus, b + c + 70° + 70° = 360° and b + c = 220°. Now, at last, we are on the right line. Again using the fact that a straight line totals 180° we see:

$$\begin{array}{rl} x + c & = 180 \\ y + b & = 180 \\ \hline x + y + b + c & = 360 \end{array}$$

Since we know b + c = 220, we can solve by substituting to get x + y + 220 = 360; thus x + y = 140.

29. **(D)** We begin by computing the capacity of the cylinder, which is πr^2 times height. Since the radius is 2 and the height is 5, the capacity of this cylinder is $\pi(2)^2 \times 5 = 20\pi$ cu. ft. It is already 40% full, which means that 60% of the capacity is left. 60% of 20π cu. ft. = 12π cu. ft., and that is the answer we seek.

30. **(A)** We are seeking c, but the given information is about the area of the triangle, while c is a distance. However, the formula for the area of triangles connects distance to area, so we should compute the area in terms of c. We know that we have a right angle in the lower right-hand corner of the figure. So, this gives us an altitude and a base. The altitude is 3c units long and the base is 4c units long. So, the area is $\frac{1}{2}ab$ or $\frac{1}{2}(3c)(4c) = \frac{1}{2}(12c^2) = 6c^2$. And this is equal to 54: $6c^2 = 54$; so $c^2 = 9$ and c = 3.

SECTION IV

1. **(C)** Of course, it is possible to perform the subtraction indicated in Column A, and to do so probably would not require more than 30 seconds: $343 - \frac{343}{2} = \frac{686 - 343}{2} = \frac{343}{2}$. A better way of solving the problem, however, is to reason: 343/2 is one-half of 343. To take any number and subtract half of that number leaves half of the number. So the two quantities must be equal. Since this is early in the subsection, look for a shortcut.

2. **(B)** First, simplify the centered information: 6x = 6; therefore x = 1. Once you know x = 1, then substitute 1 for x in each column. Column A becomes $\frac{1}{6}$ and Column B becomes $\frac{6}{1}$. Since $\frac{1}{6}$ is less than $\frac{6}{1}$, our answer choice must be (B).

3. **(B)** Since n is between p and m, we have either m < n < p or p > n > m. Since m < n, the former must be true and, thus, n must be less than p, so Column B is larger and (B) is the correct answer.

4. **(A)** It would probably take too long to actually do the indicated calculations. Therefore, we should look for a shorter method. In each column we have the same process—subtraction. We can observe that $\frac{1}{63}$ is the largest of the four fractions in the problem and that $\frac{1}{69}$ is the smallest of the four. In turn, $\frac{1}{65}$ is the second-largest, while $\frac{1}{67}$ is the second-smallest. Thus, the smallest fraction is taken away from the largest while the second-smallest is taken away from the second-largest. Therefore, Column A must be larger (just as, for exmple, 9 − 3 is larger than 7 − 5).

5. **(C)** This problem is typical of the GRE. The two quantities must be equal. The order of multiplication is irrelevant and the number of decimal places is equal in both columns:

$$.0006 \times 1.34 = .0134 \times .06$$

Or the % sign can be taken as the fraction $\frac{1}{100}$, yielding:

$$(.06)(\tfrac{1}{100})(1.34) = (1.34)(\tfrac{1}{100})(.06)$$

6. **(A)** Although there are no restrictions on the values of x, we know that it is permissible to subtract equal quantities from both columns (that will not interfere with the comparison). Here we subtract $2x^2$ from both columns. The result is

$$x^2 + 5 \qquad 4$$

Then, just to make things as simple as possible, we subtract 4 from both columns and the result is:

$$x^2 + 1 \qquad 0$$

We must now ask what values x might have. Since there is no restriction on the values x might assume, x can range over the entire set of real numbers. But no matter what x is, so long as x ≠ 0, x^2 will be positive. Even if x is 0, $x^2 + 1$ will be greater than 0 (0 + 1 > 0), and if x has a value greater than 0, that will just make x^2 even larger. So Column A is always greater than Column B.

Another, shorter way of approaching this problem would be to note that we have the same process in both columns—addition. The 5 in Column A is bigger than the 4 in Column B, so if the $3x^2$ is also bigger than $2x^2$, A will be larger. Since x^2 must be positive, more often it will yield a larger number.

7. **(B)** If you were schooled in the "new math," you may find this problem easy; otherwise, it takes a bit longer to work out. The key to the problem is that the number 423,978 is equal to 400,000 plus 20,000 plus 3,000 plus 900 plus 70 plus 8. Now each of these terms can be expressed using powers of ten: $4 \times 10^5, 2 \times 10^4, 3 \times 10^3, 9 \times 10^2, 70 \times 10^1$, and 8. The digit 2 then is used in the slot for 10^4; therefore, b must be 4. 5 is greater than 4, so Column B is greater.

8. **(B)** One sure way of solving the problem is to substitute the values -3 and -5 for x and y, respectively. Before we do that, however, the following word of warning is in order for the students well versed in math: in this case the fact that x and y are negative means that the absolute value of $x - y$ will be *less* than the absolute value of $x + y$. Consequently, when we square $x - y$ and $x + y$, both will be positive, but Column B will be greater. Now, with that note to the mathematicians, we can solve the problem by substituting—a direct, simple, and sure way of getting a right answer:

$$(-3 - -5)^2 \qquad (-3 + -5)^2$$
$$2^2 \qquad\qquad -8^2$$
$$4 \qquad\qquad +64$$

9. **(D)** This problem teaches a very important lesson: It is better to rely on your intuitive knowledge of geometry than to try to memorize formulas. In this case, many students will pick answer (B). Their justification will be the well-known principle that "the larger the angle of a triangle, the larger the opposite side." The rule is absolutely correct, but it is incompletely stated and really applies only within a given triangle. Since the angles belong to *different* triangles it doesn't apply here. Studying principles of math is a good idea, but knowing when to apply the principles is absolutely essential. The following group of drawings should make it clear that no comparison is possible:

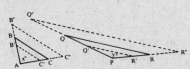

10. **(C)** The formula for computing the volume of a rectangular solid such as a box is width times length times height. For Column A, this is $2 \times 3 \times \frac{1}{6} = 1$. For Column B this is $4 \times 2 \times \frac{1}{8} = 1$. So the two volumes are equal.

11. **(C)** We begin our solution by dividing 13 into 208, with 16 the result. Now we know that either 13 is the largest prime factor of 208 or that the largest prime factor of 208 is paired as a multiple with some number between 1 and 208. The following consideration leads us to this conclusion. First, neither 14 nor 15 are factors of 208 (and in any event are not prime numbers). This lets us know that 13 and 16 are the pair of factors which are most nearly equal. Any other pair of factors will be spread farther apart. Importantly, however, whether we find that 208 is factorable by 104, for example, we know that the other element of that pair will be a number between 1 and 13. So, though 104 and 2 are factors, we can quickly isolate all pairs of factors by working our way up from 1 to 13. They are 1 and 208, 2 and 104, 4 and 52, 8 and 26, and 13 and 16. Although 208 has some factors that are larger than 13, e.g., 208, none of these are prime. So the largest prime factor is 13, and the two columns are equal.

Another way of approaching this problem would be to use the important principle of doing what you know how to do. Since 208 is even, we could simply divide it by 2, getting 104. Dividing by 2 again gives us 52. Doing it again yields 26, and once again leaves 13, which is a familiar prime, and equal to Column B.

12. **(D)** In this equation, we have no powers, roots, radicals, or the like. But the equation is not just letters; we also have a number in the equation since the numbers could be consolidated all on one side or the other, such as $x + .7 = 2y$. Since there are two variables and only one equation, we do not have a definite solution to the situation as it stands. If it had been that x plus a number equalled just y with no multiplier, then we would know for sure how x and y relate. What you are most concerned about is whether this relationship is definite, whether one of the variables is ALWAYS greater, less than, or equal to the other. It should be fairly clear to you that this equation permits x and y to be different, so you might ask yourself if they could be the same, and the answer here is "yes," since if both were equal to .7, the equation would work. Since x and y could be different and they could be the same, the relationship cannot be tied down.

Alternatively, you could substitute some simple positive and negative numbers and compute that x is sometimes greater than y and sometimes smaller. It's better if you can just see it quickly.

For the mathematicians, there is yet another possible solution (among many others) which we can show. First, it should be clear that the .7 makes no difference to the comparison—we could as easily use 1 or even 0. The only difference will be the precise point at which x and y are equal. Having simplified the problem, say, to $x + 1 = 2y$, which is $y = \frac{1}{2}x + \frac{1}{2}$ (the numbers are easier), one can sketch the line roughly on a graph:

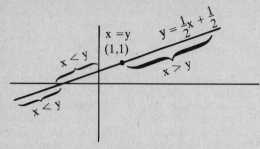

In the second quandrant, x is negative and y is positive, so x is less than y. In the first quadrant, though both x and y are positive, since the slope of the line is $\frac{1}{2}$, the values for x climb more rapidly than do the values for y.

13. **(A)** In the last problem we mentioned the coordinate axis for the mathematicians. Here, everyone will need to understand the use of the axis. In this case, we have the graph of the equation x = y, which is a straight line passing through the origin (0,0). Since (m,n) is in the first quadrant, both m and n must be positive. Then, since (m,n) is below the line x = y, the x coordinate must be greater than the y coordinate. Had they been equal, the point (m,n) would have fallen on the line. Since it fails to fall on the line, it is as though one went over x units on the x axis, but did not go up quite as far in the vertical direction, so the point fell short. Thus, x must be greater than y, and so, too, m must be greater than n.

14. **(C)** In problems involving some defined operations, such as ∗, the best attack is usually to substitute the values suggested. In the case of Column A, we use 1 for x and 2 for y. Looking at the centered information, we substitute: $\frac{1 + 2}{(1)(2)} = \frac{3}{2}$. For Column B, we reverse x and y: $\frac{2 + 1}{(2)(1)} = \frac{3}{2}$. So the two columns are equal.

It might happen to strike you that Columns A and B are simply swapping the x and y in the input to the ∗ function. If we look at the operations that ∗ is calling for, we see that one is addition and the other multiplication. In both of those operations, order doesn't matter: xy = yx and x + y = y + x. (We say that both addition and multiplication are "commutative"—order is not important.) Therefore, the answers would be the same for both columns. If something like that strikes you, it is worth a little following up. However, if what you think is a shortcut doesn't seem to be getting you anywhere, drop it!

15. **(D)** The easiest way to solve this problem is to try to redraw the figure in a way that preserves the specified relationships but also shows that a definite answer cannot be reached:

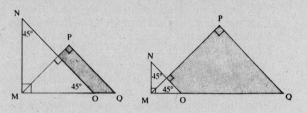

Both configurations are permissible. We still have the right angles preserved, and we still have the 45° angles preserved. This shows that the given information is not sufficient to allow us to reach a conclusion about the relationship between the sizes of the regions.

16. **(E)** This is a very easy problem. One need only do the indicated operation. Multiply 1.50 by 2: (1.50)(2) = 3.00 = 3.

17. **(B)** Again, we have a relatively easy problem. We must substitute −2 for x, and then multiply: (−2 − 5)(−2 + 5). (−2 − 5) = −7, and (−2 + 5) = 3. Then, (−7)(3) = −21, since a negative number times a positive number gives a negative number. Thus, answer (B) is correct.

18. **(D)** While it is possible to set up a formula for this problem: Original Price − Discount = Discounted Price, a little common sense is a better attack. The discount is 25% of the original price, and 25% of $90 is $22.50. If the item originally cost $90, and we are getting a discount of $22.50, the new price will be $67.50.

19. **(A)** This is a fairly straightforward chart question. We need only count the number of years in which the dotted line ("Sophomores") exceeded (was above) the heavy black line ("Freshmen"). This first occurred in 1959 and continued in 1960, 1961, 1962, 1963, and 1964 (when "Sophomores" was barely larger than "Freshmen"). It came to an end in 1965, when the two were equal. "Sophomores" remains well below "Freshmen" until 1977 when it almost reached the level of "Freshmen," but not quite. So, in only six years did the attrition rate for Sophomores exceed that of Freshmen.

20. **(B)** In 1965 the attrition rate for Juniors was 40 per 1000. In 1970, it was 60 per 1000. So, it increased by 20 during that time. To compute that increase, we take the difference, 20, and divide by the original, or starting, quantity, which is 40. $\frac{20}{40} = \frac{1}{2}$, or a 50% increase, answer choice (B).

21. **(E)** Reading the chart carefully is an important part of the exercise. In this case, the chart gives

the attrition rate, that is, the number of students per 1000 who left the college. The chart does not provide any information about the actual number of students leaving. For example, in 1970 the attrition rate for freshmen was 90 students per every 1000, but that does not say how many freshmen actually left. If there were 1000 freshmen, we could conclude 90 left. If there were 2000, we would know that 180 left, and so on. But without the additional information regarding the size of the classes, we cannot conclude anything about the numbers of students who left. And without that information, we cannot compute a ratio between the number of freshmen leaving and the number of juniors leaving.

22. **(D)** The reasoning of our explanation to question 21 provides the key to this question and an important reminder of the importance of attending carefully to the title, margins, and footnotes of the chart as a source of information. Neither I nor II can be inferred since we have no information about the *numbers* involved. We have the attrition *rate*—that is, the number per 1000 who left. But without additional information we can conclude nothing about the actual numbers involved. III is, however, inferable from the graph. During that period, only the dashed line ("Seniors") declined on the graph.

23. **(C)** We are looking for those categories, if there are any, where the drop from 1970 to 1980 was $\frac{1}{4}$ of the 1970 total, for that will indicate a decrease of 25%. (After a 25% decrease, the new total will be 25% less than the old total.) For freshmen the drop was from 90 to 75, a difference of 15 over a starting value of 90; $\frac{15}{90}$ is much less than $\frac{1}{4}$. For sophomores, the value drops from 80 to 50, a difference of 30 over a starting value of 80; $\frac{30}{80}$ is greater than 25%. For juniors, the drop was from 60 to 45, a difference of 15 over a starting value of 60, $\frac{15}{60}$—the 25% decrease we seek. Finally, the senior attrition rate dropped from 23 to 20, such a small percentage change that eyeballing the line would be enough. Only the juniors' rate decreased by 25% from 1970 to 1980—III only.

24. **(C)** Let us begin our solution by dropping a perpendicular from the upper vertex of the triangle:

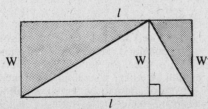

This divides the rectangle into two other rectangles, each with a diagonal running across it:

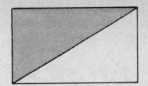

It should be intuitively clear that the diagonal of a rectangle divides the rectangle in half since all sides and angles are equal. Therefore, the left shaded area is equal to the left unshaded area and the right shaded area is equal to the right unshaded area, which means the total shaded area is equal to the total unshaded area. Thus, the triangle has half the area of the rectangle. This is actually the proof of the formula you use to find the area of a triangle—A = (height)(base)$\frac{1}{2}$. Remember this situation since it could easily come up in one problem or another.

25. **(B)** Since Earl and Ellen will be working together we add their work rates:

$$\frac{\text{Number of tasks}}{\text{Time}} + \frac{\text{Number of tasks}}{\text{Time}}$$
$$= \frac{\text{Number of tasks together}}{\text{Time}}$$

In this case:

$$\frac{45 \text{ envelopes}}{60 \text{ seconds}} + \frac{45 \text{ envelopes}}{90 \text{ seconds}} = \frac{300 \text{ envelopes}}{x \text{ seconds}}$$

Or: $\frac{45}{60} + \frac{45}{90} = \frac{300}{x}$
To make the arithmetic simpler, we reduce fractions:

$$\frac{3}{4} + \frac{1}{2} = \frac{300}{x}.$$

Then we add: $\frac{10}{8} = \frac{300}{x}$.
And solve for x: $x = 300(\frac{8}{10}) = 240$ seconds.
Since 240 seconds is equal to 4 minutes, our answer is (B).
If you are not comfortable with fractions, you could have kept to minutes.

Another way to approach this problem would be to try to get the rate of each worker in envelopes per minute. Earl is already known to work at 45 envelopes per minute. Ellen takes $1\frac{1}{2}$ minutes for the same work. Thus, 45 envelopes are done in three half-minutes. 45 divides by 3 nicely, as we often find on the GRE, so Ellen does 15 envelopes in $\frac{1}{2}$ minute or 30 envelopes per minute. 45 per minute + 30 per minute = 75 per minute, which means $\frac{300}{75} = 4$ minutes.

26. **(D)** First, let us count the number of subjects having characteristic X. The first two categories are those subjects having X (25 which also have Y, 10 which do not have Y but do have X), which is a total of 35. Then those subjects having Y are entered in the first and third categories (25 also

have X, 25 have Y but lack X), for a total of 50. Our ratio is $\frac{35}{50}$, which, when reduced by a factor of 5, is equal to $\frac{7}{10}$.

27. **(D)** This problem is a bit tricky, but not really difficult. When dealing with a ratio, say 4 to 1, it is important to remember that the number of parts is the sum of these two numbers. So we might say we have five parts—four parts are passenger vehicles, one part is all other vehicles—and that is how we get a ratio of 4 to 1. But this means that 4 parts out of the total of 5 parts are passenger vehicles, and 4 out of 5 is $\frac{4}{5}$, or 80%. Answer (E) makes the mistake of forgetting that although there are four times as many passenger cars as all other vehicles, the passenger vehicles constitute only $\frac{4}{5}$ of the total number.

28. **(D)** Let us logically approach this problem before even trying to calculate it. Although we have a 10% increase and then a 10% decrease, we must always ask ourselves "10% of what?" The increase was 10% of the original price, but the decrease was 10% of the higher price and consequently the decrease is bigger than the increase and the result at the end is less than the starting price, which eliminates answer choices (A), (B), and (C). Similarly, on logical grounds, it is hard to see how a 10% decrease from a 10% higher price could be equal to an 11% decrease from the starting price; that seems too much, which leaves (D) as the answer.

If we wish to compute the answer, let us start by saying that the original price of the item is x. A 10% increase in that price will be one-tenth of x, or .1x. When we add the increase to the original price, we find our increased price is 1.1x. We must then take away ten percent of that. Ten percent of 1.1x is .11x, and subtracting .11x from 1.1x, we get .99x. We started with x; we ended with .99x, so we lost .01x, which is 1%.

29. **(D)** First, we must note that the question asks for *percentage* decrease, not simply decrease in price. And percentage change is a function of the absolute change or difference over the starting value. We begin our solution by noting that both (B) and (E) mention periods in which the price increased, so we know that neither of them could be correct. Then we run a quick calculation of percentage decrease for the remaining three:

(A) $\frac{70 - 40}{70} = \frac{30}{70}$, for slightly less than 50% decrease.

(C) $\frac{50 - 30}{50} = \frac{20}{50}$, for slightly less than 50% decrease.

(D) $\frac{30 - 10}{30} = \frac{20}{30}$, for a $66\frac{2}{3}$% decrease.

So (D) is greater than both (A) and (C).

30. **(A)** This is an interesting problem in that no formula is going to solve it. Instead, it requires the use of some good old common sense. Perhaps the solution is more easily visualized if we explode the cube.

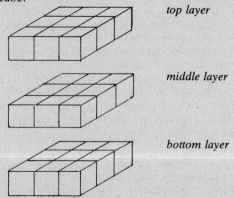

top layer

middle layer

bottom layer

All of the small cubes on the top and the bottom layers will have at least one side painted. In the middle layer, the outer eight smaller cubes encircle the center cube, which is protected on top by the top layer, on the bottom by the bottom layer, and on the remaining four sides by the outside of the sandwich layer:

middle layer

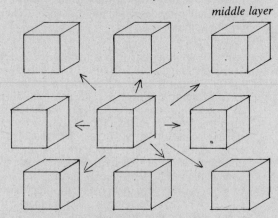

SECTION V

Questions 1–3

ARRANGING THE INFORMATION

The three question stems are all "what is it" questions, so we know that the situation is one in which the arrangement is stable or fixed, and a large proportion of the time will be spent in arranging the information. We have a setup in which there are three items of information to be sorted out about the four people: names, musical preference, and hair color. There is an auxiliary relationship in that there are two couples.

Since the situation is a fixed one, with relatively few parameters, we will do it in one chart:

NAME	Mrs. N.	Mr. N	Mrs. P	Mr. P
MUSIC				
HAIR				

Since the situation is fixed and we are using a single chart, and there are not that many pieces of information, we might consider whether there are any pieces of information which would be most helpful to enter out of order because they are fixed. The very last piece of information, that Mrs. P. has brown hair, can be the rock on which our diagram is founded.

NAME	Mrs. N.	Mr. N	Mrs. P	Mr. P
MUSIC				
HAIR			Brown	

We might now look for something which links to that information. If nothing did, we would just enter information, but there is an item which links: the wife with blond hair likes jazz. This must be Mrs. N. since we have determined that Mrs. P has brown hair. We thus learn both the hair color and musical preference of Mrs. N. This gives us the following diagram:

NAME	Mrs. N.	Mr. N	Mrs. P	Mr. P
MUSIC	Country			
HAIR	Blond		Brown	

The same sentence contains another piece of information we can now link up: the blond wife's husband (Mr. N) likes classical music. This yields:

NAME	Mrs. N	Mr. N	Mrs. P	Mr. P
MUSIC	Country	Classical		
HAIR	Blond		Brown	

We can now consider the last pieces of information—there are only two blonds and one of them likes jazz. We have previously determined that one of the blonds likes country, so we must now determine who the other blond might be. It cannot be Mr. N, for he likes classical music, nor can it be Mrs. P, since she has brown hair. Therefore, Mr. P must have blond hair and like jazz.

NAME	Mrs. N	Mr. N	Mrs. P	Mr. P
MUSIC	Country	Classical		Jazz
HAIR	Blond		Brown	Blond

We can now make the inference that Mrs. P. likes rock music since that is the only possibility left. We do not know what color hair Mr. N has except that it is not blond since the two blonds have been accounted for. So our final diagram looks like this:

NAME	Mrs. N	Mr. N	Mrs. P	Mr. P
MUSIC	Country	Classical	Rock	Jazz
HAIR	Blond	Not blond	Brown	Blond

Answering the Questions

All the answers can be read from the diagram.

1. **(C)** Music tastes are fully determined.

2. **(A)** Mr. P has blond hair and likes jazz.

3. **(D)** Mr. N likes classical music.

4. **(C)** The author is arguing that the budget cuts will not ultimately be detrimental to the poor since the adverse effects will be more than offset by beneficial ones. II and III attack both elements of this reasoning. II points out that there will be no beneficial effects to offset the harmful ones, and III notes that the harmful effects will be so harmful that they will outweigh any beneficial ones that might result. I, however, is not relevant to the author's point. The author is arguing a point of economics. How the congressmen get themselves elected has no bearing on that point.

5. **(A)** The author reasons from the premise "there are bottles of this product in the apartments" to the conclusion "therefore, these people believe the product is effective." The ad obviously wants the hearer to infer that the residents of the apartments decided themselves to purchase the product because they believed it to be effective. (A) directly attacks this linkage. If it were true that the company gave away bottles of the product, this would sever that link. (B) does weaken the ad, but only marginally. To be sure, we might say to ourselves, "Well, a person who touts a product and does not use it himself is not fully to be trusted." But (B) does not aim at the very structure of the argument as (A) does. (C) can hardly weaken the argument since it appears to be a premise on which the argument itself is built. (C) therefore actually strengthens the appeal of the advertisement. It also does not link to Painaway's effectiveness. (D) seems to be irrelevant to the appeal of the ad. The ad is designed to change the hearer's mind, so the fact that he does not now accept the conclusion of the ad is not an argument against the ability of the ad to accomplish its stated objective. Finally, (E) is irrelevant to the purpose of the ad for reasons very similar to those cited for (D).

6. **(C)** The weakness in Gerry's argument is that he assumes, incorrectly, that getting drunk is the only harm Clyde has in mind. Clyde could respond very effectively by pointing to some other harms of alcohol. (A) would not be a good response for Clyde since he is concerned with Gerry's welfare. The fact that other people get drunk when Gerry does not is hardly a reason for Gerry to stop drinking. (B) is also incorrect. That other people do or do not get drunk is not going to strengthen Clyde's argument against Gerry. He needs an argument that will impress Clyde, who apparently does not get drunk. (D) is perhaps the second-best answer, but the explicit wording of the paragraph make it unacceptable. Gerry has been drinking the same quantity for fifteen years. Now, admittedly it is possible he will begin to drink more

heavily, but that *possibility* would not be nearly so strong a point in Clyde's favor as the *present* existence of harm (other than inebriation). Finally, (E) is irrelevant, since it is white wine which Gerry does drink.

Questions 7–12

Arranging the Information

We have two separate dimensions here: sweetness and deadliness. Sweetness is presumably a surrogate for attractiveness to ants. The preview of the question stems reinforces the conclusion that these two are the basic ideas and also tells us that we have a question about redundancy, at least insofar as information about sweetness goes. Let us arrange the information about sweetness.

		←LESS—SWEET—MORE→
I.	U sweeter than V	V U
II.	V sweeter than Y	Y V U
III.	W less sweet than X— cannot enter yet	
IV.	X less sweet than Y	X Y V U
	Now enter III:	W X Y V U
V.	Y less sweet than U— ALREADY KNOWN (Q # 9)	
VI.	Z sweeter than U	W X Y V U Z

Now let us do deadliness:

		←LESS—DEADLY—MORE→
I.	U deadlier than Z	Z U
II.	V less deadly than Z	V Z U
III.	W less deadly than U	V Z U ←——W→
IV.	X deadlier than Y— cannot enter yet	
V.	Y deadlier than U	V Z U Y ←——W→
	Now Enter IV:	V Z U Y X ←——W→
VI.	Z less deadly than W	V Z W U Y X

Answering the Questions

7. **(E)** Z is the sweetest of the compounds.

8. **(D)** U and Z are sweeter than V, and both of the compounds are also deadlier than V.

9. **(D)** As noted during the arrangement phase of the problem, V added no new information to the sweetness classification.

10. **(A)** V, U, and Z are sweeter than Y, and U, Y, and X are deadlier than W. Thus, only U meets both criteria.

11. **(B)** V is the least deadly.

12. **(E)** X is the most deadly.

Questions 13–17

Arranging the Information

There are four things to know about each piece of luggage: position, type, weight, and owner. Five pieces times four kinds of information about each piece is a grid of $5 \times 4 = 20$ boxes.

Question 13 should be done first since it uses only part of the information, but since none of the questions asks about contradiction or redundancy, the order in which the particular information statements are done after question 13 is answered will not make any difference. Questions 14, 15, and 16 indicate that pretty much the entire story is known about the luggage, but question 17 indicates that at least two parts of the grid will not be definitely completed.

The grid outline from statement I:

POSITION	1	2	3	4	5
TYPE					
WEIGHT					
OWNER					

Entering item II:

POSITION	1	2	3	4	5
TYPE					
WEIGHT					10 lbs
OWNER					

Entering item III:

POSITION	1	2	3	4	5
TYPE					
WEIGHT					10 lbs
OWNER	not Sw	Sw?	Sw?	Sw?	not Sw

Entering item VI:

POSITION	1	2	3	4	5
TYPE					
WEIGHT			20 lbs		10 lbs
OWNER	not Sw	Sw?	Amer	Sw?	not Sw
	not Amer	not Amer		not Amer	not Amer

At this point Question 13 is answerable, as shown in the following "Answering the Problems" section.

Now we enter the other items of information. IV can only be partially entered since there is only the negative inference to be made that anything not 15 pounds cannot be the Turk's, which needs to be kept in mind in entering each further piece of information. V can be entered now:

POSITION	1	2	3	4	5
TYPE		box			
WEIGHT		5 lbs	20 lbs		10 lbs
OWNER	not Sw	Sw?	Amer	Sw?	not Sw
	not Amer	not Amer		not Amer	not Amer
			not Turk		not Turk

Now enter VII, since VI has already been entered. VII tells us that the hatbox weighs 10 pounds (second-from-lightest), and thus is the fifth item, and it is not owned by the German.

POSITION	1	2	3	4	5
TYPE		box			hatbox
WEIGHT		5 lbs	20 lbs		10 lbs
OWNER	not Sw	Sw?	Amer	Sw?	not Sw
	not Amer	not Amer		not Amer	not Amer
			not Turk		not Turk
					not Germ

Notice that we can now do some more with the owner line: Since 5 cannot be any of the other four, it must be Belgian.

OWNER	not Sw	Sw?	Amer	Sw?	Belg
	not Amer	not Amer		not Amer	
	not Belg	not Belg		not Belg	
		not Turk			

Now we enter VIII. Since this is the last item, we expect to have many interactions and to all but complete the remaining blanks at this point. Here is what it looks like after filling in only the direct information in VIII:

POSITION	1	2	3	4	5
TYPE	trunk	box			hatbox
WEIGHT	25 lbs	5 lbs	20 lbs		10 lbs
OWNER	not Sw	Sw?	Amer	Sw?	Belg
	not Amer	not Amer		not Amer	
	not Belg	not Belg		not Belg	

Our further deductions are these:
—Since the Turk has a 15-pound item, his cannot be in position 1, which makes position one not American or Swedish or Belgian or Turkish, and thus must be German.
—Since the weights are known for positions 1, 2, 3, and 5, position 4 must be the last possibility: 15 pounds and position 4 must, therefore, also be the Turk's item.
—Since the ownership of item 1 is German, 3 American, 4 Turkish, and 5 Belgian, 2 must be Swedish.
—The crate and the suitcase might be in either position 3 or 4. Note that question 17, which indicated that there was some uncertainty in the final grid, would not directly name the uncertain portions of the grid, but refers to them through the weights, which are certain. This is typical.

Thus, the final grid looks like this:

POSITION	1	2	3	4	5
TYPE	trunk	box	crate suitcase	suitcase crate	hatbox
WEIGHT	25 lbs	5 lbs	20 lbs	15 lbs	10 lbs
OWNER	Germ	Sw	Amer	Turk	Belg

Answering the Problems

13. **(C)** As can be seen from the preceding third diagram, these statements tell us that the Swede owns the second or fourth item since his luggage is surrounded by other luggage and had to be either 2, 3, or 4, and the American is 3. Choices (A) and (B) incorrectly allege position 1 is possible. (D) errs in saying that position 3 is possible when that is the American. (E) refers to the 10-pound box, which is position 5 and not surrounded by other luggage.

14. **(A)** This is answered from the grid. The German owns a 25-pound trunk, not a 25-pound box or crate. VIII by itself rules out answers (B) and (C). V by itself rules out items (B) and (E).

15. **(D)** The American's luggage is 20 pounds and the German's 25. Thus, (D) is false and the answer sought. (A) is true since Turk = 15 pounds and Belgian = 10. (B) is true since American = 20, German = 25, and 20 + 5 = 25. (C) is true since Turk = 15 and Swede = 5. (E) is true even though the exact location of the crate is unknown; it is position 3 or 4, while the trunk is position 1—thus, not next to it.

16. **(B)** The 10-pound hatbox is owned by the Belgian. (C) and (D) cannot be known since those items' positions are not certain. (A) and (E) are simply false.

17. **(E)** Each of the statements is sufficient. Anything which will distinguish the crate from the suitcase or tie down either one of them will do the trick. One of them is 20 pounds and owned by the American, the other is 15 pounds and owned by the Turk.

   I. works since it tells us the crate must be the 20-pound item.
   II. works since it tells us that the crate is the 20-pound item.
   III. works since it tells us that the suitcase is the 15-pound item.

Questions 18–22

Arranging the Information

The whole first paragraph is mostly background. The real meat of the setup is in the second paragraph, where the method of determining the grade of a calf from the grades of its parents is laid out.

If father = mother or +/− 1 grade, child = mother.
If father +2 or 3 from mother, child = mother +1.
If father −2 or 3 from mother, child = mother −1.
Permissible grades 2A, 3A, 4A, and 5A.

Since the question stems are largely conditional, this small amount of information in the arranging end of the job is to be expected. Most of the work will be in the questions.

Answering the Questions

18. **(A)** A 2A mother's calf will be raised one grade if the father is either 4A or 5A; hence, answer choice (A) yields a 3A child.

    Since the calf's grade must always be within one grade of its mother's grade, a 3A calf could not have had a 5A mother. This eliminates answer choices (B) and (D). Count the A's carefully.

    (C) fails because although the father is higher than the 2A mother, he is only one grade higher, and thus cannot lift the calf to 3A. (E)'s breeding will produce a 4A calf, which, while preferable from the Bellman's perspective perhaps, is not a preferable answer choice when you are trying to explain a 3A result.

19. **(D)** The least resistant grades will be those that could not possibly have had 2A or 3A fathers, if any. 5A offspring can only be the result of 5A mothers and 5A or 4A fathers. Any other father would be sufficiently below the 5A mother to lower the offspring to 4A. By the same sort of reasoning, the 2A offspring would be the most resistant since they must have had a 2A or 3A father. The others would be in-between since it is likely that some of them did have 2A or 3A fathers. As the discussion shows, it is not true that all of the grades will have the same resistance; thus, (E) fails.

20. **(B)** Answer choices (A), (B), and (C) all have some merit since they will each result in all of the next generation of cattle having at least one 4A parent, and thus presumably be more gentle. Though (D) does improve the milk-producing qualities of the herd, it will do nothing to enhance gentleness. Thus, (D) is eliminated. (E) could not be correct since a random breeding program would leave some non-gentle offspring, which (B) avoids.

    Since (A), (B), and (C) all have good results on gentleness, you must tell them apart and choose the best answer on the basis of their effect on milk quality and quantity. (A) will upgrade the 2A cows' offspring, but the other cows will have the same grade calves as they are themselves. (C), on the other hand, will eliminate 5A grades from the herd altogether.

    (B) is preferable to either (A) or (C) because it will preserve 5A grades, unlike (C), and it will improve the herd more than (C)—since it is using higher-grade cows rather than higher-grade bulls, and the cows will pull up the grades more than the bulls, according to the given information.

21. **(A)** Statement I has no basis whatever in the problem set, so it cannot be known to be true. II is not true because a 2A bull and a 4A cow produce a 3A offspring, and so does the breeding of a 4A bull to a 3A cow. III is also false since a 2A bull and a 5A cow will produce a 4A calf. Thus, all three statements are false.

22. **(A)** The key to this problem is the phrase at least, which permits you to assume the most favorable permissible conditions without worrying about what might actually happen down on the dairy farm. Since we want to raise the grade rapidly, and a high-grade mother will raise grade more rapidly than a high-grade father, we will assume that we start with a 2A hide color bull which is bred to a 5A cow, producing a 4A bull offspring. That is the first generation. This 4A hide color bull is then bred to another 5A cow to produce a 5A hide color offspring in the second generation after the first hide color animal.

23. **(B)** The chief failing of the argument is that it draws a false analogy. Since prisons are required to feed and maintain as well as house prisoners (not to mention the necessity for security), the analogy to a hotel room is weak at best. (C) focuses on this specific shortcoming. Remember, in evaluating the strength of an argument from analogy it is important to look for dissimilarities which might make the analogy inappropriate. Thus, (A) and (E) are also good criticisms of the argument. They voice the general objection of which (C) is the specification. (D) is also a specific objection—the argument compares two numbers which are not at all similar, but that does not apply here. (B) is not a way in which the argument can be criticized, for the author never cites any authority.

24. **(E)** The author cites a series of similarities between the two diseases, and then, in his last sentences, he writes, "So . . . ," indicating that his conclusion that the causes of the two diseases are similar rests upon the other similarities he has listed. Answer (E) correctly describes the basis of the argument. (A) is incorrect, for nothing in the passage indicates that either disease is a public health hazard, much less that one disease is a greater hazard than the other. (B) is unwarranted for the author states only that the scientists are looking for a cure for *aphroditis melancholias*. He does not state that they will be successful; and even if there is a hint of that in the argument, we surely would not want to conclude on that basis that scientists will eventually find a cure for *every* disease. (C), like (A), is unrelated to the conclu-

sion the author seeks to establish. All he wants to maintain is that similarities in the symptoms suggest that scientists should look for similarities in the causes of these diseases. He offers no opinion of the ultimate goal of modern technology, nor does he need to do so. His argument is complete without any such addition. (D) is probably the second-best answer, but it is still completely wrong. The author's argument, based on the assumption that similarity of effect depends upon similarity of cause, would neither gain nor lose persuasive force if (D) were true. After all, many diseases occur in both man and other animals, but at least (D) has the merit—which (A), (B), and (C) all lack—of trying to say something about the connection between the causes and effects of disease.

25. **(A)** The form of the argument can be represented using letters as:
    I. All R are either O or W. (All non-Readers are non-Opinionholders or Wrong.)
    II. All O are R.

    If II is true, I might be either false or true, since it is possible that there are some who have not read the report who hold right opinions. That is, even if II is true and all O are R, that does not tell us anything about all the R's, only about the O's. The rest of the R's might be W's (wrong opinion-holders) or something else altogether (right opinionholders). By this reasoning we see that we cannot conclude that I is definitely true, so (B) must be wrong. Moreover, we have no ground for believing I to be more or less likely true, so (C) can be rejected. As for (D), even if we assume that all the R's are *either* O or W, we are not entitled to conclude that all O's are R's. There may be someone without an opinion who has not read the report. Finally, (E), if it is false that all the O's (non-opinionholders) are not R's, tells us nothing about all R's and their distribution among O and W.

SECTION VI

Questions 1–4

Here we have a linear ordering problem, a type now very familiar. We begin by summarizing the information:

N = 1 and P = 7
L > K
J > M
K > O > M or K < O < M

1. **(B)** We begin by processing the additional information. For J and O to be separated by exactly two grades, it must mean that they are in grades 2 and 5 or grades 3 and 6, though not necessarily in that order:

1	2	3	4	5	6	7
N	J			O		P
N	O			J		P
N		O			J	P
N	J				O	P

We can eliminate all but the third possibility. The first arrangement is not possible because we cannot honor the requirement J > M. The second is not possible because we cannot place O between K and M. The fourth is not possible for the same reason. Using only the third possibility, we know further:

1	2	3	4	5	6	7
N	K	O	M	L	J	P

OR: N K O L M J P

OR: N M O K L J P

This proves (B) is necessarily true. The diagram further shows that (A), (C), (D), and (E) are only possibly, though not necesarrily, true.

2. **(B)** We begin by processing the additional information:

1	2	3	4	5	6	7
N	M	J	O	K	L	P

With J in grade 3, M must be in grade 2. And we know that L must be a higher grade than K and, further, that O must go between K and M. This means that O, K, and L must be in grades 4, 5, and 6, respectively. The diagram shows that (B) is necessarily true, and that each of the remaining choices is necessarily false.

3. **(D)** The proper means of attack on this question is to test each of the three statements. Since there are only three, this can be done in a reasonable amount of time. As for statement I:

1	2	3	4	5	6	7
N	K	M	J			P

We see there is no place for O between K and M. So this is not possible. As for statement II;

1	2	3	4	5	6	7
N	K		M	J		P

This will allow us to place O between K and M, and placing L in grade 6 ensures that L is in a grade higher than K. So statement II is possible. As for statement III:

1	2	3	4	5	6	7
N	K		M		J	P

This allows us to place O in grade 3, and therefore between K and M. And we can place L in grade 5, which respects all other conditions. So statement III is also possible. Our correct answer must therefore be (D), II and III are possible, though I is not possible.

4. **(A)** We begin by processing the additional information:

$$1 \quad 2 \quad 3 \quad 4 \quad 5 \quad 6 \quad 7$$
$$N \quad M \quad J \quad O \quad K \quad L \quad P$$

We separate J from M by one grade by placing J in grade 3, which means that M, to be in a lower grade, must be in grade 2. Next, we reason that for L to be in a grade higher than K, and yet allowing that O must be between K and M, we have O, K, and L in grades 4 through 6, respectively. The diagram, therefore, proves that (A) is correct while each of the other choices is necessarily false.

5. **(B)** Notice that there is much common ground between the jockey and the veterinarian. The question stem asks you to uncover the areas on which they are in agreement by asking which of the answer choices is NOT a shared assumption. Note that the exception can be an area neither has as well as an area only one has. Examine the dialogue. Both apparently assume that human emotions can be attributed to animals since they talk about them being loyal and brave (C), and both take those characteristics as being noble—that is, admirable (A). Neither speaker offers scientific evidence but rests content with an anecdote (E) and (D). As for (B), it would seem that some kind of study of animal behavior might resolve the issue. We could find out how horses and dogs would react in emergency circumstances—do they show concern for human beings, or do they watch out for themselves? Importantly, it may be wrong to attribute such emotions to animals, but whatever behavior is taken by the speakers to be evidence of those emotions can be tested. So their claims—animals behave in such a way—are, in principle, testable.

6. **(D)** Note the question stem very carefully: We are to find the answer choice *from which* we can deduce the sample argument. You must pay very careful attention to the question stem in every problem. (D) works very nicely as it gives us the argument structure: "All post-1974 students are required. . . . George is a post-1974 student. Therefore, George is required. . . ." Actually, the middle premise is phrased in the conditional (with an "if"), but our explanation is close enough, even if it is a bit oversimplified. (A) will not suffice, for while it describes the situation before 1974, it just does not address itself to the post-1974 situation. And George is a post-1974 student. (B) also fails. We cannot conclude from the fact that all of those who took the course graduated after 1974 that George was one of them (anymore than we can conclude from the proposition that all airline flight attendants lived after 1900 and that Richard Nixon, who lived after 1900, was therefore one of them). (C) fails for the same reason that (A) fails. (E) is a bit tricky because of the double negative. It makes the sentence awkward. The easiest way to handle such a sentence is to treat the double negative as an affirmative. The negative cancels the negative, just as in arithmetic a negative number times a negative number yields a positive number. So (E) actually says that before 1974 the course was not required. That is equivalent to (A) and must be wrong for the same reason.

7. **(D)** The author's recommendation that public schools should have computerized reading programs depends upon the correctness of his explanation of the present deficiency in reading skills in the public schools. His contrast with private-school students shows that he thinks the deficiency can be attributed to the lack of such a program in the public schools. So, one of the author's assumptions, and that is what the question stem is asking about, is that the differential in reading skills is a result of the availability of a computerized program in the private-school system and the lack thereof in the public-school system. (E) is, of course, irrelevant to the question of reading skills. (C) tries to force the author to assume a greater burden than he has undertaken. He claims that the reading skills of public-school children could be improved by a computerized reading program. He is not concerned to argue the merits of having good reading skills. (A) and (B) are wrong for the same reason. The author's claim must be interpreted to mean "of children who are able to learn, all would benefit from a computerized reading program." When the author claims that "public-school children can be good readers," he is not implying that all children can learn to be good readers nor that all can learn to read equally well.

Questions 8–12

Arranging the Information

At first, this looks like it is going to be a map problem, but reading the question stems and the given information shows that there is really only one direction that is at issue: north–south. Furthermore, there is a numerical aspect in that the streets are laid out regularly with a regular distance between them. Thus, the real situation is similar to a ladder or musical scale and we have only to worry about one direction. Perhaps a good first step is to lay out a series of slots which symbolically will all be a quarter of a mile from each other, and which will alternate roads and streets.

```
                    ←SOUTH——————NORTH→
                    __ __  __ __  __ __ __  __   __ __
                    St Rd  St Rd  St Rd St  Rd   St Rd
Easy—1 mile
north of            __ __  __ __  __ Main __ __  __ Easy __
Main St.            St Rd  St Rd  St Rd St  Rd   St Rd

Main—¾ mile
south of            __ __  __ __  __ Main __ __ Abbey Easy __
Abbey Rd.           St Rd  St Rd  St Rd St  Rd   St Rd

Tobacco Rd—¾
mile south          __ Tob __ __  __ Main __ __ Abbey Easy __
of Main St.         St Rd  St Rd  St Rd St  Rd   St Rd

Mean St—½
mile south          __ Tob Mean __ __ Main __ __ Abbey Easy __
of Main St.         St Rd  St Rd  St Rd St  Rd   St Rd
```

Answering the Questions

8. **(A)** As the diagram shows, Easy Street is farthest.

9. **(D)** The diagram shows that all of the cited locations are as yet unnamed thoroughfares, but the reason that (D) is correct is that this location cannot be a road. This is why the diagram should be drawn to include all of the information at your disposal, which in this case includes the idea that roads and streets alternate.

10. **(C)** Abbey Road is five steps of the ladder from Mean Street, with each step being a quarter of a mile for a total distance of 1¼ miles.

11. **(D)** Although we have a north–south thoroughfare being named in the problem, it is only being used as a surrogate for distance and the problem is essentially no different than problem 10. Just count the steps and figure out the distance. It is six steps to Tobacco Road and three more back to Main Street. Nine steps equals 2¼ miles.

12. **(C)** Easy Street is the northernmost street and Tobacco Road is the southernmost. They are seven steps away, which equals 1¾ miles. If you don't want to do any work with fractions, just count up ¼, ½, ¾ . . . .

Questions 13–17

Arranging the Information

The major issue is who can and can't be on the team with particular other candidates.

    WEST CAMPUS   EAST CAMPUS
      (TWO FROM EACH CAMPUS)
          X   P
    Y←NOT WITH→L←NOT WITH→
    Y←NOT WITH→N

Answering the Questions

13. **(E)** The rejection of Y requires the selection of X and Z. The selection of Z forbids N. The selection of M bars L, leaving only M, N, X, and Z, choice (E).
    (C) and (D) fail for lack of two West campus members. (A) puts L and M together, which is wrong, and (B) puts Z and N together, which is forbidden.

14. **(E)** L's inclusion bars Y and M, Y's omission requires the inclusion of X and Z to have two West campus members, leaving only (E).
    (A) and (D) wrongly put L with M and Y, respectively. (B) has Z and N, which is not permitted, while (C) has only one West campus member.

15. **(B)** The selection of Y and Z excludes L and N, respectively, thus assuring the selection of P and M, choice (B).
    (A), (C), and (D) wrongly claim the selection of excluded members, and (E) omits the necessity of having M.

16. **(E)** The answer to problem 15 gives an example of M, P, and Z being on the same team, thus falsifying statements I and III. N, P, Y, and X is a possible team which shows the error of II, hence, (E).

17. **(B)** I is not true since we can select team Y, Z, P, and M. II is true since N's selection eliminates Z, requiring the selection of both X and Y to ensure that there are two West campus members. III is false since the rejection of L and N, while not requiring the selection of X, still permits it: M, P, X, and Z.

Questions 18–22

Arranging the Information

O will not go next to T or E. The condition of not forming a common three-letter word cannot be usefully listed out. A simple alertness to the words formed is sufficient. English words are formed only left to right, however.

Answering the Questions

18. **(C)** I is true because O is in the middle, it will be next to T, which is forbidden. II is a little more complicated. If M, O, and T are on one wall, then H, E, and R are the paintings on the other wall.

These will form the word *her* if H and R are the left and right paintings on the east wall.

III, however, is not required since the east wall could be REH, which is not a common English word.

19. **(B)** O cannot be the center painting since it would then be between R and T, placing it next to T, which is forbidden. Also, both ROT and TOR are words, though TOR is not so common.

(A) is not correct since MEH is possible. (C) is possible with:

T	R	O
E	M	H

(D) is possible with:

M	H	E
T	R	O

(E) is possible with:

M	H	E
T	R	O

20. **(D)** The diagram is this:

M	O	T
R	E	H

Since the word runs from left to right as you turn around in the middle of the room, (A), (B), and (C) are true, while (D) is false. (E) fails when (D) succeeds.

21. **(A)** If H, M, and R are on the one wall, this leaves only E, O, and T for the other wall, which is incorrect since O would have to be next to at least one forbidden partner.

(B) is possible if the wall is arranged E H T, so no word is formed. (C) is possible:

H	T	E
M	O	R

(D) is also possible:

T	M	E
R	O	H

E is possible too:

E	R	T
O	M	H

22. **(C)** After the trade Jon has O, O, T, H, E, and R. Note that the new O painting is the same color as the original, and thus also cannot go next to T or E.

(C) is impossible since to have the O's in the middle of both walls would guarantee that they would be next to the T and the E, which is not permitted. The diagram looks like this:

O	O	
		R/H
T	E	

However, the order on each side could be different.

The O's cannot be on the same side as the T or E. Answers (A) and (B) both turn on the same idea that either the R or the H will be on one side or the other.

(D) can be false, but is not necessarily false, and thus is not the answer sought.

23. **(E)** Now, it must be admitted that a liar can abuse just about any word in the English language, and so it is true that each of the five answer choices is *conceivably* correct. But it is important to keep in mind that you are looking for the BEST answer, which will be the one word which, more than all the others, is likely to be abused. As for (A), while there may be different ways of doing a random selection, we should be able to decide whether a sample was, in fact, selected fairly. Although the ad may be lying about the selection of participants in the study, we should be able to determine whether they are lying. In other words, though they may not have selected the sample randomly, they cannot escape by saying, "Oh, by *random* we meant anyone who liked the Goblin." The same is true of (C), "first." That is a fairly clear term. You add up the answers you got, and one will be at the top of the list. The same is true of (D)—a "response" is an answer. Now, (B) is open to manipulation. By asking our question correctly, that is, by finagling a bit with what we mean by handling, we can influence the answers we get. For example, compare: "Did you find the Goblin handled well?" "Did you find the Goblin had a nice steering wheel?" "Did you find the wheel was easy to turn?" We could keep it up until we found a question that worked out to give a set of "responses" from "randomly" selected drivers who would rank the Goblin "first." Now, if the one category itself is susceptible to manipulation, imagine how much easier it will be to manipulate a "composite" category. We have only to take those individual categories in which the Goblin scored well, construct from them a "composite" category, and announce the Goblin "first" in the overall category. There is also the question of how the composite was constructed, weighted, added, averaged, etc.

24. **(C)** The problem with this argument is that it contains no argument at all. Nothing is more frustrating than trying to discuss an issue with someone who will not even make an attempt to prove his case, whose only constructive argument is: "Well, that is my position. If I am wrong, you prove I am wrong." This is an illegitimate attempt to shift the burden of proof. The person who advances the argument naturally has the burden of giving some argument for it. (C) points out this problem. (A) is incorrect because the author uses no group classifications. (B) is incorrect because the author does not introduce any analogy. (D) is

a weak version of (C). It is true the author does not provide statistical evidence to prove his claim, but neither does he provide any kind of argument at all to prove his claim. So if (D) is a legitimate objection to the paragraph (and it is), then (C) must be an even stronger objection. So any argument for answer (D)'s being the correct choice ultimately supports (C) even more strongly. The statement contained in (E) may or may not be correct, but the information in the passage is not sufficient to allow us to isolate the theory upon which the speaker is operating. Therefore, we cannot conclude that it is or is not discredited.

25. **(A)** If II is true, then both independent clauses of II must be true. This is because a sentence which has the form "P and Q" (Eddie is tall and John is short) can be true only if both sub-parts are true. If either is false (Eddie is not tall or John is not short) or if both are false, then the entire sentence makes a false claim. If the second clause of II is true, then I must also be true, for I is actually equivalent to the second clause in II. That is, if "P and Q" is true, then Q must itself be true. On this basis, (B) and (C) can be seen to be incorrect. (D) is wrong, for we can actually define the interrelationship of I and II as a matter of logic: We do not have to have recourse to a probabilistic statement; i.e., it is *unlikely* (E) is incorrect since a statement of the form "P and Q" might be false and Q could still be true—if P is false "P and Q" is false even though Q is true.

SECTION VII

1. **(C)** The two words or phrases which give us something to work with are admiration and getting into the front pages. An instinct for publicity is not generally admired and thus one would look first for a word in the first blank that expresses some sort of diminution of the admiration felt for the Senator. (C) has such a word and is the only one to have it. The second blank is not that helpful in this case since all of the answer choices except (B), perhaps, have reasonable alternatives, although (C) and (E) are the best. Overall, the first blank guides us, and (C) is the best answer choice.

2. **(A)** The sentence contains two similar ideas— growth and expansion—and they are both moving rapidly. The blank is the link between them, the verb that relates the two. Therefore, it should be a verb that shows that they are similar, which (A), parallels, does very well. The other choices do not convey any similar idea and have no merit. (E) might work if the sentence were reversed.

3. **(D)** The structure of the sentence is telling you that both blanks are verbs which connect you with fairy tales and myths ("them"). Thus, the two words chosen will have to have some compatible relationship to each other. (A) fails since you will not esteem something if you reject it. Similarly, (C) and (E) have opposite ideas for the two blanks and thus fail. (B) and (C), then, are the best choices. In order to distinguish them, we rely on the tone of the sentence as expressed by the word might. This gives a somewhat tentative tone to the whole thing, and thus we would prefer the weaker of the two statements, which is given by (D). In (D) all that is sought is understanding, and if something is studied, it seems relatively reasonable to infer that understanding might follow. (B), on the other hand, implies that the mere reading of the fairy tales will lead to your coming to uphold them. Thus, (D) is the best answer.

4. **(A)** There is a contrast being drawn between the past status of diseases and the current situation. Since the current situation is that they are treated successfully, the former situation must have been that they were not treatable. Only choices (A) and (E) come close to this idea. (C) has a little merit since the treatment of the disease is not possible if it is mysterious, generally speaking. However, it is much more direct to speak of incurable. (B) and (D) have none of the correct idea and are eliminated. The distinction between (A) and (E) is that incorrigible, while meaning uncorrectable, is used to mean uncorrectable in a moral or ethical way, as beyond reform. Thus, (A) is the best answer.

5. **(A)** The sentence is negative about the consequences of the establishment of the colonies. Everything that we are told about the results is bad: rapid and careless, suffering. For the first blank, (D) is thus not a very good choice. (B) and (E) fail since cancellation and disintegration are not things that happen to natural resources in general. (C) is also poor in this regard. For the second blank, (C) and (E) are too strong. There is no indication that the human suffering was either planned or compelled. The words careless and rapid, though describing the depletion of the natural resources, indicate a situation in which (C) and (E) do not work for the second blank. (D) is also a little strong and not quite to the point. (A) does make the point that the suffering was appalling, which completes the idea of error and bad result the sentence requires. Thus, (A) is the best for both blanks and the best answer choice.

6. **(E)** The sentence has a contrast between business something and government practices. No matter what the relationship is between the two, they must be things that have enough in common to be contrasted. Procedures is precisely the same idea as practices, and affairs is possible. The other

three choices are not well suited to comparison nor contrast with practices. In the second blank, we need a word of comparison or connection, describing the way in which we are to put the two ideas together. Since the whole of the sentence has the form of "this even though that," we see that the second half of the sentence, which contains both of the blanks, will somehow be opposed to the first half of the sentence. Since the first half of the sentence equates business and public affairs, the second half will probably show how they are different, but note the qualifier "only slightly" preceding the second blank. Choices (A) through (D) all try to say that one is better than the other, but there is no information in the sentence to permit that. The issue is not better or worse, but similar or different. Only (E) addresses the issue of whether business and government are similar or different, and thus (E) is the best answer.

7. **(C)** Here the first blank is fairly difficult to approach until the second is understood. The first part is too wide open to be tied down right away. The second part of the sentence shows a sequence. At first, we do not know what the sequence will be, though the first part is the prayer that business conditions improve. (E) and (B) are words which do not describe something that would occur to dozens of firms daily. The firms might become confused or distressed, but the words should not be used in the way the sentence is currently constructed. Now we see that what is happening to the firms is either they are dying (demise or bankruptcy) or they are starting. These have to be compared with the statements that better conditions are needed. This means conditions now are not good, so it is not too likely that dozens of firms will be opening up. If they are closing because of presidential policies, this is inconsistent with presidential statements, and (E) is the best answer.

8. **(C)** A caboose is the last car on the train, and the idea of being the end of something is the most common way in which the term caboose is used. However, the original meaning of the word and the original purpose of the caboose was to be the home and sleeping place of the train's crew as the train travelled along. It is still used in this way, though it is less important than it once was. Thus, the original pair is one of a special house for the use of a special type of person or worker. A brakeman lives in a caboose when he is on the job and a wrangler lives in a bunkhouse when he is on the job. Furthermore, these structures are specifically for these types of persons. (A) and (B) fail to show the idea of anyone living in a particular place. (D) fails because the castle is for the king or noble and the footman lives there only for the convenience of the castleowner. (E) is the second-best answer since the bear is typically in a cave.

However, the original pair has a particular individual living in a house constructed particularly for that type of individual. This is much closer to (C) than to (E). Thus, (C) is the best answer.

9. **(E)** The original pair are synonymous physical characteristics, and there is some greater intensity in the first term of the pair. (B) is not of this mold since tawny refers to color, not shape or size. The association between tawny and other characteristics stems from the fact that tawny is the color of healthy tanning and thus is associated with the outdoor life. (C) is not a synonymous pair and is eliminated. (D) might have some merit since a chicken is sometimes used as a metaphor for scrawniness. A bull is not, however, a metaphor for leanness. (A) and (E) have real merit. Brawny means muscular and strong. Massive, when referring to bodies, usually means thick and wide. The nod goes to (E) since it is more likely that two words meaning thin will relate the same way as two words meaning thick than two words meaning strong. The reason is that the ideas of thick and thin are more closely related and more likely to work in the same way. Thus, (E) is the best answer.

10. **(B)** This is somewhat similar to the previous problem in that it has somewhat synonymous words in the original pair. (A) and (E) may be eliminated since they have no synonym relationship within the pairs. (C) likewise can be eliminated since a razor is not the same as a butter knife, when seen in terms of sharp and blunt. We are left with (B) and (D). In choosing between them we must consider how these words are used—that is, to what situations they apply. Stupid and moronic in (D) apply only to mental properties; acute and sharp in (B) can apply both to mental and physical properties. This difference is helpful when compared to the original pair. Obtuse can be both a physical and a mental description, meaning stupid or unintelligent. Blunt, however, has a mental reference that is quite different. A blunt person is not stupid, but merely says things very directly and without concern for tact and discretion. This is not the same as (D), but the physical ideas related by obtuse and blunt will work in just the same ways as the physical ideas related by acute and sharp. There is also an echo of a relationship between obtuse and acute in that they are both used in geometry, but that is not carried through by the other parts of the pairs and is irrelevant.

11. **(C)** In the original pair and all of the answer choices the first term is a structure of some sort and the second term is a material that may be used in its construction. (D) and (E) are the first to be eliminated on the grounds that an igloo is a house and these two are about machines or modes of transportation. An igloo has the connotation of

being a primitive house, which would eliminate (A). (B) and (C) can be distinguished on the grounds that a tepee is made out of skins and was the original method of making a tent in "primitive" cultures. A tent made out of canvas is not primitive. Thus, (C) is the best answer.

12. **(D)** Languor is the opposite of vigor. All of the answer choices have some oppositeness, but (E) and (B) have very little and can be eliminated. (D) is precisely the same relationship as the original since it contains precisely the same pair of meanings. Both are states of being.

13. **(C)** The relationship is between an animal and its classification or type. A clam is a type of mollusk. (A) and (B) are mixed with each other: A lobster is a crustacean and a whale is a cetacean, not the other way around. (E) is simply false since a bat is not a bird. (D) has some possibilities, but a lion has the characteristic of being a predator, but that is not the group to which it belongs. A wolf is a canine, along with dogs, foxes, and some other animals. Thus, (C) is the best answer.

14. **(B)** Feral means wild and untamed. Frenzied means wild and uncontrolled. It is more than merely an opposition; there is an implication of danger and wildness in the first word. (D) is fine for the first word, but staid is more a question of propriety than danger. (E) is not opposite. (C) has opposites, but they are not good and bad. (A) has the appeal of referring to animals, which the original pair may be used to do. However, the issue of temperament is not necessarily related to diet, which is the relationship in (A). Thus, (B) is the best available answer choice.

15. **(D)** The only issue here is to choose the correct plural form. Stratum is the singular and strata is the plural. Criterion is the singular and criteria is the plural. (A) is a bit tricky since the singular of mores, meaning social and ethical customs, is mos, which is almost never used. The singular of phyla is phylum, which is a major division of taxonomy. A phratry is a grouping of clans within a tribe. The plural is phratries. (C) is particularly tricky, but specie is coined money, while a species is a singular word. (E) has two unrelated words.

16. **(A)** Feckless means cowardly, and heedless means not taking notice of anything. Cowardly and careless have the same relationship. This sort of structure is rare in a GRE analogy problem, but it will sometimes appear to you that there is more of an echo or secondary relationship than anything else. Usually this indicates that you have not fully plumbed the depths of the problem. In this case, we have constructed the problem with only a secondary or echo relationship so that you would be forced to make a guess on that basis. This is proper, provided that the entire relationship holds

up for all four words and that no regular or horizontal relationship can be found.

17. **(C)** I is stated in the passage. The only possible objection is that it may sometimes be the case that unemployment can be reduced through the operation of forces other than government intervention. The word excessive copes with that.

II is the result of I and the idea that taxation to produce the revenue needed for public spending would defeat the purposes of the spending.

III, however, is not advanced by Keynes as the author explains him. This refers to the author's discussion of the ideas which preceded Keynes.

18. **(D)** (D) is essentially the same idea as 17, I and II, while (A) is similar to III in the same problem. (B), (C), and (E), like (A), refer to the ideas that preceded Keynes.

19. **(C)** There is not much in the passage which yields tone or attitude. This lack of strong attitude is itself the best reason for eliminating (A), (D), and (E), which are all strong attitudes that would need some strong evidence. (B), questioning, is not supported since there is no statement of doubt, nor is there any questioning. The reference to Keynes' work having some "fascinating obscurity" could mean many things, depending on the tone of voice with which it is delivered. Unfortunately, as written, there is no tone, so we must take it straight as an indication of the difficulty of the work, and of its fascination. Thus, this becomes more a support of (C) than of (B).

20. **(A)** (A), (B), and (E) make a good contrast. Their difference, the question of whether Keynes would favor forcing people to work or not, is resolvable from the passage which refers to willing workers. (C) fails because nowhere is it even hinted that Keynes is opposed to private spending. Actually, the passage indicates that insufficient private spending can be one of the causes of unemployment. (D) is simply false.

21. **(D)** (B), (C), and (E) are relatively easy to dispose of as being, respectively, unfounded, irrelevant, and too distant from the passage as well as too strong. (A) and (D) are more difficult. (A) is somewhat too strong since it is only in certain circumstances that unemployment is far enough advanced to require government intervention, but such remedy is the final remedy proposed by Keynes. The real key is to remember that this question has a certain focus in the passage—the very beginning—where the term at issue was used. In the first paragraph, the sentence immediately after the one including the term central thesis discussed the previous theory's assumption that the equilibrium point of an economy was full employment. Since the two theories are being contrasted—"until it appeared"—this is the point of difference.

22. **(B)** Only (B) has any basis in the passage. Keynes' theory is stated to be the successor to certain prior classical or non-socialist theories; hence, he is a non-socialist theoretician.

23. **(E)** The passage states that it is necessary to give interest in order to get people to let go of their cash—hence (E).

24. **(B)** If Redi wished to test the hypothesis that the flies' eggs were the source of the maggots, then he needed to provide access to the meat for the flies. It is true that the other side of the coin is that when flies do not have access to the meat, maggots do not develop, but both parts are needed.

25. **(D)** The passage states that Redi repeated his experiment many times to avoid the possibility that his results were just luck. This is what (D) says.
    (A) has the merit that this is what Redi did in this particular experiment; but the question is asking about experiments in general, so this is not general enough to be the correct answer. (B) is a reasonable idea about the construction of experiments, but it is not something that can be deduced from the passage since the experiments described used only one substance. (C) also has some merit, but the word guarantee is open to some question. Simply varying the conditions does not by itself guarantee good results, no matter how you define good results. So (C) fails. (E) also grabs at a portion of Redi's experiment and tries to generalize it, in this case too much. Redi did not watch everything that happened to the living creatures in his experiment, but only the development of maggots and the egg-laying behavior of the flies.

26. **(D)** Although Redi was a scientist, his primary impulse in the experiments described in the passage was the idea that living things could not come from dead things. Thus, he would not be predisposed to accept the theory in the question stem which holds precisely that. (C) is a possibility, but (D) is much more to the point since it relates to one of the basic things that we know about Redi's beliefs. (E), like (C), is something that he might say, but it is a comment that is not directed to the specific theory presented, while (D) is. Thus, (D) is the best answer choice.

27. **(C)** The passage holds that a working hypothesis gives direction to the scientist's work; thus, (C). (A) and (D) are hardly serious answers. (B) and (E) are partly true in that the hypothesis is a model, for the purposes of testing, and a scientist believes that testing and experiments are the road to truth, but these interpretations are somewhat removed from the passage. Also, (B) has the idea of the hypothesis being a model of what the universe actually is (true universe), which is clearly not the function of the working hypothesis.

28. **(A)** A schism is a split of a group into two or more parts. An amalgamation is taking several separate parts and making a unity of them. A paradox is a statement that is self-contradictory or absurd. Doctrine is ideology. Faith might be appealing since schisms often occur in religious groups; however, it is not only religious groups which have schisms.

29. **(D)** A dilettante is someone who dabbles in a field, while a professional has a much higher level of commitment. An adept is someone who is very good at an activity and this has some merit. However, the essence of a dilettante is not that he is poorly skilled, but rather that he has a lower level of commitment to the enterprise. Thus, professional is preferable to adept.

30. **(C)** To procrastinate is to delay doing something. To expedite is to make something go easier and more quickly. To eulogize is to heap praise on, especially on a dead person. To insinuate is to imply something, literally to slip something in between one's stated words. To mediate a dispute is to find the middle (media-) ground.

31. **(A)** To venerate is to revere or have great regard for. To abominate is to detest or hate. To instigate means to cause something to start or occur. To correlate means to have an orderly relation to something, such as two trends correlating with each other because they both go up and down together, or when one goes up, the other goes down.

32. **(B)** To embellish is to make prettier or add to the beauty of. To disfigure is to make ugly or to mar the beauty of. Because embellish has the idea of "adding" to the beauty of, trim, which means taking away or reducing, has some appeal. However, the root meaning of embellish is beauty and the addition aspect of the word is only in relation to the beauty; thus, trim is not a good opposite, and certainly not as good as disfigure. Demolish, meaning to tear down totally, and derogate, meaning to speak ill of, also have reducing ideas in them and might appeal for those reasons. They fail for the same reason as trim. Suffice means be sufficient.

33. **(C)** A disciple is a follower, particularly one who believes in the same system of beliefs and supports it. A renegade is someone who has broken away from some system and now opposes it. Devil and criminal have some appeal since the word disciple brings to mind the Christian disciples or other religious contexts, thus leading to an erroneous association between the word disciple and a moral connotation which does not exist. A craven is a coward, and an artisan is a craftsman of high skill, even an artist at his trade.

4. **(D)** A terminus is an end point or an ending; thus, beginning is an excellent opposite. Either end of a railway might be referred to as a terminus in the sense that it is the end of the line in that direction. It is also the beginning of the trip in the opposite direction. Roadway and marina might appeal to the sense of travelling that terminus vaguely implies. Spontaneity is natural, unpremeditated behavior. A replica is a duplicate.

35. **(B)** A stoic person represses emotions and passions, while a passionate person gives them freer rein. An anemic person has a low level of iron in the blood; pliable means flexible and able to be bent and shaped; gossamer means thin or delicate, like a spider's web.

36. **(B)** Bucolic means rural or pastoral. Urban is a good opposite. Bucolic is sometimes mistakenly thought to mean jolly and pleasant, but that is an attempt at a derived meaning based on certain stereotypes and is incorrect. Circumspect means discreet and cautious; abortive means brought to an early end without useful result; laconic means terse and using few words; punctilious means extremely conscientious.

37. **(A)** Lugubrious means sad and gloomy. Cheerful is a perfect opposite. There is no way to make an informed guess between these answer choices if you have no idea what lugubrious means, so do not waste time on it.

38. **(C)** Inexorable means unyielding or unalterable, not capable of being changed. Resistable is not a perfect opposite, but something that cannot be changed or altered and that does not yield in any way is also irresistible in a very direct way. Impregnable has much the same meaning as inexorable, except that it is passive as in an impregnable defense fating an inexorable advance. Erudite means learned, very educated or well read. Perspicacious means mentally sharp. Quixotic derives from Don Quixote, who tilted at windmills and took on generally hopeless causes.

ANSWER SHEET—PRACTICE EXAMINATION 5

Section I

1 Ⓐ Ⓑ Ⓒ Ⓓ Ⓔ   8 Ⓐ Ⓑ Ⓒ Ⓓ Ⓔ   15 Ⓐ Ⓑ Ⓒ Ⓓ Ⓔ   22 Ⓐ Ⓑ Ⓒ Ⓓ Ⓔ   29 Ⓐ Ⓑ Ⓒ Ⓓ Ⓔ   36 Ⓐ Ⓑ Ⓒ Ⓓ Ⓔ

2 Ⓐ Ⓑ Ⓒ Ⓓ Ⓔ   9 Ⓐ Ⓑ Ⓒ Ⓓ Ⓔ   16 Ⓐ Ⓑ Ⓒ Ⓓ Ⓔ   23 Ⓐ Ⓑ Ⓒ Ⓓ Ⓔ   30 Ⓐ Ⓑ Ⓒ Ⓓ Ⓔ   37 Ⓐ Ⓑ Ⓒ Ⓓ Ⓔ

3 Ⓐ Ⓑ Ⓒ Ⓓ Ⓔ   10 Ⓐ Ⓑ Ⓒ Ⓓ Ⓔ   17 Ⓐ Ⓑ Ⓒ Ⓓ Ⓔ   24 Ⓐ Ⓑ Ⓒ Ⓓ Ⓔ   31 Ⓐ Ⓑ Ⓒ Ⓓ Ⓔ   38 Ⓐ Ⓑ Ⓒ Ⓓ Ⓔ

4 Ⓐ Ⓑ Ⓒ Ⓓ Ⓔ   11 Ⓐ Ⓑ Ⓒ Ⓓ Ⓔ   18 Ⓐ Ⓑ Ⓒ Ⓓ Ⓔ   25 Ⓐ Ⓑ Ⓒ Ⓓ Ⓔ   32 Ⓐ Ⓑ Ⓒ Ⓓ Ⓔ

5 Ⓐ Ⓑ Ⓒ Ⓓ Ⓔ   12 Ⓐ Ⓑ Ⓒ Ⓓ Ⓔ   19 Ⓐ Ⓑ Ⓒ Ⓓ Ⓔ   26 Ⓐ Ⓑ Ⓒ Ⓓ Ⓔ   33 Ⓐ Ⓑ Ⓒ Ⓓ Ⓔ

6 Ⓐ Ⓑ Ⓒ Ⓓ Ⓔ   13 Ⓐ Ⓑ Ⓒ Ⓓ Ⓔ   20 Ⓐ Ⓑ Ⓒ Ⓓ Ⓔ   27 Ⓐ Ⓑ Ⓒ Ⓓ Ⓔ   34 Ⓐ Ⓑ Ⓒ Ⓓ Ⓔ

7 Ⓐ Ⓑ Ⓒ Ⓓ Ⓔ   14 Ⓐ Ⓑ Ⓒ Ⓓ Ⓔ   21 Ⓐ Ⓑ Ⓒ Ⓓ Ⓔ   28 Ⓐ Ⓑ Ⓒ Ⓓ Ⓔ   35 Ⓐ Ⓑ Ⓒ Ⓓ Ⓔ

Section II

1 Ⓐ Ⓑ Ⓒ Ⓓ Ⓔ   8 Ⓐ Ⓑ Ⓒ Ⓓ Ⓔ   15 Ⓐ Ⓑ Ⓒ Ⓓ Ⓔ   22 Ⓐ Ⓑ Ⓒ Ⓓ Ⓔ   29 Ⓐ Ⓑ Ⓒ Ⓓ Ⓔ   36 Ⓐ Ⓑ Ⓒ Ⓓ Ⓔ

2 Ⓐ Ⓑ Ⓒ Ⓓ Ⓔ   9 Ⓐ Ⓑ Ⓒ Ⓓ Ⓔ   16 Ⓐ Ⓑ Ⓒ Ⓓ Ⓔ   23 Ⓐ Ⓑ Ⓒ Ⓓ Ⓔ   30 Ⓐ Ⓑ Ⓒ Ⓓ Ⓔ   37 Ⓐ Ⓑ Ⓒ Ⓓ Ⓔ

3 Ⓐ Ⓑ Ⓒ Ⓓ Ⓔ   10 Ⓐ Ⓑ Ⓒ Ⓓ Ⓔ   17 Ⓐ Ⓑ Ⓒ Ⓓ Ⓔ   24 Ⓐ Ⓑ Ⓒ Ⓓ Ⓔ   31 Ⓐ Ⓑ Ⓒ Ⓓ Ⓔ   38 Ⓐ Ⓑ Ⓒ Ⓓ Ⓔ

4 Ⓐ Ⓑ Ⓒ Ⓓ Ⓔ   11 Ⓐ Ⓑ Ⓒ Ⓓ Ⓔ   18 Ⓐ Ⓑ Ⓒ Ⓓ Ⓔ   25 Ⓐ Ⓑ Ⓒ Ⓓ Ⓔ   32 Ⓐ Ⓑ Ⓒ Ⓓ Ⓔ

5 Ⓐ Ⓑ Ⓒ Ⓓ Ⓔ   12 Ⓐ Ⓑ Ⓒ Ⓓ Ⓔ   19 Ⓐ Ⓑ Ⓒ Ⓓ Ⓔ   26 Ⓐ Ⓑ Ⓒ Ⓓ Ⓔ   33 Ⓐ Ⓑ Ⓒ Ⓓ Ⓔ

6 Ⓐ Ⓑ Ⓒ Ⓓ Ⓔ   13 Ⓐ Ⓑ Ⓒ Ⓓ Ⓔ   20 Ⓐ Ⓑ Ⓒ Ⓓ Ⓔ   27 Ⓐ Ⓑ Ⓒ Ⓓ Ⓔ   34 Ⓐ Ⓑ Ⓒ Ⓓ Ⓔ

7 Ⓐ Ⓑ Ⓒ Ⓓ Ⓔ   14 Ⓐ Ⓑ Ⓒ Ⓓ Ⓔ   21 Ⓐ Ⓑ Ⓒ Ⓓ Ⓔ   28 Ⓐ Ⓑ Ⓒ Ⓓ Ⓔ   35 Ⓐ Ⓑ Ⓒ Ⓓ Ⓔ

Section III

1 Ⓐ Ⓑ Ⓒ Ⓓ Ⓔ   6 Ⓐ Ⓑ Ⓒ Ⓓ Ⓔ   11 Ⓐ Ⓑ Ⓒ Ⓓ Ⓔ   16 Ⓐ Ⓑ Ⓒ Ⓓ Ⓔ   21 Ⓐ Ⓑ Ⓒ Ⓓ Ⓔ   26 Ⓐ Ⓑ Ⓒ Ⓓ Ⓔ

2 Ⓐ Ⓑ Ⓒ Ⓓ Ⓔ   7 Ⓐ Ⓑ Ⓒ Ⓓ Ⓔ   12 Ⓐ Ⓑ Ⓒ Ⓓ Ⓔ   17 Ⓐ Ⓑ Ⓒ Ⓓ Ⓔ   22 Ⓐ Ⓑ Ⓒ Ⓓ Ⓔ   27 Ⓐ Ⓑ Ⓒ Ⓓ Ⓔ

3 Ⓐ Ⓑ Ⓒ Ⓓ Ⓔ   8 Ⓐ Ⓑ Ⓒ Ⓓ Ⓔ   13 Ⓐ Ⓑ Ⓒ Ⓓ Ⓔ   18 Ⓐ Ⓑ Ⓒ Ⓓ Ⓔ   23 Ⓐ Ⓑ Ⓒ Ⓓ Ⓔ   28 Ⓐ Ⓑ Ⓒ Ⓓ Ⓔ

4 Ⓐ Ⓑ Ⓒ Ⓓ Ⓔ   9 Ⓐ Ⓑ Ⓒ Ⓓ Ⓔ   14 Ⓐ Ⓑ Ⓒ Ⓓ Ⓔ   19 Ⓐ Ⓑ Ⓒ Ⓓ Ⓔ   24 Ⓐ Ⓑ Ⓒ Ⓓ Ⓔ   29 Ⓐ Ⓑ Ⓒ Ⓓ Ⓔ

5 Ⓐ Ⓑ Ⓒ Ⓓ Ⓔ   10 Ⓐ Ⓑ Ⓒ Ⓓ Ⓔ   15 Ⓐ Ⓑ Ⓒ Ⓓ Ⓔ   20 Ⓐ Ⓑ Ⓒ Ⓓ Ⓔ   25 Ⓐ Ⓑ Ⓒ Ⓓ Ⓔ   30 Ⓐ Ⓑ Ⓒ Ⓓ Ⓔ

Section IV

1 Ⓐ Ⓑ Ⓒ Ⓓ Ⓔ	6 Ⓐ Ⓑ Ⓒ Ⓓ Ⓔ	11 Ⓐ Ⓑ Ⓒ Ⓓ Ⓔ	16 Ⓐ Ⓑ Ⓒ Ⓓ Ⓔ	21 Ⓐ Ⓑ Ⓒ Ⓓ Ⓔ	26 Ⓐ Ⓑ Ⓒ Ⓓ Ⓔ
2 Ⓐ Ⓑ Ⓒ Ⓓ Ⓔ	7 Ⓐ Ⓑ Ⓒ Ⓓ Ⓔ	12 Ⓐ Ⓑ Ⓒ Ⓓ Ⓔ	17 Ⓐ Ⓑ Ⓒ Ⓓ Ⓔ	22 Ⓐ Ⓑ Ⓒ Ⓓ Ⓔ	27 Ⓐ Ⓑ Ⓒ Ⓓ Ⓔ
3 Ⓐ Ⓑ Ⓒ Ⓓ Ⓔ	8 Ⓐ Ⓑ Ⓒ Ⓓ Ⓔ	13 Ⓐ Ⓑ Ⓒ Ⓓ Ⓔ	18 Ⓐ Ⓑ Ⓒ Ⓓ Ⓔ	23 Ⓐ Ⓑ Ⓒ Ⓓ Ⓔ	28 Ⓐ Ⓑ Ⓒ Ⓓ Ⓔ
4 Ⓐ Ⓑ Ⓒ Ⓓ Ⓔ	9 Ⓐ Ⓑ Ⓒ Ⓓ Ⓔ	14 Ⓐ Ⓑ Ⓒ Ⓓ Ⓔ	19 Ⓐ Ⓑ Ⓒ Ⓓ Ⓔ	24 Ⓐ Ⓑ Ⓒ Ⓓ Ⓔ	29 Ⓐ Ⓑ Ⓒ Ⓓ Ⓔ
5 Ⓐ Ⓑ Ⓒ Ⓓ Ⓔ	10 Ⓐ Ⓑ Ⓒ Ⓓ Ⓔ	15 Ⓐ Ⓑ Ⓒ Ⓓ Ⓔ	20 Ⓐ Ⓑ Ⓒ Ⓓ Ⓔ	25 Ⓐ Ⓑ Ⓒ Ⓓ Ⓔ	30 Ⓐ Ⓑ Ⓒ Ⓓ Ⓔ

Section V

1 Ⓐ Ⓑ Ⓒ Ⓓ Ⓔ	6 Ⓐ Ⓑ Ⓒ Ⓓ Ⓔ	11 Ⓐ Ⓑ Ⓒ Ⓓ Ⓔ	16 Ⓐ Ⓑ Ⓒ Ⓓ Ⓔ	21 Ⓐ Ⓑ Ⓒ Ⓓ Ⓔ
2 Ⓐ Ⓑ Ⓒ Ⓓ Ⓔ	7 Ⓐ Ⓑ Ⓒ Ⓓ Ⓔ	12 Ⓐ Ⓑ Ⓒ Ⓓ Ⓔ	17 Ⓐ Ⓑ Ⓒ Ⓓ Ⓔ	22 Ⓐ Ⓑ Ⓒ Ⓓ Ⓔ
3 Ⓐ Ⓑ Ⓒ Ⓓ Ⓔ	8 Ⓐ Ⓑ Ⓒ Ⓓ Ⓔ	13 Ⓐ Ⓑ Ⓒ Ⓓ Ⓔ	18 Ⓐ Ⓑ Ⓒ Ⓓ Ⓔ	23 Ⓐ Ⓑ Ⓒ Ⓓ Ⓔ
4 Ⓐ Ⓑ Ⓒ Ⓓ Ⓔ	9 Ⓐ Ⓑ Ⓒ Ⓓ Ⓔ	14 Ⓐ Ⓑ Ⓒ Ⓓ Ⓔ	19 Ⓐ Ⓑ Ⓒ Ⓓ Ⓔ	24 Ⓐ Ⓑ Ⓒ Ⓓ Ⓔ
5 Ⓐ Ⓑ Ⓒ Ⓓ Ⓔ	10 Ⓐ Ⓑ Ⓒ Ⓓ Ⓔ	15 Ⓐ Ⓑ Ⓒ Ⓓ Ⓔ	20 Ⓐ Ⓑ Ⓒ Ⓓ Ⓔ	25 Ⓐ Ⓑ Ⓒ Ⓓ Ⓔ

Section VI

1 Ⓐ Ⓑ Ⓒ Ⓓ Ⓔ	6 Ⓐ Ⓑ Ⓒ Ⓓ Ⓔ	11 Ⓐ Ⓑ Ⓒ Ⓓ Ⓔ	16 Ⓐ Ⓑ Ⓒ Ⓓ Ⓔ	21 Ⓐ Ⓑ Ⓒ Ⓓ Ⓔ
2 Ⓐ Ⓑ Ⓒ Ⓓ Ⓔ	7 Ⓐ Ⓑ Ⓒ Ⓓ Ⓔ	12 Ⓐ Ⓑ Ⓒ Ⓓ Ⓔ	17 Ⓐ Ⓑ Ⓒ Ⓓ Ⓔ	22 Ⓐ Ⓑ Ⓒ Ⓓ Ⓔ
3 Ⓐ Ⓑ Ⓒ Ⓓ Ⓔ	8 Ⓐ Ⓑ Ⓒ Ⓓ Ⓔ	13 Ⓐ Ⓑ Ⓒ Ⓓ Ⓔ	18 Ⓐ Ⓑ Ⓒ Ⓓ Ⓔ	23 Ⓐ Ⓑ Ⓒ Ⓓ Ⓔ
4 Ⓐ Ⓑ Ⓒ Ⓓ Ⓔ	9 Ⓐ Ⓑ Ⓒ Ⓓ Ⓔ	14 Ⓐ Ⓑ Ⓒ Ⓓ Ⓔ	19 Ⓐ Ⓑ Ⓒ Ⓓ Ⓔ	24 Ⓐ Ⓑ Ⓒ Ⓓ Ⓔ
5 Ⓐ Ⓑ Ⓒ Ⓓ Ⓔ	10 Ⓐ Ⓑ Ⓒ Ⓓ Ⓔ	15 Ⓐ Ⓑ Ⓒ Ⓓ Ⓔ	20 Ⓐ Ⓑ Ⓒ Ⓓ Ⓔ	25 Ⓐ Ⓑ Ⓒ Ⓓ Ⓔ

Section VII

1 Ⓐ Ⓑ Ⓒ Ⓓ Ⓔ	8 Ⓐ Ⓑ Ⓒ Ⓓ Ⓔ	15 Ⓐ Ⓑ Ⓒ Ⓓ Ⓔ	22 Ⓐ Ⓑ Ⓒ Ⓓ Ⓔ	29 Ⓐ Ⓑ Ⓒ Ⓓ Ⓔ	36 Ⓐ Ⓑ Ⓒ Ⓓ Ⓔ
2 Ⓐ Ⓑ Ⓒ Ⓓ Ⓔ	9 Ⓐ Ⓑ Ⓒ Ⓓ Ⓔ	16 Ⓐ Ⓑ Ⓒ Ⓓ Ⓔ	23 Ⓐ Ⓑ Ⓒ Ⓓ Ⓔ	30 Ⓐ Ⓑ Ⓒ Ⓓ Ⓔ	37 Ⓐ Ⓑ Ⓒ Ⓓ Ⓔ
3 Ⓐ Ⓑ Ⓒ Ⓓ Ⓔ	10 Ⓐ Ⓑ Ⓒ Ⓓ Ⓔ	17 Ⓐ Ⓑ Ⓒ Ⓓ Ⓔ	24 Ⓐ Ⓑ Ⓒ Ⓓ Ⓔ	31 Ⓐ Ⓑ Ⓒ Ⓓ Ⓔ	38 Ⓐ Ⓑ Ⓒ Ⓓ Ⓔ
4 Ⓐ Ⓑ Ⓒ Ⓓ Ⓔ	11 Ⓐ Ⓑ Ⓒ Ⓓ Ⓔ	18 Ⓐ Ⓑ Ⓒ Ⓓ Ⓔ	25 Ⓐ Ⓑ Ⓒ Ⓓ Ⓔ	32 Ⓐ Ⓑ Ⓒ Ⓓ Ⓔ	
5 Ⓐ Ⓑ Ⓒ Ⓓ Ⓔ	12 Ⓐ Ⓑ Ⓒ Ⓓ Ⓔ	19 Ⓐ Ⓑ Ⓒ Ⓓ Ⓔ	26 Ⓐ Ⓑ Ⓒ Ⓓ Ⓔ	33 Ⓐ Ⓑ Ⓒ Ⓓ Ⓔ	
6 Ⓐ Ⓑ Ⓒ Ⓓ Ⓔ	13 Ⓐ Ⓑ Ⓒ Ⓓ Ⓔ	20 Ⓐ Ⓑ Ⓒ Ⓓ Ⓔ	27 Ⓐ Ⓑ Ⓒ Ⓓ Ⓔ	34 Ⓐ Ⓑ Ⓒ Ⓓ Ⓔ	
7 Ⓐ Ⓑ Ⓒ Ⓓ Ⓔ	14 Ⓐ Ⓑ Ⓒ Ⓓ Ⓔ	21 Ⓐ Ⓑ Ⓒ Ⓓ Ⓔ	28 Ⓐ Ⓑ Ⓒ Ⓓ Ⓔ	35 Ⓐ Ⓑ Ⓒ Ⓓ Ⓔ	

PRACTICE EXAMINATION 5

SECTION I

30 minutes
38 questions

Directions: Each of the questions below contains one or more blank spaces, each blank indicating an omitted word. Each sentence is followed by five (5) lettered words or sets of words. Read and determine the general sense of each sentence. Then choose the word or set of words which, when inserted in the sentence, best fits the meaning of the sentence.

1. Politics, because of its overemphasis on expediency, often places candidates in the _____ position of supporting candidates they attacked only months before.
   (A) anomalous
   (B) piquant
   (C) succulent
   (D) strategic
   (E) embarrassing

2. Often criticism may be more effectively made by _____ than by direct censure.
   (A) writing
   (B) malignity
   (C) innuendo
   (D) illusion
   (E) collusion

3. In the face of an uncooperative Congress, the Chief Executive may find himself _____ to acomplish the political program to which he is committed.
   (A) impotent
   (B) permitted
   (C) neutral
   (D) contingent
   (E) equipped

4. Because of his _____ sense of his own importance, Larry often tried to _____ our activities.
   (A) exaggerated—monopolize
   (B) inflated—autonomize
   (C) insecure—violate
   (D) modest—dominate
   (E) egotistic—diffuse

5. After such _____ meal, we were all quick to _____ Arlene for her delicious cooking.
   (A) a fearful—congratulate
   (B) an enormous—console
   (C) a delightful—avoid
   (D) a heavy—thank
   (E) a wonderful—applaud

6. The use of color to express feeling is so _____ in Van Gogh's paintings that the canvas seems to fairly _____ the museum-goer.
   (A) ingenious—fall
   (B) emphatic—insult
   (C) subtle—echo in
   (D) sensitive—seduce
   (E) successful—cry out to

7. The monopoly capitalists of the early 1900's saw both the factories and the workers as _____ without rights or feelings, whose only useful purpose was to _____ profits.
   (A) animals—assist
   (B) machinery—increase
   (C) beings—garner
   (D) resources—guarantee
   (E) objects—allow

Directions: In each of the following questions, you are given a related pair of words or phrases in capital letters. Each capitalized pair is followed by five (5) lettered pairs of words or phrases. Choose the pair which best expresses a relationship similar to that expressed by the original pair.

8. MOUTH : ORIFICE ::
   (A) eye : sight
   (B) nose : odor
   (C) ear : projection
   (D) touch : felt
   (E) taste : tongue

9. WORKER : BONUS ::
   (A) capitalist : dividends
   (B) banker : interest
   (C) sports : winning
   (D) horse : spur
   (E) actor : applause

10. RIGID : FLEXIBLE ::
    (A) hard : brittle
    (B) stubborn : yielding
    (C) steel : rubbery
    (D) hostile : honest
    (E) muscle : tone

11. EATING : GOBBLE ::
    (A) speaking : jabber
    (B) drinking : guzzle
    (C) running : sprint
    (D) seeing : believing
    (E) shoving : pushing

12. SIN : FORGIVE ::
    (A) error : mistake
    (B) reign : authority
    (C) debt : release
    (D) wrong : code
    (E) accident : intentional

13. SENSATION : ANESTHETIC ::
    (A) breathe : lung
    (B) reaction : drug
    (C) sound : muffler
    (D) poison : detoxicant
    (E) disease : vaccine

14. GUN : HOLSTER ::
    (A) foot : shoe
    (B) ink : pen
    (C) books : shelf
    (D) sword : scabbard
    (E) shot : cannon

15. MIST : RAIN ::
    (A) fog : cloud
    (B) shadow : sun
    (C) snow : hail
    (D) breeze : gale
    (E) foam : sea

16. PHARMACIST : DRUGS ::
    (A) psychiatrist : ideas
    (B) mentor : drills
    (C) mechanic : troubles
    (D) chef : foods
    (E) nurse : diseases

Directions: Below each of the following passages, you will find questions or incomplete statements about the passage. Each statement or question is followed by five lettered words or expressions. Select the word or expression that most satisfactorily completes each statement or answers each question in accordance with the meaning of the passage. After you choose the best answer, blacken the corresponding space on the answer sheet.

Shams and delusions are esteemed for soundest truths, while reality is fabulous. If men would steadily observe realities only, and not allow themselves to be deluded, life, to compare it with such things as we know, would be like a fairy tale and the Arabian Nights' entertainments. If we respect only what is inevitable and has a right to be, music and poetry would resound along the streets. When we are unhurried and wise, we perceive that only great and worthy things have any permanent and absolute existence—that petty fears and petty pleasures are but the shadow of the reality. This is always exhilarating and sublime. By closing the eyes and slumbering, and consenting to be deceived by shows, men establish and confirm their daily life of routine and habit everywhere, which still is built on purely illusory foundations. Children, who play life, discern its true law and relations more clearly than men, who fail to live it worthily, but who think that they are wiser by experience; that is, by failure.

I have read in a Hindu book that there was a

king's son who, being expelled in infancy from his native city, was brought up by a forester, and, growing up to maturity in that state, imagined himself to belong to the barbarous race with which he lived. One of his father's ministers, having discovered him, revealed to him what he was, and the misconception of his character was removed, and he knew himself to be a prince. "So soul," continues the Hindu philosopher, "from the circumstances in which it is placed, mistakes its own character, until the truth is revealed to it by some holy teacher, and then it knows itself to be *Brahme*."

We think that that *is* which *appears* to be. If a man should give us an account of the realities he beheld, we should not recognize the place in his description. Look at a meeting-house, or a court-house, or a jail, or a shop, or a dwelling-house, and say what that thing really is before a true gaze, and they would all go to pieces in your account of them. Men esteem truth remote, in the outskirts of the system, behind the farthest star, before Adam and after the last man. In eternity there is indeed something true and sublime. But all these times and places and occasions are now and here. God himself culminates in the present moment, and will never be more divine in the lapse of all ages. And we are enabled to apprehend at all what is sublime and noble only by the perpetual instilling and drenching of the reality that surrounds us. The universe constantly and obediently answers to our conceptions; whether we travel fast or slow, the track is laid for us. Let us spend our lives in conceiving, then. The poet or the artist never yet had so fair and noble a design but some of his posterity at least could accomplish it.

17. The writer's attitude toward the arts is one of
    (A) indifference
    (B) suspicion
    (C) admiration
    (D) repulsion
    (E) reluctant respect

18. The author believes that children are often more acute than adults in their appreciation of life's relations because
    (A) children know more than adults
    (B) children can use their experience better

    (C) children's eyes are unclouded by failure
    (D) experience is the best teacher
    (E) the child is father to the man

19. The passage implies that human beings
    (A) cannot distinguish the true from the untrue
    (B) are immoral if they are lazy
    (C) should be bold and fearless
    (D) believe in fairy tales
    (E) have progressed culturally throughout history

20. The word fabulous in the second line means
    (A) wonderful
    (B) delicious
    (C) birdlike
    (D) incomprehensible
    (E) illusion

21. The author is primarily concerned with urging the reader to
    (A) meditate on the meaninglessness of the present
    (B) look to the future for enlightenment
    (C) appraise the present for its true value
    (D) honor the wisdom of past ages
    (E) spend more time in leisure activities

22. The passage is primarily concerned with problems of
    (A) history and economics
    (B) society and population
    (C) biology and physics
    (D) theology and philosophy
    (E) music and art

23. Which of the following best describes the author's idea of the relationship between man and the universe?
    (A) Each person's mind can control the galaxies.
    (B) What you see is what you get.
    (C) Our lives are predetermined.
    (D) We may choose to live quickly or slowly.
    (E) Poets cannot conceive of their posterity.

A glance at five leading causes of death in 1900, 1910, and 1945, years representing in some measure the early and late practice of physicians of that time, shows a significant trend. In 1900 these causes were (1) tuberculosis, (2) pneumonia, (3) enteritis, typhoid fever, and other acute intestinal diseases, (4) heart diseases, and (5) cerebral hemorrhage and thrombosis. Ten years later the only change was that heart disease had moved from fourth to fifth place, tuberculosis now being second, and pneumonia third.

In 1945, however, the list had changed profoundly. Heart diseases were far out in front; cancer, which had come up from eighth place, was second; and cerebral hemorrhage and thrombosis, third. Fatal accidents, which had been well down the list, were now fourth, and nephritis was fifth. All of these are, of course, composites rather than single diseases, and it is significant that, except for accidents, they are characteristic of the advanced rather than the early or middle years of life.

24. On the basis of the paragraph, which of the following statements is most tenable?
   (A) A cure for cancer will be found within this decade.
   (B) Many of the medical problems of today are problems of the gerontologist (specialist in medical problems of old age).
   (C) Older persons are more accident-prone than are younger persons.
   (D) Tuberculosis has been all but eliminated.
   (E) Heart disease will be conquered within this decade.

25. Which one of the following trends is *least* indicated in the paragraph?
   (A) As one grows older, one is more subject to debilitating disease.
   (B) Pneumonia has become less common.
   (C) Relative to mortality rates for acute intestinal diseases, the mortality rate for cancer has increased.
   (D) The incidence of heart disease has increased.
   (E) Cancer has become more prevalent.

26. Which one of the following statements is most nearly correct?
   (A) Such mortality trends are caused by decreased infant mortality.

   (B) The changes in the data reported are a function of improved diagnosis and reporting.
   (C) The mortality data are based on the records of physicians who practiced continuously from 1900 to 1945.
   (D) There appears to be a greater change in the mortality patterns from 1910 to 1945 than in the decade ending in 1910.
   (E) none of the above

27. It can be inferred from reading this passage that
   (A) longevity increased between 1900 and 1910
   (B) longevity increased steadily between 1910 and 1945
   (C) longevity increased significantly between 1900 and 1945
   (D) longevity was not a factor in these findings
   (E) the causes of death listed did not effect any increase in longevity

Directions: Each of the following questions consists of a word printed in capital letters, followed by five (5) lettered words or phrases. Select the word or phrase which is most nearly *opposite* to the capitalized word in meaning.

28. RESTITUTION:
   (A) inflation
   (B) cataclysm
   (C) deprivation
   (D) constitution
   (E) anonymity

29. PARSIMONY:
   (A) closely held
   (B) free spending
   (C) acting apishly
   (D) poorly expressed
   (E) modish frugality

30. PERSPICUITY:
   (A) homelike ambiance
   (B) precise meaning
   (C) vague memory
   (D) partial fulfillment
   (E) mental dullness

31. PREPOSTEROUS:
    (A) complaisant
    (B) conceited
    (C) apologetic
    (D) credible
    (E) sincere

32. SANCTIMONIOUS:
    (A) proud
    (B) stubborn
    (C) wealthy
    (D) devout
    (E) impervious

33. EXTIRPATE:
    (A) preserve
    (B) inseminate
    (C) ingratiate
    (D) enter
    (E) daub

34. CAPRICIOUS:
    (A) redoubtable
    (B) constant
    (C) phlegmatic
    (D) solitary
    (E) ignominious

35. CASUISTRY:
    (A) resultant
    (B) interior
    (C) sediment
    (D) verity
    (E) beauty

36. CONTUMELY:
    (A) willingness
    (B) sporadically
    (C) praise
    (D) augmented
    (E) tractability

37. SEDULOUS:
    (A) vociferous
    (B) derelict
    (C) concomitant
    (D) itinerant
    (E) onerous

38. IMPERTURBABLE:
    (A) militant
    (B) cynical
    (C) conical
    (D) agitated
    (E) flattering

STOP

END OF SECTION. IF YOU HAVE ANY TIME LEFT, GO
OVER YOUR WORK IN THIS SECTION ONLY. DO NOT
WORK IN ANY OTHER SECTION OF THE TEST.

SECTION II

30 minutes
38 questions

Directions: Each of the questions below contains one or more blank spaces, each blank indicating an omitted word. Each sentence is followed by five (5) lettered words or sets of words. Read and determine the general sense of each sentence. Then choose the word or set of words which, when inserted in the sentence, best fits the meaning of the sentence.

1. With _____ a thought for his own safety, Gene _____ dashed back across the courtyard.
    (A) even—quickly
    (B) scarcely—courageously
    (C) barely—cautiously

(D) seldom—swiftly
(E) hardly—randomly

2. The _____ of the *Titanic* could have been avoided if more safety _____ had been taken.
    (A) tragedy—precautions
    (B) embargo—preservers
    (C) disaster—reservations
    (D) crew—measures
    (E) fiasco—inspectors

3. We are _____ going to have to face the reality that the resources of Earth are _____.
    (A) finally—worthless
    (B) gradually—limitless
    (C) eventually—finite
    (D) quickly—unavailable
    (E) seldom—vanished

4. Though many thought him a tedious old man, he had a _____ spirit that delighted his friends.
    (A) perverse
    (B) juvenile
    (C) meek
    (D) leaden
    (E) youthful

5. _____, the factories had not closed, and those who needed work most were given a chance to survive during the economic disaster.
    (A) Unintentionally
    (B) Mercifully
    (C) Blithely
    (D) Importunately
    (E) Tragically

6. There was a _____ all about the estate, and the _____ concerned the guards.
    (A) pall—shroud
    (B) focus—scrutiny
    (C) hush—quiet
    (D) coolness—temper
    (E) talent—genius

7. Some works of literature hold one's interest to the very last page, but others serve only as a _____, to be kept handily at a bedside table.
    (A) resource
    (B) reference
    (C) soporific
    (D) pleasure
    (E) reminder

Directions: In each of the following questions, you are given a related pair of words or phrases in capital letters. Each capitalized pair is followed by five (5) lettered pairs of words or phrases. Choose the pair which best expresses a relationship similar to that expressed by the original pair.

8. KARATE : FOOT ::
    (A) judo : chop
    (B) bridge : hand
    (C) fencing : foil
    (D) boxing : ring
    (E) baseball : bat

9. INCISOR : MOLAR ::
    (A) canine : bicuspid
    (B) scissor : file
    (C) upper : lower
    (D) sharp : foolish
    (E) knife : hammer

10. GOURMAND : GOURMET ::
    (A) wisdom : epicureanism
    (B) spaghetti : chopped liver
    (C) atrophy : empathy
    (D) good : plenty
    (E) indiscriminate : selective

11. TRESS : HAIR ::
    (A) pat : butter
    (B) slice : lox
    (C) bevy : beauties
    (D) land : cotton
    (E) skein : wool

12. LIBEL : SLANDER ::
    (A) telephone : telegraph
    (B) copier : plagiarist
    (C) intentional : unintentional
    (D) written : oral
    (E) printed : handwritten

13. WATER : COLANDER ::
  (A) dust : broom
  (B) chaff : sifter
  (C) sand : dune
  (D) fluid : pipette
  (E) shale : flat

14. DECIBEL : SOUND ::
  (A) calorie : weight
  (B) volt : electricity
  (C) temperature : weather
  (D) color : light
  (E) area : distance

15. ASTUTE : STUPID ::
  (A) scholar : idiotic
  (B) agile : clumsy
  (C) lonely : clown
  (D) dunce : ignorant
  (E) intelligent : smart

16. QUEUE : PEOPLE ::
  (A) gaggle : geese
  (B) pile : sand
  (C) stack : books
  (D) string : pearls
  (E) file : letters

Directions: Below each of the following passages, you will find questions or incomplete statements about the passage. Each statement or question is followed by lettered words or expressions. Select the word or expression that most satisfactorily completes each statement or answers each question in accordance with the meaning of the passage. After you have chosen the best answer, blacken the corresponding space on the answer sheet.

When an animal is presented with food he will salivate. If a bell is repeatedly presented shortly before the food is administered, the animal will begin to salivate soon after the sound of the bell, even if the food is not offered. With repeated trials of the bell followed by the food (conditioning trials), the latency of the response (that is, the time interval between the advent of the bell and the beginning of salivation) decreases. This process is called conditioning, and salivation to the sound of the bell is termed the conditioned response. The conditioned response may be unlearned or extinguished if the bell is presented a number of times without being followed by food (extinction trials).

Under such conditions, the latency of the conditioned response gradually increases until it does not take place at all. One theory holds that after each conditioning trial a finite amount of excitation is left which facilitates the occurrence of the conditioned response, and also that a finite amount of inhibition is left which inhibits the occurrence of the conditioned response.

17. If the conditioned response, salivation, is extinguished
  (A) its latency decreases
  (B) the food was presented without the bell

  (C) the amount of inhibition is greater than the amount of excitation
  (D) the animal is no longer hungry
  (E) none of these

18. According to the theory advanced at the end of the passage, which of the following is NOT possible?
  (A) Continued training will have no effect whatever.
  (B) A response can get so well established that it will never fail.
  (C) Responses other than salivation will not necessarily differ in the amount of training required to achieve a response.
  (D) No matter how many times an extinction trial is run, retraining is still possible.
  (E) The measurement of residual excitation and inhibition can be measured in all cases, though some measurements might be indirect.

19. As used in the passage, the term "latency" most nearly means
  (A) unfulfilled potential
  (B) delayed excitation
  (C) tendency for an action to not occur
  (D) improvements in response time
  (E) experimental deviations from the norm

Suppose you go into a fruiterer's shop, wanting an apple—you take up one, and on biting it you find it is sour; you look at it, and see that it is hard and green. You take up another one, and that, too, is hard, green, and sour. The shopman offers you a third; but, before biting it, you examine it, and find that it is hard and green, and you immediately say that you will not have it, as it must be sour, like those that you have already tried.

Nothing can be more simple than that, you think; but if you will take the trouble to analyse and trace out into its logical elements what has been done by the mind, you will be greatly surprised. In the first place you have performed the operation of induction. You find that, in two experiences, hardness and greenness in apples went together with sourness. It was so in the first case, and it was confirmed by the second. True, it is a very small basis, but still it is enough from which to make an induction; you generalize the facts, and you expect to find sourness in apples where you get hardness and greenness. You found upon that a general law, that all hard and green apples are sour; and that, so far as it goes, is a perfect induction. Well, having got your natural law in this way, when you are offered another apple which you find is hard and green, you say, "All hard and green apples are sour; this apple is hard and green; therefore, this apple is sour." That train of reasoning is what logicians call a syllogism, and has all its various parts and terms—its major premises, its minor premises, and its conclusion. And, by the help of further reasoning, which, if drawn out, would have to be exhibited in two or three other syllogisms, you arrive at your final determination. "I will not have that apple." So that, you see, you have, in the first place, established a law by induction, and upon that you have founded a deduction, and reasoned out the special particular case.

Well now, suppose, having got your conclusion of the law, that at some times afterwards, you are discussing the qualities of apple with a friend; you will say to him, "It is a very curious thing, but I find that all hard and green apples are sour!" Your friend says to you, "But how do you know that?" You at once reply, "Oh, because I have tried them over and over again, and have always found them to be so." Well, if we were talking science instead of common sense, we should call that an experimental verification. And, if still opposed, you go further, and say, "I have heard from the people in Somersetshire and Devonshire, where a large number of apples are grown, and in London, where many apples are sold and eaten, that they have observed the same thing. It is also found to be the case in Normandy, and in North America. In short, I find it to be the universal experience of mankind wherever attention has been directed to the subject." Whereupon, your friend, unless he is a very unreasonable man, agrees with you, and is convinced that you are quite right in the conclusion you have drawn. He believes, although perhaps he does not know he believes it, that the more extensive verifications have been made, and results of the same kind arrived at—that the more varied the conditions under which the same results are attained, the more certain is the ultimate conclusion, and he disputes the question no further. He sees that the experiment has been tried under all sorts of conditions, as to time, place, and people, with the same result; and he says with you, therefore, that the law you have laid down must be a good one, and he must believe it.

20. The writer is probably
   (A) French
   (B) English
   (C) American
   (D) Italian
   (E) none of the above

21. "All giraffes are beautiful and graceful.
   Twiga is a giraffe.
   Twiga is beautiful and graceful."

   According to the passage, the above reasoning is a(n)
   (A) empirical verification
   (B) induction from cases
   (C) syllogism
   (D) experimental conclusion
   (E) developmental sequence

22. Apples are used
   (A) in order to convince the reader that fruit has no intellect
   (B) to illustrate the subject of the passage
   (C) to give color to the story
   (D) to show how foolish logic is
   (E) to compare various types of persons

23. The author has the approach of a(n)
   (A) scientist
   (B) artist
   (C) novelist

(D) economist
(E) businessman

24. The term "natural law" as it appears in the text refers to
(A) common sense
(B) the "honor system"
(C) the result of an induction
(D) the order of nature
(E) a scientific discovery

25. Which of the folloing would be the best title for the passage?
(A) Discovering the Natural Laws of Apples
(B) The Uses of Induction
(C) Syllogistic Reasoning in Common Circumstances
(D) Experimental Verification As an Adjunct to Reasoning
(E) The Logic of Everyday Reasoning

26. If you find a hard and green apple that is not sour, you should
(A) try more apples to see if the natural law has changed
(B) eat the rest of the apple at once
(C) reject the law stating that hard and green apples are usually sour
(D) conduct further investigations and make adjustments to the law of apples as necessary
(E) all of the above

27. According to the above passage, the significance of "extensive verification" of a general law is that

I. general laws are difficult to disprove
II. the more extensively a law is tested, the truer it is
III. if a law holds up in a variety of situations, then it is more than likely based on some general characteristic of the world

(A) I only
(B) II only
(C) III only
(D) II and III only
(E) I, II, and III

Directions: Each of the following questions consists of a word printed in captial letters, followed by five (5) lettered words or phrases. Select the word or phrase which is most nearly *opposite* to the capitalized word in meaning.

28. PROFUSION:
(A) travesty
(B) validity
(C) scarcity
(D) retraction
(E) antidote

29. TEMPERATE:
(A) aged
(B) unlimited
(C) truncated
(D) productive
(E) inebriated

30. MITIGATION:
(A) aggravation
(B) verdancy
(C) obscenity
(D) restriction
(E) imposition

31. INIQUITY:
(A) fairness
(B) rectitude
(C) peace
(D) apostasy
(E) calmness

32. PROTUBERANCE:
(A) cadence
(B) habitation
(C) indentation
(D) attachment
(E) recession

33. EFFULGENCE:
(A) murky
(B) harshness
(C) mercenary
(D) quiet
(E) mundane

34. AMELIORATE:
(A) increase
(B) worsen
(C) clasp
(D) dissemble
(E) curl

35. BENIGN:
    (A) sick
    (B) poor
    (C) damaged
    (D) evil
    (E) morose

36. SALUTARY:
    (A) noxious
    (B) objectionable
    (C) moderate
    (D) farewell
    (E) antiseptic

37. ALIENATE:
    (A) go native
    (B) say clearly
    (C) make friends
    (D) give freely
    (E) promise solemnly

38. DROLLERY:
    (A) firm warning
    (B) serious statement
    (C) incredible threat
    (D) witty aside
    (E) frank admission

STOP

END OF SECTION. IF YOU HAVE ANY TIME LEFT, GO
OVER YOUR WORK IN THIS SECTION ONLY. DO NOT
WORK IN ANY OTHER SECTION OF THE TEST.

SECTION III

30 minutes
30 questions

Directions: For each of the following questions two quantities are given, one in Column A and one in Column B. Compare the two quantities and mark your answer sheet with the correct lettered conclusion. These are your options:

    A: If the quantity in Column A is the greater;
    B: if the quantity in Column B is the greater;
    C: if the two quantities are equal;
    D: if the relationship cannot be determined from the information given.

Common Information: In any question, information applying to both columns is centered between the columns and above the quantities in columns A and B. The common information applies to both columns. Any symbol that appears in both columns represents the same idea or quantity in both columns.

Numbers: All numbers used are real numbers.

Figures: Assume that the position of points, angles, regions and so forth are in the order shown. Figures are assumed to lie in a plane unless otherwise indicated. Figures accompanying questions are intended to provide information you can use in answering the questions. However, unless a note states that a figure is drawn to scale, you should solve the problems by using your knowledge of mathematics and *not* by estimating sizes by sight and measurement.

Lines: Assume that lines shown as straight are indeed straight.

COLUMN A	COLUMN B

1.

Value of 4 coins	Value of 5 coins

2.

$$x + 7 = 8$$
$$x + y = 6$$

x	y

3.

$\sqrt{9}$	3

4.

Jack is taller than Kate.
Kate is taller than Linda.
Linda is taller than Mike.

$\dfrac{\text{Jack's height}}{\text{Mike's height}}$	4

5.

$$n > 1$$

$n + n + 1 + n + 2 + n + 3$	$n(n + 1)(n + 2)(n + 3)$

6.

The area of a circle with a diameter of 2 yards	The area of a circle with a radius of 3 feet

7.

The negative of -4	-4

8.

The weight of a pound of feathers	The weight of a pound of lead

9.

x is the greatest integer less than -10

x^2	100

10.

$\left(\frac{34}{68}\right)^2$	$\frac{1}{2}$

11.

$$x = \left(\tfrac{1}{2}\right)\left(\tfrac{2}{3}\right)\left(\tfrac{3}{4}\right)\left(\tfrac{4}{5}\right)$$

x	$\frac{1}{5}$

12.

PQRS is a rectangle

Perimeter of shaded area	Perimeter of PQRS

13.

$-2(-x - 2)$	$-4 + 2x$

14.

$$x > 1$$
$$y > 1$$

xy	x + y

COLUMN A   COLUMN B

15.

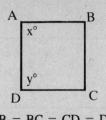

AB = BC = CD = DA

x   y

Directions: For each of the following questions, select the best of the answer choices and blacken the corresponding space on your answer sheet.
Numbers: All numbers used are real numbers.
Figures: The diagrams and figures that accompany these questions are for the purpose of providing information useful in answering the questions. Unless it is stated that a specific figure is not drawn to scale, the diagrams and figures are drawn as accurately as possible. All figures are in a plane unless otherwise indicated

16. There are just two ways in which 5 may be expressed as the sum of two different positive (nonzero) integers, namely, 5 = 4 + 1 = 3 + 2. In how many ways may 9 be expressed as the sum of two different positive (nonzero) integers?
   (A) 3
   (B) 4
   (C) 5
   (D) 6
   (E) 7

17. A board 7 feet 9 inches long is divided into three equal parts. What is the length of each part?
   (A) 2 ft. 7 in.
   (B) 2 ft. $6\frac{1}{3}$ in.
   (C) 2 ft. $8\frac{1}{3}$ in.
   (D) 2 ft. 8 in.
   (E) 2 ft. 9 in.

18. What is the smallest possible integer K > 1 such that $R^2 = S^3 = K$, for some integers R and S?
   (A) 4
   (B) 8
   (C) 27
   (D) 64
   (E) 81

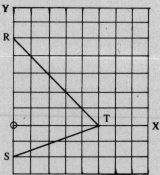

19. Triangle RST is superimposed on a coordinate system in which all angles are right angles. The number of square units in the area of triangle RST is
   (A) 10
   (B) 12.5
   (C) 15.5
   (D) 17.5
   (E) 20

20. Which of the following has the same value as $\frac{P}{Q}$?
   (A) $\frac{P - 2}{Q - 2}$
   (B) $\frac{1 + P}{1 + Q}$
   (C) $\frac{P^2}{Q^2}$
   (D) $\frac{3P}{3Q}$
   (E) $\frac{P + 3}{Q + 3}$

21. In the accompanying figure, ACB is a straight angle and DC is perpendicular to CE. If the number of degrees in angle ACD is represented by x, the number of degrees in angle BCE is represented by
   (A) 90 − x
   (B) x − 90

(C)   90 + x
(D)   180 − x
(E)   45 + x

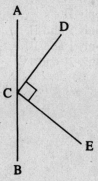

22.   The diagonal of a rectangle is 5. The area of the rectangle
   (A)   must be 12
   (B)   must be 24
   (C)   must be 25
   (D)   must be 50
   (E)   Cannot be determined from the information given.

Questions 23–24 refer to the accompanying circle graph, which shows how a certain family distributes its expenditures.

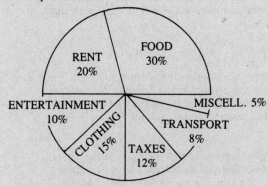

23.   If the family spends a total of $650 per month, how much are its monthly taxes?
   (A) $78.00
   (B) $72.22
   (C) $66.30
   (D) $48.00
   (E) $12.00

24.   How many degrees should there be in the central angle showing clothing, taxes, and transportation combined?
   (A)   100
   (B)   110
   (C)   120

(D)   126
(E)   130

25.   A boy takes a 25-question test and answers all questions. His score is obtained by giving him 4 points for each correct answer, and then subtracting 1 point for each wrong answer. If he obtains a score of 70, how many questions did he answer correctly?
   (A)   17
   (B)   18
   (C)   19
   (D)   20
   (E)   21

26.   A man travels a certain distance of 60 miles per hour and returns over the same road at 40 miles per hour. What is his average rate for the round trip in miles per hour?
   (A)   42
   (B)   44
   (C)   46
   (D)   48
   (E)   50

27.   Six tractors can plow a field in 8 hours if they all work together. How many hours will it take 4 tractors to do the job?
   (A)   9
   (B)   10
   (C)   11
   (D)   12
   (E)   14

28.   Which of the following numbers is the smallest?
   (A) $\frac{1}{5}$
   (B) $\sqrt{5}$
   (C) $\frac{1}{\sqrt{5}}$
   (D) $\frac{\sqrt{5}}{5}$
   (E) $\frac{1}{5\sqrt{5}}$

29.   The cost of 30 melons is d dollars. At this rate, how many melons can you buy for 80 cents?
   (A) $\frac{24}{d}$
   (B) $\frac{240}{d}$

(C) 24d

(D) $\dfrac{3d}{8}$

(E) $\dfrac{8d}{3}$

30. The sum of three consecutive odd numbers is always divisible by I. 2, II. 3, III. 5, IV. 6
    (A) only I
    (B) only II
    (C) only I and II
    (D) only I and III
    (E) only II and IV

STOP

END OF SECTION. IF YOU HAVE ANY TIME LEFT, GO
OVER YOUR WORK IN THIS SECTION ONLY. DO NOT
WORK IN ANY OTHER SECTION OF THE TEST.

SECTION IV

30 minutes
30 questions

Directions: For each of the following questions two quantities are given, one in Column A and one in Column B. Compare the two quantities and mark your answer sheet with the correct lettered conclusion. These are your options:
  A: If the quantity in Column A is the greater;
  B: if the quantity in Column B is the greater;
  C: if the two quantities are equal;
  D: if the relationship cannot be determined from the information given.
Common Information: In any question, information applying to both columns is centered between the columns and above the quantities in columns A and B. The common information applies to both columns. Any symbol that appears in both columns represents the same idea or quantity in both columns.
Numbers: All numbers used are real numbers.
Figures: Assume that the position of points, angles, regions and so forth are in the order shown. Figures are assumed to lie in a plane unless otherwise indicated. Figures accompanying questions are intended to provide information you can use in answering the questions. However, unless a note states that a figure is drawn to scale, you should solve the problems by using your knowledge of mathematics and *not* by estimating sizes by sight and measurement.
Lines: Assume that lines shown as straight are indeed straight.

COLUMN A	COLUMN B
1.	$x = -1$	
$x^3 + x^2 - x + 1$	$x^3 - x^2 + x - 1$
2. The edge of a cube whose volume is 27	The edge of a cube whose total surface area is 54

	COLUMN A	COLUMN B

3.

$$\frac{\frac{1}{2} + \frac{1}{3}}{\frac{2}{3}}$$

$$\frac{\frac{2}{3}}{\frac{1}{2} + \frac{1}{3}}$$

---

4. $.02$ $\sqrt{.02}$

5.

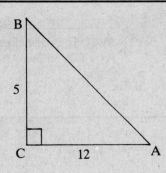

$(AB)^2$ $(AC)^2 + 5CB$

---

6. Area of circle   Area of a square
with radius 7   with side 7

7.

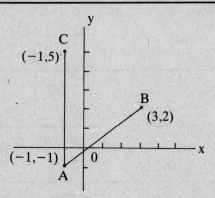

The length of AB   The length of AC

8.

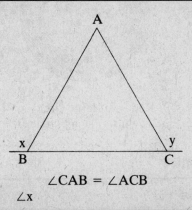

$\angle CAB = \angle ACB$

$\angle x$ $\angle y$

COLUMN A	COLUMN B

9.

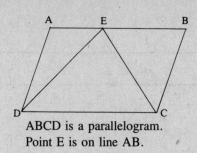

ABCD is a parallelogram.
Point E is on line AB.

area of △DEC

area of △AED
+ Area △EBC

10.

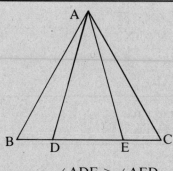

∠ADE > ∠AED

∠B

∠C

11.

$a < 0 < b$

a^2

$\dfrac{b}{2}$

12.

$rt > 0$

r

t

13.

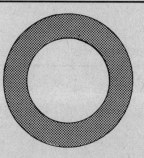

Radius of large circle = 10
Radius of small circle = 7

Area of shaded
portion

Area of small circle

14.

4% of .003

3% of .004

COLUMN A   P   COLUMN B

15.

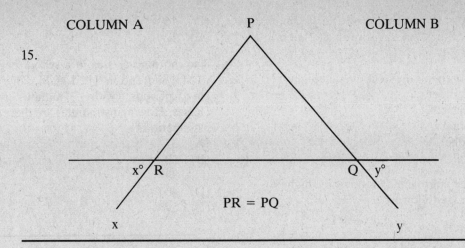

PR = PQ

x	y

Directions: For each of the following questions, select the best of the answer choices and blacken the corresponding space on your answer sheet.

Numbers: All numbers used are real numbers.

Figures: The diagrams and figures that accompany these questions are for the purpose of providing information useful in answering the questions. Unless it is stated that a specific figure is not drawn to scale, the diagrams and figures are drawn as accurately as possible. All figures are in a plane unless otherwise indicated.

16. In the figure, a rectangular piece of cardboard 18 inches by 24 inches is made into an open box by cutting a 5-inch square from each corner and building up the sides. What is the volume of the box in cubic inches?

(A) 560
(B) 1,233
(C) 1,560
(D) 2,160
(E) 4,320

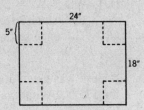

17. The figure below represents the back of a house. Find, in feet, the length of one of the equal rafters PQ or QR, if each extends 12 inches beyond the eaves.

(A) 19
(B) 21
(C) 23
(D) 25
(E) 43

art

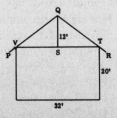

18. The scale of a certain map is $\frac{3}{4}$ = 9 miles. Find, in square miles, the actual area of a park represented on the map by a square whose side is $\frac{7}{8}$ inch.

(A) $10\frac{1}{2}$
(B) 21
(C) $110\frac{1}{4}$
(D) 121
(E) $125\frac{2}{3}$

19. If t represents the ten's digit and u the unit's digit of a two-digit number, then the number is represented by

(A) t + u
(B) tu
(C) 10u + t
(D) 10t + u
(E) ut

Answer Questions 20–22 with reference to the graph below.

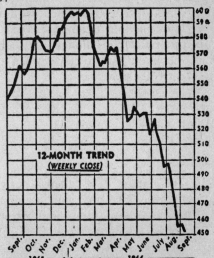

The graph shows the *New York Times* Industrial Stock Averages over a 12-month period.

20. In what month was the stock average highest?
    (A) December
    (B) January
    (C) February
    (D) October
    (E) April

21. What is the approximate ratio of the highest stock average to lowest?
    (A) 4 : 3
    (B) 5 : 3
    (C) 2 : 1
    (D) 3 : 2
    (E) 5 : 2

22. During what 3-month period did the stock market experience the greatest decline?
    (A) Sept.–Nov.
    (B) Nov.–Jan.
    (C) Feb.–April
    (D) May–July
    (E) July–Sept. '66

23. The pages of a typewritten report are numbered from 1 to 100 by hand. How many times will it be necessary to write the number 5?
    (A) 10
    (B) 11
    (C) 12
    (D) 19
    (E) 20

24. A clock that gains two minutes each hour is synchronized at midnight with a clock that loses one minute an hour. What will be the difference, in minutes, between the times shown on the two clocks when a third clock correctly shows noon?
    (A) 36
    (B) 24
    (C) 14
    (D) 12
    (E) 0

25. The number 6 is called a perfect number because it is the sum of all its integral divisors except itself. Another perfect number is
    (A) 36
    (B) 28
    (C) 24

(D) 16
(E) 12

26. The morning classes in a school begin at 9 A.M., and end at 11:51 A.M. There are 4 class periods, with 5 minutes between classes. How many minutes are there in each class period?
    (A) $37\frac{3}{4}$
    (B) $38\frac{1}{2}$
    (C) 39
    (D) 40
    (E) 59

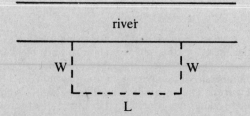

27. A man plans to build a fenced-in enclosure along a riverbank, as shown in the figure. He has 90 feet of fencing available for the three sides of the rectangular enclosure. All of the following statements are true EXCEPT
    (A) L + 2W = 90
    (B) The area of the enclosure is LW.
    (C) The area of the enclosure is 90W − 2W².
    (D) When W = 20, the enclosed area is 1000 square feet.
    (E) The enclosed area is greatest when L = W.

28. A desk was listed at $90.00 and was bought for $75.00. What was the rate of discount?
    (A) 15%
    (B) $16\frac{2}{3}\%$
    (C) 18%
    (D) 20%
    (E) 24%

29. In the figure below, a running track goes around a football field in the shape of a rectangle with semicircles at each end, with dimensions as indicated on the figure. The distance around the track in yards is
    (A) $100 + 60\pi$
    (B) $200 + 30\pi$
    (C) 320
    (D) $200 + 60\pi$
    (E) $100 + 30\pi$

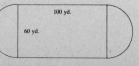

30. In the figure below, if angle **P** may take on values between 90° and 180°, exclusive, which inequality best expresses the possible values of the base x?

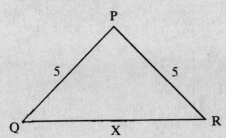

(A) $5 < x < 10$
(B) $5\sqrt{3} < x < 10$
(C) $7 < x < 10$
(D) $5\sqrt{2} < x < 10$
(E) $5\sqrt{2} < x < 5\sqrt{3}$

STOP

END OF SECTION. IF YOU HAVE ANY TIME LEFT, GO OVER YOUR WORK IN THIS SECTION ONLY. DO NOT WORK IN ANY OTHER SECTION OF THE TEST.

SECTION V

30 minutes
25 questions

Directions: Each of the following questions or groups of questions is based on a short passage or a set of propositions. In answering these questions it may sometimes be helpful to draw a simple picture or chart. When you have selected the best answer to each question, darken the corresponding circle on your answer sheet.

Questions 1–3

A slot player may possess only one token at a time.

A blue token in slot 19 produces a prize and one yellow token.

A blue token is obtained by putting a yellow or green token in slot 10, or a pink token in slot 15.

Pink tokens are obtained by putting a white token in slot 8.

A white token can be obtained from the cashier only by exchanging another token other than a yellow one for it.

1. The procedure fails to specify how to get which of the following?
   (A) a prize without first getting a yellow token
   (B) as many prizes as one wants
   (C) a green token
   (D) a prize without first getting a green token
   (E) a yellow token

2. Once a player has won a prize, which of the following is possible as the player's next play?
   (A) obtaining a white token from cashier
   (B) playing slot 10
   (C) playing slot 15
   (D) playing slot 19
   (E) playing slot 8

3. If you have a green token, what other colors of token can you get?
   (A) blue only
   (B) pink, blue, or yellow only
   (C) green, blue, or yellow only

(D)' blue or yellow only

(E) all the other colors

4. Why pay outrageously high prices for imported sparkling water when there is now an inexpensive water carbonated and bottled here in the United States at its source—Cold Springs, Vermont. Neither you nor your guests will taste the difference, but if you would be embarrassed if it were learned that you were serving a domestic sparkling water, then serve Cold Springs Water—but serve it in a leaded crystal decanter.

The advertisement rests on which of the following assumptions?

I. It is difficult if not impossible to distinguish Cold Springs Water from imported competitors on the basis of taste.

II. Most sparkling waters are not bottled at the source.

III. Some people may purchase an imported sparkling water over a domestic one as a status symbol.

(A) I only

(B) II only

(C) III only

(D) I and II only

(E) I and III only

5. In our investigation of this murder, we are guided by our previous experience with the Eastend Killer. You will recall that in that case the victims were also carrying a great deal of money when they were killed, but the money was not taken. As in this case, the murder weapon was a pistol. Finally, in that case the murders were also committed between six in the evening and twelve midnight. So we are probably after someone who looks very much like the Eastend Killer who was finally tried, convicted, and executed: 5'11" tall, a mustache, short brown hair, walks with a slight limp.

The author makes which of the following assumptions?

I. Crimes similar in detail are likely to be committed by perpetrators who are similar in physical appearance.

II. The Eastend Killer has apparently escaped from prison and has resumed his criminal activities.

III. The man first convicted as the Eastend Killer was actually innocent, and the real Eastend Killer is still loose.

(A) I only

(B) I and II only

(C) II only

(D) I and III only

(E) III only

6. The main ingredient in this bottle of Dr. John's Milk of Magnesia is used by nine out of ten hospitals across the country as an antacid and laxative.

If this advertising claim is true, which of the following statements must also be true?

I. Nine out of ten hospitals across the country use Dr. John's Milk of Magnesia for some ailments.

II. Only one out of ten hospitals in the country do not treat acid indigestion and constipation.

III. Only one out of ten hospitals across the country do not recommend Dr. John's Milk of Magnesia for patients who need a milk of magnesia.

(A) I only

(B) II only

(C) I and III

(D) I, II, and III

(E) None of the statements is necessarily true.

Questions 7–11

The tribe of Ater is divided into three clans—first, second, and third.

Only men and women of the same clan may marry.

On maturity, sons of couples in the first and second clans move down one rank, while sons of the third clan join the first.

On maturity, daughters of the second and third clans move up a rank and daughters of the first clan join the third.

Only mature Ater may marry.

7. Is it ever possible for an Ater woman born of the first clan to marry her nephew?
   (A) Yes, but only the son of her brother.
   (B) Yes, but only the son of her sister.
   (C) Yes, but only the daughter of her brother.
   (D) Yes, but only the daughter of her sister.
   (E) No.

8. Into what clans were the parents of an adult second clan male born?
   (A) father first clan, mother first clan
   (B) father first clan, mother third clan
   (C) father second clan, mother third clan
   (D) father second clan, mother first clan
   (E) father third clan, mother second clan

9. If a baby is born into the third clan, its mother's mother's mother could have been born to adult parents of what clan(s)?
   (A) first, second, or third
   (B) first and second only
   (C) first and third only
   (D) second only
   (E) third only

10. An Ater man has a granddaughter who is married to a man in the second clan. In what clan(s) could he be?
    (A) first only
    (B) second only
    (C) third only
    (D) first or second
    (E) second or third

11. Which of the statements about the Ater may be inferred from the information given?
    I. A sister and brother may not marry.
    II. A man may not marry his mother.
    III. A woman may not marry her grandson.
    (A) I only
    (B) II only
    (C) I and II only
    (D) I and III
    (E) I, II, and III

Questions 12–16

J, K, L, M, N, P, and Q get on an empty express bus at 10th Street. The bus only stops

every ten blocks. No one else gets on the bus, and no one leaves and gets back on. Nobody gets off at 30th Street or at 60th Street. When the bus pulls away from 80th Street, there are three people left on the bus.

Both P and Q get off before 80th Street, with P getting off at an earlier stop than Q.

12. If J gets off the bus on the second stop after M does, at which street(s) could J have gotten off?
    (A) 20th and 40th
    (B) 20th, 40th, and 70th
    (C) 40th and 70th
    (D) 50th, 70th, and 80th
    (E) 70th and 80th

13. If L, M, and N are on the bus after 80th Street, which of the following is true?
    I. Each of the other passengers could have gotten off at separate stops.
    II. There was at least one stop at which no one got off.
    III. No one got off at 80th Street.
    (A) I only
    (B) I and II only
    (C) I and III only
    (D) II and III only
    (E) I, II, and III

14. If K and L get off at separate stops before 80th Street, which of the following must be false?
    (A) J did not get off the bus.
    (B) M did not get off the bus.
    (C) N did not get off the bus.
    (D) Q did not get off the bus.
    (E) None of the above.

15. If P left the bus after M did, and no one got off at 70th Street, then
    (A) everyone who left the bus left at a different stop
    (B) Q left at either 50th or 80th Streets
    (C) P left at either 50th or 80th Streets
    (D) M left after J
    (E) Q left after J

16. If X, Y, and Z got on the bus at 20th, 30th, and 40th Streets, respectively, and stayed on

the bus for 3, 4, and 5 stops, respectively, how many persons were on the bus when it arrived at 90th Street?

(A) 1
(B) 2
(C) 3
(D) 4
(E) Cannot be determined from the information given.

Questions 17–23

A philosophical foundation presents six once-a-month lecture series, with no dates conflicting:

Metaphysics—August through January

Epistemology—April through October

Ethics—January through September

Esthetics—March through June

Political Philosophy—October through April

Philosophy of Science—October through December

17. During which month are the fewest lectures given?
    (A) January
    (B) February
    (C) June
    (D) August
    (E) September

18. What is the largest number of lectures that can be attended in a single month?
    (A) 7
    (B) 6
    (C) 5
    (D) 4
    (E) 3

19. What two series taken together fill the year without overlap?
    (A) Metaphysics and Esthetics
    (B) Political Philosophy and Epistemology
    (C) Epistemology and Metaphysics
    (D) Political Philosophy and Ethics
    (E) Ethics and Philosophy of Science

20. During how many months of the year must a student attend to hear all the lectures on Metaphysics, Epistemology, and Esthetics?
    (A) 11

(B) 10
(C) 9
(D) 8
(E) 7

21. How many lecture series last more than 6 months?
    (A) 1
    (B) 2
    (C) 3
    (D) 4
    (E) 5

22. How many different lecture series can be attended in September, October, and November?
    (A) 2
    (B) 3
    (C) 4
    (D) 5
    (E) 6

23. How many different lectures can be attended in January, February, and March?
    (A) 12
    (B) 10
    (C) 8
    (D) 6
    (E) 4

24. Is your company going to continue to discriminate against women in its hiring and promotion policies?

    The above question might be considered unfair for which of the following reasons?

    I. Its construction seeks a "yes" or "no" answer where both might be inappropriate.
    II. It is internally inconsistent.
    III. It contains a hidden presupposition which the responder might wish to contest.

    (A) I only
    (B) II only
    (C) I and II only
    (D) I and III only
    (E) I, II, and III

Ms. Evangeline Rose argued that money and time invested in acquiring a professional degree are totally wasted. As evidence supporting her argument, she offered the case of a man who, at considerable expense of money and time, completed his law degree and then married and lived as a house-husband taking care of their children, and worked part time at a day care center so his wife could pursue her career.

25. Ms. Rose makes the unsupported assumption that

(A) an education in the law is useful only in pursuing law-related activities
(B) what was not acceptable twenty-five years ago may very well be acceptable today
(C) wealth is more important than learning
(D) professional success is a function of the quality of one's education
(E) only the study of law can be considered professional study

STOP

END OF SECTION. IF YOU HAVE ANY TIME LEFT, GO OVER YOUR WORK IN THIS SECTION ONLY. DO NOT WORK IN ANY OTHER SECTION OF THE TEST.

SECTION VI

30 minutes
25 questions

Directions: Each of the following questions or groups of questions is based on a short passage or a set of propositions. In answering these questions it may sometimes be helpful to draw a simple picture or chart. When you have selected the best answer to each question, darken the corresponding circle on your answer sheet.

Questions 1–3

3 Masters, L, M, and N, and 3 experts, O, P, and Q, compete in a special tournament.

All the competitors play all the other players once.

1 point is gained for defeating an expert.

2 points are gained for defeating a master.

Masters lose 2 points for each game lost.

Experts lose 1 point for each game lost.

1. What is the highest score that a master can obtain if he loses 2 games?
   (A) 0

(B) 1
(C) 2
(D) 3
(E) 4

2. How many games does an expert have to win to be sure of coming in ahead of a master who lost to the other masters?
   (A) 1
   (B) 2
   (C) 3
   (D) 4
   (E) 5

3. If P wins all his games except the one against L, and did not lose to the winner of the tournament, which of the following could have been the winner?
   (A) L or P
   (B) M or N
   (C) O or Q
   (D) any one of M, N, O, or Q
   (E) any player except L or P

4. SPEAKER: The great majority of people in the United States have access to the best medical care available anywhere in the world.

   OBJECTOR: There are thousands of poor in this country who cannot afford to pay to see a doctor.

   A possible objection to the speaker's comments would be to point to the existence of
   (A) a country which has more medical assistants than the United States
   (B) a nation where medical care is provided free of charge by the government
   (C) a country in which the people are given better medical care than Americans
   (D) government hearings in the United States on the problems poor people have getting medical care
   (E) a country which has a higher hospital bed per person ratio than the United States

5. It is sometimes argued that we are reaching the limits of the Earth's capacity to supply our energy needs with fossil fuels. In the past ten years, however, as a result of technological progress making it possible to extract resources from even marginal wells and mines, yields from oil and coal fields have increased tremendously. There is no reason to believe that there is a limit to the Earth's capacity to supply our energy needs.

   Which of the following statements most directly contradicts the conclusion drawn above?
   (A) Even if we exhaust our supplies of fossil fuel, the earth can still be mined for uranium for nuclear fuel.
   (B) The technology needed to extract fossil fuels from marginal sources is very expensive.
   (C) Even given the improvements in technology, oil and coal are not renewable resources, so we will sometime exhaust our supplies of them.
   (D) Most of the land under which marginal oil and coal supplies lie is more suitable to cultivation or pasturing than to production of fossil fuels.

(E) The fuels which are yielded by marginal sources tend to be high in sulphur and other undesirable elements that aggravate the air pollution problem.

6. Statistics published by the State Department of Traffic and Highway Safety show that nearly 80% of all traffic fatalities occur at speeds under 35 miles per hour and within 25 miles of home.

   Which of the following would be the most reasonable conclusion to draw from these statistics?
   (A) A person is less likely to have a fatal accident if he always drives over 35 miles per hour and always at distances greater than 25 miles from his home.
   (B) There is a direct correlation between distance driven and the likelihood of a fatal accident.
   (C) The greater the likelihood that one is about to be involved in a fatal accident, the more likely it is that he is driving close to home at a speed less than 35 miles per hour.
   (D) If it were not the case that a person were about to be involved in a fatal traffic accident, then he would not have been driving at the speed or in the location he was, in fact, driving.
   (E) Most driving is done at less than 35 miles per hour and within 25 miles of home.

Questions 7–11

Coach Nelson is putting together a four-member handball team from right-handed players R, S, and T and left-handed players L, M, N, and O. He must have at least two right-handed players on the team, and all players must be able to practice with each other.

S cannot practice with L.
T cannot practice with N.
M cannot practice with L or N.

7. If L is on the team, what other individuals must also be on the team?
   (A) R and T only
   (B) R, T, and N
   (C) R, T, and O

(D) R only

(E) M and O only

8. If O is not on the team, which of the other players must be on the team?
   (A) No other particular player must be on the team if O is not chosen.
   (B) M only
   (C) R and S only
   (D) R, S, T, and M
   (E) S only

9. If both S and T are chosen for the team, what other individuals must be on the team with them?
   (A) L only
   (B) M only
   (C) M and O only
   (D) O only
   (E) none of the above

10. How many different teams can be formed without R?
    (A) 0
    (B) 1
    (C) 2
    (D) 3
    (E) more than 3

11. If T were to become a left-handed player, how many different teams could be formed?
    (A) 0
    (B) 1
    (C) 2
    (D) 3
    (E) more than 3

Questions 12–16

   I. A cube has six sides, each of which is a different one of the following colors: black, blue, brown, green, red, and white.
  II. The red side is opposite the black.
 III. The green side is between the red and the black.
 IV. The blue side is adjacent to the white.
  V. The brown side is adjacent to the blue.
 VI. The red side is the bottom face.

12. Which statement adds no information that is not already given by the statements above it?
    (A) II

(B) III

(C) IV

(D) V

(E) VI

13. The side opposite brown is
    (A) white
    (B) red
    (C) green
    (D) blue
    (E) black

14. The four colors adjacent to green are
    (A) black, blue, brown, red
    (B) black, blue, brown, white
    (C) black, blue, red, white
    (D) black, brown, red, white
    (E) blue, brown, red, white

15. Which of the following can be deduced from statements I, II, and VI?
    (A) Black is on the top.
    (B) Blue is on the top.
    (C) Brown is on the top.
    (D) Brown is opposite black.
    (E) None of the above can be deduced.

16. If the red side is exchanged for the green side, and blue is swapped for black, which of the following is false?
    (A) Red is opposite black.
    (B) White is adjacent to brown.
    (C) Green is opposite blue.
    (D) White is adjacent to green.
    (E) White is adjacent to blue.

Questions 17–22

   I. Four contestants, P, Q, R, and S, will each receive one of four prizes. They are, in descending order of value: a new car, a vacation to Europe, a stereo system, and a year's supply of dog food.
  II. If P gets the car, then Q gets the dog food.
 III. If Q gets the stereo, then P gets the dog food.
 IV. P will get a more valuable prize than R.
  V. If S doesn't get the car, then P will get the vacation.
 VI. If Q gets the vacation, then R won't get the dog food.
 VII. If Q gets the car, then R gets the vacation.

17. Based on the above information, which of the following conclusions must be false?
    (A) R will get a more valuable prize than Q.
    (B) No two people will get the same prize.
    (C) Q gets the vacation and R gets the dog food.
    (D) P gets a less valuable prize than S.
    (E) Q will get one of the two least valuable prizes.

18. Which of the contestants will get the dog food?
    (A) P
    (B) Q
    (C) R
    (D) S
    (E) none of the above

19. Which of the contestants will get the car?
    (A) P
    (B) Q
    (C) R
    (D) S
    (E) none of the above

20. Which of the following combinations of the above statements are sufficient to deduce that Q will not receive the car?
    (A) I, II, and VI
    (B) II, VI, and VII
    (C) III and V
    (D) VI and VII
    (E) I, IV, and VII

21. Which of the seven statements merely gives information available from previous statements?
    (A) IV
    (B) V
    (C) VI
    (D) VII
    (E) none of the above

22. Which of the contestants will not receive a stereo?
    A) Q and S only
    B) P, Q and R
    C) P, S and R
    D) P, S and Q
    E) P and R only

23. A study published by the Department of Education shows that children in the central cities lag far behind students in the suburbs and the rural areas in reading skills. The report blamed this differential on the overcrowding in the classrooms of city schools. I maintain, however, that the real reason that city children are poorer readers than non-city children is that they do not get enough fresh air and sunshine.

Which of the following would LEAST strengthen the author's point in the argument above?
    (A) Medical research which shows a correlation between air pollution and learning disabilities.
    (B) A report by educational experts demonstrating there is no relationship between the number of students in a classroom and a student's ability to read.
    (C) A notice released by the Department of Educaiton retracting that part of their report which mentions overcrowding as the reason for the differential.
    (D) The results of a federal program which indicates that city students show significant improvement in reading skills when they spend the summer in the country.
    (E) A proposal by the federal government to fund emergency programs to hire more teachers for central city schools in an attempt to reduce overcrowding in the classrooms.

24. Some judges have allowed hospitals to disconnect life-support equipment of patients who have no prospects for recovery. But I say that is murder. Either we put a stop to this practice now or we will soon have programs of euthanasia for the old and infirm as well as others who might be considered a burden. Rather than disconnecting life-support equipment, we should let nature take its course.

Which of the following are valid objections to the above argument?

    I. It is internally inconsistent.

II. It employs emotionally charged terms.
III. It presents a false dilemma.

(A) I only
(B) II only
(C) III only
(D) II and III only
(E) I, II, and III only

25. PUBLIC ANNOUNCEMENT: When you enroll with Future Careers Business Institute (FCBI), you will have access to our placement counseling service. Last year, 92% of our graduates who asked us to help them find jobs, found them. So go to FCBI for your future!

Which of the following would be appropriate questions to ask in order to determine the value of the preceding claim?

I. How many of your graduates asked FCBI for assistance?
II. How many people graduated from FCBI last year?
III. Did those people who asked for jobs find ones in the areas for which they were trained?
IV. Was FCBI responsible for finding the jobs or did graduates find them independently?

(A) I and II only
(B) I, II, and III only
(C) I, II, and IV only
(D) III and IV only
(E) I, II, III, and IV

STOP

END OF SECTION. IF YOU HAVE ANY TIME LEFT, GO OVER YOUR WORK IN THIS SECTION ONLY. DO NOT WORK IN ANY OTHER SECTION OF THE TEST.

Section VII

30 minutes
38 questions

Directions: Each of the questions below contains one or more blank spaces, each blank indicating an omitted word. Each sentence is followed by five (5) lettered words or sets of words. Read and determine the general sense of each sentence. Then choose the word or set of words which, when inserted in the sentence, best fits the meaning of the sentence.

1. Wild beasts roamed the deserted country, which had not been _____ for hundreds of years.
   (A) temperate
   (B) active
   (C) winnowed

(D) lived in
(E) civilized

2. Paul's _____ at work is a natural product of his _____ nature.
   (A) wastefulness—unpleasant
   (B) thoughtfulness—rarefied
   (C) diligence—sedulous
   (D) candor—familial
   (E) stubbornness—intrepid

3. Blustery winds knocked off hats and rattled windows, and the adventurous children were _____.
   (A) frightened

(B) terrified
(C) improved
(D) anxious
(E) delighted

4. At night, the inn turned into a theater, not one of actors and actresses, but one of the _____ of real people.
   (A) sciences
   (B) psychologies
   (C) dramas
   (D) jokes
   (E) novels

5. The stubborn families feuded for generations, and _____ feelings are still fixed in their _____.
   (A) begrudging—acceptance
   (B) bitter—generosity
   (C) inimical—antagonism
   (D) suspicious—relief
   (E) wary—helplessness

6. Her feeling of _____was so _____ that all the other patients were soon smiling or laughing.
   (A) contrition—repulsive
   (B) embolism—catastrophic
   (C) melancholia—cataclysmic
   (D) ebullience—contagious
   (E) rehabilitation—paranoiac

7. His _____ was so great that he became the _____ of all our disputes about art and music.
   (A) euphony—censor
   (B) irascibility—object
   (C) wealth—reimburser
   (D) erudition—arbiter
   (E) pomposity—cause

Directions: In each of the following questions, you are given a related pair of words or phrases in capital letters. Each capitalized pair is followed by five (5) lettered pairs of words or phrases. Choose the pair which best expresses a relationship similar to that expressed by the original pair.

8. VALVE : FLOW ::
   (A) faucet : shower

(B) tub : bath
(C) major : promotion
(D) mores : conduct
(E) throttle : speed

9. LEE : WINDWARD ::
   (A) port : larboard
   (B) upstream : downstream
   (C) sheltered : harbored
   (D) starboard : larboard
   (E) port : starboard

10. QUARRY : MARBLE ::
    (A) timber : forest
    (B) game : preserve
    (C) mine : coal
    (D) tungsten : wolframite
    (E) igneous : metamorphic

11. WRITER : MANUSCRIPT ::
    (A) artist : description
    (B) cooper : barrel
    (C) fletcher : weapon
    (D) glazier : roof
    (E) blacksmith : forge

12. WATTLE : TURKEY ::
    (A) feet : squid
    (B) beard : lady
    (C) crown : king
    (D) core : apple
    (E) jowls : man

13. WAYWARD : DELINQUENT ::
    (A) false : eternal
    (B) heavenly : infernal
    (C) tardy : late
    (D) spastic : retarded
    (E) youth : age

14. WHIM : PREMEDITATED ::
    (A) purpose : impressed
    (B) caprice : deliberate
    (C) lark : consolidated
    (D) book : studied
    (E) impromptu : extemporaneous

15. WHET : HONE ::
    (A) sharpen : dull
    (B) moisten : residence
    (C) desiccate : dehumidify
    (D) weigh : pound
    (E) strap : stone

16. QUAFF : SIP ::
    (A) conflagration : blaze
    (B) press : quash
    (C) slam : punish
    (D) gorge : nibble
    (E) gallop : trot

Directions: Below each of the following passages, you will find questions or incomplete statements about the passage. Each statement or question is followed by lettered words or expressions. Select the word or expression that most satisfactorily completes each statement or answers each question in accordance with the meaning of the passage. After you have chosen the best answer, blacken the corresponding space on the answer sheet.

This chemical method of classifying substances is interesting as an example of a logical argument. A single experiment in which a substance is decomposed into two or more other substances or is alone formed from them proves that it is a compound; this conclusion is inescapable. The failure of such an experiment, however, does not prove that the substance is an element. It is, indeed, not possible to prove that a substance is an element by tests of this kind, no matter how many are made. It may be convenient to assume it to be an element, in case there is no evidence to the contrary; but if this is done, it should not be forgotten that the assumption is not necessarily true.

17. According to this passage, proving a substance to be a compound is feasible
    (A) only theoretically
    (B) without controls
    (C) by the null hypothesis
    (D) to a limited degree of certainty
    (E) by a decomposition reaction

18. Which one of the following statements is best supported by the information given in the paragraph?
    (A) It is impossible to determine whether a substance is an element or a compound.
    (B) Not proving an unknown to be a compound does not thereby prove it to be an element.

(C) The inherent uncertainty of the chemical method, as described in the passage, is primarily responsible for the introduction of errors encountered in chemical analysis.
(D) The present classification of elements is inaccurate.
(E) None of these.

19. From this passage it may be inferred
    (A) there is no experimental way to prove that a given substance is an element
    (B) any substance which cannot be separated into two different substances is not a compound
    (C) the decomposition of a substance will never yield an element
    (D) there is no known way of proving a substance to be a compound
    (E) none of the above are true

When the television is good, nothing—not the theatre, not the magazines, or newspapers—nothing is better. But when television is bad, nothing is worse. I invite you to sit down in front of your television set when your station goes on the air and stay there without a book, magazine, newspaper, or anything else to distract you and keep your eyes glued to that set until the station signs off. I can assure you that you will observe a vast wasteland. You will see a procession of game shows, violence, audience-participation shows, formula comedies about totally unbelievable families, blood and thunder, mayhem, more violence, sadism, murder, Western badmen, Western goodmen, private eyes, gangsters, still more violence, and cartoons. And, endlessly, commercials that scream and cajole and offend. And most of all, boredom. True, you will see a few things you will enjoy. But they will be very, very few. And if you think I exaggerate, try it.

Is there no room on television to teach, to inform, to uplift, to stretch, to enlarge the capacities of our children? Is there no room for programs to deepen the children's understanding of children in other lands? Is there no room for a children's news show explaining something about the world for them at their level of understanding? Is there no room for reading the great literature of the past, teaching them the great traditions of freedom? There are some fine children's shows, but they are drowned out in the massive doses of cartoons, violence, and more violence. Must these be your trademarks? Search your conscience and see whether you cannot offer more to your young beneficiaries whose future you guard so many hours each and every day.

There are many people in this great country, and you must serve all of us. You will get no argument from me if you say that, given a choice between a Western and a symphony, more people will watch the Western. I like Westerns and private eyes, too—but a steady diet for the whole country is obviously not in the public interest. We all know that people would more often prefer to be entertained than stimulated or informed. But your obligations are not satisfied if you look only to popularity as a test of what to broadcast. You are not only in show business; you are free to communicate ideas as well as to give relaxation. You must provide a wider range of choices, more diversity, more alternatives. It is not enough to cater to the nation's whims—you must also serve the nation's needs. The people own the air. They own it as much in prime evening time as they do at six o'clock in the morning. For every hour that the people give you—you owe them something. I intend to see that your debt is paid with service.

—excerpt from speech by Newton H. Minow, chairman of the Federal Communications Commission, before the National Association of Broadcasters.

20. The wasteland referred to by the author describes
    (A) western badlands
    (B) average television programs
    (C) morning television shows
    (D) television shows with desert locales
    (E) children's programs generally

21. The author's attitude toward television can best be described as
    (A) sullenness at defeat
    (B) reconciliation with the broadcasters
    (C) righteous indignation
    (D) determination to prevail
    (E) hopelessness over the size of the problem

22. The author is primarily concerned to tell broadcasters that
    (A) the listener, not the broadcaster,

should make the decisions about which programs are aired
    (B) all children's shows are worthless
    (C) mystery programs should be banned
    (D) they had better mend their ways
    (E) televised instruction should become a substitute for classroom lessons

23. Concerning programs for children, it may be inferred that Minow believes that such programs should
    (A) include no cartoons at all
    (B) include ones which provide culture
    (C) be presented only during the morning hours
    (D) be presented without commercial interruption
    (E) not deal with the Old West

24. The statement that "the people own the air" implies that
    (A) citizens have the right to insist on worthwhile television programs
    (B) television should be socialized
    (C) the government may build above present structures
    (D) since air is worthless, the people own nothing
    (E) the broadcasters have no right to commercialize on television

25. It can be inferred from the passage in regard to television programming that the author believes
    (A) the broadcasters are trying to do the right thing but are failing
    (B) foreign countries are going to pattern their programs after ours
    (C) there is a great deal that is worthwhile in present programs
    (D) the listeners do not necessarily know what is good for them
    (E) six o'clock in the morning is too early for a television show

26. Which of the following would NOT be inferable from the passage?
    (A) The needs of minorities must be met by television.
    (B) Minow would probably favor more

television stations being established, if they were responsible stations.
(C) Violence is not a good ingredient for children's television shows.
(D) Children's television is uniformly terrible.
(E) Minow believes that better shows are possible.

27. Minow believes that his tastes are
(A) better than most people's
(B) better than those of the television industry
(C) the same as most people's
(D) better than the average child's
(E) less demanding of television than of other art forms

Directions: Each of the following questions consists of a word printed in capital letters, followed by five (5) lettered words or phrases. Select the word or phrase which is most nearly *opposite* to the capitalized word in meaning.

28. CATEGORICAL:
(A) unchosen
(B) doglike
(C) vague
(D) unregenerate
(E) voluptuous

29. PREMEDITATED:
(A) superannuated
(B) tractable
(C) diagnosed
(D) impromptu
(E) aroused

30. PROPINQUITY:
(A) distance
(B) succulence
(C) antiquity
(D) tedium
(E) justice

31. ADJURE:
(A) judge harshly
(B) give into

(C) ask facetiously
(D) jump quickly
(E) remove instantly

32. POSTULATE:
(A) undulate
(B) prove
(C) peculate
(D) palpitate
(E) disenchant

33. ABRIDGE:
(A) wade
(B) encourage
(C) lengthen
(D) edit
(E) retain

34. AVERSION:
(A) serenity
(B) contact
(C) affinity
(D) pleasance
(E) valance

35. PROCLIVITY:
(A) insipidity
(B) disinclination
(C) effrontery
(D) antithesis
(E) contingency

36. ETHEREAL:
(A) conscious
(B) advantageous
(C) tangible
(D) contagious
(E) clear

37. EXTRANEOUS:
(A) doubled
(B) native
(C) germane
(D) neutral
(E) sequential

38. ASSUAGE:
(A) corrugate
(B) detest
(C) exacerbate
(D) impede
(E) reverberate

STOP

END OF SECTION. IF YOU HAVE ANY TIME LEFT, GO
OVER YOUR WORK IN THIS SECTION ONLY. DO NOT
WORK IN ANY OTHER SECTION OF THE TEST.

PRACTICE EXAMINATION 5—ANSWER KEY

Section I

1.	E	10.	B	19.	A	28.	C	37.	B
2.	C	11.	B	20.	E	29.	B	38.	D
3.	A	12.	C	21.	C	30.	E		
4.	A	13.	C	22.	D	31.	D		
5.	E	14.	D	23.	B	32.	D		
6.	E	15.	D	24.	B	33.	A		
7.	B	16.	D	25.	A	34.	B		
8.	C	17.	C	26.	D	35.	D		
9.	E	18.	C	27.	C	36.	C		

Section II

1.	B	10.	E	19.	C	28.	C	37.	C
2.	A	11.	E	20.	B	29.	E	38.	B
3.	C	12.	D	21.	C	30.	A		
4.	E	13.	B	22.	B	31.	B		
5.	B	14.	B	23.	A	32.	C		
6.	C	15.	B	24.	C	33.	A		
7.	C	16.	D	25.	E	34.	B		
8.	E	17.	C	26.	D	35.	D		
9.	E	18.	B	27.	C	36.	A		

Section III

1.	D	7.	A	13.	A	19.	D	25.	C
2.	B	8.	C	14.	D	20.	D	26.	D
3.	C	9.	A	15.	D	21.	A	27.	D
4.	D	10.	B	16.	B	22.	E	28.	E
5.	B	11.	C	17.	A	23.	A	29.	A
6.	C	12.	C	18.	D	24.	D	30.	B

Section IV

1.	A	7.	B	13.	A	19.	D	25.	B
2.	C	8.	D	14.	C	20.	C	26.	C
3.	A	9.	C	15.	C	21.	A	27.	E
4.	B	10.	D	16.	A	22.	E	28.	B
5.	C	11.	D	17.	B	23.	E	29.	D
6.	A	12.	D	18.	C	24.	A	30.	D

Section V

1.	C	6.	E	11.	C	16.	D	21.	C
2.	B	7.	A	12.	C	17.	B	22.	D
3.	E	8.	E	13.	B	18.	D	23.	C
4.	E	9.	E	14.	D	19.	E	24.	D
5.	A	10.	D	15.	B	20.	A	25.	A

Section VI

1.	B	6.	E	11.	E	16.	B	21.	E
2.	B	7.	C	12.	B	17.	C	22.	D
3.	C	8.	D	13.	A	18.	B	23.	E
4.	C	9.	E	14.	D	19.	D	24.	E
5.	C	10.	B	15.	A	20.	E	25.	E

Section VII

1.	E	10.	C	19.	E	28.	C	37.	C
2.	C	11.	B	20.	B	29.	D	38.	C
3.	E	12.	E	21.	D	30.	A		
4.	C	13.	C	22.	D	31.	C		
5.	C	14.	B	23.	B	32.	B		
6.	D	15.	C	24.	A	33.	C		
7.	D	16.	D	25.	D	34.	C		
8.	E	17.	E	26.	D	35.	B		
9.	B	18.	B	27.	C	36.	C		

EXPLANATORY ANSWERS

SECTION I

1. **(E)** If you are now supporting a candidate whom you have attacked only a month before, your position must be embarrassing. Anomalous is the second-best answer, but it means deviating from the norm or, here, irregular. This has appeal since one would like to think that such things as those described in the sentence are deviations from the norm, but the sentence says that these things often occur. Thus, (A) is the best answer. Piquant means sharp, spicy-tasting, or flavorful; succulent means juicy.

2. **(C)** The sentence structure tells us that we are looking for a better and different way of communication than direct censure. You do not really need to know what censure means to answer the question, since it is clearly some form of criticism. Thus, we seek an answer that is an *indirect* form of communication criticism. (C), innuendo, is precisely that. (A) might have some appeal since one might suppose that writing is less direct than speaking to someone face to face; however, writing is not necessarily indirect, only not oral. Furthermore, writing is not necessarily a form of criticism, as censure and innuendo are. (B), (D), and (E) are not really forms of communication. (D) and (E) appeal since they remind you of allusion, which is a form of indirect reference and communication and would therefore be a fairly good answer choice, though still not as good as innuendo, which carries the particular connotation of making an indirect, critical remark.

3. **(A)** If the Congress is uncooperative, the Chief Executive may lack the power to accomplish his program. There is some outside knowledge required here, in that you need to know that power in the government is likely divided between the Congress and the Chief Executive. If the Chief Executive had all the power, there would be no point to worrying about whether the Congress was cooperative or not. (A) means powerless and is thus just the right word. (C) and (D) do not even fit into the sentence and are eliminated.

   (B) and (E) have only a little merit. (E)'s appeal is from a mental extension of the sentence to say something like: "He is equipped to do the program, but is not allowed to do it." This is a fine idea, but not the one that is presented in the problem. (B) has the same slight merit if it is interpreted to mean that he is permitted by the

grace of the Congress to do something, as opposed to being able to do it based on his own power. However, this is a derivative meaning and first depends on the idea that the Chief Executive is impotent; thus, (A) remains the better answer.

4. **(A)** Someone with a high opinion of his own importance tends to try to run others' activities. Choice (A) best reflects this attitude. (E) is good for the first blank, but diffusion would not flatter Larry's ego.

5. **(E)** If we accept that Arlene's cooking was delicious, one doesn't generally avoid or console someone for a tasty meal. Thus, (E) is the only logical answer.

6. **(E)** The color is expressing feeling, so something implying feeling should be in the way that the painting relates to the museum-goer. This is a sentence in which none of the answer choices is eliminated by reference to only one of the blanks. The sentence structure shows that the first blank—the way in which the paintings are done—will produce a result described by the second blank. Therefore, the solution to the question is to see how well each answer choice will work in this structure. Painting techniques might be ingenious, (A), but that would not make it fall on the viewer, hence (A) fails. (B) has some merit since too emphatic a technique might insult the viewer, though it is not a strong answer choice. (C) is unacceptable since something that echoes in your mind is very strong, and not very subtle. "Creep up on" would express being subtle, but it is not available. (D) has some merit since a sensitive expression of feeling might be very appealing, although seduce has more meaning than merely sensitivity of feeling. (E) is quite strong for two reasons. First, if the technique is successful, it will "say" something to the viewer. Second, if the expression of feeling is "so" successful, some strong result is appropriate and cry out is a strong result. (E) is preferable to (D) primarily because crying out is a better way to express feeling than seduction. Both of these are preferable to (B) since there is no reason to suppose that emphatic feeling in a painting is universally insulting, and we do know that Van Gogh is revered today. Thus, (E) is the best answer.

7. **(B)** The structure of the sentence tells us that the factories and the workers were regarded in the same way by the monopoly capitalists. Thus, the

first blank must be filled with a word that could apply to both factories and workers in order to express their lack of rights or feelings. It is, of course, correct and natural to say that a factory has no rights or feelings, so the qualifier—without rights or feelings—will primarily apply to the workers.

In (A), the workers are seen as animals, which does not deny their feelings and is an unlikely view of a factory. (B) is strong because in equating the workers and factories to machinery, the workers' rights and feelings are denied. (C) fails since beings likely do have the rights and feelings which the sentence says were denied. (D) and (E) are acceptable since they both conform to the idea that there is something that has no rights or feelings.

The second blank must be filled with a word that relates the use to which we would expect a monopoly capitalist of the early 1900's might put to something that had no rights or feelings. The capitalist clearly wishes to increase his profits; thus (B) is superior to (D) or (E). (D)'s use of the word guarantee is deceptive. While the capitalist would certainly like to guarantee his profits, there is no reason to suppose that the workers and factories, no matter how regarded by him, would, in fact, guarantee that he would have profits. Thus, that purpose, while desirable, would not be reasonably expected in this context. Thus, (B) is the best answer choice.

8. **(C)** The original pair, mouth and orifice, have the relationship that a mouth can be described physically as an orifice. Similarly, an ear can be described physically as a projection. All the other answer choices relate a sense to the type of thing sensed, such as a nose sensing odors. Thus, (C) is the best answer.

9. **(E)** A worker earns a bonus and the bonus is an extra, something over and above his regular earnings, a reward, say, for a job well done. (D) has some small attraction since one could conceive of a bonus as a spur to better efforts; however, to use the old image of the stick and the carrot, the spur is a stick to the horse, while the bonus is a carrot to the worker. Thus, (D) fails. (C) has winning in the second position, but that is a goal and not a reward, so (C) fails. (A), (B), and (E) are all attractive since they are all types of rewards or earnings. (A) and (B) are appealing since they continue the theme of monetary reward. However, when there is an overlapping situation, you must have an even more precise relationship. The dividends of the capitalist and the interest of the banker are their regualr receipts, while the similar idea for the worker would be his wages. Thus, (A) and (B) are not as good as (E), where the actor is receiving a reward, a "bonus" of applause. Also, it is a little difficult to tell the difference between (A) and (B). Thus, (E) is the best answer.

10. **(B)** Rigid and flexible are opposites that describe a physical property, and that are also used to describe personalities. (A) is eliminated since it is a pair of synonyms. (E) is eliminated since muscle and tone are not opposites, but an object (muscle) and a typical characteristic of it (tone). (D) is not a real pair of opposites, and therefore fails. This leaves (B) and (C). (C) is an example of something that is relatively unusual. (C) is wrong because it has the noun steel instead of the adjective steely, which would make it quite as good as (B). As written, however, (B) is the best answer.

11. **(B)** We have here another special word, gobble, which means to eat quickly and in large pieces. Guzzling is to drink quickly and in large draughts. A good first approximation of this relationship might have been that these are synonyms with differences of degree. This would eliminate (D) and possibly (E). (A), (B), and (C) all have the idea of the second term being a hurried form of the first, but then we have the additional concept of it being some sort of eating or drinking, and thus the idea of doing it in large pieces/draughts. Hence, (B) is the best answer.

12. **(C)** A sin requires forgiveness and a debt requires release. (A) is wrong since the two terms represent the same idea and do not, therefore, mirror the stem-pair relationship of having the second undo the first. The other answers also lack this idea. Thus, (C) is the only answer that carries out this idea of undoing, or forgiving. It is perfectly proper to speak of forgiving a debt, but it is not the only way of referring to the situation in which the debt is undone.

13. **(C)** The function of an anesthetic is to reduce or even obliterate sensation. The purpose of a muffler is to reduce or even obliterate sound. Note that one would use the meaning of muffler relating to sound and not that of the muffler which goes around the neck. (A) and (B) have no idea of the second word working against the first. (D) and (E) do share some of the idea with (C). In (E) we have, however, a vaccine, which is a preventative measure only, and in (D) we have a curative, or palliative, measure. Actually, a detoxicant is not necessarily correct for a particular poison. (E) is not as good as (C) because of the need to use the vaccine prior to the crisis, while an anesthetic could be used at any time. But even more important than any details of usage, sound is a sensation and the muffling of it is more like the idea of an anesthetic. One could even speak of muffling the pain.

14. **(D)** A holster is the special device which holds the gun in readiness for use. The scabbard is the special device which holds the sword in readiness for use. All the answer choices have the idea of

the first term being in the second one. However, (A), (B), and (C) lack the idea of a weapon, and in (E) the cannon is itself the weapon. Thus, (D) is the best answer.

15. **(D)** A mist is a mild rain in that it is composed of the same material and does the same thing—make you wet—but does so very gently. A breeze is a mild wind and a gale is a strong one. (B) fails since it is a pair of opposites, not a matter of difference in degree. (A), (C), and (E) all have some idea of the two items being the same or similar, but a fog is a cloud, and the foam is not really a kind of sea. (C) is the second-best answer choice since both snow and hail are made of ice. However, while hail might be seen as icier than snow, a rain is not really wetter than mist. More to the point, snow is not necessarily as gentle as a mist or breeze are. Thus, (D) is the best answer choice.

16. **(D)** A pharmacist prepares drugs, just like a chef prepares foods. None of the other answer choices have the idea of the first term being in charge of the creation and preparation of the second term.

17. **(C)** The author first uses a comparison to the Arabian Nights as a positive example, and then uses music and poetry in the streets as an example of true bliss. At the end he refers to artists having "fair and noble" designs. The focus on reality should not be seen as antithetical to arts, which can be seen as mirrors of reality rather than as "mere" fictions.

(E), perhaps the second-best answer, fails because there is no reluctance to be found in the admiration. The indifference, suspicion, and repulsion in the passage are all for lies and fictions, not art, thus (A), (B), and (D) fail.

18. **(C)** The end of the first paragraph equates experience with failure, an unusual thought that should stand out to your eye. This directly eliminates (B) and (D), and argues for (C). (A) is wrong because it is in discernment that children excel, not in amount of knowledge, which the author feels may even interfere with discernment. (E) means that childhood sets many patterns for the adult that is to come, but here the author is saying that the adult is less able than the child.

19. **(A)** The first sentence says just what (A) says. (D) is incorrect because the reference to Arabian Nights is to show the wonder of reality. (B), (C), and (E) have no basis in the passage.

20. **(E)** The first sentence describes the situation that the author sees as actually going on in the world—delusions are seen as real and reality as delusion—everything is backward. Thus, (E) makes the best sense. Note that he is speaking of the perceptions of the actual reality. (A) is a common meaning of the word fabulous, but not the one used in this sentence. The whole passage is about how to comprehend reality. Hence, (D) fails while (C) and (B) are entirely unrelated.

21. **(C)** In the last paragraph all the true and sublime are stated to be true now and the emphasis is on the value of properly and truly perceiving the present, hence (C) rather than (A), (B), or (D). (E) is an attempt to lure the unwary into thinking that children and Arabian Nights refers to leisure.

22. **(D)** The issues dealt with in the passage are the good, the true, and the soul—hence, (D). (C) and (A) have little connection to the passage. (B)'s word society connects, but population does not. (E)'s reference to the arts confuses the celebration with the cause for celebration.

23. **(B)** (B) is admittedly a little glib and has a lighthearted tone not entirely in keeping with the passage, but it is the only choice which conveys the meaning of the passage, albeit by using this expression somewhat differently than common usage does. The passage indicates that we can achieve what we see, but we will be limited by our false perceptions of the world if we let ourselves be blinded. The universe's answering to our perceptions is just that—the limits are set by us, not the universe.

(A) plays on the universe-answering idea; however, physical control is not the issue, but rather spiritual matters. (C) is opposite to the theme of the passage and a trap for those who think of any reference to Eastern religion as meaning all is fated. (D) plays with the fast and slow tracks, which we may choose, but it is not physical speed, but mental life which is referred to. Perceiving fully makes us experience more and more quickly. (E) is simply false since the last sentence has posterity, in fact, doing what the poet conceived.

Questions 24–27

Since several of the questions turn on somewhat similar parts of the passage, it is simplest first to discuss them together to some extent. The change in the ranking of the causes of death does not, by itself, indicate that there has been any change in the rates of any particular disease. If pneumonia, for instance, continued at the same rate, a large increase in heart disease, for example, could cause heart disease to become ranked higher than pneumonia. Conversely, a constant rate of heart disease combined with a drastically falling rate of pneumonia could cause the same change in rankings. In fact, any absolute movement of either of the two diseases is compatible with the change in rank order, provided that the other disease rate changes in the proper fashion. However, there is one other significant fact about the changes in the diseases which is mentioned in the passage: the diseases of the old have become the top-ranked causes of death. Either the old are dying much more rapidly or the young are dying much less rapidly. Since we do know, as common knowledge, that the population of the United States has increased significantly over the period 1900–1945, it is clear that the young people are dying less frequently—that is, there is less death than before. Let us now consider the specific problems.

24. **(B)** Since the diseases that are most common now are those of advanced years, this implies (B) rather directly. (A) and (E) are clearly not within the scope of the passage and are thus untenable, based on the passage. Sadly, (D) is not true in the real world, but, more importantly, the descending of tuberculosis on the ranking of causes of death does appear to mean that it is less common, but it does not mean that it is all but eliminated, which is a very strong statement and not at all supported in the passage. (C) has some real merit since fatal accidents are part of the list which is referred to as being typical of the advanced years. Thus, you must determine whether (B) or (C) is best. Both suffer from the difficulty that the paragraph only deals with causes of death, while the answer choices concern total medical practice or total "accident-proneness." In order to distinguish these answer choices, one must ask which of the two is least likely to lead to the mortality statistics cited. Since (B) merely says that many problems are, while (C) compares older and younger persons, in the absence of any statement in the passage about younger persons, (B) is less demanding and thus the best answer.

25. **(A)** The form of the question stem tells us that four of the answer choices will be strongly indicated and one will not be indicated as strongly. The correct answer choice may not be indicated either because it refers to some information that is not in the passage or because the passage makes it clear that the choice is false.

   As developed in the general discussion above, the passage does seem to imply that young persons are suffering from less disease than the elderly. However, despite the fact that mortality statistics are being used, there is no reference to debilitating disease as opposed to other disease. This is probably a true statement in the world, but it is not indicated in the passage. Thus, (A) is the answer we seek. The other answers are all indicated, as developed in the general discussion.

26. **(D)** (D) is known to be true from the data presented and the judgment of the author that the changes in the period 1910–1945 are referred to as being profound.

   (A) fails since nothing is stated about infant mortality. (B) fails for the same lack of reference in the passage. (C) is a typical wrong answer in that it overstates a piece of evidence in the passage. All that is said in the passage is that this data would span the possible early and late practice of certain physicians, but it does not state

that the data is from those physicians. (E) fails, of course, when (D) succeeds.

27. **(C)** As the general discussion above notes, there is some inference that the relative changes in the causes of death were a function of the young dying less frequently rather than of the old dying more frequently. In short, the argument is that more people are living long enough to suffer from diseases that afflict the elderly. This argument is not absolutely dominant, but it is strong enough to support (C). (A) fails since the first decade of the period did not show as profound a change as the last 35 years. (B) fails because of the word steadily. We have no information about how these changes operated between the dates cited. (D) and (C) are arguable, as noted above, but (C) is a better choice.

28. **(C)** Restitution means to return something that one had taken, probably wrongly. Deprivation means to take something away from someone, and there is some idea of the action not being good. None of the other answers speaks at all to the issue of taking or giving. Inflation means getting bigger, like a balloon or prices; a cataclysm is a catastrophe; and the constitution of something is its makeup or its ingredients; anonymity means literally having no name (from the Greek *onyma* and thus being unknown in one's true self. Although constitution shares a considerable number of letters with restitution, knowledge of prefixes could help you if you needed it. *Con-* means with and *re-* means again. These are not really opposite ideas and thus you should not be tempted by constitution.

29. **(B)** Parsimony is thriftiness. Free spending is a perfect opposite. The others are unconnected. To ape means to imitate without understanding, so acting apishly would be acting imitatively, without understanding. Frugality is a synonym of parsimony, though not as strong. Modish would simply mean fashionable, so the result is not opposite to parsimony.

30. **(E)** Perspicuity means mental sharpness, and mental dullness is a perfect opposite. Perspicacious is the adjective and is somewhat more common than the noun given in the problem. Some of the other answer choices refer to mental attributes, but none to the same attribute.

31. **(D)** Preposterous means directly contrary to reason or good sense, and comes from a root meaning with the back part foremost. Something that is credible is inherently believable and sensible. The connection is not perfect, but preposterous does have the connotation of unbelievability that is directly related to its primary meaning.

   Complaisant means agreeable in the sense of being willing to go along with someone else's plans or ideas. This is not a matter of whether something is believable. Conceited means having an exaggerated opinion of one's own worth. Sincere, like complaisant, has a vague connection to preposterous. Sincere means truthful and with full intention to mean what you say. A sincere statement is perhaps more believable than an insincere one, which is probably meant to mislead. This is not the same as saying that something is inherently believable or not.

32. **(D)** Sanctimony is hypocritical devoutness. Thus, devout refers to the real thing, and sanctimonious describes a false show of religious feeling. Impervious, meaning unable to be breeched or broken through, might appeal to an echo of sanctuary, but that is a different word from sanctimony.

33. **(A)** To extirpate something means to hunt it down and destroy it utterly. To preserve something is an active stance of helping the thing to survive—a perfect opposite. To inseminate is to either fertilize or to put something where it can grow, which only establishes the capacity for growth; to ingratiate is to act so as to obtain the gratitude and favor of someone else, but usually in a petty or unworthy way; daub means to smear with.

34. **(B)** Capricious is whimsical and arbitrary changing, presumably for little or no reason. Constant means to be steady and sure, and always the same. Phlegmatic means to have a slow or apathetic nature, to not be easily excited. Naturally, a phlegmatic person will not be too likely to be capricious since he will not likely do much of anything or change much from his apathy. However, this is a derivative meaning and, while possessing some real merit as an answer choice, is not nearly as good as constant, which addresses the heart of the matter, the changeability. Ignominious means disgraceful and unworthy.

35. **(D)** Casuistry is the misapplication of general ethical principles and often has the connotation of being a deliberate misapplication, and thus a lie or deceit. Verity is not a perfect opposite, but at least it opposes the deceitful aspects of casuistry. This is not a problem that provides many clues for guessing. If you had an echo of its being an ignoble or bad thing, then the first three answer choices would not be attractive. Do not confuse sediment, meaning precipitated deposits at the bottom of a liquid, with sentiment, meaning feeling.

36. **(C)** Contumely is a humiliating insult. Despite the *-ly* ending, it is a noun and not an adverb. When there is a mixture of word types in the answer choices, you might think twice before relying only on a word ending to make eliminations. There are a number of words which have misleading endings, and some may appear on the test.

Praise is the best opposite to insult. Tractability means the ability to be easily directed onto a particular course or track.

37. **(B)** Sedulous means to be very conscientious in taking care of duty. To be derelict in one's duty is to abandon it and fail to carry it out. Vociferous means loud and assertive; concomitant means typically accompanying; itinerant means traveling; and onerous, from onus, means difficult and burdensome.

38. **(D)** Imperturbable is a good example of a word whose word parts can help you to understand it. The stem portion of this word is perturb, which means disturb, so imperturbable means undisturbable, calm. Thus, agitated, meaning in motion and, by extension, upset or disturbed, is a nearly perfect opposite. Militant means aggressive or combative; cynical is distrustful of other people's motives; conical means shaped like a cone; and flattering means something which puts you in the best light and makes the best of what you have.

SECTION II

1. **(B)** If Gene dashed across the courtyard, he might have run quickly; but since he didn't take time to think of his safety, courageously is better. Quickly only repeats what the dash already says.

2. **(A)** The loss of the *Titanic* is best described as a tragedy or a disaster. Precautions, not reservations, is the second word that is required, making (A) the correct response.

3. **(C)** As the Earth's resources are not limitless, worthless, or unavailable, only (C) logically completes this sentence.

4. **(E)** A meek spirit may comfort or console people, but it won't delight them. A juvenile spirit is immature and thus is also inappropriate. A youthful spirit, however, may be mature as well as vigorous.

5. **(B)** According to the sense of this sentence, it was merciful, not unintentional, blithe, importunate, or tragic, that the factories remained open.

6. **(C)** It follows that a hush or a quiet about an estate would concern the guards, not a pall, focus, coolness, or talent.

7. **(C)** The sentence structure tells us that one type of book is interesting but another is only good for the blank. The blank, then, is some characteristic of books that are not interesting. Furthermore, this special function of being uninteresting is

carried out near a bedside table, in other words in bed. The likely function is to help one to get to sleep, a notorious effect of uninteresting books; thus soporific, which means something that makes one sleepy, is the ideal answer. All of the other answers are ideas which could apply to books, but not particularly because they are uninteresting or at the side of a bed. Thus, (C) is the best answer.

8. **(C)** In karate the foot is a weapon. In fencing the foil—a type of sword—is a weapon. (B) has an echo of hand to foot in the second position, but this is just flack and has no merit. In (D), the ring is the arena, not any sort of equipment, thus it fails. In (A), which appeals at first because of the relationship between karate and judo, we could have had a relationship based on the fact that karate uses the foot as a weapon and judo uses the hand as a weapon. This would have some appeal even though it is not strictly accurate. However, the term chop does not refer to the weapon, but the movement of the weapon. In fencing, the equivalent of the judo chop would be the thrust or parry. Thus, (A) fails for addressing a different part of the process involved. (E) is probably the second-best answer, though it is quite poor. A bat is a piece of equipment used in the sport of baseball, but this does not say it is better than (C), but only shares some merit with (C). In addition to that equipment aspect, (C) has the idea of weapon, which is important since both karate and fencing are combat sports.

9. **(E)** The incisor and the molar are both teeth. The difference is that they have different functions. The incisor cuts and the molar grinds. The knife cuts and the hammer, being blunt like the molar, bashes and breaks up things, even if it does not quite grind. (A) is attractive since it would result in a completed analogy with four teeth. However, the canines do not cut, but rather rip, and the bicuspids are not molars but work more like the canines. It is still attractive, but does not fit very precisely. (C) is eliminated since both incisors and molars are upper and lower. (D) fails since an incisor and molar will have a much more complex relationship than merely being opposites. Even though incisive can mean sharp in a mental sense, one would not speak of someone being a molar-mind to mean they are foolish. (B) and (E) both present tools which could relate to the original pair's functions. The first word in both (B) and (E) is fine. In (B), however, the second word, file, has little to do with the action of the molars. Hammer, in (E), is not perfect, but is at least the action of a blunt instrument like the molar.

10. **(E)** Both the gourmand and the gourmet are interested in food. The gourmand is interested in quantities of food, while the gourmet is interested in the quality of food. Thus (D) expresses,

in admittedly abstract terms, the relationship between the original pair quite well. The only problem is that it is backward. However, (E) is even better since the difference between the two types of eaters is that the one will eat anything while the other, because he is interested in quality, will be selective. So the sharper difference is the indiscriminate eater versus the selective eater. Wisdom disqualifies (A), and (B) and (C) are totally unrelated. The specific food is irrelevant.

11. **(E)** A tress of hair is a lock of hair. A skein of wool is an amount of wool, probably more than a tress's worth of hair, but at least it is a special word for describing an amount. (D) does not have the relationship of an "amount" word to the thing of which there is an amount. (A), (B), and (C) are all "amount" or group words. (C) is a group word, like a gaggle of geese, and that is not the same as an amount of something. The best distinction between (A), (B), and (E) is that wool is hair and thus a tress is a collection of thin fibers (of probably human hair), and a skein is a collection of thin fibers (of wool). The other words refer to solid objects, which are a piece of something, but tress and skein refer to something consisting of many little parts. Thus, (E) is the best answer.

12. **(D)** Libel and slander are both offensive statements that are presumably incorrect and untrue, even malicious. The difference between them is that libel is written and slander is spoken. (D) perfectly catches that difference in the abstract. (A) has some of the same distinction, but is backward. Both parts of (B) and (E) refer to written work. (C) is irrelevant. Thus, (D) is the best answer.

13. **(B)** A colander is a kitchen utensil that is used to drain water off of or out of something. A sifter separates the wheat from the chaff, although in that case the wheat is the part that falls through, and the waste product, chaff, remains in the sifter. (C), (D), and (E) lack the idea of separation of the useful part of something from the waste product or non-useful part. (A) has some idea of cleaning up, but the broom does not separate dust from, say, the floor in the same way that a sifter and colander do their work. The broom merely rubs the surface and brushes dust away. The sifting action is key to the utility of the colander. Thus, (B) is the best answer.

14. **(B)** A decibel is the unit used to measure sound. Similarly, the volt is used to measure electricity. Both decibel and volt measure the "force" of the sound and electricity, but this need not be considered since none of the other choices presents a measurement and the thing measured. A calorie is not a measure of weight, but of energy. The fact that a decibel is used to measure some

quantities other than sound and that a volt is not the only measure of electricity do not disqualify the choice, but merely make it less than perfect. (B) is still clearly the best answer choice.

15. **(B)** The original pair present opposites, which are positive and negative attributes in terms of intelligence. (E) fails for being synonyms, and (D) has much the same problem. (A) has some idea of mental ability and oppositeness, but even if it had scholarly rather than scholar, the oppositeness is not very precise, and the original pair are very precise opposites indeed. (C) has no opposite meaning. This leaves (B), which has precisely opposite parts and which also has a positive and negative connotation in the same direction as the original pair. Thus, (B) is the best answer.

16. **(D)** A queue is a line of people in a particular order, such as a line waiting to get something. All of the answer choices have the meaning of a grouping of things, but (A) and (B) are merely undifferentiated groupings. (E) has no feel of being a line of anything. (D) and (C) both have some idea of being stretched out, but (D) does this much more than (C). (E) presents the problem of the idea of order that is present in a queue. A file of letters need not be in order, but even if it is, the image of a queue, which is a physical concept, is much more like a string than a file.

17. **(C)** Since the excitation is the force leading to the occurrence of the response, and the inhibition is the force leading to the non-occurrence of the response, the fact that the response does not occur indicates that the inhibition is greater than the excitation. (B) and (D) are outside the scope of the passage, and thus incorrect. (A) fails since once a response does not occur, its latency period is not relevant, nor does it exist. (E) fails when (C) succeeds.

18. **(B)** Since the theory holds that there is always a finite amount of inhibition and that the inhibition can be increased by the right experimental actions, it can be inferred that there is always some possibility of getting the response to fail, given enough time and energy. In other words, continuing support is required, even if there can be occasional lapses.

(A) is incorrect since training can include training to reduce the response or to increase it at any point. After the twists and turns of (C) are plumbed, what it means is that responses might not differ, which is certainly possible. (D) is certainly possible, for the same reason that (B) is not. (E) is the second-best answer choice since the issue of measurement is not directly addressed in the passage. There is a finite amount of the two forces at all times. From that, it can be concluded that it can be measured, though we do not need to meet the claim that it is currently known how to measure it, but only that it is measurable in principle.

19. **(C)** Latency is, of course, defined in the passage, and the most usual situation would be for the correct answer to be either the passage's definition or some paraphrase of that. Sometimes, as in this case, the correct answer is a somewhat derived concept. If latency is the time that it takes for an action to occur after the stimulus is applied, then it is a measure of the tendency for the action not to occur at all. In addition, the passage itself explicitly says that there is such a connection; thus, (C) is the best answer. The others are all either not specifically related to the passage or wrong.

20. **(B)** The references to the shires and London are detailed and imply a closeness to hand. (A), France, is only mentioned with one reference, and thus is not as good as (B). America, (C), is only supported by a reference to North America, which is insufficiently detailed to override the English references. (D) is nowhere mentioned.

21. **(C)** The only trick here is to remember that the third line of a syllogism does not always have the word thus or its equivalent. The other methods are all in the passage, but not for this sort of reasoning. (See also the instructional materials for the Logical Reasoning questions).

22. **(B)** While it is true that the use of apples gives the story a pedestrian flavor, this is merely to exemplify the author's view that there is real reasoning even in very ordinary events. The apples are the subject of an analogy between the situation with them and all everyday reasoning, which is likened and explained through that example. (C) has a little merit, but (B) is far better since it goes with the basic ideas of the passage. (D) is attractive, but it is false since the author shows how common logic is, not how foolish. (A) and (E) are merely flack.

23. **(A)** While the answer choice of "philosopher" would be better yet, the scientist's reference to experimental method and logic make (A) the best available choice. All the others may use logic and experiment, of course, but the topic here is science—in the sense of its root, meaning knowing—not art, fiction, economics, or business, nor the distinguishing methods of those fields.

24. **(C)** The passage notes that you establish a natural law as the result of the induction in just those words—hence, (C). (D) and (E) are other meanings of the term natural law, but not the ones used in this particular passage. (A) and (B) have little connection to the passage.

25. **(E)** All the answer choices reflect part of the

passage, but (E) covers the largest portion of the passage, and thus is best. Each of the others can be subsumed under it since (A) is the example used, and (B), (C), and (D) are the methods of everyday reasoning brought out through the use of the example of apples.

26. **(D)** The law of apples is a construct based, as noted in the passage, on experimental verification of an induction. If further verification should show that the law is not perfect, then it must be modified as (D) suggests. (C) is particularly attractive, but the word usually makes it fail, since it is still the case that hard and green apples are usually sour. If (C) had said always, it would have been hard to refuse.

(A) is subsumed under (D) and is incorrect in supposing that the nature of apples has changed, when it is only that our original understanding of them proved to be inadequate. (B), while attractive in the real world, where tasty apples are all too rare, has little to do with standardized tests. Since (A), (B), and (C) are faulty, (E) does not apply.

27. **(C)** Extensive verification is brought up in the last part of the passage as something that makes an argument or proposed general law more attractive. Proposition I is just flack. There is nothing in the passage that says whether general laws are harder or easier to prove or disprove than any other kind of law. Proposition III is precisely what the passage does say. This is why the friend will find it persuasive for you to show him that the law has been tested in a variety of situations. Proposition II is a bit of precision reading that turns on the word tested. Tested means that something is put to some sort of test; it does not mean that the something passed the test. The reason that II is attractive is that a law or proposal that was not passing its tests would soon be dropped and no longer subjected to tests. Thus, there is a potential for erroneously leaping from the fact that something was widely tested to the conclusion that it passed most of its tests. This is, however, based on an idea not present in the passage.

28. **(C)** A profusion is a great number, even an overabundance. A scarcity is an excellent opposite. A travesty is a bizarre and vastly inferior imitation. Antidote, meaning something which counteracts some poison or disease, might have some appeal if profusion were misinterpreted to be a medical term of some sort.

29. **(E)** Temperate means moderate, but is not a general synonym for moderate. Temperate applies to passions, appetites, and temperature and has a special meaning of not drinking alcohol. This special meaning derives from the temperance movement and supports inebriated as an opposite.

A more general opposite, such as extreme, would be stronger, but is not present. Unlimited has some appeal since it has a non-moderate feel to it, but without limit is not as good as inebriated because temperate is not as general a word as is unlimited. This is a fairly tough choice. Truncated means cut off short.

30. **(A)** Mitigation means amelioration or lessening of some harm or evil. Aggravation means increasing some harm or evil—one would not speak of aggravating one's love for something. Verdancy means greenness, especially with plants. Imposition has some opposite feel to mitigation since mitigating a condition can reduce the burden or even lift the burden. But this is a derived, or two-step, connection, which is only rarely a sound basis for a correct answer.

31. **(B)** Iniquity means a gross injustice, hence evil. There is a definite moral tone. Fairness and rectitude are both strong answers. Fairness is a weaker level of moral correctness than is rectitude. Rectitude means great goodness, and iniquity means great evil. Apostasy is a total abandonment of one's principles or cause.

32. **(C)** A protuberance is something that sticks out. An indentation is the opposite since it is a portion of a surface that recedes or is forced inward. Recession itself has merit, but is a more general word in which one would speak of the entire sea or wave receding as opposed to a portion sticking out. Cadence is rhythmic modulation or the beat of something, usually a voice. A habitation is a place that is lived in or inhabited, such as a home or house.

33. **(A)** Effulgence means a bright shining or radiance. Murk is darkness. Harshness may erroneously appeal if effulgence is confused with indulgence. A mercenary is someone who is hired, usually to fight. Mundane means commonplace or ordinary.

34. **(B)** To ameliorate is to mitigate or make less severe, as in to ameliorate the effects of a disease. Worsen is the precise opposite. Dissemble means to deceive or lie.

35. **(D)** Benign means harmless or well intentioned. Evil is a clear opposite. Sick may appeal because of the association to benign tumors not usually being as serious as malignant tumors. Morose means sad.

36. **(A)** Salutary means healthful and noxious means unhealthful or even poisonous. Objectionable has a negative connotation which opposes the positive connotation of salutary, but there is no specific meaning of health. Moderate has no real connection. Neither does farewell, but it might be

attractive if you thought that salutary had something to do with a salute or greeting. Actually, a salute originally meant a wish for good health, but no longer. Antiseptic is, if anything, similar to the stem word.

37. **(C)** Alienate means, literally, to make an alien of someone, which is the opposite of making friends of them. (A) is an attempt to appeal to the oppositeness of alien and native, but alienate does not mean to go alien.

38. **(B)** A drollery is an amusing statement since droll means amusing. (D) has some appeal since witty has to do with drollness, perhaps. However, there is no necessary idea of a drollery being an aside.

SECTION III

1. **(D)** Since we do not know the value of any of the coins, we cannot know the value of 2, 3, 4, or even of a dozen coins. For that reason, our answer must be (D). We don't even know they are U.S. coins.

2. **(B)** Since the first equation shows only one variable, it makes sense to start our attack there, solving for x. If x + 7 = 8, then x = 1. Once we know that x = 1, we can substitute that value into the second equation:

$$x + y = 6$$
$$1 + y = 6$$
$$y = 5$$

Now that we have determined that x = 1 and y = 5, we can conclude that Column B is greater than Column A.

3. **(C)** The $\sqrt{9} = 3$. Thus the two columns must be equal. (Note that a printed $\sqrt{}$ sign should be interpreted as a positive root.)

4. **(D)** We can deduce that Jack is taller than Mike. But the information we are given does not allow us to reach any conclusion about the *difference* between their heights. Consequently, we do not know how much taller Jack is than Mike.

5. **(B)** Although we do counsel performing an indicated operation, e.g., multiplication, we have also cautioned against undertaking unwieldy or hopelessly complicated arithmetic or algebra. In this case, it would probably require too much time to perform the multiplication indicated in the right-hand column. A quick glance should show that there will be a n^4 term, some n^3's, some n^2's, some n's and 6. That realization shows that the multiplication is much too involved for the time allowed by the section. It also provides the

answer. We can see that even if we used just the last two expressions, we sould have $n^2 + 5n + 6$. The expression in Column A is only $3n + 6$. Since n> 1, more n's makes Column B greater than Column A.

6. **(C)** Since there are three feet in a yard, the radius of the circle mentioned in Column A is equal to the radius of the circle mentioned in Column B. Circles with radii which are equal must have areas which are equal, so our answer is (C). You did not need to compute the areas and should not have tried until trying this method.

7. **(A)** The negative of a negative number is a positive number. So the negative of negative 4 is a positive 4. Column B is negative while Column A is positive, so Column A must be the larger.

8. **(C)** This is a variation on the standard children's riddle, "Which weighs more, a pound of feathers or a pound of lead?" Of course, they both weigh the same. A pound of any substance is a pound. Surprisingly, however, just such a problem has appeared on the GRE, so we remind students of the importance of carefully reading each question.

9. **(A)** We must begin by determining the greatest integer or whole number less than −10. Since the larger the absolute value (the numerical value) of a negative number, the smaller the actual value of that number, the greatest integer which is less than −10 is −11. That is the largest integer which is still less than −10. When we square −11, we get a positive 121. So Column A is greater than Column B.

10. **(B)** Try to find a way of comparing the fractions without doing extra work. We can reduce $\frac{34}{68}$ to $\frac{1}{2}$. Then, when we square $\frac{1}{2}$, Column A becomes $\frac{1}{4}$ while Column B is $\frac{1}{2}$, so Column B is greater. Any number multiplied by a fraction gets smaller.

11. **(C)** In this case, before performing any multiplication, we must try to cancel like terms. This simplifies the problem to such an extent that no multiplication is really needed:

$$1/2 \times 2/3 \times 3/4 \times 4/5 = x$$
$$1/5 = x$$

And our two columns are equal.

12. **(C)** To discuss this problem clearly, let us add the points T and U. QR and SR are the same for both perimeters, so we don't need to consider them further. The same applies to ST and QU. This leaves the four sides of PUVT. PUVT must be a rectangle since angle P and angle V are right angles. Since PUVT is a rectangle, the opposite sides are equal, which is to say that PT = UV and

UP = RS. Thus the two perimeters are equal.

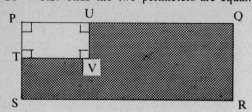

13. **(A)** In this problem it is best to do the indicated operation in Column A so that the comparison is easier.

$$-2(-x - 2) = 2x + 4$$

Now we can strip the 2x from both sides of the comparison (technically by subtracting 2x from both sides). Then we are left comparing +4 in Column A with −4 in Column B, so Column A must be greater.

14. **(D)** The common information simply makes both x and y positive and greater than 1. This means that both columns are positive. You are always trying to see what connections can be made between the quantities in the two columns. In this case, it is possible for x to equal y. In that case we would have x² versus 2x, which is a (D) answer.

Another approach, which is also quite effective and efficient in this sort of problem, is substitution. When you are considering substitution, you should be choosing numbers that are both easy to compute with and usefully varied. Normally, positive and negative numbers are good to substitute with; but we only have positive numbers, so we want to use numbers at the ends of our available range. Since x and y can be equal, it is easiest to start the substituting with both the same. First try 1.1 for each, which yields (1.1)(1.1) = 1.21 in Column A and 1.1 + 1.1 = 2.2 in Column B. Since B is greater, answer choices (A) and (C) are eliminated.

A second substitution could be 10, yielding (10)(10) = 100 in Column A and 10 + 10 = 20 in Column B. Since A is larger, that eliminates B as an answer choice, leaving (D).

15. **(D)** We cannot assume that the figure is a square:

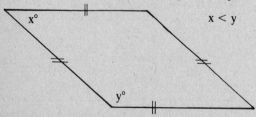

Still, all four sides are equal, but x is not equal to y.

16. **(B)** There is no mystical math formula which you

are supposed to know in order to solve this problem. It is merely a matter of counting up the possibilities. Thus there are four ways of getting nine as the problem specifies. (8 + 1 is the same thing as 1 + 8.)

17. **(A)** This problem asks you to divide feet and inches. You could convert the whole length into inches, getting 93 inches divided by three and giving an answer of 31 inches, or 2 feet 7 inches. Alternatively, you could divide three into seven feet, getting two feet, and then carry the other foot over into the inches as 12 inches. Twelve inches plus the nine inches is 21 inches, which yields seven inches when divided by three. The latter approach is a little more direct, but also has more opportunities for error.

18. **(D)** Since all three variables are integers, we know that K is a number that is both a perfect square and a perfect cube (perfect means that a number is the square or cube of an integer). Eight and 27 are not perfect squares and 4 is not a perfect cube. 64 does work, since $8^2 = 4^3 = 64$.

19. **(D)** The only formula for the area of a triangle that you need on this test is A = bh/2. The base is the distance from R to S, which is 7 units. The height is the distance from T to the Y axis, which is 5 units. Using the formula we get (7)(5)/2 = 17.5 units.

20. **(D)** Since the test will permit only one answer to be correct, give the choices a once-over to try and find some simple answer. (D) is it since 3 can be cancelled from the top and bottom of the fraction to give P/Q. (C) may have some attraction, but it yields (P/Q)² not P/Q.

21. **(A)** Since ACB is a straight line, ∠ACD + ∠DCE + ∠ECB = 180°. You are told that $\overline{DC}$ is perpendicular to $\overline{CE}$, which means that ∠DCE = 90°. If ∠ACD = x°, then the first equation looks like this: x° + 90° + ∠ECB = 180°. Moving x and the 90° to the right leaves ∠ECB = 180° − 90° − x = 90° − x.

22. **(E)** Knowing the length of the hypotenuse of a right triangle does not tell you what the sides are as the diagrams below indicate:

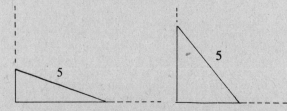

There might be some temptation to think that because the hypotenuse is 5, the other two sides must be 3 and 4. However, 3, 4, and 5 represent a special case of the right triangle not because they are the only solutions with a hypotenuse of 5, but because they are the only way to have the lengths of the sides be integers. The following is an acceptable right triangle with a hypotenuse of 5: $5^2 = (\sqrt{5})^2 + (\sqrt{20})^2$; so the sides could be 5, $\sqrt{5}$, $\sqrt{20}$.

23. **(A)** Taxes are 12% of monthly income. If monthly income is $650, then taxes are 12% × $650 = $78.00.

24. **(D)** In a pie chart, the entire circle represents 100%. The total number of degrees around the center of a circle is 360. Thus 100% = 360°. Clothing, taxes, and transportation total 35%. 35% × 360° = 126°.

25. **(C)** It is important to note that the boy answered all of the questions. This gives you a way of relating the total correct answers and total wrong answers. Before setting up a system of equations, let us try a shortcut. The heart of the matter is that the boy did not get them all right. If he had gotten them all right, he would have scored 100. If he missed one, then he would have lost the 4 plus points AND he would have another point taken off. This means that, compared to 100, he loses 5 points for each of the 25 problems he got wrong instead of right. Since he actually scored 70, he actually lost 30 points. 30 points divided by 5 points per error means he made 6 errors. 25 questions − 6 errors leaves 19 correct. A system of equations would look like this:

Let x = number of questions correct. 25 − x = number of questions wrong.
$$\text{Then } 4x - 1(25 - x) = 70$$
$$4x - 25 + x = 70$$
$$5x = 95$$
$$x = 19$$

26. **(D)** The temptation here is to simply average 40 MPH and 60 MPH and choose the wrong answer, (E). The reason that you cannot just average the speeds is that speed is PER HOUR and the hours are different. The trip took longer at 40 MPH than at 60 MPH. A speed is a fraction with some number of miles on top and some number of hours underneath. If you travelled for one hour at 40 MPH and one hour at 60 MPH, then you would have gone 100 miles in 2 hours and would have averaged 50 MPH. This case is very different.

You should think of what information you need to compute an average rate of speed. You need the total miles and you need the total time. To find the total time and hours, you have to add together the time and the hours respectively for the two legs of the trip, and then make the division of miles per hour.

Let the number of miles traveled each way = M

$$\text{The time going} = \frac{\text{distance}}{\text{rate}} = \frac{M}{60}$$

$$\text{The time coming} = \frac{M}{40}$$

$$\text{Total time for round trip} = \frac{M}{60} + \frac{M}{40}$$

$$= \frac{2M + 3M}{120} = \frac{5M}{120} = \frac{M}{24}$$

Average rate =

$$\frac{\text{total distance}}{\text{total time}} = \frac{2M}{\frac{M}{24}} = 48 \text{ miles per hour.}$$

27. **(D)** The total work that is to be done is six tractors times 8 hours = 48 tractor-hours of work.

Four tractors will thus take $\frac{48 \text{ tractor-hours}}{4 \text{ tractors}} = 12$ hours.

28. **(E)** In comparing fractions, one important separation is between the fractions which are larger than 1 and those which are smaller. (B), $\sqrt{5}$, is larger than 1. All the others have bottom parts larger than their tops and thus are smaller than 1. (A), (C), and (E) can be compared directly since they all have the same top, 1. When fractions have the same top, the largest bottom will denote the smaller fraction since the same quantity is being divided into more parts. $5\sqrt{5} > 5 > \sqrt{5}$; therefore, (E) is smaller than (A) or (C) or, as previously established, (B). All that remains is to compare (E) to (D). (E) has both a larger bottom and a smaller top than (D) and thus (E) is smaller. Note that, in this case, you did not have to actually compute the values of any of the possibilities.

29. **(A)** Since your money available with which to buy melons is in cents, it is probably easiest to put the price of melons into cents as well. The cost of melons is $\frac{100d \text{ cents}}{30 \text{ melons}}$, which is to say $\frac{100d}{30}$ cents per melon. We know that the purchasing power of our 80 cents will be 80 cents divided by the cost per melon. We now have the cost per melon and can go ahead.

$$\frac{80 \text{ cents}}{\frac{100d \text{ cents}}{30 \text{ melon}}}$$

To divide by a fraction, the rule is to invert the fraction and multiply: 80 cents $\times \dfrac{30 \text{ melon}}{100d \text{ cents}} = \dfrac{2400 \text{ melon}}{100d \text{ cents}} = \dfrac{24}{d}$ melon. Those partial to the ratio method might work this way: Let x = the number of melons you can buy for 80 cents. Then $\dfrac{30}{100d} = \dfrac{x}{80}$, 100dx = 2400, and $x = \dfrac{24}{d}$.

30. **(B)** Consecutive odd numbers, where n is an integer, may be represented as

$$2n + 1$$
$$2n + 3$$
$$\underline{2n + 5}$$

Sum = 6n + 9

Always divisible by 3. Thus, only II.

The key is to remember that an odd number is always one more than an even number. Another, similar approach would be to represent the three numbers as x + (x + 2) + (x + 4) = 3x + 6, which is always divisible by 3.

SECTION IV

1. **(A)** The simplest approach is to substitute (−1) for x:

Col. A: $x^3 + x^2 - x + 1 = (-1)^3 + (-1)^2 - (-1) + 1$
$= -1 + 1 + 1 + 1$
$= 2$

Col. B: $x^3 - x^2 + x - 1 = (-1)^3 - (-1)^2 + (-1) - 1$
$= -1 - 1 - 1 - 1$
$= -4$

You might have omitted the x^3 term in evaluating each column since it is the same in each column.

2. **(C)** Setting the edge length as e, we get:

Col. A   Col. B
$e^3 = 27$ $6e^2 = 54$
$e = 3$ $e^2 = 9$
        $e = 3$

3. **(A)** You know it cannot be (D) since it is all numbers. In addition, looking, as always, for connections between the columns, you see that the two columns are reciprocals. So knowing one will give you the other. You could calculate Column A, for instance:

$$\frac{1}{2} + \frac{1}{3} = \dfrac{\dfrac{3 + 2}{6}}{\dfrac{2}{3}}$$

$$= \dfrac{\dfrac{5}{6}}{\dfrac{2}{3}}$$

$$= \dfrac{\dfrac{15}{12}}{1} \quad \text{multiplying numerator}$$
$$\text{and denominator by } \tfrac{3}{2})$$

$$= \dfrac{15}{12}$$

But you don't need to do this if you can see that in Column A the top of the fraction ($\frac{1}{2} + \frac{1}{3}$) is bigger than the bottom ($\frac{2}{3}$). That means Column A is > 1, and Column B, its reciprocal, must be < 1, giving answer (A).

4. **(B)** When you square a fraction, you are multiplying it by a fraction, so it gets smaller. Conversely, taking the square root of a fraction or other number between zero and +1 gets larger. Thus:

$$.02 = \sqrt{.0004}$$
$$\sqrt{.02} > \sqrt{.0004}$$

5. **(C)** Since you have squares of the lengths of the sides and a right triangle, the Pythagorean Theorem should leap to mind. Column A is the hypotenuse squared, so we must see if Column B is the sum of the squares of the other two sides. $(AC)^2$ is one side squared and 5CB is the other because CB = 5.

6. **(A)** This is not a computational question. The real issue is noticing how the two figures would fit together. As the diagram below makes clear, the circle is much larger.

7. **(B)** Column B is simply the distance from −1 to +5, which is 6. For Column A we can construct a right triangle in this way:

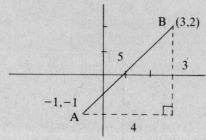

As often is the case, it is a 3–4–5 right triangle, leaving Column A as 5. Thus, (B) is the answer.

8. **(D)** If we had been told the two bottom angles of the triangle, ∠B and ∠C, were equal, then we would know x = y by subtraction from the straight line. As it is, the knowledge that ∠C = ∠A does not tell us anything about ∠B, which we would need in order to know x.

9. **(C)** Since the heights and bases of the triangle DEC and the parallelogram are the same, △DEC is equal in area to one-half the parallelogram.

Therefore, the area of △DEC equals the combined areas of △ADE and △EBC.

10. **(D)** Nothing is tying down B or C, so the joints are flexible and no fixed relationship between ∠B and ∠C is to be found.

11. **(D)** While both sides are positive, since a negative squared is positive, no size information is given. For example a could be −1 and b could be 2 or a could be −1 and b could be 12.

12. **(D)** We only know that both r and t are the same sign, but no magnitudes are known.

13. **(A)** This is one of the rare Quantitative Comparison computational problems. Shaded areas are usually found by subtracting one area from another or by addition. Here, the shaded area is the outer circle minus the inner one.

$$\begin{pmatrix} \text{Area of} \\ \text{shaded} \\ \text{portion} \end{pmatrix} = \begin{pmatrix} \text{Area of} \\ \text{larger} \\ \text{circle} \end{pmatrix} - \begin{pmatrix} \text{Area of} \\ \text{smaller} \\ \text{circle} \end{pmatrix}$$

$$= \pi(10^2) - \pi(7^2)$$
$$= 100\pi - 49\pi$$
$$= 51\pi$$

$$\begin{pmatrix} \text{Area of} \\ \text{smaller} \\ \text{circle} \end{pmatrix} = \pi r^2$$
$$= \pi(7^2)$$
$$= 49\pi$$
$$51\pi > 49\pi$$

14. **(C)** No calculation is needed. Just set it up: $(4)(\frac{1}{100})(\frac{3}{1000})$ versus $(3)(\frac{1}{100})(\frac{4}{1000})$.

15. **(C)** Since PR = PQ, angles PRQ and PQR are equal. Since ∠PRQ = x and ∠PQR = y, x = y as well.

AB ‖ DF and BD ‖ FG, but x° ≠ y°.

16. **(A)** The dimensions of the open box become:

length = 24 − 10 = 14 in.
width = 18 − 10 = 8 in.
height = 5 in.
V = h · l · w

Hence, V = 14 · 8 · 5 = 560 cu. in.

17. **(B)** VT = 32 feet so that ST = $\frac{1}{2}$TV = 16 feet. Thus, in right triangle QST, the legs are 12 = 4(3) and 16 = 4(4), so that hypotenuse QT = 4(5) = 20 feet. Add 1 foot for the extension and we get QR = 21 feet.

18. **(C)** Form the proportion $\frac{\frac{3}{4}}{9} = \frac{\frac{7}{8}}{x}$, where x is the side is miles. Then $\frac{3}{4}x = \frac{7}{8} \cdot 9$. Multiply both sides by 8.

$$6x = 7 \cdot 9 = 63$$
$$x = 10\tfrac{1}{2} \text{ miles}$$

Area = $x^2 = \frac{21}{2} \cdot \frac{21}{2} = \frac{441}{4} = 100\tfrac{1}{4}$ square miles.

19. **(D)** The tens digit of a number has a place value which is ten times the value of the digit. Hence, the number may be represented as 10t + u.

20. **(C)** Highest point of curve occurred in February, when it reached 600.

21. **(A)** Highest was 600.
Lowest was about 450.

Ratio = $\frac{600}{450} = \frac{4}{3}$

22. **(E)** From July '65 to Sept. '66, the average dropped from 525 to 450, about 75 points, which was the steepest decline.

23. **(E)** 5 is written ten times in the units column of the pages: 5, 15 . . . 95; and ten times in the tens column: 50, 51 . . . 59.

24. **(A)** The key here is to focus on the minute hands alone. The fast clock gains 24 minutes. The slow clock loses 12 minutes. The fast clock reads 12:24. The slow clock reads 11:48.

25. **(B)** The divisors of 28 are 14, 7, 4, 2, 1. The sum of these is 28, making it a perfect number. This does not apply to the other numbers listed.

26. **(C)** Let x = number of minutes per period. There are 4 class periods and 3 passing periods from 9 A.M. to 11:51 A.M., or in 2 hr. 51 minutes. Hence:

$$4x + 3(5) = 120 + 51$$
$$4x = 15 = 171$$
$$4x = 156$$
$$x = 39$$

27. **(E)** Since the perimeter involves 3 fenced-in sides, it is true that L + 2W = 90. Also, the area is LW. If we solve the first equation for L, we obtain L = 90 − 2W. Now substitute in area = LW, giving area = W(90 − 2W) = 90W − 2W². Let W = 20 in this equation, giving area = 1000. Hence, A, B, C, D are all true.
   Now substitute L = W in the first equation;
W + 2W = 90, 3W = 90, W = 30
When W = 30, area = 90(30) − 2(30²)
= 2,700 − 1,800 = 900
But this area is less than when W = 20.
   Hence, E is not true.

28. **(B)** Discount = 90 − 75 = $15
Rate of Discount = $\frac{15}{90} = \frac{1}{6} = 16\frac{2}{3}\%$

29. **(D)** The two semicircles make up the circumference of one circle of diameter 60 yd. Hence, the circumference = $\pi60$. The sum of the two lengths of the rectangle is 200. Thus, the perimeter is equal to $200 + 60\pi$.

30. **(D)** No matter what happens, x cannot quite equal the sum of the other two sides, or 10. If $\angle P = 90°$, then we have a 45–45–90 right triangle, so $x = 5\sqrt{2}$. Any time you have a range on the GRE, you need concern yourself only with the ends of the range.

SECTION V

Questions 1–3

Arranging the Information

This is clearly a process situation with some element of transformation since one puts in one color of token and gets another. Thus, a labelled-arrow method seems appropriate. The restriction that a player may possess only one token at a time is not essential in making the diagram, but must be kept in mind for the questions.

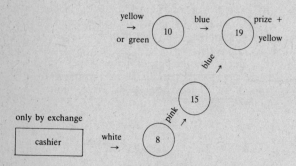

Answering the Questions

1. **(C)** There is no specification about getting a green token. (A) is specified in several ways. (B) is specified since the yellow token which is obtained with the prize can be used to get another prize. (D) is specified since any other color of token may start one enroute to a prize, and a yellow token may be obtained along with a prize. The most salient thing not specified is how to get your first token. However, the question does not present that as an available answer choice, so you must look for something else that is not specified, which is (C).

2. **(B)** After winning a prize, a player is in possession of one yellow token. (Remember, only one token per customer at a time.) With only a yellow token, a player cannot play slots 15, 19, or 8; so (C), (D), and (E) are wrong. (A) is incorrect since the cashier will not exchange a white token for a yellow token. (B) is possible since slot 10 uses yellow tokens.

3. **(E)** Just follow through the diagram. If you have a green token, you can go through the slots 10 and 19, or you can go and exchange the green token for a white one and go through that branch of the procedure, following up by going through the 10, 19 cycle. Thus, you can get whichever color of token you want. You could, of course, stop at any point and keep that token. The phrase all the other colors refers to all the other colors that are mentioned in the problem.

4. **(E)** The main point of the advertisement is that you should not hesitate to buy Cold Springs water even though it is not imported. According to the ad, you will not be able to taste the difference. Thus, I is an assumption of the ad: "Neither you nor your guests will taste the difference," and it is explicitly mentioned. We know it is an assumption for if there were a taste difference, the appeal of the ad would be seriously undermined. III is an assumption, too—but it is hidden or suppressed. Implicit in the ad is a rebuttal to the objection: "Yes, but it is not imported?" Whether it is imported or not can have only to do with status since the ad also states (assumes) that the tastes of Cold Springs and imported waters are indistinguishable. II is not an assumption. Although it is mentioned that Cold Springs is bottled at the source, the ad does not depend on whether other imported or domestic waters are bottled. They could be bottled fifty miles away from the source, and that would not affect the appeal of the ad.

5. **(A)** The argument makes the rather outlandish assumption that the physical characteristics of the criminal dictate the kind of crime he will commit. But as unreasonable as that may seem in light of common sense, it *is* an assumption made by the speaker. (We did not make the assumption, he did.) II is not an assumption of the argument, since the paragraph specifically states that the killer was executed—he could not have escaped. III does not commit the blatant error committed by II, but it is still wrong. Although III might be a better explanation for the crimes now being committed than that proposed by our speaker, our speaker advances the explanation supported by I, not III. In fact, the speaker uses phrases such as "looks very much like" which tells us that he assumes there are two killers.

6. **(E)** The ad is a little deceptive. It tries to create the impression that if hospitals are using Dr. John's Milk of Magnesia, people will believe it is a good product. But what the ad actually says is that Dr. John uses the same *ingredient* that hospitals use (milk of magnesia is a simple suspension of magnesium hydroxide in water). The ad is something like an ad for John's Vinegar which claims it has "acetic acid," which is vinegar. I falls into the trap of the ad and is therefore wrong. II is not inferable since there may be treatments other than milk of magnesia for these disorders. Finally, since I is incorrect, III must certainly also be incorrect. Even if I had been true, III might still be questionable since use and recommendation are not identical.

Questions 7–11

Arranging the Information

Since the transfer from clan to clan takes place upon reaching adulthood, a person can be referred to either by the clan into which they were born or by the one in which they are adults. The requirement that only mature Ater may marry simply keeps order. The basic information can be organized in this way

MEN		WOMEN	
BORN	ADULT	BORN	ADULT
1	2	1	3
2	3	2	1
3	1	3	2

Answering the Questions

7. **(A)** Answers (C) and (D) are flack and can be dismissed.

The nephew we are seeking is the son of a sister OR of a brother. Since marriage is permitted only within a clan, the question is whether the nephew can ever be the same clan.

The woman and her brother or sister would have been born into the same clan—the first. Sisters born into the first clan would both become third-clan adults and the son of a third-clan person becomes a first-clan adult and is not able to marry the third-clan adult woman who is the subject of the question. This eliminates (B).

A brother and sister born into the first clan would be in separate clans as adults, the woman moving to the third and the man to second. The brother's son would be born second clan and be a third-clan adult, who is eligible to marry his aunt. Hence, (A). (E) is eliminated by this reasoning also.

8. **(E)** An adult second-clan male was born into the first clan, thus, both parents must be first-clan adults. The father, as an adult first-clan male, must have been born third clan, which gives the answer (E). The mother, as a first-clan adult, must have been born into the second clan.

9. **(E)** Tracing the lineage:

BABY 3 → MOTHER 3 ADULT → 1 BORN → GRANDMOTHER 1 ADULT → 2 BORN → GREATGRANDMOTHER 2 ADULT → 3 BORN.

10. **(D)** Tracing the lineage possibilities:

GRANDDAUGHTER 2 ADULT → 3 BORN → (branch here)

because the subject of the question could be related through either the father or the mother of the granddaughter.

→ FATHER/SON ADULT 3 → BORN 2, AND THUS GRANDFATHER IS A 2 OR → MOTHER/DAUGHTER ADULT 3 → BORN 1, THUS GRANDFATHER IS A 1

Note that we are concerned only with the adult status of the subject of the question since he is clearly an adult now.

11. **(C)** I is inferable since a sister and brother are born into the same clan and move in different directions, they cannot marry each other.

II is inferable since a son will move out of his birth clan and his mother will stay in it. Thus, they cannot marry.

III is not inferable since it is possible for the grandson to be the same clan as the grandmother, and clan membership is the only restriction on who may marry whom. For example:

woman adult 3 → daughter born 3 → adult 2 → grandson born 2 → adult 3, same as grandmother.

Questions 12–16

Arranging the Information

This is similar to an elevator problem or any other sequence or arrival and departure problem. You can refer to the express stops as 1 through 8, with 3 and 6 not used. P gets off earlier than Q, with three on after 8.

10	20	30	40	50	60	70	80	
		xx			xx			3 left
		P < Q						

Answering the Questions

12. **(C)** J is M + 2. At first it seems as though M can get off anywhere except 30th and 60th (10th is not possible). But since there is the two-stop differential, J cannot get off at 10th, 20th, 30th, 50th, (because M can't leave at 30th), 60th, or 80th (because M can't get off at 60th). This leaves only 40th and 70th.

13. **(B)** The seeming addition of information actually does nothing except to specify which were the three who were still on the bus after 80th. There are four passengers and five available exit stops (20th, 40th, 50th, 70th, and 80th), so I and II are both possible. III however is not known for sure since the unused stop could have been any other available stop. Hence, (B).

14. **(D)** Learning that K and L got off before 80th, coupled with the information that P and Q also got off before 80th, means that J, M, and N are still on the bus. Thus, (A), (B), and (C) are true. The original information tells us that (D) must be false.

15. **(B)** If M precedes P, and therefore Q, this couples with the original information that P preceded Q to produce M P Q. Since Q had to wait through at least two available stops, he could not have exited at either 20th or 40th, but used 50th, 70th, or 80th, but the question stem rules out 70th, leaving (B).
    (A) is not necessarily true since the fourth departing passenger may have left at the same time as M, P, or Q.
    (C) is not necessarily true since P could have left as early as 40th. (D) and (E) fail since we do not even know that J left at all.

16. **(D)** We know from the original information that three of the original persons were still on the bus after 80th Street, so the answer cannot be (A) or (B).

    X enters on 20th and leaves at 50th, Y enters at 30th and leaves at 70th, but Z enters at 40th and leaves at 90th, thus, adding one to the three otherwise known to be on the bus after 80th. Hence, (D).

Questions 17–23

Arranging the Information

Previewing the question stems and the information set shows that the concern of this question is the schedule of events at the foundation. You really don't care what the names of the courses are, though the fact that three of them begin with E and two with P means that you need at least two letter abbreviations. Probably a syllable is best, so you can recognize the answer choices most easily.

Since the schedule is organized by the months of the year, the diagram should be too:

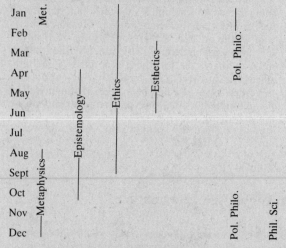

Answering the Questions

Most of these answers will be matters of checking the chart:

17. **(B)** February has the fewest available classes of any of the answer choices available. July also has only two classes, but is not an available answer choice.

18. **(D)** The phrase a single month refers to a single calendar month since that is the way that month is used in the problem. October and April both have four lectures in each month.

19. **(E)** The qualification "without overlap" is the key here. (A), (B), and (C) do not fill the year, and (D) fills the year with an overlap during January to April. (E) fills the year neatly.

20. **(A)** The simplest way to figure this out is just to take any one of the courses and then check the remaining months. Metaphysics covers August through January, leaving February through July. Epistemology covers April through June of that and Esthetics adds March, leaving only February uncovered. Hence, 11 months are needed to hear the three series.

21. **(C)** This is just a matter of counting. Epistemology, Ethics, and Political Philosophy all last longer than six months.

22. **(D)** This question is asking just what it says: how many of the series can be attended, not how many lectures. In September there are three series running and in October two more start, for a total of 5.

23. **(C)** Here the issue is how many different lectures can be heard. Three are available in January, two in February, and three more in March, for a total of 8.

24. **(D)** The question contains a hidden assumption: that the person questioned agrees that his company has, in the past, discriminated. So I is applicable since the speaker may wish to answer neither "yes" or "no." He may wish to object to the question: "But I do not admit that our company has ever discriminated, so your question is unfair." III is just another way of describing the difficulty we have just outlined. II is not applicable to the question. Since a simple question never actually makes a statement, it would seem impossible for it to contradict itself. A contradiction occurs only between statements or assertions.

25. **(A)** There are two weaknesses in Ms. Rose's argument: she reaches a very general conclusion on the basis of one example and her argument overlooks the possibility that an education can be valuable even if it is not used to make a living. Importantly, Rose may be correct in her criticism of the man she mentions—we need make no judgment about that—but the assumption is nonetheless *unsupported* in that she gives no arguments to support it. (B) plays on the superficial detail of the paragraph—the inversion of customary role models. But that is not relevant to the structure of the argument; the form could have been as easily shown using a woman with a law degree who decided to become a sailor, or a child who studied ballet but later decided to become a doctor. (D) also is totally beside the point. Rose never commits herself to so specific a conclusion. She simply says professional education is a waste; she never claims success is related to quality of education. (E) is wrong because Rose is making a general claim about professional education—the man with the law degree was used merely to illustrate her point. (C) is, perhaps, the second-best answer, but it is still not nearly as good as

(A). Her objection is that the man she mentions did not use his law degree in a law-related field. She never suggests that such a degree should be used to make money. She might not have objected to his behavior if he had used the degree to work in a public interest capacity.

SECTION VI

Questions 1–3

Arranging the Information

We are interested in the scores of the various participants in the tournament. We have two groups of three members each and we have a process. Each player will play five games, but these games are not entirely symmetrical since each master will play two other masters and three experts, while each expert will play two experts and three masters.

Since the questions are all conditional, we do not expect to spend much time on the diagram. The questions will be the thing.

EXPERTS—L, M, N
MASTERS—O, P, Q
All play two of the same category and three in the other category.

Scoring depends on classification of the loser. If loser is a master, winner scores 2, loser loses 2. If loser is an expert, the winner scores 1 and the loser loses 1.

Answering the Questions

1. **(B)** Since the most is gained from beating masters, the master will wish to lose to experts so that he can beat masters. His loss of points is the same whether he loses to a master or to an expert—2 games at 2 points each = loss of 4 points. By beating two masters, he will gain back these four points and by winning his match against the third expert, he will end up with a score of +1.

2. **(B)** We are speaking now of minimums. If a minimum number of games are to yield a best result, then it is masters who must be beaten. We have two things to figure out: First, the master's maximum score under the circumstances must be determined; then the expert's score must be worked out.

   If the master has lost two games to the other masters, he has lost 4 points. The best he can do is win his other three games against the experts and gain back 1 point for each victory, yielding a net score of $-4 + 3 = -1$.

   Thus, all the expert has to do is to end up with a net score greater than -1. We figured out the master's score first so that we would know the limits for our work on the expert's score. If the expert wins only one game, he could get +2, but losing four games would be -4, yielding a total of

−2, which is not enough. Winning another game against a master would result in a swing of 3 points—two for beating the master and one for not losing the game as first projected. This would increase the score from −2 to +1, which is enough to beat the master. Hence, (B) is the correct answer.

3. **(C)** Since P has lost to L and did not lose to the winner, the first inference is that L is not the winner, which eliminates answer (A). Here, our reference point is P's score. He has lost to one master (−1) and beaten two masters (+4) and two experts (+2), for a total score of +5. Clearly the final winner must have won all of his games except the one he lost to P. This means that the final winner must have scored at least 6 points total, which means that the winner must have gained at least 7 points in the four games he won. The only way to do that would be to have played and beaten all of the masters and one of the experts (2 + 2 + 2 + 1 = 7). This means that the winner must have been an expert rather than a master since the masters only got to play two masters—hence, answer choice (C).

4. **(C)** There are really two parts to the speaker's claim. First, he maintains that the majority of Americans can get access to the medical care in this country; and, second, that the care they have access to is the best in the world. As for the second, good medical care is a function of many variables: number and location of facilities, availability of doctors, quality of education, etc. (A) and (E) may both be consistent with the speaker's claim. Even though we have fewer assistants (A) than some other country, we have more doctors and that more than makes up for the fewer assistants. Or, perhaps, we have such good preventive medicine that people do not need to go into the hospital as frequently as the citizens of other nations (E). (B) is wrong for a similar reason. Although it suggests there is a country in which people have greater access to the available care, it does not come to grips with the second element of the speaker's claim: that the care we get is the best. (C), however, does meet both because it cites the existence of a country in which people are *given* (that is the first element) *better* (the second element) care. (D) hardly counts against the speaker's claim since he has implicitly conceded that some people do not have access to the care.

5. **(C)** The author's claim is that we have unbounded resources, and he tries to prove this by showing that we are getting better and better at extracting those resources from the ground. But

that is like saying "I have found a way of getting the last little bit of toothpaste out of the tube; therefore, the tube will never run out." (C) calls our attention to this oversight. (A) does not contradict the author's claim. In fact, it seems to support it. He might suggest, "Even if we run out of fossil fuels, we still have uranium for nuclear power." Now, this is not to suggest that he would. The point is only to show that (A) supports rather than undermines the author's contention. (B) is an attack on the author's general stance, but it does not really *contradict* the particular conclusion he draws. The author says, "We have enough." (B) says, "It is expensive." Both could very well be true, so they cannot contradict one another. (D) is similar to (B). Yes, you may be correct, the technology is expensive or, in this case, wasteful, but it will still get us the fuel we need. Finally, (E) is incorrect for pretty much these same reasons. Yes, the energy will have unwanted side effects, but the author claimed only that we could get the energy. The difficulty with (B), (D), and (E) is that though they attack the author's general *position*, and though they undermine his general suggestion, they do not *contradict* his *conclusion*.

6. **(E)** Common sense dictates that where one is driving in relationship to his home (within or without a 25 mile radius) has little or nothing to do with the safety factor. Moreover, common sense also says that a person driving under 35 miles per hour is (usually) safer than one driving at 60 miles per hour. The explanation, then, for the fact that most traffic fatalities occur under conditions contrary to those which would be suggested by common sense is that more driving is done under those conditions. Just as common sense indicates, the driving is safer per mile, but there are so many more miles driven under those conditions that there are many fatalities. (A) is obviously inconsistent with common sense. And the directions for the Logical Reasoning section explicitly say that the BEST answer will be one which does not require you to make such assumptions. (B) is incorrect since the statistics mention the location of the accident—how far away from home—not how far the driver had driven at the time of the accident. Even though the accident occurred, say, 26 miles from home, you would not want to conclude the driver had driven 26 miles. (C) compounds the error made by (A). Not only does it take the general conclusion regarding fatalities and attempt to apply it to a specific case without regard to the individual variety of those cases, but it commits the further error of conditioning the speed of driving on the occurrence of an accident. (D) does exactly the same thing and is also wrong.

Questions 7–11

Arranging the Information

LEFT-HANDED   RIGHT-HANDED

M← NOT WITH→ { L← NOT WITH→ S
N← NOT WITH→ T   4 TOTAL

O   R

MUST BE 2

Answering the Questions

7. **(C)** If L is on, that eliminates M and S, and thus choice (E) is out. The elimination of S means that T and R must be on the team since two right-handers are needed, which eliminates (D). The inclusion of T means the exclusion of N, and thus choice (B). Thus, L, O, R, and T are the team, answer choice (C).

8. **(D)** This is a little tricky since you have to remember that the only handedness limitation is that at least two right-handers must be on the team. It is OK if only one left-hander is on the team.

    If O is omitted, then the only way to have two left-handers is to have L and N, since neither of those can go with M. But if L and N are used, then S and T can't be, which leaves only one right-hander, R, and a team of only three players. This means that L and N cannot be right, so the left-hander component must be M only, since M cannot go with L or N. (Note that using only L or N will still leave only three players even though two right-handers will be achieved.)

    If only M is taken from the left-handers, then all three right-handers must be used, hence (D). The key was to start with the information you had—about left-handers—and build on that.

9. **(E)** If S and T are chosen, then L and N are excluded. At first glance, this seems to require M and O also to be chosen, but remember that, as discussed in 8, there can be three right-handers, so any two of M, O, and R could be chosen, which means (E) is correct since none of the answer choices has sufficient flexibility.

10. **(B)** If R is omitted, S and T are chosen. If S and T are chosen, then L and N are out and only M and O are left, which is only one possibility, M, O, S, and T—answer choice (B).

11. **(E)** Changing T to a left-handed player does not eliminate the restriction that T cannot go with N, or any other restriction or condition. If T is left-handed, then S and R must be on the team as the two needed right-handers. S eliminates L and we are left with R, S, and two of the others. Let us count the ways:

    If N is chosen, T and M are out, giving R, S, N and O—1.

    If T is chosen, N is out, but it could be combined with either M or O giving R, S, T, and M/O for two more—3 so far.

    If M is chosen, N is out leaving T and O. R, S, M, and T/O. The combination with T has already been counted, but R, S, M, and O is a fourth possibility, thus answer choice (E).

Questions 12–16

Arranging the Information

Some people can easily either visualize or draw a cube and label the sides accordingly. However, such powers are not necessary to the solution of the problem. Simply note that a cube, like a room, has a top, a bottom, and four sides, and draw the diagram as follows:

TOP   _____

SIDES _____

BOTTOM _____

At first it is not clear how this information is to be arranged, since the top and bottom are not clear until the end of the information. If you noticed that the last statement gave the bottom side's color, you could have done that first. If not, just assign one side to the top or bottom and then shift if it turns out to be wrong.

Since question 12 asks about redundancy from the top down, it is best to do the statements in that order, at least until 12 is solved.

Problem 12 is solved by noting that if red and black are opposite sides, all of the other sides are between them, so that statement III must be true, given II, and, thus, (B) is the answer to 12.

Code in I:

TOP   BLACK

SIDES _____

BOTTOM   RED

As previously noted, III adds nothing new.

Code in IV. Note that these other sides are all in the middle of the diagram, so even though they are not specifically related to red/black, we still do know where in the diagram they go.

TOP   BLACK

SIDES BLUE WHITE

BOTTOM   RED

Code in V:

TOP			BLACK		
SIDES		BROWN	BLUE	WHITE	
BOTTOM			RED		

From the preceding diagram we can put the last color, green, next to white and between white and brown—since that is the only place left.

TOP			BLACK		
SIDES		BROWN	BLUE	WHITE	GREEN
BOTTOM			RED		

The colors of the sides could be rotated in any way, as long as their relative order is preserved. VI places red on the bottom, so this is the final diagram.

Answering the Questions

12. **(B)** This is analyzed in "Arranging the Information."

13. **(A)** Sides that are separated by one other side are opposite, just as the wall in front of you is one wall away from the wall in back of you (if you are in a box-like room). Thus, white is opposite brown.

14. **(D)** Since green is one of the side colors, the top and bottom—red and black—are adjacent to it, eliminating (B) and (E). From the diagram, we can see that white and brown are adjacent sides, thus (D).

15. **(A)** Since the statements in the question mention specific positions only of red and black, answers (B), (C), and (D) cannot be supported. If red is the bottom (VI) and black is opposite it (II), then black must be the top—(A).

16. **(B)** This problem calls for a readjustment of the diagram, which now becomes:

TOP		GREEN		
SIDES	BROWN	BLACK	WHITE	RED
BOTTOM		BLUE		

This was a tricky but easy question since the statement that is false, (B), was false in the original configuration. The diagram shows that (A), (C), (D), and (E) are all true. (A) is also a little tricky since this very important original relationship is preserved.

Questions 17–22

Arranging the Information

The question stems tell us that the situation is a stable, or fixed, one. You will end up knowing pretty much which contestant won which prize. This conclusion follows from the fact that the questions are all descriptive and do not add any further information before asking you who won the dog food, etc. Knowing that it can be figured out is a help since you may wish to try certain assumptions and see if they work.

Question 21 is a redundancy question, which inclines us to do the propositions in order, though 20 seems to require otherwise.

Question 20 is a form of partial information question, though not as simple to deal with as the usual form in which the propositions are listed and the conclusion is at issue. Here the conclusion is listed and we must see what could lead us to that conclusion. Question 20 is unusual. The question stem gives a specific part of the final diagram which makes it clear that the original setup does tell you that Q does not receive the car. You will probably not see a stem like this on the actual test, and we will not use its piece of information in solving the problem. This is such an unlikely situation that we urge you to not believe it when you think you see it on the test.

This problem could be diagrammed as an information table, provided that you write in all of the back-and-forth connections. Another way of doing this problem would be to make a scorecard with arrows connecting the various boxes indicating how they are connected. This tends to be a bit messy.

The simplest approach would be to search for a general statement as a good starting point and then to consider all of the ramifications of each of the statements. All of the statements except I and IV are specific statements about particular prize–contestant relationships. I is the setup and IV covers the total relationship between P and R.

First, however, let us turn to the partial information question (20). Choices (B), (C), and (D) are highly unlikely since they exclude the situation given in I. Between the other two, (E) has a better case on its face since it includes VII, the only statement to directly address the issue of Q and the car. Under VII, if Q gets the car, which is the most valuable prize, R gets the vacation, which is the second-most-valuable prize. This would mean that P could not have gotten a more valuable prize than R. Since we know that the result of Q getting the car would lead to something impossible, Q does not get the car. Note that IV is not a conditional statement, but a statement of definite fact. Thus, I, IV, and VII are enough by themselves to tell us that Q does not get the car.

Note that we have not established that R doesn't get the vacation, but only that Q does not get the car. If P got the car, then R could have the vacation.

Let's get down to the situation. We have four statements that could bear on the disposition of the car: II, IV, V, and VII, so that looks like a good place to start.

Under IV, R cannot win the car since it is the most valuable, and P must receive a more valuable prize than R.

Under IV and VII together, as described above, Q cannot win the car.

Under V, we see that P cannot get the car. If S gets it, then P doesn't, and if S doesn't get it, then P gets something other than the car. Thus, S gets the car.

Since we have a powerful general principle in IV, we might as well work our way down the list in decreasing order of value. Thus, the vacation is next. VI addresses the vacation directly. If Q gets the vacation, then R won't get the dog food, which means he would get the stereo and P would take the dog food. That, however, is impossible since it would have R getting a more valuable prize than P, which is forbidden by IV. Thus we find that Q did not get the vacation. Similarly, we know that R cannot have it since he must be below P. This leaves only P to have the vacation.

The stereo and dog food must be distributed between R and Q. III refers to one of those possibilities and states that if Q gets the stereo, P will get the dog food, but P is, in fact, getting the vacation, so Q is not getting the stereo. This means that R is getting the stereo and the final allocation is:

S   Car
P   Vacation
R   Stereo
Q   Dog food

There are other routes of deduction that could have been followed. The redundancy issue is discussed in the answer to question 21.

Answering the Questions

17. **(C)** This is largely a matter of checking the final solution. (B) is true from the setup of the situation. (C) contradicts the fact that Q got the dog food and R the stereo.

18. **(B)** This is also a look-up question. (E) is absurd since the whole premise of the situation is that each of the four prizes was awarded to a different contestant.

19. **(D)** Again, our work was done in the arranging. S gets the car.

20. **(E)** This was discussed in "Arranging the Information." I, IV, and VII yield the conclusion that Q will not receive the car.

21. **(E)** Having previewed this question, we would at first be expecting to do the statements in numerical order. However, that did not seem to be the way things were going, especially under the impetus of question 20. Another way of keeping track of the question of redundancy is to see if any of the statements are not used in the working out of the problem. In this case, all of them were used and we could have checked them off as we used them for different deductions. Even more to the point, the kinds of statements given are not likely to be redundant since they are one-way statements

only—if A, then B—which would only be redundant if there were other statements saying, essentially: if A then C; if C then B. There is no such overlap in the statements given. Hence, there is no wasted information.

22. **(D)** This question is just a backhanded way of asking which of the contestants did win the stereo. Since all is known, (A) and (E) are not possible. Since R won the stereo, P, S, and Q did not, answer choice (D).

23. **(E)** The question stem asks us to find the one item which will not strengthen the author's argument. That is (E). Remember, the author's argument is an attempt (to be sure, a weak one) to develop an alternative causal explanation. (A) would provide some evidence that the author's claim—which at first glance seems a bit far-fetched—actually has some empirical foundation. While (B) does not add any strength to the author's own explanation of the phenomenon being studied, it does strengthen the author's overall position by undermining the explanation given in the report. (C) strengthens the author's position for the same reason that (B) does: It weakens the position he is attacking. (D) strengthens the argument in the same way that (A) does, by providing some empirical support for the otherwise seemingly farfetched explanation.

24. **(E)** Perhaps the most obvious weakness in the argument is that it oversimplifies matters. It is like the domino theory arguments adduced to support the war in Vietnam: Either we fight Communism now or it will take us over. The author argues, in effect: Either we put a stop to this now, or there will be no stopping it. Like the proponents of the domino theory, he ignores the many intermediate positions one might take. III is one way of describing this shortcoming: The dilemma posed by the author is a false one because it overlooks positions between the two extremes. II is also a weakness of the argument: "Cold-blooded murder" is obviously a phrase calculated to excite negative feelings. Finally, the whole argument is also internally inconsistent. The conclusion is that we should allow nature to take its course. How? By prolonging life with artificial means.

25. **(E)** This advertisement is simply rife with ambiguity. The wording obviously seeks to create the impression that FCBI found jobs for its many graduates and generally does a lot of good for them. But first we should ask how many graduates FCBI had—one, two, three, a dozen, or a hundred. If it had only twelve or so, finding them jobs might have been easy; but if many people enroll at FCBI, they may not have the same success. Further, we might want to know how many people graduated compared with how many enrolled. Do people finish the program, or does

FCBI just take their money and then force them out of the program? So II is certainly something we need to know in order to assess the validity of the claim. Now, how many of those who graduated came in looking for help in finding a job? Maybe most people had jobs waiting for them (only a few needed help), in which case the job placement assistance of FCBI is not so impressive. Or perhaps the graduates were so disgusted they did not even seek assistance. So I is relevant. III is also important. Perhaps FCBI found them jobs sweeping streets—not in business. The ad does not say what jobs FCBI helped its people find. Finally, maybe the ad is truthful—FCBI graduates found jobs—but maybe they did it on their own. So IV also is a question worth asking.

SECTION VII

1. **(E)** This sentence concerns a wilderness and an absence of people or civilization. Lived in has a meaning similar to civilized, but it implies a home or a town and not a countryside.

2. **(C)** "Natural product" in this sentence means "logical extension or outgrowth of" and joins like characteristics. Diligence and sedulousness are synonyms.

3. **(E)** Adventurous children will be delighted by blustery winds and rattling windows.

4. **(C)** The concept of theater is satisfied by dramas, not sciences, psychologies, jokes, or novels.

5. **(C)** This sentence describes enmity and a persistence of ill will. Answer (C) best completes the thought of this sentence.

6. **(D)** The sentence structure shows us that the first blank describes a feeling and the second blank an adjective that might apply to that feeling. More significantly, since only (E) has serious problems meeting that first criterion, the result of this situation was to make the other patients feel good. At first glance, all of the second words in the answer choices are highly negative and not likely to make anyone feel good. But some are worse than others. (A) is poor since nothing that is repulsive will make people feel good, even (or especially) contrition, which means feeling guilty. A catastrophic blood clot, embolism, will certainly not make anyone feel good, so (B) fails. (C) would have us believe that one patient's feeling extremely depressed, melancholic, would cheer up the other patients, so (C) fails. (D)'s second word, contagious, is good or bad, depending on what is being spread. If it is ebullience, high spirits, then it well might make the other patients feel good. (E) has some positive aspect in the first

word, rehabilitation, but a darkly suspicious, or paranoiac, rehabilitation will not cheer up anyone. Thus, (D) is the best answer choice.

7. **(D)** The second blank must be something that can be connected to disputes. Object, arbiter (judge), and cause certainly are ideas that relate well to disputes. Censor could also relate to a dispute in the sense of someone who would forbid certain disputes, but it is not strong. Reimburse, in (C), is unacceptable, and (C) is eliminated.

   The sentence tells us that the first word is the reason that he had the status defined in the second word. Thus, we must ask ourselves whether having the characteristic described in the first word would justify the status granted in the second word. (A) fails because having euphony, good sound, does not justify being a censor. (B) has some merit since being irritable or irascible might cause one to be the object of disputes, but cause would be better, though it is not available in (B). (C), already eliminated on other grounds, is also poor in this way. Wealth may permit reimbursing, but not of disputes. (D) is very good since great erudition, or learning, is a basis for being appointed to judge disputes. (E) is probably the second-best answer since great pomposity might well cause disputes, but it is not clear why the disputes should be about art and music. Thus, (D) is the best answer.

8. **(E)** A valve controls flow. Similarly, a throttle controls speed. There is a control device and the measure of the things being controlled. (A) has some merit since a faucet can control a shower, but what it actually controls is the flow of water in the shower, and through that perhaps the temperature. (B) and (C) are unconnected. (D) has some merit since the mores of a community are its ethical conventions and they will control the conduct of the community, but this is really the same structure as (A) in that the second term of the pair is the general item being controlled rather than the measure of the thing being controlled or the specific aspect being controlled. If (E) were not present, (D) would be plausible, though a little weak. As it is, (E) is the best answer.

9. **(B)** The lee side is the side downwind of something, like the lee side of an island or a boat. The windward is the upwind side. The relationship to (B) is clear once the analogy of a wind and a stream is seen. (A) fails since port and larboard are the same side of the boat. (D) and (E) have some merit in that they are both nautical terms and both opposites; however, they are both saying the same thing and there is no specific direction to the oppositeness, while (B) does have a specific directional aspect, which is the same as the original pair. (C) starts out very well with sheltered, since the lee, or downwind, side of something is sheltered from the wind. However,

the second term of (C) completely fails to carry this idea through. If it said exposed, or something like that, it might be an even better answer than (B) since there would be an extra dimension to it that is lacking in (B). As it is, harbored is nearly a synonym in this context, and thus (B) is the best answer available.

10. **(C)** A quarry is the place where marble is found, and where it is taken from the earth. A mine is the source of coal. (E) fails for lack of any connection to the idea of source or place of location. (D) fails since tungsten is derived from the ore wolframite, but that is a chemical connection rather than one of location. (A) and (B) are places where things are found and (A), particularly, has some idea of the forest being the source of timber. In choosing between (A) and (C), aside from the fact that (A) is backward, the fact that marble is a rock and comes from the earth, just like coal, is the deciding factor in seeing that the action of quarrying marble is closer to that of mining coal than to lumbering timber from the forest. Thus, (C) is the best answer.

11. **(B)** A writer creates or makes a manuscript. A cooper is a maker of barrels. (A) fails since there is no idea of the maker and the product since an artist is not defined by producing descriptions of things. A fletcher is someone who puts feathers on arrows; a glazier makes glass and puts in windows. (E) has a superficial appeal but a blacksmith uses a forge rather than making it, as a writer makes the manuscript or a cooper makes the barrel. Thus, (B) is the best answer.

12. **(E)** The wattle of a turkey is the name for that area of its body that is called jowls on a person. The others are simply different parts of the body or different ideas altogether. If you knew no more than that a turkey has a wattle as part of his regular physical equipment, you could eliminate (A), (B), and (C). In guessing between (E) and (D), (E) would be better here since it is a part of an animal to a part of an animal and might be the right part. If the full meaning of wattle is known to you, there is no debate that (E) is the best answer.

13. **(C)** The two words in the original pair are synonyms and the only synonyms in the answer choices are (C). (D) is not a pair of synonyms since spastic refers to a physical muscle problem and not to a mental one, as retarded does.

14. **(B)** A whim is an action that is not premeditated. A caprice is an action that is not deliberate. None of the other pairs have the same oppositeness. (E) has a pair of synonyms.

15. **(C)** The original pair are synonyms since they both mean to sharpen. Desiccate and dehumidify both mean to dry out. None of the other answer

choices have any synonym aspect and (A) has a pair of opposites. The only issue here, as in a small proportion of the analogy questions, is the vocabulary.

16. **(D)** To quaff is to drink quickly in big gulps. This is the opposite of sip, which means to drink in small quantities. To gorge is to eat quickly, while to nibble is to take small bites. (B) and (C) have no idea of being the same thing, though (B) has an opposite aspect to it. In (A) and (E), the first word is a greater intensity of the second word, but they do not have the additional idea of being ways of eating and drinking or things that people do, though the latter is truer of quaff and sip than of gorge and nibble. Thus, (D) is the best answer.

17. **(E)** This question asks about an explicit statement by the author. He states that a single example of decomposition *proves* that the substance is a compound. It is true that he is describing a theory, but that is not to say that the idea is not practical. Answer choice (A) says only theoretically, and that limitation is not in the passage. Similarly, (C) and (D) might have some merit in the world, but the passage does not permit them. In the real world it is sometimes difficult to know that a decomposition reaction has taken place rather than some other form of reaction, but that difficulty is not referred to in the passage, which only deals with the consequences of knowing that you do have a decomposition reaction.

(B) has some merit in that controls are not necessarily needed in the methods described in the passage, but they are not forbidden nor stated to be unnecessary.

18. **(B)** The passage makes it clear that it is impossible to prove that something is an element by techniques having to do with whether it is a compound or not (tests of this kind). (A) is false since the passage does say that the compound nature of substances can be determined. (C) is wrong since the only uncertainty is the reference to convenience, but that is not even clearly part of the chemical method. (D) may well be true, if the only method available were decomposition reactions, but the passage does not impose that limitation and even implies that there are other sorts of tests. (E) fails when (B) succeeds. Thus, (B) is the best answer.

19. **(E)** (A) fails as described for 18 because the limitations of the method under discussion are not generalized by the passage, and the existence of other methods is implicit in the idea of convenience and the references to other methods. (B) fails since the passage explicitly limits the things that can be proved by the method discussed to the fact of some substance's being a compound. (C) is incorrect since the passage merely states that you

cannot be certain that you have found an element, not that it is not, in fact, an element. (D) fails for the same reason as described for (B). Thus, (E) must be the answer.

20. **(B)** The author states that there are some good shows, but from the start to the end of the television day, the average is bad.

21. **(D)** He is telling the industry what it must do, "I intend . . . ." Hence (D). He is not defeated, (A), nor hopeless, (E). While he is righteous, (C), the intention to prevail is dominant. There is no reconciliation, (B), at all.

22. **(D)** The whole thing is an extended shape-up-or-else statement, with justifications. (A) is not intended, and while there is an obligation to the listener or viewer, it is in seeking only to please the viewer that the author sees error; thus (A) is incorrect. (B) and (C) fail since good children's shows are said to exist and it is only the steady diet of mystery, etc., which is objectionable. (E) fails because the teaching referred to is not classroom instruction.

23. **(B)** Literature and great traditions of freedom are urged as subjects for children's shows and these are certainly culture. None of the others are objected to, except cartoons, and there it is the massive doses only. The entire speech is a plea for moderation.

24. **(A)** (C) and (D) wrongly refer to air as the thing we breathe, while the author is referring to the broadcasting of television programs. (E) fails since the author nowhere opposes commercial television, but only insists that it should provide real service in return for using the common property that the airwaves represent. Thus, (E) fails. (B) has some merit since clearly the idea that the airwaves are owned by the people could be part—though only part—of an argument to say that the people should actually run everything to do with the airwaves through their government, but this is not part of the author's speech, and only if government oversight is to be equated with socialism can (B) ultimately be supported. We are, thus, left with (A), which is correct. While other rights may accrue to the people from their "ownership" of the airwaves, the right to have worthwhile use made of their property is certainly a permissible inference.

25. **(D)** The author states explicitly that the popularity of shows should not be the only criterion for selecting them. Since he has separated merit from popularity, he must believe that not all listeners or viewers know what is good for them. (A) and (C) have some appeal, but the author accuses the networks of catering to the nation's whims, which is hardly consonant with trying to do the right thing. He certainly does agree that they are failing, but that is not enough to justify choosing (A). The author's statements that there are some worthwhile shows is not enough to justify (C). (B) and (E) are flack.

26. **(D)** The citation of some good children's shows, even though they are overwhelmed by trash, is sufficient to choose (D). While (A) is not currently fashionable, the author is talking about meeting the needs of all of the population. (C) and (E) are directly stated, while (B) can be derived from the author's emphasis on opportunity of choice.

27. **(C)** There are two ways in which Minow refers to his own tastes in comparison to those of other people. First, he says that he finds little merit during the entire broadcasting day and says that the broadcasters to whom he is speaking would reach the same judgment if they sat and watched an entire day's shows. So, he does not claim that he has better taste than the broadcasters, but rather that they, like he, would find the shows appalling. The second connection is between Minow's tastes and those of the general public. He says that most people would rather watch a Western than a symphony, and then he states that he likes Westerns and spy shows himself. What he objects to is the lack of choice, not the rank order or popularity as such. Thus he does not hold himself as having better taste than anyone, eliminating (A) and (B), and (D) since he does not speak of children's tastes at all. The appeal of (E), to the extent that it does appeal, is his first statement that television can be better than anything else, when it is good. But he means that in a simple and direct way and it is not some sort of complicated sneer. Don't exercise your imagination unnecessarily.

28. **(C)** A categorical statement is explicit and unqualified. Vague means unclear and is quite the opposite. Unregenerate means remaining at odds with God or otherwise morally unimproved. Voluptuous means full of luxurious or sensuous enjoyment. Doglike is a simplistic play on cat- in categorical.

29. **(D)** Premeditated means something that has been thought about before being done. Impromptu means without prompting or planning, and thus without premeditation. Superannuated means having too many years (*annu-*), and thus being too old or out of date. Tractable means able to be handled or directed.

30. **(A)** Propinquity means physical nearness. Distance is exactly the opposite, as in keeping one's distance. Antiquity, meaning of great age, "looks like" an opposite since it has an "anti" to oppose the "pro" of propinquity. However, this is not

enough to make an antonym answer. The stems look similar in that they both have q's and end in "quity." However, the "pin" of propinquity is ignored in this analysis. It is never a good guess to go on word parts alone—and then not consider one part of the word. "Antipinquity" might, if such a word existed, be a good opposite on structural grounds, but it is not available. Succulence means juiciness. Tedium is the state of being dull and wearisome.

31. **(C)** Adjure means to command earnestly and solemnly. "Ask facetiously" is very opposite since facetiously means not seriously. "Ask" itself can present some problems since it is used here in the sense of requesting some performance of someone. (E) might have some appeal because *ad* means "to," as in adhere. (A) could also appeal because of the stem *-jure*, meaning law, and the fact that judges are called jurists. Adjure literally means giving the law to someone, thus telling them what they must do.

32. **(B)** To postulate something is to accept it without proof, at least for the purposes of discussion; thus, to prove something is the opposite. Undulate, meaning to move up and down like an undulating wave in the ocean and peculate, meaning to embezzle money or goods, both have a similar ending, but that is not enough. Palpitate means to beat unusually rapidly, like your heart after intense exercise.

33. **(C)** Abridge means to shorten something, generally a writing or presentation. Lengthen is just the opposite. It is not quite a perfect opposite in that abridge applies only to some types of situations, while lengthen could apply to a sewer, which abridge would not. Wade is a crude attempt to get you to think about going under "a-bridge" instead of over it.

34. **(C)** An aversion is a turning away from something, a strong dislike for it. An affinity is a strong connection to something, a desire to come close to it. These are not perfect opposites. An affinity is not quite the same as a strong liking for something, which would be the perfect opposite of the broad meaning of aversion; but affinity is a good opposite to the literal meaning of aversion. Serenity is great calmness and sureness of self. Pleasance sounds like pleasant and thus has some appeal as an opposite to aversion, meaning dislike. However, a pleasance now refers only to a laid-out walk with trees and plants, which presumably is pleasant. A valance is a short, ornamental drapery. The chemical term valence, with an *e*, refers to the electrochemical properties of atoms that govern their combinations into molecules.

35. **(B)** A proclivity is a tendency or inclination to do something. Thus, a disinclination is a good opposite. Insipidity means dullness and commonness. Effrontery is rude presumption; antithesis is the total opposite; and a contingency is something that depends on chance, or is one possibility of several.

36. **(C)** Something ethereal is insubstantial, only existing in the "ether." A tangible item is touchable (a tangent line touches the circle). Contagious means able or likely to be spread (by touch).

37. **(C)** Extraneous means unrelated, and germane means meaningfully related. Native might have some appeal since *extra-* means outside of or in addition to.

38. **(C)** To assuage some hurt is to make it less painful. To exacerbate something is to make it worse. Corrugate means to make ridges in something, like a corrugated tin roof. Impede means to delay or prevent progress or change. This might have some feeling of opposite since to impede the progress of a disease, for instance, might help to assuage its effects, but this is a derived meaning.